INSI

MW01253843

Structuring M&A Transactions

Leading Lawyers on Negotiations, Due Diligence, and Deal Strategies for Mergers & Acquisitions

Mat #40677850

BOOK & ARTICLE IDEA SUBMISSIONS

If you are a C-Level executive, senior lawyer, or venture capitalist interested in submitting a book or article idea to the Aspatore editorial board for review, please email AspatoreAuthors@thomson.com. Aspatore is especially looking for highly specific ideas that would have a direct financial impact on behalf of a reader. Completed publications can range from 2 to 2,000 pages. Include your book/article idea, biography, and any additional pertinent information.

WRITING & EDITORIAL ASSISTANCE

In select instances Aspatore will assist in helping our authors generate the content for their publication via phone interviews. Aspatore editors create interview questions that help generate the main content for the book or article. The content from the phone interviews is then transcribed and edited for review and enhancement by the author. If this method could be of assistance in helping you find the time to write an article or book, please email AspatoreEditorial@thomson.com for more information, along with your biography and your publication idea.

ISBN 978-1-59622-646-3   Library of Congress Control Number: 2007921618

For corrections, updates, comments or any other inquiries please email AspatoreEditorial@thomson.com.

First Printing, 2007
10 9 8 7 6 5 4 3 2 1

Praise for *Inside the Minds*

"Need-to-read inside information and analysis that will improve your bottom line—the best source in the business." – Daniel J. Moore, Member, Harris Beach LLP

"The *Inside the Minds* series is a valuable probe into the thoughts, perspectives, and techniques of accomplished professionals…" – Chuck Birenbaum, Partner, Thelen Reid & Priest

"Aspatore has tapped into a goldmine of knowledge and expertise ignored by other publishing houses." – Jack Barsky, Managing Director, Information Technology and CIO, ConEdison Solutions

"Unlike any other publisher—actual authors that are on the front lines of what is happening in industry." – Paul A. Sellers, Executive Director, National Sales, Fleet and Remarketing, Hyundai Motor America

"A snapshot of everything you need…" – Charles Koob, Co-Head of Litigation Department, Simpson Thacher & Bartlet

"Everything good books should be—honest, informative, inspiring, and incredibly well written." – Patti D. Hill, President, BlabberMouth PR

"Great information for both novices and experts." – Patrick Ennis, Partner, ARCH Venture Partners

"A rare peek behind the curtains and into the minds of the industry's best." – Brandon Baum, Partner, Cooley Godward

"Intensely personal, practical advice from seasoned deal-makers." – Mary Ann Jorgenson, Coordinator of Business Practice Area, Squire, Sanders & Dempsey

"Great practical advice and thoughtful insights." – Mark Gruhin, Partner, Schmeltzer, Aptaker & Shepard PC

"Reading about real-world strategies from real working people beats the typical business book hands down." – Andrew Ceccon, CMO, OnlineBenefits Inc.

"Books of this publisher are syntheses of actual experiences of real-life, hands-on, front-line leaders—no academic or theoretical nonsense here. Comprehensive, tightly organized, yet nonetheless motivational!" – Lac V. Tran, Senior Vice President, CIO, and Associate Dean, Rush University Medical Center

"Aspatore is unlike other publishers…books feature cutting-edge information provided by top executives working on the front lines of an industry." – Debra Reisenthel, President and CEO, Novasys Medical Inc.

www.Aspatore.com

Aspatore Books is the largest and most exclusive publisher of C-Level executives (CEO, CFO, CTO, CMO, partner) from the world's most respected companies and law firms. Aspatore annually publishes a select group of C-Level executives from the Global 1,000, top 250 law firms (partners and chairs), and other leading companies of all sizes. C-Level Business Intelligence™, as conceptualized and developed by Aspatore Books, provides professionals of all levels with proven business intelligence from industry insiders—direct and unfiltered insight from those who know it best—as opposed to third-party accounts offered by unknown authors and analysts. Aspatore Books is committed to publishing an innovative line of business and legal books, those which lay forth principles and offer insights that, when employed, can have a direct financial impact on the reader's business objectives, whatever they may be. In essence, Aspatore publishes critical tools—need-to-read as opposed to nice-to-read books—for all business professionals.

Inside the Minds

The critically acclaimed *Inside the Minds* series provides readers of all levels with proven business intelligence from C-Level executives (CEO, CFO, CTO, CMO, partner) from the world's most respected companies. Each chapter is comparable to a white paper or essay and is a future-oriented look at where an industry/profession/topic is heading and the most important issues for future success. Each author has been carefully chosen through an exhaustive selection process by the *Inside the Minds* editorial board to write a chapter for this book. *Inside the Minds* was conceived in order to give readers actual insights into the leading minds of business executives worldwide. Because so few books or other publications are actually written by executives in industry, *Inside the Minds* presents an unprecedented look at various industries and professions never before available.

Structuring M&A Transactions

Leading Lawyers on Negotiations, Due Diligence, and Deal Strategies for Mergers & Acquisitions

CONTENTS

Managing Mergers & Acquisitions as a Business Process

John C. Grosvenor

Partner

Manatt, Phelps & Phillips LLP

Now (2017.11.26) EVP & General Counsel
at First Pactrust Bancorp, Inc.
(aka Banc of California, Inc.)

Most mergers and acquisitions don't maximize the potential economic benefits of the deal. In many cases, that failure can be attributed to the fact that mergers and acquisitions are usually handled as unique events as opposed to using a methodical approach to manage the transaction as a business process. Although lawyers, financial advisers, and accountants provide essential contributions, much of the success of a merger or acquisition in maximizing economic benefits is determined more by the use of methodical processes that foster realistic objectives and a disciplined implementation of the transaction, neither of which can occur without a conscious business management approach to doing the deal. Although that idea may seem obvious, it is seldom followed in practice.

This chapter focuses primarily on the benefits of using such processes in the typical kind of mergers and acquisition (M&A) transaction: a negotiated combination of two enterprises that together have more value than either alone would have. This additional value, or "synergy value," is shared between the two stockholder groups, some in the form of a premium to stockholders of the acquired entity and the rest as potential future value to be derived from cost savings, revenue enhancements, or other economic benefits the combined entity can enjoy.

An illustration of how economic benefits from an M&A transaction can be lost due to the absence of a coherent management process that focuses on realistic synergy values and effective integration planning is provided by the following scenario.

Case Study

The chairpersons of two publicly traded banks meet and discuss a possible combination of their respective companies. Bank A is an acquisition-oriented regional bank, and Bank B is a local community-based bank. Their two market areas complement one another, and they engage in similar types of lending. Both banks are represented by experienced attorneys, accountants, and financial advisers. They enter into a letter of intent and conduct due diligence about each other. They negotiate a comprehensive, definitive merger agreement that addresses all of the issues identified in due diligence. The merger agreement provides a sophisticated pricing mechanism and exhaustive representations, warranties, covenants, and conditions. Proxy statements are prepared and mailed to both stockholder groups, which overwhelmingly approve the merger. Everything is done precisely the way it's supposed to work, but the economic benefits expected to be achieved are not fully realized after the merger. How could this happen?

The reason it happened is that one of the anticipated synergies did not actually materialize. Bank A expected that Bank B's unusually low cost of funds from their local deposit base would continue after the merger. As it turns out, Bank B's low cost of funds was due to its community-based banking culture in which local depositors were willing to accept a lower return on their deposits because of the value placed on their personal relationships with Bank B's local management. Consequently, as these local depositors went elsewhere, the combined entity experienced liquidity pressures that forced it to raise deposit rates much higher than had been previously paid, thereby reducing its net interest margin for the foreseeable future.

The relevant questions for this analysis are: should this synergy value have been discounted in the initial assessment of the perceived benefits of doing the deal or, in the alternative, could this synergy value have been captured if, during integration planning, the risks of capturing it had been identified and plans for dealing with those risks put in place before closing? In addition, if it had been identified as such a "soft" synergy value earlier in the transaction, would the process discipline have been in place to provide a meaningful opportunity for Bank A to decide whether to withdraw from the deal or seek to change the price it was willing to pay? Finally, even if the softness of this synergy value had not been recognized until after closing, would the existence of an effective integration team have provided feet on the ground to quickly deal with the unexpected need to woo at least some of those local relationship-based depositors to stay in the fold. Once gone, those deposits could not be easily recaptured and this significant synergy value expected to be gained through the merger was lost forever.

In this scenario, legal, accounting, and financial due diligence had been effective. What was missing was something accountants, lawyers, and financial advisers are not well equipped to provide: management of the transaction as a business process in the context of the respective strategic needs of each of the two banks. Outside professionals follow their client's directions to accomplish a desired goal. Their job is to get the deal done, not to decide whether the deal is good. That decision belongs solely to directors and management who, as representatives of the company's stockholders, have been elected and appointed to exercise their judgment in deciding whether the transaction is in their company's best interests. Although lawyers, accountants, and financial advisers consult with and advise their clients in order to assist directors and management in making the best decisions, they cannot substitute their judgment for that of the duly elected and appointed representatives of the stockholders. Besides, not many boards or chief executive officers would employ outside professionals who frustrate the exercise of their legitimate authority.

How Could an M&A Process Have Helped?

The important processes, which I will call "enhanced due diligence" and "effective integration planning," that are usually missing in most M&A transactions are driven by strategic planning as part of the business of managing a merger or acquisition. Even though outside professionals can't provide those processes, they should be included and can make significant contributions to the effectiveness of those processes in capturing realistic synergy values.

I am not suggesting that experienced outside professionals are not important in an M&A transaction. They are critical to the success of a deal. What I am suggesting is that the expertise of those professionals is most valuable when it is harnessed to serve a comprehensive management-driven business planning process. All too frequently, the efforts of people conducting due diligence are insufficiently coordinated to permit the companies involved to leverage the collected information for the purpose of effective business planning. As an example, traditional due diligence will identify where third-party consents are required to complete a deal or where completing the deal would breach a third-party agreement. But, there are always material agreements for products or services that will be duplicative once the two businesses have been combined. Lawyers working with their clients in a process method of managing an M&A transaction as part of business planning can assist in the business decision of which of the duplicative vendors will best serve the interests of the combined entity. If the telecommunications vendor for one company operates under a contract that, like the other vendor's contract, does not require consent but, unlike the other vendor's contract, imposes severe penalties upon termination, there may be a synergy cost of choosing that company's vendor for post-combination services. Lawyers who participate in a management-driven M&A process can help both with the assessment of the realistic net synergy value of choosing one vendor over another as well as developing strategies for overcoming anticipated obstacles to choosing the best vendor.

The dilemma for many companies, especially middle-market companies like Bank A and Bank B, is how to create a business process for what might be a one-time event. Mergers and acquisitions involving middle-market companies are the most frequent kind of M&A transaction, and most of those are negotiated transactions. But unlike large, experienced acquirers, middle-market companies usually do not have an institutionalized business development function and the principal responsibilities for completing an M&A transaction usually fall on the chief executive officer, chief financial officer, and general counsel, who may or may not have relevant past transaction experience but certainly have other ongoing roles and responsibilities that make it difficult to assemble an internal team of professionals who can be dedicated to the process of managing a merger or acquisition. In addition, many companies are reluctant to put processes in place that may increase the cost of doing what may be regarded as a one-time transaction that is already expensive enough to begin with. In those cases, they end up taking the gamble that everything will work out fine. What they frequently don't realize is that the margin for error, both in assessing synergy values and in capturing them, is narrow enough that even small errors can wipe out significant economic benefits. With those practical problems in mind, it is still nonetheless advisable that companies strive to create as much process discipline as possible to maximize the economic benefits of doing the deal.

Regardless of whether a company has any prior experience in mergers and acquisitions, and regardless of whether it is the acquirer or the acquired company, the economic benefits from an M&A transaction need to be realistically assessed, and the post-combination follow-through necessary to capitalize on those benefits must be in place to maximize the economics of the deal. For companies experienced in mergers and acquisitions, those skills may already exist. For those with little or no prior M&A experience, it is still important to develop that capability to have a successful transaction.

What Is an "M&A Process"?

The best way to maximize the economic benefits of a merger or acquisition is to first understand what actual synergy values may exist and then manage the M&A transaction as a business process in order to ensure that those realistic synergy values are captured. The typical M&A transaction usually lacks the two management processes necessary for maximizing economic benefits: enhanced due diligence and effective integration planning.

The first of the improved processes, enhanced due diligence, is the same phase of the transaction during which typical due diligence is performed, but during enhanced due diligence, strategic needs are affirmed, synergy values are verified, relationship capital is created, and effective integration teams coalesce. These attributes normally do not occur during traditional due diligence.

The second of the improved processes, effective integration planning, is a phase that functions as the natural extension of enhanced due diligence and builds upon the benefits of that earlier phase in order to plan how and when realistic synergy values can and should be captured upon the combination of the two businesses. Effective integration planning begins early and extends well past closing until all of the necessary integration activities have been completed. Integration is the important phase when synergy values are either captured or lost.

Few M&A transactions are managed under these processes, and therefore the companies involved lose significant economic benefits that were either overoptimistic to begin with or lost because they were not captured timely after closing.

This type of M&A process promotes discipline in reaching objective assessments of realistic synergy values by creating a higher level of purpose-driven analysis covering a broader range of information than traditional due diligence is designed to cover. It also recognizes the obvious importance, usually overlooked in most M&A transactions, of using that comprehensive understanding about both companies as the basis for the ultimate integration of the two businesses once the combination has occurred. Both of these processes will either reflect (for those companies that perform routine strategic planning) or should trigger (for those companies that do not) a realistic self-assessment of the strategic goals that support the need for a merger or acquisition.

The question of whether and to what extent an M&A transaction is beneficial will always depend upon the strategic needs and goals of both companies. A deal that looks good may not actually be needed, and a premium that seems too high for others may be appropriate for some depending upon the potential synergy contribution of the M&A transaction to a company's strategic gaps. These management processes also help guard against the risk of emotional attachment to a deal that does not satisfy genuine needs, a risk that can otherwise result in overpaying for a company that does not offer sufficient synergy values.

Mergers and acquisitions can occur on either a planned or opportunistic basis. In either case, the determination to pursue a merger or acquisition must always be grounded on a realistic strategic plan in which obstacles to achieving desired goals for each company can be effectively addressed by a merger or acquisition. Companies that do not engage in ongoing strategic planning can still review a potential transaction strategically as part of the management of the M&A process. It's more than price that will determine whether a merger or acquisition is really advantageous, and sophisticated structuring and pricing mechanisms don't change the fact that realization of the maximum post-closing value of the combined entity will always depend on methodical management of an M&A process that has been driven by a thoughtful strategic assessment.

One should never underestimate how easy it can be to lose sight of strategic relevance. In one proposed acquisition, a large telecommunications acquirer wanted to acquire a broadband wireless company that utilized a proven technology capable of distributing information and video signals. The target company, as well as its technology, was fully vetted, but the acquisition did not suit the strategic needs of the acquirer: most of its market areas, unlike the market areas where the technology was being successfully used, had variable topographies of rolling hills and wooded terrain that made it unsuitable for obtaining the necessary line of sight to potential customers. Even though the engineers were fascinated with the strategic benefits of the technology for fast and cheap deployment, the technology failed to fill the strategic need for cost-effective marketing since it could not be known which customers could actually receive the service until an installer showed up to determine whether line of sight could be acquired. As simple as this sounds, the debate over which elements of the acquisition strategy were more important, cheap deployment or cost-effective marketing, was ultimately resolved only after extensive discussion of the acquirer's strategic needs for pursuing the acquisition at all.

Since mergers and acquisitions usually occur under intense time pressures, completing the transaction can sometimes become the driving objective. The discipline of the business processes of enhanced due diligence and effective integration planning helps promote the objectivity and prioritization necessary to ensure that the deal is a good one, and it provides a basis for balancing the urgency of doing the deal quickly with the wisdom of doing the deal at all. These enhanced processes promote that balancing by injecting, throughout the process, opportunities for critical analyses based upon an increasingly deeper level of information and understanding about the companies, the realistic synergy values both may enjoy from a combination, and the actual strategic needs served by doing the deal at all.

What Are "Synergy Values"?

There can be many reasons why the economic benefits of an M&A transaction may not be maximized, including an emotional attachment to a bad deal, a myopic focus on getting the "best" price, or a single-minded determination to just get the deal done. However, the enhanced business processes I've described make that much less likely to occur. These enhanced processes recognize that there is no single correct price and that the key to mutual success is knowing the amount of synergy value available to be shared, and having the discipline to walk away if there are insufficient synergy values to satisfy the strategic needs and goals of both parties.

Simply stated, synergy values represent the difference between the aggregate intrinsic values of the two companies standing alone compared to the perceived enhanced value of the post-closing combined entity. That difference, or synergy value, can come from projected cost savings, anticipated revenue enhancements, or other synergies such as potential tax benefits that otherwise would not exist for either company independently.

It is essential for maximizing economic benefits that synergy values are rigorously calculated based upon realistic assumptions. No matter how "strategic" the deal may appear to be, if the numbers don't offer compelling evidence of tangible synergy values to the combined businesses, management should look closely at the wisdom of proceeding. Although many companies perform detailed financial and operating analyses as part of their traditional due diligence, few do a comprehensive risk analysis that examines what the best- and worst-case outcomes could be, which is not surprising in light of the tendency in most deals to "find" synergy values that justify the deal.

In calculating synergy values, cost savings are the most obvious and usually the easiest to quantify because historical cost information is readily available for identifying functions, personnel, or facilities that may be deemed unnecessary when the businesses are combined. The principal concern in calculating projected cost savings is the tendency to underestimate one-time costs that may accompany the projected savings. The example given above for choosing between two duplicative vendors, when one of the contracts includes termination penalties, is an example.

Revenue enhancements are much harder to quantify because they involve external variables that are difficult to predict or control. As a result, the assumptions used require much more rigorous scrutiny. It is in cases like revenue enhancements where best- and worst-case analyses can be particularly valuable. Despite the difficulty in coming up with hard values for revenue enhancements, they can nonetheless be sources of very significant synergy value.

Other forms of potential synergy values, including financial re-engineering, tax benefits, or the like, are too unique to a particular transaction to discuss generally, but like any other synergy value they must be accurately predicted and efficiently captured to maximize the economic benefits of the deal.

What Is "Enhanced Due Diligence"?

It is important to note what traditional due diligence is and what it is not. Typical due diligence is an investigation, usually conducted primarily by outside advisers, into relevant facts and circumstances associated with an M&A transaction to ensure that obstacles to accomplishing the deal can be addressed and resolved. It seldom includes comprehensive critical analysis of the information gained in that investigation to verify that anticipated economic benefits are realistic and serve strategic needs, and it is rarely used as a basis for planning how those realistic values can be captured upon integration. As such, traditional due diligence serves a more limited purpose than the suggested forms of enhanced M&A processes can serve.

The first phase of these enhanced processes is enhanced due diligence, which can provide a way to build relationship capital in the combined corporate culture, serve as a vehicle for honing the calculation of realistic synergy values and affirming strategic goals, and establish a platform for effective post-closing integration. Few companies use the traditional due diligence process to achieve these kinds of benefits.

For instance, the success of an M&A transaction depends to a great extent on surmounting cultural obstacles by creating a shared sense of common goals. Most M&A transactions are some form of negotiated combinations, and it is important to remember "they" will become "us" once the deal is done. Managing the transaction as a business process, and focusing on the synergies the combined businesses will enjoy, provide an important first step in establishing the relationship capital that will become increasingly important as the transaction progresses. In addition to building cultural bridges during the early stages of the deal, an enhanced due diligence team, operating under a management process that contemplates a transition to integration planning, will also aid in promoting effective integration by a group that embodies the "new" combined business culture.

In addition, culture is something that is often overlooked but can be an important element in the acquisition process, even where there is no carry-over of personnel or stockholders of the acquired company. In an all-cash acquisition of a small record label, the strategic need of the acquirer was limited to obtaining the music rights to the target company's library of music. However, that little company had been built by a small group of individuals throughout their careers, and they cared very much about the culture of the company acquiring that library. Throughout the acquisition process, the chief executive officer of the acquirer astutely gave respectful attention to the sellers' emotional concerns and persuaded them that their life's work would be in good hands. In the end, he was able to convince them not only that the price being offered was fair, but that their company would be in better hands than it would be in the hands of a competing bidder who was offering more money.

Using the due diligence team during the first phase of a business process that will extend well past closing, produces a higher level of analysis of realistic synergy values, since these people will be looking at facts and circumstances during due diligence with an eye toward the eventual integration they will be responsible for performing, and a more disciplined and effective post-closing integration of the expected economic benefits of the deal once the time for that has come. Since there is only so much information and time available to calculate preliminary synergy values, the additional information gleaned during an enhanced due diligence phase, by people who will be planning how to capture those synergies, allows companies to constantly refine their assessment concerning what realistic synergy values actually exist. In some cases, a deal that might have looked good at first may turn out to be bad and, as mentioned before, the risk of emotional attachment in the face of genuine problems is much less likely to occur.

What Is "Effective Integration Planning"?

All too often, upon the closing of a merger or acquisition, management, lawyers, accountants, and financial advisers relax in satisfied exhaustion after an intense period of activity, celebrate at a closing dinner, and then pretty much forget about what is perhaps the most important activity for realizing the economic benefits they are celebrating: capturing synergy values through prompt and effective integration.

If the M&A transaction has been managed as a business process, the people who had been involved in the enhanced due diligence phase, where synergy values were confirmed and honed, have also put comprehensive integration plans into place long before the closing to ensure that there will be prompt implementation to capture the expected economic benefits.

Enhanced integration planning also helps ensure that unexpected costs do not arise and furthers the building of post-closing relationship capital that any successful business combination must have. It can also allow the combined entity to react quickly and with better intelligence to the inevitable post-closing problems that unexpectedly occur, such as challenges that can arise from a competitor trying to capitalize on the transaction as an opportunity to steal customers or employees. Enhanced integration planning can also minimize the kind of personnel disruption that can occur when a sudden post-closing silence follows the loud noises of months of pre-closing activity. That personnel disruption is frequently due more to anxiety and uncertainty, and less from prompt and respectful integration actions.

To maximize economic benefits from a merger or acquisition, companies need to view post-closing integration as a manageable process. That process requires that planning for integration starts early, with roots in the enhanced due diligence phase, and extends well beyond closing. Many aspects of effective integration planning, such as communications, occur throughout the entire process of managing the transaction. In addition, as a general matter, changes necessary for integration should occur sooner rather than later. Synergy values, whether in the form of cost savings or revenue enhancements, erode or disappear if not realized quickly and effectively. Changes in management structure or reporting relationships, and layoffs, should be announced and implemented as soon as possible. Further, the integration process should be used to integrate not only business operations but also corporate cultures, as well as dealing with important stakeholders. Although most companies generally do a good job of communicating with employees, effective integration planning also includes communication plans to the various external stakeholders involved, including capital markets, customers, suppliers, regulatory bodies, and geographic communities, explaining the benefits of the deal and how the various stakeholders would be affected. If Bank A and Bank B had planned properly before closing their merger, the integration process would have anticipated competitive response and included activities for branding, product offerings, marketing communications, and personal contact with important customers that would have allowed it to be nimble in reacting to those relationship-based depositors who decided to take their money elsewhere.

How Does an M&A Process Work?

M&A opportunities can occur unexpectedly and must be evaluated quickly. As described above, adopting a business management approach to an M&A transaction can help balance urgency with judgment.

Many large and experienced acquirers frequently have an institutional capability for managing M&A transactions. Most middle-market companies do not. Although a process can be built around an unexpected M&A opportunity, it is better to think ahead about process as part of a corporate strategic plan that identifies areas where strategic goals can be served through mergers or acquisitions. Regardless, once that process is established, even if it arose as a result of a company's first M&A experience, that company will thereafter have a competency that can provide competitive advantage going forward.

The sequence of most M&A transactions proceeds through customary and predictable stages, starting with an agreement in principle that typically sets a price and provides a basis for both sides to feel that the investment of additional time and significant costs is justified. Then begins the traditional due diligence phase in which reams of documents are reviewed and hours of discussions occur focusing on financial statements, public reports, material documents, and other facts and circumstances, as a basis for ferreting out undisclosed potential obstacles to accomplishing the transaction. At the same time, the drafting of definitive agreements begins in anticipation of final negotiations of the specific terms and conditions once due diligence has been completed. Upon execution of definitive agreements, attention turns to satisfying the parties' obligations to completing the deal, including obtaining the approval of stockholders. Once all of those conditions have been satisfied and the transaction closes, the deal is usually considered done.

So how does an M&A process differ from that model? Although each transaction has its own unique problems and circumstances, there is a sequence of broad, observable differences between M&A transactions that are "processes" and those that are not.

Stage One: Preliminary Synergy Values

Before anything else can occur, there must be an initial assessment of the potential synergy values that may arise from an M&A transaction, how those values support strategic needs, and how those values may be captured. The problem is that these preliminary decisions, especially as to price, are always made with less information than is needed to be reliable.

The key to determining the "best" price is based upon how much synergy value actually exists. There is no single correct price. The more synergy values an M&A transaction can generate, the higher the maximum price can be, as long as the business discipline is in place to accurately calculate synergy values or change course if the numbers don't make sense. Many companies get locked into a price before they know enough to make intelligent decisions about synergy values. It is important to recognize that the initial assessment of synergy values will probably change as the transaction progresses, so it is important to leave enough room for final pricing to reflect the outcome of the enhanced due diligence phase.

Where the target company is public, an initial assessment of potential synergy values can be made based upon publicly filed reports and financial statements, and industry data. When a non-public company is the subject of interest, confidential information must be made available for review before any meaningful assessment of interest can be made. Sometimes a non-public company has retained financial advisers to solicit interest under a confidential marketing document. Where that does not occur, pursuing an M&A transaction with a non-public target company that is not contemplating being acquired will require that there be some arrangement to share a limited amount of non-public information, under a confidentiality agreement, to allow a prospective acquirer to make an informed assessment of whether sufficient potential synergy value exists to support a decision to proceed further.

It's also important for acquirers to note that auction opportunities, even though confidential information is always provided in those transactions, are nonetheless risky since the bidder may find itself competing with the most careless of its competing bidders. To win that battle is to lose the war and end up owning a company at an inflated price above that which only the dumbest bidder was willing to pay. For that reason, many experienced acquirers will not participate in auction opportunities, or if they do, they do so with rigorous discipline, prepared to walk away the moment the price exceeds the perceived synergy values involved.

Stage Two: Preliminary Discussions

Most M&A transactions among middle-market companies are negotiated combination transactions in which the benefits, or disappointments, of the combination will be shared. Although it is usually unwise to establish a firm price early in the process, it is important to address certain critical issues, one of which is the decision to pursue the transaction as a process in which both companies will participate. Despite the desire to nail down the "best" price as soon as possible, the "best" price is not always clear until there is confidence in the likely synergy value.

As a result, companies using a process management approach to M&A transactions view early negotiations as a time to work together to determine whether there is a price at which the deal is mutually advantageous. Developing good personal relationships early on will reap benefits in the later stages of the deal, especially at final negotiations. Therefore, despite the temptation to get detailed, it is better at this stage to enter into preliminary understanding on certain critical items, including perhaps a preliminary pricing estimate based upon a review of confidential information, and otherwise only agree to pursue exclusive negotiations, during a specified period of time, while enhanced due diligence commences.

Stage Three: Enhanced Due Diligence

The next stage, due diligence, is customarily a time-consuming and mundane process. Not surprisingly, therefore, much of the work at this stage usually gets delegated to accountants, lawyers, and financial advisers. In most cases, traditional due diligence is usually an information-gathering process delegated to a group of people toiling away in back rooms. The traditional process is usually not used for its potential to formulate strategy or build valuation. In addition, the people doing the due diligence investigation seldom participate in negotiations or the integration process.

The management process approach of enhanced due diligence is different. Under that business process approach, the due diligence team, under the supervision of an M&A manager, can tie their investigation to business planning, deepen knowledge about the other company, and test preliminary assumptions about potential synergy values. The team members participate in due diligence as part of the business planning associated with the M&A process.

Under this approach, the due diligence team serves an entirely different function from traditional due diligence. Instead of disbanding, never to be heard from again, upon completion of the typical information-gathering exercise, the team that performs enhanced due diligence under the business process model provides continuity to the transaction in many important respects. Maintaining continuity among those who have done the enhanced due diligence, those who negotiate the final terms, and those who will ultimately be involved in achieving the anticipated benefits contributes significantly to maximizing the economic benefits of the deal.

Stage Four: Final Negotiations

A typical mistake in many M&A transactions is the failure to prioritize among critical issues during negotiations. Under the business process model, the importance, and therefore the priority among those concerns, will have been considered during the process of enhanced due diligence tied to business planning, and members of that team will be at the negotiating table to support negotiations and explain how synergy values are tied to the open issues list. Negotiations frequently stall in many mergers and acquisitions over terms for which, in many cases, there are clearly identifiable and objective tradeoffs involved in one approach or another, but the negotiators aren't aware of the underlying synergies at stake.

The business model approach facilitates fruitful negotiations in two ways. First, the relationship capital built up in the earlier stages provides a basis of goodwill that may be important in surmounting obstacles during negotiations. Second, both parties are operating with better knowledge about the amount and nature of the synergy values to be shared in the business combination, with members of the due diligence team at the negotiating table to discuss those values. These attributes tend to make for intelligent negotiations between people who are striving to find a mutually beneficial basis for reaching agreement.

This negotiating approach is sometimes disliked because it makes it more difficult to gain a negotiating advantage over someone who is deemed to be less well informed. However, experience shows that, particularly in the kind of combination transaction that typically occurs, those negotiating advantages are usually illusory. Realistically assessing synergy values and capturing them through effective integration planning are much more difficult to do without full participation by both parties.

It is important to remember that getting a "good" deal is more than obtaining the "best" purchase price. High-premium deals can be more economically beneficial than low-premium deals. What matters more is what the deal is actually worth to the two parties involved based upon a realistic assessment of synergy values and strategic needs.

Stage Five: Effective Integration

Usually, once definitive documents have been finalized, much of what was learned in traditional due diligence is set aside and forgotten. The better practice for ensuring that anticipated benefits are realized is to commence comprehensive integration planning as soon as negotiations have been completed. While others focus on the formal steps necessary to close the transaction, the due diligence team can transition into developing plans for capturing the synergy values it identified during the enhanced due diligence phase. If there is continuity between the team doing enhanced due diligence and the team planning for integration, the odds favor a successful maximization of economic benefits because the integration team, under the supervision of the M&A manager, started thinking about integration while they were verifying synergy values during the earlier phase.

Synergy values can be fully realized only if they are quickly captured. Obviously, capturing particular synergies may take longer or require different timing than others, but the general rule remains true: the sooner the better. In addition, effective integration includes communication planning throughout the M&A process to ensure that the concerns of interested stakeholders are addressed with relevant information at the appropriate time. Once the deal is signed, it needs to be "sold" to stockholders, regulators, the capital markets, suppliers, customers, and others. Remember those relationship-based depositors of Bank B who were not sold on the reasons they should stay.

If the business process model has been followed throughout the transaction, a fully articulated integration plan, which includes specific actions under a proposed timetable, will be immediately implemented at closing by an integration team that has been thinking about synergies since the early stages of the deal. It is not unusual for integration to take a full year to implement, and during that period, the combined company is in the best position to address the unanticipated problems that inevitably arise during integration under what has, by that time, become an institutionalized business process for successfully managing an M&A transaction to maximize the economic benefits of the deal.

John C. Grosvenor is a partner in the law firm of Manatt, Phelps & Phillips LLP. His practice focuses on the representation of public and private companies, primarily in the areas of mergers and acquisitions, corporate finance and securities, and business transactions.

Apart from law practice, Mr. Grosvenor has also had broad business experience as a senior executive in both middle-market and Fortune 100 companies, managing business development, marketing, and external affairs functions.

Navigating the Process Toward the Right Result

Gus M. Dixon

Partner

Nelson Mullins Riley & Scarborough LLP

My Background

Our transactions generally involve representing private companies, although we have represented some public companies in merger and acquisition (M&A) transactions. Most of the deals we have worked on in South Carolina are in the $10 to $100 million range, and that is generally where my practice area focuses.

For the last few years, I have helped give a seminar in South Carolina with a partner at another law firm here in town, an investment banker who focuses mainly on the middle market, and an accountant who focuses on the middle market. We usually bring in a businessperson or two, a chief financial officer or chief executive officer, who have been through a recent M&A deal, because they help confirm the accuracy of our comments regarding M&A transactions. Most businesspeople are used to getting some level of advice, and then they make their own business decisions. However, in the M&A area, the lawyer's view of things takes on more significance because there are lawyers on the other side of the deal and we generally know how the lawyers for the other side are going to think and approach the deal. The businessperson in his or her day-to-day business dealings does not necessarily have to interface as much with lawyers, but the M&A area is very lawyer-intensive.

I give this as background because when people ask what we do and how we can help them in the M&A area, I answer that, on a global basis, we help people effectively buy or sell a business. When you examine it further, what we do is help a client better understand the process so the client can have the appropriate expectations and so we are better able to work with the client to manage and navigate the process so the process gets to the right result. Business folks need to realize that an M&A transaction is typically filled with lawyers and other professionals. To that extent, in order to more effectively assist clients, if possible, we need to be able to get with them before the letter of intent stage to help them better posture themselves. We need to help them find what their strengths and weaknesses are, to hopefully clean up as many of the weaknesses as we can and then figure out a strategy for emphasizing the strengths and addressing the weaknesses that exist. In addition, many significant decisions are sometimes made at the letter of intent stage, and it is important that a client obtain appropriate advice before these decisions are made.

The M&A Practice

Primarily, we aid with the overall process. We help a client understand, "Here is what you are going to be presented with, here are the issues that will need to be addressed, and here are the things you are going to have to talk about." When we are able, we typically meet with the client with typical M&A documents, and to varying degrees we walk the client through a sample due diligence list, letter of intent, and acquisition agreement, including the representations and warranties, and we explain that the representations and warranties will likely need to be backed up by indemnities. We explain to them that the indemnities really have three primary purposes:

1. To help the buyer understand what they are buying (The buyer has an idea, but the representations and warranties help the buyer firm up exactly what it is—what good things the buyer is getting and what bad things the buyer is exposed to.)

2. To make sure the sellers have the appropriate focus and attention to detail (It is easy for a seller to say things about the seller's business, but it gets harder when the seller starts getting pinned down and understands that the seller will potentially be financially liable if the seller is wrong.)

3. To generally allocate known and unknown risks between the buyer and the seller

As part of having this conversation with the client, what we are really doing is breaking it down to the nuts and bolts of where lawyers spend a large amount of their time in M&A transactions and helping the client understand the significance of these areas to getting the deal closed and the financial significance to the client. We help the client understand that the legal language reflects the business deal. We explain that the diligence and the representations and warranties that result from the diligence will be a significant part of the buyer's decision to buy the business, and that the overall process will help the seller decide whether these are people the seller really wants to sell the business to. The more we discuss that on the front end and help clients better understand the roadmap, the better off they are. Overall, what we point out to them is that M&A deals are very much relationship-driven and that the process significantly impacts the relationship. We try to help them better understand the process so they hopefully are (1) not caught by surprise by issues that upset or irritate them, (2) better prepared to address what their positions are on sensitive issues, and (3) in a position to best interface with the buyer or the seller, as applicable.

In this regard, it is critical that the client assemble the right team and use that team effectively. Sometimes we are asked by the client to help assemble the team, which we are glad to do. It is important for the client to determine who is going to negotiate the deal points. Do they use an investment banker as an intermediary, do the owners negotiate themselves, or do they use a non-owner officer, if available? There are almost always difficult deal points to negotiate, and these can place a strain on a newly developing relationship. It is important to remember that usually if a deal is going to be successful after closing, the relationship needs to work. Accordingly, having the right person negotiating can be very important.

As part of the introductory process, we generally provide the client a general estimate of timing and costs. Although these are difficult to predict (and certain aspects of this are out of the client's control, particularly if the client is the seller), it is important for the client to have as good a sense as possible with respect to these issues.

We have done some deals in the private area that involve stock of the buyer as the consideration, although most of the deals we do involve cash. In the public deals we have worked on, the stock generally worked out well. A good number of those were banks acquiring smaller banks. One of the challenges associated with stock consideration is that the deals can get much more expensive because you have the securities overlay, particularly in the public company context. You also have issues on the selling side, among other things, as to whether you are getting a good deal on the stock. And you have opposite issues on the buying side, among other things, as to whether you are giving the stock at too low of a price.

In the private company context, we are relatively leery of stock, particularly these days. A good number of the deals we did for stock were roll-ups that were ultimately going to go public, or sell, and these generally did not turn out well. We saw people who basically sold a good company, lost control of it, and ended up with pieces of paper in a larger but illiquid company. Generally these days, we are seeing more cash deals and more of a focus on employment agreements and covenants not to compete.

Our market is driven primarily by strategic buyers such as buyers looking to expand geographically, looking for complimentary products, or filling a part of their supply or distribution chain. As a result, we have not found our market in South Carolina for M&A work to be particularly sensitive to the economy either way. Obviously, buyers need to have the cash, because typically our deals are cash deals, so companies either need to be in favorable cash positions or need to be able to borrow or raise money. The willingness of banks or other sources of funds to loan these buyers money or invest in them is different in different economic climates, and that does affect the deals being made. Four or five years ago, we were doing a good number of technology M&A deals, some for stock and some for cash. We are not doing a lot of those these days, but that is more because of the general state of the technology industry. What drives the economic climate in our area these days, more than anything, is how a particular industry is doing at the time.

The Process of an M&A Transaction

As previously discussed, if a client came to us on the front end and wanted our help to buy or sell a business, we would advise the client to assemble the right team and conduct an analysis of the client's business, including an analysis of its strengths and weaknesses. Then the client would need to determine the overall approach as to how the client is going to go out and find appropriate candidates. Then the client would need to determine how to appropriately contact those candidates. After that, you get into the documenting aspects of the deal, which includes a confidentiality agreement, an appropriate letter of intent with the right level of detail, due diligence, and negotiation of the acquisition agreement. Then comes the closing with the attendant closing documents, and the post-closing.

The different steps to structuring the deal and the factors that affect the deal all have some financial impact on the end result. Our firm attempts to assist clients by guiding them through the pitfalls and problem areas that could easily result in a negative financial impact to them.

One of the areas in which we can add value to our clients, particularly if we are involved before they even decide to sell, is enabling them to structure things properly. Among the top legal mistakes we frequently see is unclear ownership of the company, or not having your technology properly licensed or protected. We have been involved in deals where it was unclear who owned what. Generally, the cleaner your company is, the better you are able to sell it and the better price you are able to obtain for it.

Another thing we help clients do is strategically think through where they think they fit in and who the best buyers for them might be. As discussed above, we also help them figure out who the right team is to help them get where they need to go. Does the chief executive officer try to find a buyer, or does the company bring in an investment banker? What is the team that will be used to help market the company, and how is the company going to be marketed? We help on the front end with these issues, which can significantly impact the ultimate value received for the company.

We can also help clients with how they are structured from a capitalization perspective. It is generally easier to sell a company that is owned by a few people than one owned by many. Addressing these types of issues on the front end can help posture a company much more effectively for a sale.

When we get into the deal on the selling side, we prefer to talk to a client on the front end to help them better understand that not dealing with problems up front may be worse than letting them wait. However, there are a variety of strategies and approaches to selling a company and dealing with the different issues.

We have generally found that at the beginning of the deal, the buyer is usually more desirous of buying than at the end of the deal. Businesspeople frequently prefer to push hard issues off until the end, but the problem is that at the end, the seller has the momentum of the deal pushing the seller to closing, but the buyer has likely found problems and may be starting to get a little uncertain. We find that if we can pin things down better on the front end and put deals on a relatively short fuse, there is a much better chance of closing and you have a much better chance of getting an economically advantageous deal than if you let those issues float. We are seeing buyers generally spending more time and money on diligence, and we are generally seeing the momentum of the deal not carrying deals through, particularly on the buying side, as much as they used to. Accordingly, we are seeing fewer deals close. We are seeing that if deals do close, if the sellers have not properly positioned themselves for the sale and properly managed the process to get the buyer to close, the sellers are selling at a lower price than they expected when everything started.

Part of this is that as a transaction drags on, the seller gets distracted from running the business and the business can significantly suffer. Accordingly, getting a deal to closing as soon as practical not only helps ensure the previously agreed-to purchase price, but it also better protects the business itself. A critical mistake a seller can make is assuming a deal is done at the letter of intent stage. There is still a great deal of work and negotiation to do after the letter of intent is signed.

Handling Problems that Make Deals Fail

A failure to integrate the two businesses is often a contributor to deals failing to succeed. Recently, there seems to have been a lot of press about synergies not working out between businesses as people anticipated. Integrating different businesses is much more difficult than people expect. Many acquisitions now are in areas that involve technology, which can be more complicated and can lead to expensive mistakes. We have done deals where people do not conduct appropriate diligence and end up paying significant amounts of money attempting to fix these problems post-closing. Because of this, I think buyers have grown much more sensitive on the diligence side. The more diligence you do on something, the more problems you are likely to find. We try to explain to clients that it is not personal, but the buyer is getting ready to spend a significant amount of money and wants to kick the tires pretty hard. I think M&A deals have not gone as well for people as they expected, so there is a lot more work done both on the diligence side and on the synergy side than there used to be.

You can only do so much with paper. The relationship and the cultures have to be there or the paper does not seem to matter that much.

Many strategies to make sure the deals do go through are client-driven and dependent upon the client understanding and accepting the process. One of the reasons I enjoy giving my aforementioned seminar is giving people a chance to sit and hear business folks say, "Look, they are not making this up." Businesspeople can view lawyers as impediments, thinking the lawyers are in the way of the deal. They come to lawyers and sometimes it appears as though all the lawyers want to do is slow and complicate their deal. What we try to do is help the businessperson understand that we are here to help and we know how to get deals done. However, the client needs to have a realistic understanding of what the process is going to be and that, unlike most types of business deals, there is a component of the lawyers being involved that you are only going to be able to drive so hard, particularly if it is a small business selling to a large business. If we can get the client to understand the process, what issues are going to arise, and what positions the client wants to take on those issues, we try to address many of them up front at the letter of intent stage. If they realize early on that when raising these issues they are not getting the responses or the comfort level they want, they can stop the process early rather than spending a great deal of time, money, and energy on a process that ultimately fails.

We have seen deals start with a high price and then go down, compared to a belief of some businesspeople that if they can get the sale in the door, they can sell up from there. We do not really see that often in M&A transactions. You do not see many M&A prices going up, so we try to get them to address those issues up front to be sure this really is the deal they want to do and that they are comfortable with it. After that, we drive the deal very hard, because in my opinion, the longer you let a deal float, the more problematic it becomes. People start expressing more concerns about it, and more issues start coming up.

What you have to do is drive hard but be reasonable. M&A deals do take time, and buyers are generally going to take the time they need to get comfortable. During this process, it is important for the seller to stay as focused as possible under the circumstances on the seller's business. We see deals where the owners get so distracted that the business falls apart, then the buyer wants a big discount, the seller refuses to provide the discount, and the seller is left with a much worse business than it had before starting the process. If we can get everyone on board and get the right team together, get a good understanding of the process and what the important deal points are, we try to get through those important deal points quickly with an established closing. However, we also try to get our clients to realize you have to be willing to walk away and you have to keep yourself in a position where you can.

The Role of Due Diligence

Due diligence can contribute to keeping a deal alive or warn the participants away from pursuing the deal. If we are on the buying side, one of our first questions is: Why are you buying this business, and what are you expecting to get out of it? That is where you want to focus. For example, assume we have a buyer who wants certain technology it believes the target company owns. After we get involved in diligence, it turns out the seller does not have any protected technology. We ask the buyer, "Do you think it is these people's know-how you are buying, or did you think they had actual property with certain protections?" If they say it is the people, we focus on the people. If they say it was protected technology, the buyer may need to walk away.

Although some diligence, such as ownership of the company, will generally apply in any transaction, certain diligence will be more deal-specific. For example, with respect to a bank acquisition, you spend a great deal of time with the customer base, the risks of the market, the quality of the loan portfolio, and the bank's relationship with its regulators. It depends a great deal on the industry and what is perceived to be the value of the business.

There are also considerations like risk management, which involves discovering what skeletons might be in the closet. These items may be related to the business's industry or may be more general business problems such as an employee benefit plan that does not comply with applicable law, a problematic business venture, or the headquarters building having been built where a gas station used to be. Often, the client will say, "We can go in and look at the business issues, such as the loan loss ratio or the medical cost ratio, but we want you to look at the other risks." For example, we frequently look at risks relating to the ownership of the business. Does it look like the person who originally owned 50 percent of the business and was supposedly bought out years ago still owns the business?

There are a myriad of ways to approach due diligence. I have seen clients send in due diligence lists with a request that documents be sent back indexed to the list. I have seen data rooms set up where the company being acquired puts the requested documents and the acquirer's team comes to do its diligence. I have seen large teams of people come on-site and visit. Recently, virtual data rooms have become more frequently used where information is uploaded and remotely accessible. There are pros and cons to all of these approaches. What I generally like to see is a large data dump on the front end, whether through hard copy or virtual, followed by in-person interviews and visits. This approach enables the diligence team to be much more up to speed before the interviews, so hopefully the diligence interviews are more efficient and effective.

Strategies and Factors Affecting the Financial Bottom Line

Along with good research and preparation, one strategy we use to ensure a successful deal and financial success for the resulting company in an M&A transaction is to focus heavily on the relationship.

If you are on the buying side and you begin to get the idea you are significantly irritating the people you are acquiring, or if the people you are acquiring are not real cooperative and spend more time worrying about their vacation time than implementing the business strategy, you need to look at whether the deal is going to work. These deals work or do not work primarily because the people you are acquiring are properly integrated. Frequently, you are obtaining people and their know-how, so if those people are not going to properly integrate, you really need to think about whether to do the deal. I think what you find, over and over, is that the deals worked on paper, the synergies were there, the business plan was there, but you did not have the right people implementing it.

We represented a large, publicly held company that bought many smaller privately held companies, and I remember thinking in some of those deals that the personalities would not mesh. It was clear some of the more entrepreneurial sellers would not do well in a larger and more bureaucratic environment, and this did create a number of difficulties post-closing.

Some banks seem to have figured out the relationship issues a while ago. I remember a successful bank chief executive officer telling me the first issues he addressed in a possible merger transaction were the "social issues." Are the executives being acquired comfortable with their jobs and with the culture of the organization? Will the acquired company's people fit with the acquiring company's culture? He told me there were certain banks that, although attractive on paper, he would not approach, because they did not fit with his bank's culture. It appears the ones who got it right in the banking industry did well, and the ones that did not focus as much on the culture ended up with some significant challenges.

Government rules and regulations need to be taken into account, because the limitations or requirements they impose can influence the success of an M&A transaction. There is the Hart-Scott-Rodino filing relating generally to antitrust concerns, but that threshold has been pushed up so high we seldom in our market have to deal with it. Hart-Scott is a global regulatory requirement that needs to be dealt with if your transaction falls within its applicability. In addition, if securities are involved in the transaction, you may need to deal with state and federal securities regulations.

Our focus on regulatory approvals is typically more industry-based. If you do something in the banking area, you have state and federal banking regulators to deal with. If you do something in the insurance area, you have the state insurance regulators and you have a lot of federal laws relating to the insurance industry. In the health care area, you have a lot of state and federal laws.

As I said before, for us it is more industry-specific as to what regulations relate to the M&A transaction, and those vary significantly between notices, approvals, and other requirements.

Technology industry deals can be relatively straightforward from a regulatory perspective. Sometimes we will have copyright, patent, or trademark issues that need to be worked through. From a diligence perspective, those have become much more important, such as whether you are infringing and similar issues, but from the perspective of having a regulator hold up a deal, in our deals there generally have not been that many issues to deal with.

In addition to the costs and issues associated with the regulatory approvals, the problems with a long, detailed regulatory process are primarily twofold. First, it can cause the public to know you are doing your deal, and it gives people plenty of time to cause you problems. Second, it is very difficult to walk away from the deal, because it is tough to say, "We are going to compete with this company," while the world knows, at least at one point, you were going to sell to them. It can be very challenging to consider M&A deals in an industry where drawn-out regulatory approvals can make it much more difficult to get a deal done and walk away from a deal once that deal begins.

Publicity, whether press releases or rumors, can have both positive and negative impacts on a deal. At the last seminar where I spoke, informing employees about a pending deal was probably the most hotly discussed issue. Business owners feel a great deal of loyalty to their employees and generally like to keep them informed. However, there is also the issue that generally as soon as two people know something, it is going to get out. One of the more interesting answers I heard was that a chief executive officer of a small business generally should tell his or her constituents the business is always for sale if the right offer comes along. That way, if someone came in and asked if the chief executive officer was considering selling the company, he or she could honestly answer, "Yes, if the right offer came along."

Generally, what we suggest is if the owner has a couple of executives he or she trusts, the owner should keep it relatively close with them until he or she reaches the letter of intent stage. At the letter of intent stage, based on a variety of factors, including the likelihood of the deal and the competitive disadvantages that may arise if word gets out that you are potentially selling, clients should consider calling an employee meeting and telling them about the letter of intent and why the client is excited about it. Sometimes we advise them to include only the next level of managers and try to keep it as quiet as possible. It really is a fact-specific question, but it can be very important.

In making this decision, however, the client needs to be aware that it is very difficult to keep things confidential. I am not sure we have ever seen a deal get to closing without news of the sale spreading at least somewhat through rumor. Secrecy is very difficult. We do tell clients they ought to work to properly inform the right people at the right time, but you have to assume the word is going to get out, and if you want to control the spin on it, you have to make sure you get the word out before it otherwise leaks.

Another factor that affects the financial results is the size of the acquired company. In the technology area, a number of the clients we represent were relatively small, and what you were really acquiring were the people. I would see a lot of diligence spent on things that, in my opinion, did not matter, and all it really did was upset people until I expect some were thinking, "I just cannot wait until the deal is done and then coast until I can quit." If the acquirers knew that, they never would do the deal, because they wanted the people. So when buying a company where the people are really important, you need to remember while conducting diligence and negotiating that those people are important to you and those relationships matter.

On the flip side, a lot of times when smaller companies are being bought by larger companies, you have to decide whether the small company is going to fit individually, operationally, and otherwise. For example, culturally, will the personalities of the people work within the organization? As mentioned previously, it can be very difficult integrating entrepreneurial owners into a larger, more structured organization. Another example of cultural challenges can occur with banks. In a small bank, a loan officer may better be able to deal with people based on relationships and past experiences. In a large organization, more objective criteria may need to be used.

In addition, operational issues can arise on a number of fronts. For example, one of the more unsuccessful deals I have seen was when a large company bought a small company that dealt with products in a particular area where the large company was held to a higher manufacturing standard. This led to a great deal of the acquired product not being able to be sold. Obviously, this led to post-closing difficulties between the buyer and seller.

These issues have to be anticipated and dealt with ahead of time to prevent negative financial impact on the deal.

One strategy for financial success in a deal is to have an overall solid integration plan before the deal closes. Frequently, the buyer and seller know the company better than they will ever know it when a deal is getting ready to close because of all the due diligence that has been done. If the parties, as part of that process, can hammer out the integration plan and how they are going to address various issues, there is a much greater likelihood of the deal being successful.

The problem is that if you are selling your company, you want to deal with the issues that are important to a successful sale of the company, which does not necessarily mean at that point you are going to want to talk about difficult integration issues. You may decide to worry about protecting your key people and other issues once the deal closes. What you do not want is for the buyer to say, "Fine, if you want to keep that operations facility open, we will need to take $1 million off the purchase price."

My firm does sometimes get involved in advising clients regarding what the resulting company will look like, but the depth of the involvement depends on the relationship with the client. Clients use us in different ways, and much of that depends on whether this is a long-standing client or someone relatively new to us. Many times, clients come to us after they have signed a letter of intent and they just want us to get their deal closed. The sellers decide to let the buyer worry about how the synergies work out.

On the buying side, we sometimes spend a lot more time discussing the shape of the resulting company because typically, if you have a client who is looking to do an acquisition, that client is doing it as part of an overall growth strategy. We help them on the front end and then we learn from each deal, so we are much more actively involved in that process.

One thing we emphasize is that, particularly from the buyer's side, integration should be considered before the deal closes. There should be a plan on how everything is being integrated and who is doing what and talking to whom. However, we generally still do not see that consistently being done well. I have seen some companies do it very well, particularly companies that have strong, savvy human resources departments. You see some human resources departments where they generally see only the problems, and then you see some pretty sophisticated human resources departments that come in with practical can-do attitudes. These latter departments really help make things work, because if the acquired employees are happy, generally they are more likely to listen when people talk about the synergies and grand plans for a win-win situation. If the employees are unhappy, they are not real receptive. As previously discussed, it needs to be remembered that M&A deals involve putting people together.

Clauses or points regarding integration can be negotiated into the deal. The typical things we see, sometimes much more detailed than others, are the human resources issues. Often, a seller will negotiate making the seller's employees whole, covering things such as accrued vacation, years of service, vesting, bonus plans, and other such matters. In some deals, a good deal of time is spent negotiating human resources issues. Those issues are very significant, and you see them worked through in different levels of detail, but they are almost always significant issues.

Frequently, but not always, you see provisions relating to how the deal is going to be announced and who goes to and speaks at the announcement meetings.

Another frequent integration area you see addressed is customers and vendors. How do you roll the transaction out to customers and vendors? Sometimes it is nothing more than agreeing to cooperate when the deal closes. Sometimes, particularly when there are representations from the seller regarding customers and vendors, a seller says, "These are the five most important clients, and I want you contractually obligated to take me to talk to them to tell them I am still here and nothing is going to change."

Merger of Equals

I remember someone telling me a while ago there is no such thing as a merger of equals, and that pretty well in any purported merger of equals, somebody is going to be in charge when it is all done. You will see people go to great lengths sometimes to make it look like it is a merger of equals, but generally you will see sooner or later one side or the other ultimately prevails. At the end of the day, many mergers of equals are being done for efficiencies, which means, for example, somebody's operations center is going to get closed or somebody's information technology staff is going to get laid off. As much as it is attempted to be a merger of equals, some people and operations are generally going to get cut, and somebody wins in those and somebody loses.

Example Transactions

A win-win situation I saw was a bank that had been taken over by a couple of seasoned bank executives. They wanted to take the bank to the next level and jump-start themselves by moving significantly into a new geographical location. They found a smaller bank, well connected in its community, and bought that smaller bank for stock. They did a good job of integrating the smaller bank into the larger one. The deal was profitable, provided the bank good publicity, and gave it a good platform to grow. The deal was a good opportunity for the bank's operations team to learn how to grow and integrate the new business. Ultimately, the bank was successful enough where it was noticed by a larger bank and was sold profitably to that larger bank. The seasoned executives who had come to the bank and the people who sold the smaller bank for stock all were financially successful.

A transaction that did not work particularly well was a large manufacturer of equipment trying to acquire networking organizations run by entrepreneurs. Although on paper the transaction made sense, it was very difficult to get the entrepreneurs to function effectively in the larger, more bureaucratic organization.

Although it is likely an unfair generalization, in my experience, lose-lose deals I have most frequently seen are roll-ups. A number of people owning small businesses decide they are going to roll their business up to form a big business and either go public or get bought. The idea, among other things, is to get bigger and maximize and take advantage of efficiencies. These deals are usually very expensive and time-consuming, and they are usually done with stock because the participants are counting on the ultimate payout. Unfortunately, many times the cost, timing, and complexity of the deal are underestimated and the possible opportunities for a successful liquidity event are overestimated. If it does not work, businesses find themselves in this big thing that never really works, it is difficult to get cashed out, and the economies of scale are never realized. So, everybody is in a marriage none of them want to be in, and they are difficult to untangle. These are probably the most common lose-lose situations I have seen.

Summary

In conclusion, understanding the M&A process is critical whether you are on the buy or sell side of a transaction. As part of this, it is very important that the proper team be assembled to assist with the transaction, including the appropriate legal support. Working with an experienced M&A attorney can make a significant difference in the ultimate success of a transaction. Such a lawyer should not only be well versed in the M&A process, but must understand that he or she will have a direct impact on the development of the relationship between the buyer and the seller both during the transaction and thereafter. As discussed above, developing a strong working relationship between buyer and seller is critical to the ultimate success of an M&A transaction.

Gus M. Dixon is a partner of Nelson Mullins Riley & Scarborough LLP and practices in Columbia in the areas of securities, corporate, corporate finance, mergers and acquisitions, outsourcing, and technology. A former chairman of the corporate, banking, and securities law section of the South Carolina Bar, Mr. Dixon frequently writes and lectures on significant corporate, securities, and technology-related issues.

A member of the South Carolina Bar and the Virginia Bar, Mr. Dixon served as an adjunct professor of legal writing at the University of South Carolina School of Law from 1998 to 2002. He has been recognized in Chambers USA: America's Leading Lawyers for Business *for his experience in corporate law/mergers and acquisitions, and in* The Best Lawyers in America *for his expertise in corporate law, mergers and acquisitions law, and securities law.*

In 1988, Mr. Dixon earned a juris doctor, cum laude, from the University of South Carolina School of Law, where he served as articles editor of the South Carolina Law Review *and was a member of the Order of the Coif and the Order of Wig and Robe. He earned a bachelor's of arts degree in American government, cum laude, from the University of Virginia in 1985.*

Factors in Closing a Successful Deal

John F. Cinque

Partner

Fox Rothschild LLP

The M&A Law Practice

For the most part, my firm acts as in-house counsel for smaller companies, both public and private, assisting them in the various stages of a transaction. The main steps of a financially successful transaction are the pre-deal preparation, due diligence, negotiating of the actual deal, and the post-closing items.

Pre-Deal and Due Diligence

The pre-deal is a matter of keeping the company operating on the straight and narrow before getting into negotiations on a deal. This makes things easier when you do get into a deal, and it makes the company more attractive to a potential buyer. Often, the buyer will discount the purchase price for any uncertainties. To the extent that a seller can minimize the risk and eliminate uncertainties, it goes a long way to get the deal done on terms most favorable to the seller.

Negotiating the Deal

The next stage on the selling side is when you have entered into negotiations with a potential buyer. It could be an auction process or a one-on-one sale. When the board decides to sell the company, many public companies, and even certain private companies, will be counseled to put the company up for bid. In this instance, my firm would advise the company to engage an investment banker, put together a confidential memorandum that describes the business and why it would be attractive to a buyer, put together a due diligence or data room, and then go out and solicit bids for the company through its investment banker. This helps the directors satisfy their fiduciary duty to get the best deal possible for the shareholders, and in theory it will drive the price up, which is better from a seller's standpoint.

Once they have engaged the banker, we work with the client to create a data room. Today, most data rooms are created electronically by scanning all of the seller's documents into a secure data site that is password-protected. When creating a data room, a client must balance its desire to retain its important non-public information as confidential against a potential buyer's legitimate interest in understanding the seller's business. We strongly advise that clients have potential buyers sign a confidentiality agreement prior to being granted access to the data room. These agreements usually prohibit the use of the information in the data room (and other information disclosed during the due diligence process) for any purpose other than evaluating the proposed transaction. In addition, these agreements may contain non-solicit provisions whereby, subject to certain limited exceptions, the potential buyer would agree not to solicit the seller's customers or employees. This helps prevent a potential buyer from "stealing" the company's customers and/or employees. With respect to truly sensitive information, we counsel clients to hold such information back until later in the process when they are more certain of a deal. If something is really sensitive or critical to the ongoing success of the company, we do not want to rely solely on the injunctive relief provided for in the confidentiality agreement to protect the company's confidential information. Most buyers understand the sensitive position a seller is in at this stage of the process and will agree to review such sensitive information at a later time. Of course, it would be unreasonable to expect a potential buyer to enter into a binding acquisition agreement without having the opportunity to review all material documents related to the seller's business. A seller must come to grips with this reality if they are serious about completing a transaction. At some point in the process, the seller will have to reveal its most sensitive information to the buyer. We believe a complete and orderly data room makes the company more attractive to potential buyers and may result in a higher purchase price for the seller.

In order to create a data room, we would provide our client with a full-blown due diligence checklist setting forth the corporate information a potential buyer would typically like to review. This information includes:

- A basic organizational structure of the company
- The company's charter, bylaws, or other governing documents
- The company's capital structure, including an ownership table
- Material contracts
- Lists of significant customers, suppliers, and the like
- Lists of the company's assets, including equipment, real property, and intellectual property
- Financing arrangements, if any

A buyer may be very interested in the intellectual property rights of the seller. For instance, if it is a technology business, does the company own or have the rights to use its intellectual property, and does it have appropriate patent and trade secret protections? If it is more of a retail brand consumer-oriented company, are the trademarks adequately protected? Are the trademarks registered with the U.S. Patent and Trademark Office, or is the company relying on common law protections? If it is a manufacturing business, environmental considerations can kick in. Environmental liabilities can create substantial risks for a buyer. If the seller has had environmental issues in the past, it must be prepared to answer a number of questions that will be raised by the buyer and its counsel. Employee matters are also very important and would include:

- Collective bargaining agreements
- Employment agreements, particularly with the company's management team
- Stipulations, obligations, and guidelines in the employee handbook
- Severance provisions if someone is fired
- A list of employees including titles, duties, and compensation
- Parachute payments, if any, in a change of control scenario
- Option plans and how they are affected in doing this deal

In addition to providing information to the potential buyer regarding the seller's business, the due diligence process helps identify the conditions that must be satisfied to close the deal. A number of questions that are relevant to both buyer and seller must be answered prior to closing. For instance, do all employee options accelerate? Is the consent of creditors, material customers, governmental agencies, or other third parties required to do the deal? What kind of approvals do you need under the applicable state's corporate statute? Does the transaction require shareholder approval? If so, can the company act by shareholder consent, or is a shareholder meeting required? If a shareholder meeting is required, the parties will need to build in a window of time (usually about thirty days) between the signing of the definitive acquisition or merger agreement and the closing of the transaction.

If we are on the buying side, we would review the documents in the seller's data room with the buyer to determine what risks or liabilities may be imposed on the buyer after the closing and to understand what consents and approvals will be required to close the deal. This review also helps determine how the deal is structured (i.e., whether it is a stock deal, asset deal, or merger) and what kind of capital structure the company has. Many of these factors dictate how the deal will be structured and what hurdles must be overcome to consummate the transaction.

Negotiating the Deal and Post-Closing Matters

If the seller has decided to conduct an auction, the seller's counsel will often prepare a form of purchase agreement to be reviewed and revised by the potential buyers. A mark-up with proposed revisions to the purchase agreement will be submitted by the potential buyers along with their bid. If a seller is fortunate, they may end up with multiple bids from interested buyers. Besides purchase price and the form of consideration, the prime areas of concern for the parties in the transaction typically center around the breadth and scope of the seller's representations and indemnification obligations, the amount of the purchase price held back as escrow or subject to earn-out, and post-closing covenants such as non-compete provisions. As counsel, we would review the bids, together with the mark-ups to the purchase agreement, to determine which was best, taking into account financial considerations, legal impediments, and likelihood of closing the deal with each particular bidder (e.g., is there a financing condition?). A bidder may give you a top-dollar offer but then impose restrictions or obligations in the agreement that are not attractive. Most sellers want to be sure the buyer does not come after them after the closing, whether for indemnification payments or to enforce restrictive covenants. A seller may reasonably conclude that a little less money today may be a better deal going forward. We assist sellers in making that determination. If we are on the buying side, we would assist in putting together the bid proposal, marking up the form of purchase agreement, and identifying the important legal points for the buyer to consider.

If the buyer and seller are negotiating on a one-to-one basis, we would recommend the parties enter into a letter of intent prior to entering into a definitive agreement. Typically, letters of intent are non-binding on the parties except for certain limited provisions, including confidentiality provisions and "no shop" clauses that are intended to prevent the buyer from shopping the buyer's offer to other potentially interested buyers. As non-binding agreements, letters of intent are helpful in setting forth the basic business terms the parties have agreed to, but not obligating the parties to close the transaction if definitive agreements are not reached. However, most, if not all, states require that the parties proceed in good faith to consummate the transaction.

Once a bid is accepted or the letter of intent is executed, you negotiate the deal. Ultimately, this is what most people view as the role of the lawyers: negotiating the definitive agreements. Typically, these agreements include:

- The definitive acquisition or merger agreement
- The escrow agreement
- Employment or consulting agreements for the seller's management team
- Any other agreements that may be part of a particular transaction, such as distribution or manufacturing agreements

In addition, the parties will also negotiate the content of the disclosure schedules to the definitive acquisition or merger agreement. Generally, the disclosure schedules list exceptions to the representations and warranties made by the seller to the buyer. The disclosure schedules are important to inform the buyer of the current state of the seller's business. From the seller's standpoint, it is important to disclose as much as possible on the disclosure schedules to avoid disputes down the road and to limit the indemnification claims a buyer may have against the seller post-closing.

Even after the definitive agreements are negotiated and the transaction is closed, there may be some post-closing items to attend to, whether clean-up of some pending matters, working capital adjustments, or earn-out payments. Lawyers are usually involved in that process as well. There may be some post-closing conditions or covenants that have to be seen to and often just general corporate and transactional clean-up.

We serve our clients diligently in each stage of the process, because each stage is important for different reasons. It is important even prior to the deal to have everything in order. Many deals have failed because a company did not have its house in order and a buyer came in, was anxious to do a deal, saw a mess, and moved on. It is important to be ready, because even if the market is hot, that can change, and if your house is not in order and you lose an opportunity to make a deal, that can cost you and your shareholders a lot of money.

Factors Affecting Transactions

The way a transaction is structured and the consideration paid can differ depending on the size of the companies involved and whether they are public or private. For public companies that are in the position of buying, many want to use their stock as currency so it does not adversely affect their balance sheet. Instead, they may prefer to keep their cash on hand. If they are cash flush, which sometimes happens, they may not want to sit on the cash, and they may believe they can get a better return by buying a company. In other instances, the buyer may decide to pay a combination of stock and cash for the business. From the seller's standpoint, the required consideration may depend on the owners' personal situations. Is it a family-owned or venture-backed business looking to cash out? Is the management team expecting to remain employed by the buyer? If so, they might be more willing to take stock as part of the purchase price, hoping the stock value appreciates significantly over time.

In any event, I think it is important for a seller to get as much as possible in writing with tightly drafted language, particularly with respect to how the business will be operated post-closing if the purchase price includes an earn-out payment. In that case, a seller will want to make sure it has maximum flexibility to operate the business without unreasonable interference from the buyer. Often, this is the biggest area of contention between the parties. Obviously, a buyer has the right to operate its business, including the business it just purchased, in its own best interest. However, this approach may have a short-term negative impact on the seller's business. If not addressed prior to closing, a seller may become very unhappy with the buyer if it feels the earn-out payments are at risk due to a broader corporate initiative. In an ideal world, the buyer would agree to let the seller continue to manage the business as it deems appropriate in order to give the seller the best opportunity to achieve the earn-out objectives. Unfortunately for sellers, this hurdle is often difficult to overcome. I think in the current economy, M&A transactions have become very attractive for a couple of reasons. I think there is a large amount of cash in the private equity area. In order to satisfy their investors, private equity fund managers often feel compelled to put that cash to work. They certainly do not want to return it to their investors. When that is combined with the fairly small opportunities for initial public offerings and the significant expenses associated with Sarbanes-Oxley compliance in the U.S. public markets, M&A transactions have become a much more viable alternative, particularly in the middle-market space where I do most of my work. With valuations very high right now, many sellers (and their financial backers) believe an M&A liquidity event is the best way to go.

Financial implications are always a large consideration when contemplating a merger or acquisition. However, the parties must consider more than just the up-front purchase price when negotiating the terms of an agreement. Everyone knows of the up-front purchase price reported in the newspapers, but there are more details behind that number to consider. How much is in escrow? There is a big difference between 5 percent of the purchase price being held in escrow and 25 percent. Another consideration is the indemnities. What kind of indemnification exposure do you have, and how long is the indemnification period? Is it capped at a certain percent of the purchase price, or is it limited to just escrow? How long do the representations and warranties survive, particularly tax and environmental indemnities? The reported purchase price may also be subject to adjustments. Is there a working capital adjustment, which is fairly common, or are there earn-out payments? A deal might have the potential to be worth $150 million, but if you only get $20 million up front, maybe it is not so good. How likely is an earn-out payment to be earned? Who controls the operation of the business post-closing? Ultimately, the answers to these questions may determine what you actually get in your pocket for selling the business.

If you are on the selling side, the idea is to get as much guaranteed money as possible, with less money in escrow and less money subject to earn-out payments and indemnification claims. You want to try to minimize your exposure on these issues. Other factors to consider include whether you stay on in the company or leave, if there will be a division of the company in which you have full control, or if you will now have to answer to fourteen layers of management. These are all questions that are specific to a particular deal, but my advice is generally to try to get as much up front as you can. Try to avoid earn-outs if possible, unless the earn-out is similar to a bonus payment. For example, say the deal is for a $100 million purchase price delivered at closing, plus a $10 million per-year earn-out for five years. If you were willing to sell on the $100 million and you are satisfied with that price, you should not have a problem with the earn-out provisions. I often advise clients to assume they will not receive the earn-out payments, because so many things could happen to interfere with them. Rather, the question I ask is simple: Assuming you will get no other payments for the sale of this business, would you do the deal at this purchase price? If not, a seller should reconsider the transaction and try to negotiate a better deal before entering into a definitive agreement to sell the company.

If you are on the buying side, you want a larger escrow amount, earn-out payments as opposed to purchase price delivered at closing, and longer survival periods for representations and warranties. These factors greatly minimize the risk for a buyer.

Although preferable, it is not exactly necessary for a target company to be financially strong in order for an M&A transaction to be financially successful on both sides. For instance, the target company may have great technology, including valid patents, and great people, but it has not yet turned the corner financially for any number of reasons. If a seller's technology is valuable, a larger competitor could come in and want to buy the company just for its technology and personnel as opposed to its past financial performance. A buyer may still be willing to pay a premium for that type of business, even if the price is not justified based on the seller's financial statements. If you own or operate a company that is not financially strong yet owns a valuable product or technology, to get what you want in the deal, you must accentuate the positives. You also want to know who the potential buyers are. Are they financial buyers such as private equity firms or operational buyers who may be competitors? Different types of buyers may have different reasons to buy a business. It is important for a seller to "tell the story" in a way that is most attractive to a particular type of buyer. This may mean a seller focuses on different aspects of its business for different types of buyers. That is why you hire investment bankers. Investment bankers can help a seller identify potential buyers and formulate the seller's story for each particular type of buyer. They can help enhance the value of a seller's business by finding interested buyer candidates and presenting the business to them in a way that is most appealing to them. Sometimes struggling companies make attractive targets from a buyer's standpoint, because they think they can get a better deal now rather than later. For instance, if the struggling company turns things around, the seller will want more money in a future sale.

The Financial Benefits and Consequences of Stock versus Cash

Many different things come into play if there is stock or cash or some combination of both involved in a merger or acquisition. The biggest issue is often the tax consequences that arise based upon the type of consideration paid by the buyer to the seller.

A stock-for-stock transaction is usually done on a tax-free basis (or more accurately, a tax-deferred basis), which means the seller's shareholders would likely not have a taxable event upon the sale of the shares. If they receive cash, it will typically result in a taxable event.

When structuring these deals, you have to be careful. I always recommend that a tax expert be involved. If you try to do a stock-for-stock deal and do not do it right, you could create a significant tax liability for the individuals, depending on the value of the stock. If you received $100,000 in cash as the purchase price consideration, at least you have the cash to pay the taxes if you have a tax liability, but if you receive stock as the purchase price consideration and end up with a tax liability, you may have to come out of your own pocket to satisfy the liability. I have seen instances where a seller ended up with a tax liability with no cash from the transaction to pay the taxes. Obviously, this is a bad result for a seller. Maybe the stock received by the seller was from a privately held company or a public company with very little public float and not very liquid, or the price of the stock starts to decline. When your taxes become due, you may not have the cash on hand to satisfy your obligations. Selling shareholders must carefully consider all of the tax consequences of a transaction and the liquidity of the stock if they are going to receive stock as part of the deal. If it is a private company, they could be locked into that investment for a long time. Even if it is a public company, the stock may not be very liquid. If possible, you want to make sure the stock is registered, which will give the recipient a greater opportunity to liquidate the position in the future. However, this increases the cost of the transaction for the buyer and could delay the closing.

Stock is a viable option if those involved in the deal want it to be a tax-free transaction. Take a scenario where the buying company is an attractive company going forward and its stock is at a reasonable price today. You could see how the sellers would be willing to take their chances and take a ride with the buying company, because they may think the stock is going to be worth a lot more two years from now. If so, they will have stock that is worth far more than what they would have gotten in cash.

Strategies to Maximize Value

Many of the strategies and practices discussed above should help maximize the value of a business being sold. In my view, the less risky a company appears to the buyer, the better off you will be. If there are questions about receivables, potential litigation, or protection of the intellectual property, for instance, the buyer may want to reduce the purchase price to take into account the risk associated with these issues. Some buyers may be willing to take on more risk but then not pay as much. The more you can flush out any questions they have and try to anticipate and be prepared for them, the more comfortable a buyer will be with your business. In theory, this should be reflected in a higher purchase price for the seller.

In addition, the structure of the deal may increase the value to a seller. For instance, is it a tax-free deal? Does the purchase price include earn-out payments? If so, are the targets easily achieved? Also, will management be employed by the buyer post-closing? If so, will they receive employment agreements with severance arrangements? We help identify important issues for the seller to ensure that they receive the best package of consideration possible.

My personal negotiation strategy for obtaining the highest cash value for the selling company is simply to try to be up front. I try to identify the issues my client has deemed important and work with the seller to make sure they get what they want. I am not confrontational or abusive. I am trying to get a deal done, so my approach is to be reasonable and accommodating to the extent I can be. Hopefully, my reasonableness will be considered by the buyer and its counsel when I am taking a strong position with respect to an important issue to my client.

This strategy does not change, regardless of what side I am on. I always try to be reasonable. I think it is important for the lawyer to understand both sides of the transaction. Part of what we do is educate our client. Most times, our client has not gone through this before and will ask if the other side's position is reasonable. I will tell them what is commercially reasonable in my experience. However, even if a client's position is not commercially reasonable, we are advocates for our clients, so it is our responsibility as counsel to fight for the things they deem important.

Legal Aspects and Considerations

Government Regulation

Along with knowing what the clients want, it is necessary to stay on top of developments in the laws that govern M&A transactions. These rules and regulations can influence the financial success of any deal. For the most part, M&A transactions are subject to state law. However, in some instances, the transaction may be subject to federal laws such as the Securities Act of 1933 or the Hart-Scott-Rodino Act, which relates to U.S. antitrust laws. The parties to the transaction may be required to make a filing with the Department of Justice and the Federal Trade Commission if a transaction and the parties are of a particular size. Typically, the required approvals are received within thirty days of filing. However, if the regulatory agencies make a second request for information, it could take much longer. Second requests are often substantial undertakings and can cost the parties a significant amount of money and cause the closing of a transaction to be pushed back for months, sometimes longer. The good news, however, is that only a small percentage of filers are required to provide more information through a second request.

The Securities and Exchange Commission (SEC) may get involved if the transaction includes a public company. For instance, if the buyer is using stock as consideration for the transaction, the seller may require that the stock be registered so it may be freely traded by the seller after the closing.

Also, the seller may have many shareholders, which makes it more difficult for a buyer to rely on a private offering exemption under the securities laws to issue shares of its stock as consideration in the transaction. In either case, the buyer would file a registration statement with the SEC to register the shares prior to issuance. Depending on the scope of the SEC's review, this process could delay the closing for three or four months. Also, if the public company requires shareholder approval, it will need to file a proxy statement with the SEC. Again, depending on the SEC's review and the time required to conduct a shareholder meeting, the parties must be prepared to delay the closing for at least a few months.

Finally, there may be industry-specific government regulations that affect the deal. For example, a merger between two utilities may require the approval of a state's department of energy before the deal can be consummated. This could postpone the closing of the transaction indefinitely. It is important for the parties to understand what approvals are required from the outset of the transaction and to adjust their expectations accordingly.

Representations and Indemnities

When trying to sell their business, sellers often feel uncomfortable disclosing the negative aspects of the business. Rather, they try to focus on only the positive. As discussed above, this is a good approach when marketing the company to potential buyers. However, in the context of the definitive acquisition or merger agreement, full disclosure is the best approach. Too often, sellers will not want to disclose problems because they think it will hurt the deal. If a seller thinks it is important enough to withhold, it is very likely that a buyer would find that information relevant. I do not believe a good foundation for an ongoing business relationship is created by withholding important information from the other party. In addition, disclosure of such problems on a disclosure schedule is a form of insurance policy for the seller. If the problem is adequately disclosed to the buyer prior to the signing of the definitive agreement, typically the buyer is precluded from seeking an indemnity from the seller if the problem creates a post-closing liability for the buyer. At the end of the day, most buyers understand there is good and bad with any business. If a potential problem is significant, I believe it is better to resolve it before the closing. If not, the parties could end up in litigation if the problem arises post-closing. This is not an ideal situation for businesses that have agreed to combine, and it could prove costly to both sides.

If you are honest and open and disclose all details, you can protect yourself against future problems. Full disclosure makes it more likely the deal will get done. This is particularly important when there is a gap between the signing of the definitive agreement and the closing. A buyer will often include a provision in the definitive agreement relieving the buyer of its obligation to close the transaction if there is any material breach of the seller's representations and warranties. A seller can help prevent this by disclosing more at the time of signing, which makes it less likely that a buyer could invoke this provision at the time of closing. As a result, the deal is more likely to close.

Defining Success

When all is said and done, our success is based on our client's success. If a client is anxious to get the deal closed, anything we do that helps facilitate getting that deal closed is a success. If they want to get a deal done, our job is to get them there. Of course, we also have to ensure that they get the benefit of their bargain and that their post-closing liability is minimized. We must understand the client's objectives and determine the best way to accomplish these objectives.

A company engaged in an M&A transaction should never lose sight of its business, especially small businesses. These deals can seem all-consuming. For many of these companies, they are make-or-break transactions, but you still have to service your customers and maintain your relationships with your employees. It is extremely important to continue to operate the business so you can maximize the value of the company when it does finally get sold.

John F. Cinque is a partner with Fox Rothschild LLP. He focuses his practice in the areas of corporate finance, mergers and acquisitions, venture capital, securities, and corporate governance. His experience includes the representation of (i) private and public companies in commercial transactions such as mergers and acquisitions, private placements, public offerings, and loan transactions; (ii) companies on securities law compliance and corporate governance matters including rules and regulations related to 1934 Act periodic filings, the Sarbanes-Oxley Act, and fiduciary duties of boards of directors; and (iii) venture capitalists with respect to portfolio investments and fund formation matters.

Mr. Cinque earned his B.A. from Hobart College, his M.B.A. from the Pace University Lubin School of Business, and his J.D. from the Rutgers School of Law-Newark. While attending law school, he served as managing production editor of the Rutgers Computer and Technology Law Journal. *He is admitted to the bars of New York and New Jersey and is admitted to practice before the U.S. District Court for the District of New Jersey and the U.S. District Court for the Southern District of New York.*

The M&A Lawyer:
A Diverse and Critical Role

William B. Payne

Senior Partner

Dorsey & Whitney LLP

Structuring M&A Transactions

I have been practicing merger and acquisition (M&A) law for a long time, and in my experience, I have represented both buyers and sellers of businesses of all types in connection with M&A transactions as well as handling special assignments. Representations include private companies and public companies, as well as private equity funds and investment banks. In terms of mainstream M&A practice, I am typically involved in the preparation and negotiation of major documents. However, any transaction of consequence is supported by the various specialists we have at our disposal, including antitrust specialists, benefit law specialists, and tax practitioners. This allows us to bring a true team approach to the practice.

Any particular M&A transaction may be approached in many different ways. Some transactions are completed through an extensive process in which a company is marketed by investment bankers (or the country club), which necessitates preparing sales materials, contacting possible buyers, and so on. Others may be initiated privately between parties that happen to be acquainted with one another through industry contacts. Since the approach will depend upon the individual case, it is difficult to point to a single process used in M&A transactions and in turn a single role for the M&A lawyer.

A lawyer's involvement in any particular process may vary significantly. For example, we have many clients who regularly participate on the buy side of transactions, and they are routinely contacted by investment bankers to determine their interests in pursuing potential acquisitions. The bankers send out various teasers and general information, and based upon that information our clients may determine they have no real interest in pursuing that particular opportunity. Those clients never speak with us as lawyers about their determination of whether to pursue a transaction, so we are totally uninvolved in the preliminary decision of whether to move forward.

With other clients, however, we may be asked to become part of the acquisition team in a buy-side transaction from the beginning (or at any point along the way) once the decision has been made to pursue a transaction. How early or late our involvement may come and the scope of our involvement will depend upon the client, the nature of the transaction, and many other factors.

Failing to enlist us early on a sell-side assignment may be a particularly egregious mistake. Too often, the structure of the deal, the materials presented to the other side in due diligence, and imperfections in the business may have adverse consequences to a seller. Some of those problems could have been avoided by advance preparation if we had been involved.

The Financial Implications of M&A Law: Adding Value

To the extent that we are successful in representing our clients in reducing price (on the buy side) or increasing price (on the sell side) through the negotiation process, an M&A lawyer can have a significant financial impact. However, in my experience, lawyers do not typically become involved in price negotiations, which are usually handled by investment bankers and other businesspeople. In certain transactions, and particularly in cases involving inexperienced clients, a lawyer may take the lead in price negotiations, but this is not the norm.

What we need to do as lawyers is take a step back to determine what it means to add value for a client in an M&A transaction. There are numerous studies indicating that, on the whole, M&A transactions are not successful, while there are other studies that indicate these transactions are successful. Fairly recently, an economist who specializes in the M&A field attempted to survey the literature, and he arrived at the conclusion that M&A transactions do generally add value to shareholders. Part of his conclusion, however, was that the sellers of business tend to do much better in these transactions than perhaps they ought to, while buyers of business on average at best are only marginally successful. Of course, when you mix both the sell and the buy side together, M&A transactions clearly produce shareholder value, but that does not support the proposition that strategic buyers of business, on average, are particularly successful.

This is an interesting phenomenon, especially considering that strategic buyers continue to buy businesses despite ample indication that they are not successful. There are many real-world examples, but perhaps the poster child in terms of economic reality was the Quaker Oats acquisition of Snapple several years ago. In this example, Quaker Oats bought a business for billions of dollars and sold it two or three years later for ten cents on the dollar. Quaker Oats lacked the ability to integrate the business acquired and take real advantage of the synergies, and so the strategic acquisition of Snapple did not make good business sense.

There are many such examples of acquisitions gone wrong. How can a lawyer help a client who is bent on making a bad acquisition do a better job of it? This is likely a difficult if not impossible task, but around the margins, lawyers can assist their clients in these transactions by making sure they are thoughtful in moving forward. Lawyers often participate in due diligence on behalf of clients, but more often than not the lawyer is merely a player and does not lead the process. Due diligence should be done thoroughly, and the consequences of the acquisition should be fully thought through, but because these are business decisions—particularly the ability to integrate an acquisition into a strategic buyer—the issues are almost wholly out of the hands of the lawyer.

While a lawyer can offer a client special expertise in certain situations, such as addressing concerns about employee benefits and explaining employment agreements, it is not a matter of what you pay employees, but rather what benefits you realize from the acquired business, that makes all the difference in the world. Lawyers are simply not typically involved in that aspect of an acquisition.

One way lawyers can offer a significant contribution is by involving themselves in negotiating the details of the acquisition agreement, where they can properly set client expectations about the strength of their negotiated agreement and whether courts are likely to enforce its provisions. There are numerous cases in which buyers, feeling aggrieved and believing the business they purchased was not the business they bargained for, have sued sellers. Buyers typically lose these cases. Thus, a critical role of the lawyer is making sure the buyer understands the reluctance of courts to enforce the purchase agreement and, if possible, to maximize the leverage a client has in enforcing the agreement through skillful negotiation and careful wording. On the other side, any lawyer representing a seller should carefully negotiate the agreement to minimize the risk that a complaint could be made successfully against the seller of the business.

A typical claim brought against a seller might contend that the business that was bought was not the business the buyer believed it was buying. Last year, there was a district court decision involving an acquisition of the energy trading business from Merrill Lynch in which the buyer of the business paid a great deal of money and was unable to benefit from the business. The buyer claimed many misrepresentations were made by the seller and brought a suit. Eventually, the court held that the buyer had ample opportunity to do due diligence and should not have relied upon the vague representations it had extracted from the seller, and therefore its claim of being defrauded was nonsense.

Courts are particularly skeptical about sophisticated buyers who had ample opportunity to make their own investigation of a business prior to an acquisition. Courts will simply not accept a suit that is based upon either boilerplate or vague representations that are always contained in agreements. My advice to clients is that if you truly want to be able to prevail in litigation over those agreements, you will have to develop very explicit language to support the strength of your claim against the seller.

Common Buyer Mistakes

For the most part, sellers believe themselves to be most vulnerable to claims asserted against them. Sellers worry that since they have received a great deal of money for a business, should trouble arise, they will be sued by the buyer. However, because sellers typically prevail on those claims, it is in fact the buyers who more often find themselves in trouble in connection with an acquisition.

While buyers often overpay for acquired businesses without having adequate legal recourse against sellers, more importantly, buyers buy businesses when they should not be. They often outrun their capabilities of either evaluating a business to be purchased or of effectively integrating the business that is purchased with their own. The definition of "trouble" for the buyer is often completing a deal that, in hindsight, did not make sense.

Buyers should also be concerned about what would happen once a transaction has been announced but the target business simply goes awry. The buyer should make sure there is a material adverse change condition in the agreement that it can enforce. The problem with material adverse change conditions lies in the fact that if the target's business is in fact headed in the wrong direction, the courts will be reluctant to enforce the termination right. Therefore, any buyer should carefully think through its ability to rely on these conditions, and the provision must be carefully drafted to make it truly enforceable. Too often, buyers erroneously believe a so-called "MAC clause" is tantamount to a unilateral termination right.

I am not suggesting that strategic buyers do not often make great deals. However, the number of deals that are done and do not pan out in the end overshadows the totality of the buy side experience for strategic buyers in M&A transactions. Private buyers and strategic buyers are much different in their approach, and for the most part private buyers do a better job of buying businesses. Although the success formula for private equity fund buyers is certainly not 100 percent, they are playing the odds and are able to gamble that a runaway acquisition will make them a great deal of money. The track record of private equity funds and the returns they have been able to produce for their investors demonstrate objectively that private equity funds on average are doing the right thing.

Influential Agencies in M&A Transactions

There are three main agencies whose rules and regulations are a concern in doing M&A deals. The most obvious and direct is the Federal Trade Commission and Department of Justice in administrating the Hart-Scott-Rodino Anti-Trust Improvements Act of 1976, in which they need to approve transactions of a certain size. However, antitrust enforcement is fluid to some degree. At times it is a high priority, and at times it is a fairly low priority. Basically, the enforcement of Hart-Scott-Rodino in the United States has not proven to be much of an obstacle in recent years. The European Union's enforcement of antitrust provisions is somewhat more dramatic—for example, the recent fine of Microsoft and the rejection of GE's acquisition of Honeywell—and this is something everyone in the business sector needs to be conscious of. Ultimately, however, it is more a hoop to jump through than a true stop sign. For example, some antitrust officials can require that an acquiring business agree to spin off part of the acquired business in order to avoid defined overlapping markets, but that sort of thing is relatively rare.

Another agency that affects the economics of an M&A transaction is tax law. Buyers want to create the highest possible tax basis in the business purchased, because the depreciation and amortization of assets having a high tax basis will produce tax benefits (an expense for tax purposes that will lower taxes) in future years. On the other hand, sellers want to minimize the present payment of taxes. These goals are usually at odds with each other. Buyers are nevertheless willing in certain circumstances to accommodate the desires of sellers, such as constructing a transaction so it is a tax-free reorganization. Careful tax planning is always required to assure that the parties have their expectations satisfied.

The third agency of concern to M&A transactions is the Securities and Exchange Commission (SEC). The SEC only affects a small number of transactions that are done, but it very likely affects a much larger value of transactions that are done. That is to say, most M&A transactions tend to be small, privately negotiated deals in which the SEC has no real jurisdiction. However, with respect to the acquisition of a public company that is registered with the SEC, there are certain points a public company making the acquisition must be aware of. Typically, these have to do with the filing obligations, which are not usually a very heavy burden but can lead to significant delays. For example, when a public company is being sold or when a buyer is using its stock and requires stockholder approval, there is a regulatory scheme by which the SEC will require additional disclosure. This involves a bulky proxy statement that must be submitted to and ultimately approved by the SEC, which can mean jumping through a number of hoops. The proxy statement itself usually does not result in any substantive change in the transaction, but the approval process requires an additional three or four months.

SEC influence becomes more substantive in the case of a tender offer that must meet certain SEC standards. A tender offer must be done pursuant to the SEC rules, and the provisions include a minimum time it must be kept open and the method for approaching the marketplace, among others. While these provisions will likely not affect the value of the transaction, they need to be built into the process. The greatest cost in terms of lost time and risk is due to the delays required by the SEC approval process in the case of a proxy statement, not the tender offer process, which moves rather quickly and typically is not subject to SEC-imposed delay.

The Impact of Publicity

It is becoming increasingly possible for institutional investors, particularly hedge funds that command influence over whether a particular transaction is approved, to affect transactions through publicity or public statements. For instance, there was a transaction announced last fall in which hedge funds and institutional investors publicly disparaged the value of the deal, and ultimately the transaction was abandoned by the parties.

It used to be that stockholders voted with their feet. Upon announcement of a transaction, they might sell off their holdings, but they did not involve themselves in voting against it. That has changed in this day and age, and so it has become increasingly important to demonstrate to the marketplace the value of a particular transaction where a stockholder vote will be involved. Stockholder votes are involved in cases where the buying company is using its stock and issuing a significant number of shares, or in cases where the target company is publicly held, except in the rare circumstance where an exchange offer might be made. A stockholder vote can be avoided, but those instances are rare.

The ability to provide information to the marketplace has become increasingly important. We were involved in a transaction several years ago that I believe represents a dramatic indication of the consequences of this shift. At the time, we were representing a publicly traded target when it agreed to be acquired by another public company. Upon the announcement of the transaction, the acquirer's shares fell dramatically, and by the time the transaction was done, shares were worth 60 percent of what they were worth before the transaction. This was due to the fact that the marketplace considered it a bad deal, and the marketplace was ultimately proven correct when the acquirer went bankrupt.

These are the kinds of forces acquirers must be equipped to handle these days. In fact, the rules now accommodate the ability to feed significant information into the marketplace so it can understand the circumstances surrounding a transaction. This allows the marketplace to see the true value rather than reacting blindly to a perceived and perhaps misunderstood value.

There are a few ways to approach advising companies on making public statements. Those statements need to comply with SEC pronouncements, since public companies are always subject to legal review, and it is the lawyer's job to make certain they comply with the legal standards. In terms of the true content of the statements, what is divulged to the investment community and what is emphasized is a matter of the business case for that particular acquisition. Lawyers will of course caution issuers not to be false or misleading about their business, but typically, the company makes its own business case.

Structuring a Deal: Merger versus Acquisition

In structuring a deal, there are some mechanical points lawyers may be concerned about. For example, if a lawyer is representing a selling corporation in a stock-for-stock deal, there is always the question of how the exchange ratio will be determined. Is it a fixed exchange ratio, whereby my stockholders get two shares of your stock and you get one share of my stock? Is it a fixed value proposition, whereby my shareholders will get $100 million of your stock regardless of how many shares there are? From there, each of these alternatives begets further issues. If we decide upon a fixed exchange ratio, for example, you might impose a "collar" so if at some point in time the value of the stock being used in the deal becomes too imbalanced, either one side or the other can walk away from the transaction. Since this may force a renegotiation, lawyers need to be concerned about the structure of a stock-for-stock deal.

Deal structuring changes in the case of a merger of equals, and the merger normally has some governance issues associated with it that will make the difference. For example, if a giant company acquires a smaller company, it would be unusual for the smaller company to have much leverage over the buying company. However, as the companies become more equal in size, there is usually a willingness to accommodate the needs of the two companies. This may result in a governance structure in which representation is provided from both sides.

A merger of equals used to be thought of as a consolidation, and sometimes in these cases, an entirely new corporation would be set up so the resulting entity would not be perceived as a cultural extension of either of the constituent entities. However, that is fairly rare today due to the tax and regulatory issues that typically favor one of the entities over the other. It is typical to select the favored entity to survive, even though it may not be the controlling corporation. Representation on the board of directors is usually split between the two constituent entities, and in some strange cases, the business might be run by co-chief executive officers, or an agreement might be struck whereby one chief executive officer would be elevated to chairman of the board at some future time with a promise that the chief executive officer of another firm would succeed him or her. There are various ways of structuring these governance issues to keep both parties satisfied that, despite the fact that it is usually one entity surviving over the other, it does in fact appear more like a merger of equals.

Successful Integration: The Importance of Due Diligence

As referred to earlier, a large company is responsible for doing appropriate due diligence before acquiring a smaller company in order to ensure a profitable investment. The process of doing due diligence is often difficult for strategic buyers, and this is one reason why so many transactions fail. What often passes for due diligence is simply an economic or financial analysis that makes various assumptions about how the business that is purchased will be integrated. This is usually done by financial and M&A types. In fact, many strategic acquirers have a separate M&A group upon which they depend for financial analysis.

Since so many assumptions are made about the integration of the business, most buyers don't truly plan for integration or adequately test whether those assumptions can be achieved. By contrast, GE has a process in which integration becomes key to making the acquisition. If it is serious about an acquisition, the person who will be leading the integration becomes part of the M&A team at a very early stage. Rather than simply making the handoff, as many businesses do, GE starts with the proposition, determines how the integration is going to proceed, and has the person involved with the integration continue to lead that unit to be sure it proceeds properly. Eventually, once things are running smoothly, the integrator is reassigned to their integration team. Thus, there is no handoff involved.

The GE example stands in stark contrast to the many clients who do not give proper thought to how integration will work until the deal is closed. In my mind, this is the key to success or failure. I see it as an extension of due diligence, as it forces the company to look at whether it is in fact possible to integrate and achieve the successes that have been postulated in the business. This is a very difficult thing to do, since so often success or failure of integration will depend upon cultural values in the business. While these cultural values are difficult to see and understand, that does not make proper analysis any less vital to the process. Often, those who are doing due diligence need to accept that the business model of the business to be acquired simply cannot fit within the acquiring organization. If the value of the business to be acquired depends upon changing the business model to harmonize with the acquiring organization, and if that change cannot be made, the acquisition will fail.

Other concerns that can arise in due diligence have to do with understanding the basics of what drives the success of the business, and in turn determining whether those driving factors are extendable and will continue to grow in the future. This is not simply a matter of looking at the past financial results, but of being able to create appropriate models that will be able to extend those results into the future. Doing so requires an understanding of where a particular marketplace is going. It often seems to me that financial models are done as a simple extrapolation of what has been achieved in the past, which is an inadequate approach.

The M&A Timeline

Because M&A transactions are tremendously variable, a transaction could take days or years, and it could require one or many steps to get there. Today, companies are typically sold and not bought. There are significant obstacles to identifying and then buying a business. A possible target might be either a subsidiary or a business unit of a public company, or privately owned. As a result, there is no public information regarding the target, and it becomes very difficult for buyers to identify acquisition candidates and initiate a process on the buy side. Further, the buyer can never know whether after a difficult process of identifying such a target, the potential seller would even entertain the notion of a sale (at least at a reasonable price).

Most businesses are sold through a seller-initiated process, which is typically handled with the involvement of an investment banker. The investment banker is hired by the seller of a business to prepare marketing materials describing what the company has to offer, identify a list of entities that might have an interest in purchasing the business (such as industry players, private equity funds, and so on), and contact each of those potentially interested players. At this point, the name of the target is not generally revealed. There is some general information to describe the business, and based upon this information the contacted companies will indicate whether they have any interest in pursuing a transaction.

If there is indeed an interest, the interested company will be asked to sign a confidentiality agreement that protects the information that will be presented. There may be as few as one or as many as dozens of companies who sign this agreement. Those who do will be given a copy of the sales materials that have been prepared by the investment banker. Based upon their review of those sales materials, they will again be asked to indicate whether they have an interest in acquiring that particular business and what their possible range of values might be.

While many businesses will indicate they are not interested, the seller hopes a handful of parties will come forward with a range of values, for example, $200 to $250 million. Investment bankers will then rank the responses, trying to determine who would truly be interested in the acquisition at the best possible price. Through this process, some bidders may be eliminated for having a low bid price or a bad track record of follow-through.

The benefit of being selected as one of the true potential bidders is being granted access to management. Potential bidders will be able to listen to a management presentation in which management will lay out the specifics of the business, and they will be given access to a data room that will contain much of the confidential information about the business. Between talks with management and data room visits, the players will be able to put forth a final bid for the business. Of course, some potential bidders will drop out, but the seller hopes there will be enough left to spark a healthy bidding process. From there, one bidder is selected with which to negotiate the final transaction.

There are numerous variations on the theme of how to conduct a limited auction today, depending on how many bidders you are able to attract and whether there is sincere interest in the target. Many of the steps can be avoided in some transactions, as there is a limited universe of buyers. Assuming there is no public company involved, and depending upon whether the buyer needs financing, the process outlined above can take anywhere from four to six months. If a public company is involved that will require shareholder approval, the process can be longer. There will certainly be cases that are unsuccessful at the end of the day, as no bidder has come forth with an acceptable price, in which case the seller may think about putting the entire business back on the shelf.

A Success Story

Success in M&A transactions is most easily defined as those cases where the seller has received a huge price for a relatively small business that was started from scratch, family-owned, or entrepreneur-owned. This is often like hitting the jackpot in a lottery, simply in the sense that a great deal of money can be made.

One such example from my own experience involved a business that started in a small town and was sold for a large price to a national banking firm. The banking firm was in a business that had a true need for the service model the individual was offering, and as such it was willing to pay a large amount of money. This is another example of how an investment banker can drive value by identifying appropriate buyers and making certain those buyers understand the value of the business. Starting a bidding war is sometimes the best way to ensure that the buyers understand the value of the product or service to the exclusion of other competitors in the same business. Therefore, I would say this example of success was not so much a matter of having a superb lawyer, but a superb investment banker.

William B. Payne is the head of Dorsey & Whitney LLP's mergers and acquisitions practice. He represents buyers and sellers in the purchase and sale of businesses.

A Step-by-Step Overview of the M&A Process

J. Franklin Cable

Partner

Miller Nash LLP

The Components of Mergers and Acquisitions

Depending on the requirements and wishes of our clients, our firm provides the following services to aid in the development and process of a merger or acquisition.

Analyze and Structure the Transaction

We help clients examine their goals for the transaction and develop a structure that meets the goals. Goals vary with the type of buyer and seller. Although the goals of buyers vary widely, they are generally categorized as "strategic" and "financial."

Strategic buyers are generally already active in the target's industry or a related industry, but their goals can vary widely, from simply eliminating industry capacity in a commodity product to augmenting market share of the buyer with an integrated enterprise to expanding a thriving brand the buyer wants to keep differentiated from its own brand. In an acquisition to eliminate capacity, a buyer would be well served by a structure such as a stock acquisition followed by a dissolution that keeps the target as independent as possible in an attempt to protect the buyer from unknown liabilities. In an integrated transaction, even if the target is initially acquired as a subsidiary, it may be subsequently merged into the buyer for operational or cultural reasons and an asset acquisition may be better initially. In a transaction motivated by brand expansion, cultural if not operational considerations may call for a subsidiary structure that maintains an element of independence for the target while, of course, providing for ultimate control in the buyer. Financial buyers are generally operating in a limited timeframe with an exit strategy as an important element in their overall plan. They generally wish to acquire a going concern with cash, maintain or improve it, and sell again in a limited timeframe such as five to seven years. They may be more concerned with a structure that allows equity participation for management and retention of management in general.

Sellers' goals are at least as varied as those of buyers. A simple cash deal may serve the needs of a buyer who just wants out, perhaps with an earn-out component to bridge valuation issues. But many sellers want to "have their cake and eat it too" by gaining liquidity for themselves or additional capital for the enterprise while maintaining control of, or at least participation in, the enterprise. For those who want to remain active in the enterprise, more complicated solutions may be necessary involving issuance of structured securities to private equity firms or, for larger enterprises, perhaps a public offering.

Develop an Implementation Plan

We help find and select other members of the transaction team such as accountants, investment bankers, proxy solicitation agents, media and public relations consultants, environmental consultants, risk management experts, and others who can form a cohesive team. We develop a time and responsibility schedule that assigns duties and lays out the steps of the transaction and the anticipated timing.

Negotiate the Terms of the Transaction

We work with the client's management team and other advisers to negotiate with the other party to try to meet the needs of both sides in the transaction. For example, a public company doing an acquisition may need extensive due diligence to meet fiduciary and regulatory obligations, while a private seller may have privacy concerns and concerns about the effect of due diligence on the business together with limited patience for the process the buyer feels is required. We work to draft letters of intent, access agreements, and confidentiality agreements that allow the deal to go forward and keep it moving as quickly as possible. We interact with counsel for the other party to establish reliable channels of information based on a relationship of trust and mutual interest. The parties may have agreed on the essential elements of the transaction, but they need experienced professionals to deal with the legal, regulatory, and accounting issues that arise from due diligence investigations and document preparation.

Structure and Conduct Due Diligence

We assist in developing a due diligence plan and checklist to structure the due diligence process, and we implement appropriate portions of the plan relating to legal issues. We coordinate the efforts of various parties involved in the process. Typical areas of focus in due diligence are environmental issues, real property title issues, personal property lien issues, Employee Retirement Income Security Act issues, intellectual property issues, corporate governance and security issuance issues, accounting issues, and internal control issues, to name a few. Some of the issues, particularly environmental issues, real property title issues, and personal property lien issues, are investigated initially through third-party experts who provide reports that form the basis for further negotiation by the parties and their counsel to resolve issues raised by the reports. Other issues, such as corporate governance and security issuance issues, are generally investigated directly by counsel. Due diligence is generally the concern of the buyer initially, although it can raise issues that become of concern to the target, and the target is well advised to look for and resolve significant issues in advance to keep the transaction from losing momentum. In a stock-for-stock merger, due diligence goes both ways and is a concern of both parties, particularly in a "merger of equals."

Draft Documents

We draft or review the transaction documents setting out the terms of the transaction and related documents for financing the transaction and obtaining necessary regulatory approvals. This frequently includes coordinating negotiation among a number of parties. Typical transaction documents include letters of intent, confidentiality agreements, acquisition agreements, loan agreements, security agreements, regulatory filings, and closing documents. Public transactions involve other documents such as proxy statements, registration statements, and registration rights agreements. Regulatory filings vary widely from industry to industry, but one common to larger transactions is a Hart-Scott-Rodino filing for antitrust purposes.

Close the Transaction

We orchestrate the timely completion of various aspects of the transaction to meet the closing deadline and conclude the transaction. We also develop a post-closing checklist of ongoing items related to the transaction that will require attention in periods following the closing. While many regulatory filings must be made on a prospective basis, some are done on an informational basis following closing. The same is true of some contractual obligations. For example, some contracts such as leases may require advance notice and consent of the other party, but other contracts may merely require notice following completion of the transaction.

The common denominator in merger and acquisition (M&A) transactions is the pursuit of profit. The financial implications, beyond the basic consideration of purchase price, make it imperative that the deal will be handled with care and consideration for all the variables involved, for both the buyer and the seller. Time is an important factor, whether it is facilitating a speedy and smooth negotiation process or simply reducing the number of man hours expended in research, preparation, or dealing with complications.

Our firm's services are valuable to our clients during an M&A transaction in several ways. First, we help by developing innovative or efficient ways of structuring a transaction that result in transactions that are more likely to occur and be completed more quickly at considerable cost savings. "Time is money" in many ways in an M&A transaction. Of course, many professionals charge based on time, and their fees can be significant. Management time is also money, as is distraction from other aspects of the business. And deals that drag on frequently collapse of their own weight, resulting in a write-off of expense. We may develop structures that avoid regulatory burdens, are more tax-efficient, or otherwise result in significant savings of time or expense.

Another way we help our clients is by organizing the progress of a transaction and selecting other members of the transaction group so the transaction proceeds quickly in an organized fashion. Also, we provide value to our clients through relationships with advisors for the counterparty that are constructive and help us avoid unnecessary friction and loss of time or, possibly, loss of the entire transaction.

Variables Affecting the Deal Structure

There is no way to ensure that a target company will be a profitable investment. There is always an element of risk, because buying an enterprise is not analogous to buying treasury bills. The risk must be evaluated and an appropriate level of return anticipated. Experienced advisers and organized procedures can help reduce the risk, but it will always exist to some extent due to unavoidable business risks. It is not necessary for the target company to be financially strong. The acquiring company can, and frequently does, bring capital or access to capital markets and financial expertise the target lacks, which may account for why the target is the target. Financial buyers in particular seek out struggling companies that need the capital, access to capital, or management expertise they can provide with the goal of improving the value of their investment. Typically in the past, these buyers have insisted on at least a majority interest in the target and a well-defined exit strategy, but market conditions can allow greater flexibility in this area when available capital gives sellers greater leverage.

The integration process is critical to achieving the anticipated financial benefits of a transaction. This involves the integration of physical systems (such as information technology, distribution systems, etc.), the integration of organizational and administrative structures (such as sales and accounting), and the integration of management structures and entity cultures. Culture is frequently overlooked, and its effect is difficult to quantify, but it must be dealt with to avoid distraction or inefficiency in the combined entity. The buyer should plan for integration early in the transaction so preparation for integration can be worked into the due diligence process. The buyer needs a clear plan prior to closing of how all elements of the acquired enterprise, from accounting and intellectual property systems to benefit plans and personnel, can be integrated promptly following the closing. But the seller needs to keep the process from going so far that its employees develop the mentality that they are already working for the buyer. Legal issues can also arise, particularly in an antitrust context, if the buyer in effect gains control of the target prior to closing. These countervailing considerations can be balanced to some extent in the letter of intent or the acquisition agreement, but many of them are so detailed and operational that they must be worked out on a practical basis by the parties. This is another example of the need for the parties and the professionals to maintain a civil and business-like relationship throughout the transaction.

Other financial implications of an M&A transaction need to be considered, besides future profit or the sale price. If the companies involved in the deal are public companies, the effect of the deal on the value of shares needs to be considered. This is especially important if the purchase is accomplished through an exchange of stock rather than cash. Sometimes those involved are concerned over the transaction creating a "discounted" share price. However, a discounted price is relative.

With a public company, the price is generally judged by its relationship to the market price, and a discount seldom occurs. The question is usually how large the premium will be. With a private company, various "comparables" can be developed, but they are never precisely comparable. Discounted prices can result from bad timing for the sale, failure to have adequate records and financial information, unresolved administrative, regulatory, or legal proceedings, or a random approach to the sale process. Retaining experienced and innovative advisors, "detailing" the enterprise before putting it up for sale, and conducting an organized sale process can result in an improved price.

The shape of the company that will emerge from the deal can have an impact on the deal structure. Sometimes an acquisition is publicized as a merger of equals because there are benefits to be had for both the buyer and seller. In theory, a merger of equals could create economies of scale, synergies in operations, and savings in administrative costs that would make one plus one equal to more than two. In practice, cultural issues can offset these benefits. Transactions described as mergers of equals frequently turn out to be something else as one party gains control.

I advise clients considering a merger of equals to focus more on cultural issues at all levels than would normally be necessary, and to spend extensive time with senior management of the other company. It is a rare instance when two chief executive officers can share ultimate authority, and with good reason, as this arrangement can result in loss of management focus. Mergers of equals are more likely to be a success if senior management at one of the companies does not intend to remain with the combined entity or intends to assume some other role in the combined entity. Even in transactions not billed as mergers of equals, the buyer may have a stated goal of incorporating significant parts of the culture or business procedures of the target to modify the buyer's culture or procedures. This is very difficult to accomplish, particularly if the buyer is significantly larger than the target. If articles of merger are filed, the merger is accomplished as a legal matter but the anticipated benefits come only from continuing management efforts. Even the most arduous efforts will not suffice if the structure is wrong in the first place or the relationship of the people involved has been poisoned by a rancorous acquisition process. For example, an inadequately designed contingent compensation arrangement can lead to a failure of integration despite goodwill on both sides.

The size of the companies involved also has an impact on the structure of the deal. Simplicity in the deal structure is an advantage in a deal of any size, but it is critical in a small transaction. Small transactions can be more difficult for a number of reasons, including the emotional involvement of the parties, particularly sellers. This makes speed and simplicity essential, so that sellers who may have mixed emotions about the deal in the first place do not "freeze in the headlights" when confronted with complicated terms they cannot or will not understand. Simplicity also helps keep costs in line with the size of small transactions.

As stated earlier, the sale can be accomplished using stock or cash. There are advantages and disadvantages to either choice, depending on what end results the buyer and seller hope to achieve.

The benefits of using stock include avoiding depletion of liquidity or increased debt. There may also be tax advantages. For example, a true stock-for-stock merger may be a tax-free reorganization, or a corporate seller who gets preferred stock of the buyer may have advantageous treatment of the dividends. The benefits of cash are simplicity and sometimes bargaining power. Which one is best depends on the financial position of the parties in a particular situation. Some buyers may not have cash and may be unwilling or unable to utilize debt, and so they need to use stock. Other buyers may not wish to issue stock at the current valuation and prefer to use cash if they have it or leverage if they can. Innovative financing techniques can provide an almost infinite gradation of vehicles, including options, warrants, different types of preferred stock, and various tranches of debt that can be developed to meet the parties' needs in each transaction. Hybrid securities with some of the elements of equity and some of the elements of debt can be developed to meet financial and structural needs in a tax-efficient manner.

Government Involvement in M&A Transactions

Various agencies of the government, on both state and federal levels, impact M&A transactions beyond tax concerns. The agencies influencing the success of an M&A transaction are numerous and varied. Most large transactions involve the Securities and Exchange Commission for federal securities issues and the Federal Trade Commission or Department of Justice for antitrust issues. There are a number of other federal regulatory agencies that may affect a transaction in a particular industry, including the Federal Communications Commission, the Environmental Protection Agency, the Alcohol and Tobacco Tax and Trade Bureau, and a host of others.

Similar regulatory agencies at the state level frequently will be implicated in a number of states. Early identification of the relevant agencies and planning for the lead times required by each is essential, as is coordination of dealings with various agencies, particularly in multi-state transactions.

Many areas of law affect M&A transactions, including corporate law, securities law, antitrust law, environmental law, tax law, and many others. The increasing complexity in many of these areas has made M&A transactions much more complicated. One example is the enactment of the Sarbanes-Oxley Act of 2002. This act makes it awkward for a public company to acquire a private company that does not have adequate internal controls, even if the public company considers the risks worthwhile after extensive due diligence. This also affects the planning a private company should do before running a sale process. In order to maximize the potential universe of buyers, a seller who might be acquired by a public company may be well advised to comply with key provisions of Sarbanes-Oxley even though it is not legally required to do so. This may give comfort to a potential public company buyer and make acquisition by such a buyer smoother, quicker, and more profitable.

Example Transactions

Probably the most financially successful M&A transaction I was involved in concerned the acquisition of a manufacturing facility in Mexico by a U.S. public company. An extensive due diligence process helped make it successful, but the principal factor leading to success was astute business analysis by management, coupled with a management plan for ongoing operations that utilized the skills, and met the needs, of the sellers who continued to be active in the business. The sellers needed capital to expand the business, access to better sources of supply, and support for an intergenerational change of management. But the sellers were key to management of the company in the local culture, so it would have been very difficult for the buyer to make a success of the acquisition without the continued involvement of the sellers. Particularly in foreign acquisitions, the ability to manage and utilize the skills of existing personnel is critical to avoiding financially punishing missteps and maintaining the momentum of the acquired entity. Of course, if the acquired entity does not have momentum, sweeping personnel changes may be necessary, but this can be more difficult in foreign jurisdictions.

One unsuccessful transaction I can recall was the acquisition of a U.S. company by a European company attempting to expand into a related industry. The lack of success mostly came from reasons related to developments in the economy, not to the acquirer's very thorough and organized M&A process. This example shows the ever-present risks of M&A transactions. Adequate due diligence can reduce, but not eliminate, the risk.

Another transaction, where I represented the target, was ultimately unsuccessful for the acquirer due to excess use of financial leverage. The transaction closed and the target struggled on for some time but was ultimately unable to carry the debt load from the acquisition even though it was operated competently.

Success for an M&A lawyer is often defined as closing a transaction. But it is not really success if the transaction is not economically successful because of issues such as unanticipated problems arising from inadequate due diligence, use of financial or transaction structures that will not support the enterprise, or the existence of cultural problems unresolved or even created by the acquisition process A few of the key points to be kept in mind during the process are:

1. *Be thorough.* Discover issues early while there is time to resolve them before the transaction implodes.
2. *Be creative and flexible.* Be willing to change structures, documents, and procedures to deal with issues that arise. And they will arise.
3. *Be civil.* M&A transactions often involve stress that can degenerate into personal animosity among the parties and even the advisors. There can be an adversarial element to transactions, but they are not litigation. There is a much greater chance of the transaction occurring and succeeding if lines of communication are kept open and negotiations are conducted in a civil and business-like manner.

J. Franklin Cable, a partner, joined Miller Nash in 1967. He serves as general counsel to businesses and provides representation in a variety of areas including corporate and contract matters, mergers and acquisitions, corporate finance, and intellectual property matters. He served as general counsel to Willamette Industries before its acquisition by Weyerhaueser Company and has in-depth knowledge of the forest products industry. Major transactions in which Mr. Cable has acted as counsel include roll-up transactions, leveraged buyouts, tender offers, mergers, acquisitions of foreign enterprises, acquisitions of domestic enterprises by foreign enterprises, and acquisitions of retail stores, radio stations, newspapers, vineyards, and transportation companies.

Mr. Cable is included in The Best Lawyers in America, Chambers USA, Who's Who in America, *and* Who's Who in American Law. *He is a member of the Oregon State Bar's securities and business law sections and has served on the executive committee of both sections. He has also served as chairman of the client security fund committee of the Oregon State Bar.*

Mr. Cable is an emeritus member of the Portland metropolitan advisory board of the Salvation Army and a member of the board of directors of the Christie School, an institution for the care of mentally disabled children. He earned his bachelor's degree, with distinction, at Stanford University in the honors program in economics, and his law degree at Harvard Law School.

It's About Much More Than Just Money

Barry J. Siegel

Partner and Co-Chairman, Corporate Department

Klehr, Harrison, Harvey, Branzburg & Ellers LLP

The Practice

Practicing merger and acquisition law requires patience and people skills, technical knowledge, and the ability to organize large amounts of information and people. We spend a great deal of time with shareholders, owners, and managers to understand their specific goals for the transaction and their appetite for risk. We then manage the transaction with these goals in mind and have as our driving force the accomplishment of these goals.

We negotiate and document the purchase price and other economic terms of the letter of intent, merger, stock or asset purchase, or other definitive agreement, and employment or other agreements with management. We organize and manage the due diligence process and the delivery of business information. We manage the business executives, investment bankers, and specialist lawyers (e.g., tax, employee benefits, environmental, intellectual property) so each party knows their role and there is consistent and coordinated communication throughout the process. We also manage the consent and approval process with shareholders, regulators, and other government officials and other third parties.

The most important strategy in all this is to provide clear, concise, but complete communication on all issues. Often, we must force clients to slow down enough to fully appreciate and analyze an issue.

Along with staying on top of the latest developments in laws affecting the transaction, we focus on understanding people and human nature and finding compromises to issues and problems to provide a win for everyone. All people want to be understood and acknowledged. While you do not necessarily have to agree with the other person, if you work to understand his or her point of view and even in the face of disagreement, you acknowledge validity in his or her point, you have a much better chance of reaching compromise. In any event, the person on the other side of the deal will have much better feelings toward you and will likely be more sympathetic to your points on that particular issue and others.

Having the courage of your convictions and finding solutions to problems instead of merely warning about risks is another value lawyers can bring to a transaction. While clients make business decisions and lawyers advise, generally lawyers serve their clients best by bringing their own views and opinions to a problem and telling clients when and why they are making mistakes, and why a particular resolution to an issue should be acceptable.

Finding solutions to problems that are difficult takes discipline, fortitude, and concentrated thought. In trying to attain a successful outcome for my clients, the thing I most focus on is communication. I make sure my client understands the issue and proposed outcome and that we have fully analyzed the upside and downside of all possible solutions and agree on the proposed solution. My firm places a strong value on careful due diligence and finding creative solutions to difficult problems. By working hard to analyze a potential issue, you can determine all underlying facts and give an accurate assessment of the potential risk.

Staying on top of developments in the business world and law is important. To do that, I read *The Wall Street Journal*, business magazines, and publications geared to legal issues to keep on top of current news and trends. I talk to friends, clients, and partners about issues they have encountered in their business dealings and how they have solved problems.

Major Client Issues in Mergers and Acquisitions

Some problems clients face before and during the process of a deal can be avoided. Some are self-generated, and a lawyer can only give advice on how to prevent it. Loose lips sink ships. Clients need to strictly keep the potential of a transaction under wraps if possible. This avoids insider trading issues and potential problems with valuation if the companies are public and rumors concerning a deal affect the stock price. In many public deals, it seems the amount of rumors surrounding a deal naturally increase as a deal comes closer to fruition.

Many clients track closely the conversation occurring on financial Internet chat boards. While this can often be frustrating because of the detailed inside information often discussed amongst the participants, most clients feel that tracking Internet conversations is necessary in order to keep abreast of developments in the marketplace. Much speculation surrounds trading activity prior to a transaction's announcement. Substantial increases in trading volume often indicates that word is on the street that a transaction is about to be announced. In one transaction I was working on, trading volume increased substantially immediately prior to the record date for the meeting to approve the deal. In that situation, we were very concerned that a competitor of the target was purchasing substantial blocks of stock with the intent of voting against the deal and thereby ensuring that its competitor would not be acquired by a company with greater financial resources. Because of Securities and Exchange Commission requirements that all holders of 5 percent or more of a public company's outstanding securities must make public filings, companies can typically assess anyone purchasing large blocks of stock and thereby plan better for any potential difficulties in the proxy solicitation process.

Following are three major aspects of a transaction we handle for and with our clients before and during the deal process:

Due Diligence

This is the factual examination of a target company. We help clients manage the diligence process and are responsible for analyzing specific aspects of a target. Some things lawyers are typically responsible for are the company's legal agreements and contracts, intellectual property, existing and threatened litigation, and environmental issues. We also help coordinate the receipt and analysis of information we specifically are not responsible for analyzing. For example, an acquirer may hire investment bankers or accountants to help analyze financial aspects of a target. We make sure these experts receive all information that is necessary for their analysis and help resolve any issues that arise from their review of the target.

Negotiation and Documentation of a Transaction

We draft (typically when representing buyers) or review (typically when representing sellers) all agreements necessary to consummate a transaction, including purchase agreements, employment agreements, non-compete and non-solicitation agreements, and registration rights agreements. We negotiate issues in connection with the definitive agreements, including the representations and warranties, covenants, and restrictions on the company and parties, and the indemnification obligations for misrepresentations and breaches of covenants.

Social Issues

When representing the seller, we help management negotiate a satisfactory employment or termination arrangement for themselves and the employees. When we represent the buyer, we make sure the buyer makes satisfactory arrangements with the management and employees of the seller, whether they intend to remain with the company, provide services for a limited transition period, or leave the company.

Managing Specific Legal Issues

The financial implications of the legal aspects of merger and acquisition transactions can be significant. The violation of federal securities laws could have a significant negative impact on a company, including fines, penalties, and orders restricting the company from affecting securities registration (and raising capital) for a period of time. Antitrust rulings that require a divesture could have significant economic impact. We add value to our client service through skillful navigation of the regulatory approval process.

A mergers and acquisitions practice consists of both legal and non-legal aspects. While various state and federal laws govern certain matters, the economic transaction between the parties is largely a negotiated business transaction and is not subject to laws, rules, and regulations. The various legal aspects are described below:

Federal Securities Laws

Under federal securities laws, all issuances of securities must be either registered under the Securities Act of 1933, as amended, or there must be an exemption available for such issuance. In transactions where the consideration to be issued consists of securities, we ensure compliance with these securities law provisions, including the preparation of registration statements and merger proxies on Form S-4. When shareholder approval is required and the company solicits proxies for such approval, we ensure that the proxy statement complies with the complicated and detailed requirements of the proxy rules, and we help manage the printing, mailing, and proxy solicitation process. We help clients comply with the public disclosure requirements of the securities laws. We also advise clients with respect to insider trading law.

State Securities and Corporate Law

State securities or "blue sky" laws also govern the issuance of securities by a company. We analyze relevant state securities laws to ensure compliance. State law also provides for the fiduciary duties and obligations owed by the board of directors (or the managing member/partner for limited liability companies/partnerships) to its shareholders and other constituents. Many states have detailed anti-takeover laws that typically are designed to discourage hostile takeovers. We ensure that the process and procedures followed by the board, or a special committee of the board, comply with their duties of care and loyalty, and that anti-takeover statutes are not triggered. These include carefully structured "no shop" provisions and break-up fees. We also advise companies with respect to "dissenter's rights" and similar state laws designed to ensure that shareholders receive a fair price for their shares.

Antitrust Laws

The Hart-Scott-Rodino Anti-Trust Improvement Act of 1986 requires that buyers and sellers of businesses provide detailed information to the Federal Trade Commission and the antitrust division of the Justice Department, and wait a minimum of thirty days (unless early termination of the waiting period is requested and granted) after such filing to consummate the transaction. These departments use this period to determine whether the business combination or acquisition will be anti-competitive, and they often request additional information or require divesture of certain businesses prior to permitting such acquisition to be completed. Lawyers typically produce the Hart-Scott application and negotiate and/or litigate with federal authorities over particular document requests or divesture plans and requirements.

Other Applicable Laws

State and/or federal authorities regulate entities in various industries. The approval of these regulators is often necessary to transfer an applicable license in connection with a change of control. Examples of these include banks, thrifts, and insurance companies. Lawyers guide clients through the applicable regulatory approval process.

Self-Regulated Organizations

Public companies must adhere to the rules and regulations of the exchange or market on which their securities are traded. The New York Stock Exchange, the American Stock Exchange, and the NASDAQ have rules and regulations requiring, among other things, shareholder approval in connection with certain transactions.

Navigating the legal requirements and obtaining the best possible deal for my clients is not the full measure of success. Just as understanding people facilitates the transaction, the trust my client places in me facilitates our lawyer/client relationship. The more a client trusts me, the more successful the transaction is.

Strategies for Profitability

When negotiating or structuring a deal, I advise following three key steps to ensure that the new company is as profitable as possible. First, spend as much time as possible analyzing the issues and problems created by integrating two companies and their personnel. Companies are much more than the products or services they sell. They consist of people who form a very specific culture and work environment. Most unsuccessful transactions are not caused by inadequate financial or other terms in the transaction, but by a bad fit between the companies and their cultures. A good integration team is worth more than their weight in gold.

Next, ensure that the personnel responsible for completing the transaction have a vested interest in its success. Develop strategies to make sure all the hard work of the people responsible for the acquisition is rewarded through cash or stock bonuses, recognition, or otherwise.

And last, ensure thorough financial and market due diligence. If necessary, hire financial experts or consultants who have deep and specific knowledge of the target company's market. Money spent prior to an acquisition can save a company a tremendous amount, either through avoiding costly mistakes or by enabling the acquirer to better value the target.

Establishing good relations with the personnel of the other company is never wasted effort. I encourage clients, in their public statements, to acknowledge the skills and talents of the management team of the other side. This is an easy and cost-free way to make people feel good about themselves and their potential role in a combined company. Even if the acquiring party does not intend to keep these people on, public recognition works as a powerful force to make friends and invest everyone in the success of a transaction. This can and should pay huge dividends when difficult issues arise later in a transaction.

Advice for Profitable Mergers and Acquisitions

A merger of equals involves a business combination as opposed to one company acquiring another. While the name implies companies of roughly equal size combining and sharing power, in reality there is usually one company that is stronger. This may be reflected in the result that one company's management may maintain control, or the headquarter operations of one company may serve as headquarters for the combined entity.

Mergers of equals are designed to strategically grow the business of both parties. Presumably, the value of the combined companies should exceed the sum of the two. This is achieved through various synergies of the combined companies. Some ways these can be created are through cost savings by eliminating duplicate functions (e.g., financial staff, marketing), through greater purchasing power as a larger entity, or increased leverage with customers as market share increases.

My advice for the best financial outlook in a merger of equals is to first deal with the social issues. What management team/combination/board will govern the company? If synergies through staff reductions are planned, where are these cuts intended? What financial gains through option accelerations, stay bonuses, or otherwise are planned for the personnel?

When a client wants to acquire another company, I advise the buyer to remember the seller will be focused primarily on maximizing value and returns for shareholders, and this is in direct conflict with the buyer's goal of paying as favorable a price as possible. In a merger, companies are much more concerned about the synergies between the companies and the combined value. While pricing is important in how much stock a shareholder will receive, the success of the deal will often hinge on whether additional value was created through the combination.

If a client wants to sell a company, my advice concerns maximizing the value of the company to maximize the financial gain in the transaction. In a private transaction, minimizing the indemnification obligations maximizes the value. This can be done through a thorough review of all representations, warranties, and disclosure schedules. The indemnity obligation should also be subject to a basket and cap. If a significant part of the value of the business relates to the future, earn-outs can significantly increase a shareholder's return.

Similarly, if a buyer wants to reduce the purchase price as a result of certain items discovered during diligence (e.g., a questionable large receivable), a seller can take certain risk regarding that issue. For example, if a large receivable appears to be uncollectible, the seller could take an assignment of that receivable or receive additional consideration if the receivable is collected. In a recent transaction I worked on, the seller believed strongly that the company was owed approximately $3 million from a prior customer. The seller's accountants, however, did not believe in the validity of this receivable and therefore did not reflect it on the seller's financial statements. Thus, the buyer did not account for this receivable in valuing the business. This was difficult for the seller to accept, however, and it threatened to kill the transaction. As a compromise, the buyer and seller agreed that the seller's shareholders would receive $0.50 for every $1 the company collects on account of this receivable. If the company is subject to a lawsuit, additional consideration could be given to the seller if the outcome of the suit is favorable to the company.

Considering the needs and goals of the other side of any transaction is a major step toward success and both sides being satisfied with the results.

Doing the homework and considering issues other than money will result in satisfaction and profit for both sides.

Barry J. Siegel concentrates his practice in mergers and acquisitions, securities, venture capital and private equity financings, e-commerce, corporate restructuring, and general corporate counseling for a wide range of clients from emerging growth businesses to public companies.

Mr. Siegel frequently acts as outside general counsel to his clients, representing them on all corporate and financial matters and coordinating other legal issues ranging from litigation to intellectual property to regulatory matters.

Mr. Siegel has built a significant practice representing venture capital funds, hedge funds, and other institutional investors in venture capital and private equity financings. His corporate restructuring and merger and acquisition experience is significant, having participated in numerous refinancings, workouts, and purchases and sales of companies, both public and private.

How to Succeed in M&A: Do It Right, Not Right Away

Stephen M. Quinlivan
Shareholder

Marci K. Winga
Shareholder

Leonard, Street and Deinard PA

Our role as merger and acquisition (M&A) lawyers is to structure, negotiate, and document the purchase or sale of a business to maximize the value of the transaction to our clients. Price is an obvious and important part of that process, but it is often only one of many variables that significantly affect the value of the deal to the buyer and seller. The challenge for us as lawyers is to identify those variables, provide you with the information you need to understand and assess the risks from a business perspective, and then assure that the transaction is structured and documented so you get what you've bargained for.

When clients approach us to represent them in an M&A transaction, they have generally already developed business and financial goals for the proposed transaction. The five major M&A-related transaction steps to accomplish those goals are (i) evaluation of transaction structure considerations, (ii) due diligence and risk management, (iii) employment and business transition issues, (iv) negotiation and preparation of transaction documents, and (v) corporate governance and related ownership issues.

Legal counsel can add the most value by analyzing and structuring the transaction in a manner that accomplishes your goals and minimizes unforeseen costs that would materially reduce the value to you.

The Legal Components of M&A Law

Tax Implications

At the outset of any M&A transaction, we recommend thoroughly reviewing and considering the tax impact of the transaction on various participants such as the buyer, seller, shareholders, management, and employees, to make sure there aren't any surprises that would be likely to derail the deal or reduce the value to our client. Then we consider whether there are any creative ways we can increase the value to our client. Also, there may be preliminary work that needs to be done to get regulatory assurance that a particular tax structure will not be challenged, like requesting a private letter ruling from the Internal Revenue Service. These types of issues need to be addressed very early in the process, because they can take a long time to resolve. They can also be very expensive to revisit later in the process in terms of reduced leverage at the bargaining table.

Employment and Benefits

Nearly every business has employees, and with that comes employment issues and benefits considerations that need to be addressed upon sale. The structure of the sale (e.g., asset sale, stock sale, or merger) can have a significant impact on what needs to be done to transition employees, although nearly every transaction has some employment and benefits aspect. At a minimum, the buyer will want to complete due diligence on legal compliance, any outstanding claims, and expense issues. At the other end of the scale, employment and benefits issues can drive the transaction in certain situations, such as where the seller has unionized facilities, where an employee stock ownership plan controls a significant portion of the seller's equity, or where retaining key employees or non-competition provisions are critical.

Real Estate

Nearly every business also leases or owns one or more physical locations. Transferring real property is a complicated process that requires a high level of attention to detail. Where real estate is a significant asset of the company, the value of the deal can change considerably if it is not handled properly. While leases can be less complicated to transfer, there can be substantial risks to either the buyer or seller that can result in a significant impact on value if not carefully addressed. Further, there is the added complication that the landlord's consent will generally be required to accept the buyer as tenant, and that can often lead to a renegotiation of terms. If a seller's real property leases or ownership are substantial, the costs and risks associated with transfer can be a significant factor in determining the structure of the deal.

Environmental

Many companies mistakenly believe environmental laws do not affect them, but in reality they touch on most businesses at some level. If the seller conducts a business that involves significant handling of hazardous substances, the legal compliance implications and risks are more obvious. For example, there are often Environmental Protection Agency and other regulatory compliance requirements for transferring licenses, among other things. However, even where a business does not handle materials traditionally viewed to be toxic, environmental considerations can still be a factor in a sale. If the seller owns any land that is part of the sale, the seller and buyer will be in the chain of title and could be responsible for clean-up. Old tanks on the property and underground contamination can be particularly expensive to remedy. Even where no land is being transferred, the seller can be held responsible for anything done while occupying the property that contributed to any contamination. This can include things as common as leaking oil or gasoline from company cars, paint, or cleaning substances. Further, emissions and processing of all sorts of seemingly innocuous substances are regulated, including clean waste water.

Intellectual Property

Protecting intellectual property rights—such as patents, trademarks, and copyrights—is a very important factor in certain types of businesses. In technology-driven and creative industries, assuring that intellectual property rights are properly transferred can be the most critical element of value in the transaction and can sometimes turn on seemingly insignificant language in the conveyance documents and compliance with precise registration procedures. Also, it is important to evaluate during due diligence whether there is any infringement or other factors that could reduce value or prevent enforcement.

Contracts

In every deal, the buyer and sellers have to consider what will happen to their contracts with third parties. Will they continue, or will they end? Will the transaction result in a breach of the contract? Will consent of the other parties be required? Sometimes the contracts themselves make that very clear. In other cases, the contracts do not provide the answer and we have to consider the legal and practical implications of various courses of action. Where there is a contract, the other party to the contract always has to be considered. Even if that party cannot change the legal outcome of a particular course of action, there may be other ways the party can affect the acquired business and decrease value to the buyer or seller if that party is displeased with the result. Identifying and considering these issues early on can facilitate the sale and business transition process.

Insurance

Every transaction involves payment of actual costs and the assumption of various risks and contingencies. Certain types of risks can be insured against so they do not become deal-breakers. Property and casualty insurance, employment practices coverage, product liability coverage, director and officer policies, professional liability coverage, or malpractice coverage can all be critical elements in assuring that the value of the transaction isn't affected by unknown or hard-to-value risks.

Corporate Governance

M&A transactions generally need to be approved by the owners of the seller, and there may be other significant considerations like payment of preferences, exercise of options or warrants, or rights of first refusal or co-sale that can affect the seller's ability to complete the transaction and the value to various parties. Determining what these requirements are early on and confirming there are no obstacles to completing the deal can be critical.

International

Where one of the parties is foreign or the business involves material international elements such as overseas customers, suppliers, or facilities, considering international law implications is important for both parties. The acquisition or sale of such a business can involve tax issues, Patriot Act concerns, import/export regulations, employment and immigration factors, and differences in contracting and regulatory requirements and practices. Some of these can be addressed from the United States, but it is often advisable to hire local counsel in the overseas jurisdiction where the business is conducted to avoid surprises.

Securities/Securities and Exchange Commission Compliance

Depending on the nature of the consideration to be paid and whether any of the parties are public reporting companies, state securities law requirements and compliance with Securities and Exchange Commission regulations can be a crucial, time-consuming, and expensive part of the deal. This is a very specialized area of law, and the consequences of noncompliance can be particularly severe, ranging from enforcement actions to monetary penalties, rescission, or criminal sanctions against the individuals involved in the deal.

Other Regulatory Compliance

Depending on the nature of the industry and type of transaction, regulatory compliance can range from being a mere formality to being the primary obstacle to getting the transaction completed. The sheer breadth and depth of authority of the numerous state and federal agencies that regulate businesses prevents an in-depth discussion of specific requirements, but establishing a good record of compliance and respectful relationship with the regulators in the context of operations often facilitates the compliance process in the context of a sale. Some of the agencies that are particularly active in substantive evaluation of various aspects of M&A transactions include the Federal Communications Commission, the Federal Trade Commission, the Department of Justice, and the Federal Energy Regulatory Commission. In certain situations, being able to effectively manage that process can be the key to a successful transaction.

The Financial Implications of M&A Law

When you are buying or selling a business, there are three basic kinds of financial implications:

1. There are the actual costs and expenses that will have to be paid— the purchase price, whether in cash, stock, or other consideration, plus additional actual costs, such as expenses to transition and operate the business, salaries and benefits to the employees hired to operate the business, and legal, accounting, and consulting costs to complete the transaction.

2. There will be non-cash costs and benefits to you that may not constitute out-of-pocket cash expenses but will affect your bottom line depending upon how the transaction is structured and accounted for—for example, tax savings, utilizing loss carry-forwards, or booking up assets that have been depreciated.

3. Finally, you will take on numerous different risks and contingencies that may end up resulting in cost to you at some point or may not, but you won't know until after you buy the business. These include things like potential litigation claims by customers, suppliers, or employees, unknown problems relating to the condition of the seller's property or equipment, or lapses in regulatory or legal compliance.

As lawyers, we help identify the factors that have important financial implications to the client and develop a comprehensive approach to maximize the overall value. Attempting to negotiate a transaction before engaging legal, tax, and financial advisers is generally a mistake unless the client has sophisticated M&A experience. Clients also tend to grossly underestimate the time needed to participate in due diligence and understand the documents, often leading to less-than-optimal results.

Tax implications are often the most significant non-purchase price financial considerations and are often the primary financial driver of the transaction structure, but there are other significant considerations, like regulatory compliance or being able to realize economies of scale and efficiencies through consolidation. While not applicable to every business or industry, these factors can be critical, and taking the time to fully understand and evaluate them can significantly affect value.

To achieve success for you, as the client, your lawyer should guide you in considering these issues in light of your individual circumstances. How we do that for you depends upon a variety of factors. If we have a prior working relationship with the client and management, we understand your likes and dislikes and have a mutual confidence and trust, which is important for fulfilling the role of legal adviser. If we do not have a prior working relationship, it is necessary to understand your chemistry early and develop mutual confidence and trust as soon as possible.

Understanding your business is always critical. Often, we can leverage off our existing industry experience, but every client is different and it takes a certain amount of effort to understand the particular facts and circumstances. We try to avoid using a one-size-fits-all approach.

We also stay up to date by sharing knowledge within our firm, attending seminars, reading M&A-related news sources, and networking with other financial professionals. These resources can play a fundamental role in enhancing the efficiency and success of the transaction.

Negotiation and Structuring Strategies

There are three primary strategies M&A clients should use when negotiating or structuring a deal to ensure maximum profitability to the resulting larger company:

1. Before starting to negotiate, plan ahead, be proactive, and develop coordinated goals and expectations not only for the transaction, but also for the business transition/integration and future operations. These plans and goals will likely change as you learn more about the other party, but the earlier you get the right people to start thinking about it, the less likely you will be faced with unpleasant surprises later.

2. Spend the necessary time and money on the front end doing due diligence and considering all the relevant options and material issues with your financial and legal advisers. It may seem like a waste if you think you have already figured it out and want to minimize fees by just having the lawyer document the deal you've negotiated, but it can be a lot more expensive (or impossible) to fix a legal, accounting, or tax issue down the road than if it had been identified and addressed at the beginning of the process.

3. In terms of negotiating indemnification and risk allocation provisions, focus on identifying uninsured risks that may not be significant individually but are relatively common and could cause material costs in the aggregate. These are the contingencies that are most likely to materially affect profitability and financial success. It is important to consider risks that are potentially catastrophic also, but they are less common and more likely to be insured against.

Following these strategies keeps the parties focused on their goals and reduces unknown factors that are most likely to cause the actual cost of the deal to exceed expectations.

M&A transactions are often fast-paced, and there is significant internal and external pressure to act quickly or risk losing the deal. Often, such pressure is not warranted, but sometimes there are real limitations imposed by market conditions, regulatory deadlines, investor expectations, or other factors. When such pressures exist, focusing on too many "what if" scenarios in the beginning can derail the parties' enthusiasm and the momentum of the deal. Sometimes keeping the deal moving is more important, even if it means some issues may have to be revisited later.

Communication Strategies

For both public and private companies, customers and employees must be informed in a way that explains the benefits of a transaction without causing customers to flee or employees to quit. Acquisition transactions cause great uncertainty for both customers and employees. Keeping this in mind is very important.

Consider carefully the message to customers who will sense uncertainty as to continuation of duplicate product lines. Managing the business between signing and closing may be difficult if customers refuse to invest in either product for fear it will be discontinued. Consider also that antitrust restrictions may prevent a pre-closing announcement of a surviving product line to assure that the companies continue to compete until closing.

When speaking to public markets after the closing, public companies should use extreme caution in making statements explaining the benefits of a transaction.

Federal and State Regulation of M&A Deals

The rules and regulations of various federal and state agencies and governmental organizations can significantly influence the costs and financial success of an M&A transaction. The following is a summary of the roles of the primary agencies involved in M&A transactions.

Securities and Exchange Commission

When securities are bought and sold, the role of the Securities and Exchange Commission depends on whether there is a public offering or a shareholder vote of a public company, where the agency will often be integrally involved, or whether it is a private placement, where the agency has less of a role and may just serve as a repository for routine notice filings.

Department of Justice/Federal Trade Commission

Certain mergers require pre-filing clearance if the Hart-Scott-Rodino thresholds are met. Often, the approval is routinely granted, but if the agencies decide to investigate the transaction with a "second request," they play a big role (at great expense to the client).

Federal Communications Commission

The Federal Communications Commission has jurisdiction over telecommunications and other matters. Often, its approval is needed in conjunction with the Department of Justice/Federal Trade Commission, and the Federal Communications Commission will also consider anti-competitive aspects in a separate inquiry. Since approval for major transactions requires the approval of the commissioners themselves, it may turn into an unpredictable political process with the split being determined along party lines. The recent AT&T transaction is a good example of this.

Federal Energy Regulatory Commission

Because of the public interest aspects of utility and energy-related transactions, Federal Energy Regulatory Commission approval is often required and can involve extended waiting periods. Success can be severely hampered if the agency has any significant or ongoing concerns about compliance of the parties' respective operations.

State Attorney General

Often, the state attorney general has statutory authority to enforce the state's own antitrust and other laws, and may play a separate role in acquisition approval.

European Union/Other Foreign Approvals

Regulatory bodies in different countries may have approval requirements over significant M&A deals. This is particularly true where the business has national defense implications or involves state-operated or -regulated businesses or utilities.

Internal Revenue Service

Tax laws and regulations can affect the financial aspects of a transaction. In addition to influencing transaction structure, sometimes the parties ask for a private letter ruling from the Internal Revenue Service prior to completing a transaction to determine if desired tax benefits will be available.

Achieving Success through Timing, Managing Expectations, and Avoiding Common Mistakes

When to buy? When to sell? Who to work with? What to pay? How you answer these questions plays a significant role in how successful the transaction will be. The following is a list of practical considerations and common mistakes to avoid when making these decisions:

- M&A deals boom with a growing economy. During those times, there is plenty of financing and willing sellers. Buyers need to be sensitive to overpaying. In a recession, there is less activity. Uncertainty in economic outlook leads people to be cautious. However, there can be circumstances where it pays to be aggressive in a down market if the proper opportunity presents itself.

- For closely held private companies, it is a mistake to think you can hire an investment bank and go to market tomorrow. First, the sale process will be best if there are audited financial statements. If companies want to sell and do not have an audit, it is time to get one. Second, there needs to be depth in the management team. If there is no proprietary process and the founding shareholder has to stay around to run everything, he or she often has nothing to sell. Third, get your house in order. Deals are priced off a multiple of historical earnings before interest, taxes, depreciation, and amortization. For every dollar you eliminate, you add $4 to $10 in sale price. Get your company lean now, and run it for a couple of years so you have attractive financial statements to support pricing expectations.

- If your investment banker is going to run an auction, do it right. That requires a lot of advance preparation for the seller. The most effective technique is to provide the potential buyers with a draft agreement together with the related disclosure schedules. Many sellers do not bother to send the schedules with the draft agreement because they have not invested the time to prepare the schedules. That is a serious mistake. You want the bidders to be able to see the schedules before they bid so they cannot claim unfair surprise later when they see the schedules. It also allows the transaction to be rapidly consummated once the final bidder is selected, since there is less work to be done.

- Do not be impressed by investment banks that tout how many potential buyers they will provide with a confidential information memorandum. The confidential information memorandum includes all kinds of key details about your company that could harm you if they fell into a competitor's or another adverse party's hands. Make sure the potential buyer list is targeted toward entities that will have a significant interest in buying your company, not just learning your secrets.

- Integration planning needs to be done decisively so the benefits accrue as fast as possible. Antitrust restrictions may again play a role in the extent to which integration planning can be done before the closing.

- As a buyer, entering into a transaction to acquire a business that requires the special skills or resources of any individuals or key employees without reasonable assurances that they will be willing and able to perform is a big mistake. This generally requires appropriate financial incentives, but that is not the only factor. Among other things, change in corporate style or opportunities for advancement can have an adverse effect on job performance. The transaction will only be profitable to you if the acquired business continues to perform as well or better following closing. Look to key employee retention plans to retain the employees you need to make the transition a success. It is important to be honest with employees, as they will sense if management is making unrealistic promises.

- As a seller, the corollary mistake is to enter into a transaction with a significant amount of the consideration to be speculative (e.g., debt or equity of the buyer instead of cash) without a reasonable degree of confidence as to whether or how you will be able to realize the value. Keep in mind the old saying, "A bird in the hand is worth two in the bush."

- Timing is everything. If you want to sell right away and are ready to go, think hard about waiting if current pricing seems reasonable. Two years from now, purchase price multiples may be down because of lack of financing or other macroeconomic concerns. Or, your business can decline because of a lost customer or other factors. If you sell now, you might not get the windfall you are dreaming of, but you might be better off in the long run.

Making a Profitable Investment

Conducting a thorough due diligence investigation and analysis is the best way to assess the current value of the business or assets you are acquiring and the size and likelihood of risks that have the potential to adversely affect value. This will generally require the involvement of your legal counsel and financial and tax advisers, and depending upon the size and nature of the transaction, it may involve other professional advisers as well.

Whether the target is ultimately a profitable investment for you will also depend upon a number of other factors, including how well you transition the business and operate it following the acquisition.

Fit, planning, and execution are more important than the size or type of business in an M&A transaction. However, as a general matter, small companies are worth less than big companies. There is less diversification of revenues and less of a platform to spring off of. Often, there is no depth in management and financial and operational controls are not sophisticated, increasing integration costs.

It is not necessary for the target company to be financially strong for the transaction to be financially successful, but it generally helps. If the target is already financially strong, you know as a buyer that it is possible to operate it as a profitable business and, in the absence of significant changes in the market, that gives you some degree of assurance that you should be able to operate it profitably if you simply continue the seller's proven business practices and policies. As a result, this type of acquisition is generally considered less risky than acquiring a financially insecure target. All else being equal though, the price will generally be higher. It also assumes you can bring to the table skills and resources that are comparable to the seller's.

If the target is not financially strong, you will have to do something different from prior management to turn it around. This could involve significant additional investment on your part, and there is no guarantee that whatever you do will be successful. On the other hand, the corollary is that the price will be lower, and if you have superior resources to address the deficiencies in the target's business and financial condition, there may be a greater opportunity to create additional value to the buyer and achieve significant gain.

Stock versus Cash

Purchasing a business primarily with stock of the buyer instead of cash allows the buyer to acquire a company without issuing additional debt or depleting working capital reserves. If structured properly, being paid in stock instead of cash consideration can also allow the seller to defer taxes on capital gains until the stock acquired in the transaction is sold, whereas the taxes on gain would be due immediately upon receipt of cash consideration.

For the seller, getting paid in stock is often not the most attractive option, because it is riskier than getting cash. If the buyer is a private company, there will be a limited market, if any, in which to sell the stock issued to the seller. If the buyer is a public company and the stock issued to the buyer is registered, the seller would have more liquidity, but registration can be expensive, and there are often still significant restrictions on resales. If the seller or its owners become officers, directors, or 10 percent owners of the buyer after the transaction, they will be subject to legal restrictions on sales by affiliates. In addition, the buyer often insists on being able to limit or suspend the sale of the stock issued in the transaction upon recommendation of its analysts if they believe it will flood the market and depress the buyer's stock price.

Getting paid in stock also subjects the seller to the more obvious risk that the stock price could go down following the transaction, which could significantly decrease the value of the consideration paid to the seller. The flip side to this is that getting paid in stock can provide the seller the opportunity to realize a higher price if the price of the buyer's stock goes up following the sale. The seller will also have certain rights as a shareholder of the buyer. Essentially, the seller has to make a decision as to whether the buyer's stock is a good investment given the seller's individual financial circumstances and risk tolerance.

It is easy for sellers to get caught up in the belief that their business will add value to the buyer's business beyond the purchase price and cause the buyer's stock price to rise. While this may sometimes be the case, there is no guarantee. If market analysts believe the buyer has overpaid for the transaction, it can have an immediate depressive effect on stock prices. The buyer's plans for the acquired business and whether the seller will continue to be involved and have an impact on the buyer's operation of the acquired business could be additional factors to consider.

The actual results the buyer is able to achieve in its existing business and the acquired business, and corresponding changes in market price, will also depend on outside factors that neither buyer nor seller can necessarily control, such as changes in the industry, supply costs, or customer expectations. If the buyer pays in stock, the seller will become a stockholder and share that risk.

The primary benefits to paying and getting paid in cash instead of stock is that the actual cost is calculable at the time it is paid and there are fewer unknowns that can affect the value to either party. As a seller, once you get paid in cash, it is in your control and you can reinvest or spend it as you will. As a buyer, once you pay in cash, you have few if any continuing obligations to the seller, in contrast to having the seller as a shareholder. The downside to the seller is that there is little opportunity, if any, to delay capital gains tax on cash consideration and the seller doesn't get the benefit of rising stock prices if the market thinks the deal was undervalued. For the buyer, paying in cash will mean incurring debt or depleting cash reserves, in contrast to issuing stock.

Whether to recommend cash or stock consideration depends upon who the parties are and the size of the transaction. However, as a general rule, if cash is an option, it provides significant benefits in terms of flexibility and finality to both parties. From the buyer's perspective, issuing stock can be attractive if the transaction price is high enough that raising the necessary cash would be cost-prohibitive. The sellers can benefit too if they can negotiate a premium over the cash price they would otherwise be able to obtain. However, that same premium can cause the market to conclude that the buyer overpaid, depress stock prices, and eliminate the premium. Ironically, if the buyer is large enough and its stock is stable enough that receiving stock is an attractive alternative to the seller, the buyer is more likely to be able to pay in cash.

Preventing Discounted Share Price in M&A Transactions

A discounted share price is the result of a market that does not believe the touted benefits of a deal will occur. For instance, companies like Cisco have a great deal of experience acquiring and integrating companies. They know how to do it right. Others do not, and the market may not believe management has the expertise.

Reading the financial press, half of all deals destroy shareholder value. Management either thinks it's too easy, thinks they know more than the next guy, or does not do their homework. M&A transactions need to be carefully thought out and implemented to avoid, at the best case, getting nowhere for a lot of work and money, or at worst case, a disaster. The M&A track record is full of disasters from AOL/Time Warner to Boston Scientific/Guidant.

Steps to Successful M&A Transactions

The five main steps of an M&A transaction are:

1. Planning, transaction structure, and strategy
2. Due diligence
3. Negotiating consideration, risk management, and other terms
4. Document preparation
5. Business transition

Planning, Transaction Structure, and Strategy

Planning, transaction structure, and strategy should be started in the very initial stages of discussions with interested buyers or sellers. Meeting with financial, accounting, and legal advisers to assess transactions and structure alternatives and strategies early on will help you stay focused on your goals and can facilitate finding a buyer or seller with compatible goals and maximizing the value to you. Generally, the party with the clearest idea of what it wants to accomplish and who is willing to put the extra time and money into being proactive instead of reactive in terms of structuring the transaction, establishing terms, and document preparation is likely to get closer to its desired outcome.

Due Diligence

For a prospective buyer, due diligence involves getting to know the target's owners and management, reviewing the target's business, financial, and legal records, inspecting the target's property and equipment, and evaluating its operations and internal controls. The initial formal step is generally to send a due diligence request list asking for copies of all contracts, financial statements, tax records, minute books, benefit plans, reports, and other business and financial records. Then the buyer and its legal counsel and other professional advisers review and analyze the information, identify risks that could affect value, and consider business transition issues.

The three primary types of due diligence a company should engage in to help ensure maximum financial returns when contemplating an M&A transaction are legal, accounting, and operational.

- *Legal.* Are there change of control provisions that will cause contracts to terminate? Is there litigation, environmental exposure, or other contingent liabilities? What kinds of benefit plans are there, and what will be done with them post-closing? Is there real property, and what is the state of title? Is there intellectual property, and what are the risks?

- *Accounting.* Are the seller's financials in accordance with generally accepted accounting principles? Does the seller have proper financial controls? Has the seller recently engaged in aggressive accounting practices to increase earnings and therefore purchase price? How will the transaction be accounted for post-closing? What sort of write-offs will be involved?

- *Operational.* How is the purchase price justified, and what assumptions are made? Those assumptions should be verified to the extent possible. Are the seller's projections realistic? Are there any customer issues or customer concentration issues? What will be done with the seller's contracts? Are they needed, and if not, can they be terminated? How will product lines be rationalized? How will the work force be rationalized? What costs and expenses can be eliminated to provide for synergies?

For a prospective seller, conducting due diligence on the buyer is often overlooked, but it can be equally important, particularly if the buyer is issuing debt or equity to the seller as all or part of the consideration to be paid in the transaction.

Negotiating Consideration, Risk Management, and Other Terms

Negotiating the nature and timing of the consideration to be paid in the deal is often the heart of the deal, and it can be one of the simplest or one of the most complex elements of the transaction. Consideration can be paid in cash, stock, debt, or any conceivable combination of the three. Further, the consideration may be paid at closing or in the future and may be fixed or contingent upon future performance or other factors. Sometimes there are factual circumstances that make certain types of consideration appropriate in certain transactions. For example, if the buyer cannot pay cash, the seller may have to settle for debt or equity. The nature and timing of the consideration can also have significant tax implications that can materially change the value to either party. Although clients will often lead the negotiations on many of these terms, discussing the alternatives with accounting and legal advisers early on is helpful so there are no surprises.

Negotiating other terms, like indemnification, survival, and representations and warranties, focuses more on the risk allocation elements of a transaction and tends to fall to the lawyers to resolve.

Document Preparation

Careful and thoughtful document preparation can add significant efficiencies to the transaction process by minimizing the amount of time spent on corrections and clarifications. It can also protect the client by making it clear what happens in the event there is a disagreement between the parties in the future. Generally, one party's lawyers will prepare most of the documents and solicit comments from the other side. Typically, the party who prepares the documents will incur higher costs in legal fees than the party who is reviewing and commenting. However, the tradeoff is that the final document is likely to more closely reflect the view of the party who prepares the documents than the party who reviews and comments, particularly with respect to terms like indemnification and warranty language that do not have immediate cash implications.

The initial document is generally some kind of letter of intent. Then a purchase agreement or merger agreement is started during or after due diligence is completed. Other closing documents will depend upon the structure of the transaction but often include employment agreements, leases, notes, assignments, and consents.

Business Transition

Business transition is principally conducted by the buyer, but lawyers are typically involved in employment, benefits, real estate, and regulatory matters related to changes in ownership, as well as assuring that contracts affected by the sale are handled in accordance with their terms.

Finding the Most Valuable Deal

Finding the right buyer or seller and walking away from the wrong ones is one of the most important aspects of an M&A transaction. Finding a buyer or seller who is motivated, reasonable, and has compatible goals is a critical factor in achieving financial success. This combination generates a greater opportunity to leverage the value to both parties.

Understanding the Buyer's Goals and Resources

For example, consider an entrepreneur who has decided he's ready to sell the business he founded ten years ago. Although the company has suffered losses over the last few years, the technology he's developed is cutting-edge and he has an excellent reputation and market acceptance. He loves the business and thinks it still has a lot of potential for growth, but he realizes he doesn't have the resources required to take the business to the next level, and his investors, who own about 60 percent of the company, are putting pressure on him for some return on capital. His financial advisers think the business is worth approximately $15 million, net of $10 million of outstanding debt and taking into account $5 million of loss carry-forwards. Most of the target's equipment is in good condition but has been almost completely depreciated on the books.

Three prospective buyers have made preliminary offers:

1. *A prominent venture capital firm.* The venture capital firm thinks this is a hot new industry and that this would be an attractive opportunity to diversify its portfolio. Despite recent losses, their analysts think

the target is financially sound and has significant potential. They are interested in adding the company to their portfolio and would like the founder to continue running it. They have offered to pay up to $18 million for the stock of the target, consisting of $6 million in cash at closing, plus an earn-out of up to $12 million over five years subject to meeting certain performance criteria, and a five-year employment agreement with a very competitive salary and incentive bonus program. The venture capital firm also requires that 25 percent of the initial cash payment be held in escrow for a year to cover potential indemnification claims.

2. *An up-and-coming competitor in the industry.* The competitor has similar technology and personnel to manage the business and is primarily interested in acquiring the target's customer relationships and equipment to expand its operations. The competitor cannot take advantage of any of the loss carry-forwards and desires to do an asset purchase so it can book up the equipment. The competitor has offered a total of $22 million for the assets but is short on cash and has limited borrowing capacity, so it proposes to pay $17 million in cash at closing (resulting in $7 million of cash to the seller after paying off the target's debt) and the $5 million balance in the form of a subordinated five-year promissory note at a rate of 8 percent *per annum*. In the past, the entrepreneur has had trouble with this competitor trying to hire away his employees, and he worries they may just be trying to get a look at the target's confidential information.

3. *An established public company in a related industry.* The public company is interested in expanding into the target's industry and desires to jump-start its operations and market penetration by taking advantage of the target's developed technology and name recognition. The public company could develop the line of business itself from scratch, but it would prefer to acquire an established business at a reasonable price if possible. It would like the entrepreneur to be available for a year on a part-time consulting basis at a competitive rate, but it does not require his long-term participation. The public company can take immediate advantage of the loss carry-forwards and refinance the debt at a lower rate. It

proposes to do a merger in the form of a tax-free reorganization. The public company is offering aggregate consideration of $15 million, consisting of $2 million in cash at closing and stock with a market value of $13 million on the closing date. The stock of the public company has been strong historically, but it has experienced some significant fluctuations in recent months.

So, which of these buyers is offering the best deal financially? Obviously, it depends on the seller's financial considerations and risk tolerance.

Understanding the Seller's Goals and Expectations

In the above example, consider the following scenarios and some of the key financial and legal considerations affecting the seller and how that affects the decision-making process:

- If the entrepreneur is a thirty-year-old and desires to stay involved in the business, he can realize the most gain in the long run by selling to the venture capital firm, but if the business fails, he may earn no more than his 40 percent share of the initial cash payment. Further, his investors may not find this alternative very attractive because the return is so heavily dependent upon the entrepreneur's continued performance. If we represented the entrepreneur, we would want to make sure he was well protected in terms of the objective performance criteria under which the earn-out and incentive bonus program would be calculated and that he would be adequately protected from involuntary termination. If we represented the entrepreneur's investors, we would want to maximize the amount of the incentive consideration that flows through to investors through the earn-out as opposed to being paid in bonus to the entrepreneur as an employee.

- If the entrepreneur is a forty-year-old with a family who wants to maximize his immediate cash return so he can set aside a small nest egg for retirement and use the rest to launch a related new business, he may be most interested in the competitor's offer. It is the smallest total consideration, but it is the most cash up front, and if the competitor is successful, it will result in a consistent stream of cash over five years while he is starting the new business. It is also simple to distribute cash to the entrepreneur's investors, but there are other legal issues such as making sure the entrepreneur's new business plans will be compatible with any non-compete or solicitation entered into as part of the transaction. In addition, we would need to address the entrepreneur's concern about whether the competitor is in good faith interested in the transaction or just trying to gain access to the target's confidential information. A non-disclosure agreement provides some protection against the competitor sharing the information with other third parties or other inappropriate uses of the information, but it is often very difficult to prove and a seller should always be very circumspect about sharing information with anyone he or she doesn't trust.

- If the entrepreneur is a sixty-year-old who desires to retire and has no immediate need for cash, the public company's offer may be the most desirable to him. It has a slightly higher price than the competitor's offer, but it only requires him to continue working for a limited time and allows him to defer some taxes until he sells the stock. He takes the risk that the stock will lose value, but if he has time to wait out the market and strategically time his sales with the rest of his retirement portfolio, he could realize additional gain on the stock. This may provide him the most attractive mix of return versus risk. If we represented the seller in this scenario, we would want to minimize restrictions on liquidity and make sure the seller is adequately protected from fluctuating stock prices prior to the closing date (for example, by placing a "collar" around the share price—a minimum and maximum price that constitutes a condition to closing).

While the foregoing examples may be overly simplistic, they demonstrate how important it is to find a buyer and seller who have compatible goals. Where the goals are incompatible, the highest value to the parties cannot be realized.

Other Buyer/Seller-Related Considerations

<u>Buying from an Entrepreneur</u>

Entrepreneurs often have an emotional attachment and expectation of growth for the business that exceeds the fair market value determined by traditional financial modeling. This can be particularly true if it is his or her first successful business venture. In approaching the negotiation process, entrepreneurs need to learn to manage their expectations, and buyers need to understand that a completely objective valuation approach may not be persuasive. Often, there is a middle ground, like structuring a significant portion of the consideration as an earn-out that can reasonably balance the goals and expectations of both sides.

<u>Selling to Private Equity Groups</u>

When management sells to private equity groups, they often overlook and fail to appreciate the potential downside. Management often rolls a portion of their stake into the acquisition vehicle. Many make the mistake of not looking beyond closing and payment of the purchase price. Management often gives the private equity group overly optimistic projections of future operations in order to increase the purchase price. Then when management is later unable to meet those projections, the private equity group becomes dissatisfied and either replaces management or reduces their scope of authority and compensation.

<u>Mergers of Equals</u>

A merger of equals often involves two companies with similar or related product lines. The similarity often leads to those situations where synergies are greatest. By combining the best of both companies and eliminating redundant costs, significant value can often accrue to shareholders. Merger of equal transactions are often the most difficult to negotiate. Every decision requires a consensus, because neither party views themselves as being acquired. It is not just about price, but the post-closing roles for directors and management.

When It Works, When It Doesn't

We recently represented an entrepreneur who sold her business to a national manufacturer and distributor in a related industry. Much like some of the elements in the example above, she developed her product line over the last fifteen years, developed significant regional name recognition in a niche industry, and concluded that the next step was to expand nationally. After reflecting on her initial efforts to expand the business, she realized her greatest contribution to the business was in product development and marketing and that she needed a broader network to expand production, sales, and distribution.

After talking with several potential bidders with different business models, she decided to sell to the national manufacturer. From the seller's perspective, the thing that gave her significant leverage and that ultimately led to a very attractive financial deal for her was that the buyer wanted to buy more than the seller wanted or needed to sell. The seller had a profitable business, no immediate need to sell, and other prospective buyers who had made competitive offers. While the basic price was set from the initial stages, through the negotiation process we were able to minimize our client's indemnification obligations, restructure some of the consideration so it would qualify for capital gains treatment instead of ordinary income treatment, narrow the non-compete and non-solicitation provisions, and reduce our client's overall risk. The shareholders of the seller received their respective proportion of the total consideration in cash, and the extra incentive consideration to the entrepreneur to continue working for the business was reflected in the employment agreement instead of through an earn-out that would have reduced the transaction consideration immediately payable to all shareholders.

The transaction was an all-cash asset sale and incentive compensation to the entrepreneur under an employment agreement to stay and work for the buyer to continue growing the acquired target business.

Again, it must be emphasized that it's not just about price, but finding the right buyer. Other bidders in the above example offered similar prices, but they could not provide some of the assurances that minimized the seller's risk or as desirable a mix for the entrepreneur and the shareholders of up-front cash and future incentive consideration. Also, this particular buyer had a very practical approach and respectful appreciation for the business and the entrepreneur that facilitated the efficiency of the transaction and the parties' mutual satisfaction with the process and results.

There are also a lot of horror stories. We saw one company pay $150 million for a client, only to sell the business five years later for $20 million. They apparently underestimated what it would take to transition and run the business successfully. We saw another company pay $30 million to a client, only to literally give the company back a little over a year later. After such significant internal and external cost, they re-evaluated and determined they had to return to their core business and focus on it.

Some hardships cannot be avoided even when the highest degree of caution is taken, but to the extent such obvious disasters can be avoided or lessened through more thorough front-end integration planning, these examples demonstrate how important that can be. Achieving success requires addressing integration issues at the outset, working with your legal counsel and accountants and other advisers to handle the financial and legal considerations relating to the transaction, and making contingency plans for those challenges and misfortunes that cannot be avoided.

Stephen M. Quinlivan practices primarily in the areas of mergers and acquisitions, sports law, securities, and international transactions. His mergers and acquisition experience includes numerous cross-border transactions, assets purchases, public and private mergers, and tender offers. His securities experience includes all types of offerings including private placements, initial public offerings, high-yield offerings, investment-grade debt, securitizations, and international offerings by foreign private issuers.

Mr. Quinlivan joined Leonard, Street and Deinard in 1997 after seven years of corporate transactional practice in the New York, London, and Hong Kong offices of Cravath, Swaine & Moore. He also has five years of experience as a certified public accountant with Peat Marwick/KPMG Main Hurdman and previously worked as an audit manager.

Mr. Quinlivan is a member of the American Institute of Certified Public Accountants, the American Bar Association, and the Minnesota State Bar Association. He earned his B.S. in accounting and finance in 1982 from the University of Utah and his J.D. in 1990 from the University of Utah College of Law, where he was a member of the Order of the Coif. He is admitted to practice in Minnesota, Colorado, New York, and the District of Columbia.

***Marci Winga** focuses her practice in the areas of mergers and acquisitions, securities law, and general corporate representation. Her experience includes various types of business acquisitions; sales and reorganizations involving public and private companies, including tender offers and going private transactions; as well as venture capital financing, initial public offerings, investment-grade and high-yield debt deals, private placements, and other types of debt and equity offerings. She also counsels clients regularly regarding securities disclosure requirements, contracts, fiduciary obligations, and corporate governance matters. In her practice, she has worked with domestic and foreign clients in a variety of industries ranging from heavy industrial manufacturing to food, retail, medical device, agriculture, auto dealer, Internet, software, and investment companies.*

Ms. Winga is a member of the American Bar Association, the Minnesota State Bar Association, and the Wisconsin State Bar Association. She is a frequent lecturer for the Minnesota Institute of Legal Education and the Wisconsin State Bar Association. She earned her B.S., with high distinction, in economics in 1992 from the University of Iowa, her L.L.M. in international and comparative law in 1995 from the Duke University School of Law, and her J.D. in 1995 from the Duke University School of Law. She is admitted to practice in Minnesota and Wisconsin.

The Benefits of Getting Involved Early

Garth A. Osterman

Partner

Reed Smith LLP

Understanding Your Client's Goals

In a mergers and acquisitions (M&A) practice, we help our clients buy and sell businesses, assets, and/or companies by structuring the transaction, protecting the interests of our clients, drafting and negotiating documents, and helping to consummate the final transaction. As an M&A lawyer, I am most able to add value with regard to the "non-business" financial components of the process. That is, ensuring that the client receives the value that was bargained for. This includes tax issues, indemnification issues, and other matters that protect the client's deal. Much of what drives the structuring of M&A transactions is related to tax and client protection issues, and it is my job to ensure that the transaction is structured to achieve the most efficient tax treatment and to protect the economics negotiated by the client. While I myself am not a tax lawyer, I bring in specialists, troubleshoot issues, and discuss tax implications with my clients. As for the protection issues, those are the issues I specifically focus on and utilize others as necessary.

Because M&A lawyers are charged with protecting our clients, whether one is representing a buyer or a seller, it is the M&A lawyer's duty to make certain the client is getting the transaction he or she bargained for. When we drive a deal to the finish line, we do so with the goal of making sure the deal not only gets done, but gets done and achieves the client's goals.

The Financial Structure of M&A Transactions

Although M&A transactions can be structured in a variety of ways, three general structures are most common: a stock purchase (or, in the case of partnerships or limited liability companies, an equity purchase), an asset purchase, or the merger of two entities. The choice of structure is often dependent on the desired tax treatment, although there are often other considerations. As for merger transactions, depending on the structure of the merger, the merger itself might be treated as a stock purchase or an asset purchase.

In the world of corporate transactions, structuring a transaction as an asset deal can often be a benefit to the buyer but a detriment to the seller, as it means any cash gained from selling assets must first go into the target corporation and then be distributed to the owners. In this process, the cash is taxed by the Internal Revenue Service first when it goes into the corporation, and second when it is distributed to the owners as a dividend or in liquidation of the target corporation. On the other hand, selling a company's stock results in only a single event of taxation for the seller, most likely at the low capital gains rate.

However, from the buyer's side, it is typically better to structure an asset deal. Buying up the stock of a company means the purchased company becomes a wholly owned subsidiary of the buyer, with the assets "stuck" in that entity. Additionally, in buying the target company, all of the liabilities of the target company become the liabilities of the buyer (through the chain of ownership). On the other hand, if the buyer completes an asset deal and brings those assets into the buyer, the buyer will receive a step up in basis of the assets, as well as have the opportunity to exclude certain negotiated liabilities of the target.

The Impact of Protections

Another major financial component of M&A transactional structuring is dealing with client protections such as indemnifications, hold-backs, earn-outs, and either the exclusion or transferring of unwanted liabilities (depending on what side of the transaction you represent). Each of these issues affects the amount of dollars the buyer must pay or the seller receives. In the past, I have been involved in transactions in which a seller believes it is receiving a great deal of money, but the deal is structured such that much of the money is back-ended in terms of an earn-out. The seller often does not realize this or appreciate the effect of an earn-out in the negotiation of the term sheet if the client chooses not to involve a lawyer throughout the process. Obtaining indemnifications from the seller's side can also be of great value to a buyer, as we are able to protect the buyer's interests by ensuring that they are not walking into unknown liabilities, which can add considerable expense to a transaction. Of course, each of these issues affects both sides. Buyers can protect the value of their deal by having earn-outs, hold-backs, and strong indemnifications, while sellers can protect the value of their deal by receiving most, if not all, the sale price up front, limiting the size of any hold-backs, and either limiting the indemnifications or the survival of the indemnifications. I have been involved in several transactions in which the buyer had been lulled into a false security by the fact that they were already acquainted with the seller, only to later realize, once I was brought into the transaction and was able to conduct due diligence, that the seller's business had greater risk or larger liabilities than originally anticipated. In a few of those instances, I was brought in too late to effectively change the structure and the client was stuck with a deal that no longer made economic sense. In short, having an M&A lawyer on board from the beginning stages of the transaction ensures that the client ultimately gets a fair deal with fewer surprises along the way.

Common Client Mistakes

I think it is fair to say most of the clients I deal with are risk-takers. Whether they are selling or buying, my clients look at a business to see whether it will suit their purposes and, if so, they would be happy to close the deal on a napkin or a handshake. As a lawyer, on the other hand, I tend to be risk-averse. Clients consistently fail to anticipate the potential risks involved in any transaction, whether tax risks, liability risks, or protection risks. When I step in, it is not my intention to hinder or slow a deal, but rather to protect the deal my clients believe they are getting. While I am not suggesting businesspeople should stop taking risks, I do believe they should be more thorough in evaluating risks, and M&A lawyers can help in this area.

Bringing a lawyer into the fold sooner can help mitigate or avoid many of the structural problems that can sidetrack deals later down the road. As M&A lawyers, we often become involved in a transaction late in the day because the deal has been handled mostly in-house, and often by non-lawyers. More often than not, there are fundamental problems with the transaction that make it impossible for my client to get the deal they want, and so much of my time is taken up with damage control. I believe the costs of fixing these problems would be lessened by bringing in a lawyer earlier in the process and front-ending the structuring costs.

Elements of Success: Early Involvement

Early in my career, I was very lucky to have excellent mentors in this business, each of whom has helped me develop checklists at the front of each transaction to help clients structure the deals they are looking for. Doing this allows clients to have a set of options at their fingertips from the beginning. More often than not, critical questions that should be addressed up front have not been properly considered by the client, even by the time I become involved in the deal. Making certain these issues are carefully considered helps focus the deal and reduce headaches later in the process.

The sooner I am brought into a transaction, the more successful I am in my role. If my client were to call me the moment after their first phone call with the other side, I am most effective because I am able to focus the negotiation process immediately. Many clients seem not to realize this, and so a lawyer must have a good working relationship with his or her client so the client respects and trusts him or her to add value to the transaction. If a client does not trust that my early involvement is necessary, my role is limited in terms of what I am ultimately able to do for that client. My best client relationships are those based on trust, as the client is more likely to bring me into the deal at an early stage.

Keeping Informed

In order to keep my edge in my field, I read M&A periodicals, deal lists, and daily articles. I read Securities and Exchange Commission publications and keep up to date on continuing legal education, which is released annually, for various types of transactions. Being an avid reader helps keep me on top of current trends in the business.

Structuring M&A Transactions

The five main steps in any successful transaction are identifying the client's goals, structuring for tax issues, conducting effective due diligence, ensuring regulatory compliance, and handling integration issues post-closing. If each of these steps is given proper time and care early in the process, the resulting business will move forward more smoothly and efficiently. The key is to start early. It is ineffectual to do due diligence at the end of the process, or to identify integration problems after the deal is complete. Bringing in an M&A lawyer early in the transaction will facilitate the handling of any issues up front, as a lawyer will be able to bring in the appropriate professionals, line up the due diligence team, and get employment lawyers on board to troubleshoot from the beginning.

The Regulatory Bodies of M&A Law

The most important agencies that influence the financial success of M&A transactions are the Securities and Exchange Commission and the Federal Trade Commission (in regards to Hart-Scott-Rodino compliance). When doing large transactions, it is critical to identify the need for antitrust approval early on. In addition, there are a great many securities regulations that must be complied with in connection with M&A deals on the public level. Even on the private level, where multiple shareholders are involved, the Securities Act of 1933 plays an important role. Using these laws to their maximum financial benefit is a matter of hiring people who understand the potential pitfalls that can trip up a transaction in its later stages.

Understanding the ins and outs of the rules and regulations is crucial to the ultimate success of a deal. Outlining safe harbors and pitfalls to the client should be a front-end event. This is another reason why it is important to get involved with the client early on in the transaction. If a client proposes a structure that does not work from a regulatory standpoint, the issues must be addressed as early and quickly as possible. For example, if a client is looking to close a deal in thirty days due to a quarterly reporting requirement, one may need to factor in Hart-Scott-Rodino waiting periods, and so on, and advise the client accordingly. Troubleshooting regulatory issues is where M&A lawyers are poised to add great front-end value for their clients.

Of course, the laws governing M&A deals are constantly evolving. The Internal Revenue Service Code goes through various changes each year as the government decides what tax breaks will be given and what loopholes must be closed. For example, in 2003, the tax rate on dividends qualifying was dropped, which allows for asset sale transactions to be more profitable to the sellers. Furthermore, with the advent of Sarbanes-Oxley, along with the traditional Securities and Exchange Commission compliance requirements for public companies, there are enhanced rules and regulations in connection with acquisitions that have made the process more complex than ever. Although there has been significant criticism of some aspects of the Sarbanes-Oxley Act, in the context of M&A transactions, Securities and Exchange Commission compliance, as well as Federal Trade Commission approval, will continue through this decade and the foreseeable future. In fact, as private equity firms continue their fevered pace of acquisitions, enhanced regulatory scrutiny is inevitable.

Types of Mergers

M&A transactions come in a number of forms, with one category being mergers. Mergers can be legally structured in a variety of ways, some structures driven by tax goals, others driven by integration needs, and even others driven by the need to resolve one or more deal issues that require unique structuring. Further, from a commercial context, the term "merger" means more than just the legal structure of the transaction, but instead describes the bringing of two companies together. In the commercial context, terms such as "horizontal merger," "vertical merger," "market extension merger," "product extension merger," and "conglomeration" are used, which do not necessarily describe the legal form of a merger, but more of the commercial purposes of the merger.[1]

Regardless of the different types of merger structures and commercial descriptions, the most beneficial type of merger will depend upon the nature of the transaction and the client's ultimate goals in consummating the transaction. It is understanding the client's goals that allows an M&A attorney to bring his or her experience to the table and add value to a transaction. The types of mergers are as diverse as the motivations behind them, and choosing the most beneficial type is a function of the individual circumstances of the buying and selling companies. Whether a transaction is considered a "horizontal merger" or a "product extension merger," it is more important to understand what the client's goal is and help structure the transaction to achieve maximum profitability.

---

[1] A "horizontal merger" typically involves the combining of two companies that are in competition with one another. A "vertical merger" typically involves the merger of a customer and a company or a supplier and a company. A "market extension merger" typically involves the combination of two companies that sell the same products in different markets. A "product extension merger" typically involves the merger of two companies that sell different, but somewhat related, products in a common market. A "conglomeration" is generally the merger of two companies that have no related products or markets (i.e., they have no common businesses).

Obtaining Maximum Profitability

A key approach to structuring a deal to ensure maximum profitability is to give due consideration to the issue of post-closing integration. Combining companies into a single entity raises integration issues for employees and management from both ends. Successful integration is dependent upon the compatibility of the cultures of the two entities into a single unified identity. I have seen a number of deals go badly post-transaction because the two sides continued to fight over which company had the better identity. The most successful mergers are those in which both sides look at the combined entity at the front end of the transaction (that is, envision the combined entity and the "identity" of that entity) and move forward with creating that identity (whether it is a new identity, a combined identity, or one party's identity). From a lawyer's perspective, this translates into executive compensation issues, employee agreements, equity incentive plans, and other employment-related matters. It is often the case that the target company will receive either restricted stock or part of the cash payment as an earn-out, or a combination of both, and I council my buyer clients to not just think about squeezing every penny out of the target entity, but ensuring that the employees and executives of the target company are properly incentivized to make the most of the larger company. In representing the buyer, on the other hand, I spend a good deal of time counseling clients on structuring the integration of their team into the bigger entity to avoid potential conflicts of interest down the road.

Tax is another area that demands careful attention, as a lack of good tax counsel from the start will translate into tax problems that will ultimately affect the economics of the deal. In this area, it is imperative that M&A counsel involve tax specialists at the term sheet stage of the transaction, as once the deal is moving down a certain path, it can be difficult (or embarrassing) to advise the client to change structure due to a tax issue that could have been identified early in the transaction. Of course, this is another reason clients should and need to involve M&A counsel early. Changing structures can be very expensive and time-consuming, something clients do not always appreciate. For example, a relatively unsophisticated client of mine (along with a relatively unsophisticated target company) negotiated a transaction that contemplated a triangular merger of a limited liability company (as the target) and corporation (as the acquirer). The client believed the structure, because it involved stock instead of cash as consideration, would result in a non-taxable transaction (such as when two corporations enter into a triangular merger for stock consideration). The client spent time and energy on this structure and set a closing schedule that was aggressive, assuming all that was left was documenting the transaction. Of course, once I was brought into the transaction (and counsel for the target became involved), the fatal flaws in the transaction were quickly identified. However, the deal then had to be renegotiated due to the tax implications and other items that were identified by counsel. The result was that the closing took much longer than expected, and counsel fees were larger than expected due to the need for restructuring. In the end, had counsel been involved from the beginning, a proper structure would have been put in place and the closing achieved in the timeframe originally projected. It's not that there are common oversights in transactions that could be avoided if the client was sophisticated, it's that the common oversight is failing to involve tax counsel early in the deal.

Non-tax-driven structuring is another critical area in making the most out of the two combining companies. Given that the companies are separate entities with unique cultures and often multiple divisions of businesses, one must determine how the assets are to be utilized in the combined entity to achieve maximum flexibility in gaining economic benefit from the assets. This also includes identifying liabilities in the deal, which are often part of the buying process. Properly structuring the deal means determining which liabilities must be paid off, which liabilities are excluded, who is responsible for the liabilities, and so on.

Achieving the best financial outlook in any acquisition will depend upon its purpose. To that end, it is necessary to identify clear reasons for doing the deal, and then to structure and plan according to those objectives. I have often worked with clients who have no identifiable post-merger plan once the deal is complete, which results in competing objectives between the buyer and the seller that can ultimately hinder the buyer's ability to handle its assets post-closing.

For example, I once handled a transaction in which an acquiring company bought a target merely because the target was extremely profitable, and the buyer was able to incorporate those profits into their current business in order to offset the buyer's liabilities, which in turn helped them in seeking out new funding. However, the buyer had no other goal for the target company, and once merged, in-fighting and a lack of identity and integration resulted in the failure of both businesses.

On the other hand, in buying a company with only assets, as opposed to an operating company with employees, for example, we will attempt to structure the deal according to the client's end goal in order to get the maximum benefit to the client of the assets being acquired. If the buyer intends to hold the assets for the short term, the deal structure will differ than if their intention was to integrate those assets into their own business. We also deal with strategy plays, such as buying a company in order to put an end to the competition, which again is a very different deal than one in which the target is intended to enhance an existing business. In each of these cases, it is crucial to know the end goal of the acquisition in order to ensure that the client will reach its goals. And, as mentioned earlier, if the client's goal is to end competition with a competitor by buying that competitor, understanding that goal is critical to advising on the regulatory aspects of the transaction.

Expanding Due Diligence in M&A Transactions

Another area in which clients sometimes get into trouble is in the context of due diligence or the lack thereof. Companies contemplating an M&A transaction should engage in substantive due diligence, including corporate due diligence, intellectual property due diligence, asset due diligence, and business due diligence. While most clients understand the need for solid intellectual property due diligence, clients cannot forget the need for due diligence in other areas of the business. This not only includes employment due diligence to ascertain what the employment agreements and equity incentive grants look like, and financial due diligence including historical tax returns and balance sheets, but also market due diligence to determine the viability of the market the buyer is entering. Even a company that looks good on paper, both in terms of financials and products, may prove to be unsustainable in the marketplace over the long term. Thus, due diligence should be a careful and cautious process.

Building the Public Image of a Merger

In the case of a merger between two operating companies, typically it is economically beneficial to both sides for any acquisition to be publicized as a merger of similar cultures, and sometimes as a merger of equals. The idea in most mergers of operating companies is that the sum of the whole is greater than the sum of the parts, which is the driving force behind many M&A deals. Regardless of how the parties see themselves—whether as equals, one more dominant, or one culture being better than the other—it is important to publicize it as a merger of two companies that creates synergies, which will allow the combined entity to leap to the next level of business.

Of course, dealing with public company mergers involves compliance with the Securities Exchange Act of 1934, and there are very specific requirements as to what kind of statements should and can be made regarding any transaction. And, although most clients want to make bold statements about their merger transactions, I discourage my clients from making grandiose statements about the merger, as these can be highly problematic, especially if the ultimate results are not what were represented in the statement. While it is good to be positive about any merger, it is an understatement to say one must be careful not to run afoul of public disclosure rules.

The Aftermath: Preventing Discounted Share Prices

The discounted share price that often results from an M&A transaction is very much a market factor analysis. Some excellent M&A transactions have resulted in an immediate drop in share price, but the shares will increase in value thereafter. Generally, the uncertainty period following any deal creates an initial impulse to sell, and the severity of the drop in share price will depend on the debt load in the transaction as well as the market perception of the acquisition's value.

While it is difficult to prevent the market uncertainty that correlates to a drop in share price, it is important to gauge the temperature of the market to ensure that the merger is seen as financially beneficial. The best way to do this is to have the client evaluate the acquisition's potential, and then structure around it. Anticipating market perception is more than a matter of press releases. Rather, it requires a true understanding of the market in order to determine how share prices will be affected, whether positively or negatively.

It is also important to remember that entering into an M&A transaction often brings with it new markets that the buyer and seller alone did not previously have access to. Although clients will often focus on short-term drops in share price (and that may well be a legitimate concern), one must focus on the ultimate potential benefit of a larger market base and the larger revenue that comes with it. However, it is of course essential to ensure that the new revenues received are not overwhelmed by any additional costs the transaction may have created.

The Successful M&A Transaction: Case Example

One of the most rewarding transactions I have been involved in occurred just before the bubble burst in 2001. A young man from a relatively modest background founded a business that became highly successful, and he ultimately sold his company for $60 million to another company. The seller, my client, benefited highly from the sale. I think of this deal with particular fondness because his success was well deserved, and he has gone on to make great charitable contributions with the money he made.

This deal was also handled in a particularly efficient manner. The buyer involved me from the beginning and explained his objectives for the deal, which established a solid up-front understanding of where the transaction was headed. We were able to bring in tax experts early in the game to ensure a sound tax structure for the transaction; we conducted thorough due diligence of the client's business to anticipate issues that might (and eventually did) arise; we involved employment counsel to help negotiate the executive employment agreements that were put in place; and we drove the negotiation process from the beginning (ensuring that we drafted the agreement and proposed the initial structure). Importantly, in talking candidly with the client at the beginning of the transaction, we determined his ultimate desire was to work for the buyer for only a short period of time and transition the management of what would become the new division in the buyer to some of the client's employees. The result of understanding this ultimate goal was negotiation of a set of documents that allowed my client to retire from the buyer early without penalty or affecting the economics of the sale price. In short, my client was able to maximize the up-front value with as little earn-out hold-back as possible, and on the day of closing he did not have to be concerned with his financial position. My client's trust in me was a big part of the success of that deal.

Of all the different strategies in M&A transactions, whether in negotiating deals, drafting documents, or structuring the transaction, the greatest advantage an M&A attorney can gain in a transaction is understanding the client's goals up front, clearly fleshing out those goals, and then proceeding accordingly. The failure to do so can sometimes result in a less-than-satisfactory end to a deal.

Garth A. Osterman regularly serves as lead counsel for clients of all sizes in merger, acquisition, and divestiture transactions, and has served as lead counsel for developers and lenders in project finance transactions. In the project finance arena, his practice includes structured finance transactions and the acquisition, sale, and restructuring of assets for clients participating in the renewable energy industry. His energy practice also includes the development and operation of power generation facilities. In addition, he counsels private owners, banks, and other financial institutions on leveraged leasing transactions involving personal property, including the financing, purchasing, leasing, and selling of aircraft, railcars, container ships, and various types of equipment.

Prior to practicing in the corporate department, Mr. Osterman was a business and commercial litigator, focusing on all types of complex business litigation including commercial transactions, class action litigation, and other business torts.

Mr. Osterman earned his B.A. in English literature in 1993 from the University of Washington, and his J.D., cum laude, in 1996 from the University of San Francisco, where he was managing editor of the University of San Francisco Law Review *and recipient of the American Jurisprudence Award in legal research and writing, and criminal law.*

Dedication: *I would like to dedicate this chapter to my wife, Jacqueline R. Mijuskovic, for all her love and support.*

Risk Assessment: The Deal Lawyer's Perspective

William G. Lawlor

Partner

Dechert LLP

M&A Law: An Overview

As a mergers and acquisitions (M&A) lawyer, I act in three principal capacities:

- As a business counselor, addressing business issues that commonly arise in M&A matters
- As a strategic counselor, addressing tactical and negotiating strategies
- As a legal counselor, addressing legal and contractual issues

As an M&A lawyer, there are three areas of particular focus:

- Valuation (What areas affect value? How do you define value?)
- Certainty of closing (What obstacles are in the way to closing? These might involve anything from competitive bids to legal or business restraints.)
- Speed to closing (How can we structure the deal in a way that gets the deal done as soon as possible?)

In essence, I identify and try to eliminate risk.

Valuation Issues

I assist my clients in analyzing purchase price metrics. For instance, if there is an investment banker involved, I will review the analyses and assumptions made by the banker to make sure they are appropriate based on my experience with deals. Or if there are synergies, I inquire as to the types of synergies and test their achievability (e.g., can you really restructure the labor contract?). I also look for value leakage in the deal. For instance, does there need to be a purchase price adjustment mechanism? An inventory or accounts receivable protection mechanism? What about undisclosed liabilities? Are there breakage costs or transaction expenses that can be avoided? What needs to be bridged to the financials?

Certainty of Closing Issues

When handling the certainty of closing issues, I ask several questions. What are the obstacles to closing? Is there a way to structure the transaction to avoid or mitigate these obstacles? If there are obstacles, do they create leverage for or against my client, and how can these be dealt with? What incentives can you create to motivate the other side to get to the closing? Clients often underrate the certainty of closing issues, which sounds counterintuitive in that no deal can be worth very much if it cannot reach the finish line. Often, this lack of focus by the businesspeople arises from the sometimes technical or legal nature of the issues that can crop up. Probability analysis can sometimes be used to overcome this by translating the risk to a value proposition for the businessperson. Say a client runs an auction and ultimately agrees to sell a business to a buyer who has a particular antitrust problem that must be cleared before the deal can go through. The purchase price is $100 million, and there is a 25 percent chance of the deal failing because of this risk. Applying basic probability theory, the value of this risk is $25 million, and the "real" value of the deal to the seller may be worth just $75 million. What does this tell the client? Maybe the slightly less rich alternative deal he or she may have turned down that had less antitrust risk was really better. Or, maybe the risk is so great that the seller needs to require the buyer to agree to take whatever actions are required to make the antitrust problem go away, or pay a special fee to the seller if they don't.

Certainty of closing issues also are important value drivers from a leverage perspective. Let's take another common example that occurs from time to time. A seller represents in the contract that between the signing and closing of the transaction, there will not be a material adverse change in the business that is being sold. If this condition is not met, the buyer can elect not to close the deal. However, in the real world, this problem usually results in price renegotiations, not busted deals. A buyer can renegotiate (downward) the purchase price in exchange for closing the deal. So, here is an example of a certainty of closing principle leading to leverage leading to value extraction.

Speed to Closing Issues

Lastly, making sure the deal is structured such that it is completed in a timely fashion is very important. This really feeds off of certainty of closing issues and is often handled the same way in terms of identification and management of issues. Valuing speed to closing is very subjective. Sure, there is the time value of money in terms of the nominal purchase price, but there are other parameters as well. From the buyer's perspective, getting the target assets sooner rather than later can be critical in terms of integration or restructuring plans. Or from the seller's perspective, shortening the period between signing and closing a contract alleviates the uncertainties that can crop up in the target business over a period of time, which could complicate a closing condition. Think of the material adverse change issue discussed in the section above, and how a quick closing might alleviate that problem.

The Financial Implications

There are numerous areas with financial implications that arise in a transaction beyond the purchase price (for instance, whether it is appropriate to hire an investment banker and, if so, for what purpose and for how much). We advise clients on the situations that really cry out for a banker and when a client can actually dispense with this engagement. We advise clients on fee amounts and structures based on various databases. We also assist in non-purchase price due diligence matters where valuation efforts come into play. For example, valuation of assumed liabilities such as environmental liabilities, employee costs, and litigation are very important to consider. Finally, winning the deal and getting it completed has an effect on what the financial outcomes are. For instance, if you represent a buyer, you have to consider how best to position the client to get the deal signed up, when to ask for exclusivity, and how to anticipate what other competing bidders might do.

I've found that some clients fall victim to what I call "deal heat." In the excitement of the deal, a buyer or seller might lose perspective as to why they are doing the deal. For instance, issues that seem small when they are conceded to get the deal done often loom large a year later after the dust settles. A lawyer who has been through the thick and thin of a deal cycle can bring balance to the situation and give real-life examples of problems that arise down the road. I once represented a buyer who was thinking of assuming some innocuous-sounding litigation as part of the purchase of a business. I explained how I once saw a company do this and the litigation ended up costing the client more than the purchase price. The point is not that assumption or non-assumption is the right answer. It obviously depends on the situation. The point is rather to slow down and truly reflect on what you know and don't know about a potential problem and how to appropriately value it.

Successful M&A Strategies

My principle strategy in handling M&A transactions is to take the time to understand what the client really wants to accomplish in doing the deal, what his or her pain threshold is, and finally what his or her risk and reward philosophy is. There are literally thousands of issues that can arise during a transaction, and good lawyers can help the client triage decisions if they occupy the same mindset.

After making sure my client and I are on the same page, I translate as much as I can into dollars and cents, because that's how the businesspeople look at things. Risk can be quantified.

Sellers may have more at stake in failed deal, as uncertainty could mean loss of key managers and portray the seller as "damaged goods" – resulting in the next deal likely being at a lower value.

Is the highest bid always the best price? Take for example, these two bids:

1) $1.25 billion
   – 40% chance that deal will survive antitrust review
   – 6 months till closing
2) $1.1 billion
   – No antitrust issues
   - 30 days till closing

- Using formula to factor in probability, and time of value of money:

$$(P \times B1) + ((1 - P) \times (B2 - E))$$

B1	=	Present value of bid from high bidder with regulatory risk
B2	=	Present value of bid from highest bidder without regulatory problem at second auction
E	=	Additional transaction expenses from failed B1 transaction
P	=	Probability that B1 transaction will close

- Result of formula
  - Value of risky bid
    $(0.40 \times \$1,250,000,000/1.045) + ((1-0.40) \times (\$1,000,000,000 / 1.09 - \$2,000,000))$
    $= \underline{\$1,027,727,615}$

  - Value of safe bid (present value of second highest bid with no regulatory problem)
    $\$1,100,000,000 / 1.0075$
    $= \underline{\$1,091,811,414}$

  - Assumptions
    - 9% discount rate
    - Second auction price = $1,000,000,000
    - Additional transaction expenses from failed bid = $2,000,000

Breakup Fees and Regulatory Risk
- Contractual arrangements may not be enough
  - Divestitures
  - Commitment to litigate
- Break fees typically range 2% to 4% of equity value where seller exercises fiduciary out
- In seller's market, you may be able to obtain a break fee if failure is due to regulatory problem.

- Compensate seller for lost value
- Deter buyer walk-away option

- What should the fee amount be?
  - If buyer views deal as having 50% chance of obtaining approval, consider adjusting fee for risk ($20 million fee should be $40 million)

I can feel pretty confident I've been successful in an M&A transaction when I've helped the client look at value in ways he or she might not have thought of.

Changes in M&A Law

Over the last several years, the Securities and Exchange Commission has attempted to streamline its rules governing transactions to make them more consistent and not dependent on the form of deal structure (e.g., tender offer versus merger). They have also tried, with some success, to reduce the regulatory red tape in completing transactions. For the most part, I give the Securities and Exchange Commission high marks in this area.

The Sarbanes-Oxley rules have been a double-edged sword. On the one hand, they have brought more integrity and transparency to the disclosure and governance process, and this is efficient from an M&A standpoint. On the other hand, the rules' burdensome costs of compliance can negatively affect M&A transactions. For instance, a public company subject to the Sarbanes-Oxley rules might take a pass on a company that had inadequate internal controls or other financial reporting issues if the cost of remediating these problems under the rules outweighs the benefits of the transaction. Sarbanes-Oxley has materially increased compliance costs, and these are ultimately borne by the buyers of the businesses.

Over time, deals have become more complicated in their structure and implementation. This is due to several factors, including a proliferation of various laws that impact an M&A transaction, the increasingly global footprint of buyers, sellers, and their businesses, the cumulative effect of deal precedents, and the increasing sophistication of deal participants.

This trend has led to increasingly complex legal documentation, which has increased the costs of doing deals for buyers and sellers. Looking into the crystal ball, it will be interesting to see if the advent of M&A insurance affects deal practice in a paradoxical way despite this increasing complexity. This insurance essentially provides protection for a buyer or seller with respect to representations, warranties, and indemnities in the purchase and sale agreements, or gaps therein. It could be that as the insurance model takes further hold, agreements may become more standardized. Different risk tolerances of buyers or sellers can be addressed via customized insurance policies.

Mergers of Equals

An acquisition that is publicized as a merger of equals can be beneficial to both the acquiring and target companies because synergies can be emphasized. An underrated aspect in many mergers is the people resource. Mergers of equals are often, but not always, in-market transactions. The companies get an opportunity to reshuffle the talent deck and study in depth what their competitors do, for better or worse.

A "merger of equals" should really be a merger of "equals." A disguised takeover of one company by another can lead to confusion in management expectations as well as shareholder concerns about the strategic direction of the businesses.

I encourage my clients to avoid fluff and "corpspeak," and to articulate the most important strategic and operational strategies when making public statements about an M&A transaction. Forward-looking information is an important part of this equation, but the information provided must be reasonable and the assumptions must be well articulated. This transparency helps avoid disconnects between the marketplace and the deal participants about the purpose of the deal and the value that ultimately comes out of it.

The Prepared Seller

In order for a target company to maximize its financial gain in an M&A transaction, it must have the patience and time to set up a very professional sales and due diligence process. This instills confidence in the prospective buyers that the seller knows what it is doing, and it can affect perceptions that permeate the whole negotiation process. The second-worst response a seller can give a buyer is "I don't know" or "I haven't got that information." The worst response is false information. Both problems stem from a faulty due diligence process.

Cash versus Stock

There are several variables involved with choosing stock or cash, with valuation and tax consequences often the key factors. All things being equal, an acquirer with a stock that trades at a higher multiple than a target's can create a nice arbitrage by using its stock. Stock can also be attractive for acquirers in the sense that the target shareholders will share the risks as well as the benefits of the combined company going forward. On the other hand, sometimes an acquirer will prefer cash because it is less dilutive. If tax efficiencies are important, this usually dictates that stock comprise some portion of the purchase price.

William G. Lawlor is a partner and leads the firm's mergers and acquisitions group. He focuses his practice on mergers and acquisitions, securities offerings, and general corporate representation. His work also includes representation of U.S. and foreign companies in international transactions. He is recognized as a leading lawyer in Chambers USA *as well as* Legal 500.

Mr. Lawlor regularly represents corporate clients, boards of directors, and special committees in ongoing private transactions and other assignments. His work includes both negotiated and contested transactions.

Mr. Lawlor is a graduate of the University of Pennsylvania (B.A., 1977) and Stanford Law School (J.D., 1980).

Mergers & Acquisitions:
A Practical Perspective

Richard S. Green

Partner

Thelen Reid Brown Raysman & Steiner LLP

The main focus of a mergers and acquisitions (M&A) lawyer is helping clients understand M&A deals as a sales process. It is critical to understand not only what is being bought or sold, but also why it is being bought or sold and the objectives of the client in the context of the transaction. I have worked with a number of clients who have a great deal of experience in operating businesses, but who have little or no experience in purchase and sale transactions, and I help these clients manage the legal risks and challenges in accomplishing the transaction they have in mind. I add the most value for clients in clarifying the M&A process with knowledge and experience.

From a legal point of view, risk management is the most significant challenge in the context of M&A deals. Proper risk management requires an understanding of what is to be gained by consummating the transaction as well as the consequences of not completing the transaction. For example, if I am representing a buyer whose expectations are not met, it will become necessary to consider whether the buyer will have any recourse against the seller and, if so, how and to what extent. One must understand the rights of a buyer not to close, the rights of a seller to compel a closing, and the consequences of not reaching a closing if one party determines the deal did not proceed as promised.

The Main Areas of M&A Law

Contract law is the basis of virtually all my client work, as every M&A transaction involves a contract. The key issues we help our clients with are pricing, contract terms, statements about the business, the operation of the acquired business pending closing, the conditions (outs), and the consequences of a failure to close. The transaction is structured taking into accounts terms of the deal and the facts of the business, the warranties, and the covenants, wherein each party agrees to perform certain duties by the closing of the transaction. Furthermore, termination provisions must be agreed upon, including post-closing remedies and rights of recovery. These are the fundamentals of risk allocation. Therefore, it is critically important for the client to understand how an M&A agreement is put together and why it's important.

Secondly, tax issues play a significant role in M&A deals, as taxes are integral to any acquisition transaction. If the transaction is not taxable, the acquisition structure must conform to the requirements of the applicable tax code provisions. If a transaction is intended to be non-taxable but turns out to be taxable, the seller may be liable for taxes it doesn't have the cash to pay. In taxable transactions, the impact of the transaction on the tax attributes of the acquired entity, such as the incurrence of entity-level gain and step-ups in tax basis, need to be considered. Although I have acquired a working knowledge of many of the basic tax principles involved in structuring acquisitions, given the complexities of tax law, I believe it is always prudent to involve a tax lawyer at an early stage in connection with any acquisition transaction.

Corporate governance issues also can be important in M&A transactions. This is particularly true of public companies, in which it is the duty of directors to decide whether to sell the business. It is the M&A lawyer's responsibility to help directors manage that process and ensure compliance with the applicable legal standards. This is true both in terms of assessing alternatives to a transaction as well as authorizing a transaction, and the process may continue through to closing if another bidder arises along the way.

Securities law is also particularly relevant to M&A practice if securities are used as a consideration in the transaction. Where a shareholder vote is required, disclosure issues will arise. In particular, it is always a challenge to present the material facts of the background of the transaction, the history of the negotiations, and the board's reasons for recommending the transaction, while safeguarding confidential facts to the maximum extent possible.

Understanding Your Motivation: The Importance of Due Diligence

The financial concerns of M&A deals begin with the basic question of why the client is proposing to engage in the transaction. In this respect, selling a business can be likened to selling a house. One must decide when to sell, why to sell, and what the expected price is. Whereas one person may decide to sell a house because he or she is moving away, another may have gone bankrupt and must sell in order to raise money.

The same is true of acquisition transactions generally. It is always important to determine the reasons behind the acquisition, whether it is to enter a market, obtain a product, hinder competition, or simply take advantage of an irresistible price. Investigation and due diligence are, therefore, highly important in helping a client manage the financial implications of an M&A deal. We help the client look at the business thoroughly and address any questions so our clients will emerge with the best transaction possible.

Due diligence usually involves a consideration of the fundamentals of the business (which the client itself must assess), finance and accounting matters, human resources and benefits matters, regulatory matters, key contracts and liabilities, litigation, and other contingencies that can have a direct effect on value. Sophisticated clients will usually rely upon a team of advisers, including not only their own personnel (who may possess valuable, practical experience in looking at a business) and legal counsel, but also accountants, investment advisers, and other consultants with specialized expertise. The client benefits from the perspectives each of these experts brings.

For instance, some years ago we worked on a transaction in which our client was a large, publicly traded company that had signed a contract to purchase a significant subsidiary of another company. The seller company became fairly well known through the headlines when the parent company filed for bankruptcy, triggering tax, pension, and securities law liabilities the parties had not contemplated at the time they signed the acquisition agreement. We found ourselves embroiled in months of negotiations and discussions in an attempt to demonstrate to the bankrupt seller that it could not deliver at the closing what was promised at the signing. Meanwhile, our client had obtained substantial financing commitments in order to fund the purchase price to be paid in the transaction. Our main goal was to ensure that our client could get out of the deal without incurring any further financial loss. The seller's business team was eventually persuaded that the transaction now had a very low probability of closing, and that it would be in the best interests of both sides for them to terminate the agreement.

Avoiding "Deal Fever"

In my experience, clients can develop "deal fever." In other words, clients have a tendency to acquire an ardor for a quick closing that makes them grow impatient with the process. This can happen particularly in auction situations, where a business is put up for sale in a competitive bidding process. Clients may be reluctant to ask all the questions they should in order to grow comfortable with the contours of the acquisition. Furthermore, there can be a great deal of impatience with the negotiation process, especially at the chief executive officer or chief financial officer level. While senior executives may simply want to get the deal done, that may not always be the best outcome. From a legal standpoint, patience is a virtue.

In order to help a client through deal fever, I have learned to keep my own temper and emotions in check at all times so I am better able to focus on the client's needs and interests. Lawyers are advisers, not principals, and I have found it critical to remember this throughout the transaction. I also diligently try to ensure that the deal being made is the deal the client wants, not necessarily the deal I believe the client should make. While there are times when those deals may be one and the same, other times I may feel strongly based on my experience that a particular point ought to be resolved in a different manner. However, while I am willing to bring these points to my client's attention, the ultimate decision is the client's and not mine.

Achieving Success as an M&A Lawyer

My success is dictated by how well I help my clients define their goals and objectives from the beginning. Some clients may be highly sophisticated and experienced in the M&A area, in which case my role will be more technical and supportive. Many clients, however, are less familiar with the process, and for those clients I may play a much broader role in helping them shape their final decisions. I take a proactive stance to working with clients, and even when they have no questions of their own, I try to elicit thinking on topics they may not have previously considered (or haven't discussed with me).

In successfully negotiating a deal, it is critical to make certain the economic terms are clear, as imprecise pricing terms can have real financial implications for a client. I once worked with a client on a major transaction that ended in a very expensive litigation because the client agreed to amend the acquisition agreement without clearly understanding the terms embodied in the amendment. Unfortunately, that amendment was the one document my client had signed while I was on vacation. After closing, the client was excited to receive a large down payment, but was expecting further payments after the closing based upon the signed amendment. In fact, the buyer and seller had two very different understandings of how the post-closing arrangements were to proceed, and the result was litigation.

Furthermore, I have come to believe that in the M&A business, one can never be too well prepared. The only circumstance in which I ever feel anxious is when I enter a negotiation for which I feel less prepared than I ought to be. While it is true an M&A deal is an economic transaction in which money changes hands, it is also important to remember that businesses are organizations composed of people. It is critical to size up the other side, since the behavior of the people across the table can provide a good indication of how the deal will proceed.

Lastly, I do my best to understand my clients' concerns fully and to keep those concerns at the forefront of any deal. Legal issues should never eclipse business issues, and the business objective should always be held as the ultimate goal. Ordinarily, this will involve helping the client identify and understand the true "deal-breakers" and "walk-away points."

Structuring Successful M&A Transactions

The initial role of a lawyer in any M&A deal is developing the right structure for the transaction. In structuring a transaction, M&A lawyers first and foremost identify the key issues at hand, such as the challenges, opportunities, and unconventional and conventional risks of the deal. These issues affect how prices are driven as well as whether the deal structure will be tax-free.

Ordinarily, the structuring state will be followed by due diligence, in which one tests to see how well the assumptions hold up.

From there, the process proceeds to the contract negotiation and execution stage, in which the parties embody their understandings in a binding contract. In this stage, risk is allocated and the conditions to closing are set forth precisely and in detail.

The parties then work together to satisfy the conditions to closing. This may be quick, or it may take substantial time. For example, regulatory approvals in some industries may require many months.

Next comes the closing itself, in which the conditions of the contract are met, the transaction is completed, and the acquiring and acquired businesses come together.

The final stage, and perhaps most important from the client's perspective, is post-closing, in which the buyer must make the most of the newly acquired business. While lawyers may not be heavily involved in the life that begins the day after the closing, it is critical that clients anticipate and fully consider the issues that may arise.

The Rules and Regulations in M&A Law

In M&A law, regulation is a big question. There are those who suggest the rules and regulations of the Securities and Exchange Commission can influence the outcome of an M&A transaction. However, I disagree with that position. Securities laws deal mainly with disclosure, and as such, in general, I perceive that Securities and Exchange Commission rules are something to be managed, and usually those rules should not represent an insurmountable impediment that changes the outcome of the deal.

In reality, the substantive regulations applicable to particular businesses or industries can be much more significant. For instance, I have worked a great deal in the utilities sector, in which the implication of utility rate making can make or break a deal. Consequently, there is a high level of deal mortality in utility mergers. Furthermore, antitrust can be particularly influential in terms of whether assets must be disposed of in order for the transaction to pass regulatory muster. Lastly, cross-border transactions may be subject to local governmental rules concerning currency repatriation, change of control restrictions, restrictions on foreign ownership, and so on. These issues can have real implications for any M&A deal, as they may mean the buyer may not be unable to keep certain parts of a business.

Furthermore, the adoption of the Sarbanes-Oxley Act in 2002 caused a number of acquirers to stop and consider how the chief executive officer of an acquiring company would be able to give certifications on the financial statements that include a newly acquired company. The adoption of Sarbanes-Oxley has also placed significantly more emphasis on disclosure and internal control than in the past. Speaking optimistically, Sarbanes-Oxley has forced publicly traded acquiring companies to be more sober and careful about the buying process, potentially giving acquirers sounder footing in understanding and integrating the acquired business.

Types of Mergers: Risks and Benefits

There are several types of business combinations, such as horizontal versus vertical mergers, and market extension or product extension acquisitions. While no one category of transaction is necessarily more beneficial than the others, each has its own considerations. In any business combination merger, one must first look at antitrust issues, as the market position of the combined companies may be so powerful that antitrust laws come into play. If one is able to realize cost production and the economics of scale, it is possible to become a powerful player in the market.

The core question at the heart of any M&A deal is how the merger will make the combined company stronger. A horizontal merger will allow the acquiring company to cover more of the market, while a vertical merger can presumably strengthen the acquiring company's source of supply. Market extension mergers may allow products to be sold together, as with product extension mergers. In structuring the deal, one must pursue the path that will strengthen the company while keeping realistic expectations of the benefits. Therefore, there is no mathematical equation for choosing which type of merger will yield the most benefit, as it is dependent upon the nature of the specific opportunity.

A useful exercise is to turn the question around and ask oneself why the acquired company is pursuing a sale transaction. Looking at the deal from both sides allows the buyer to see the opportunity more clearly, which ultimately can produce the best result.

The Effect of Company Size on Deal Structure

In general, when a smaller acquisition (in relation to the size of the combined business) goes sour, there will be less of a negative impact. On the flip side, a smaller acquisition that goes well will have less of a positive impact. Because going for big deals involves more risk, the potential upside and downside are greater. On one hand, small businesses have a need for capital and corporate support that can make them excellent candidates for acquisitions. The resources of a larger enterprise may be better able to provide capital resources, management resources, infrastructure, and access to markets. As a result, the small business will be able to grow as part of a larger enterprise, achieving goals it may not have been capable of achieving on its own. On the other hand, large companies may be under pressure to produce a strong increase in stockholder value in the short term, which also can make them excellent candidates for acquisition.

It is my opinion that separating the concept of a "merger of equals" from a so-called "acquisition" can be an artificial distinction. Rather, one ought to look at business combination transactions as part of a continuum. At one end of the spectrum are very large businesses acquiring very small businesses for cash. Under these circumstances, the post-closing direction is clearly in the hands of the buyer. At the other end of the spectrum is what might be considered true mergers of equals, in which the management and stockholder groups of both combining companies participate on a relatively similar basis in the combined enterprise. The latter is, however, a relatively very rare situation, because the two combining companies must be seen to be of roughly equal value. Between those two end points lies a whole range of transactions, the conditions of which are dictated by how much cash is in the transaction relative to the amount (if any) of stock, as well as the relative sizes and values of the combining businesses. Also significant will be the relative roles of the two management teams in the combined enterprise.

The deal structure itself should be approached as a solution to a problem. For example, the seller of a small business may prefer cash to stock. Likewise, in a larger transaction, a public company may not wish to concentrate ownership of stock in only a few hands, and may therefore prefer to pay for acquisitions in cash. At the same time, most public companies are concerned about earnings dilution, and therefore will take care to limit the number of shares to be issued in an acquisition transaction. Therefore, one must look at the needs of the seller and the buyer, taking into consideration the nature of the shareholders as well as the risks and opportunities involved *vis-à-vis* the size of the business. Ultimately, the benefits of an M&A deal depend heavily on the individual facts and merits of the companies involved. I would not say big businesses can never benefit from being taken over, nor would I say small businesses should always remain independent.

Negotiation Strategies

The most important day for a client in any transaction is the day after the closing. The buyer must be able to answer the question of what the buyer will do with the acquired business after closing. The strategic reason driving the acquisition in the first place will dictate the buyer's approach to integration, and if the client does not understand the motivations for the transaction, such that effective integration does not occur, the prospects of achieving financial success are limited. Likewise, sellers have different motives when pursuing a deal, and those motives should be considered in the integration plan. Thus, the heart of M&A practice goes back to understanding the clients' objectives in doing the deal.

Any client looking to acquire another company must be able to answer the question of why they are entering into the transaction, what the expected benefits are, and how the risks and benefits balance out. I often ask my clients to consider the consequences of not doing the transaction in contrast to the consequences of going ahead. This discussion often helps flesh out the risks and opportunities involved in the deal. Lawyers are in an excellent position to bring their experience to bear in helping clients think beyond legal issues.

In the situation of a company that is being acquired, maximizing financial gain is a question of balancing near-term price with allocation of legal risk. When a public company is acquired, for example, the representations and warranties in the acquisition agreement do not survive the closing. When the transaction closes, the public shareholders receive the purchase price, and that is the end of the discussion. In a private company acquisition, however, shareholders are typically asked to make representations and warranties about the acquired business that will survive the closing. The buyer will have the ability to make a claim against the sellers if any of those representations or warranties turn out not to be accurate. Thus, it is necessary, as part of the negotiation of the purchase contract, to determine the scope of those representations and warranties, as well as the bounds of exposure.

Two years ago, I was representing a certain acquirer. In the negotiations, the seller's lawyer told me that what was most important to him was not how much my client was offering to pay at the time, but rather what the potential benefits would be a year in the future. I never forgot those words, because it was a wonderful learning experience and it allowed me to see how a seller thinks. The process is akin to buying a car in that the buyer must decide whether to pay more for a car that comes with a warranty. One must consider not only how much to spend, but also the likelihood that the warranty will apply and whether the person behind the warranty will make good on it.

Economic Success Factors

The economic situation of the acquired company can have a significant impact on the financial success of an M&A transaction. A target company does not necessarily need to be in a strong financial position for the transaction to be a success. However, a buyer must be extremely realistic in dealing with a company in financial trouble, not only in terms of the capital that will be required to shore up the target company's finances, but also in terms of the management time and resources that will be needed to address the target's weaknesses. Businesses are often on the block because of strategic or financial weakness, and while they may present a good business opportunity, the limits of that opportunity must be completely understood from the beginning.

There is also a question of whether to conduct a transaction with stock versus with cash. In the past, when one could account for business combination transactions on the "pooling of interests" accounting method, the potential benefits of using stock as acquisition currency were greater. Now that this is no longer the case and all transactions must be accounted for on using the "purchase" method, tax considerations will play a more central role in determining whether to proceed with cash versus stock. One must determine not only whether the seller can obtain favorable tax treatment, but also what the relative cost of capital will be for the acquiring company. Stock is equity, and as such has an equity cost of capital. Depending upon the company's cash situation, cash may or may not have the same cost.

Lastly, the state of the economy itself may affect the financial benefits of a transaction. In a strong economy, prices tend to be higher, there is more optimism in the market, and acquirers are willing to take more risk. Furthermore, acquired companies that see the opportunity for higher prices may be more willing to sell. In a weak economy, on the other hand, there are more opportunities to buy businesses poised for the next upturn, and buyers may be able to purchase at more advantageous prices. Supply and demand also dictates the amount of capital and competition for certain targets irrespective of the economy. For example, there is currently a tremendous amount of private equity looking for deals, and that will tend to keep prices high.

Preventing Discounted Share Price

Preventing a discounted share price in the wake of an M&A transaction will depend upon execution (integration) to assure that the acquired company will perform as projected. Similarly, the accuracy of projected performance can depend upon the quality of the due diligence investigation. Unsuccessful transactions, whether due to poor assessment of the opportunity or failure to realize expected results in the marketplace, will depress share prices. The AOL-Time Warner merger is an example of a deal in which post-closing business performance simply did not measure up to market expectations, and as a result, the market value of shares of Time Warner common stock languished.

There are several aspects of the transaction that have a direct impact on the financial benefits of the companies involved. Risk allocation, representations and warranties, the quality of the management team, and the tenure of the management all affect the success of the new enterprise in the marketplace. Once the issues that are in need of attention are identified, one is in a position to affect the results of the integration tremendously.

One of the most sobering exercises a company can perform is to look at a deal a year later and ask whether the company has lived up to the expectations of the deal. Consequently, identifying and addressing risk allocation and dealing with management should be central to the lawyer's role in any transaction.

Example Deals: Positive and Negative

The most financially rewarding M&A transactions in which I have been involved have entailed the acquisition of assets that have become very hard to duplicate—for example, buying a power plant in an area in which no new permits for plants will be issued. Because there are barriers to entry and the property is unique, the margin is high and the transaction has a great possibility of success. The trick is to know the market, the business, and the trends. There may be assets that are so unique they will confer pricing power on their owner. In these instances, it is critical to understand the opportunities such unique properties can present.

A recipe for disaster in any transaction is dishonest people selling a company that has hidden liabilities. If the people behind the deal are not trustworthy, the contract itself may be of limited value after the closing. (Resolution of post-closing claims is difficult even in the best of circumstances.) Clients must be willing to walk away from greedy and dishonest people, which can mean leaving a deal on the table. This is very difficult to do, particularly if the asset seems to be worth owning. Of course, this is a business decision. I once worked on the acquisition of a construction company that had a hidden liability, the amount of which ended up greater than the purchase price paid for the whole business. The chief executive officer of our client company described the deal as the worst acquisition they ever made.

In the end, it is most important for clients to keep sight of the basic strategic reasons underlying the transaction and to remain disciplined in achieving that objective. Lawyers often tend to focus on problems when businesspeople want to focus on solutions. In M&A transactions, it's been my experience that clients tend to become fixated on the rewards and such that they may lose sight of the risks that must be considered if the transaction is to be successful. I feel most successful when I have been able to assist clients in balancing the risks and rewards.

Richard S. Green is a partner in the law firm of Thelen Reid Brown Raysman & Steiner LLP, resident in its New York office. A member of the firm's business department, he also serves as chair of the firm's opinion committee. Mr. Green, who has practiced law since 1979, specializes in corporate and securities matters, with an emphasis on mergers and acquisitions and related financing, as well as on strategic planning. He possesses specialized expertise in strategic transactions involving regulated electric and gas utilities, engineering and construction companies, and infrastructure projects. He also has extensive experience in the formation and termination of partnerships, joint ventures and consortia, and strategic alliances. His experience in corporate financing transactions includes public offerings and private placements of debt and equity securities, as well as securitizations and structured financings.

Mr. Green, a member of the New York and District of Columbia Bars, received a B.A. from Harvard University, an M.B.A. from the Wharton School of the University of Pennsylvania, and a J.D. from the University of Pennsylvania Law School.

The Roles of
an M&A Lawyer

Byron F. Egan
Partner
Jackson Walker LLP

As a mergers and acquisitions (M&A) lawyer, my first responsibility in any transaction is to listen to my client to learn what my client wants to achieve, how far my client has progressed with the deal, and what role my client wants me to play in the particular matter.

My client usually has thought about deal and structure before contacting me, but the depth of the client thought processes varies from client to client and deal to deal. My client typically has thought about the role they want me to play in the transaction. Sometimes I play the role of the general counsel in handling or supervising all aspects of the transaction, in which case I may have the discretion to put together the legal team from my firm or elsewhere. Sometimes I play the role of M&A specialist whose client is really the company's general counsel, and sometimes I am special Texas counsel whose role is focused on Texas law issues.

Whatever my designated role may be and whether I am reporting to a client's regular counsel or its businesspeople, I usually feel free to challenge all assumptions and decisions made to date. That way, I can better understand what my client wants and whether the client has focused on all of the issues I see. Clients appreciate this approach, even if it does not change the client's game plan.

Typically, an M&A transaction requires the client to consult with other professionals such as accountants, investment bankers, and consultants. The client often puts the deal team together, but sometimes I can help the client choose the people to perform specified deal roles. However the team is put together, I must adapt to the team my client has approved and work as a seamless unit with the other components of the team to achieve the result sought by the client.

Most of the time the client has a good idea of the value of the entity or assets the client is proposing to acquire (the "target") as well as the amount and form of the consideration the client is prepared to pay for the target. In the process of listening to the client, I try to be an engaged listener, testing what alternatives the client has considered and the client's reasoning behind various decisions. In this process I not only learn, but also contribute value for my client, because in the process of learning what my client has considered, my questions may also cause the client to recognize issues and alternatives that were not initially considered or not fully appreciated. While at this stage my client usually has thought more about the deal and understands it better than I do, my disciplined questions help the client's own cognitive processes and lead to a more fully reasoned deal strategy.

M&A Law and Structure

To be a complete M&A lawyer, one should be a corporate and securities lawyer skilled in corporate governance and process, the drafting and negotiation of acquisition agreements, financing arrangements, and applicable securities laws. I bring to any transaction a knowledge of the business entity statutes governing the formation, governance, and combination of entities, including corporations and "alternative entities" such as partnerships (general, limited, and registered limited), the applicable federal and state securities laws, and relevant case law. In the M&A arena, state court decisions largely define the fiduciary duty principles, which in turn drive how many M&A agreements are structured.[1] I also understand enough federal and state tax, environmental, intellectual property, labor, and real estate law to interface with the team experts in those and other disciplines. I also understand the Sarbanes-Oxley Act of 2002 [2] and how it is currently affecting clients' dealings with their accountants. In short, an M&A lawyer is both a specialist and a generalist, and must in any event be capable of dealing with experts in other areas, both inside and outside of the lawyer's firm, in helping the client coordinate the legal aspects of the M&A transaction. My focus in any particular transaction will be determined by both the nature of the transaction and the role my client expects me to play in the deal.

---

[1] Byron F. Egan, "Recent Developments with Respect to Director and Officer Fiduciary Duties and Other Issues Affecting M&A Activity," 28th Annual Conference on Securities Regulation and Business Law Problems, Dallas, February 10, 2006, available at www.jw.com/site/jsp/publicationinfo.jsp?id=557.

[2] Byron F. Egan, "Effect of Sarbanes-Oxley on M&A Transactions," ABA's 10th Annual National Institute on Negotiating Business Acquisitions, Washington, D.C., November 11, 2005, available at www.jw.com/site/jsp/publicationinfo.jsp?id=527; Byron F. Egan, "Communications with Accountants After the Sarbanes-Oxley Act (including Attorney Letters to Auditors re Loss Contingencies, Attorney Duties under SOX §§ 303 and 307, Options Backdating)," UCLA Law Third Annual Institute on Corporate, Securities, and Related Aspects of Mergers and Acquisitions, New York, October 24, 2006, available at www.jw.com/site/jsp/publicationinfo.jsp?id=624.

Securities Laws

The foregoing is generally applicable whether either the target or the acquiring company (i) is required to file periodic reports with the Securities and Exchange Commission (SEC) under the Securities Exchange Act of 1934 and has a class of equity securities for which there is a public trading market (a "public company") or (ii) is not a public company (a "private company"). If the transaction involves a public company, compliance with the Securities Exchange Act of 1934 overlays the entire M&A process, beginning with when the act will require the disclosure of the transaction. If the transaction would be material to the public company and possible leaks regarding the proposed transaction cause increased trading activity such that a stock exchange or securities regulator makes inquiries, the public company may be forced to make disclosures regarding the transaction even before a binding agreement to effect the transaction has been executed. Such premature disclosure could in turn require further disclosures during the course of negotiations. None of the parties wants to negotiate a transaction in a fishbowl where transactional negotiating developments may require a press release or SEC Form 8-K Report, which could exacerbate otherwise intense negotiating pressures and perhaps provide an opening for a rival bidder to emerge. Thus, an M&A lawyer is sensitive to both developments that could require disclosure and advising clients as to ways to minimize the risks. The acquirer and the target will typically enter into an agreement between themselves to maintain the confidentiality of information received by one from the other. The M&A lawyer will recognize the risks of leaks from financing sources and others, and seek assurances of confidentiality from them as well.

Once the transaction is announced, the public company will have to promptly issue press releases and make SEC filings disclosing the transaction. In the event that the public company is required to submit the transaction to a vote of its shareholders, the company will have to file its proxy materials with the SEC under the SEC's proxy rules under the Securities Exchange Act of 1934. I work on all of these SEC filings for clients.

Structuring

For both public company and private company deals, the M&A lawyer advises the client in structuring the transaction.[3] The considerations involved in the structuring of a sale of a business include federal income taxes; state sales, use, and transfer taxes; federal and state environmental laws; federal and state securities laws; accounting treatment; state takeover laws; problems involving minority shareholders; the purchaser's liability for the seller's debts and contingent liabilities; insolvency and creditors' rights laws; problems in transferring assets; state corporation laws; stock exchange rules; pension, profit-sharing, and other employee benefit plans; antitrust laws; foreign laws; employment, consulting, and non-compete agreements; union contacts and other labor considerations; insurance; pending and threatened litigation and other target loss contingencies; and the purchaser's remedies for breach of seller's representations and warranties and ability to reach seller assets to satisfy seller liabilities to purchaser for such breaches.

The analysis of these and other factors helps the M&A lawyer advise the client as to which of the three basic forms of business acquisition appears most suited to the proposed transaction:

- Statutory business combination (i.e., a merger, consolidation, or statutory share exchange)
- Purchase of shares
- Purchase of assets

Mergers and Consolidations

Mergers and consolidations involve a vote of shareholders, resulting in the merging or disappearance of one corporate entity into or with another corporate entity and the surviving corporation being vested in the assets of, and liable for the obligations of, the constituent corporations. Mergers and consolidations can be structured to be taxable or non-taxable for federal income tax purposes. If stock is the consideration for the acquisition of the

---

[3] See Byron F. Egan and H. Lawrence Tafe III, "Private Company Acquisitions: A Mock Negotiation," UCLA Law Third Annual Institute on Corporate, Securities, and Related Aspects of Mergers and Acquisitions, New York, October 24, 2006, available at www.jw.com/site/jsp/publicationinfo.jsp?id=625.

non-surviving corporation, the merger can qualify as an "A" reorganization (Section 368(a)(1)(A) of the Internal Revenue Code of 1986, as amended) in which a shareholder of the target corporation may receive stock in the purchasing corporation without recognizing gain or loss at the time under the Internal Revenue Code. However, a shareholder of the target who receives only "boot" (i.e., consideration other than purchaser's stock or other purchaser securities under certain circumstances) is normally taxed as if the shareholder had sold his or her stock in the target corporation in a taxable transaction. Generally stated, a shareholder who receives both stock and boot is not taxed on the stock received (so, as in the merger, at least approximately half the target stock is converted into acquiring company stock), but is taxed on the boot. The boot is taxed either as a dividend or as a capital gain, but not in excess of the gain that would have been realized if the transaction were fully taxable.

Purchases of Shares

The purchase of shares of the target, which only changes who owns the target's stock and thus does not change the assets or liabilities of the target at the time of the acquisition, can likewise be handled on a taxable or non-taxable basis. In a negotiated stock purchase, the acquiring corporation must generally negotiate with each selling shareholder individually. An exception to this is a mechanism known as the "share exchange" permitted by certain state business corporation statutes under which the vote of holders of the requisite percentage (but less than all) of shares can bind all of the shareholders to exchange their shares pursuant to the plan of exchange approved by such vote.

Generally speaking, under §368(a)(1)(B) of the Internal Revenue Code, if the purchaser acquires the stock of the target solely in exchange for the purchaser's voting stock and, after the transaction the purchaser owns stock in the target possessing at least 80 percent of the target's voting power and at least 80 percent of each class of the target's non-voting stock, the transaction can qualify as a tax-free "B" reorganization. One disadvantage of such an acquisition of the target's stock is that the purchaser ordinarily does not obtain a "step-up" in the basis of the target's assets for tax purposes.

Asset Purchases

Generally speaking, asset purchases give the buyer the advantage of specifying the target assets to be acquired and the target liabilities to be assumed. A disadvantage involved in asset purchases in recent years, however, is that the seller is subject to corporate-level taxation on the sale of its assets to a third party in connection with a complete liquidation of the corporation and the distribution of the proceeds to its shareholders. Further, the shareholders of the target are taxed as if they had sold their stock for the liquidation proceeds (less the target's corporate tax liability). Absent available net operating losses, if the sale is a gain, an asset sale is less advantageous for the shareholders than a merger or stock sale.

Generally, under Code §368(a)(1)(C), an acquisition of assets may be non-taxable if the purchaser acquires "substantially all" of the target's assets solely in exchange for the voting stock of the purchaser and then distributes the purchaser's stock, securities, and other properties it receives, as well as its other properties, to its shareholders pursuant to the plan of reorganization.

An acquisition might be structured as an asset purchase for a variety of reasons. It may be the only structure that can be used when a non-corporate seller is involved or where the buyer is only interested in purchasing a portion of the target's assets or assuming only certain of its liabilities. If the target is a public company or if it is likely that one or more of the shareholders will not consent, a sale of stock (except perhaps by way of a statutory merger or share exchange) may be impractical. In many cases, however, an acquisition can be structured as a merger, a purchase of stock, or a purchase of assets.

As a general rule, often it will be in the buyer's best interests to purchase assets, but in the seller's best interests to sell stock or merge. Because of these competing interests, it is important that counsel for both parties be involved at the outset in weighing the various legal and business considerations in an effort to arrive at the optimum, or at least an acceptable, structure. Some of the considerations are specific to the business in which a company engages, some relate to the particular entity structure of the buyer and the seller, and others are more general in nature.

Evaluating the Asset Purchase Alternative

Set forth below are some of the more typical matters to be addressed in evaluating an asset purchase as an alternative to a merger or share exchange ("statutory combination") or a stock purchase.

Purchased Assets

Asset transactions are typically more complicated and more time-consuming than stock purchases and statutory combinations. In contrast to a stock purchase, the buyer in an asset transaction will only acquire the assets described in the acquisition agreement. Accordingly, the assets to be purchased are often described with specificity in the agreement and the transfer documents. The usual practice, however, is for buyer's counsel to use a broad description that includes all of the seller's assets, while describing the more important categories, and then to specifically describe the assets to be excluded and retained by the seller. Often excluded are cash, accounts receivable, litigation claims or claims for tax refunds, personal assets, and certain records pertaining only to the seller's organization. This puts the burden on the seller to specifically identify the assets that are to be retained.

A purchase of assets also is cumbersome because transfer of the seller's assets to the buyer must be documented and separate filings or recordings may be necessary to affect the transfer. This often will involve separate real property deeds, lease assignments, patent and trademark assignments, motor vehicle registrations, and other evidences of transfer that cannot simply be covered by a general bill of sale or assignment. Moreover, these transfers may involve assets in a number of jurisdictions, all with different forms and other requirements for filing and recording.

Contractual Rights

Among the assets to be transferred will be the seller's rights under contracts pertaining to its business. Often these contractual rights cannot be assigned without the consent of other parties. The most common examples are leases that require consent of the lessor and joint ventures or strategic alliances that require consent of the joint venturer or partner. This can be an opportunity for the third party to request confidential information regarding the financial or operational capability of the buyer and to extract concessions in return for granting its consent. This might be avoided by a purchase of stock or a statutory combination. Leases and other agreements often require consent of other parties to any change in ownership or control, whatever the structure of the acquisition. Many government contracts cannot be assigned and require a novation with the buyer after the transaction is consummated. This can pose a significant risk to a buyer.

Asset purchases also present difficult questions about ongoing insurance coverage for risks insured against by the seller. Most insurance policies are, by their terms, not assignable and a buyer may not be able to secure coverage for acts involving the seller or products it manufactures or services it renders prior to the closing.

Governmental Authorizations

Transfer of licenses, permits, or other authorizations granted to a seller by governmental or quasi-governmental entities may be required. In some cases, an application for a transfer or, if the authorization is not transferable, for a new authorization may involve hearings or other administrative delays in addition to the risk of losing the authorization. Many businesses may have been "grandfathered" under regulatory schemes and are thereby exempt from any need to make costly improvements to their properties. The buyer may lose the grandfather benefits and be subject to additional compliance costs.

Income Taxes

The income tax consequences to the buyer and to the seller and its shareholders are important factors in determining the structure of the transaction. The seller will prefer a structure that will generate the highest after-tax proceeds to it, while the buyer will want to seek ways to minimize taxes after the acquisition. The ability to reconcile these goals will depend largely on whether the seller is a C or an S corporation or is an entity taxed as a partnership.

In a taxable asset purchase, the buyer's tax basis in the purchased assets will be equal to the purchase price (including assumed liabilities). An important advantage to the buyer of an asset purchase is the ability to allocate the purchase price among the purchased assets on an asset-by-asset basis to reflect their fair market value, often increasing the tax basis from that of the seller. This "step-up" in basis can allow the buyer greater depreciation and amortization deductions in the future and less gain (or greater loss) on subsequent disposition of those assets.

A significant disadvantage of an asset sale to a C corporation and its shareholders is that a C corporation will generally recognize gain on a sale of assets to a third party or on the in-kind distribution of its appreciated assets in a complete liquidation. Thus, if a buyer purchases assets and the seller liquidates, the seller will recognize gain or loss on an asset-by-asset basis, which will be treated as ordinary income or loss or capital gain or loss, depending on the character of each asset. However, corporations do not receive the benefit of a lower rate on long-term capital gains, and the gains can be taxed at a rate as high as 35 percent. Its shareholders then will be taxed as if they had sold their stock for the proceeds received in liquidation (after reduction by the seller's corporate tax liability). Gain or loss to the shareholders is measured by the difference between the fair market value of the cash or other assets received and the tax basis of the shareholders' stock.

Absent available net operating losses, this can make an asset transaction significantly less advantageous for the shareholders of a C corporation. A sale of stock would avoid this "double tax." However, a buyer purchasing stock of a C corporation will obtain a stepped up basis only in the stock, which is not an asset it would be able to amortize or depreciate for tax purposes, and the buyer generally would not want to succeed to the seller's presumably low tax basis in the acquired assets.

The preceding discussion, which relates only to federal income taxes under the Internal Revenue Code in the case of a C corporation, illustrates the complexity of the tax analysis that may be required for an M&A transaction. By helping the client appreciate how the Internal Revenue Code provisions affect alternative structuring decisions, the M&A lawyer can add value for the client.

Transfer Taxes

Many state and local jurisdictions impose sales, documentary, or similar transfer taxes on the sale of certain categories of assets. For example, a sales tax might apply to the sale of tangible personal property, other than inventory held for resale, or a documentary tax might be required for recording a deed for the transfer of real property. In most cases, these taxes can be avoided if the transaction is structured as a sale of stock or a statutory combination. Responsibility for payment of these taxes is negotiable, but it should be noted that the seller will remain primarily liable for the tax and that the buyer may have successor liability for them. It therefore will be in each party's interest that these taxes are timely paid.

State or local taxes on real and personal property may also require examination, as there may be a reassessment of the value for tax purposes on transfer. However, this can also occur in a change in control resulting from a sale of stock or a merger.

Employment Issues

A sale of assets may yield more employment or labor issues than a stock sale or statutory combination, as the seller will typically terminate its employees who may then be employed by the buyer. Both the seller and buyer run the risk that employee dislocations from the transition will result in litigation or, at least, ill will of those employees affected. The financial liability and risks associated with employee benefit plans, including funding, withdrawal, excise taxes, and penalties, may differ depending on the structure of the transaction. In a stock purchase or statutory combination, any collective bargaining agreements generally remain in effect. In an asset purchase, the status of collective bargaining agreements will depend upon whether the buyer is a "successor," based on the continuity of the business and work force or provisions of the seller's collective bargaining agreement. If it is a successor, the buyer must recognize and bargain with the union.

Assumed and Excluded Liabilities

In any acquisition, regardless of form, one of the most important issues to be resolved is what liabilities incurred by the seller prior to the closing are to be assumed by the buyer. Most such liabilities will be known and dealt with in the representations and warranties of the seller in the acquisition agreement and in the exhibits thereto, reflected in the seller's financial statements, or otherwise disclosed by seller to buyer during the course of the negotiations and due diligence in the acquisition. For such known liabilities, the issue as to which will be assumed by the buyer and which will stay with the seller is resolved in the express terms of the acquisition agreement and is likely to be reflected in the price. For unknown liabilities, the solution is not so easy, and lawyers representing principals in acquisition transactions spend significant time and effort dealing with the allocation of responsibility and risk in respect of such unknown liabilities.

While all of the foregoing would pertain to an acquisition transaction in any form, the legal presumption as to who bears the risk of undisclosed or unforeseen liabilities differs markedly depending upon which of the three conventional acquisition structures has been chosen by the parties.

- In a stock acquisition transaction, since the acquired corporation simply has new owners of its stock and has not changed in form, the corporation retains all of its liabilities and obligations, known or unknown, to the same extent as it would have been responsible for such liabilities prior to the acquisition. In brief, the acquisition has had no effect on the liabilities of the acquired corporation.

- In a merger transaction, where the acquired corporation is merged out of existence, all of its liabilities are assumed, as a matter of state merger law, by the corporation that survives the merger. Unlike the stock acquisition transaction, a new entity will be responsible for the liabilities. However, the practical result is the same as in a stock transaction (i.e., the buyer will have assumed all of the pre-closing liabilities of the acquired corporation as a matter of law).

- By contrast, in an asset purchase, the contract between the parties is expected to determine which of the assets will be acquired by the buyer and which of the liabilities will be assumed by the buyer. Thus, the legal presumption is very different from the stock and merger transactions: the buyer will not assume liabilities of the selling corporation that the buyer has not expressly agreed to assume by contract.

There are a number of business reasons for structuring an acquisition as an asset transaction rather than as a merger or purchase of stock. Some are driven by the obvious necessities of the deal (for example, if less than all of the assets of the business are being acquired, such as when one acquires a division of a large corporation). However, there is probably no more important reason for structuring an acquisition as an asset transaction than the desire on the part of the buyer to limit by express provisions of a contract the liabilities—particularly unknown or contingent liabilities—the buyer does not intend to assume.

Unlike a stock purchase or statutory combination, where the acquired corporation retains all of its liabilities and obligations, known and unknown, the buyer in an asset purchase has an opportunity to determine which liabilities of the seller it will contractually assume. Accordingly, one of the most important issues to be resolved is what liabilities incurred by the seller prior to the closing are to be assumed by the buyer. It is rare in an asset purchase for the buyer not to assume some of the seller's liabilities relating to the business (for example, the seller's obligations under contracts for the performance of services or the manufacture and delivery of goods after the closing). Most of the seller's liabilities will be set forth in the representations and warranties of the seller in the acquisition agreement and in the seller's disclosure letter or schedules, reflected in the seller's financial statements or otherwise disclosed by the seller in the course of the negotiations and due diligence. For these known liabilities, the issue as to which will be assumed by the buyer and which will stay with the seller is reflected in the express terms of the acquisition agreement.

For unknown liabilities or liabilities that are imposed on the buyer as a matter of law, the solution is not so easy, and M&A lawyers spend a significant amount of time and effort dealing with the allocation of responsibility and risk with respect to such liabilities. Many acquisition agreements provide that none of the liabilities of the seller, other than those specifically identified, are being assumed by the buyer, and then give examples of the types of liabilities not being assumed (i.e., tax, products, and environmental liabilities). There are, however, some recognized exceptions to a buyer's ability to avoid the seller's liabilities by the terms of the acquisition agreement, including the following:

- Bulk sales laws permit creditors of a seller to follow the assets of certain types of sellers into the hands of a buyer unless specified procedures are followed.

- Under fraudulent conveyance or transfer statutes, the assets acquired by the buyer can be reached by creditors of the seller under certain circumstances. Actual fraud is not required and a statute may apply merely where the purchase price is not deemed fair consideration for the transfer of assets and the seller is, or is rendered, insolvent.

- Liabilities can be assumed by implication, which may be the result of imprecise drafting or third-party beneficiary arguments that can leave a buyer with responsibility for liabilities of the seller.

- Some state tax statutes provide that taxing authorities can follow the assets to recover taxes owed by the seller. Often, the buyer can secure a waiver from the state or other accommodations to eliminate this risk.

- Under some environmental statutes and court decisions, the buyer may become subject to remediation obligations with respect to activities of a prior owner of real property.

- In some states, courts have held buyers of manufacturing businesses responsible for tort liabilities for defects in products manufactured by a seller while it controlled the business. Similarly, some courts hold that certain environmental liabilities pass to the buyer that acquires substantially all the seller's assets, carries on the business, and benefits from the continuation.

- The purchaser of a business may have successor liability for the seller's unfair labor practices, employment discrimination, pension obligations, or other liabilities to employees.

- In certain jurisdictions, the purchase of an entire business where the shareholders of the seller become shareholders of the buyer can cause a sale of assets to be treated as a "de facto merger." This theory would result in the buyer becoming responsible for all of the seller's liabilities.

None of these exceptions prevents a buyer from attempting to limit the liabilities to be assumed. Thus, either by compliance with a statutory scheme (i.e., the bulk sales laws or state tax lien waiver procedure) or by careful drafting, a conscientious buyer can take comfort in the fact that most contractual provisions of the acquisition agreement should be respected by the courts and should protect the buyer against unforeseen liabilities of the seller.

Determining the Risk of an Asset Purchase

The first step in determining whether a proposed asset purchase will involve any substantial risk of successor liability is to analyze the facts involved in the particular transaction in light of the developments of the various theories of successor liability discussed above. Product liability and environmental liability pose the most serious threats, as virtually all of the significant developments in the law of successor liability seem to involve either product liabilities or environmental liabilities.

It may well be that the company whose assets are the subject of the transaction will not have any product liability problem by reason of the nature of its business. Moreover, even if the company to be acquired does sell products that create some potential liability issues, in the course of due diligence the buyer may be able to make some reasonable judgments with respect to the potential for problems based upon the past history of the selling company. A buyer might also be able to rely on insurance, on an occurrence basis if previously carried by the seller and on a claims-made basis with respect to insurance to be carried by the buyer. It may also be possible to acquire a special policy relating only to products manufactured by the seller prior to the closing and to build in the cost of that policy to the purchase price.

On the environmental front, a similar analysis must be made. There are obviously some types of businesses that present very high-risk situations for buyers. As previously noted, there are both federal and state environmental statutes that will impose liabilities on successors regardless of the form of the transaction.

In addition to analyzing the particular facts that might give rise to successor liability for either products or environmental concerns, one should obviously also review the laws that might be applicable if a successor liability issue were to arise. While choice of law problems may deny complete comfort, the more expansive doctrines of successor liability have been adopted by a relatively small number of states, and it may well be that in any particular transaction, one can determine that the risk of such doctrines applying in the aftermath of a particular acquisition transaction is very low.

If a transaction is likely to be subject to one or more of the doctrines of successor liability, it might be possible to structure the asset purchase in a manner that avoids one or more of the factors upon which courts rely in finding successor liability. In all likelihood, the business considerations will dictate most of the essential elements of how the transaction will be put together—and, in particular, how the business will be run by the buyer in the future. However, since continuity of the seller's business into the buyer's period of ownership is a common theme in all of the current successor liability doctrines, it may be possible for the buyer to take steps to eliminate some of the elements upon which a successor liability case could be founded. Thus, continuity of management, personnel, physical location, trade names, and the like are matters over which the buyer has some control after the asset purchase and might be managed in a way to reduce the risk of successor liability in a close case.

It is important to recognize that in a sale of assets the seller retains primary responsibility for satisfying all its liabilities, whether or not assumed by the buyer. Unlike a sale of stock or a statutory combination, where the shareholders may only be liable to the buyer through the indemnification provisions of the acquisition agreement, a creditor still can proceed directly against the seller after an asset sale. If the seller is liquidated, its shareholders may remain subject to claims of the seller's creditors under statutory or common law principles, although this might be limited to the proceeds received on liquidation and could expire after a period of time. Under state corporate law statutes, a seller's directors may become personally liable to its creditors if the seller distributes the proceeds of a sale of assets to its shareholders without making adequate provision for its liabilities.

In determining what liabilities and business risks are to be assumed by the buyer, the M&A lawyers drafting and negotiating the acquisition agreement need to be sensitive to the reasons the transaction is being structured as a sale of assets. If the parties view the transaction as the acquisition by the buyer of the entire business of the seller, as in a stock purchase, and the transaction is structured as a sale of assets only for tax or other technical reasons, it may be appropriate for the buyer to assume most or all liabilities, known and unknown. If instead the transaction is structured as a sale of assets because the seller has liabilities the buyer does not want to assume, the liabilities to be assumed by the buyer will be correspondingly limited.

A buyer may be concerned about successor liability exposure and not feel secure in relying on the indemnification obligations of the seller and its shareholders to make it whole. Under these circumstances, it might also require that the seller maintain in effect its insurance coverage or seek extended coverage for pre-closing occurrences that could support these indemnity obligations for the benefit of the buyer.

Purchase Agreement Provisions

The form of agreement for the sale of a business can involve many variations. The principal segments of a typical agreement for the sale of a business include:

- Introductory material (i.e., opening paragraph and recitals)
- The price and mechanics of the business combination
- Representations and warranties of the buyer and seller
- Covenants of the buyer and seller
- Conditions to closing
- Indemnification

- Termination procedures and remedies
- Miscellaneous (boilerplate) clauses

Special Asset Purchase Agreement Provisions

An asset purchase agreement has some unique provisions that provide an opportunity for the M&A lawyer to add value for the client.

Liabilities Excluded

To avoid unexpected liabilities in an asset transaction, the contract between the buyer and the seller must be unambiguous as to what liabilities the buyer is and is not assuming. In any transaction in which a buyer is acquiring an ongoing business, the buyer is likely to be assuming certain of the seller's liabilities, especially obligations incurred by the seller in the ordinary course of the seller's business. Indeed, it is likely to be very important to the buyer in dealing with the seller's creditors, vendors, customers, and so on that the asset purchase be viewed in a seamless process in which the buyer hopes to get the benefit of the seller's goodwill for which the buyer has paid. Under these circumstances, however, it is most important that the contract be very clear as to which liabilities the buyer is expressly not assuming.

Indemnification

Comprehensive indemnification by the seller, particularly if indemnification is backstopped by a portion of the purchase price held in escrow, can give the buyer protection against liabilities it did not agree to assume.

Selling Corporation Survival

The dissolution of the selling corporation is a factor the courts have consistently taken into account in successor liability cases. Thus, if the seller's dissolution were delayed, one of the elements of the successor liability rationale would at least be in doubt and the potential claimants would have a greater opportunity to satisfy its claims out of the seller's assets without resorting to the successor liability theories in an effort to gain recourse against the buyer.

Limitation on Assets

In creating an entity structure for the asset purchase, the buyer may be able to limit the assets of the acquired enterprise that might be accessible to a plaintiff in a future successor liability case. Thus, if in the last analysis the buyer is to be charged with a liability created by the seller or a predecessor of the seller, it would be helpful to the buyer if assets available to satisfy that claim were limited in some manner. For example, if the particular line of the seller's business with serious product liability concerns were acquired by a separate corporation and thereafter operated consistently with principles that would prevent veil piercing, at least the buyer would have succeeded in placing a reasonable cap on the successor liability exposure.

Fiduciary Duties

The M&A lawyer also advises clients in both public and private company deals regarding the appropriate corporate processes to follow in structuring and negotiating an M&A transaction.[4] The directors of both the buyer and the seller have fiduciary duties to act with due care and in the best interest of the entity they serve.

The concepts that underlie the fiduciary duties of corporate directors have their origins in English common law of both trusts and agency from more than 200 years ago. The current concepts of those duties are still largely matters of evolving common law.

The corporate statues of the various states provide that the business and affairs of a corporation are to be managed under the direction of its board of directors. While the statues provide statutory guidance as to matters such as the issuance of securities, the payment of dividends, the notice and voting procedures for meetings of directors and shareholders, and the ability of directors to rely on specified persons and information, the nature of a director's fiduciary duty to the corporation and the shareholders has been largely defined by the courts through damage and injunctive actions.

---

[4] Byron F. Egan, "Recent Developments with Respect to Director and Officer Fiduciary Duties and Other Issues Affecting M&A Activity," 28th Annual Conference on Securities Regulation and Business Law Problems, Dallas, February 10, 2006, available at www.jw.com/site/jsp/publicationinfo.jsp?id=557.

These fiduciary duties include those of loyalty, care, and good faith. Importantly, the duties of due care, good faith, and loyalty give rise to a fourth important precept of fiduciary obligation: the so-called "duty of disclosure," which requires the directors to disclose full and accurate information when communicating with stockholders.

Loyalty

The duty of loyalty mandates that there shall be no conflict between duty and self-interest. It demands that the best interests of the corporation and its stockholders take precedence over any personal interest or bias of a director that is not shared by stockholders generally.

Conflicts of interest do not *per se* result in a breach of the duty of loyalty. Rather, it is the manner in which an interested director handles a conflict and the processes invoked to ensure fairness to the corporation and its stockholders that will determine the propriety of the director's conduct and the validity of the particular transaction.

The duty of loyalty may be implicated in connection with numerous types of corporate transactions, including the following: contracts between the corporation and directors or entities in which directors have a material interest; management buyouts; dealings by a parent corporation with a subsidiary; corporate acquisitions and reorganizations in which the interests of a controlling stockholder and the minority stockholders might diverge; usurpations of corporate opportunities; competition by directors or officers with the corporation; use of corporate office, property, or information for purposes unrelated to the best interest of the corporation; insider trading; and actions that have the purpose or practical effect of perpetuating directors in office. A director can be found guilty of a breach of the duty of loyalty by approving a transaction in which the director did not personally profit, but did approve a transaction that benefited the majority stockholder to the detriment of the minority stockholders.

Care

Directors have an obligation to inform themselves of all material information reasonably available to them before making a business decision and, having so informed themselves, to act with the requisite care in making such decision. Directors are not required, however, to read *in haec verba* every contract or legal document, or to know all particulars of the legal documents they authorize for execution. Although a director must act diligently and with the level of due care appropriate to the particular situation, the courts have held that action (or inaction) will constitute a breach of a director's fiduciary duty of care only if the director's conduct rises to the level of gross negligence.

Compliance with the duty of care requires active diligence. Accordingly, directors should attend board meetings regularly. They should take time to review, digest, and evaluate all materials and other information provided to them. They should take reasonable steps to assure that all material information bearing on a decision has been considered by the directors or by those upon whom the directors will rely. They should actively participate in board deliberations, ask appropriate questions, and discuss each proposal's strengths and weaknesses. They should seek out the advice of legal counsel, financial advisers, and other professionals, as needed. They should, where appropriate, reasonably rely upon information, reports, and opinions provided by officers, experts, or board committees. They should take sufficient time (as may be dictated by the circumstances) to reflect on decisions before making them.

In many cases, of course, the directors' decision may be not to take any action. To the extent that decision is challenged, the focus will be on the process by which the decision not to act was made. Corporate directors' obligations to be reasonably informed concerning the corporation includes a duty to attempt in good faith to assure that a corporate information and reporting system, which the board concludes is adequate, exists.

The courts tend to defer to the informed business judgment of independent and disinterested directors. Since the business judgment rule dictates that courts defer to the business judgment of independent and disinterested directors, the judicial focus is on independence, information, and decisional process.

Process Framework for Friendly M&A Transactions

State corporation statutes permit corporations to merge with other corporations by their respective boards of directors adopting a plan of merger and obtaining the requisite shareholder approval.

Responsibilities of Directors

Serious proposals for a business combination received from a third party require serious consideration. The chief executive officer and management will usually be called upon to make an initial judgment as to the level of seriousness. A written, well-developed proposal from a credible prospective acquirer should be studied. In contrast, an oral proposal, or a written one that is incomplete in material respects, should not require management efforts to develop the proposal further. In no event does management's response need to indicate any willingness to be acquired.

When a board addresses a pending takeover bid, it has an obligation to determine whether the offer is in the best interests of the corporation and its shareholders. Just as all proposals are not alike, board responses to proposals may differ. A proposal that is incomplete in material respects should not require serious board consideration. On the other hand, because more developed proposals may present more of an opportunity for shareholders, they ought to require more consideration by the board.

Where an offer is perceived as serious and substantial, an appropriate place for the board to begin its consideration may be an informed understanding of the corporation's value. This may be advisable whether the board's ultimate response is to "say no," to refuse to remove pre-existing defensive measures, to adopt new or different defensive measures, or to pursue another strategic course to maximize shareholder value.

That is not to say, however, that a board must "price" the corporation whenever a suitor appears. Moreover, it may be ill advised even to document a range of values for the corporation before the conclusion of negotiations. However, should the decision be made to sell or should a defensive reaction be challenged, the board will be well served to have been adequately informed of intrinsic value during its deliberations from the beginning. In doing so, the board may also establish, should it need to do so under enhanced scrutiny, that it acted at all times to maintain or seek "the best value reasonably available to the stockholders." This may also be advisable even if that value derives from remaining independent.

In assessing the bid and the bidder's responsibility, a board may consider, among various proper factors, the adequacy and terms of the offer; its fairness and feasibility; the proposed or actual financing for the offer, and the consequences of that financing; questions of illegality; the impact of both the bid and the potential acquisition on other constituencies, provided it bears some reasonable relationship to general shareholder interests; the risk of non-consummation; the basic stockholder interests at stake; the bidder's identity, prior background, and other business venture experiences; and the bidder's business plans for the corporation and their effects on stockholder interests.

Although there is no one blueprint for being adequately informed, the courts do value expert advice, the judgment of directors who are independent and sophisticated, and an active and orderly deliberation. The fact that the board of directors relies on expert advice to reach a decision provides strong support that the board acted reasonably.

Addressing the value of a corporation generally entails obtaining investment banking advice using techniques or methods that are generally considered acceptable in the financial community. Although fairness opinions by independent investment bankers are not required as a matter of law, in practice, investment banking advice is obtained for any decision to sell and for many decisions not to sell. In the non-sale context, such advice is particularly helpful where there may be subsequent pressure to sell or disclosure concerning the board's decision not to sell is likely. The advice of investment bankers is not, however, a substitute for the judgment of the directors.

Assessing the Impartiality of the Board

One of the first tasks of M&A counsel in a takeover context is to assess the independence of the board. In responding to a suitor, a corporation that has significant independent directors may have an advantage over companies without such independent directors. In a sale of control transaction, the role of outside, independent directors becomes particularly important because of the magnitude of a sale of control transaction and the possibility, in certain cases, that management may not necessarily be impartial. Active participation of the independent members of the board is important in demonstrating that the board did not simply follow management.

When directors or shareholders with fiduciary obligations have a conflict of interest with respect to a proposed transaction, the use of a special committee is recommended. A special committee is also recommended where there is only the appearance of a conflict, as the mere appearance of a conflict may be sufficient to invoke application of the entire fairness standard of review. Accordingly, use of a special committee should be considered in connection with any going-private transaction (i.e., management buyouts or squeeze-out mergers), asset sales or acquisitions involving entities controlled by or affiliated with directors or controlling shareholders, or any other transactions with majority or controlling shareholders. If a majority of the board is disinterested and independent with respect to the proposed transaction, a special committee may not be necessary, since the board's decision should be accorded deference under the business judgment rule (assuming, of course, that the disinterested directors are not dominated or otherwise controlled by the interested party). In that circumstance, the disinterested directors may act on behalf of the company and the interested directors should abstain from deliberating and voting on the proposed transaction.

Where a majority of the board is disinterested, a special committee may be useful if there are reasons to isolate the deliberations of the non-interested directors. Where a majority of the directors have some real or perceived conflict, however, formation of a special committee may still be useful. Ideally, the special committee should be formed prior to the first series of negotiations of a proposed transaction, or immediately upon receipt of an unsolicited M&A proposal. Formation at a later stage is acceptable, however, if the special committee is still capable of influencing and ultimately rejecting the proposed transaction. As a general rule, however, the special committee should be formed whenever the conflicts of fellow directors become apparent in light of a proposed or contemplated transaction. Rather, the disinterested directors should select the committee members and the committee members should elect their chairperson. To the extent possible, however, the interested party should not be permitted to influence the selection of the members of the special committee or its chairperson.

In selecting the members of a special committee, care should be taken to ensure not only that the members have no financial interest in the transaction, but that they have no financial ties, or are otherwise beholden, to any person or entity involved in the transaction. In other words, all committee members should be independent and disinterested. To be disinterested, the member cannot derive any personal (primarily financial) benefit from the transaction not shared by the stockholders. To be independent, the member's decisions must be based on the corporate merits of the subject before the committee rather than extraneous considerations or influences.

If a committee member votes to approve a transaction to appease the interested director/shareholder, to stay in the interested party's good graces, or because he or she is beholden to the interested party for the continued receipt of consulting fees or other payments, such committee member will not be viewed as independent.

Although there is no legal requirement that a special committee retain legal and financial advisers, it is highly advisable that the committee retain advisers to help them carry out their duties. The selection of advisers, however, may influence a court's determinations of the independence of the committee and the effectiveness of the process.

Selection of advisers should be made by the committee after its formation. Although the special committee may rely on the company's professional advisers, perception of the special committee's independence is enhanced by the separate retention of advisers who have no prior affiliation with the company or interested parties. Accordingly, the special committee should take time to ensure that its professional advisers have no prior or current, direct or indirect, material affiliations with interested parties.

Retention of legal and financial advisers by the special committee also enhances its ability to be fully informed. Because of the short timeframe of many of today's transactions, professional advisers allow the committee to assimilate large amounts of information more quickly and effectively than the committee could without advisers. Having advisers that can efficiently process and condense information is important where the committee is asked to evaluate proposals or competing proposals within days of their making. Finally, a court will give some deference to the committee's selection of advisers where there is no indication that they were retained for an "improper purpose."

From a litigation standpoint, one of the most important documents when defending a transaction that has utilized a special committee is the board resolution authorizing the special committee and describing the scope of its authority. Obviously, if the board has materially limited the special committee's authority, the work of the special committee will not be given great deference in litigation since the conflicted board will be viewed as having retained ultimate control over the process. Where, however, the special committee is given broad authority and permitted to negotiate the best possible transaction, the special committee's work and business decisions will be accorded substantial deference.

Committee members need to rely upon, interact with, and challenge their financial and legal advisers. While reliance is often important and necessary, the committee should not allow an adviser to assume the role of ultimate decision-maker.

Without board planning and oversight to insulate the self-interested management from improper access to the bidding process, and to ensure the proper conduct of the auction by truly independent advisers selected by, and answerable only to, the independent directors, the legal complications a challenged transaction faces are unnecessarily intensified.

The cases repeatedly emphasize the importance of the process followed by directors in addressing a takeover proposal. The courts have frowned upon board decision-making that is done hastily or without prior preparation. Counsel should be careful to formulate and document a decision-making process that will withstand judicial review from this perspective.

The Process

Early in the process, the board should be advised by counsel as to the applicable legal standards and the concerns expressed by the courts that are presented in similar circumstances. Distribution of a memorandum from counsel can be particularly helpful in this regard. Management should provide the latest financial and strategic information available concerning the corporation and its prospects. If a sale is contemplated or the corporation may be put "in play," investment bankers should be retained to advise concerning comparable transactions and market conditions, provide an evaluation of the proposal in accordance with current industry standards, and, if requested, render a fairness opinion concerning the transaction before it is finally approved by the board. The board should meet several times, preferably in person, to review reports from management and outside advisers, learn the progress of the transaction, and provide guidance. Directors should receive reports and briefing information sufficiently before meetings so they can be studied and evaluated. Directors should be active in questioning and analyzing the information and advice received from management and outside advisers. A summary of the material provisions of the merger agreement should be prepared for the directors and explained by counsel.

A board may determine to reject an unsolicited proposal. It is not required to exchange the benefits of its long-term corporate strategy for short-term gain. However, like other decisions in the takeover context, the decisions to "say no" must be adequately informed. The information to be gathered and the process to be followed in reaching a decision to remain independent will vary with the facts and circumstances, but in the final analysis, the board should seek to develop reasonable support for its decision.

A common ground for rejection is that the proposal is inadequate. Moreover, the proposal may not reflect the value of recent or anticipated corporate strategy. Another ground is that continued independence is thought to maximize shareholder value. Each of these reasons seems founded on information about the value of the corporation and points to the gathering of information concerning value.

A decision based on the inadequacy of the proposal or the desirability of continuing a pre-existing business strategy is subject to the business judgment rule, in the absence of the contemporaneous adoption of defensive measures or another response that proposes an alternative means to realize shareholder value. Defensive measures are subject to enhanced scrutiny, with its burden on the directors to demonstrate reasonableness. An alternative transaction can raise an issue as to whether the action should be reviewed as essentially a defensive measure. Moreover, the decision not to waive the operation of a poison pill or the protection of a state statute restricting business combinations can be viewed as defensive.

When a board makes a decision to reject an offer considered inadequate, the board may adopt defensive measures in case the suitor becomes unfriendly, but the responsive action taken should be reasonable in relation to the threat posed.

When a board decides to pursue a sale of the corporation, whether on its own initiative or in response to a friendly suitor, ordinarily it must seek the best value reasonably available to the stockholders.

During the course of acquisition negotiations, it may be neither practicable nor possible to auction or actively shop the corporation. Moreover, even when there has been active bidding by two or more suitors, it may be difficult to determine whether the bidding is complete. In addition, there can remain the possibility that new bidders may emerge that have not been foreseen. In these circumstances, it is generally wise for the board to make some provision for further bidders in the merger agreement. Such a provision can also provide the board with additional support for its decision to sell to a particular bidder if the agreement does not forestall competing bidders, permits the fact gathering and discussion sufficient to make an informed decision, and provides meaningful flexibility to respond to them. In this sense, the agreement is an extension of, and has implications for, the process of becoming adequately informed.

In considering a change of control transaction, a board should consider whether the circumstances afford a disinterested and well-motivated director a basis to reasonably conclude that if the transactions contemplated by the merger agreement close, they will represent the best available alternative for the corporation and its shareholders. This inquiry involves consideration, *inter alia*, of the nature of any provisions in the merger agreement tending to impede other offers; the extent of the board's information about market alternatives; the content of announcements accompanying the execution of the merger agreement; the extent of the company's contractual freedom to supply necessary information to competing bidders; and the time made available for better offers to emerge. Management will, however, have to balance the requirements of the buyer against these interests in negotiating the merger agreement. The buyer will seek assurance of the benefit of its bargain through the agreement, especially the agreed-upon price, and the corporation may run the risk of losing the transaction if it does not accede to the buyer's requirements in this regard. The relevant cases provide the corporation and its directors with the ability, and the concomitant obligation in certain circumstances, to resist.

No-Shop Clauses, Lock-Ups, and Break-Up Fees

The assurances a buyer seeks often take the form of a "no shop" clause, a "lock-up" agreement for stock or assets, or a break-up fee. In many cases, a court will consider the effect of these provisions together. Whether the provisions are upheld may depend, in large measure, on whether a court finds that the board has adequate information about the market and alternatives to the offer being considered. The classic examples of no shop clauses, lock-ups, and break-up fees occur, however, not in friendly situations, where a court is likely to find that such arrangements provide the benefit of keeping the suitor at the bargaining table, but rather in a bidding war between two suitors, where the court may find that such provisions in favor of one suitor prematurely stop an auction and thus do not allow the board to obtain the highest value reasonably attainable. The fact that a buyer has provided consideration for the assurances requested in a merger agreement does not end the analysis.

The term "no shop" is used generically to describe both provisions that limit a corporation's ability to actively canvas the market (the "no shop" aspect) or to respond to overtures from the market (more accurately, a "no talk" provision). No shop clauses can take different forms. A strict one allows no solicitation and prohibits a target from facilitating other offers, all without exception. Because of the limitation a strict no shop clause imposes on the board's ability to become informed, such a provision is of questionable validity. A customary and limited no shop clause contains some type of "fiduciary out" that allows a board to take certain actions to the extent necessary for the board to comply with its fiduciary duties to shareholders. Board actions permitted can range from supplying confidential information about the corporation to unsolicited suitors, to negotiating with unsolicited suitors and terminating the existing merger agreement upon payment of a break-up fee, to actively soliciting other offers. Each action is tied to a determination by the board, after advice of counsel, that it is required in the exercise of the board's fiduciary duties. Such fiduciary outs, even when restrictively drafted, will likely be interpreted by the courts to permit the board to become informed about an unsolicited competing bid.

Although determinations concerning fiduciary outs are usually made when a serious competing suitor emerges, it may be difficult for a board or its counsel to determine just how much of the potentially permitted response is required by the board's fiduciary duties. As a consequence, the board may find it advisable to state the fiduciary out in terms that not only address fiduciary duties, but also permit action when an offer, which the board reasonably believes to be "superior," is made.

Lock-ups can take the form of an option to buy additional shares of the corporation to be acquired, which benefits the suitor if the price for the corporation increases after another bidder emerges and discourages another bidder by making the corporation more expensive. Lock-ups can also take the form of an option to acquire important assets (a company's "crown jewels") at a price that may or may not be a bargain for the suitor, which may so change the attractiveness of the corporation as to discourage or preclude other suitors. Lock-ups and related agreements are permitted where their adoption is untainted by director interest or other breaches of fiduciary duty. The courts tend to look askance at lock-up provisions when such provisions, however, impede other bidders or do not result in enhanced bids.

Break-up fees generally require the corporation to pay consideration to its merger partner should the corporation be acquired by a competing bidder who emerges after the merger agreement is signed. As with no shop clauses and lock-ups, break-up fees are not invalid unless they are preclusive or an impediment to the bidding process, and such fees that bear a reasonable relation to the value of a transaction so as not to be preclusive have been upheld. In practice, counsel are generally comfortable with break-up fees that range up to 4 percent of the equity value of the transaction, and a fee of up to 5 percent may be justified in connection with certain smaller transactions. However, the jurisprudence has not yet resolved whether the appropriate basis for calculating a termination fee is equity or enterprise value. For this purpose, the value of any lock-up given by the corporation to the bidder should be included.

M&A Strategies

M&A transactions typically involve bright businesspeople, lawyers, and other advisers on both sides. As discussed above, my first responsibility is to understand my client's objectives and strategies and, in the process of understanding them, I try to provide a reality check and test what alternatives have been considered. I also try to anticipate what the other side's motives and objectives are. Objectives, strategies, motives, and their factual underpinning evolve as the transaction progresses, and I try to help my client be sensitive to this reality.

Lessons from Experience

Both public and private company deals can benefit from the following lessons I have learned over the years from M&A deals:

1. *Pigs get fat and hogs get slaughtered.* You can make good money in dealing with someone, but if you are too greedy, you will not get away with it and may end up in trouble.

2. *Never let go for a better grip.* When you have a good deal, don't keep trying to make it better, for the whole thing may backfire when you give up a good deal to reach for a better one.

3. *Humor can help a lot when you are at the "licklog."* A "licklog" is a difficult issue that must be resolved before the deal can go forward.

Rather than telling the other side "when hell freezes over" or "what part of 'no' don't you understand," say something disarming like "don't cry down my back, or you'll rust my spurs" or "if wishes were horses, beggars would ride."

Also, in this post-Sarbanes-Oxley era, it is important to remember the first law of holes: when you find yourself in a hole, stop digging. Otherwise, you will dig a deeper hole for yourself. This is another way of saying the cover-up can be worse than the first crime and is often easier to prove.

There are three great lies in the M&A world:

1. "The check is in the mail."
2. "I am from the government and here to help you."
3. "We are buying this business for its people, not for its customer base or tangible assets."

The first two "lies" may be substituted for others in various M&A deals, but statements that the buyer is doing the deal to get the target's people recurs in most deals.

Repeatedly, there is no up-front discussion of the social issues—where target company personnel will fit in the organization chart of the acquiring company. Often, there is a group that does a merit selection process from the two companies to put names with job descriptions, but a year after closing, the organization chart of the surviving company often looks a lot like the purchaser's organization chart before the acquisition, and there has been an exodus of target company personnel. Directors' fiduciary duties require that the focus must be on what is in the best interests of the shareholders and what maximizes the value the shareholders receive, and that the officers negotiating the deal must work out the economics of the deal for the benefit of the shareholders before focusing on the social issues. However, the reality is that the social issues lurk below the surface of most deals, and influence the timing and outcome. History tends to repeat itself.

Adding Value

An M&A lawyer adds value to a transaction by advising the client in structuring, negotiating, and documenting transactions, and in complying with applicable disclosure requirements under SEC rules and applicable state law statutory and fiduciary duty requirements. The client sets its economic objectives. The lawyer assists the client in negotiating transaction documents that allow the client to receive the benefit of its bargain and avoid legal pitfalls that would frustrate consummation of the transaction or realization of its intended benefits.

The measure of success of an M&A lawyer in a transaction depends upon his or her role and the role of the client. Sometimes there is a big closing dinner where the principals will toast to the successful completion and make toasts to the lawyers, without whose labors in the trenches the transaction would not have been completed. Other times, success for the client is measured by nothing happening (for example, the failure of a proposed business deal the client opposed). The M&A lawyer, in the final analysis, is a team player in the M&A process, and the success of his or her efforts are silently measured by the sagacity of the advice provided. A lawyer ultimately can do no more than the client's bargaining positioning in the deal will allow.

Changes in M&A Law

The laws and deal practices relating to M&A transactions are constantly evolving. The chancery and supreme courts in Delaware, where many of the larger corporations are incorporated, issue a considerable volume of scholarly opinions regarding Delaware corporate statutes and fiduciary principles, or interpret laws relevant to M&A transactions, including securities, tax, and environmental laws, as well as other substantive provisions governing the formation, governance, and fundamental transactions of entities. Federal courts and state courts in other jurisdictions also regularly issue opinions that should be considered when rendering M&A advice. Congress, the state legislatures, and federal and state agencies also change the legal framework within which an M&A lawyer must operate.

Keeping up with new court decisions, as well as changing statutes and regulations, is a daunting and time-consuming challenge for all M&A lawyers. I stay on top of M&A developments by regularly writing law journal articles and continuing legal education papers, speaking at continuing legal education programs around the country, and activities associated with the committee on negotiated acquisitions of the business law section of the American Bar Association.

I serve as a vice chair of that committee, which is now the second largest committee of the ABA business law section with more than 2,200 members from more than forty-five states and twenty-five other countries. The committee has produced a number of significant works dealing with M&A deals and sponsors a variety of continuing legal education programs dealing with current M&A topics, including an Annual National Institute on Negotiating Business Acquisitions at which I regularly speak.

When one speaks or writes on M&A topics, one helps educate one's peers and competitors, but in the process one learns far more than the audience can assimilate. Further, in the crucible of debating these concepts with one's peers, one's skills can be forged into something stronger.

Regulatory Influence

When a public company is involved in an M&A transaction, the SEC may have the most pervasive influence over the timing and success, although the SEC's role is ultimately only to assure full and fair disclosure to investors. By its rules, interpretations, and enforcement practices that affect when and what level of disclosure is required of a public company involved in an M&A transaction, the SEC can affect whether an M&A transaction can be done. From the buyer's perspective, premature disclosure can allow an opposing transaction time to develop. Of course, from the seller's perspective, its shareholders can benefit from a rival bidder that forces the buyer to raise its bid to remain competitive.

Antitrust review of a proposed M&A transaction by the Federal Trade Commission and the U.S. Department of Justice under the Hart-Scott-Rodino Antitrust Improvements Act can also affect the economics of a transaction. Under Hart-Scott-Rodino, generally the parties to an M&A

transaction make a filing thereunder with the Federal Trade Commission and the Department of Justice if the value of the proposed transaction exceeds $53 million in order to give them an opportunity to assess the anti-competition aspects of the transaction. Once the filings are complete, there is a thirty-day waiting period. By requesting additional information, the Department of Justice or Federal Trade Commission can delay a potential transaction. They can also raise antitrust objections that could require changes to the transaction (for example, the divestiture of assets) before it will approve it.

Merger of Equals

A "merger of equals" is technically defined as a combination of two businesses, rather than an acquisition of the other, with the result that equity owners of both companies remain shareholders of the combined company, little or no premium is paid for the share of either, and the directors and executive officers of both companies are represented in the management of the combined company. In my experience, most mergers of equals are in reality an acquisition of one entity by another but are advertised as a merger of equals for a variety of reasons, including (i) allowing the buyer to pay little or no premium for control in acquisition, (ii) allowing management of the target to be represented in the management of the combined companies, thereby delaying the inevitable exodus of key personnel following a merger and allowing a representative of target management to step into the chain of command of the buyer with less damage to employee morale at buyer, and (iii) to give assurances of continuity of operations to local customer, civic, political, and regulatory constituencies. By treating a business combination as a merger of equals, the parties may each achieve or compromise their economic objectives at less cost than would have otherwise been required.

When advising a client considering a merger of equals, I focus on the principles with respect to merger of equals transactions and director fiduciary duties outlined above, and then concentrate on getting the transaction documentation to reflect the business deal. Sometimes the social issues relating to the management of the combined companies must be left to the good faith of the individuals involved over an extended period, and often events do not play out as expected as to the social issues.

When I review client press releases and scripts with respect to business combinations, I typically counsel clients to consider all of the consequences and constituencies. My principal objective is to temper the optimism of the parties after they have made a big deal so they will not create potential liability for their statements under applicable securities laws. Sensitivity to the reaction of important constituencies (i.e., customers, employees, and regulators) is also critical.

Strategies for Maximizing the Economics of M&A Deals

Who Is the Client?

An M&A lawyer's strategy with respect to the resulting larger company of course depends on which side the lawyer is representing. If one's client is the seller and is not receiving equity securities of the resulting larger company, the profitability of the resulting larger company is important only to extent that it motivates the buyer to consummate the transaction. If the client is the seller and is receiving equity securities, the M&A lawyer will focus particularly on the due diligence on the surviving company, the client's ability to resell the shares acquired, and any provisions or restrictions that would be applicable to the client. Thus, the focus of an M&A lawyer is less on the profitability of the resulting larger company than on the legal issues that would affect his or her client economically. If the client is the buyer, the M&A lawyer recognizes the foregoing interests of the seller and endeavors to accommodate them without impairing the profitability of the resulting larger company on the market for its stock. In each case, the M&A lawyer also considers the other factors discussed below.

Whether or how soon an acquisition would be accretive to the buyer from a financial reporting standpoint turns principally on the purchase price paid and in part on how the purchase price is allocated to the acquired assets, which are accounting questions beyond the purview of the M&A lawyer. The lawyer, however, can be sensitive to how the buyer's advisers on these matters are analyzing the structure and to how the acquisition agreement mirrors the financial terms.

The client, whether as buyer or seller, makes the fundamental decisions underlying a business combination, beginning with whether the client wants to do a deal with the other side and generally, what the client expects to get out of the transaction. The lawyer adds value principally by helping to structure the transaction and negotiate the applicable acquisition agreements and related documents in a way that permits the client to achieve its objectives. From the lawyer's perspective, the driving forces are whether the client wants to acquire the entire business with all of its assets and liabilities, which would suggest a stock purchase or a merger, or whether the client only is willing to take part of the assets and liabilities, in which case an asset purchase is often chosen.

Acquisition Agreement Provisions

Whether the target company is a public or private company, the target's objective will be to have an acquisition agreement with minimum seller representations, covenants, and conditions to the buyer's obligations to close the transaction. If the target is a public company, there would ordinarily be no representations or covenants that survive closing and, thus, in negotiating the acquisition agreement, in addition to the matters referenced in the preceding sentence, the M&A lawyer's focus is upon getting fiduciary out provisions that will enable the target to terminate the agreement in the event a third party makes a superior proposal to acquire the target. If the target is a private company, the acquisition agreement will typically provide that the target's representations and covenants survive the closing, and the target and its shareholders will indemnify the buyer for losses suffered as a result thereof. The target's M&A counsel will seek to add provisions to the acquisition providing a deductible amount before any damages are recoverable, capping the damages the buyer may recover and limiting the time period after closing within in which to make an indemnification claim.

Economics Are the Driver

Whether a public company buyer's stock will trade at a discount after the transaction is a function of the economics of the deal. If the buyer pays too much, or if the target's business declines after the transaction or is subjected to unexpected third-party claims, the buyer of a public company is ordinarily stuck with its bargain as the representations, warranties, and covenants of a public company target typically do not survive the closing and the buyer does not have the benefit of any indemnification arrangements. An exception would be if the buyer can make a claim that it was defrauded and perhaps rescind the transaction under common law equitable principles or recover damages under the anti-fraud provisions of applicable securities laws.

Diversification from an acquisition is beneficial only if the acquired business performs better than the acquiring company's previous business lines. Often, diversification results in the acquisition of a business that does not perform well, or that the buyer does not know how to manage effectively, and works out poorly for the acquiring company.

The Most Beneficial Type of Merger

When considering a horizontal merger versus a vertical merger, or a market extension merger versus a product extension merger, it is important to keep in mind that the type of merger does not matter as much as how well the acquired business performs and can be integrated into the buyer's other operations. Often, this is as much a function of the individuals involved as the nature of the business. Mergers tend to be more beneficial to the acquiring company when the acquired business is similar enough to the buyer's existing business that management can run it effectively and staffing reductions are possible due to the elimination of overlaps and redundancies. Likewise, the public securities markets tend to value larger targets more highly than smaller ones, which suggests that more economies of scale are possible in such a transaction.

A larger public company transaction typically involves companies in which much is known about the target and materiality will render unimportant many issues that would be important in a smaller deal. Conversely, in a smaller private company acquisition, smaller issues may be more material to the viability of the transaction, but the deal size may limit the amount that can be paid for expert advice.

Financial Benefits

The financial benefits of an M&A transaction are primarily driven by the price paid and what synergies exist, which are business rather than legal issues. The M&A lawyer can maximize the financial benefits through assistance in due diligence prior to closing and in the negotiation of acquisition agreement provisions that will enable the buyer to terminate the agreement if bad facts emerge between signing and closing, and to be indemnified if it suffers damages thereafter.

The financial strength of the acquiring company is not a prerequisite to the financial success of an acquisition, but a buyer that overextends itself with acquisition debt may find itself financially harmed as a result.

An acquisition in which the purchase price is paid in buyer stock will likely result in a financially stronger buyer than if debt had been incurred to pay a cash purchase price, and may enable the shareholders of the target to avoid recognizing taxable income in the transaction. The buyer's existing shareholders may find their ownership of the combined company diluted.

An acquisition using cash rather than buyer stock may be less dilutive to the buyer's stockholders than a stock acquisition and, as it does not require the registration of buyer stock under the Securities Act of 1933, may be effected more quickly and with less transaction costs. Whether to use cash or stock turns on what the seller wants, what the buyer can pay, and timing considerations.

In a strong economy, acquisition financing may be more readily available, but there may be more competition for deals and target values may be higher. The converse may be true in a weak economy. The relative financial strength of the buyer and seller will likely be more important in a weak economy, and may enable a stronger buyer to effect acquisitions more cheaply.

The Five Main Steps of a Financially Successful M&A Transaction

The five main steps of an M&A transaction after the buyer's identification of, and initial communications with, the target are:

1. Negotiation of the confidentiality agreement
2. Due diligence
3. Negotiation of the acquisition agreement
4. Satisfy the conditions to closing
5. Close the transaction

Confidentiality Agreement

A confidentiality agreement is usually drafted by the seller's counsel and contains the buyer's promise to maintain the confidentiality of the information provided by seller.[5]

Due Diligence

The due diligence process in an M&A transaction is the buyer's investigation of the business, financial, and legal affairs of the target, and is conducted by a team that typically includes buyers inside and outside accounting, business, financial, and legal people.[6] The M&A lawyers often play a critical coordinating and summarizing role in an effort to present the legal issues presented in terms that are understandable by the buyer's executive team.

If the seller is receiving securities of the buyer in the transaction, the seller will also perform a due diligence investigation of the buyer. The seller's due diligence investigation of the buyer, particularly if the buyer is a much larger company, is typically much more limited.

Negotiation of the Acquisition Agreement

Negotiating the acquisition is often preceded by a term sheet or non-binding letter of intent that sets forth what were at the time perceived to be

---

[5] See the form of confidentiality agreement that appears as Ancillary Document 1 to the *ABA Model Asset Purchase Agreement with Commentary* (2001).

[6] The due diligence process is described in two publications of the committee on negotiated acquisitions of the business law section of the American Bar Association: *Manual on Acquisition Review* (1995) and *The M&A Process: A Practical Guide for the Business Lawyer* (2005).

the principle terms of the deal. Typically, the buyer's counsel is tasked with preparing the first draft of the acquisition agreement in consultation with the buyer's other advisers. The seller's counsel, in consultation with the seller's other advisers, prepares a response, which typically is after a marked-to-show-changes revised draft of the draft submitted by the buyer's counsel. From there, negotiations proceed until there is either an agreement or the deal dies.

Out of the five steps, the negotiation of the acquisition agreement is the most critical aspect of any negotiated acquisition, as it sets forth the financial agreement of the parties.

Satisfying the Conditions to Closing

The conditions to closing typically include obtaining the required regulatory approvals; required consents of third parties (i.e., the consents to the transaction by other parties whose consent is necessitated by the terms of the lease or other contract); further due diligence; obtaining of any financing on which the transaction is conditioned; and the absence of any material adverse change in the business or affairs of the seller.

Closing

The closing of the transaction is a process by which the parties confirm that the requirements for the closing of the transaction specified by the acquisition agreement, which presumably would include all actions required by law, have been properly satisfied and then exchange the consideration specified in the acquisition agreement. Counsel assists in the closing process by preparing or reviewing the documents required for the closing and supervising the execution and delivery thereof.

The Laws behind the Financials of M&A Transactions

Since the acquisition agreement sets forth the bargain of the parties and it is principally governed by the common law of contracts, contract law principles establish how the acquisition agreement is to be construed and enforced. Tax, securities, environmental, tort, and other laws discussed above provide a critical overlay and sometimes trump the agreement of the parties. Knowing how these laws apply and intersect enables the M&A lawyer to help the client appreciate the risks and opportunities in the transaction.

As discussed above, M&A transactions are affected by both state and federal laws. State law fiduciary duty and SEC disclosure concepts are constantly evolving, and as a result, the practices of M&A lawyers must change and adapt.

Buyers and sellers negotiate vigorously in order that the definitive agreement will make the other party responsible in the event that post-closing the transaction does not work out for the buyer as anticipated. This is accomplished in large part through due diligence and detailed representations, warranties, and covenants in the acquisition agreement and, in the case of the acquisition of a private company, provisions that a party will indemnify the other party against its breaches of the agreement.

Defining Success

Whether an M&A transaction is financially successful often depends upon whether you are the buyer or seller. When the seller is able to sell before an economic downturn in its business, it may conclude that the transaction was successful, while the buyer may have the opposite view.

The buyer's ability to integrate the acquired business with its existing business is also critical. This in turn depends to a large extent on the people involved and the extent they can work together. In most acquisitions, the parties talk of how good their personal chemistry has been and will be post-closing, but things often do not turn out that way.

Whether a buyer or the target, a company in the midst of an M&A transaction must never lose sight of their respective economic objectives in the transaction. During negotiations, the focus of the parties and their counsel tends to center on the aspects of the deal over which there is disagreement. The protagonists, however, must not let the heat of the negotiations overcome their overall objectives.

Byron F. Egan is a partner in the business transactions section of Jackson Walker LLP. He is principally engaged in corporate, partnership, securities, mergers and acquisitions, and financing practice.

For more than ten years, Mr. Egan has been listed in The Best Lawyers in America *under corporate, merger and acquisition, and securities law. He won the Burton Award for Legal Achievement in 2005 and 2006. He has been recognized as one of the top corporate and merger and acquisition lawyers in Dallas and Texas by* Corporate Counsel Magazine, D Magazine, Texas Monthly, *and the* M&A Journal, *which profiled him in 2005. He has more than thirty-five years of experience in business entity formation and governance matters, mergers and acquisitions, and financing transactions. The entities included corporations, limited liability companies, and partnerships, and many had publicly traded securities.*

These transactions have included representation of clients in energy, financial services, insurance, manufacturing, real estate, technology, utility, and other sectors. Mr. Egan has represented banks, brokerage firms, investment advisers, and investment companies. In addition to handling transactions, he advises boards of directors and their audit, compensation, and special committees with respect to fiduciary duty, the Sarbanes-Oxley Act, special investigations, and other issues. His financing practice has included representation of companies and lenders in a wide spectrum of secured and unsecured transactions, both in the United States and abroad.

Acknowledgment: *The author wishes to acknowledge the contributions of Brian L. Dethrow of Jackson Walker LLP in Dallas.*

A Detailed Look at the Elements of an M&A Practice

Victor A. Hebert

Shareholder

Heller Ehrman LLP

M&A Basics

A merger and acquisition (M&A) lawyer assists clients, whether acquirers or targets, in clearly defining their objectives from the proposed transaction, and then to optimize the structure so as to achieve the objectives.

In representing an acquirer, it is important to understand both the acquirer's business and the target's business, and to understand what the acquirer hopes to achieve with the acquisition. Is the purpose to add new or complimentary products? To acquire a new distribution channel? To strengthen the business vertically as with a new technology? To strengthen the business horizontally as to expand geographically in a domestic or foreign market? To strengthen management by acquiring skilled managers whose skills are complimentary to those of the acquirer? The objectives of the acquirer will have a major impact in how the M&A lawyer works to facilitate the proceedings.

In representing a target, it is vital to assist the sellers in understanding what they hope to accomplish financially and otherwise. Is the acquirer a good home for the target's business? If stock is part or all of the consideration, will it be a good investment over time, restricted or freely tradable, received tax-free, and so on? Will the target's constituencies of employees, customers, and suppliers be treated well and fairly?

The Value of an M&A Lawyer

The M&A lawyer adds value by bringing to the attention of the acquirer or target the important characteristics of the proposed transaction. The M&A lawyer will describe and rank in priority those issues that are important to both parties. He or she will predict the timing, nature, and scope of the negotiations. Most importantly, based upon experience, the M&A lawyer will describe with particularity the range of likely outcomes on important issues. The client, therefore, whether the acquirer or target, is prepared to focus clearly upon the end game and is positioned to avoid minutiae and optimize outcomes.

Specifically, an M&A lawyer assists clients in the following areas:

- Explaining the process and timing of the proposed transaction and factors that will accelerate or delay the transaction

- If stock is a component of the consideration, explaining to acquirers what is required from a corporate and securities law perspective in connection with issuance of shares, and explaining to sellers what restrictions might apply to their shares

- Structuring and explaining relevant tax and accounting issues that may apply to the acquirer, target, and target shareholders

- Identifying business and legal risks inherent in the transaction and creating structures or solutions to deal appropriately with legacy liabilities that affect value

M&A Law and Its Components

M&A law has several distinct areas an effective M&A lawyer needs to be familiar with. The following is a brief rundown of those areas:

- Corporate and securities laws, particularly as they relate to the issuance of shares (For instance, is approval required from the shareholders of the acquirer, the target, or both? What are the requirements for registration of shares with federal, state, or international securities regulations, the listing of shares for trading on stock exchanges, and so on?)

- Contract law as it relates to the principal acquisition agreement and related agreements, such as employment and non-compete agreements (The validity or enforceability of certain provisions can be different from state to state.)

- Tax laws at all levels (federal, state, local, and international) affecting the acquirer, the target, and shareholders, including those resulting from the transaction itself or to be dealt with post-acquisition

- Antitrust laws, which might require domestic or international filings with regulatory bodies or negotiation and structuring to permit a proposed transaction to proceed in connection with regulatory concerns

- Laws affecting regulated industries such as banking, insurance, securities, communications, food and drug, or other regulatory regimes

Each of these particular areas is examined below in detail, with a focus on the legal questions an M&A lawyer would be expected to deal with.

Corporate and Securities Laws

<u>When Representing the Acquirer</u>

If shares are to be issued, are sufficient shares available pursuant to the charter document, or will approval be necessary to authorize additional shares? Will shareholder consent be required by the laws of the jurisdiction of the acquirer or by the rules of the stock exchange upon which its shares are listed? Will the nature of the target and its shareholders require registration of shares with the Securities and Exchange Commission or with state or foreign securities regulators, or are there exemptions available under applicable securities laws to enable issuance of shares without registration? Are there attributes of a special class of securities proposed to be issued, such as preferred stock, which require consideration, structuring, or refinement to achieve desired objectives?

If cash is to form part of the consideration, does the acquirer have the cash available? Will the acquirer borrow the funds, and if so, will the borrowing be under existing or new credit facilities? If new facilities are to be obtained, what restrictions exist under existing facilities, and will the new debt be sold privately or publicly with or without underwriters?

<u>When Representing the Target and Its Shareholders</u>

Will the shares to be issued by the acquirer be lawfully issued and freely tradable upon receipt? If there are restrictions, such as with shares issued under a private offering exemption, what is the track to and timing of subsequent registrations to enable trading? If there are restrictions upon affiliates, such as with the shares issued to a controlling person of the target, does the affiliate understand the nature of the restrictions, and are there things that can be done to minimize the impact or risk associated with such restrictions? If preferred stock or a debt security is to be issued, the lawyer should advise on the nature and extent of protections to the holders that can be included in the terms of the security.

Contract Law

The M&A lawyer must determine whether desired terms of a proposed contract are valid and enforceable under the laws applicable to the jurisdiction governing the transaction. For example, laws affecting employment or non-compete agreements can vary widely. This might suggest attempting to agree that a more favorable state law will control. In some instances, such attempts themselves may fail because it is against a state's public policy to enforce laws of other states against its citizens.

Tax Law

For the Acquirer

The lawyer should determine whether the transaction is tax-free to the shareholders of the target. If taxable, the lawyer should also determine what is necessary for the acquirer to get a stepped-up basis in the assets of the target, such as a Section 338(h)(10) election. Do any taxes result from the transaction such as transfer taxes, sales taxes, franchise taxes, excise taxes, and so on? If so, how much and who bears the economic burden?

The lawyer must identify legacy tax liabilities as risks associated with the manner in which the target conducted its business, perhaps resulting from improper filing in states, inadequate treatment or funding of pension or retirement plans, transfer pricing among subsidiaries of target, and so on.

Finally, is there a tax at the corporate level of the target?

For the Target and Shareholders, Settle the Following Questions:

- Is the transaction tax-free in whole or in part?
- Can the conduct post-closing of the acquirer, the target, or shareholders affect the taxability of the transaction? If so, how do you avoid or minimize risk?
- Will employees of the target with stock options or other stock-based compensation get substitute options with appropriate carry-over of economic and tax characteristics?
- Is there a mechanism or procedure to deal adequately with post-closing tax issues that survive the closing?
- If the target has been an S corporation, are there issues of built-in gain or other issues peculiar to S corporations?
- If debt forms a portion of the consideration, are sellers entitled to installment sale treatment?
- Is there any risk from the structure proposed by the acquirer of a double tax (tax at both the corporate and shareholder levels) when both parties assumed a single tax at the shareholder level? If so, can the structure be altered to achieve the objective?

Antitrust Law

The lawyer must determine whether the size and nature of the transaction will require notice filings such as under Hart-Scott-Rodino or foreign jurisdictions, and whether there is a substantive issue with respect to industry concentration, and if so, what is the strategy to minimize impact on the transaction and the businesses of the acquirer and target?

Regulatory Laws

- Are the constituent parties to the merger in a regulated industry? If so, what are the special requirements to proceed as desired?

- Are there aspects of the target's business or the nature of the acquirer that require special attention and filings under the Exxon Florio Act if a foreign company seeks to acquire a domestic defense company?

The Financial Implications of an M&A Event

There are numerous aspects of an M&A transaction with financial implications to the parties. Most obviously, price tops the list, but there are many other things to consider as well.

Price

If shares are used, how are the shares to be valued? For a public company, it is customary for the share price to be tied to an average over a trading period. A buyer normally desires a longer period, perhaps twenty to thirty trading days, to reduce the risk of a sudden run-up in price just prior to the merger date. Sellers usually prefer a shorter period to ensure that the value of shares when received is likely to be close to the average price. For a private buyer, shares may be valued in any number of ways, such as a formula tied to net asset value or multiples of earnings or revenues.

Often, the consideration is based upon performance criteria applied to the target. A seller will prefer the price to be based upon performance that has occurred prior to the signing of the merger agreement to avoid uncertainty. A buyer might prefer applying the criteria to more recent performance so as to ensure that value is based on current numbers.

In many mergers, a fixed ratio of shares of the buyer is used, perhaps because one or both parties desire to own a certain percentage of the outstanding shares of the buyer after the merger. Or more commonly, the buyer doesn't want to take the risk that a reduction in the share price prior to the merger would require the issuance of more shares. Depending upon the parties' expectations of share price performance leading up to the merger, they will be more or less sanguine about a fixed ratio. For instance, the sellers may believe circumstances make it more likely than not that the share price will increase. If so, a fixed ratio will result in higher consideration received than a fixed-dollar amount tied to a fluctuating stock price.

Some buyers and sellers cannot agree on a value for the merger at the time of the transaction. They may have differing views of how the target's business will perform after the merger. In these cases, the parties may agree to an earn-out (i.e., they may agree that additional consideration will be paid after the closing based upon a formula applied to agreed-upon performance criteria). In such cases, it is extremely important to negotiate clear and precise terms so both parties' expectations will coincide with the realities post-acquisition. Such terms may include limitations on what the buyer can do in operating the business post-closing or on what can be charged for corporate overheads, and so on.

Indemnification

One area of merger agreements with significant financial implications is the indemnification provisions. Sellers will want to minimize the risk associated with their agreement to protect the buyer from known or unknown liabilities. In connection with the acquisition of a public company, it is customary that the representations and warranties made by the target do not survive the closing of the merger, and thus there are no post-closing indemnification provisions. The rationale for this is that it is cumbersome to set up a mechanism for the buyer to hold back a portion of the purchase price or to otherwise seek recovery from a disparate group of public shareholders.

For acquisition of private companies, sellers will want to limit the period for which their representations and warranties survive to the shortest time possible or, as is common, to negotiate a range of survival periods with tax liabilities usually the longest, financial representations the shortest, and others, such as environmental filings, in between. Sellers will want a so-called "threshold" or "basket" where if claims in the aggregate are within the basket amount, sellers will have no liability, and if they exceed the amount, sellers are responsible for the excess (or in some cases, the entire amount from dollar one).

Limitations may be set upon the total amount for which sellers might be responsible. Sellers of a particularly desirable business may limit their exposure to a percentage (say 10 or 20 percent) of the total purchase price. If sellers aren't able to obtain a limitation as a percentage of their consideration, they will uniformly request, and the buyer will agree, to limit their liability to the total consideration they receive in the deal.

Just as there might be a range of survival periods, there can be a range of limitations where sellers will accept full responsibility for back taxes (perhaps above the basket) but otherwise limit exposure to a percentage of the total price.

Other Provisions of Agreements

Many other aspects of merger agreements can have financial implications. Expenses can be borne in whole or part by buyers. In public-to-public deals, the agreement will provide that each party bears its own expenses, but as an economic matter, the buyer is paying because the expenses reduce the asset value of the target. Parties will negotiate over transfer taxes such as state taxes on the sale of equipment. Taxable transactions to sellers normally result in elections giving stepped-up basis in assets to the buyer and depreciation recapture to the sellers. Materiality as it applies to specific representations and warranties or other provisions can affect the economics of the transaction. The nature and extent of the disclosure in disclosure schedules can have economic effects. If a seller describes a specific dispute such that there is no liability and successfully excludes all similar disputes by category, there won't be protection to the buyer even for unknown matters of that description.

Avoiding Obvious Mistakes

Most major mistakes in the M&A process can be avoided by paying attention to the experts. Clients should avoid negotiating key aspects of the acquisition arrangements, including economic terms, before consulting their advisers (financial, legal, and accounting). If the client gets too far ahead, a structural or substantive position can be taken that would not have been considered with appropriate advice. When the advisers do get involved and it appears desirable to change aspects of the deal, it may be too late to convince sellers to change or something major will have to be traded away to get where you should have been in the first place. For example, a buyer might agree on the purchase of stock when circumstances suggest an asset purchase would be preferable. A buyer might forego a hold-back of a portion of the purchase price to protect against liabilities or agree to limitation of liabilities prematurely or in inadvisable amounts. Advisers should be consulted early in the process. Clients should also appreciate the special expertise of each adviser and not permit one adviser to advocate structures or positions as to which they are not expert.

The M&A lawyer is a key part of any network of experts. For sellers, it is critical to be confident that when an agreement is signed the parties are obligated to proceed and the buyer's ability to back out or negotiate a different deal has been minimized. Among other things, the buyer should have completed all due diligence prior to signing, and the material adverse change clause should have been carefully crafted so as to minimize those things that give the buyer a chance to withdraw. Public company sellers will want fiduciary out clauses that permit consideration of unsolicited superior offers subsequent to signing the agreement. Sellers should retain as much flexibility as possible to react to changed circumstances, but they too want to be certain the deal will go through as negotiated. Thus, buyers will want tight "no shop" clauses with substantial break-up fees if sellers accept a superior offer.

Undue complexity should be avoided. Complex contract provisions lead to ambiguities and widen the possibility of varying interpretations. This may lead to disputes that could have been avoided or are difficult to resolve. A lawyer can identify and prepare appropriate language to address likely areas of dispute, such as with calculation of price, earn-outs, net worth or working capital adjustments, post-closing audits and adjustments, resolutions of scheduled or contingent liabilities, and so on. Clear and concise dispute resolution clauses and procedures can result in substantial value to all parties.

Strategies of M&A Law

Over the years, I have honed some particular approaches to M&A problems that have proven effective. In any situation, I seek to understand quickly the objectives of my client, and to assess the likely motivations of the opposite party. I focus on the likely difficult issues, whether involving structure, price, or terms. I evaluate those from the client's perspective and the likely perspective of the other party. I explain carefully and completely the entire process including screening of bids (if applicable), initial meetings, letters of intent (whether to have one and, if there is one, what should be included), negotiation of the merger agreement and collateral agreements (such as employment and non-compete agreements), regulatory and shareholder approvals, and closing. This permits the client to focus on important things and to avoid time spent on peripheral or unimportant issues. It also assists the client by creating realistic expectations and avoiding disappointment when things do not go as smoothly as hoped.

Success in M&A Law

A successful M&A event is all about meeting the client's goals. Hopefully, each client is instilled with confidence early in the transaction that my experience is sufficiently broad and diverse to permit an appropriate and thoughtful response to the variety of issues that inevitably arise in merger transactions. The client should feel comfortable that I can and will bring considerable skill and judgment to every situation in a thoughtful and professional manner. It is helpful if a client keeps his or her ego in check and continuously focuses upon important matters. Convincing clients at the outset to seek advice sooner rather than later and on a broad range of issues will facilitate the process and, most likely, enhance the outcome.

It is helpful at the outset to learn about the opposing party's business. Careful reading of its financial statements can give insight to the reasons for and ability to effect the transaction. It is also helpful to understand those aspects of the business that are more inherently risky than others. For example, technology companies frequently have inventory issues because rapidly changing technology can result in obsolescence, while declining parts prices can affect the carrying value of inventories. Consumer products companies frequently experience issues with distribution channels or the supply chain.

Staying Up to Date

There is a wealth of material an M&A attorney can use to stay informed and current. Right at the top, I read *The Wall Street Journal* every day. This is particularly useful when innovative structures or financing techniques are described.

I also regularly read legal publications, including the WSB Publications *SEC Today* and the *BNA Securities Reporter*. Occasional reading includes the *Daily Deal* and *Jesse Brill's Securities Regulation Report*.

Beyond reading, personal contacts are an invaluable part of staying informed. Consultation with my partners about unusual situations is helpful. Also, my firm has numerous topical presentations by my colleagues who are expert in their areas (such as tax, employee benefits, antitrust, etc.).

Regulations and Regulatory Bodies

For public companies issuing securities in M&A transactions, the Securities and Exchange Commission is the principal governmental agency affecting such transactions. It can principally affect the timing of the deal. If the proposed transaction is reviewed, it can take considerable time and effort to respond to and satisfy the commission's comments. If the comments involve close scrutiny of financial statements of the acquirer or target, a great deal of time and effort might be required. Securities and Exchange Commission review will not usually affect whether a deal gets done, but delays can allow other circumstances to impact the deal, such as intervening performance issues affecting either party or litigation that arose during the delay.

If the transaction requires filings with the Justice Department and Federal Trade Commission under the Hart-Scott-Rodino Antitrust Improvements Act, most transactions will not be affected adversely. Rarely is the time of Hart-Scott-Rodino review a gating issue in a transaction. Many transactions receive early termination of the thirty-day period to two or three weeks. However, if the constituent parties are competitors with significant market shares, Hart-Scott-Rodino review can be very important. If one of the agencies requests additional information, the additional waiting period does not commence until both parties have submitted all of the requested information. If a substantive antitrust issue is raised, prolonged negotiations can ensue over what conditions might be required to receive approval, such as the divestiture of a portion of the acquirer's or target's businesses. Occasionally, the agency will object to the transaction in total, indicating it will litigate to prevent the transaction. Most often this will kill a deal, but once in a while the matter will be litigated. One example of this was when

Oracle Corporation successfully fought the government over its intended acquisition of PeopleSoft.

Increasingly, foreign antitrust authorities are affecting multinational mergers. The U.S. focus is on anti-competitive effects on consumers, whereas the European focus is on such effects on competitors. So a merger might be approved in the United States but denied in Europe, as happened with General Electric's proposed acquisition of Honeywell.

State attorneys general can also get involved in proposed mergers. Most often, the focus is upon the alleged anti-competition effect of the merger upon consumers in violation of state antitrust law. Sometimes the state attempts to protect companies incorporated in their state based upon legislation in their state designed to insulate domestic companies from hostile takeovers.

Mergers involving regulated industries such as banking, insurance, securities, communications and broadcasting, and so forth can be affected greatly by the requirements of the agency having jurisdiction. The timing of review by industry regulators can be long and the process arduous. Among the most time-consuming and arduous is the Federal Communications Commission, the members of which often have strongly held and opposing points of view.

The Merger of Equals: Mutually Beneficial?

An announced merger of equals is most economically beneficial to both parties if there is an excellent strategic bit. When Morgan Stanley combined with Dean Witter, Morgan had leading investment banking and trading operations, whereas Dean Witter had large retail operations and diversity in the insurance and credit card industries. The combined balance sheets of both companies gave financial strength to the other. A stronger balance sheet ostensibly aided Morgan Stanley's trading operations and Dean Witter's insurance and credit card operations. Dean Witter's retail brokerage operations were ostensibly strengthened by having product to distribute from Morgan Stanley's underwriting of securities. Morgan Stanley gained additional distribution of its underwritings through Dean Witter's retail network.

When Nations Bank and Bank of America combined as a merger of equals, both became national institutions with geographical expansion to both coasts. In addition, combination in the same industry, such as banking, should permit the combined company to reduce costs through streamlining of operations and reduction of personnel.

Sometimes the shareholders of one constituent party benefit economically by acquiring a stock that has large trading volume and thus greater liquidity, or perhaps a higher dividend than was being paid prior to the combination. Both constituents might economically benefit by reduction of risk associated with their particular business (i.e., risk reduction occasioned by portfolio diversity). The effects of cyclicality should be reduced by a more diverse portfolio of businesses.

The first advice to give a client proposing a merger of equals is to remind them of George Orwell's line in *Animal Farm*: "All animals are equal, but some animals are more equal than others."

Merger of equals is usually applied to combinations where the value of each constituent company is approximately equal, and the shareholders of each company will own after the merger close to 50 percent of the combined enterprise. But, regardless of governance or other mechanisms in place, one party usually emerges as the "more equal" party in the combination.

The advice given is to design the transaction to have the appearance of a merger of equals and to ensure that at least for a time the appearance reflects reality. Thus, the board of directors should be divided equally, the senior management ranks should be populated with representatives of both parties, the implementation plans should not favor the employees or operations of one over the other, and so forth.

Publicity and Its Financial Implications

Generally speaking, I do not encourage clients to make more than required public statements. With that said, there can be situations where a public statement explaining the rationale for a merger can be useful. If the target is in a different business, it assists the public to understand the benefits of the transaction that motivated the buyer. If the premium to the target is high or unusually high, it may be useful to explain the benefits, such as reduced costs that will make the combination accretive or strengthen the combined business. Such statements, if made, are usually designed to forestall criticism or bolster the acquirer's stock price in the face of skepticism.

Structure and Strategy

There are no strategies in structuring or negotiating merger agreements that will ensure profitability of the combined enterprise. However, for most combinations retention of key personnel is essential to the continued health and profitability of the acquired company. Two strategies are almost uniformly used to assist in retention. The first is to require employment contracts with designated key employees. The second is to devise compensation arrangements designed to retain key, and perhaps an expanded group of, employees. Sellers resist designating a large group to receive employment contracts because they don't want to invest these employees with too much power, actual or perceived, in the negotiations. Buyers may not have an existing culture of using employment contracts, but may need to change their culture to ensure retention. Special compensation arrangements can adversely affect attitudes of the target's important employees who do not receive such packages and of the acquirer's employees who feel disadvantaged relative to their soon-to-be colleagues.

Specific strategies can be utilized depending upon the business involved in the acquisition in order to ensure further profitability. For example, if an investment management company is acquiring another investment manager, two strategies might be proposed. One would adjust the price being paid to the retention of clients of the acquired company. Another would create special compensation arrangements to retain key personnel. Both strategies could have the adverse effect of creating a "we/they" attitude among the personnel of each company. The target's personnel may feel under pressure to retain clients to the detriment of portfolio performance and customer service. The acquirer's personnel who do not receive such compensation may feel disadvantaged and resent the target's personnel, hampering a collegial atmosphere post-combination.

Advising a Target Company

A target company should seek to avoid announcement of a transaction until a binding agreement is signed. Otherwise, the inertia of a proposed transaction favors the buyer who has announced a possible transaction to which it isn't bound, and the target must deal with its employees, customers, and suppliers before it knows it has a deal.

Targets should seek to minimize deductions that can arise from the acquisition agreement, such as from a representation of minimum working capital or minimum net worth. Thresholds to indemnity payments should be as high as possible, and the limitation on the total amount of potential indemnification liability should be as low as possible as a percentage of the overall deal.

If possible, the deal value should be calculated on known numbers at the time of signing and not subject to adjustment after signing or post-closing.

If stock is to be received, the stock price should be determined in a way to maximize the probability that the deal price will be equal to the market price at closing. Also, the target shareholders should be able to sell stock received as soon as possible after the closing.

Discounted Share Prices

A discounted share price will be more or less important to the acquirer or target depending upon the structure of the transaction. If there is a fixed ratio of shares to be issued for each target share, a discounted acquirer's share price is very important to the target, because less value is paid as the discount increases. However, the acquirer is less concerned, because it knows a set number of shares are to be issued regardless of movement in its share price.

Conversely, if there is a deal value upon which to calculate the number of shares to be issued, the acquirer is very concerned about discounted share prices, resulting in the issuance of more shares and the acquirer's shareholders owning a lower percentage of the combined company.

Discounted share prices can occur from numerous circumstances (for instance, a perception among analysts and the market that the target is not a good fit for the acquirer, or that the acquirer is paying too high a price). Performance issues at either the acquirer or the target post-announcement can cause the price to go down. The acquirer's sector might be out of favor, causing stock prices of most companies in that sector to fall.

While there can be no guarantee that a particular course of action will avoid a discounted share price, several things might be done to attempt to prevent a decline. At the time of the announcement, disclose sufficient detail about the rationale for the merger and the nature of the target's business to persuade analysts and the market to see the transaction in the same light as the acquirer. Such action may result in an increase rather than a decrease in share price. The acquirer can embark on a road show to explain to institutional holders, analysts who follow the stock, and potential new shareholders the transaction and how the acquirer's prospects will be improved by the proposed acquisition.

Diversification

When an acquirer proposes a merger that results in diversification of its products and markets, it believes economic gains will result to the combined company. Such gain is most likely to result when the synergies of the combined companies permit immediate cost reductions in purchasing, manufacturing, distribution, or overhead, particularly when both companies are in the same business. Gains are harder to achieve if cost reductions are not available, because the diversification is of different products, different markets, or strictly geographical. The acquisition could result in higher costs, perhaps temporarily, to assimilate the target's personnel and businesses. If there are different products, different markets, and different distribution channels, the combined company's business will be more complex and less likely to produce large gains. Some acquisitions resulting in diversification are proposed to bring to the acquirer new technology or innovations in situations where acquisition is necessary to avoid or prolong obsolescence or decline. Diversification for diversification's sake is rarely a good reason for an acquisition, unless the acquirer's goal is to become a conglomerate, or perhaps to take advantage of an inflated stock price by buying companies that will add substance to the acquirer with a cheap currency.

Merger Types

A vertical merger is more likely to be financially beneficial than a horizontal merger, because it is more likely that cost reductions and business efficiencies will result for the combined company. A market extension merger is more likely to produce greater economic results than a product extension merger, because the scale will be larger in the market-extension. However, a market extension can entail more risk than a product extension, because the new market might not develop as planned or to a suitably large scale, whereas the product extension will rely on the same customer base and distribution channel, resulting in lower risk.

Vertical mergers almost always result in the greatest combined gain. This is no doubt due in part to the fact that the acquirer has a better understanding of the target's business and can bring to bear more knowledge and experience sooner to achieve the desired synergies of the businesses.

Merger Sizes

It is often said that doing a large merger is just as easy as a small one. By and large, a merger requires a comparable amount of time, effort, and documentation regardless of size, so it is cost-efficient to do a large merger. A larger target also provides more opportunity to extract value through cost reductions and so forth. Of course, the relative sizes of the constituent parties are relevant. A small company normally can't acquire a larger company, so its universe of potential targets is limited by its own size. Many acquisitions result from the "make or buy" analysis. A company will evaluate that it could invest capital to develop a product or market, and it will calculate the time and capital that will be required and evaluate the risks of failure and the rewards of success. It may conclude that "making" the product is more risky than "buying" it. Buying reduces the time and removes development risk, but may cost more in the short run. The "make or buy" analysis can be relevant to many sizes and types of business.

There is no particular size or type of business that one can generalize benefits more or less from acquisition. However, a small company may be constrained by its personnel and infrastructure such that an acquisition can pose significant risks. Thus, generally, mergers are better proposed by companies that are large enough to deal effectively with the myriad issues involved in an acquisition. A small company's personnel may get so involved in a merger that its management loses focus upon its core business.

Businesses most likely to benefit from acquisitions are those with a clear vision of where they want to be and a clear strategy to get there. By having this vision and strategy, the acquirer is prepared to act quickly and opportunistically to potential acquisitions. If a proposed deal fits the vision and strategy, the acquisition is simplified and a deal can be made or rejected promptly. It is vitally important for the acquirer to understand its and the target's businesses, and how they will fit to benefit the combined company.

Integrating the Target Business

The integration of the target to the acquirer's business is vitally important. The acquirer can often achieve the best results by taking a *laissez faire* attitude to the target: leave it alone to do what it already has proven it can do. Sometimes, growth of the target's business can be accelerated by bringing capital or other resources of the acquirer to the target that have minimal impact on the target's organization. The more changes proposed by the acquirer to the target, the higher the risk that the acquirer will get it wrong and destroy some of the capabilities it has acquired. Thus, personnel decisions are critical. The acquirer must make the target's employees comfortable and excited to be part of the combined company.

The best way for an acquirer to ensure that its investment in acquiring the target will be profitable is to understand clearly and well the target's business. This is accomplished by conducting a thorough due diligence process. Business due diligence will include an evaluation of all aspects of the target's business, such as its products or services, research and development, customer and supplier relationships, manufacturing, distribution channels, human resources, industry position and competition, and so forth. Financial due diligence will be designed to understand the financial policies and procedures, adequacy of internal controls, appropriateness and adequacy of reserves (related to accounts receivable, inventories, litigation, taxes, and contingencies), and the areas of risk inherent in the financial statements. Legal due diligence will be complete and designed to illuminate and quantify actual and potential problems.

The acquirer should prepare a list of the target's strengths and weaknesses and evaluate risks. It should analyze projected performance in light of known risks and possible favorable and unfavorable post-closing developments.

There are no particular characteristics of the target that must be present, including financial strength. Quite often, the target is a relatively new or small company that is growing rapidly and does not have the resources to finance increasing needs.

In the end, there is no way to ensure that any investment in a target will be profitable, though good investigation and appropriate knowledge and analysis can increase the likelihood of a favorable outcome.

Stock versus Cash in an M&A Transaction

The financial benefits of a stock transaction instead of cash need to be considered from the perspective of the buyer and the seller.

By issuing stock, the buyer is able to conserve its cash to support the combined business post-acquisition, perhaps avoiding a financing that might not be available on favorable terms or at all. If the buyer's stock is highly valued as a multiple of earnings or revenues relative to the valuation of the target, the transaction can be immediately accretive to the buyer. The buyer's shareholders have benefited by acquiring revenues and earnings on a favorable basis with the buyer's shareholders retaining a disproportionately higher percentage of the combined company than might be indicated by the relative revenues and earnings of the constituent parties. Transactions of this sort can accelerate appreciation of the buyer's market capitalization through a perception that the buyer has made a smart acquisition. This in turn will further enhance the buyer's ability to create additional acquisitions for stock, or to sell stock to the public on favorable terms. Another benefit to a buyer might be that the stock transaction results in a larger public float of its stock. Also, the enterprise value of the combined company would be higher with a stock transaction than a cash transaction. In the stock transaction, the enterprise value of the combined company will reflect the value of stock issued and net cash (cash less debt) of the buyer. By definition, this is a higher value than if the buyer uses cash.

Sellers will look at stock versus cash from a tax and investment perspective. Most stock transactions can be structured to be tax-free to the selling shareholders, where no gain is recognized when shares are received. This defers tax until the shares are sold. If the acquirer's stock pays a dividend, the selling shareholders will receive dividends on the entire value of shares received, not just an after-tax amount.

The selling shareholders may perceive that they are receiving the acquirer's shares on a favorable basis, or that the combination will accelerate appreciation in the acquirer's stock price, and thus the shares will be an excellent investment, especially if received tax-free.

A buyer might prefer cash to stock because of the speed and simplicity of a cash transaction compared with stock, particularly if the cash is already in the company treasury. The buyer may perceive that its stock is valued too low, perhaps because current market conditions are depressed overall. If large cash resources are on hand and are earning a low interest return, the cash acquisition can increase the buyer's return on invested capital. A cash transaction will be taxable to the sellers and thus result in the buyer's ability to step up the tax basis of the assets acquired with favorable tax consequences. Use of cash will avoid dilution that might occur from the issuance of shares, particularly if the acquisition price as a multiple of the target's earnings is higher than the multiple of earnings associated with the buyer's share price. Use of cash will avoid the necessity of compliance with securities laws, particularly if the transaction does not require approval of the buyer's shareholders and the target is a private company with few shareholders. The selling shareholders may be motivated to accept and close a cash transaction more readily than a stock transaction.

It is said that "cash is king." Many sellers of businesses believe this. They favor cash over stock, because they understand it and are not willing to accept the risk associated with taking stock for their company. By taking cash, they can pay their tax and invest the net proceeds in a diverse portfolio. If they choose to own some of the buyer's shares, they can make that investment decision independent of the decision to sell the company. Selling shareholders may not perceive the value of the buyer's shares in the same way, but except for tax consequences, all will have a uniform view of cash.

The decision to use stock or cash is driven by the financial circumstances of the acquirer and the willingness of the selling shareholders to accept shares. Lawyers do not make these decisions, but can influence the direction of a transaction by explaining the pros and cons of the different forms of consideration. I am never driven to recommend cash over stock unless the facts and circumstances suggest the client's objectives are better met by one over the other.

The Right Economy for an M&A Transaction

An M&A transaction can work well in any economy. As a general proposition, the costs of an M&A transaction are higher in a strong, growing economy because valuations are higher and there will be more money chasing fewer deals. By the same token, acquirers using stock are likely to have a higher stock price with which to acquire the target.

In a strong economy, targets have more options available to them, which may make it more difficult to effect an M&A deal. If a target requires more capital for growth or its owners want liquidity, the public market may be available and more attractive than a merger. Capital can be raised by private equity or venture capital on favorable terms. Also, the growth of the target's business in the strong economy may make it very expensive to buy.

Some of the most successful and profitable M&A transactions occur in weak economies. Targets have fewer options. If the nature of the economy involves risk to the target of declining revenues and profits, owners may be encouraged to seek the safety and liquidity offered by a merger. Many successful acquirers focus more attention on M&A transactions in weak economies, because they perceive bargains to be available or they have more time to devote to longer-term strategic transactions. Also, if the target is performing well (or adequately) in a weak economy, it can be expected to grow when the economy rebounds. This might be especially true if the integration can be effected during the weak economy in order to increase prospects when the economy rebounds.

In the end, circumstances are so varied for any particular transaction that timing to take advantage of particular economic conditions is difficult. Acquirers may prepare a list of potential targets and periodically evaluate whether conditions are right to optimize results.

The Steps to a Successful M&A Deal

The steps to a financially successful M&A transaction can be different for the acquirer and target. For the acquirer, the first step is always the identification of the target and developing the business case for the deal. Then the acquirer must do enough preliminary work, including negotiation, to get to the general framework of a deal: structure, price, and terms. This is followed by extensive diligence: business, financial, and legal. Then comes the negotiation of the merger agreement and preparation of proxy materials (if needed). The last stage is selling the deal to the acquirer's shareholders and to the market so there is a good understanding of the benefits and minimal adverse effects (or maximum positive effect) on the acquirer's stock price, followed in a timely manner by the closing.

For the target, the first step might be to evaluate the advantages and disadvantages of a merger and to develop a clear understanding of value, objectives, and possible problems. If the target is initiating the process instead of reacting to an unsolicited offer, it will need to select its team, including interviewing and engaging appropriate financial, legal, and accounting advisers. Thirdly, the target should understand what aspects of a transaction are important and have a good understanding of relative importance so as to increase the likelihood of achieving most of them. Negotiation of the merger agreement and preparation of proxy materials, if needed, are common to both target and acquirer. Upon negotiation of the agreement and public awareness of it, the target must focus upon its constituencies. Shareholders need to be informed, particularly significant shareholders. Employees need to understand the transaction and how they will be treated as part of and after the merger. Customers and suppliers will need to be dealt with appropriately. The final objective of the target will be to ensure that the approval and closing process go as quickly and smoothly as possible. Delay and uncertainty are the enemies of merger transactions, particularly for targets.

Recent Changes in M&A Law

The largest changes in regulations affecting M&A transactions in the past ten years have occurred in the accounting area. The elimination of the pooling of interests method of accounting dramatically affected the evaluation, approval, and structuring of transactions. Associated changes in the accounting for goodwill at the time of and after the acquisition are very important. Accounting matters associated with Sarbanes-Oxley, especially the focus upon internal controls, reportable events, and material weaknesses, have increased the cost and time required to effect a merger, both for the acquirer and the target.

Securities and Exchange Commission disclosure in M&A transactions is more detailed, particularly as it relates to the reasons for the merger and the description of the background and nature of the meetings among the parties prior to signing of the merger agreement.

Antitrust laws have been less vigorously enforced, with the result that there are fewer restructurings or dispositions required than might have been necessary ten years ago and before.

A Case Example of Success

One of my most successful M&A transactions occurred a few years ago in unusual circumstances. The target held a franchise from a local government. It was a well-established company in a rapidly growing area and it was profitable, but the target and several of its officers were under criminal indictment for tax fraud. The target needed to be sold quickly before trial in order for the shareholders to receive the value of the business, because a criminal conviction of the target would forfeit the franchise, destroying value. From several potential national acquirers in the same business, one decided it would make an offer sufficiently attractive as to be pre-emptive, an offer that could not be refused. The price offered was three and a half times revenue and thirty-eight times earnings. The target's shareholders would hold 5 percent of the acquirer's shares. The target wanted to acquire assets because it did not want a corporation that was tainted with a criminal indictment and possible conviction. The buyer also wanted pooling of interests accounting treatment (which was then available), since the value of the merger consideration far exceeded the asset value of the target. The selling shareholders wanted tax-free treatment so gain would only be recognized when the shares were sold. Obtaining tax-free treatment was complicated by the sale of assets, because it was important to avoid a separate tax at the target's corporate level.

Speed of negotiating and closing the transaction was imperative to both the acquirer and target. The tax trial was scheduled for early October. Negotiations began in June, a definitive agreement was signed in July, and the closing occurred in late August.

The transaction was structured as a sale of assets by the target in exchange for the acquirer's stock, which was distributed to the target's shareholders in liquidation. The acquirer achieved its objective of acquiring the assets, and the business of the target, and pooling of interests accounting. The target achieved its objective of no tax at the corporate level and tax-free treatment to the shareholders. The closing and issuance of shares occurred well within the time allowed.

For both accounting and tax reasons, the affiliate officers and shareholders restricted their ability to sell shares for a period of time. In the end, most shareholders were able to sell their shares in the market at or above the strike price of the shares at the time of the acquisition.

An Unsuccessful Transaction

Success as described above is not usually so easily achieved. In some instances, quite the opposite can occur. In one instance, a client acquirer, a U.S.-based telecommunications infrastructure company, sought to acquire a publicly held U.K. company that also had products in the telecommunication infrastructure industry. The transaction was complex because of the need to comply with the laws and securities regulations of both the United States and the United Kingdom. The transaction went smoothly, with both parties in full agreement and with both appearing to have achieved their respective objectives. However, it was ultimately and within a relatively short time not financially beneficial for a variety of reasons, mostly having to do with design and manufacturing issues of the target. Also, competition was a factor. Some of the adverse effects could have been avoided if more time and due diligence had been spent at the front end to better understand the target's technologies, products, and markets, and to properly assess the risks of the acquisition. This might have resulted in no transaction or a transaction at a price that more clearly reflected long-term value.

Crucial Mistakes

Some mistakes need to be avoided at all costs.

For a target, the biggest financial mistake is agreeing to a fixed ratio of shares that decline appreciably before the closing and with no downside protection or minimum value. This will create a large gap between the expected deal value at the time of signing and the real value at the time of closing.

For an acquirer, the biggest potential financial mistake might come from having known and assumed legacy or contingent liabilities that turn out to be much larger than expected. In acquiring a public company, this risk assumption is usually required so the protection comes, if at all, from properly assessing the risk and reflecting this risk in the price paid.

Also, acquirers should never lose sight of the fact that negotiation and consummation of a merger transaction is a relatively small part of a successful merger. More important is the integration and management of the business post-acquisition to the maximum potential advantage.

Victor A. Hebert joined the firm in 1962 and has a business practice. He is a member of the corporate securities, merger and acquisition, and life sciences practice groups.

Mr. Hebert is a business lawyer with extensive experience in mergers and acquisitions, corporate finance, and corporate governance matters. He has been involved in public and private offerings of debt and equity securities for issuers, underwriters, and purchasers. He has represented issuers and investors in venture capital transactions. He has handled numerous mergers and acquisitions for public and private clients including leveraged buyout transactions. He has also been involved in a variety of domestic and international joint ventures.

Clients for which Mr. Hebert has responsibility are in numerous industries, including aluminum, steel, telecommunications, financial services, semiconductor equipment and services, analytical instruments, computer software and hardware, forest products, biotechnology, solid waste disposal, and food and beverages.

Mr. Hebert served as co-chairman of the firm from 1987 to 1993. He serves as a director or officer of several corporations and non-profit organizations. He earned his A.B. degree in 1958 and his L.L.B. in 1961, both from the University of California at Berkeley. Early in his career, he served as a law clerk to the late Honorable O.D. Hamlin Jr. of the U.S. Court of Appeals for the Ninth Circuit.

Appendices

CONTENTS

APPENDIX A

ACQUISITION AGREEMENT

THIS ACQUISITION AGREEMENT (the "Agreement"), is made as of this ____ day of _____, _____, by and among _____, a _____ corporation ("Purchaser"), _____, a _____ corporation ("the "Acquisition Sub"), _____, a _____ corporation ("Acquired Company") and the Shareholders as defined in the Glossary.

WITNESSETH:

WHEREAS, the parties hereto desire to enter into this Agreement pursuant to which the Acquisition Sub will merge with Acquired Company upon the terms and subject to the conditions set forth herein thereby causing Acquired Company to become a direct or indirect wholly-owned subsidiary of Purchaser;

NOW, THEREFORE, in consideration of the foregoing and the respective representations, warranties, covenants and agreements set forth herein, the receipt, sufficiency and adequacy of which are hereby acknowledged, and intending to be legally bound hereby, the parties hereto agree as follows:

I.   DEFINITIONS.

Unless the context requires otherwise, capitalized terms used in this Agreement shall have the meaning set forth in the Glossary attached to this Agreement.

II.   THE MERGER.

2.1   The Merger. Subject to the terms and conditions of this Agreement and the Plan of Merger, Acquired Company shall be merged with and into the Acquisition Sub, and the Acquisition Sub shall be the surviving corporation (the "Surviving Corporation") in the Merger. The terms and effect of the Merger are set forth in the Plan of Merger, which is attached hereto as Exhibit 2.1 and incorporated herein by reference. The Merger shall become effective upon the filing with the Secretary of State of _____ of a Certificate of Merger, and with the Secretary of State of _____ of Articles of Merger (collectively, the "Articles of Merger"), executed in accordance with the relevant provisions of the _____ and the _____ (the time the Merger becomes effective being referred to as the "Effective Time"). As of the Effective Time, the Surviving Corporation shall be a direct or indirect wholly-owned subsidiary of Purchaser. It is intended by the parties hereto that this transaction qualify as a tax free reorganization pursuant to section 368(a)(2)(D) of the Internal Revenue Code of 1986, as amended.

2.2   Conversion of Shares.

Each Outstanding Share issued and outstanding immediately prior to the Effective Time shall, at the Effective Time, by virtue of the Merger and without any action on the part of the holder thereof, be converted into the right to receive its pro rata share of the Merger Price as specified on Exhibit 2.2, when and, with respect to the contingent part of the Merger Price, if applicable, if, payable without any interest thereon, upon the surrender of the certificates formerly representing such Outstanding Share. For purposes of calculating such pro rata share all shares of Common Stock underlying the Options or that can be acquired through any other conversion rights, if any, (whether or not the Options or other conversion rights are currently exercisable or available) shall be deemed to be outstanding.

2.3   Options.

(a)   Purchaser, the Acquisition Sub, the Acquired Company and the Shareholders agree as follows with respect to the Options:

(i)   On and after the date of this Agreement, the Acquired Company (its Board of Directors or any committee thereof) shall not issue any additional Options or similar rights or, except as contemplated in Section 5.9 amend the terms of any outstanding Option.

(ii)   At the Effective Time, the holder of an Option (whether or not it is currently exercisable) shall be entitled to receive, if such Option has not been previously exercised, for each share of Common Stock into which such Option would have been convertible upon exercise, an amount in cash equal to the excess, if any, of the pro rata portion of the Merger Price over the per share exercise price of such Option, less all applicable withholding taxes. The payments under this Subsection (ii) shall be made at the Effective Time.

(b)   At the Effective Time, and as a result of the Merger, the Stock Option Plans and Options shall be cancelled and shall thereafter not confer any rights whatsoever.

2.4   <u>Payment of the Merger Price; Surrender of Certificate</u>. At the Closing, upon surrender to the Purchaser of the outstanding certificate or certificates which immediately prior to the Effective Time represented Outstanding Shares (the "Certificates") together with any other required documents, the holder of such Certificate shall be entitled to receive in exchange therefor the consideration set forth in Section 2.2, and such Certificate shall forthwith be cancelled. No interest will be paid or accrued on the Merger Price. If payment is to be made to a Person other than the Person in whose name the Certificate surrendered is registered, it shall be a condition of payment that the Certificate so surrendered shall be properly endorsed or otherwise in proper form for transfer and that the Person requesting such payment shall pay any transfer or other taxes required by reason of the payment to a Person other than the registered holder of the Certificate surrendered or establish to the satisfaction of the Surviving Corporation that such tax has been paid, or will be paid within a reasonable period of time, or is not applicable. Until surrendered in accordance with the provisions of this Section 2.4, each Certificate shall represent for all purposes only the right to receive the consideration set forth in Section 2.2, without any interest thereon.

2.5   <u>Holdback Escrow</u>. At the Closing, the appropriate parties shall execute and deliver an Escrow Agreement in the form attached hereto as Exhibit 2.5 and the Management Shareholders shall deposit into escrow on a pro rata basis a total of _____ shares(representing _____% of the

Purchaser Preferred Stock being received by the Management Shareholders as part of the Merger Price as specified on Exhibit 2.2)(the "Holdback).

2.6   Transfers After Effective Time. After the Effective Time, except as contemplated by Section 2.4, there shall be no transfers on the stock transfer books of the Acquired Company of the shares of Common Stock that were outstanding immediately prior to the Effective Time. If, after the Effective Time, Certificates representing shares of Common Stock which were outstanding immediately prior to the Effective Time are presented to the Surviving Corporation, they shall be cancelled and exchanged for the consideration provided in Section 2.2.

III.   REPRESENTATIONS AND WARRANTIES OF ACQUIRED COMPANY AND THE MANAGEMENT SHAREHOLDERS.

The Acquired Company and the Management Shareholders, jointly and severally, represent and warrant to Purchaser and the Acquisition Sub as follows:

3.1   Organization, Standing and Foreign Qualification.

(a)   Acquired Company is a corporation duly organized, validly existing and in good standing under the laws of the State of _____ and has the requisite corporate power and authority to carry on its business in the places and as it is now being conducted and to own and lease the properties and assets which it now owns or leases.

(b)   Acquired Company is duly qualified and/or registered to transact business and is in good standing as a foreign corporation in the jurisdictions listed in Exhibit 3.1, and the character of the property owned or leased by the Acquired Company and the nature of the business conducted by it does not require such qualification and/or registration in any other jurisdiction, whether domestic or foreign.

3.2   Authority and Status.

(a)   Acquired Company has the capacity and authority to execute and deliver this Agreement, to perform hereunder and to consummate the transactions contemplated hereby without the necessity of any act or consent of any other Person, except as set forth on Exhibits 3.10 or 3.11.

(b)   The execution, delivery and performance by Acquired Company of this Agreement and each and every other agreement, document and instrument provided for herein have been duly authorized and approved by the Board of Directors of Acquired Company.

(c)   This Agreement and each and every agreement, document and instrument to be executed, delivered and performed by Acquired Company in connection herewith constitute or will, when executed and delivered, constitute the valid and legally binding obligations of Acquired Company enforceable against it in accordance with their respective terms.

(d)   True, correct and complete copies of the Articles of Incorporation and Bylaws of Acquired Company are attached hereto as Exhibit 3.2(d).

3.3   Capitalization; Ownership.

(a)   The entire authorized capital stock of Acquired Company consists of _____ (_____) shares of stock, all of which are designated Common Stock, no par value per share. Acquired Company has no preferred stock authorized or issued. Exhibit 3.3 contains a true, accurate and complete listing of the total number of each class of capital stock of Acquired Company outstanding as well as the total number of Options outstanding. Exhibit 3.3 also contains a true, accurate and complete listing of all the shareholders of Acquired Company, along with the number of shares owned by each shareholder and such shareholder's full name and mailing address. In addition, Exhibit 3.3 contains a true, accurate and complete listing of all the holders of the Options along with the number of Options held by each holder, the exercise price for each such Option, and such holder's full name and mailing address.

(b)   All of the currently outstanding shares of capital stock of Acquired Company are duly authorized, validly issued, fully paid and nonassessable. Any shares that may be issued pursuant to the Options have been duly authorized, and when issued and the Option price is paid, will be validly issued, fully paid and nonassessable. None of the capital stock of Acquired Company is entitled to or subject to preemptive rights or any right of first refusal or other similar right (whether statutory, contractual or otherwise) and none of the capital stock of Acquired Company has been issued in violation of any such rights in favor of any Person, including current or former shareholders of Acquired Company.

(c)   Other than the requisite board of directors vote (which has already been obtained) and the requisite shareholder vote to consummate the Merger, the authorization or consent of no other Person or entity is required in order to consummate the transactions contemplated herein by virtue of any such Person or entity having an equitable or beneficial interest in the Acquired Company or the capital stock of the Acquired Company.

(d)   Except as set forth on Exhibit 3.3, there are no outstanding options, warrants, calls, commitments or plans by the Acquired Company to issue any additional shares of its capital stock, to pay any dividends on such shares or to purchase, redeem, or retire any outstanding shares of its capital stock, nor are there outstanding any securities or obligations which are or may become convertible into or exchangeable for any shares of capital stock of the Acquired Company. There are not now, and at the Effective Time there will not be, any voting trusts or other Contracts to which the Acquired Company or any of the Shareholders is a party or is bound with respect to the voting of the capital stock of the Acquired Company.

(e)   The Acquired Company has not granted, and there are not outstanding, and the Acquired Company has not promised to grant (whether by Contract or otherwise) any equity participation rights, phantom stock rights, stock appreciation rights or other similar rights of the Acquired Company.

3.4   Absence of Equity Investments. Except as described in Exhibit 3.4, the Acquired Company does not, either directly or indirectly, own of record or beneficially any shares or other equity interests in any corporation, partnership, limited partnership, joint venture, trust or other business enterprise. Except as described in Exhibit 3.4, none of the

Shareholders, directly or indirectly, own of record or beneficially any shares or other equity interests in any corporation (except as a stockholder holding an interest of less than one percent (1%) in a corporation whose shares are traded on a national or regional securities exchange or in the over-the-counter-market), partnership, limited partnership, joint venture, trust or other business enterprise, all or any portion of the business of which is competitive or complementary with that of the Acquired Company.

3.5   Corporate Records. The minute books of the Acquired Company accurately reflect all corporate action taken by the Board of Directors and shareholders of the Acquired Company and contain true and correct copies of all charter documents, including all amendments thereto and restatements thereof, all minutes of meetings, resolutions and other proceedings of the Board of Directors and shareholders of the Acquired Company duly signed by appropriate officers or directors, and are otherwise complete and current in all respects, and the stock record book of the Acquired Company is complete and current. The minute books of the Acquired Company have been made available to the Purchaser.

3.6   Financial Statements; Liabilities and Obligations of the Acquired Company.

(a)   Attached hereto as Exhibit 3.6(a) are true, correct and complete copies of Acquired Company's unaudited balance sheet as of _____ and the related statements of income for the year then ended (the "_____ Financial Statements") and _____'s unaudited balance sheets as of _____ and _____ and the related statements of income for the years then ended (respectively, the "_____ and _____ Financial Statements"). Also attached are true, correct, and complete copies of the Acquired Company' unaudited balance sheet as of _____ and the related unaudited statement of income for the two month period then ended (the "Interim Financial Statements"). The ____, ____ and ____ and Interim Financial Statements are complete, and after _____, have been prepared in accordance with generally accepted accounting principles (except that the Interim Financial Statements do not contain any notes thereto and are subject to normal year-end audit adjustments, which individually and in the aggregate, will not deviate adversely from the Interim Financial Statements) consistently applied, and fairly present the financial condition of the Acquired Company as of the respective dates thereof.

(b)   The Acquired Company has no liability or obligation (whether accrued, absolute, contingent or otherwise) except for (i) the liabilities and obligations of the Acquired Company that are disclosed on Exhibit 3.6.(b) or reserved against in the Interim Financial Statements, to the extent and in the amounts so disclosed or reserved against, and (ii) liabilities incurred or accrued in the ordinary course of business since the date of the Interim Financial Statements, which liabilities do not, either individually or in the aggregate, have an adverse effect on the businesses, properties, rights, operations or financial condition of the Acquired Company, and (c) liabilities incurred in connection with the transactions referred to herein.

(c)   Except as disclosed in the Interim Financial Statements or Exhibit 3.6(b), the Acquired Company is not in default with respect to any liabilities or obligations, and all such liabilities or obligations shown or reflected in the Interim Financial Statements or Exhibit 3.6(b) and such liabilities incurred or accrued subsequent to the date of the Interim Financial Statements have been, or are being, paid and discharged as they become due, and all such liabilities and obligations were incurred in the ordinary course of business except as indicated on Exhibit 3.6(b).

(d)   Except as disclosed on Exhibit 3.6(d), there are no loans, advances or other like amounts, including any interest due thereon, from any shareholder, director, employee or former shareholder of the Acquired Company. Except as set forth on Exhibit 3.6(d), the Acquired Company does not have any off-balance sheet undertakings, including, but not limited to, any guarantees (in any form whatsoever, including as a comfort letter), sureties, warranties or securities with regard to the performance of obligations contracted by third parties (including partners, shareholders, corporate officers or members of its staff). The Acquired Company is not participating in any portage operations, interest rate or exchange rate swap Contracts, or derivative transactions, nor is it bound by any Contracts made on a futures market.

(e)   All of the accounts receivable of the Acquired Company reflect actual transactions, have arisen in the ordinary course of business, are not subject to offset, deduction or counterclaim and will be collectible within three (3) months after the Closing Date at the aggregate recorded amounts thereof.

3.7   Tax Returns.

(a)   The Acquired Company has, as of the date hereof, and will have as of the Effective Time, timely and accurately filed all returns and reports as required by Applicable Laws with respect to Taxes and has timely paid, or will prior to the Effective Time timely pay, all Taxes shown on such returns as owed for the periods of such returns, including all withholding or other payroll related taxes shown on such returns. All such returns and reports are or will be correct and complete.

(b)   The tax basis of all assets of the Acquired Company as reflected on its books and records is correct and accurate for use in tax periods ending after the Effective Time.

(c)   Except as described on Exhibit 3.7, the Acquired Company is not, and will not become, subject to any additional Taxes, interest, penalties or other similar charges as a result of the failure to file timely or accurately, as required by any Applicable Laws, any such return or report or to pay timely any amount shown to be due thereon, including, without limitation, any such Taxes, interest, penalties or charges resulting from the obtaining of an extension of time to file any return or to pay any Taxes.

(d)   No assessments or notices of deficiency or other communications have been received by the Acquired Company with respect to any such return or report for Taxes which have not been paid, discharged or fully reserved against in the Interim Financial Statements or disclosed on Exhibit 3.7, and no amendments or applications for refund have been filed or are planned with respect to any such return or report.

(e)   There are no agreements between the Acquired Company and any Regulatory Authority waiving or extending any statute of limitations with respect to any return or report for Taxes, and the Acquired Company has not filed any consent or election including, without limitation, any election under Section 341(f) of the Code, other than such consents and elections, if any, reflected in _____'s federal income tax return for its taxable year ended _____, a true, correct and complete copy of which is included in the Disclosure Materials.

    3.8   <u>Ownership of Tangible Assets and Leases</u>.

    (a)   <u>Exhibit 3.8</u> sets forth a true, accurate and complete list and a brief description of all real property and tangible personal property, owned, leased or licensed by the Acquired Company or otherwise used in its business (such list identifying which of such properties are owned by the Acquired Company and all of the leases, licenses or agreements under which the Acquired Company is lessee or licensee of or holds or operates any property, real or personal and the location of such property).

    (b)   The Acquired Company has good and marketable title to all of its property and assets, other than leased or licensed property, including those listed and described on <u>Exhibit 3.8</u> as owned property and assets, in each case free and clear of any liens, security interests, claims, charges, options, rights of tenants or other encumbrances, except as disclosed or reserved against in the Interim Financial Statements or as disclosed on <u>Exhibit 3.8</u> (to the extent and in the amounts so disclosed or reserved against).

    (c)   Each Contract for the leased or licensed property listed on <u>Exhibit 3.8</u> is in full force and effect and constitutes a legal, valid and binding obligation of the Acquired Company and the other respective parties thereto and is enforceable in accordance with its terms, and there is not under any of such Contracts any material default of the Acquired Company or of any other parties thereto (or event or condition which, with notice or lapse of time, or both, would constitute a material default). A true, complete and correct copy of each such Contract is contained in the Disclosure Materials.

    (d)   Neither the Acquired Company nor any of the Shareholders has received any payment from a lessor or licensor in connection with or as inducement for entering into a Contract in which the Acquired Company is a lessee or licensee. All buildings, machinery and equipment owned or leased by the Acquired Company are in good operating condition and reasonable state of repair, subject only to ordinary wear and tear. The inventories of the Acquired Company consist of items of supplies of a quality and quantity readily usable or readily salable, at prices equal to the values at which such items are reflected in the Acquired Company's books in the normal course of the Acquired Company's business and are valued so as to reflect the normal valuation policy of the Acquired Company in accordance with generally accepted accounting principles applied on a basis consistent with prior years, but not in excess of the lesser of cost or net realizable value.

(e)   The Acquired Company has not received any notice of violation of any Applicable Laws relating to its operations and properties, whether owned or leased, and to the knowledge of the Acquired Company and the Management Shareholders, there is no such violation or grounds therefor.

(f)   Except pursuant to this Agreement, the Acquired Company has not granted to anyone an absolute or contingent right to purchase, obtain or acquire any rights in any items of the assets, properties or operations which are owned by the Acquired Company or which are used in connection with the business of the Acquired Company.

3.9   <u>Agreement Does Not Violate Other Instruments</u>. Except as listed on <u>Exhibit 3.9</u>, the execution and delivery by the Acquired Company and the Shareholders of this Agreement and the other agreements and instruments to be executed and delivered in connection with the transactions contemplated hereby or thereby does not, and the consummation of the transactions contemplated hereby or thereby will not violate or conflict with (i) any provision of the Articles of Incorporation, as amended, or Bylaws, as amended, of the Acquired Company; (ii) any Applicable Laws to which the Acquired Company or any of the Shareholders is subject; (iii) any judgment, ruling, order, writ, injunction or decree of any court or of any Regulatory Authority to which the Acquired Company or any Shareholder is a party or bound or by which the Acquired Company's assets or business are affected; (iv) or constitute an occurrence of default under any provision of, or result in acceleration of any obligation under, or give rise to a contractual right by any party to terminate its obligations under any mortgage, deed of trust, conveyance to secure debt, note, bond, loan, lien, lease, agreement, instrument, or other Contract, to which the Acquired Company or any Shareholder is a party or is bound or by which the Acquired Company's assets or business are affected.

      3.10   <u>Required Governmental Consents</u>. Except as listed or described on <u>Exhibit 3.10</u>, no consent, approval, order, certification, permission or authorization of, notice to, exemption by, or registration, declaration, recording or filing with, any Regulatory Authority is required to be obtained or made by the Acquired Company, any shareholder of the Acquired Company or any assets, properties or operations of the Acquired Company in connection with the execution and delivery by the Acquired Company and the Shareholders of this Agreement or the consummation of the transactions contemplated hereby, the failure of which to obtain or make would have a material adverse effect on the Purchaser, the Acquired Company or the consummation of the transactions contemplated hereby.

      3.11   <u>Other Required Consents</u>. Except as set forth in <u>Exhibit 3.11</u> and for the approval of the Board of Directors of the Acquired Company (which has already been obtained) and the approval of the Shareholders of the Acquired Company, no approval, authorization, consent, permission, or waiver to or from, or notice, filing, or recording to or with, any Person (other than the governmental authorities addressed in Section 3.10) is necessary for (a) the execution and delivery of this Agreement and the other agreements and instruments to be executed and delivered in connection with the transactions contemplated hereby or thereby by the Acquired Company and the Shareholders or the consummation by the Acquired Company and the Shareholders of the transactions contemplated hereby; or (b) the merger or liquidation of the Acquired Company.

      3.12   <u>Absence of Changes</u>. Since _____, the Acquired Company has not, except as disclosed on <u>Exhibit 3.12</u>:

      (a)   Transferred, assigned, conveyed or liquidated into current assets any of its assets or business or entered into any transaction or incurred any liability or obligation, other than in the ordinary course of its business;

(b) Suffered any adverse change in its business, properties, rights, operations or financial condition (whether absolute, accrued, contingent or otherwise), or become aware of any event or state of facts which may result in any such adverse change;

(c) Suffered any destruction, damage or loss, whether or not covered by insurance;

(d) Suffered, permitted or incurred the imposition of any lien, charge, encumbrance (which as used herein includes, without limitation, any mortgage, deed of trust, conveyance to secure debt or security interest) or claim upon any of its assets, except for any current year lien with respect to personal or real property ad valorem taxes not yet due and payable;

(e) Committed, suffered, permitted or incurred any default in any liability or obligation;

(f) Made or agreed to any adverse change in the terms of any Contract or instrument to which it is a party;

(g) Waived, canceled, sold or otherwise disposed of, for less than the face amount thereof, any claim or right which it has against others;

(h) Declared, promised or made any distribution or other payment to its shareholders of the Acquired Company (other than reasonable compensation for services actually rendered) or issued any additional shares or rights, options, warrants or calls with respect to the Acquired Company's shares (except as listed on Exhibit 3.3), or redeemed, purchased or otherwise acquired any of the Acquired Company's shares, or made any change whatsoever in the Acquired Company's capital structure;

(i) Paid, agreed to pay or incurred any obligation for any payment for any contribution or other amount to, or with respect to, any employee Benefit Plan (except for the payment of health, disability and life insurance premiums which became due pursuant to the terms of applicable policies), or paid any bonus to, or granted any increase in the compensation of, the Acquired Company's directors, officers, agents or employees, or made any increase in the pension, retirement or other benefits of its directors, officers, agents or other employees;

(j)   Committed, suffered, permitted or incurred any transaction or event which would increase its tax liability for any prior taxable year;

(k)   Incurred any other liability or obligation or entered into any transaction other than in the ordinary course of business;

(l)   Received any notices, or had reason to believe, that any supplier or customer has taken or contemplates any steps which could disrupt the business relationship of the Acquired Company with said supplier or customer or could result in the diminution in the value of the Acquired Company as a going concern;

(m)   Paid, agreed to pay or incurred any obligation for any payment of any indebtedness, except current liabilities incurred in the ordinary course of business and except for payments as they become due pursuant to Contracts referred to in Section 3.16;

(n)   Changed any accounting methods, practices or principles or systems of internal accounting controls or added to the Acquired Company's capitalized software costs;

(o)   Written off as uncollectible any notes or accounts receivable in excess of $10,000.00 in the aggregate;

(p)   Written down the value of any asset or investment on its books or records, except for depreciation and amortization taken in the ordinary course of business and consistent with past practice;

(q)   Adopted or made any change in any Benefit Plan; or

(r)   Entered into any Contract to take any action described in this Section 3.12.

3.13   Litigation. Except as otherwise set forth in Exhibit 3.13, there is no litigation, suit, action, indictment, claim, investigation, or administrative, arbitration or other proceedings (including grand jury investigations, actions or proceedings and workers' compensation suits, actions or proceedings) pending or, to the best knowledge of the Acquired Company and the Shareholders, threatened against or affecting the Acquired Company or its shareholders, officers, directors or employees and, to the best knowledge of the Acquired Company and the Shareholders, there exists no basis or grounds for any such suit, action, proceeding, claim or investigation. None of the items described in Exhibit 3.13, singly or in the aggregate, if pursued and/or resulting in a judgment, would have an adverse effect on the businesses, properties, rights, operations or financial condition of the Acquired Company or the right of the Acquired Company or any shareholder of the Acquired Company to consummate the transactions contemplated hereby, and neither the Acquired Company nor any of the Shareholders are aware of any valid grounds for the assertion of any such claim.

3.14   Permits. The Acquired Company holds all Permits from all Regulatory Authorities necessary for the conduct of its business and the use of its assets. All such Permits held by the Acquired Company are listed on Exhibit 3.14. Neither the execution and delivery of this Agreement nor the consummation of the transactions contemplated hereby will result in the termination of any Permit held by the Acquired Company and all such Permits will remain in full force and effect after consummation of the transactions contemplated by this Agreement. All applications for renewal of currently existing Permits for which renewal applications are required, have been timely filed.

3.15   Court Orders; Compliance with Laws. Except as noted in Exhibit 3.15, the Acquired Company has conducted and is presently concluding its business so as to comply in all respects with all Applicable Laws. There is no outstanding judgment, order, writ, injunction, decree, stipulation or award (whether rendered by a court, a Regulatory Authority or by arbitration pursuant to a grievance or other procedure) against, affecting or relating to the Acquired Company, its business or its assets. The Acquired Company neither is presently charged with nor, to the knowledge of the Acquired Company and the Shareholders, is under investigation by any Regulatory Authority with respect to any actual or alleged violation of any Applicable Laws, nor is presently the subject of any pending or threatened adverse proceeding by any Regulatory Authority having jurisdiction over its business, assets or operations.

3.16   Contracts, Etc. Exhibit 3.16 hereto consists of a true and complete list of all Contracts (other than those Exhibits referenced in Sections 3.8, 3.17, 3.19, 3.20 and 3.22), to which the Acquired Company is a party. Except as set forth in those Exhibits referenced in Sections 3.8, 3.17, 3.19, 3.20 and 3.22, the Acquired Company is not a party, or subject to, any of the following:

(a)   Any Contracts, the consummation or performance of which would, either singly or in the aggregate, have a material adverse impact upon its businesses, properties, rights, operations or financial condition;

(b)   Any Contract that is outside of the normal, ordinary and usual requirements of its business or, for Contracts involving amounts in excess of $10,000.00, at a price or prices in excess of those otherwise available at the time such Contract was entered into;

(c)   Any Contract that requires services to be provided or performed by the Acquired Company or which authorizes others to perform services for, through or on behalf of the Acquired Company;

(d)   Any Contract involving amounts in excess of $10,000.00 and involving an obligation that cannot be terminated on thirty (30) days notice;

(e)   Any note receivable;

(f)   Any Contract providing for payments based in any manner upon the sales, purchases, receipts, income or profits of the Acquired Company or any other Person;

(g)   Any single Contract or sales or purchase order, which involves future payments, performance of services or delivery of goods and/or materials, to or by the Acquired Company with an amount or value in the aggregate in excess of Three Thousand Dollars ($3,000.00) (other than trade accounts payable incurred in the ordinary course of business with an amount or value not in excess of Six Thousand Dollars ($6,000.00));

(h)   Any franchise agreement, marketing agreement or royalty agreement, and with respect to each such agreement, Exhibit 3.16 sets forth the aggregate royalties or similar payments paid or payable by the Acquired Company as of the date hereof;

(i)   Any Contract with a creditor not made in the ordinary course of business;

(j)   Any Contract regarding employees or independent contractors (including without limitation any standard form contracts such as employee nondisclosure agreements or Software consultant/employee agreements), or for any continuing payment of any type or nature, including, without limitation, any severance, termination, parachute, or other payments (whether due to a change in control, termination or otherwise) and bonuses and vested commissions. Exhibit 3.16 also includes a listing of any such agreements for which the standard form was modified. Other than the standard form agreements listed on Exhibit 3.16 and those listed variations from the standard form agreements, there are no other agreements of the type referred to in this Section 3.16(j);

(k)   Any plan or other arrangement providing for life insurance, pensions, stock rights, distributions, options, deferred compensation, retirement payments, profit sharing, medical reimbursements or other benefits for directors, officers, employees or independent contractors;

(l)   Any Contract restricting the Acquired Company or any other Person from carrying on any business anywhere in the world;

(m)   Any Contract evidencing or related to indebtedness for money borrowed or to be borrowed, whether directly or indirectly, by way of purchase money obligation, guaranty, subordination, conditional sale, lease-purchase, chattel mortgage or otherwise. Except as disclosed in

Exhibit 3.16, no such indebtedness of the Acquired Company provides for any prepayment penalty or premium;

(n)   Any Contract with any labor organization;

(o)   Any policy of life, fire, liability, medical or other form of insurance;

(p)   Any order or written approval of any Regulatory Authority required to conduct the business;

(q)   Any licensing, development, data processing, maintenance, service, consulting, educational, training or other Contract relating to the licensing, installation, servicing, maintenance or use or operation of Software;

(r)   Any Contract with any programmer, independent contractor, non-employee agent or other entity (other than an employee) to perform services relating to Software for the Acquired Company;

(s)   Any Contract between any shareholder and the Acquired Company; or

(t)   Any Contract, not of the type covered by any of the other items of this Section 3.16, that is not in the ordinary course of business or that has an adverse impact on the business or assets of the Acquired Company.

A true, correct and complete copy of each such Contract is contained in the Disclosure Materials. All of the Contracts, policies of insurance or instruments described in Exhibits 3.8; 3.16; 3.17(c), (d), (h), (j) and (k); 3.19; 3.20 or 3.22 are valid and binding upon the Acquired Company and the other parties thereto and are in full force and effect and enforceable in accordance with their terms, and neither the Acquired Company, nor, to the knowledge of the Acquired Company and the Management Shareholders, any other party to any such Contract has breached any provision of, or is in material default under, the terms thereof. There are no existing facts or circumstances that would prevent the work in process of the Acquired Company or its Contracts from maturing upon performance by the Acquired Company into fully collectible accounts receivable. Except for terms specifically described in Exhibit 3.16, neither the Acquired Company nor any Shareholder has received any payment from any contracting party in connection with or as an inducement for entering into any Contract, policy of insurance or instrument.

3.17   Intellectual Property; Computer Software.

(a)   Patents, Trademarks, Tradenames, Etc. Exhibit 3.17(a) hereto sets forth a true, accurate and complete list and summary description of all trademarks, tradenames, service marks, service names, brand names, copyrights and patents, registrations thereof and applications therefor, applicable to or used in the business of the Acquired Company, together with a complete list of all licenses granted by or to the Acquired Company with respect to any of the above. All such trademarks, tradenames, service marks, service names, brand names, copyrights, patents or registrations thereof and applications therefor are owned by, and may be used by, the Acquired Company free and clear of any third party rights, liens, claims, security interests or encumbrances of any nature whatsoever. Neither the Acquired Company nor any Shareholder has knowledge of any violation of, and the Acquired Company is not violating, the rights of others in any trademark, tradename, service mark, service name, copyright, patent, trade secret, know-how or other intangible asset. Acquired Company does hereby assign unto Acquisition Sub all right, title and interest in and to the marks set forth in Schedule 3.17(a) (the "Marks"), together with the goodwill of the business in connection with which the Marks are used and which is symbolized by the Marks, including the right to recover damages and profits for past infringements thereof.

(b)   Owned Software. Exhibit 3.17(b) contains a complete and accurate list of all Software owned by the Acquired Company (the "Owned Software"). Except as set forth on Exhibit 3.17(b), the Acquired Company has sole, full and clear title to the Owned Software, free of all claims including claims or rights of employees, independent contractors, agents, consultants, customers, licensees or other parties involved in the development, creation, marketing, maintenance, enhancement or licensing of such Software. Except as disclosed in Exhibit 3.17(b), the Owned

Software is not dependent on and does not contain any Licensed Software or any other Software, or derivatives of any of the foregoing, in order to fully operate in the manner in which it is intended. The Acquired Company has the right to use, market, distribute, sublicense, modify, and copy the Owned Software, free and clear of any limitations or encumbrances (including any obligations to pay royalties) except as may be set forth on Exhibit 3.17(b).

(c)   Licensed Software. Exhibit 3.17(c) contains a complete and accurate list of all Software for which the Acquired Company is a licensee, lessee or otherwise has obtained from a third party the right to use, market, distribute, sublicense or otherwise transfer the right to use such Software (the "Licensed Software"). Exhibit 3.17(c) also sets forth a list of all license fees, rents, royalties or other charges that the Acquired Company is obligated to pay relating to Licensed Software. The Acquired Company has the right and license to use, market, distribute, sublicense, modify and copy the Licensed Software, free and clear of any limitations or encumbrances (including any obligations to pay royalties), except as may be set forth in any license agreements listed in Exhibit 3.17(c) or, in the case of licensed "shrink-wrap" Software as identified as such on Exhibit 3.17(c) as may be set forth in the documentation attendant with such Software. The Acquired Company is in full compliance with all provisions of any license, lease or other similar agreement pursuant to which it has rights to use the Licensed Software. The Acquired Company has not published or disclosed any Licensed Software to any other party except, in the case of Licensed Software which the Acquired Company leases or markets to others, in accordance with and as permitted by the agreement relating to the Licensed Software and except pursuant to written agreements requiring such other parties to keep the Licensed Software confidential. No party to whom the Acquired Company has disclosed the Licensed Software has breached such obligation of confidentiality.

(d)   Third Party Software. Exhibit 3.17(d) contains a true, accurate and complete list of all Third Party Software in the possession of the Acquired Company which the Acquired Company has developed. Except as disclosed on Exhibit 3.17(d), the Acquired Company has not incorporated any Third Party Software or parts thereof into any other

Software in any manner which would infringe the rights of any third parties in such Third Party Software or other Software.

(e)   Software Used in Business. The Acquired Company Software constitutes all Software used in the business of the Acquired Company. The transactions contemplated herein will not cause a breach or default under any Contract relating to the Acquired Company Software or the Third Party Software or impair the Acquired Company's ability to use the Acquired Company Software in the same manner as such Software is currently used in the business of the Acquired Company. None of the Shareholders have an interest in any Software that has been used by, or for the benefit of, the Acquired Company.

(f)   Third Party Components in Owned Software. Except as disclosed on Exhibit 3.17(f), none of the Licensed Software has been incorporated into or made a part of any Owned Software or any other Licensed Software.

(g)   Confidential Information. The Acquired Company has taken all steps reasonably necessary to protect its right, title and interest in and to, and the confidentiality of, the Confidential Information. Further, no Owned Software has been published or disclosed to any other parties, except as set forth in Exhibit 3.20, and except pursuant to written agreements requiring such other parties to keep the Owned Software confidential. To the knowledge of the Acquired Company and the Management Shareholders, no such other party has breached any such obligation of confidentiality.

(h)   Personnel Agreements. All personnel, including employees, agents, consultants, and contractors, who have contributed to or participated in the conception and development of any Software, Technical Documentation, Confidential Information or related intellectual property on behalf of the Acquired Company either (i) have been party to a "work-for-hire" arrangement or agreement with the Acquired Company, in accordance with Applicable Laws, providing the Acquired Company full, effective, exclusive and original ownership of all tangible and intangible property thereby arising, or (ii) have executed appropriate instruments of assignment in favor of the Acquired Company as assignee that have conveyed to the Acquired Company full, effective, and exclusive ownership of all tangible and intangible property thereby arising. Exhibit 3.17(h) sets forth a list of all contract programmers, independent contractors, non-employee agents and Persons or other entities (other than employees) who have performed computer programming services on behalf of the Acquired Company relating to any Software and identifies all Contracts pursuant to which such services were performed.

(i)   Noninfringement of Other's Rights. The Acquired Company is not infringing any intellectual property rights of any other Person with respect to the Acquired Company Software, and no other Person is infringing any intellectual property rights of Acquired Company with respect to the Acquired Company Software. The Acquired Company has not infringed any intellectual property rights of any other Person with respect to any Third Party Software.

(j)   Contracts. The Acquired Company and all other parties to any Contract under which the Acquired Company is the licensor, lessor or has otherwise granted the right to use the Acquired Company Software are in full compliance therewith and are not in breach of their obligations with respect thereto. Except for licenses listed on Exhibit 3.20, the Acquired Company has not granted any licenses, leases or other rights and has no obligations to grant licenses, leases or other rights with respect to the Acquired Company Software. Except as set forth in Exhibit 3.20, all Contracts identified in Exhibit 3.20 constitute only end-user agreements, each of which grants the end-user thereunder solely the nonexclusive right and license to use an identified Acquired Company Software for its internal purposes only. The Acquired Company has complied in all respects with its obligations to its customers, licensees and lessees in respect of the Acquired Company Software.

(k)   Marketing Rights in Software. Exhibit 3.17(k) lists and separately identifies all Contracts pursuant to which the Acquired Company has been granted rights to market Software owned by third parties and all Contracts pursuant to which the Acquired Company has granted marketing rights in the Acquired Company Software to third parties.

(l)   Adequacy of Technical Documentation. The Acquired Company owns and has in its possession all necessary Technical Documentation for all Owned Software and has in its possession, to the extent reasonably required to use such Licensed Software, the Technical Documentation for the Licensed Software.

(m)   Protection of Acquired Company Software. The Acquired Company has not taken or failed to take any actions under the law of any jurisdiction (whether domestic or foreign) where the Acquired Company has marketed or licensed Acquired Company Software that would restrict or limit the ability of the Acquired Company to protect, or prevent it from protecting, its ownership interests in, confidentiality rights of, and rights to market, license, modify or enhance, the Acquired Company Software.

(n)   Year 2000. The Owned Software and the Third Party Software can record, store, process, and present calendar dates falling on or after January 1, 2000 in the same manner and with the same functionality as the Owned Software and the Third Party Software does for calendar dates on or before December 31, 1999. To the extent the Owned Software and the Third Party Software was developed based on software platforms licensed to Acquired Company by third parties, this representation is limited only to the actual source code written by Acquired Company, its employees or consultants.

(o)   Virus. The Owned Software does not, and to the best knowledge of the Acquired Company and Shareholders the Licensed Software does not, contain any program routine, device, or other undisclosed feature, including, without limitation, a time bomb, virus, software lock, drop-dead device, malicious logic, worm, trojan horse, or trap door, that is designed to delete, disable, deactivate, interfere with, or otherwise harm such software, any deliverables to customers or hardware, data, or other programs, or that is intended to provide access or produce modifications not authorized by any customer.

A true, complete and correct copy of each Contract disclosed on the Exhibits referenced in this Section 3.17 have been provided to the Purchaser.

3.18   Labor Matters.

(a)   Exhibit 3.18 sets forth a list of all current employees and independent contractors of the Acquired Company and their current salaries or rates and the Acquired Company's salary increase guidelines. Exhibit 3.18 sets forth a true, correct and complete list of employer loans or advances from the Acquired Company to its employees.

(b)   Within the last three (3) years the Acquired Company has not been the subject of any union activity or labor dispute, nor has there been any strike of any kind called or threatened to be called against it.

(c)   There is no, and since _____, there has not been any, condition or state of facts which may affect the Acquired Company's relations with its employees and no employees of the Acquired Company, or group of employees, the loss of whom would have an adverse effect on the business of the Acquired Company, has notified the Acquired Company within the twelve-month period prior to the date hereof of his or their intent to terminate his or their relationship with the Acquired Company, or make any demand for material payments or modifications of his or their arrangements with the Acquired Company. There has not been, and the Acquired Company and the Shareholders have no knowledge of, any adverse changes in relations with employees and independent contractors of the Acquired Company as a result of the transactions contemplated by this Agreement.

(d)   The Acquired Company's relationship with each Person that the Acquired Company treats, or had treated, as an independent contractor satisfies, or satisfied, the requirement under Applicable Law for treatment as an independent contractor.

(e)   The Acquired Company has conducted its business so as to comply in all respects with all Applicable Laws relating to immigration, naturalization and work permits, including the Immigration and Nationality Act of 1952, as amended by the Immigration Reform and Control Act of 1986 and the regulations promulgated thereunder. Subject to general principles related to wrongful termination of employees, the employment of each employee of the Acquired Company is terminable at the will of the Acquired Company.

(f)   The Acquired Company is in compliance with all Applicable Laws respecting employment and employment practices, terms and conditions of employment and wages and hours, and occupational safety and health pertaining to its business and the employees involved in its business, and is not engaged in any unfair labor practice within the meaning of Section 8 of the National Labor Relations Act.

3.18   Benefit Plans.

(a)   Exhibit 3.19 lists every pension, retirement, profit-sharing, deferred compensation, stock option, employee stock ownership, severance pay, vacation, sick leave, leave without compensation, bonus or other incentive plan, any medical, vision, dental or other health plan, any life insurance plan or any other employee benefit plan or fringe benefit plan, any other written or unwritten employee program, arrangement, agreement or understanding, commitments or methods of contribution or compensation (whether arrived at through collective bargaining or otherwise), whether formal or informal, whether funded or unfunded, and whether legally binding or not, including, without limitation, any "employee benefit plan," as that term is defined in Section 3(3) of ERISA, which is currently or previously adopted, maintained, sponsored in whole or in part, or contributed to by the Acquired Company or any ERISA Affiliate of the Acquired Company, for the benefit of, providing any remuneration or benefits to, or covering any current or former employee, retiree, dependent, spouse or other family member or beneficiary of such employee or retiree, director, independent contractor, shareholder, officer or consultant or other beneficiary of the Acquired Company or any ERISA Affiliate of the Acquired Company or under (or in connection with) which the Acquired Company or an ERISA Affiliate of the Acquired Company has any contingent or non-contingent liability of any kind whether or not probable of assertion (collectively, the "Benefit Plans"). Any of the Benefit Plans which is an "employee pension benefit plan," as that term is defined in Section 3(2) of ERISA, or an "employee welfare benefit plan" as that term is defined in Section 3(1) of ERISA, is referred to herein as an "ERISA Plan."

(b)   Exhibit 3.19 also lists, with respect to all Benefit Plans listed in Exhibit 3.19: (a) all trust agreements or other funding arrangements, including insurance contracts, all annuity contracts, financial contributions, actuarial statements or valuations, fidelity bonds, fiduciary liability policies, investment manager or advisory contracts, corporate resolutions of memoranda, administrative committee minutes or memoranda or records, and all amendments (if any) thereto, (b) where applicable, with respect to any such plans or plan amendments, the most recent determination letters issued by the IRS, (c) all communications or other correspondence issued within the last six (6) years by any Regulatory Authority, including without limitation, the IRS, DOL and the PBGC with respect to such Benefit Plan, (d) annual reports or returns and audited or unaudited financial statements for the most recent three plan years and any amendments thereto, and (e) the most recent summary plan descriptions, any material modifications thereto, and all material employee communications with respect to such Benefit Plans. Contemporaneous with the delivery of the Exhibits, the Acquired Company has delivered a true and complete copy of all such Benefit Plans, agreements, letters, rulings, opinions, letters, reports, returns, financial statements and summary plan descriptions described in Sections 3.19(a) or 3.19(b) hereof, certified as such by a duly authorized officer of the Acquired Company.

(c)   All the Benefit Plans and any related trusts subject to ERISA comply with and have been administered in compliance with the provisions of ERISA, all applicable provisions of the Code relating to qualification and tax exemption under Code Sections 401(a) and 501(a) or otherwise necessary to secure intended tax consequences, all applicable state or federal securities laws and all other applicable laws, rules and regulations and collective bargaining agreements, and the Acquired Company has not received any notice from any Regulatory Authority or instrumentality questioning or challenging such compliance. All available governmental approvals for the Benefit Plans have been obtained, including, but not limited to, timely determination letters on the qualification of the ERISA Plans and tax exemption of, related trusts, as applicable, under the Code and timely registration and disclosure under applicable securities laws, and all such governmental approvals continue in full force and effect. No event has occurred that will or could give rise to disqualification of any such Benefit Plan under Sections 401(a) or 501(a) of the Code or to a tax under Section 511 of the Code.

(d)   Neither the Acquired Company nor any administrator or fiduciary of any such Benefit Plan (or agent or delegate of any of the foregoing) has engaged in any transaction or acted or failed to act in any manner that could subject the Acquired Company to any direct or indirect liability (by indemnity or otherwise) for a breach of any fiduciary, co-fiduciary or other duty under ERISA. No oral or written representation or communication with respect to any aspect of the Benefit Plans has been or will be made to employees of the Acquired Company prior to the Closing Date that is not in accordance with the written or otherwise preexisting terms and provisions of such Benefit Plans in effect immediately prior to the Closing Date, except for any amendments or terminations required by the terms of this Agreement. There are no unresolved claims or disputes under the terms of, or in connection with, the Benefit Plans and no action, legal or otherwise, has been commenced with respect to any claim.

(e)   All annual reports or returns, audited or unaudited financial statements, actuarial valuations, summary annual reports and summary plan descriptions issued with respect to the Benefit Plans are correct and accurate as of the dates thereof; and there have been no amendments filed to any of such reports, returns, statements, valuations or descriptions or required to make the information therein true and accurate.

(f)   Neither the Acquired Company nor any other "party in interest" (as defined in Section 3(14) of ERISA) or "disqualified person" (as defined in Section 4975(e)(2) of the Code) of any Benefit Plan has engaged in any "prohibited transaction" (within the meaning of Sections 503(b) or 4975(c) of the Code or Section 406 of ERISA) with respect to such Benefit Plan, for which there is no statutory, regulatory or individual or class exemption. There has been no (a) "reportable event" (as defined in Section 4043 of ERISA), or event described in Section 4062(f) or Section 4063(a) of ERISA or (b) termination or partial termination, withdrawal or partial withdrawal with respect to any of the ERISA Plans that the Acquired Company or any ERISA Affiliate of the Acquired Company maintains or contributes to or has maintained or contributed to or was required to maintain or contribute to for the benefit of employees of the Acquired Company or any ERISA Affiliate of the Acquired Company now or formerly in existence.

(g)   For any ERISA Plan that is an employee pension benefit plan as defined in ERISA Section 3(2), the fair market value of such Benefit Plan's assets equals or exceeds the present value of all benefits (whether vested or not) accrued to date by all participants in such Benefit Plan. For this purpose the assumptions prescribed by the Pension Benefit Guaranty Corporation for valuing plan assets or liabilities upon plan termination shall be applied and the term "benefits" shall include the value of any early retirement or ancillary benefits (including shutdown benefits) provided under any Benefit Plan. As of the Closing Date, full payment will have been made of all amounts which the Acquired Company is required to have made at or prior to such time, under any Applicable Laws, as a contribution to any Benefit Plan of the Acquired Company or of an ERISA Affiliate of the Acquired Company, and no accumulated funding deficiency (as defined in ERISA Section 302 or Code Section 412), whether or not waived, will exist with respect to any Benefit Plan.

(h)   Except as described on Exhibit 3.19 as of the Closing Date, the Acquired Company will have no current or future liability with respect to any events or matters occurring, arising or accruing on or prior to such date under any Benefit Plan that was not reflected in the Interim Financial Statements or that represents contributions required to be made under written terms of such Benefit Plan as of the Closing Date.

(i)   The Acquired Company does not maintain any Benefit Plan providing deferred or stock based compensation which is not reflected in the Interim Financial Statements.

(j)   Neither the Acquired Company nor any ERISA Affiliate of the Acquired Company has maintained, and neither now maintains, a Benefit Plan providing welfare benefits (as defined in ERISA Section 3(1)) to employees after retirement or other separation of service except to the extent required under Part 6 of Title I of ERISA and Code Section 4980B.

(k)   The consummation of the transactions contemplated by this Agreement will not (i) entitle any current or former employee (or any spouse, dependent or other family member of such employee) of the Acquired Company or any ERISA Affiliate of the Acquired Company to severance pay, unemployment compensation or any payment contingent upon a change in control or ownership of the Acquired Company, or (ii) accelerate the time of payment or vesting, or increase the amount, of any compensation due to any such employee or former employee (or any spouse, dependent or other family member of such employee).

(l)   All Benefit Plans subject to Section 4980B of the Code, as amended from time to time, or Part 6 of Title I of ERISA or both have been maintained in good faith compliance with the requirements of such laws and any regulations (proposed or otherwise) issued thereunder.

(m)   No liability to the PBGC has been incurred as of the Closing Date by the Acquired Company or any ERISA Affiliate of the Acquired Company, except for PBGC insurance premiums, and all such insurance premiums incurred or accrued up to and including the Closing Date have been timely paid.

(n)   Neither the Acquired Company or any ERISA Affiliate of the Acquired Company maintains or has maintained, has contributed to or has been required to contribute to, a multi-employer plan (as defined in Section 3(37) of ERISA). No amount is due or owing from the Acquired Company on account of a multi-employer plan (as defined in Section 3(37) of ERISA) on account of any withdrawal therefrom.

(o)   All annual reports (as described in Section 103 of ERISA) and all Forms 5500 relating to the applicable provisions of the Code required to be filed in connection with one or more of the Benefit Plans have been timely and properly filed in accordance with applicable law.

3.19   Customers.

(a)   Attached as Exhibit 3.20 hereto is a true and correct list of all Contracts (including those relating to the Acquired Company Software or Third Party Software) to which the Acquired Company is a party and for which, or pursuant to which, the Acquired Company is providing or is obligated to provide maintenance, support, development, consulting, educational, training, data processing or other services after the Closing. All of such Contracts are valid and binding upon the Acquired Company and the other parties thereto and are in full force and effect and enforceable in accordance with their terms. Neither the Acquired Company nor any other party to any such agreement has breached any provision of, or is in default in any respect under, the terms thereof.

(b)   Exhibit 3.20 also includes all existing license agreements relating to the Acquired Company Software or Third Party Software regardless of whether the Acquired Company is currently obligated to provide maintenance or support services relating to such license agreements. Neither the Acquired Company nor any other party to any such agreement has breached any provision of, or is in default in any respect under, the terms thereof.

(c)   Purchaser has been provided with true, correct and complete copies of all the Contracts listed on Exhibit 3.20.

(d)   Except as specifically noted on Exhibit 3.20, the Acquired Company is not a party to:

(i)   Any Contract with a customer identified in Exhibit 3.20 that involves the incurrence of expenses in excess of the revenues to be derived from such Contract;

(ii)   Any Contract which cannot readily be fulfilled by the Acquired Company, or other party thereto, in accordance with its terms and conditions;

(iii)   Any Contract pursuant to which a customer identified in Exhibit 3.20 has been granted retrospective or future discounts, credits, price reductions or other financial incentives by the Acquired Company; or

(iv)   Any Contract requiring the Acquired Company to deliver or otherwise develop a completed set of Software or other deliverables for a fixed amount or maximum amount of money.

(e)   Exhibit 3.20 also sets forth all outstanding contract proposals for license agreements or maintenance, support, development, consulting, educational, training, data processing or other service agreements.

(f)   Since the date of the Interim Financial Statements, the Acquired Company has not lost or been notified in writing that it will lose (and no customer has notified the Acquired Company in writing that it would, in the event of the sale of the Acquired Company, lose) any customer or customers that, in the aggregate, accounted for more than 5% of the revenues of the Acquired Company during the fiscal year ending _____. Except as set forth on Exhibit 3.20 hereto, since _____, the Acquired Company has not received written notice from any customer claiming unsatisfactory performance or overbilling.

3.20   Environmental Matters. No real property now or previously owned or used by the Acquired Company or now or previously owned or leased by the Acquired Company (the "Real Property") has been used by the Acquired Company or any other party for the handling, treatment, storage or disposal of any Hazardous Substance. No release, discharge, spillage or disposal into the environment of any Hazardous Substance and no soil, water or air contamination by any Hazardous Substance has occurred or is occurring in, from or on the Real Property. The Acquired Company has obtained all Permits which are required to be obtained by the Acquired Company under Applicable Laws relating to protection of the environment and has complied with all reporting requirements under any such Applicable Laws and Permits with respect to the Real Property. There are no claims, actions, suits, proceedings or investigations related to the presence, release, production, handling, discharge, spillage, transportation or disposal of any Hazardous Substance or ambient air conditions or contamination of soil, water or air by any Hazardous Substance pending or threatened with respect to the Real Property or otherwise against the Acquired Company in any court or before any Regulatory Authority or private arbitration tribunal and there is no basis for any such claim, action, suit, proceeding or investigation with respect to the Real Property or otherwise against the Acquired Company. There are no underground storage tanks on the Real Property. No building or other improvement included in the Real Property contains any asbestos or any asbestos-containing materials, and such buildings and improvements are free from radon contamination. For the purposes of this Agreement,

"Hazardous Substance" shall mean any hazardous or toxic substance or waste as those terms are defined by any Applicable Laws and petroleum, petroleum products and oil.

3.21   Insurance. Set forth in Exhibit 3.22 is a complete and accurate list and description of all insurance policies which the Acquired Company has maintained with respect to its businesses, properties or employees within the preceding thirty-six (36) months. Except as set forth in Exhibit 3.22, such policies are in full force and effect and no event has occurred that would give any insurance carrier a right to cancel or terminate any such policy. Such policies are reasonably adequate to insure fully against risks to which the Acquired Company and its properties and assets are exposed in the operation of its business in such amounts and types of coverage as are commercially reasonable and are consistent with practices in the industry in which the Acquired Company operates. The Acquired Company has not received notice of any pending or threatened cancellation or premium increase (retroactive or otherwise) with respect to any aforementioned policies and the Acquired Company is in compliance with all conditions contained therein. Exhibit 3.22 contains a correct and complete list of all pending claims by the Acquired Company (and all facts and circumstances known to the Acquired Company or the Shareholders which may give rise to any claim) under such insurance for an amount in excess of $10,000 in respect of any one claim. There are no pending claims against such insurance by the Acquired Company as to which insurers are defending under reservation of rights or have denied liability, and there exists no claim under such insurance that has not been properly filed by the Acquired Company. Included in the Disclosure Materials are all insurance policies presently in effect with respect to the properties, assets and businesses of the Acquired Company. Except as set forth in Exhibit 3.22, since the date of the Interim Financial Statements, there has not been any change in the Acquired Company's relationship with its insurers or in the premiums payable pursuant to such policies.

3.22   Related Party Relationships. Except as set forth in Exhibit 3.23, no shareholder owning greater than a five percent (5%) interest in the Acquired Company, no affiliate or member of the immediate family of any such shareholder, and no officer or director or member of the immediate family of such officer or director of the Acquired Company possesses, directly or indirectly, any beneficial interest in, or is a director, officer or employee of, or member of the immediate family of a director, officer or employee of, any corporation, partnership, firm, association or business organization that is a client, supplier, customer, lessor, lessee, lender, creditor, borrower, debtor or contracting party with or of the Acquired Company (except as a stockholder holding less than a one percent (1%) interest in a corporation whose shares are traded on a national or regional securities exchange or in the over-the-counter market).

3.23   Exhibits. All Exhibits attached hereto are true, correct and complete. Matters disclosed on each Exhibit shall be deemed disclosed only for purposes of the matters to be disclosed on such Exhibit and shall not be deemed to be disclosed for any other purpose unless expressly provided therein.

3.24   Disclosure and Absence of Undisclosed Liabilities. This Agreement and the Exhibits hereto disclose all facts material to the business, properties, rights, operations or financial condition of the Acquired Company. No representation, warranty, or statement contained in this Agreement, the Disclosure Materials or in any certificate, schedule, list, exhibit or other instrument furnished or to be furnished to Purchaser pursuant to the provisions hereof contains or will contain any untrue statement of any fact or omits or will omit to state a material fact necessary in order to make the statements contained herein or therein not misleading.

3.25   Disclosure Materials. The Acquired Company has provided the Disclosure Materials to Purchaser prior to the closing and the Disclosure Materials contain complete, true and accurate copies of what they purport to be.

III-A.   REPRESENTATIONS, WARRANTIES OF SHAREHOLDERS.

Each Management Shareholder, jointly and severally, represents and warrants to Purchaser and the Acquisition Sub as to himself and, as to his knowledge with respect to the Shareholders other than himself, and each of the Other Shareholders represents and warrants to Purchaser and to Acquisition Sub as to himself, as follows:

(a)   Each Shareholder has full power and authority to execute and deliver this Agreement and to perform such Shareholder's obligations hereunder. This Agreement, and each and every other agreement, document and instrument to be executed, delivered and performed by each Shareholder in connection herewith constitute, or will, when executed and delivered, constitute the legal, valid and binding obligation of the Shareholder, enforceable in accordance with their respective terms and conditions. Each Shareholder is not required to give any notice to, make any filing with, or obtain any authorization, consent or approval of any person, any private entity, or any governmental agency, court or other public entity in respect of entering into this Agreement or performing the Shareholder's obligations hereunder.

(b)   Neither the execution and delivery of this Agreement, nor the consummation of the transactions contemplated hereby, will: (i) violate or constitute a default under (or an event which, with notice or lapse of time or both, would constitute a default), or require notice or consent or permit the acceleration of obligations, under any Contract to which such Shareholder is a party; or (ii) violate, conflict with, or require notice or consent under any Applicable Laws to which the Shareholder or the Common Stock are subject.

(c)   Except as set forth on Exhibit 3A(c), the Shareholder has no liability or obligation to pay any fees or commissions to any broker, finder, or agent with respect to the transactions contemplated by this Agreement.

(d)   Except as set forth on Exhibit 3A(d), each Shareholder does as of the date hereof, and at Closing shall, hold of record and own beneficially the Common Stock, free and clear of any and all liens, encumbrances, security interests, options, warrants, agreements, rights, claims, demands or other interests whatsoever of third parties. Except for the Common Stock and/or Options owned by each Shareholder as set forth on Exhibit 3.3, each Shareholder has no other ownership interest, vested, contingent, or otherwise, in the Acquired Company whatsoever, whether through: (i) ownership of other capital stock; (ii) preemptive rights, rights of first refusal, buy back rights or other similar rights; (iii) outstanding subscriptions, options, rights, warrants, convertible securities or other rights, agreements or commitments which obligate the Acquired Company to issue, or transfer any of its capital stock; or (iv) otherwise.

(e)   Each Shareholder has had ample opportunity to consult with such Shareholder's legal, financial and accounting advisors concerning the sale of the Common Stock pursuant hereto, and to ask such questions, review such documents and records, and conduct such other investigations as the Shareholder and the Shareholder's advisors deemed appropriate regarding the Purchaser and its business, assets, results of operations and financial condition and the terms and conditions of the issuance of the Purchaser Preferred Stock. Without limiting the foregoing, the Shareholder has become familiar with the terms of this Agreement and has asked such questions, reviewed such documents and conducted such other investigations as the Shareholder and the Shareholder's advisors deemed appropriate relating to the Agreement and the transactions contemplated hereby. The Shareholder is able to fend for himself, can bear the economic risk of his investment in the Purchaser Preferred Stock and the undersigned, individually or through advisors, has such knowledge and experience in financial, tax and business matters to enable the undersigned to evaluate the merits and risks of the proposed sale and to make an informed decision. In making the Shareholder's decision to enter into this Agreement and sell the Common Stock, the Shareholder has not relied on any representation, warranty, or information from the Acquired Company, Purchaser or Acquisition Sub or any director, officer, employee, agent or other representative of the Acquired Company, Purchaser or Acquisition Sub other than Purchaser's representations and warranties set forth in Section 4 of this Agreement.

(f)   Each Shareholder is acquiring the shares of Purchaser Preferred Stock issuable to him hereunder for his own account and not with a view to, or for sale or other disposition in connection with, any distribution of all or any part thereof, except (1) in an offering covered by a registration statement filed with the Securities and Exchange Commission under the Securities Act of 1933, as amended (the "Securities Act") and all applicable state securities regulatory authorities that cover the Purchaser Preferred Stock or (2) pursuant to an applicable exemption under the Securities Act and applicable state securities laws.

(g)   The Shareholder acknowledges that the Purchaser Preferred Stock has been valued at $_____ per share in determining the Merger Price and agrees that such value is a fair value for the Purchaser Preferred Stock.

(h)   The Shareholder understands (1) that the Purchaser Preferred Stock will not have been registered pursuant to the Securities Act or any applicable state securities laws, (2) that the Purchaser Preferred Stock will be characterized as "restricted securities" under federal securities laws, (3) that under such laws and applicable regulations the Purchaser Preferred Stock cannot be sold or otherwise disposed of without registration under the Securities Act and applicable state laws or qualification for an exemption therefrom and (4) that stop-transfer instructions may be issued to the transfer agent for securities of Purchaser (or a notation may be made in the appropriate records of Purchasers) in connection with the Purchaser Preferred Stock.

(i)   The Shareholder agrees and understands that the certificates representing the Purchaser Preferred Stock shall each conspicuously set forth on the face or back thereof, in addition to any legends required by applicable law or other agreement, a legend in substantially the following form:

> THE SECURITIES REPRESENTED BY THIS CERTIFICATE HAVE NOT BEEN REGISTERED UNDER THE SECURITIES ACT OF 1933, AS AMENDED (THE "ACT"), OR THE SECURITIES LAWS OF ANY STATE. THE SECURITIES MAY NOT BE TRANSFERRED EXCEPT PURSUANT TO

AN EFFECTIVE REGISTRATION STATEMENT UNDER SUCH ACT AND APPLICABLE STATE SECURITIES LAWS OR PURSUANT TO AN APPLICABLE EXEMPTION FROM THE REGISTRATION REQUIREMENTS OF SUCH ACT AND SUCH LAWS OR PURSUANT TO A WRITTEN OPINION OF COUNSEL (WHICH COUNSEL AND OPINION SHALL BE REASONABLY SATISFACTORY TO THE COMPANY) THAT SUCH REGISTRATION IS NOT REQUIRED.

(j)   The Shareholder has requested Purchasers to issue the Purchaser Preferred Stock to such Shareholder as a condition to the consummation of the transactions contemplated by this Agreement. Neither Purchasers nor any of its representatives has encouraged or persuaded such Shareholder to purchase any of the Purchaser Preferred Stock. In addition, such Shareholder has not relied upon Purchaser or any of its representatives for any advice relating to the tax or other consequences of the transactions contemplated by this Agreement or the risks attendant to an acquisition of Purchaser Preferred Stock.

(k)   Such Shareholder acknowledges and agrees that the Purchaser Preferred Stock, when issued, will be subject to the shareholders agreement in effect on the date of the Closing by and among Purchaser and its shareholders (the "Shareholders Agreement"), and that such Shareholder, as a condition to the issuance of the Purchaser Preferred Stock, must become a party to and agree to be bound by the terms of the Shareholders Agreement, and that such Shareholders certificate for the Purchaser Preferred Stock will bear a legend in substantially the form set forth in the Shareholders Agreement.

IV.   REPRESENTATIONS, WARRANTIES OF PURCHASER.

Purchaser and the Acquisition Sub, jointly and severally, represent and warrant to the Acquired Company as follows:

4.1   Organization and Standing.

(a)   Each of Purchaser and the Acquisition Sub is a duly organized and validly existing corporation in good standing under the laws of the State of _____. Purchaser has the corporate power and authority to own or lease all of its properties and assets and to carry on its business as it is now being conducted, is duly licensed or qualified to do business and is in good standing in each jurisdiction in which the nature of the business conducted by it or the character or location of the properties and assets owned or leased by it makes such licensing or qualification necessary, except where the failure to be so licensed, qualified or in good standing would not have a material adverse effect on Purchaser.

(b)   All Subsidiaries of Purchaser are listed in Exhibit 4.1(b)(1) (the "Purchaser Subsidiaries"). Each Purchaser Subsidiary is duly organized and validly existing and in good standing under the laws of its state or other jurisdiction of incorporation. Each Purchaser Subsidiary has the corporate power and authority to own or lease all of its properties and assets and to carry on its business as it is now being conducted and is duly licensed or qualified to do business and is in good standing in each jurisdiction in which the nature of the business conducted by it or the character or location of the properties and assets owned or leased by it makes such licensing or qualification necessary, except where the failure to be so licensed, qualified or in good standing would not have a material adverse effect on Purchaser. Exhibit 4.1(b)(2) sets forth copies of the Articles of Incorporation and Bylaws as in effect on the date of this Agreement, of Purchaser and each of the Purchaser Subsidiaries. Except for its ownership of the Purchaser Subsidiaries, Purchaser does not own or control, directly or indirectly, any equity interest in any corporation, company, association, partnership, joint venture or other entity.

4.2   Corporate Power and Authority.

(a)   Each of Purchaser and the Acquisition Sub has the capacity and authority to execute and deliver this Agreement, to perform hereunder and to consummate the transactions contemplated hereby without the necessity of any act or consent of any other Person.

(b)   The execution, delivery and performance by Purchaser and the Acquisition Sub of this Agreement and each and every agreement, document and instrument provided for herein have been duly authorized and approved by their respective Board of Directors.

(c)   This Agreement, and each and every other agreement, document and instrument to be executed, delivered and performed by Purchaser and the Acquisition Sub in connection herewith, constitute or will, when executed and delivered, constitute the valid and legally binding obligations of Purchaser, and the Acquisition Sub, as applicable, enforceable against each of them in accordance with their respective terms.

(d)   The execution and delivery of this Agreement and the consummation of the Merger and the other transactions contemplated by this Agreement have been duly and validly approved by the Board of Directors of Purchaser in accordance with the Articles of Incorporation of Purchaser and Applicable Laws.

(e)   The execution and delivery of this Agreement and the consummation of the transactions contemplated by this Agreement have been duly and validly approved by the Board of Directors and the sole Shareholder of Acquisition Sub in accordance with the Articles of Incorporation of Acquisition Sub and Applicable Laws.

4.3   Agreement Does Not Violate Other Instruments. Except as set forth on Exhibit 4.3, the execution and delivery by Purchaser and the Acquisition Sub of this Agreement and the other agreements and instruments to be executed and delivered in connection with the transactions contemplated hereby or thereby do not, and, the consummation of the transactions contemplated hereby will not, violate or conflict with (i) any provisions of the Articles of Incorporation, as amended, or Bylaws, as amended, of Purchaser or the Acquisition Sub; (ii) any Applicable Laws to which Purchaser or the Acquisition Sub is subject; (iii) any judgment, ruling, order, writ, injunction or decree of any court or of any Regulatory Authority to which Purchaser or the Acquisition Sub is a party or bound or by which any of its assets are attached; or (iv) constitute an occurrence of default under any provision of, or result in acceleration of any obligation under, or give rise to a contractual right by any party to terminate its obligations under, any mortgage, deed of trust, conveyance to secure debt, note, bond, loan, lien, lease, agreement, instrument, or other Contract to which Purchaser or the Acquisition Sub is a party or is bound or by which any of their respective assets are affected.

4.4   Required Governmental Consents. Except as listed or described on Exhibit 4.4, no consent, approval, order, certification, permission or authorization of, notice to, exemption by, or registration, declaration, recording or filing with, any Regulatory Authority is required to be obtained or made by or with respect to Purchaser or the Acquisition Sub or any assets, properties or operations of Purchaser or the Acquisition Sub in connection with the execution and delivery by Purchaser and the Acquisition Sub of this Agreement or the consummation of the transactions contemplated hereby.

4.5   Capitalization. As of the date of this Agreement, the authorized capital stock of Purchaser consists of (a) _____ shares of Common Stock, of which _____ shares are issued and outstanding, and (b) _____ shares of preferred stock, (i) _____ shares of which are _____ Preferred Stock, of which _____ shares are issued and outstanding, (ii) _____ shares of which are _____ Preferred Stock, of which _____ shares are issued and outstanding, (iii) _____ shares of which are _____ Preferred Stock, _____ shares of which are issued and outstanding and (iv) _____ shares of which are _____ Preferred Stock, none of which shares are issued and outstanding. Set forth on Exhibit 4.5 is a true and complete list of (i) the shareholders of the Company and, opposite the name of each shareholder, the amount of all outstanding capital stock and all outstanding options, warrants, conversion privileges, or other rights to purchase or otherwise acquire any authorized but unissued shares of capital stock or other proprietary interests (collectively, "Options") owned by such shareholder and (ii) the holders of Options (other than the shareholders set forth in clause (i) above) and, opposite the name of each such holder, the amount of all outstanding Options of the Company owned by such holder. The Company has reserved a sufficient number of shares of Common Stock for issuance upon conversion of the Purchaser Preferred Stock. The Purchaser Preferred Stock is duly authorized, and, assuming the accuracy of the representations and warranties of the Shareholders set forth in Article IV, when issued and sold to the Shareholders in accordance with this Agreement, will be validly issued, fully paid and nonassessable. The shares of Common Stock issuable upon conversion of the Purchaser Preferred Stock is duly authorized and, when issued in compliance with the provisions of the Articles of Incorporation, will be validly issued, fully paid and nonassessable. The issued and outstanding shares of capital stock of the Company are all duly authorized, validly issued, fully paid and nonassessable.

4.6   Financial Statements.

(a)   Exhibit 4.6 sets forth copies of: balance sheets of Purchaser at _____, _____ and _____ and the statements of income for the periods ended _____, _____ and _____ (collectively, the "Purchaser Financial Statements") and the Purchaser's unaudited balance sheet as of _____ and the related unaudited statement of income for the two month period then ended (the "Purchaser Interim Financials"). The Purchaser Financial Statements and Purchaser Interim Financials present fairly, in all material respects, the financial position of Purchaser as of the respective dates set forth in the Purchaser Financial Statements and the Purchaser Interim Financials, and the results of Purchaser's operations for the respective periods set forth in the Purchaser Financial Statements; except that the unaudited interim financial statements are subject to normal and recurring year-end adjustments.

(b)   Since the date of the Purchaser Interim Financials, there has not been any change, occurrence or circumstance in the business, results of operations or financial condition of Purchaser or any Purchaser Subsidiary having, individually or in the aggregate, a material adverse effect on Purchaser.

4.7   Purchaser Preferred Stock. At the Effective Time, the Purchaser Preferred Stock to be issued pursuant to the Merger will be duly authorized and validly issued, fully paid and nonassessable, free of preemptive rights and free and clear of all Liens created by or through Purchaser (except as set forth in this Agreement and the documents and agreements executed in connection herewith).

4.8   Legal Proceedings. Neither Purchaser nor Acquisition Sub is a party to any, and there is no pending or, to Purchaser's or Acquisition Sub's knowledge, threatened legal, administrative, arbitral or other proceeding, claim, action or governmental investigation of any nature against Purchaser or Acquisition Sub. Neither Purchaser nor Acquisition Sub is a party to any order, judgment or decree entered in any lawsuit or proceeding that is likely to have a material adverse effect on Purchaser or Acquisition Sub.

V.   COVENANTS AND AGREEMENTS OF THE ACQUIRED COMPANY AND THE SHAREHOLDERS.

5.1   Acquired Company Actions. The Acquired Company and the Shareholders hereby consent to the Merger and represent that the Board of Directors of the Acquired Company, by unanimous vote of all directors present at a meeting duly called and held (or pursuant to a consent in lieu of a meeting), has (a) determined that the Merger is fair to the shareholders of the Acquired Company and is in the best interests of the shareholders of the Acquired Company and (b) resolved to recommend approval of the Merger to the Shareholders of the Acquired Company.

5.2   Shareholders' Meeting.

(a)   The Acquired Company shall, and the Shareholders shall cause the Acquired Company to, in accordance with _____ and any applicable securities laws: duly call, give notice of, convene and hold a special meeting of its shareholders (or execute a consent in lieu thereof) (the "Shareholders Meeting") and submit this Agreement and any related matters, as appropriate, and the Merger to a vote of the Acquired Company's shareholders as soon as practicable for the purpose of considering and taking action upon this Agreement and any such related matters. In connection with this meeting, the Board of Directors of the Acquired Company shall recommend that the shareholders of the Acquired Company vote in favor of the approval and adoption of this Agreement. The Acquired Company shall use its best efforts to obtain the necessary approval of the Merger by its shareholders.

(b)   The Acquired Company and the Shareholders represent and agree that any materials distributed to the Acquired Company's shareholders in connection with the Shareholders Meeting will comply in all respects with the requirements of Applicable Laws. Except for information supplied by Purchaser in writing for inclusion therein, none of the information will be false or misleading with respect to any material fact or will omit to state any material fact required to be stated therein or necessary in order to make the statements therein, in light of the circumstances under which they are made, not misleading.

(c)   As soon as practicable (but in no event more than three business days) after the Shareholders' Meeting, the Acquired Company shall deliver to Purchaser a certificate of the Secretary of the Acquired Company containing the names of the shareholders of the Acquired Company that either: (a) have given written notice prior to the taking of the vote on the Plan of Merger at the Shareholders' Meeting that they dissent from the Merger, or (b) have voted against the Plan of Merger ("Certificate of Objections"). The Certificate of Objections shall include the number of shares of Common Stock held by each such shareholder and the mailing address of each such shareholder.

5.3   <u>Conduct of Business—Negative Covenants</u>. From the date of this Agreement until the earlier of the Effective Time or until the termination of this Agreement, the Acquired Company and the Shareholders covenant and agree that the Acquired Company shall, and the Shareholders shall cause the Acquired Company to, carry on its business in the ordinary course and maintain and preserve its organization, goodwill and properties and not take any action inconsistent therewith or with the consummation of the transactions contemplated by this Agreement. In this connection, the Acquired Company will not, and the Shareholders shall cause the Acquired Company not to, do or agree or commit to do, any of the following without the prior written consent of Purchaser:

(a)   amend its articles of incorporation or bylaws;

(b)   repurchase, redeem, or otherwise acquire or exchange, directly or indirectly, any shares of its capital stock or any securities convertible into any shares of its capital stock;

(c)   declare or pay any dividend whether in cash, stock or otherwise or make or agree to make any other distribution to its shareholders;

(d)   organize any subsidiary, acquire any capital stock or other equity securities of any corporation, or acquire any equity or ownership interest in any business;

(e)   mortgage, pledge, or otherwise encumber or dispose of any of its assets other than in the ordinary course of business;

(f)   incur any additional indebtedness except in the ordinary course of business;

(g)   grant any general increase in compensation to its employees as a class or to its officers, except in accordance with past practice; pay any bonus; grant any increase in fees or other increases in compensation or other benefits to any of its directors; or effect any change in retirement benefits for any class of its employees or officers;

(h)   amend any existing employment Contract between the Acquired Company and any individual to increase the compensation or benefits payable thereunder or enter into any new employment Contract with any Person;

(i)   adopt any new employee benefit plan or make any change in or to any existing Benefit Plans;

(j)   (i) utilize accounting principles different from those used in the preparation of the _____, _____ and _____ Financial Statements, (ii) change in any manner its method of maintaining its books of account and records from such methods as in effect on _____, or (iii) accelerate booking of revenues or the deferral of expenses, other than as shall be consistent with past practice and in the ordinary course of business;

(k)   suffer, permit or incur any of the transactions or events described in Section 3.12 hereof, or, other than as shall be consistent with past practice and in the ordinary course of business, enter into any contract, commitment, arrangement or transaction of the type described in Section 3.16 hereof;

(l)   grant to a third party the right to market the Acquired Company's technologies, methodologies or practices; or engage in any other transaction or event which could adversely effect the value of the Acquired Company's business;

(m)   grant or agree to grant any stock option, warrant or other right to purchase any security of the Acquired Company or issue any security convertible into such securities;

(n)   make any contribution to or distribution from any employee benefit plan, pension plan, stock bonus plan, 401(k) plan or profit sharing plan (except for the payment of any health, disability and life insurance premiums which may become due and except for contributions or distributions required to be made (and not discretionary) pursuant to the terms of any Benefit Plans); or

(o)   make any change in its banking or safe deposit arrangements or grant any powers of attorney. (A list of all bank accounts, safe deposit boxes (and the contents thereof) and powers of attorney of the Acquired Company and of all Persons authorized to act with respect thereto is attached hereto as Exhibit 5.3.)

5.4   Conduct of Business—Affirmative Covenants. Unless the prior written consent of Purchaser shall have been obtained and except as otherwise contemplated herein, the Acquired Company will, and the Shareholders shall cause the Acquired Company to: (a) operate its business only in the usual, regular and ordinary course; (b) use its best efforts to preserve intact its business organization and assets and maintain its rights and franchises; (c) keep in force at no less than their present limits all existing bonds and policies of insurance or comparable replacements thereof insuring the Acquired Company and its properties; (d) promptly advise Purchaser in writing of (i) any matters arising or discovered after the date of this Agreement which, if existing or known at the date hereof, would be required to be set forth or described in this Agreement, or, (ii) the institution or the threat of any litigation involving the Acquired Company; (e) take no action which would (i) adversely affect the ability of it to obtain any necessary approvals of Regulatory Authorities required for the transactions contemplated hereby, or (ii) adversely affect the ability of the Acquired Company to perform its covenants and agreements under this Agreement; and (f) comply with all Applicable Laws.

5.5   Adverse Changes in Condition. The Acquired Company and the Shareholders shall give written notice promptly to Purchaser concerning any material adverse change in the business, properties, rights, operations or financial condition of the Acquired Company from the date of this Agreement until the Effective Time. The Acquired Company and the Shareholders shall use their best efforts to prevent or promptly remedy the same.

5.6   Resignation. If requested by the Purchaser, the Acquired Company and the Shareholders shall deliver at the Closing the resignation of each of the directors and officers of the Acquired Company and each trustee under any Benefit Plan maintained by the Acquired Company, such resignations to be effective immediately prior to the Effective Time.

5.7   Examination of Property and Records; Additional Information. Between the date of this Agreement and the Effective Time, the Acquired Company and the Shareholders will allow Purchaser, its counsel and other representatives full access to all the books, records, files, documents, assets, properties, contracts and agreements of the Acquired Company which may be requested, and the Acquired Company and the Shareholders shall furnish Purchaser and the Acquisition Sub, their officers and representatives during such period with all information concerning the affairs of the Acquired Company which may be requested. Purchaser and the Acquisition Sub will conduct any investigation in a manner which will not unreasonably interfere with the business of the Acquired Company. During the period from the date of this Agreement to the Effective Time, the Acquired Company and the Shareholders shall cause one or more of the Acquired Company's representatives to confer on a regular and frequent basis with representatives of Purchaser and to report on the general status of its ongoing operations.

5.8 <u>Agreement as to Efforts to Consummate; Consents and Approvals</u>. Subject to the terms and conditions of this Agreement and the Plan of Merger, the Acquired Company and the Shareholders shall use all reasonable efforts to take, or cause to be taken, all actions, and to do, or cause to be done, all things necessary, proper, or advisable under Applicable Laws to consummate and make effective, as soon as practicable after the date of this Agreement, the transactions contemplated by this Agreement and the Plan of Merger. Unless specifically waived by Purchaser in writing, the Acquired Company and the Shareholders shall obtain the waiver, consent and approval of all Persons whose waiver, consent or approval (a) is required in order to consummate the transactions contemplated by this Agreement or (b) is required by any Contract or Applicable Laws and (i) which would prohibit or require the waiver, consent or approval of any Person to such transactions or (ii) under which, without such waiver, consent or approval, such transactions would constitute an occurrence of default under the provisions thereof, result in the acceleration of any obligation thereunder or give rise to a right of any party thereto to terminate its obligations thereunder. All obtained written waivers, consents and approvals shall be added to the Disclosure Materials and shall be in form and content satisfactory to Purchaser. Notwithstanding the foregoing, to the extent that such a waiver, consent or approval cannot be obtained without substantial expense or difficulty, the Acquired Company and the Shareholders shall confer with Purchaser before proceeding to obtain such waiver, consent or approval and Purchaser, in its sole discretion, may waive in writing the requirement of obtaining such waiver, consent or approval.

5.9 <u>Stock Options and Similar Rights</u>. The Acquired Company and the Shareholders shall take such actions as are necessary to ensure that from and after the Effective Time neither the Acquired Company nor any ERISA Affiliates of the Acquired Company is or will be bound by any options, warrants, rights or Contracts issued, granted or entered into by the Acquired Company that would entitle any Person, other than Purchaser or its wholly-owned subsidiaries, to beneficially own, or receive any payments (other than as otherwise contemplated by Sections 2.2 and 2.3) in respect of, any capital stock of the Acquired Company or the Surviving Corporation. The Board of Directors or any applicable Committee of the Acquired Company shall pass such resolutions, provide or direct the provision of such notices, and take such other actions as are necessary or appropriate to accomplish the termination of the Stock Option Plans and the Options, including without limitation any amendments to such plans as may be necessary or appropriate.

5.10 <u>Contact with Third Parties</u>. The Acquired Company and the Shareholders recognize that Purchaser and its authorized representatives may have need to contact customers, employees, accountants, governmental bodies and other Persons having a present business or other relationship with the Acquired Company in connection with the investigation of the Acquired Company. The Acquired Company and the Shareholders consent to such contact and waive any rights they may have to inhibit or prevent such contact to the extent such contact relates to the investigation of the Acquired Company.

5.11 <u>Agreement of Shareholders</u>. By executing this Agreement, each of the Shareholders agrees to: (a) vote all shares of Common Stock owned by such person in favor of approving the Merger; (b) not sell, transfer or encumber any of such person's shares of Common Stock or any voting rights or other interest in such shares, except (i) with the consent of Purchaser; or (ii) pursuant to the Merger; and (c) not solicit, discuss or vote in favor of any proposals relating to, among other things, the sale of the business or assets of the Acquired Company or of the securities of the Acquired Company to any person or entity other than Purchaser.

5.12 <u>Supplying of Financial Statements</u>. The Acquired Company and the Management Shareholders shall deliver to Purchaser all regularly prepared audited and unaudited financial statements of the Acquired Company prepared after the date of this Agreement, in format historically published or utilized internally (as applicable), as soon as each is available.

5.13 <u>No Solicitation</u>. The Acquired Company and the Shareholders shall not, and the Acquired Company and the Shareholders shall not authorize or permit any officer, director or employee of, or any financial advisor, attorney, accountant or other advisor or representative retained by, the Acquired Company to, solicit, initiate, encourage (including by way of furnishing information), endorse or enter into any agreement with respect to, or take any other action to facilitate, any inquiries or the making of any proposal that constitutes, or may reasonably be expected to lead to, any Takeover Proposal (as hereafter defined). The Acquired Company and the Shareholders shall immediately advise Purchaser orally and in writing of any Takeover Proposal or any inquiries or discussions with respect thereto. Neither the Board of Directors of the Acquired Company nor any committee thereof shall (a) withdraw or modify, or propose to withdraw or modify, in a manner adverse to Purchaser or the Acquisition Sub the approval or recommendation by the Board of Directors of the Acquired Company, of the Merger, or (b) approve or recommend, or propose to approve or recommend, any Takeover Proposal or any other acquisition of Outstanding Shares other than pursuant to the Merger and this Agreement. As used in this Agreement, "Takeover Proposal" shall mean any tender or exchange offer, proposal, other than a proposal by Purchaser or any of its affiliates, for a merger, share exchange or other business combination involving the Acquired Company or any proposal or offer to acquire in any manner a substantial equity interest in the Acquired Company or a substantial portion of the assets of the Acquired Company. In the event of a breach of this Section 5.13, the Acquired Company agrees to promptly pay the Purchaser $_____ in cash.

VI.   ADDITIONAL AGREEMENTS

6.1   Cooperation. Subject to the terms and conditions of this Agreement, the parties hereto shall use all reasonable efforts to take, or cause to be taken, all actions, and to do, or cause to be done, all things necessary, proper, or advisable under Applicable Laws, including all relevant securities laws, to consummate and make effective, as soon as practicable after the date of this Agreement, the transactions contemplated by this Agreement. The parties hereto shall use their best efforts to obtain consents of any Regulatory Authority and other third parties or governmental bodies necessary or desirable for the consummation of the transactions contemplated by this Agreement. Each party hereto shall cooperate with the others, and execute and deliver, or cause to be executed and delivered, all such additional instruments, including instruments of conveyance, assignment and transfer and take all such other actions as may reasonably be requested from time to time in order to effectuate the provisions and purposes of this Agreement or to ensure that each party hereto receives the full benefit of the transactions contemplated by this Agreement. Each party hereto shall endeavor in good faith and cooperate one with the other to complete the Exhibits called for by this Agreement.

6.2   <u>Press Releases and Disclosure</u>. Except as may be required by Applicable Laws, the parties hereto shall maintain the terms and conditions of this Agreement and any and all other agreements and transactions contemplated hereby in confidence subject to the applicable rules and regulations of the SEC and any other applicable Regulatory Authority and shall cooperate one with the other in making adequate and controlled disclosure with respect thereto to the public. In the event that any party proposes to issue, make or distribute any press release, public announcement or other written publicity or disclosure prior to the Closing Date that refers to the transactions contemplated herein, the party proposing to make such disclosure shall provide a copy of such disclosure to the other parties and shall afford the other parties reasonable opportunity (subject to any legal obligation of prompt disclosure) to comment on such disclosure or the portion thereof which refers to the transactions contemplated herein prior to making such disclosure. The Acquired Company and the Shareholders, on the one hand, and Purchaser and the Acquisition Sub, on the other, covenant and agree that following the execution of this Agreement and prior to the Closing, except as otherwise agreed or in connection with seeking advice from counsel and other professionals, they shall not disclose to any Person any of such terms, conditions or matters and shall keep the same confidential, to the extent not otherwise publicly known and except to the extent reasonably necessary in connection with any shareholders' approval process and to obtain the consents or approvals required by the terms of the Agreement or as otherwise required by Applicable Laws. Neither the Acquired Company nor the Shareholders will issue any press release or otherwise make any public statement or respond to any press inquiry with respect to this Agreement or the transactions contemplated hereby without the prior approval of Purchaser.

6.3   Brokers and Finders. Purchaser and the Acquisition Sub represent and warrant to the Acquired Company and the Shareholders, and the Shareholders, jointly and severally, represent and warrant to Purchaser and the Acquisition Sub, that no broker or finder has acted for them or the Acquired Company or any entity controlling, controlled by or under common control with it or them in connection with this Agreement. Purchaser and the Acquisition Sub agree to indemnify and hold harmless the Acquired Company and the Shareholders against any fee, loss or expense arising out of any claim by any broker or finder employed or alleged to have been employed by them, and the Shareholders, jointly and severally, agree to indemnify and hold harmless Purchaser and the Acquisition Sub against any fee, loss, or expense arising out of any claim by any broker or finder employed or alleged to have been employed by them or the Acquired Company. This indemnification shall be separate and apart from any other indemnification provided in this Agreement and is not subject to, and is not to be included, in any limits on indemnification contained elsewhere in this Agreement.

6.4   Guarantees. Purchaser and Acquisition Sub agree that they will pay when due the scheduled payments secured by the guarantees listed on Exhibit 6.4 and that they will also pay when due the insurance premiums relating to the cars listed on Exhibit 6.4. In this regard, Purchaser and Acquisition Sub agree to use commercially reasonable efforts to have the Shareholders released as guarantors under the guarantees set forth on Exhibit 6.4.

VII.   CONDITIONS PRECEDENT TO OBLIGATIONS OF PURCHASER AND THE ACQUISITION SUB.

All of the obligations of Purchaser and the Acquisition Sub to consummate the Merger shall be contingent upon and subject to the satisfaction, on or before the Closing, of each and every one of the following conditions. The following conditions are for the sole benefit of Purchaser and the Acquisition Sub and may be asserted by Purchaser regardless of the circumstances giving rise to any such condition and may be waived by Purchaser, in whole or in part, at any time and from time to time, in the sole discretion of Purchaser. The failure by Purchaser at any time including prior to Closing to exercise any of the foregoing rights will not be deemed a waiver of any other right and each right will be deemed an ongoing right which may be asserted at any time and from time to time.

7.1   **Representations and Warranties of Acquired Company and the Management Shareholders.** The representations and warranties of the Acquired Company and the Shareholders set forth in this Agreement shall be true and correct in all respects as of the date of this Agreement and as of the Closing Date with the same force and effect as though all such representations and warranties had been made on and as of the Effective Time, except for any such representations and warranties confined to a specified date, which shall be true and correct in all respects as of such date.

7.2   **Performance of Agreements and Covenants of Acquired Company and the Shareholders.** Each and all of the covenants and agreements of the Acquired Company and the Shareholders to be performed and complied with pursuant to this Agreement, the Plan of Merger and the other agreements contemplated hereby prior to the Effective Time shall have been duly performed and complied with in all respects; and a duly authorized officer of the Acquired Company shall deliver a certificate dated as of the Closing Date certifying to the fulfillment of this condition as it relates to the Company and the condition set forth under Section 7.1 above as it relates to the Company.

7.3   **Corporate Authorization.** All corporate action, including shareholder approval, necessary to authorize the execution, delivery and performance of this Agreement, and the Plan of Merger, and the consummation of the transactions contemplated hereby, shall have been duly and validly taken by Purchaser and the Acquired Company.

7.4   **Material Adverse Change.** There shall have been no determination by Purchaser that the consummation of the Merger or the other transactions contemplated by this Agreement is not in the best interests of Purchaser or its shareholders by reason of an actual or threatened material adverse change in the business, properties, rights, operations, or financial condition of the Acquired Company.

7.5   Outstanding Stock of the Acquired Company. There shall not be more than _____ shares of capital stock of the Acquired Company on a fully diluted basis outstanding at the Effective Time.

7.6   Required Deliveries. All documents and other information required to be delivered at the Closing by the Acquired Company, including the documents and other information, required by Section 9.2(a), shall have been delivered in form, manner and substance acceptable to Purchaser and the Acquisition Sub.

7.7   Actions of Governmental Authorities; Banking Moratorium. There shall not have been instituted or pending any action, proceeding, application, claim or counterclaim by any Regulatory Authority, and neither Purchaser, the Acquisition Sub, the Acquired Company nor any shareholder of the Acquired Company shall have been notified by any such Regulatory Authority (or a representative thereof) of its present intention to commence, or recommend the commencement of, such an action or proceeding, which (a) restrains or prohibits or seeks to restrain or prohibit the consummation of the Merger or restrains or prohibits or seeks to restrain or prohibit the performance of this Agreement, or (b) prohibits or limits or seeks to prohibit or limit the ownership or operation by Purchaser or the Acquisition Sub of all or any substantial portion of the business or assets of the Acquired Company or of Purchaser or any of its subsidiaries or compels or seeks to compel Purchaser or the Acquisition Sub to dispose of or to hold separate all or any substantial portion of the business or assets of the Acquired Company or of Purchaser or any of its subsidiaries, or imposes or seeks to impose any material limitation on the ability of Purchaser or the Acquisition Sub to conduct such business or to own such assets. There shall not be in effect a declaration of a banking moratorium or any suspension of payments in respect of banks in the United States (whether or not mandatory).

7.8   Other Legal Actions. There shall not have been any statute, rule, regulation, order or injunction enacted, promulgated, entered, enforced or deemed applicable to the Merger or this Agreement by any Regulatory Authority or court, domestic or foreign, and no claim or action for such shall have been instituted before a court, or Regulatory Authority, and such shall not have been proposed before a legislative body or

Regulatory Authority that could be reasonably expected to result in any of the consequences referred to in clauses (a) or (b) of Section 7.8 above.

7.9   Legal Approvals. The execution and the delivery of this Agreement and the consummation of the transactions contemplated hereby shall have been approved by any Regulatory Authority whose approval is required by Applicable Laws and the waiting period under the HSR Act shall have expired or have been terminated.

7.10   Due Diligence. The completion of due diligence by Purchaser and Purchaser's satisfaction with the results thereof.

7.12   Cancellation of Options, Warrants and Similar Rights, if Any. All Options, Warrants or any other rights through which capital stock of the Acquired Company may be obtained, if any, shall be cancelled on terms and conditions satisfactory to Purchaser.

7.13   Covenants Not to Compete. Those Persons identified on Exhibit 7.13 shall have entered into Covenants Not To Compete substantially in the form set forth as Exhibit 7.13 hereto.

7.14   Employment Agreements. Those Persons identified on Exhibit 7.14 shall have entered into employment agreements substantially in the form set forth as Exhibit 7.14 hereto.

7.15   Financing. The closing of the Financing must have occurred on terms acceptable to Purchaser and the terms of the Financing shall permit the acquisition of the Acquired Company.

7.16   Opinion of Counsel. Purchaser shall have received from the legal counsel for the Acquired Company and the Shareholders an opinion dated as of the Closing Date, substantially in the form and substance of the opinion attached hereto as Exhibit 7.17, reasonably satisfactory to Purchaser.

VIII. CONDITIONS PRECEDENT TO THE OBLIGATIONS OF THE ACQUIRED COMPANY.

All of the obligations of the Acquired Company to consummate the transaction contemplated by the Merger shall be contingent upon and subject to the satisfaction, on or before the Closing, of each and every one of the following conditions. The following conditions are for the sole benefit of the Acquired Company and may be asserted by the Acquired Company regardless of the circumstances giving rise to any such condition and may be waived by the Acquired Company, in whole or in part, at any time and from time to time, in the sole discretion of the Acquired Company for purposes of consummating the transactions contemplated herein. The failure by the Acquired Company at any time to exercise any of the foregoing rights will not be deemed a waiver of any other right and each right will be deemed an ongoing right which may be asserted at any time and from time to time.

8.1   Representations and Warranties. The representations and warranties of Purchaser and the Acquisition Sub set forth in this Agreement shall be true and correct in all respects as of the date of this Agreement and as of the Effective Time with the same force and effect as though all such representations and warranties had been made on and as of the Effective Time, except for any such representations and warranties confined to a specified date, which shall be true and correct in all respects as of such date.

8.2   Performance of Agreements and Covenants. Each and all of the covenants and agreements of Purchaser and the Acquisition Sub to be performed and complied with pursuant to this Agreement, the Plan of Merger and the other agreements contemplated hereby prior to the Effective Time shall have been duly performed and complied with in all respects; and a duly authorized officer of Purchaser and the Acquisition Sub shall deliver a certificate dated as of the Closing Date certifying to the fulfillment of this condition and the condition set forth under Section 8.1 above.

8.3   Corporate Authorization. All corporate action necessary to authorize the execution, delivery and performance of this Agreement, and the Plan of Merger, and the consummation of the transactions contemplated hereby and thereby, shall have been duly and validly taken by Purchaser and the Acquisition Sub.

8.4   Required Deliveries. All documents and other information required to be delivered at the Closing by Purchaser and the Acquisition Sub, including the documents and other information required by Section 9.2(b), shall have been delivered in form, manner and substance acceptable to the Acquired Company.

8.5   Actions of Governmental Authorities. There shall not have been instituted or pending any action, proceeding, application, claim or counterclaim by any Regulatory Authority, and Purchaser, the Acquisition Sub, the Acquired Company or any Shareholder shall not have been notified by any such Regulatory Authority (or a representative thereof) of its present intention to commence, or recommend the commencement of, such an action or proceeding, which restrains or prohibits or seeks to restrain or prohibit the consummation of the Merger or restrains or prohibits or seeks to restrain or prohibit the performance of this Agreement.

8.6   Other Legal Actions. There shall not have been any Applicable Laws enacted, promulgated, entered, enforced or deemed applicable to the Merger or this Agreement by any Regulatory Authority or court, and no claim or action for such shall have been instituted before a court or Regulatory Authority, and such shall not have been proposed before a legislative body or Regulatory Authority that could be reasonably expected to result in any of the consequences referred to in Section 8.5 above.

8.7   Legal Approvals. The execution and the delivery of this Agreement and the consummation of the transactions contemplated hereby shall have been approved by any Regulatory Authority whose approval is required by Applicable Laws and the waiting period under the HSR Act shall have expired or been terminated.

8.8   Shareholder Approval. This Agreement and the Merger shall have been adopted and approved by the shareholder vote required by, and in accordance with, the _____ and the _____.

8.9   Opinion of Counsel. The Shareholders shall have received from the legal counsel for the Purchaser an opinion dated as of the Closing Date, substantially in the form and substance of the opinion attached here to as Exhibit 8.9, reasonably satisfactory to Purchaser.

IX.   CLOSING

9.1   Time and Place of Closing. The Closing will take place as soon as practicable following the closing of the Financing (the "Closing Date"). The Closing shall take place at the offices of _____, in _____, _____ or at such other place as the parties hereto may mutually agree.

9.2   Transactions at Closing. At the Closing, each of the following transactions shall occur:

(a)   The Acquired Company and the Shareholders' Performance. At the Closing, the Acquired Company and the Shareholders shall deliver or cause to be delivered to Purchaser and the Acquisition Sub, in addition to this Agreement, the following:

(i)   copies of the consents and waivers described in Section 3.11;

(ii)   satisfactory evidences of the approvals described in Section 3.10;

(iii)   satisfactory evidence of the termination of the Options and any other rights to acquire capital stock of the Acquired Company;

(iv)   the Officer's Certificate contemplated by Section 7.2;

(v)   a certificate of compliance or a certificate of good standing of the Acquired Company, as of the most recent practicable date, from the appropriate governmental authority of the jurisdiction of its incorporation and any other jurisdiction which is set forth in Exhibit 3.1

hereto; and a certificate of tax compliance, as of the most recent practicable date, from the appropriate governmental authority of the jurisdiction of its incorporation;

(vi)   the Certificates for the Common Stock contemplated by Section 2.4;

(vii)   satisfactory evidence of the shareholder approval required by the _____;

(viii)   Articles of Merger and a Plan of Merger, each in form and content that complies with the applicable law, executed by Acquired Company;

(ix)   certified copies of resolutions of the Board of Directors of Acquired Company approving the transactions set forth in this Agreement;

(x)   certificates of incumbency for the officers of Acquired Company;

(xi)   the Covenants Not to Compete required by Section 7.13;

(xii)   the employment agreements required by Section 7.14;

(xiii)   an Amended and Restated Shareholders Agreement executed by the Shareholders;

(xiv)   an Amended and Restated Registration Rights Agreement executed by the Shareholders;

(xv)   the Escrow Agreement contemplated by Section 2.5 executed by the Management Shareholders;

(xvi)   the opinions contemplated by Section 7.17;

(xvii)   such   other   documents   as   may   be   required hereunder; and

(xviii)   such other evidence of the performance of all covenants and satisfaction of all conditions required of the Acquired Company and the Shareholders by this Agreement, at or prior to the Closing, as Purchaser or its counsel may reasonably require.

(b)   <u>Performance by Purchaser and the Acquisition Sub</u>. At the Closing, Purchaser and the Acquisition Sub shall deliver, or cause to be delivered, to the Acquired Company and the Shareholders, in addition to this Agreement, the following:

(i)   satisfactory evidence of the approvals described in Section 4.4;

(ii)   the Officer's Certificate contemplated by Section 8.2;

(iii)   certificate of incumbency of the officers of Purchaser and the Acquisition Sub who are executing this Agreement and the other documents contemplated hereunder;

(iv)   certified copy of resolutions of the Boards of Directors of Purchaser and the Acquisition Sub approving the transaction contemplated by this Agreement;

(v)   Articles of Merger and a Plan of Merger, each in form and content that complies with the applicable law, executed by Purchaser or the Acquisition Sub;

(vi)   the Covenants Not to Compete required by Section 7.13;

(vii)   Employment Agreements required by Section 7.14;

(viii)   an   Amended   and   Restated   Shareholders Agreement executed by the Purchaser;

(ix)   an Amended and Restated Registration Rights Agreement executed by the Purchaser;

(x)   the Escrow Agreement contemplated by Section 2.5 executed by the Purchaser and Acquisition Sub;

(xi)   the opinion contemplated by Section 8.9;

(xii)   the Merger Price; and

(xiii)   such other evidence of the performance of all the covenants and satisfaction of all of the conditions required of Purchaser and the Acquisition Sub by this Agreement at or before the Closing as the Acquired Company or its counsel may reasonably require.

X.   SURVIVAL (OR NON-SURVIVAL) OF REPRESENTATIONS AND WARRANTIES; INDEMNIFICATION.

10.1   <u>Non-Survival of Representations and Warranties of the Acquired Company.</u> All representations, warranties, agreements, covenants and obligations made or undertaken by the Acquired Company in this Agreement or in any document or instrument executed and delivered pursuant hereto shall not survive the Closing and, following the Closing, the Acquired Company shall have no liability whatsoever with respect to any such representations, warranties, agreements, covenants or obligations. Prior to Closing, the Acquired Company agrees to indemnify and hold Purchaser harmless from and against all liability, loss, damages or injury and all reasonable costs and expenses (including reasonable counsel fees and costs of any suit related thereto) suffered or incurred by Purchaser arising from any misrepresentation by, or breach of any covenant or warranty of the Acquired Company contained in this Agreement or any certificate or other instrument furnished or to be furnished by the Acquired Company hereunder, or any claim by a third party (regardless of whether the claimant is ultimately successful) which if true would be such a misrepresentation or breach.

10.2   Survival of Representations and Warranties of the Shareholders; Indemnification by the Shareholders.

(a)   All representations, warranties, agreements, covenants and obligations made or undertaken by the Shareholders in this Agreement or in any document or instrument executed and delivered pursuant hereto are material, have been relied upon by Purchaser, shall survive the Closing hereunder for a period of two years except for agreements, covenants and obligations and the representations and warranties in Sections 3.2, 3.3, 3.6, 3.7, 3.17, 3.19 and 3.21, which shall survive indefinitely.

(b)   The Management Shareholders, jointly and severally, agree to indemnify and hold Purchaser harmless from and against all liability, loss, damages or injury and all reasonable costs and expenses (including reasonable counsel fees and costs of any suit related thereto) suffered or incurred by Purchaser arising from (i) any misrepresentation by, or breach of any warranty, agreement, covenant or obligation of, any Shareholder contained in this Agreement or any certificate or other instrument furnished or to be furnished by any Shareholder hereunder, or any claim by a third party (regardless of whether the claimant is ultimately successful) which if true would be such a misrepresentation or breach; (ii) any suit, action, proceeding, claim or investigation pending or threatened against or affecting the Acquired Company that arises from any matter or state of facts existing at or prior to Closing, regardless of whether it is disclosed; or (iii) any claim against or liability of the Acquired Company, which accrued prior to the Closing, to the extent not accrued or reserved against in the Interim Financial Statements. In connection with this indemnification, the Shareholders agree that they will not seek, and they will not have, any right of reimbursement, indemnity, contribution or similar right against the Acquired Company.

(c)   Except for claims under Section 3.6, Purchaser may not recover from the Management Shareholders under Section 10.2(b) for any claims regarding a breach of a representation or warranty unless and until the aggregate amount of any such claims exceeds $20,000 (the "Minimum Liability Amount"). At such time as the total of all such claims exceeds the Minimum Liability Amount, the Management Shareholders shall be liable for the entire amount of all such claims, and all claims asserted by Purchaser thereafter.

(d)   Except for claims under Sections 3.2, 3.3, 3.6 and 3.17, the maximum aggregate liability of each of the Management Shareholders for indemnification under Section 10.2(b) regarding a breach of a representation or warranty is such Management Shareholder's pro rata portion of the Merger Price (the "Maximum Liability Amount"), and the obligations of each of the Management Shareholders regarding indemnification for such claims shall terminate once the Maximum Liability Amount has been paid by such Management Shareholder with respect to such claims. The amount of claims made under Sections 3.2, 3.3, 3.6 and 3.17 for which liability shall be unlimited shall not be counted for purposes of reaching the Maximum Liability Amount.

(e)   Any examination, inspection or audit of the properties, financial condition or other matters of the Acquired Company and its business conducted by Purchaser through the Effective Time shall in no way limit, affect or impair the ability of Purchaser to rely upon the representations, warranties, covenants and obligations set forth herein.

(f)   In the event this Agreement is terminated pursuant to Article XI hereof, such that the Merger is not consummated, then the provisions of Sections 10.2 and 10.3 shall not survive such termination.

(g)   The Management Shareholders hereby agree among themselves that if the Purchaser seeks indemnification as permitted by this Section 10.2 from fewer than all of the Management Shareholders (the "Indemnifying Shareholders"), in respect of any losses, claims, damages or liabilities referred to therein, then each Management Shareholder from whom Purchaser has not sought indemnification with respect to the specific loss, claim, damage or liability shall contribute to the amount paid or payable to Purchaser, by the Indemnifying Shareholders, as a result of such losses, claims, damages or liabilities, in such proportion equal to such Management Shareholder's pro rata portion of the Merger Price. The amounts actually paid by each of the Management Shareholders after any payments made in accordance with this Section 10.2(g) shall be the amounts used to determine whether a Management Shareholder has paid the

Maximum Liability Amount as contemplated by Section 10.2(d). The agreement set forth in this Section 10.2(g) is an agreement only among the Management Shareholders regarding contribution and nothing contained in this Section 10.2(g) shall prevent the Purchaser from seeking and obtaining full indemnification from one, some or all of the Management Shareholders in accordance with the other provisions of this Section 10.2.

10.3   Survival of Representations and Warranties of Purchaser; Indemnification by Purchaser.

(a)   All representations, warranties, agreements, covenants and obligations made or undertaken by Purchaser in this Agreement or in any document or instrument executed and delivered pursuant hereto are material, have been relied upon by the Acquired Company and the Shareholders and shall survive the Closing hereunder for a period of three years and shall not merge in the performance of any obligation by any party hereto.

(b)   Purchaser agrees to indemnify and hold the Acquired Company and the Shareholders harmless from and against all liability, loss, damage or injury and all reasonable costs and expenses (including reasonable counsel fees and costs of any suit related thereto) suffered or incurred by the Acquired Company or the Shareholders arising from any misrepresentation by, or breach of any warranty, agreement, covenant or obligation of Purchaser or the Acquisition Sub contained in this Agreement or any certificate or other instrument furnished or to be furnished by Purchaser hereunder, or any claim by a third party (regardless of whether the claimant is ultimately successful) which if true would be such a misrepresentation or breach.

10.4   Conditions of Indemnification For Third Party Claims. The respective obligations and liabilities of the Management Shareholders, on the one hand, and Purchaser, on the other hand (the "indemnifying party"), to the other (the "party to be indemnified") under Article 10 hereof with respect to claims resulting from the assertion of liability by third parties shall be subject to the following terms and conditions:

(a)   Within 10 days after receipt of notice of commencement of any action or the assertion in writing of any claim by a third party, the party to be indemnified shall give the indemnifying party written notice thereof together with a copy of such claim, process or other legal pleading, and the indemnifying party shall have the right to undertake the defense thereof by representatives of its own choosing and reasonably acceptable to the party to be indemnified by promptly notifying the party to be indemnified ("Notice to Defend"); provided, however, the indemnifying party shall not effect a settlement of any such claim, without the prior written consent of the party to be indemnified, which shall not be unreasonably withheld (it shall not be considered unreasonable to withhold consent if the settlement contains any admission on the part of the party to be indemnified of wrongdoing or against interest or contains any sanctions other than the payment of money that the indemnifying party agrees to and is able to pay, but it shall be unreasonable to withhold consent if such settlement consists solely of the indemnifying party agreeing and having the ability to pay money); provided, further in order to assume the defense of such claim, the indemnifying party shall first have acknowledged in its Notice to Defend its obligation to indemnify the party to be indemnified for the matter.

(b)   If the indemnifying party chooses to defend any claim as set forth above, the party to be indemnified shall cooperate and make available to the indemnifying party any books, records or other documents within its control that are necessary or appropriate for such defense, subject to reasonable steps to maintain the confidentiality or privileged nature of such information.

(c)   In the event that the indemnifying party, by the 15th day after receipt of notice of any such claim (or, if earlier, by the tenth day preceding the day on which an answer or other pleading must be served in order to prevent judgment by default in favor of the person asserting such claim), does not elect to defend against such claim as set forth above, the party to be indemnified shall (upon further notice to the indemnifying party) have the right to undertake the defense, compromise or settlement of such claim on behalf of and for the account and risk of the indemnifying party, subject to the right of the indemnifying party to assume the defense of such claim at any time prior to settlement, compromise or final determination thereof, provided that the indemnifying party shall be given at least 15 days prior written notice (including acknowledgement of its obligation to indemnify the party to be indemnified) of the effectiveness of any such proposed settlement or compromise.

(d)   Anything in this Section 10.4 to the contrary notwithstanding (i) if there is a reasonable probability that a claim may materially and adversely affect the indemnifying party other than as a result of money damages or other money payments, the indemnifying party shall have the right, at its own cost and expense, to compromise or settle such claim, but (ii) the indemnifying party shall not, without the prior written consent of the party to be indemnified, settle or compromise any claim or consent to the entry of any judgment which does not include as an unconditional term thereof the giving by the claimant or the plaintiff to the party to be indemnified a release from all liability in respect of such claim.

(e)   The failure to so notify the indemnifying party by the times set forth above shall not relieve the indemnifying party of its indemnification obligations hereunder, except to the extent its rights are thereby materially prejudiced by such late notice; provided, however, that the party to be indemnified shall provide notice to the other, in all circumstances, within one year of actually becoming aware of the claim or such claim shall be barred. The Shareholders are deemed to have notice of those items listed in the Exhibits hereto.

10.5   Direct Claims. Any claim by the party to be indemnified for indemnification other than with respect to Third Party Claims (a "Direct Claim") shall be asserted by giving the indemnifying party prompt written notice from discovery, and the indemnifying party will have a period of twenty (20) calendar days within which to respond in writing to such Direct Claim. If the indemnifying party does not so respond within such twenty (20) calendar day period, the indemnifying party will be deemed to have rejected such claim, in which event the party to be indemnified will be free to seek enforcement of its rights under this Agreement in a court of competent jurisdiction. The failure to so notify the indemnifying party by the times set forth above shall not relieve the indemnifying party of its indemnification obligations hereunder, except to the extent its rights are thereby materially prejudiced by such late notice; provided, however, that the party to be indemnified shall provide notice to the other, in all circumstances, within one year of actually becoming aware of the claim or such claim shall be barred. The Shareholders are deemed to have notice of those items listed in the Exhibits hereto.

XI.   TERMINATION.

11.1   Method of Termination. This Agreement constitutes the binding and irrevocable agreement of the parties to consummate the transactions contemplated hereby, the consideration for which is (a) the covenants set forth herein, and (b) expenditures and obligations incurred and to be incurred by Purchaser and the Acquisition Sub, on the one hand, and by the Acquired Company and the Shareholders, on the other hand, in respect of this Agreement, and this Agreement may be terminated or abandoned only as follows:

11.2   Termination. This Agreement may be terminated at any time prior to the Effective Date, whether before or after approval of the Merger by the Acquired Company's Shareholders.

(a)   by mutual written consent of the Acquired Company, the Acquisition Sub and Purchaser, properly authorized by their respective Boards of Directors;

(b)   by Purchaser or the Acquired Company, upon written notice to the other, (i) if the Effective Time shall not have occurred by _____, unless the failure of such occurrence shall be due to the failure of the party seeking to terminate this Agreement to perform or observe its agreements and conditions set forth herein required to be performed or observed by such party at or before the Effective Time; (ii) 90 days after the date on which any application for regulatory approval prerequisite to the consummation of the transactions contemplated hereby shall have been denied, or withdrawn at the request or recommendation of the applicable Regulatory Authority, unless within such 90-day period a petition for rehearing or an amended application has been filed with such applicable Regulatory Authority or a party hereto notifies the other party of its intent to file such a petition or application within such 90-day period in which event the right to terminate this Agreement shall be reinstated 60 days following the completion or abandonment of all administrative, or judicial proceedings to which any of the parties hereto is entitled; provided, however, that nothing in this subparagraph (ii) shall be construed as limiting any parties' right to terminate this Agreement in accordance with the provisions of subparagraph (i) of this paragraph if the Effective Time shall not have occurred by the date set forth above unless the failure of such occurrence shall be due to the failure of the party seeking to terminate this Agreement to perform or observe its agreements and conditions set forth herein required to be performed or observed by such party at or before the Effective Time;

(c)   by Purchaser, upon written notice to the Acquired Company, if there shall have been any breach of any covenant, representation, warranty or other obligation of the Acquired Company hereunder and such breach shall not have been remedied within 30 days after receipt by the Acquired Company of notice in writing from Purchaser, specifying the nature of such breach and requesting that it be remedied;

(d)   by the Acquired Company, upon written notice to Purchaser, if there shall have been any breach of any covenant, representation, warranty or other obligation of Purchaser hereunder and such breach shall not have been remedied within 30 days after receipt by Purchaser of notice in writing from the Acquired Company specifying the nature of such breach and requesting that it be remedied; or

(e)   by Purchaser, upon written notice to the Acquired Company, if there shall have occurred any material adverse change in the business, properties, rights, operations, or financial condition of the Acquired Company and such material adverse change shall not have been remedied within 30 days after receipt by the Acquired Company of notice in writing from Purchaser specifying the nature of such material adverse change and requesting that it be remedied.

11.3   Effect of Termination. In the event of a termination of this Agreement pursuant to Section 11.2(a) hereof, each party shall pay the costs and expenses incurred by it in connection with this Agreement, and no party (or any of its officers, directors, employees, agents, representatives or shareholders) shall be liable to any other party for any costs, expenses, damage or loss of anticipated profits hereunder. In the event of any other termination, the parties shall retain any and all rights attendant to a breach of any covenant, representation or warranty made hereunder. In the event of a termination of this Agreement, each party to this Agreement shall return all information received in due diligence or destroy all such information and shall certify to the other parties that such information has either been returned or destroyed. Each of the parties to this Agreement acknowledge that this Section 11.3 and the nondisclosure agreement between Purchaser and the Acquired Company shall each survive the termination of this Agreement.

XII.   GENERAL PROVISIONS.

12.1   <u>Notices</u>. All notices, requests, demands and other communications hereunder shall be in writing and shall be delivered by hand or mailed by certified mail, return receipt requested, first class postage prepaid, or sent by Federal Express or similarly recognized overnight delivery service with receipt acknowledged addressed as follows:

(a)   If to the Acquired Company:

_____

_____

_____

ATTENTION:_____
Facsimile:_____

with a copy to:

_____

_____

_____

_____

Facsimile:_____

(b)   If to the Shareholders, to their respective addresses as set forth on the signature page to this Agreement.

(c)   If to Purchaser or the Acquisition Sub:

_____

_____

_____

_____

with a copy to:

_____

_____

_____

_____

(d)   If delivered personally, the date on which a notice, request, instruction or document is delivered shall be the date on which such delivery is made and, if delivered by mail or by overnight delivery service, the date on which such notice, request, instruction or document is received shall be the date of delivery. In the event any such notice, request, instruction or document is mailed or shipped by overnight delivery service to a party in accordance with this Section 12.1 and is returned to the sender as nondeliverable, then such notice, request, instruction or document shall be deemed to have been delivered or received on the fifth day following the deposit of such notice, request, instruction or document in the United States mails or the delivery to the overnight delivery service.

(e)   Any party hereto may change its address specified for notices herein by designating a new address by notice in accordance with this Section 12.1.

12.2   Expenses. Except to the extent set forth in Section 11.3 hereof, all expenses incurred by the parties hereto in connection with or related to the authorization, preparation and execution of this Agreement and the closing of the transactions contemplated hereby shall be borne solely and entirely by the party which has incurred the same. In this regard, Purchaser hereby agrees that the Acquired Company may incur up to $30,000 of legal and other costs and expenses, but any additional costs and expenses, whether legal or otherwise relating to this transaction, shall be paid by the Shareholders. The Acquired Company hereby agrees to cooperate with the Purchaser and provide, or cause to be provided, to the

APPENDICES

Purchaser any information regarding costs and expenses reasonably requested by the Purchaser. Subject to the dollar and other limitations set forth in this Section 12.2, the Purchaser shall cause the Acquired Company upon the closing of the Merger to pay on the Closing Date the documented fees and expenses of _____ counsel to the Acquired Company and the Shareholders.

12.3   Risk of Loss. Purchaser shall assume no risk of loss with respect to the Acquired Company prior to the Effective Time.

12.4   Waiver. Any failure on the part of any party hereto to comply with any of its obligations, agreements or conditions hereunder may be waived by any other party to whom such compliance is owed. No waiver of any provision of this Agreement shall be deemed, or shall constitute, a waiver of any other provision, whether or not similar, nor shall any waiver constitute a continuing waiver.

12.5   Binding Effect. This Agreement shall be binding upon and inure to the benefit of the parties hereto and their respective heirs, legal representatives, executors, administrators, successors and assigns.

12.6   Heading, etc. Headings are for convenience only and do not affect interpretation of this Agreement. The following rules of interpretation apply unless the context requires otherwise:

(a)   The singular includes the plural and conversely.

(b)   A gender includes all genders.

(c)   Where a word or phrase is defined, its other grammatical forms have a corresponding meaning.

(d)   A reference to any legislation or to any provision of any legislation includes any modification or re-enactment of it, any legislative provision substituted for it, and all regulations and statutory instruments issued under it.

(e)   A reference to conduct includes, without limitation, any omission, representation, statement or undertaking, whether or not in writing.

(f)   Any statement made by a party on the basis of its knowledge, belief or awareness, is made on the basis that the party has, in order to establish that the statement is true and not misleading in any respect:

   (i)   made all reasonable inquiries of any officers, managers, employees, agents, representatives and other Persons who could reasonably be expected to have information relevant to the matters to which the statement relates; and

   (ii)   where those inquiries would have prompted a reasonable Person to make further inquiries, made those further inquiries, and that, as a result of those inquiries, the party has no reason to doubt that the statement is true and not misleading in any respect.

12.7   <u>Entire Agreement</u>. This Agreement constitutes the entire agreement among the parties hereto and supersedes and cancels any prior agreements, representations, warranties, or communications, whether oral or written, among the parties hereto relating to the transactions contemplated hereby or the subject matter herein. Neither this Agreement nor any provision hereof may be changed, waived, discharged or terminated orally, except in writing signed by the party against whom or which the enforcement of such change, waiver, discharge or termination is sought.

12.8   <u>Governing Law</u>. This Agreement shall be governed by and construed in accordance with the laws of the State of _____, without regard to choice of law principles.

12.9   <u>Counterparts</u>. This Agreement may be executed in two or more counterparts, each of which shall be deemed an original, but all of which together shall constitute one and the same instrument.

12.10   No Agreement Until Executed. This Agreement shall not constitute or be deemed to evidence a contract or agreement among the parties hereto unless and until executed by all parties hereto irrespective of negotiations among the parties or the exchanging of drafts of this Agreement.

12.11   Severability. Any term or provision of this Agreement which is invalid or unenforceable in any jurisdiction shall be ineffective to the extent of such invalidity or unenforceability without invalidating or rendering unenforceable the remaining terms or provisions hereof, and any such invalidity or unenforceability in any such jurisdiction shall not invalidate or render unenforceable such term or provision in any other jurisdiction; provided, however, that any such invalidity or unenforceability does not deny any party hereto any of the basic benefits of the bargain contemplated by this Agreement.

12.12   Time of Essence. Time is of the essence in this Agreement.

IN WITNESS WHEREOF, each party hereto has executed or caused this Agreement to be executed on its behalf, all on the day and year first above written.

"PURCHASER"

By:_____

Name:_____

Title:_____

"ACQUISITION SUB"

By:_____

Name:_____

Title:_____

"ACQUIRED COMPANY"

By:_____

Name:_____

Title:_____

"MANAGEMENT SHAREHOLDERS"

By:_____

Name:_____

Title:_____

By:_____

Name:_____

Title:_____

By:_____

Name:_____

Title:_____

_____

"OTHER SHAREHOLDERS"

By:_____

Name:_____

Title:_____

By:_____

Name:_____

Title:_____

By:_____

Name:_____

Title:_____

GLOSSARY TO THE ACQUISITION AGREEMENT

The following definitions apply unless the context requires otherwise.

Acquired Company shall mean _____, a _____ corporation and for matters prior to _____, shall include its predecessor _____, a _____ limited liability company.

Acquired Company Software is a collective reference to both the Owned Software and Licensed Software.

Acquisition Sub shall mean _____, a _____ corporation.

Agreement shall mean this Acquisition Agreement and the Exhibits attached hereto (including the Disclosure Materials).

Applicable Laws shall mean all applicable (i) statutes, ordinances or other legislative enactments of the United States of America or other country or foreign government, or of any state or political subdivision or agency thereof (including any county, municipal or other local subdivisions), (ii) rules, regulations, orders, permits, directives or other actions or approvals of any Regulatory Authority, and (iii) judgments, awards, orders, decrees, writs and injunctions of any court, Regulatory Authority or arbitrator.

Articles of Merger shall mean the Articles of Merger and the Certificate of Merger referred to in Section 2.1.

Benefit Plans shall have the meaning set forth in Section 3.19(a).

Certificate of Objections shall have the meaning set forth in Section 5.2(c).

Certificates shall have the meaning set forth in Section 2.4.

Closing shall have the meaning set forth in Section 9.1.
Closing Date shall mean the date on which the Closing occurs pursuant to Section 9.1.

Code shall mean the Internal Revenue Code of 1986, as amended.

Common Stock shall mean the common stock, no par value per share, of Acquired Company.

Confidential Information shall mean all confidential proprietary Software of the Acquired Company, any inventions, discoveries, techniques, know-how, trade secrets, ideas, designs, concepts and other similar proprietary rights and information, and all confidential business information concerning the business of the Acquired Company.

Contract shall mean any contract, lease, license, agreement, promissory note, debt instrument, commitment, arrangement, undertaking or understanding, whether written or verbal, conditional or unconditional, and including without limitation each and every amendment, modification or supplement to any of them.

Covenants Not to Compete shall mean the Covenants Not to Compete among Purchaser, the Acquired Company, and each of the Persons identified on Exhibit 7.13, substantially in the forms attached as Exhibit 7.13, each of which may be individually referred to as a "Covenant Not to Compete."

Disclosure Materials shall mean all documents provided to Purchaser.

Dissenting Shares shall have the meaning set forth in Section 2.6.

DOL shall mean the United States Department of Labor.

Effective Time shall mean the time the Merger becomes effective as set forth in Section 2.1.

ERISA shall mean the Employee Retirement Income Security Act of 1974, as amended.

ERISA Affiliate shall mean, with respect to a Person, any other Person which is required to be aggregated with such Person under Code Section 414(b), (c), (m) and/or (o) at any time prior to the Closing Date.

ERISA Plan shall have the meaning set forth in Section 3.19(a).

Financing means the financing arranged for the Purchaser by _____, which closed _____.

Hazardous Substance shall have the meaning set forth in Section 3.21.

Holdback shall have the meaning set forth in the definition of Merger Price and, if payable, shall be paid as set forth on Exhibit A.

Interim Financial Statements shall have the meaning set forth in Section 3.6(a).

IRS shall mean the United States Internal Revenue Service.

Licensed Software shall have the meaning set forth in Section 3.17(c).

Management Shareholders shall mean _____, _____, _____ and _____.

_____, _____ **and** _____ **Financial Statements** shall have the meaning set forth in Section 3.6(a).

Merger shall mean the merger of the Acquisition Sub with Acquired Company as set forth in Section 2.1.

Merger Price shall mean: (a) $_____ (b) plus _____ shares of Purchaser Preferred Stock; less any mutually agreed upon deductions for expenses relating to the transaction as contemplated by this Agreement. Of the Merger Price, _____ shares of Purchaser Preferred Stock (the "Holdback") to be paid to the Management Shareholders as part of the Merger Price shall be placed in escrow and released in accordance with the Escrow Agreement attached hereto as Exhibit 2.5.

Options shall have the meaning set forth in Section 4.5 of the Agreement.

Other Shareholders shall mean all of the shareholders and Option holders of the Acquired Company except for the Management Shareholders.

Owned Software shall have the meaning set forth in Section 3.17(b).

PBGC shall mean the Pension Benefit Guaranty Corporation established under Title IV of ERISA.

Permits shall mean approvals, consents, permissions, licenses, certificates, permits, franchises, rights and other authorizations.

Person shall include, but is not limited to, an individual, a trust, an estate, a partnership, an association, a company, a corporation, a sole proprietorship, a professional corporation or a professional association.

Plan of Merger shall have the meaning set forth in Section 2.1.

Purchaser shall mean _____, a _____ corporation.

Purchaser Preferred Stock shall mean the Series ____ Preferred Stock of Purchaser.

Purchaser Subsidiaries shall mean _____, a _____ corporation and _____, a _____ corporation; and Acquisition Sub.

Real Property shall have the meaning set forth in Section 3.21.

Regulatory Authority shall mean any national, federal, state, county, municipal or local government, department, commission, board, agency, taxing authority or other governmental, administrative or regulatory body (whether of the United States of America or any other country or foreign government).

Series ____ Preferred Stock shall mean the preferred stock designated in the Purchaser's Articles of Incorporation as Series ____ Preferred Stock. **SEC** shall mean the Securities and Exchange Commission.

Shareholders shall mean all of the shareholders and Option holders of the Acquired Company, each of whom may be referred to individually as a "Shareholder."

Shareholders Meeting shall have the meaning set forth in Section 5.2.

Software shall mean any computer software and all materials related thereto which may or may not include, without limitation, databases, documentation, flow charts, logic diagrams, source code, object code, specifications, technical information, and materials of any type whatsoever (tangible or intangible and machine or human readable) which incorporate or reflect the design, specifications, or workings of such programs and any derivatives thereof.

Stock Option Plans shall mean all option plans of the Acquired Company.

Subsidiary shall mean, as to any Person, any corporation or other entity of which securities or other ownership interests having ordinary voting power to elect a majority of the board of directors or other persons performing similar functions are at the time directly or indirectly owned by such Person.

Surviving Corporation shall have the meaning set forth in Section 2.1.

Takeover Proposal shall have the meaning set forth in Section 5.13.

Taxes shall mean all taxes, assessments, charges, duties, fees, levies or other governmental charges (including interest, penalties or additions associated therewith) including federal, state, city, county, foreign or other income, franchise, capital stock, real property, personal property, tangible, withholding, FICA, unemployment compensation, disability, transfer, sales, use, excise, gross receipts and all other taxes of any kind for which the Acquired Company may have any liability imposed by the United States or any state, county, city, or other taxing agency or jurisdiction therein, or by any other country or foreign government or subdivision or agency thereof, whether disputed or not.

Technical Documentation shall mean all technical materials (including source code, schematics, as well as other pertinent commentary reasonably necessary to render such materials understandable and useable by a trained computer programmer) and descriptive materials relating to the acquisition, design, development, use, or maintenance of Software in the business of the Acquired Company.

Third Party Software shall mean all Software which the Acquired Company has developed for a third party where either the right to use or title to such Software is retained or owned by such third party.

LIST OF EXHIBITS

<u>EXHIBITS</u>

A	Holdback
2.1	Plan of Merger
2.2	Allocation of Merger Price
2.5	Escrow Agreement
3.1	List of Jurisdiction of Incorporation and Jurisdictions Where Registered.
3.2	Articles of Incorporation and Bylaws of Acquired Company
3.3	Capitalization.
3.4	List of Equity Investments.
3.6(a)	Financial Statements of Acquired Company
3.6(b)	List of Liabilities and List of Defaults.
3.6(d)	Shareholder Loans and Off-Balance Sheet Undertakings.
3.7	List of Tax Matters.
3.8	List of Tangible Assets and Leases; List of Encumbrances.
3.9	List of Violations of Instruments.
3.10	List of Required Governmental Consents.
3.11	List of Other Required Consents.

3.12	List of Changes.
3.14	List of Permits.
3.15	List of Noncompliance with Laws.
3.16	List of Contracts.
3.17(a)	List of Trademarks, Trade Names, Service Marks, Service Names, Etc.
3.17(b)	List of Owned Software.
3.17(c)	List of Licensed Software.
3.17(d)	List of Third Party Software.
3.17(f)	Third Party Components.
3.17(h)	List of Computer Programming Services Providers.
3.17(k)	Software Marketing Agreements and Nonexclusive Software Marketing Rights.
3.18	List of Employees, Independent Contractors, Salaries, Rates, Employee Loans or Advances, and Labor Matters.
3.19	List of Benefit Plans.
3.20	List of Certain Customer Contracts and List of Terminations of Customer Contracts.
3.22	List of Insurance Matters.
3.23	List of Related Party Relationships.
3A(c)	Fees or Commissions

3A(d)	Liens on Common Stock
4.1(b)(1)	Purchaser Subsidiaries
4.1(b)(2)	Articles of Incorporation and Bylaws of Purchaser and Purchaser Subsidiaries
4.3	List of Violations of Instruments
4.4	List of Purchaser's Required Consents.
4.5	Capitalization
4.6	Financial Statements of Purchaser
5.3	List of Bank Accounts, Safe Deposit Boxes and Powers of Attorney.
6.4	Guarantees.
7.13	Persons to Enter into Covenants Not to Compete; Form of Covenant Not to Compete.
7.14	Persons to Enter into Employment Agreements; Form of Employment Agreement.
7.17	Form of Opinion of Counsel of Acquired Company and the Shareholders.
8.9	Form of Opinion of Counsel of Purchaser.

INDEX TO THE DISCLOSURE MATERIALS

1. Articles of Incorporation and Bylaws of the Acquired Company

2. Stock Record Books, Minute Books, Resolutions and Proceedings of Board of Directors and Shareholders of Acquired Company

3. _____, _____ and _____ Financial Statements and Interim Financial Statements

4. Interim Financial Statements

5. Copies of Contracts Referred to in Sections 3.8, 3.16, 3.17, 3.19, 3.20 and 3.22.

6. Written Waivers, Consents and Approvals Required Under the Agreement

7. Copy of Federal Income Tax Return for the Fiscal Year ended
    _____

8. Employee Benefit Plans and Related Documents Referred to in Section 3.19

Courtesy of Gus M. Dixon, Nelson Mullins Riley & Scarborough LLP

APPENDIX B

LETTER REGARDING PURCHASE OF CERTAIN ASSETS

[Date]

PERSONAL AND CONFIDENTIAL

[Address]

Re: Purchase of Certain Assets of _____ by _____

Dear _____:

This letter sets forth the general terms and conditions pursuant to which _____ ("Buyer"), will acquire substantially all of the assets (the "Assets") of _____, a _____ ("Seller").

1.   Proposed Transaction

The transaction will be structured as an asset purchase by Buyer from Seller. The purchase price for the Assets will be $_____ and will be paid at the closing of the transaction (the "Closing").

2.   Definitive Agreement

The parties hereto mutually agree to proceed in good faith toward negotiation and execution of an asset purchase agreement (the "Agreement"), which shall use an appropriate structure to accomplish the above transaction in the best way for all parties concerned, and shall include covenants, representations, terms, conditions, and agreements that are reasonable and customary in transactions of this nature. Until such time as the Agreement is executed, there is no legal obligation from any party to the other hereunder unless and until such Agreement is executed, and either party may refuse to execute the same. However, if the Agreement has not been executed by _____, _____, this letter shall automatically be terminated and be of no further force or effect, except that the provisions below relating to confidentiality and costs and expenses shall remain in full force and effect in accordance with their terms and shall survive any such termination. The Agreement shall provide that the transaction shall be closed no later than _____, _____.

3.   Conditions

In addition to the conditions specified elsewhere herein, this letter is, and the Agreement will be, subject to various conditions, including the following:

A.   Except as may be required in connection with the transaction contemplated herein, during the period between the date of this letter and the closing of the proposed transaction (or the earlier termination of this letter or the Agreement), Seller will continue to operate its business in the ordinary course of business consistent with past practice.

B.   The appropriate corporate approvals or consents shall have been obtained.

C.   All required regulatory approvals, if any, shall have been obtained.

D.   Any other appropriate approvals or consents shall have been obtained.

E.   Buyer shall have conducted a due diligence investigation of Seller and be satisfied with the results thereof.

F.   [Employment Agreements]

G.   [Non-Competition Agreements]

[Any other terms/conditions/assumptions]

4.   Confidentiality

Both parties agree to keep confidential all information furnished by or through the other concerning each other or this transaction and agree not to disclose any such information or the terms of this proposal or the

Agreement, other than to duly authorized representatives of each other who agree to be bound by this covenant of confidentiality. In the event the Agreement is not executed or a closing is not consummated, each party will, upon request, return promptly to the other all information concerning each other furnished in connection with the transaction.

5. Effect of This Letter

Except with respect to Sections 4, 6, 7, and 8, it is understood that this letter constitutes a statement of the mutual intentions of the parties with respect to the proposed acquisition, does not constitute an obligation binding on either side, does not contain all matters upon which agreement must be reached in order for the transaction to be consummated and creates no rights in favor of any party, except with respect to Sections 4, 6, 7 and 8. A binding commitment with respect to the proposed acquisition will result only from the execution of the Agreement.

6. Disclosure Restriction

The parties agree not to make any public announcement with regard to the transaction contemplated by this letter without the prior written consent of the other.

7. Exclusive Negotiations

Seller agrees that from the date of this letter and until such time as the transaction contemplated by this letter shall have been consummated or the parties shall have agreed to terminate the negotiation of this transaction or the negotiations otherwise terminate in accordance with this letter of intent, it will not, and will not permit any of its agents or representatives to, solicit, initiate or encourage inquiries or proposals, or provide any information or participate in any negotiations leading to any proposal concerning any acquisition or purchase of all or any substantial portion of the assets or shares of the Seller or any merger or consolidation of the Seller with any third party. The Seller agrees to give Buyer prompt notice of any such inquiries or proposals.

8.   Cost and Expenses

Each of the parties shall bear its own costs and expenses related to the transaction contemplated by this letter, including but not limited to, fees and expenses of legal counsel and accountants.

9.   Entire Agreement

This letter of intent constitutes the entire understanding or arrangement between the parties with respect to the subject matter hereof, and supersedes all prior negotiations, understandings or agreements of any nature with respect to the subject matter herein provided, except for any previously executed confidentiality or similar agreements.

If the foregoing proposal meets with your approval, please date, sign and return the enclosed copy of this letter. If this letter has not been signed by you on or before _____, _____, the offer contained herein shall be deemed to have been withdrawn.

Very truly yours,

By: _____

AGREED TO AND ACCEPTED THIS

_____ day of _____, _____.

By: _____

Its: _____

Courtesy of Gus M. Dixon, Nelson Mullins Riley & Scarborough LLP

APPENDIX C

STOCK PURCHASE AGREEMENT

among

_____,

The Sellers Named in the First Paragraph

and

_____

made as of

_____

_Buyer and Sellers have not reached an agreement for the purchase and sale of the Shares. The proposed transaction is subject to Buyer and Sellers entering into a mutually acceptable agreement and upon satisfaction of the conditions contained therein. Unless the agreement is reduced to writing and executed by such parties, regardless of the reason that the agreement is not executed, neither Buyer nor Sellers will be under any obligation to the other except as provided in _____[insert any confidentiality agreement, letter of intent or other]._

This STOCK PURCHASE AGREEMENT (this "Agreement") among
_____, a _____ corporation ("Buyer"), _____, _____ and _____
("Sellers") and _____ ("Sellers' Representative") is made as of _____.

Recitals

WHEREAS, Sellers own all of the outstanding capital stock [and other
equity interests] of _____, a _____ corporation (the "Company").

WHEREAS, Sellers desire to sell, and Buyer desires to buy [or cause one or
more of its affiliates to buy], all of the outstanding capital stock [and other
equity interests] of the Company [and to otherwise retire all other
outstanding equity interests of the Company] on the terms and subject to
the conditions set forth in this Agreement.

[WHEREAS, all other outstanding equity interests of the Company will be
canceled or redeemed immediately prior to any sale and purchase of the
outstanding capital stock.]

[WHEREAS, Sellers will be responsible for the cancellation or payment of
[describe indebtedness] of the Company prior to Closing.]

[WHEREAS, certain employees of the Company are concurrently entering
into employment agreements with the Company [Buyer] effective upon the
Closing.]

[WHEREAS, Buyer and Sellers have agreed to enter into certain
agreements to be performed after the sale and purchase of the outstanding
capital stock.]

NOW, THEREFORE, in consideration of the mutual representations,
warranties and agreements contained in this Agreement, and for other good
and valuable consideration, the receipt and sufficiency of which are hereby
acknowledged, the parties agree as follows:

I. Definitions

"Active Employee" means any employee employed on the Closing Date by the Company who is a bargaining unit employee currently covered by a collective bargaining agreement or employed exclusively by the Company, including employees on temporary leave of absence, family medical leave, military leave, temporary disability or sick leave, but excluding employees on long-term disability leave.

"Admitted Claim" has the meaning set forth in Section 10.1(d).

"Agreement" has the meaning set forth in the first paragraph of this Agreement.

"Affiliate" has the meaning set forth in Rule 12b-2 under the Exchange Act.

["Allocation Arbiter" has the meaning set forth in Section 11.8(d).]

"Ancillary Agreements" means _____, _____ and _____ in the form of Exhibits _____ through _____, respectively.

"Annual Financial Statements" has the meaning set forth in Section 4.6.

"Basket Amount" has the meaning set forth in Section 10.1(b).

"Buyer" has the meaning set forth in the first paragraph of this Agreement.

"Buyer Claim" has the meaning set forth in Section 10.1(d).

"Buyer Indemnified Parties" has the meaning set forth in Section 10.3(a).

"Buyer Losses" has the meaning set forth in Section 10.1(a).

["Buyer Material Adverse Effect" means _____.]

"Buyer Notice" has the meaning set forth in Section 6.8(c).

["Buyer Plans" has the meaning set forth in Section 7.9(b).]

["Buyer SEC Reports" has the meaning set forth in Section 5.10(a).]

["Buyer Shareholders' Meeting" has the meaning set forth in Section 7.3(a).]

"Capital Lease" means a lease on which the Company is a lessee that is a capital lease as determined in accordance with GAAP.

"Code" means the Internal Revenue Code of 1986, as amended.

"Company" has the meaning set forth in the recitals of this Agreement.

"Confidential Information" has the meaning set forth in Section 6.13(a).

"Confidentiality Agreement" has the meaning set forth in Section 6.3.

"Consent" means any authorization, consent, approval, filing, waiver, exemption or other action by or notice to any Person.

["Continuing Employee" has the meaning set forth in Section 7.9(a).]

"Contract" means a contract, agreement, lease, commitment or binding understanding, whether oral or written, that is in effect as of the date of this Agreement or any time after the date of this Agreement.

"Department" has the meaning set forth in Section 4.21(c).

"Disclosure Schedule" means the schedule delivered by Sellers to Buyer on or prior to the date of this Agreement.

"Employment Loss" has the meaning set forth in Section 10.1(a).

"Encumbrance" means any charge, claim, community property interest, easement, covenant, condition, equitable interest, lien, option, pledge, security interest, right of first refusal or restriction of any kind, including any restriction on use, voting, transfer, receipt of income or exercise of any other attribute of ownership.

"Environmental Costs" has the meaning set forth in Section 4.19(a)(i).

"Environmental Law" has the meaning set forth in Section 4.19(a)(ii).

"ERISA" means the Employee Retirement Income Security Act of 1974, as amended, and the rules and regulations thereunder.

"ERISA Affiliate" means any entity or trade or business that is treated as a member of the Company's controlled group within the meaning of Section 414(b), (c), (m) or (o) of the Code.

"Exchange Act" means the Securities Exchange Act of 1934, as amended, and the rules and regulations thereunder.

["Existing Policy" has the meaning set forth in Section 7.7(b).]

"GAAP" means United States generally accepted accounting principles, as in effect from time to time.

"Governmental Authorization" means any approval, consent, license, permit, waiver, registration or other authorization issued, granted, given, made available or otherwise required by any Governmental Entity or pursuant to Law.

"Governmental Entity" means any federal, state, local, foreign, international or multinational entity or authority exercising executive, legislative, judicial, regulatory, administrative or taxing functions of or pertaining to government.

"Governmental Order" means any judgment, injunction, writ, order, ruling, award or decree by any Governmental Entity or arbitrator.

"Hazardous Materials" has the meaning set forth in Section 4.19(a)(iii).

"HSR Act" means the Hart-Scott-Rodino Antitrust Improvements Act of 1976, as amended, and the rules and regulations thereunder.

["Indemnified Persons" has the meaning set forth in Section 7.7(a).]

"Insider" means (i) a shareholder, officer, director or employee of the Company or any Subsidiary, (ii) any Member of the Immediate Family of any shareholder, officer, director or employee of the Company or any Subsidiary or (iii) any entity in which any of the Persons described in clause (i) or (ii) owns any beneficial interest (other than less than one percent of the outstanding shares of capital stock of any corporation whose stock is listed on a national securities exchange or publicly traded on The NASDAQ National Market).

"Insured Exception" has the meaning set forth in Section 6.8(c).

"Intellectual Property Rights" means (i) rights in patents, patent applications and patentable subject matter, whether or not the subject of an application, (ii) rights in trademarks, service marks, trade names, trade dress and other designators of origin, registered or unregistered, (iii) rights in copyrightable subject matter or protectable designs, registered or unregistered, (iv) trade secrets, (v) rights in internet domain names, uniform resource locators and e-mail addresses, (vi) rights in semiconductor topographies (mask works), registered or unregistered, (vii) know-how and (viii) all other intellectual and industrial property rights of every kind and nature and however designated, whether arising by operation of Law, Contract, license or otherwise.

"IRS" means the United States Internal Revenue Service.

"Knowledge of any Seller" means the knowledge of any Seller or any director or officer of the Company or any knowledge that would have been acquired by any such Person upon appropriate [reasonable] inquiry and investigation.

"Last Fiscal Year End" has the meaning set forth in Section 4.6.

"Latest Balance Sheet" has the meaning set forth in Section 4.6.

"Latest Balance Sheet Date" has the meaning set forth in Section 4.6.

"Latest Financial Statements" has the meaning set forth in Section 4.6.

"Law" means any constitution, law, ordinance, principle of common law, regulation, statute or treaty of any Governmental Entity.

"Leased Real Property" has the meaning set forth in Section 4.10(c).

"Liability" means any liability or obligation whether accrued, absolute, contingent, unliquidated or otherwise, whether due or to become due, whether known or unknown, and regardless of when asserted.

"Licensed-In Intellectual Property Rights" means Third-Party Intellectual Property Rights used or held for use by the Company or any Subsidiary with the permission of the owner.

"List" has the meaning set forth in Section 4.19(a)(iv).

"Litigation" means any claim, action, arbitration, mediation, audit, hearing, investigation, proceeding, litigation or suit (whether civil, criminal, administrative, investigative or informal) commenced, brought, conducted or heard by or before, or otherwise involving, any Governmental Entity or arbitrator or mediator.

"Loss" means any Litigation, Governmental Order, complaint, claim, demand, damage, deficiency, penalty, fine, cost, amount paid in settlement, liability, obligation, Tax, Encumbrance, loss, expense or fee, including court costs and attorneys' fees and expenses.

"Material Adverse Effect" means any change, effect, event or condition, individually or in the aggregate, that has had, or, with the passage of time, could have, a material adverse effect on the business, assets, properties, condition (financial or otherwise), results of operations, prospects or customer, supplier or employee relationships of the Company and its Subsidiaries, taken as a whole.

"Material Contracts" has the meaning set forth in Section 4.15(a).

"Member of the Immediate Family" of a Person means a spouse, parent, child, sibling, mother- or father-in-law, son- or daughter-in-law, and brother- or sister-in-law of such Person.

"Off-the-Shelf Software" means Software that is widely commercially available for a price of less than $_____ for any number of users or less than $_____ per seat, PC, CPU or user.

"Ordinary Course of Business" means the ordinary course of business of the Company and the Subsidiaries consistent with past custom and practice (including with respect to quantity and frequency) [as it has been conducted since the Last Fiscal Year End].

"Organizational Documents" means (i) the articles or certificate of incorporation and the bylaws of a corporation, (ii) the partnership agreement and any statement of partnership of a general partnership, (iii) the limited partnership agreement and the certificate of limited partnership of a limited partnership, (iv) the limited liability company agreement and articles or certificate of formation of a limited liability company, (v) any charter or similar document adopted or filed in connection with the creation, formation or organization of a Person and (vi) any amendment to any of the foregoing.

"Owned Intellectual Property Rights" means Intellectual Property Rights owned by the Company or any Subsidiary.

"Owned Real Property" has the meaning set forth in Section 4.10(b).

["Permitted Encumbrances" means (i) Encumbrances for Taxes and other governmental charges and assessments (except assessments for public improvements levied, pending or deferred against the Owned Real Property) that are not yet due and payable or which are being contested in good faith by appropriate proceedings (provided required payments have been made in connection with any such contest), (ii) Encumbrances of carriers, warehousemen, mechanics' and materialmen and other like Encumbrances arising in the Ordinary Course of Business (provided lien statements have not been filed as of the Closing Date), (iii) easements, rights of way and restrictions, zoning ordinances and other similar Encumbrances affecting the Real Property and which do not unreasonably restrict the use thereof or Buyer's proposed use thereof in the Ordinary Course of Business, (iv) statutory Encumbrances in favor of lessors arising in connection with any property leased to the Company or any Subsidiary, (v) Encumbrances reflected in the Latest Financial Statements or arising under Material Contracts and (vi) Encumbrances that will be removed prior to or in connection with the Closing.]

"Person" means any individual, corporation (including any non-profit corporation), general or limited partnership, limited liability company, joint venture, estate, trust, association, organization, labor union, Governmental Entity or other entity.

"Plan" means every plan, fund, contract, program and arrangement (whether written or not) for the benefit of present or former employees, including those intended to provide (i) medical, surgical, health care, hospitalization, dental, vision, workers' compensation, life insurance, death, disability, legal services, severance, sickness or accident benefits (whether or not defined in Section 3(1) of ERISA), (ii) pension, profit sharing, stock bonus, retirement, supplemental retirement or deferred compensation benefits (whether or not tax qualified and whether or not defined in Section 3(2) of ERISA) or (iii) salary continuation, unemployment, supplemental unemployment, severance, termination pay, change-in-control, vacation or holiday benefits (whether or not defined in Section 3(3) of ERISA), (w) that is maintained or contributed to by the Company or any Subsidiary, (x) that the Company or any Subsidiary has committed to implement, establish, adopt or contribute to in the future, (y) for which the Company or any Subsidiary is or may be financially liable as a result of the direct sponsor's affiliation with the Company, its Subsidiaries or the Company's shareholders (whether or not such affiliation exists at the date of this Agreement and notwithstanding that the Plan is not maintained by the Company or any Subsidiary for the benefit of its employees or former employees) or (z) for or with respect to which the Company or any Subsidiary is or may become liable under any common law successor doctrine, express successor liability provisions of Law, provisions of a collective bargaining agreement, labor or employment Law or agreement with a predecessor employer. Plan does not include any arrangement that has been terminated and completely wound up prior to the date of this Agreement and for which neither the Company nor any Subsidiary has any present or potential liability.

"Process Agent" has the meaning set forth in Section 12.13.

"Property" has the meaning set forth in Section 4.19(a)(v).

"Real Property" has the meaning set forth in Section 4.10(c).

"Registered Intellectual Property Rights" means Intellectual Property Rights that are the subject of a pending application or an issued patent, trademark, copyright, design right or other similar registration formalizing exclusive rights.

"Regulatory Action" has the meaning set forth in Section 4.19(a)(vi).

"Release" has the meaning set forth in Section 4.19(a)(vii).

"Remedies Exception," when used with respect to any Person, means except to the extent enforceability may be limited by applicable bankruptcy, insolvency, reorganization, moratorium or other laws affecting the enforcement of creditors' rights generally and by general equitable principles.

"Required Consents" has the meaning set forth in Section 6.6.

"Restricted Business" has the meaning set forth in Section 6.15(a).

"Return" means any return, declaration, report, estimate, information return and statement pertaining to any Taxes.

"SEC" means the United States Securities and Exchange Commission.

["Section 338 Forms" has the meaning set forth in Section 11.8(d).]

["Securities Act" means the Securities Act of 1933, as amended, and the rules and regulations thereunder.]

"Sellers" has the meaning set forth in the first paragraph of this Agreement.

"Seller Losses" has the meaning set forth in Section 10.2(a).

"Sellers' Basket Amount" has the meaning set forth in Section 10.2(b).

"Sellers' Representative" has the meaning set forth in the first paragraph of this Agreement.

"Software" means computer programs or data in computerized form, whether in object code, source code or other form.

"Subsidiary" means any Person in which any ownership interest is owned, directly or indirectly, by another Person. When used without reference to a particular entity, Subsidiary means a Subsidiary of the Company.

"Tax Affiliate" means each of the Company and the Subsidiaries and any other Person that is or was a member of an affiliated, combined or unitary group of which the Company or any Subsidiary is or was a member.

"Taxes" means all taxes, charges, fees, levies or other assessments, including all net income, gross income, gross receipts, sales, use, ad valorem, transfer, franchise, profits, license, withholding, payroll, employment, social security, unemployment, excise, estimated, severance, stamp, occupation, property or other taxes, customs duties, fees, assessments or charges of any kind whatsoever, including all interest and penalties thereon, and additions to tax or additional amounts imposed by any Governmental Entity upon the Company or any Tax Affiliate.

"Third-Party Action" has the meaning set forth in Section 10.3(a).

"Third-Party Environmental Claim" has the meaning set forth in Section 4.19(a)(viii).

"Third-Party Intellectual Property Rights" means Intellectual Property Rights in which a Person other than the Company or a Subsidiary has any ownership interest.

"Title Objection" has the meaning set forth in Section 6.8(c).

"Treasury Regulations" means the rules and regulations under the Code.

"WARN Act" means the Worker Adjustment and Retraining Notification Act of 1988, as amended.

"Work Permits" has the meaning set forth in Section 4.21(c).

The following terms not defined above are defined in the sections of Article II indicated below:

Definition	Defined
Adjustment Escrow Account	
Adjustment Escrow Amount	
[Buyer Common Stock]	
[Buyer Common Stock Price]	
[Buyer Notes]	
[Buyer Option]	
[Buyer Warrant]	
Closing	
Closing Date	
Closing Date Balance Sheet	
Closing Date Net Book Value	
Company Common Stock	
[Company Option]	
[Company Options]	
[Company Preferred Stock]	
[Company Warrant]	
[Company Warrants]	
[Earnout Amount]	
Escrow Agent	
Escrow Agreement	
Escrow Amount	
Escrow Fund	
[Escrow Shares]	
Estimated Closing Date Balance Sheet	
Estimated Closing Date Net Book Value	
Estimated Purchase Price	
Excess Net Book Value	
[Exchange Ratio]	
Indemnification Escrow Account	
Indemnification Escrow Amount	
Net Book Value Shortfall	
Product Formulas	
Purchase Price	
Shares	
Target Net Book Value	

II. Purchase of Shares and Closing

2.1   Purchase and Sale. At the Closing and on the terms and subject to the conditions set forth in this Agreement, Sellers agree to sell to Buyer, and Buyer agrees to buy from Sellers, all of the issued and outstanding shares (the "Shares") of common stock, par value $_____ per share, of the Company ("Company Common Stock") [and the preferred stock, par value $_____ per share, of the Company ("Company Preferred Stock")]. Each Seller waives any co-sale rights, rights of first refusal or similar rights that such Seller may have relating to Buyer's purchase of the Shares, whether conferred by the Company's Organizational Documents, by Contract or otherwise.

2.2   Purchase Price. The aggregate consideration for the Shares (the "Purchase Price") is [(x)] $_____, plus the amount, if any, by which the Closing Date Net Book Value (as defined in Section 2.9(a)) exceeds $_____ (the "Target Net Book Value") or minus the amount, if any, by which the Target Net Book Value exceeds the Closing Date Net Book Value [plus (y) the Earnout Amount (as defined in Section 2.5)]. [In the case Buyer Notes are to be issued by Buyer, replace the foregoing with—The aggregate consideration for the Shares (the "Purchase Price") is [(x)] $_____ plus the amount, if any, by which the Closing Date Net Book Value (as defined in Section 2.9(a)) exceeds $_____ (the "Target Net Book Value") or minus the amount, if any, by which the Target Net Book Value exceeds the Closing Date Net Book Value [plus (y) the Earnout Amount (as defined in Section 2.5)], comprised of promissory notes from Buyer (the "Buyer Notes") in the form of Exhibit A in the aggregate principal amount of $_____ with the balance payable in cash.] [Alternate when Buyer Common Stock will be used and there will be no adjustment based on book value (Section 2.3 to be deleted)—The aggregate consideration for the Shares (the "Purchase Price") is [x] that number of shares of the common stock, par value $_____ per share, of Buyer ("Buyer Common Stock") rounded to the nearest whole share having an aggregate value, based on the Buyer Common Stock Price, equal to $_____ [plus (y) the Earnout Amount (as defined in Section 2.5)]. The Purchase Price is subject to equitable adjustment in the event that, prior to the Closing Date, there is any share split, subdivision, combination, share dividend, extraordinary dividend or reorganization involving Buyer Common Stock. "Buyer Common Stock Price" means the average closing price of Buyer Common Stock on the [insert exchange on or market in which Buyer Common Stock is traded] for the ten trading days ending on the third trading day immediately preceding the [date of this Agreement][the Closing Date].] Of the Purchase Price, $_____ will be allocated as payment for the covenants under this Agreement set forth in Section 6.15.

2.3   <u>Estimated Purchase Price</u>. At least two days prior to the Closing Date, Sellers will deliver to Buyer an estimated consolidated balance sheet (the "Estimated Closing Date Balance Sheet") for the Company and the Subsidiaries as of the close of business on the Closing Date (determined on a pro forma basis giving effect to the transactions contemplated by this Agreement and in accordance with GAAP applied on a basis consistent with the preparation of the Latest Financial Statements). The Estimated Closing Date Balance Sheet will include a determination of the Estimated Closing Date Net Book Value as of the close of business on the Closing Date. "Estimated Closing Date Net Book Value" means the excess of assets over liabilities shown on the Estimated Closing Date Balance Sheet. "Estimated Purchase Price" means an amount equal to $_____ [insert same amount inserted for the Purchase Price in Section 2.2] plus the amount, if any, by which the Estimated Closing Date Net Book Value exceeds the Target Net Book Value or minus the amount, if any, by which the Target Net Book Value exceeds the Estimated Closing Date Net Book Value.

2.4   <u>Escrow</u>. A portion of the Estimated Purchase Price (the "Escrow Amount") equal to the sum of (x) $_____ (the "Adjustment Escrow Amount") and (y) $_____ (the "Indemnification Escrow Amount") will be withheld from the Estimated Purchase Price and deposited by Buyer with _____, as escrow agent (the "Escrow Agent"), to be held in escrow (the "Escrow Fund") in separate accounts (the "Adjustment Escrow Account" and the "Indemnification Escrow Account," respectively) pursuant to the terms of the Escrow Agreement, in the form attached as Exhibit B (the "Escrow Agreement"), among Buyer, Sellers' Representative, on behalf of Sellers, and the Escrow Agent. The Adjustment Escrow Amount will be held by the Escrow Agent for payment pursuant to Section 2.9. The Indemnification Escrow Amount will be held by the Escrow Agent for payment pursuant to Article X. [Alternate when Buyer Common Stock will fund the escrow and there will be no adjustment based on book value—A portion of the shares of Buyer Common Stock constituting the Purchase

Price equal to that number of shares of Buyer Common Stock rounded to the nearest whole share having an aggregate value, based on the Buyer Common Stock Price, of $_____ (the "Escrow Shares") will be withheld from the Purchase Price and deposited by Buyer with _____, as escrow agent (the "Escrow Agent"), to be held in escrow (the "Escrow Fund") pursuant to the terms of the Escrow Agreement, in the form attached as Exhibit B (the "Escrow Agreement"), among Buyer, Sellers' Representative, on behalf of Sellers, and the Escrow Agent. The Escrow Shares will be held by the Escrow Agent for payment pursuant to Article X and the Escrow Agreement.]

2.5   [Earnout. Insert as appropriate, including definition of "Earnout Amount."]

(a)   [Illustrative disclaimer—The Seller acknowledge that upon the completion of the transactions contemplated by this Agreement, the assets of the Company will have a new basis for financial reporting purposes, that Buyer will utilize the Company in its business in any way that it deems appropriate and that it will operate its business utilizing the Company in its sole discretion, that all determinations of revenues and gross profits will be made by Buyer using its own accounting principles, practices and conventions, which may change from time to time, that the allocation of revenues and costs to any particular set of products is not exact and subject to many judgments, that in operating the Company to produce revenues and gross profits there may be overhead allocations by Buyer, that Buyer may establish transfer prices between its business units in its reasonable discretion, that Buyer has no obligation to operate the Company in order to achieve an Earnout Amount or to maximize the amount of the Earnout Amount, that Buyer is under no obligation to manufacture the Company's product line, that there can be no assurance that any Earnout Amount will be received, and that Buyer owes no fiduciary duty or express or implied duty to the Sellers, such as an implied duty of good faith and fair dealing, but instead the parties intend the express provisions of this Agreement to govern their contractual relationship.]

2.6   [Company Options. As of the Closing Date, each outstanding option to purchase Company Common Stock issued pursuant to the [Insert title of Company Plan] (each, a "Company Option") will be assumed by Buyer and converted into an option (each, a "Buyer Option") to purchase, on substantially the same terms and conditions as such Company Option, the number of shares of Buyer Common Stock equal to the number of shares of Company Common Stock that were issuable upon exercise of such Company Option immediately prior to the Closing Date multiplied by the Exchange Ratio (rounded to the nearest whole number of shares of Buyer Common Stock), at a per share exercise price equal to the exercise price per share of Company Common Stock at which such Company Option was exercisable immediately prior to the Closing Date divided by the Exchange Ratio (rounded to the nearest whole cent). For purposes of this Agreement, "Exchange Ratio" means _____. In the case of any Company Option to which Section 421 of the Code applies by reason of Section 422 of the Code, the option exercise price, the number of shares of Buyer Common Stock purchasable pursuant to such option and the terms and conditions of exercise of such option will be determined in order to comply with Section 424(a) of the Code. Buyer will reserve for issuance a sufficient number of shares of Buyer Common Stock for delivery upon exercise of the Buyer Options.]

2.7   [Company Warrants. As of the Closing Date, each outstanding warrant to purchase Company Common Stock (each, a "Company Warrant") will be assumed by Buyer and converted into a warrant (each, a "Buyer Warrant") to purchase, on substantially the same terms and conditions as such Company Warrant, the number of shares of Buyer Common Stock equal to the number of shares of Company Common Stock that were issuable upon exercise of such Company Warrant immediately prior to the Closing Date multiplied by the Exchange Ratio (rounded to the nearest whole number of shares of Buyer Common Stock), at a per share exercise price equal to the exercise price per share of Company Common Stock at which such Company Warrant was exercisable immediately prior to the Closing Date divided by the Exchange Ratio (rounded to the nearest whole cent). [For purposes of this Agreement, "Exchange Ratio" means _____.] Buyer will reserve for issuance a sufficient number of shares of Buyer Common Stock for delivery upon exercise of the Buyer Warrants.]

2.8   The Closing.

(a)   The closing of the transactions contemplated by this Agreement (the "Closing") will take place at the offices of _____ at _____, _____, _____, at 9:00 a.m. on [the later of] _____ [or the second business day following termination or expiration of the waiting period under the HSR Act] [or as soon thereafter as reasonably possible following satisfaction of the conditions set forth in Article VII] (the "Closing Date") or at such other place and on such other date as may be mutually agreed by Buyer and Sellers' Representative, in which case Closing Date means the date so agreed. The failure of the Closing will not ipso facto result in termination of this Agreement and will not relieve any party of any obligation under this Agreement. The Closing will be effective as of the close of business on the Closing Date.

(b)   [Immediately prior to the Closing, Sellers will cause all outstanding options to purchase capital stock of the Company ("Company Options") to be canceled and all outstanding warrants to purchase capital stock of the Company ("Company Warrants") to be redeemed.]

(c)   Subject to the conditions set forth in this Agreement, on the Closing Date:

(i)   Sellers will deliver to Buyer:

(A)   certificates representing all of the Shares, free and clear of all Encumbrances, duly endorsed or accompanied by duly executed stock powers with signatures guaranteed by a national bank or trust company or by a member firm of the New York Stock Exchange with requisite stock transfer tax stamps, if any, attached;

(B)   a certificate of Sellers dated the Closing Date stating that the conditions set forth in subsections (a) through (aa) of Section 8.1 have been satisfied;

(C)   an updated Disclosure Schedule, prepared as though this Agreement has been dated as of the Closing Date, a good faith draft of which will have been submitted to Buyer no later than five business days prior to the Closing Date;

(D)   the text of the resolutions adopted by the board of directors (or similar body) of any Seller that is not a natural Person authorizing the execution, delivery and performance of this Agreement, certified by an appropriate officer of such Seller;

(E)   [agreements duly executed by the holders canceling all outstanding Company Options] or— with respect to the substitution of options for Buyer Common Stock for Company Options;]

(F)   [certificates representing all outstanding Company Warrants, free and clear of all Encumbrances, duly endorsed or accompanied by duly executed stock powers with signatures guaranteed by a national bank or trust company or by a member firm of the New York Stock Exchange with requisite stock transfer tax stamps, if any, attached] [evidence of redemption of all outstanding Company Warrants;]

(G)   the minute books, stock or equity records, corporate seal and other materials related to the corporate administration of the Company or any Subsidiary;

(H)   resignations in writing (effective as of the Closing Date) from such of the officers and directors of each of the Company and the Subsidiaries as Buyer may have requested prior to the Closing Date;

(I)   [each Ancillary Agreement to which any Seller is a party, duly executed by each Seller;]

(J)   [each Ancillary Agreement to which the Company is a party, duly executed by the Company;]

(K)   the Escrow Agreement, duly executed by Sellers' Representative;

(L)   [all Required Consents, duly executed by all appropriate parties;]

(M)   any other instruments of transfer reasonably requested by Buyer, duly executed by the Sellers;

(N)   [a Noncompetition Agreement in the form of Exhibit C, duly executed by each Seller;]

(O)   [evidence of payment or cancellation of indebtedness of the Company that is to be canceled prior to Closing;]

(P)   [executed copies of all agreements, instruments, certificates and other documents necessary or appropriate, in the opinion of Buyer's counsel, to release any and all Encumbrances against the assets of the Company or any Subsidiary [, other than Permitted Encumbrances];]

(Q)   [a FIRPTA certificate in the form of Exhibit D, duly executed by the Sellers for purposes of satisfying Buyer's obligations under Treasury Regulations Section 1.1445 2;]

(R)   [title insurance, policies and endorsements, and owner's affidavits;]

(S)   [estoppel certificates;]

(T)   [a copy in written or electronic form of all formulas, recipes, know how and product and process specifications for the products currently manufactured, developed or being developed by or for the Company ("Product Formulas");]

(U)   [a Release of the Company and its Subsidiaries in the form of Exhibit E as of the Closing Date;]

(V)   a tax clearance certificate or other evidence reasonably satisfactory to Buyer from the taxing authority of the State of _____, evidencing payment in full by the Company and Subsidiaries of all sales and use taxes imposed by the State of _____ with respect to the business of the Company and Subsidiaries for all periods prior to the Closing Date; and

(W)   such other certificates, documents and instruments that Buyer reasonably requests for the purpose of (1) evidencing the accuracy of Sellers' representations and warranties, (2) evidencing the performance and compliance by Sellers with the agreements contained in this Agreement, (3) evidencing the satisfaction of any condition referred to in Section 8.1 or (4) otherwise facilitating the consummation of the transactions contemplated by this Agreement.

All actions to be taken by Sellers in connection with consummation of the transactions contemplated by this Agreement and all certificates, opinions, instruments and other documents required to effect the transactions contemplated by this Agreement will be in form and substance satisfactory to Buyer and Buyer's counsel.

(ii)   Buyer will deliver to Sellers:

(A)   the cash portion of the Estimated Purchase Price less the Escrow Amount by wire transfer of immediately available funds to the account designated by Sellers' Representative to Buyer no later than three business days prior to the Closing (allocated among Sellers in accordance with Exhibit G); [In the case Buyer Notes are to be issued by Buyer, replace the foregoing with— the cash portion of the Estimated Purchase Price, less the Escrow Amount by wire transfer of immediately available funds to the accounts designated by Sellers' Representative to Buyer no later than three business days prior to the Closing and delivery of the Buyer Notes in the aggregate principal amount of $_____ for the balance of the Estimated Purchase Price] (allocated among Sellers in accordance with Exhibit G);] [Alternate when Buyer Common Stock is to be used—the Purchase Price, less the Escrow Shares to be deposited in the Escrow Fund (allocated among Sellers in accordance with Exhibit G). No fraction of a share of Buyer Common Stock will be issued at Closing, but in lieu thereof, each holder of Shares that would otherwise be entitled to a fraction of a share of Buyer Common Stock (after aggregating all fractional shares of Buyer Common Stock to be received by such holder) will be entitled to receive from Buyer an amount of cash (rounded to the nearest whole cent) equal to the product of (x) such fraction multiplied by (y) the Buyer Common Stock Price;]

(B)   a certificate of an appropriate officer of Buyer dated the Closing Date stating that the conditions set forth in subsections (a) through (g) of Section 8.2 have been satisfied;

(C)   the text of the resolutions adopted by the board of directors of Buyer authorizing the execution, delivery and performance of this Agreement [including the issuance of the Buyer Notes [Buyer Common Stock]], certified by an appropriate officer of Buyer;

(D)   [for itself and its affiliates, including the Company and its Subsidiaries, a release of Sellers in the form of Exhibit F as of the Closing Date;]

(E)   [each Ancillary Agreement to which Buyer is a party, duly executed by Buyer;] and

(F)   the Escrow Agreement, duly executed by Buyer and the Escrow Agent.

(iii)   Buyer will deposit the Escrow Amount by wire transfer of immediately available funds into the Escrow Fund to be held by the Escrow Agent in accordance with the terms of the Escrow Agreement. [Alternate when Buyer Common Stock will fund the escrow—Buyer will deposit the Escrow Shares into the Escrow Fund to be held by the Escrow Agent in accordance with the terms of the Escrow Agreement.]

(d)   All items delivered by the parties at the Closing will be deemed to have been delivered simultaneously, and no items will be deemed delivered or waived until all have been delivered.

(e)   Notwithstanding any investigation made by or on behalf of any of the parties to this Agreement or the results of any such investigation and notwithstanding the fact of, or the participation of such party in, the Closing, the representations, warranties and agreements in this Agreement will survive the Closing.

(f)   [The Confidentiality Agreement will terminate effective as of the Closing Date.]

2.9   <u>Post-Closing Adjustment to Estimated Purchase Price.</u>

(a)   Buyer will promptly prepare and deliver within 60 days after the Closing Date, to Sellers' Representative a consolidated balance sheet (the "Closing Date Balance Sheet") for the Company and the Subsidiaries as of the close of business on the Closing Date (determined on a pro forma basis giving effect to [as though] the transactions contemplated by this Agreement [had not occurred] and in accordance with GAAP applied on a basis consistent with the preparation of the Latest Financial Statements). The Closing Date Balance Sheet will include a determination of the Closing Date Net Book Value of the Company and the Subsidiaries as of the close of business on the Closing Date. "Closing Date Net Book Value" means the excess of assets over liabilities shown on the Closing Date Balance Sheet. Buyer will make the workpapers and back-up materials used in preparing the Closing Date Balance Sheet available to Sellers' Representative and Sellers' Representative's accountants and other representatives at reasonable times and upon reasonable notice during (i) the review by Sellers' Representative of the Closing Date Balance Sheet and (ii) the resolution by Buyer and Sellers' Representative of any objections to the Closing Date Balance Sheet.

(b)   Sellers' Representative may object to the Closing Date Balance Sheet on the basis that it was not prepared in accordance with GAAP applied on a basis consistent with the preparation of the Latest Financial Statements or that the calculation of Closing Date Net Book Value contains mathematical errors. If Sellers' Representative has any objections to the Closing Date Balance Sheet or the Closing Date Net Book Value, Sellers' Representative will deliver a detailed statement describing such objections to Buyer within 10 days after receiving the Closing Date Balance Sheet. Buyer and Sellers' Representative will attempt in good faith to resolve any such objections. If Buyer and Sellers' Representative do not reach a resolution of all objections within 30 days after Buyer has received the statement of objections, Buyer and Sellers'

Representative will select a mutually acceptable accounting firm to resolve any remaining objections. If Buyer and Sellers' Representative are unable to agree on the choice of an accounting firm, they will select a nationally recognized accounting firm by lot (after excluding the regular outside accounting firms of Buyer and the Company). The accounting firm will [resolve any such objections and] determine, in accordance with GAAP applied on a basis consistent with the preparation of the Latest Financial Statements, the amounts to be included in the Closing Date Balance Sheet and the Closing Date Net Book Value. The parties will provide the accounting firm, within 10 days of its selection, with a definitive statement of the position of each party with respect to each unresolved objection and will advise the accounting firm that the parties accept the accounting firm as the appropriate Person to interpret this Agreement for all purposes relevant to the resolution of the unresolved objections. Buyer will provide the accounting firm access to the books and records of each of the Company and the Subsidiaries. The accounting firm will have 30 days to carry out a review of the unresolved objections and prepare a written statement of its determination regarding each unresolved objection. The determination of any accounting firm so selected will be set forth in writing and will be conclusive and binding upon the parties. Buyer will revise the Closing Date Balance Sheet and the determination of the Closing Date Net Book Value as appropriate to reflect the resolution of any objections to the Closing Date Balance Sheet pursuant to this Section 2.9(b).

(c)   If Buyer and Sellers' Representative submit any unresolved objections to an accounting firm for resolution as provided in Section 2.9(b), the party whose determination of Closing Date Net Book Value (calculated based on such party's position regarding the Closing Date Balance Sheet) is furthest from the Closing Date Net Book Value determined by the accounting firm (based on its resolution of the parties' objections submitted for determination) will bear its own costs and expenses, the fees and expenses of the accounting firm and the out-of-pocket costs and expenses (including legal fees and costs) of the other party. [Alternative—If Buyer and Sellers' Representative submit any unresolved objections to an accounting firm for resolution as provided in Section 2.9(b), Buyer and Sellers will each bear their respective costs and expenses and will share equally in the fees and expenses of the accounting firm.]

(d) Within 10 business days after the date on which the Closing Date Net Book Value is finally determined pursuant to this Section 2.9:

(i) If the Closing Date Net Book Value exceeds the Estimated Net Book Value (the amount of such excess, the "Excess Net Book Value"), (A) Buyer will pay to Sellers an aggregate amount equal to the Excess Net Book Value, and (B) the Adjustment Escrow Amount will be released by the Escrow Agent from the Adjustment Escrow Account to Sellers' Representative for the account of Sellers in accordance with the Escrow Agreement. The Excess Net Book Value and the Adjustment Escrow Amount will be distributed among Sellers in accordance with Exhibit G.

(ii) If the Closing Date Net Book Value is less than the Estimated Net Book Value, an amount equal to such deficiency (the amount of such deficiency, the "Net Book Value Shortfall") will be withdrawn by the Escrow Agent from the Adjustment Escrow Account, and, to the extent that the amount of the Net Book Value Shortfall exceeds the Adjustment Escrow Amount, from the Indemnification Escrow Amount and paid to Buyer. If the Net Book Value Shortfall is less than the Adjustment Escrow Amount, the amount remaining in the Adjustment Escrow Account (after release of the Net Book Value Shortfall to Buyer) will be released by the Escrow Agent to Sellers' Representative for the account of Sellers in accordance with the Escrow Agreement. The amount released from the Adjustment Escrow Account will be distributed among Sellers in accordance with Exhibit G.

(e)   All payments to be made to Buyer or Sellers pursuant to Section 2.9(b) will be made by wire transfer of immediately available funds to the accounts designated by Buyer or Sellers, as applicable, no later than three business days after the date on which the Closing Date Net Book Value is finally determined, and all such payments will include simple interest thereon at the annual rate of _____% from the Closing Date to the date of payment.

(f)   Any payment made pursuant to this Section 2.9 will not preclude any remedy provided in this Agreement or otherwise for any breach of representation, warranty or agreement, and the remedy provided in this Agreement for any breach of representation, warranty or agreement or otherwise will not preclude the adjustment provided in this Section 2.9.

(g)   Judgment upon the award rendered by the accounting firm may be entered in any court of competent jurisdiction.

2.10   <u>Sellers' Representative</u>.

(a)   Sellers appoint _____ (or any Person appointed as a successor Sellers' Representative pursuant to Section 2.10(b)) as their representative and agent under this Agreement and the Escrow Agreement.

(b)   Until all obligations under this Agreement have been discharged (including all indemnification obligations under Article X), Sellers who, immediately prior to the Closing, are entitled to receive more than 50% of the Purchase Price, may, from time to time upon written notice to Sellers' Representative and Buyer, remove Sellers' Representative or appoint a new Sellers' Representative upon the death, incapacity, resignation or removal of Sellers' Representative. If, after the death, incapacity, resignation or removal of Sellers' Representative, a successor Sellers' Representative has not been appointed by Sellers within 15 business days after a request by Buyer, Buyer will have the right to appoint a Sellers' Representative to fill any vacancy so created by written notice of such appointment to Sellers.

(c)   Sellers authorize Sellers' Representative to take any action and to make and deliver any certificate, notice, consent or instrument required or permitted to be made or delivered under this Agreement or under the documents referred to in this Agreement, to waive any requirements of this Agreement or to enter into one or more amendments or supplements to this Agreement that Sellers' Representative determines in Sellers' Representative's sole and absolute discretion to be necessary, appropriate or advisable, which authority includes the execution and delivery of the Escrow Agreement on behalf of Sellers and any amendments or supplements thereto and the performance of all obligations thereunder, including authority to collect and pay funds and dispute, settle, compromise and make all claims. The authority of Sellers' Representative includes the right to hire or retain, at the sole expense of Sellers, such counsel, investment bankers, accountants, representatives and other professional advisors as Sellers' Representative determines in Sellers' Representative sole and absolute discretion to be necessary, appropriate or advisable in order to perform this Agreement and the Escrow Agreement. Any party will have the right to rely upon any action taken by Sellers' Representative, and to act in accordance with such action without independent investigation.

(d)   Buyer will have no liability to any Seller or otherwise arising out of the acts or omissions of Sellers' Representative or any disputes among Sellers or with Sellers' Representative. Buyer may rely entirely on its dealings with, and notices to and from, Sellers' Representative to satisfy any obligations it might have under this Agreement, the Escrow Agreement or any other agreement referred to in this Agreement or otherwise to Sellers.

(e)   Sellers' Representative accepts the appointment made by this Section 2.10 and agrees to abide by the provisions of this Section 2.10.

2.11   [Buyer Notes. Each Buyer Note will be imprinted with a legend substantially in the following form:

The payment of principal and interest on this Note is subject to certain recoupment provisions set forth in a Stock Purchase Agreement dated as of _____ (the "Agreement") between the issuer of this Note, the person to whom this Note originally was issued and certain other persons. This Note was originally issued on _____ and has not been registered under the Securities Act of 1933, as amended. The transfer of this Note is subject to certain restrictions set forth in the Agreement. The issuer of this Note will furnish a copy of these provisions to the holder of this Note without charge upon written request.

Each holder desiring to transfer a Buyer Note first must furnish Buyer with (i) a written opinion reasonably satisfactory to Buyer in form and substance from counsel reasonably satisfactory to Buyer by reason of experience to the effect that the holder may transfer such Buyer Note as desired without registration under the Securities Act and (ii) a written undertaking executed by the desired transferee reasonably satisfactory to Buyer in form and substance agreeing to be bound by the recoupment provisions and the restrictions on transfer contained herein.]

2.12   [Buyer Common Stock. Each certificate representing Buyer Common Stock will be imprinted with a legend substantially in the following form:

The shares represented by this certificate have not been registered under the Securities Act of 1933, as amended, and may not be transferred without registration or an exemption therefor.

Each holder desiring to transfer Buyer Common Stock first must furnish Buyer with (i) a written opinion reasonably satisfactory to Buyer in form and substance from counsel reasonably satisfactory to Buyer by reason of experience to the effect that the holder may transfer such Buyer Common Stock as desired without registration under the Securities Act and (ii) a written undertaking executed by the desired transferee reasonably satisfactory to Buyer in form and substance agreeing to be bound by the restrictions on transfer contained herein.]

2.13   Further Assurances. On and after the Closing Date, Sellers will take all appropriate action and execute any documents, instruments or conveyances of any kind that may be reasonably requested by Buyer to

349

carry out any of the provisions of this Agreement. Effective upon the Closing, Sellers appoint Buyer, in its name, place and stead, to take all actions and to do such things as may be necessary or appropriate to carry out any of the provisions of this Agreement.

III. Representations and Warranties of Sellers

Sellers, jointly and severally, represent and warrant to Buyer that, except as described in the Disclosure Schedule, as of the date of this Agreement and as of the Closing Date (as though made then and as though the Closing Date were substituted for the date of this Agreement) as to each Seller:

3.1   Title to Shares. Such Seller owns, of record and beneficially, the number of Shares listed opposite such Seller's name on Schedule 3.1, free and clear of any Encumbrance. At Closing, Buyer will obtain good and valid title to such Shares, of record and beneficially, free and clear of any Encumbrance [other than an Encumbrance created by Buyer].

3.2   Incorporation; Power and Authority. If such Seller is not a natural Person, it is duly organized, validly existing and in good standing under the laws of the jurisdiction of its organization. Such Seller has all necessary power and authority to execute, deliver and perform this Agreement [and the Ancillary Agreements to which it will become a party].

3.3   Valid and Binding Agreement. If such Seller is not a natural Person, the execution, delivery and performance of this Agreement [and the Ancillary Agreements to which it will become a party] by such Seller has been duly and validly authorized by all necessary corporate or equivalent action. This Agreement has been duly executed and delivered by such Seller and constitutes the valid and binding obligation of such Seller, enforceable against it in accordance with its terms, subject to the Remedies Exception. [Each Ancillary Agreement to which such Seller will become a party, when executed and delivered by or on behalf of such Seller, will constitute the valid and binding obligation of such Seller, enforceable against such Seller in accordance with its terms, subject to the Remedies Exception.]

3.4   [No Breach; Consents. The execution, delivery and performance of this Agreement [and the Ancillary Agreements to which the Company will become a party] by such Seller will not (a) contravene any provision of the

Organizational Documents, if any, of such Seller; (b) violate or conflict with any Law, Governmental Order or Governmental Authorization; (c) conflict with, result in any breach of any of the provisions of, constitute a default (or any event that would, with the passage of time or the giving of notice or both, constitute a default) under, result in a violation of, increase the burdens under, result in the termination, amendment, suspension, modification, abandonment or acceleration of payment (or any right to terminate) or require a Consent under any Contract or Governmental Authorization that is either binding upon or enforceable against such Seller or any Governmental Authorization that is held by the Company; (d) result in the creation of any Encumbrance upon the Shares held by such Seller; or (e) require any Governmental Authorization; (f) give any Governmental Entity or other Person the right to challenge any of the contemplated transactions or to exercise any remedy or obtain any relief under any Law, Governmental Order or Governmental Authorization; (g) cause Buyer to become subject to, or to become liable for the payment of, any Tax; or (h) result in any shareholder of the Company having the right to exercise dissenters' appraisal rights.]

3.5   Brokerage. No Person will be entitled to receive any brokerage commission, finder's fee, fee for financial advisory services or similar compensation in connection with the transactions contemplated by this Agreement based on any Contract made by or on behalf of such Seller for which Buyer or the Company is or could become liable or obligated.

3.6   [Investment. Each Seller (a) understands that the Buyer Notes [shares of Buyer Common Stock] have not been, and will not be, registered under the Securities Act or under any state securities laws, are being offered and sold in reliance upon federal and state exemptions for transactions not involving any public offering and will contain a legend restricting transfer; (b) is acquiring the Buyer Notes [shares of Buyer Common Stock] solely for such Seller's own account for investment purposes, and not with a view to the distribution thereof; (c) is a sophisticated investor with knowledge and experience in business and financial matters; (d) has received certain information concerning Buyer and has had the opportunity to obtain additional information as desired in order to evaluate the merits and the risks inherent in holding the Buyer Notes [shares of Buyer Common Stock]; (e) is able to bear the economic risk and lack of liquidity inherent in holding the Buyer Notes [shares of Buyer Common Stock]; and (f) is an "Accredited Investor" as that term is defined under Rule 501 of the Securities Act.]

IV. Representations and Warranties Regarding the Company

Sellers, jointly and severally, represent and warrant to Buyer that, except as described in the Disclosure Schedule, as of the date of this Agreement and as of the Closing Date (as though made then and as though the Closing Date were substituted for the date of this Agreement):

4.1   Incorporation; Power and Authority.

(a)   Each of the Company and the Subsidiaries is a legal entity duly organized, validly existing and in good standing under the laws of the jurisdiction of its organization, and has all necessary power and authority necessary to own, lease and operate its assets and to carry on its business as conducted and proposed to be conducted. Each of the Company and the Subsidiaries is duly qualified to do business as a foreign corporation in each jurisdiction in which the nature of its business or its ownership of property requires it to be so qualified. Schedule 4.1 lists, for each of the Company and the Subsidiaries, the jurisdiction of its organization, its form as a legal entity and each jurisdiction in which it is so qualified. [If the Company is a party to the Agreement—The Company has all necessary power and authority to execute, deliver and perform this Agreement [and the Ancillary Agreements to which it will become a party].]

(b)   Each of the Company and the Subsidiaries is in full compliance with all provisions of its Organizational Documents.

4.2   [Valid and Binding Agreement. Use only if the Company is a party to the Agreement—The execution, delivery and performance of this Agreement [and the Ancillary Agreements to which it will become a party] by the Company have been duly and validly authorized by all necessary corporate action. This Agreement has been duly executed and delivered by the Company and constitutes the valid and binding obligation of the Company, enforceable in accordance with its terms, subject to the

Remedies Exception.] [Each Ancillary Agreement to which the Company will become a party, when executed and delivered by the Company, will constitute the valid and binding obligation of the Company, enforceable against the Company in accordance with its terms, subject to the Remedies Exception.]]

4.3   No Breach; Consents. The execution, delivery and performance of this Agreement [and the Ancillary Agreements to which the Company will become a party] will not (a) contravene any provision of the Organizational Documents of the Company or any Subsidiary; (b) violate or conflict with any Law, Governmental Order or Governmental Authorization; (c) conflict with, result in any breach of any of the provisions of, constitute a default (or any event that would, with the passage of time or the giving of notice or both, constitute a default) under, result in a violation of, increase the burdens under, result in the termination, amendment, suspension, modification, abandonment or acceleration of payment (or any right to terminate) or require a Consent under any Contract that is either binding upon or enforceable against the Company or any Subsidiary or any Governmental Authorization that is held by the Company or any Subsidiary; (d) result in the creation of any Encumbrance upon the Company or any Subsidiary or any of the assets of the Company or any Subsidiary; (e) require any Governmental Authorization; (f) give any Governmental Entity or other Person the right to challenge any of the contemplated transactions or to exercise any remedy or obtain any relief under any Law, Governmental Order or Governmental Authorization; (g) cause Buyer to become subject to, or to become liable for the payment of, any Tax; or (h) result in any shareholder of the Company having the right to exercise dissenters' appraisal rights.

4.4   Capitalization.

(a)   The authorized capital stock of the Company consists of _____ shares of Company Common Stock [and _____ shares of Company Preferred Stock], of which _____ shares of Company Common Stock [and _____ shares of Company Preferred Stock] are issued and outstanding and _____ shares of Company Common Stock [and _____ shares of Company Preferred Stock] are held in treasury. Schedule 4.4(a) lists the names and addresses of each record holder of the issued and outstanding Company

Common Stock [and Company Preferred Stock], the number of shares held by each such holder and the share certificate numbers, repurchase or redemption rights for such shares in favor of the Company, the vesting schedule and forfeiture provisions for any of such shares that are "restricted stock," and the extent to which vesting will or may be accelerated by the transactions contemplated by this Agreement and any limitations on the ability of the holder of such capital stock to vote or dispose of such shares. All issued and outstanding shares of Company Common Stock [and Company Preferred Stock] are duly authorized, validly issued, fully paid and nonassessable, free of preemptive rights or any other Third-Party rights and in certificated form, and have been offered, sold and issued by the Company in compliance with applicable securities and corporate Laws, Contracts applicable to the Company and the Company's Organizational Documents and in compliance with any preemptive rights, rights of first refusal or similar rights. The rights and privileges of the Company Common Stock [and the Company Preferred Stock] are set forth in the Company's Organizational Documents or otherwise provided by Law.

(b)   [[As of the date of this Agreement], Company Options with respect to _____ shares of Company Common Stock are outstanding. Schedule 4.4(b) lists the name and addresses of each holder of an outstanding Company Option and whether such holder is an employee of the Company and, with respect to each Company Option held, the date of grant of such Company Option, the number of shares of Company Common Stock subject to such Company Option, the exercise price of such Company Option, the vesting schedule (and any provisions for acceleration or deferral of vesting) for such Company Option, the extent vested as of the date of this Agreement, the extent to which exercisability of such Company Option will or may be accelerated by the transactions contemplated by this Agreement and whether such Company Option is an "incentive stock option." [As of the date of this Agreement], Company Warrants with respect to _____ shares of Company Common Stock are outstanding. Schedule 4.4(b) lists the name and addresses of each holder of an outstanding Company

Warrant, the number of shares of Company Common Stock subject to such Company Warrant, the exercise price of such Company Warrant, the expiration date of such Company Warrant and any effect of the transactions contemplated by this Agreement on such Company Warrant. All outstanding Company Options and Company Warrants have been offered, sold and delivered in compliance with applicable securities and corporate Laws, Contracts applicable to the Company and the Company's Organizational Documents. All shares of Company Common Stock issuable upon exercise of the Company Options and Company Warrants have been offered in compliance with applicable securities and corporate Laws, Contracts applicable to the Company and the Company's Organizational Documents and, upon issuance in accordance with their terms, will be duly authorized, validly issued, fully paid and nonassessable.]

(c)   [Except for the Company Options and Company Warrants listed on Schedule 4.4(b) and Company Preferred Stock,] there is no option, warrant, call, subscription, convertible security, right (including preemptive right) or Contract of any character to which the Company is a party or by which it is bound obligating the Company to issue, exchange, transfer, sell, repurchase, redeem or otherwise acquire any capital stock of the Company or obligating the Company to grant, extend, accelerate the vesting of or enter into any such option, warrant, call, subscription, convertible security, right or Contract. There are no outstanding or authorized stock appreciation, phantom stock or similar rights with respect to the Company. Except as contemplated by this Agreement, there are no registration rights agreements, no voting trust, proxy or other Contract and no restrictions on transfer with respect to any capital stock of the Company.

[Alternative Section 4.4 in the event that the Company has only one class of stock and no options or warrants—The authorized capital stock of the Company consists solely of _____ shares of Company Common Stock, of which _____ shares are issued and outstanding, none of which are held in treasury. Schedule 4.4 lists the names and addresses of each record holder of the issued and outstanding Company Common Stock, the number of shares held by each such holder and the share certificate numbers, repurchase or redemption rights for such shares in favor of the Company, the vesting schedule and forfeiture provisions for any of such shares that are "restricted stock," and the extent to which vesting will or may be accelerated by the transactions contemplated by this Agreement and any limitations on the ability of the holder of such capital stock to vote or dispose of such shares. All issued and outstanding shares of Company Common Stock are duly authorized, validly issued, fully paid and nonassessable, free of preemptive rights or any other third party rights and in certificated form, and have been offered, sold and issued by the Company in compliance with applicable securities and corporate Laws, Contracts applicable to the Company and the Company's Organizational Documents and in compliance with any preemptive rights, rights of first refusal or similar rights. The rights and privileges of the Company Common Stock are set forth in the Company's Organizational Documents or otherwise provided by Law. There is no option, warrant, call, subscription, convertible security, right (including preemptive right) or Contracts of any character to which the Company is a party or by which it is bound obligating the Company to issue, exchange, transfer, sell, repurchase, redeem or otherwise acquire any shares of capital stock of the Company or obligating the Company to grant, extend, accelerate the vesting of or enter into any such option, warrant, call, subscription, convertible security, right or Contract. There are no outstanding or authorized stock appreciation, phantom stock or similar rights with respect to the Company. Except as contemplated by this Agreement, there are no registration rights agreements, no voting trust, proxy or other Contract and no restrictions on transfer with respect to any capital stock of the Company.]

4.5   Subsidiaries. Except as listed on Schedule 4.5, neither the Company nor any Subsidiary owns any Subsidiary. For each of the Company's Subsidiaries, Schedule 4.5 shows the equity interests owned by the Company or any Subsidiary, the names of the Persons owning such equity interests and the percentage of the outstanding equity interests so owned.

All issued and outstanding equity interests of each Subsidiary of the Company are duly authorized, validly issued, fully paid and nonassessable, free of preemptive rights or any other third party right, free and clear of all Encumbrances, and in certificated form and have been offered, sold and issued by such Subsidiary in compliance with applicable securities and corporate Laws, Contracts applicable to such Subsidiary and such Subsidiary's Organizational Documents and in compliance with any preemptive rights, rights of first refusal or similar rights. There is no option, warrant, call, subscription, convertible security, right (including preemptive rights) or Contract of any character to which the Company or any Subsidiary is a party or by which it is bound obligating any Subsidiary of the Company or the Company to issue, exchange, transfer, sell, repurchase, redeem or otherwise acquire any equity interest of such Subsidiary or obligating the Company or such Subsidiary to grant, extend, accelerate the vesting of or enter into any such option, warrant, call, subscription, convertible security, right or Contract.

4.6   Financial Statements. The unaudited consolidated balance sheet as of _____ ("Latest Balance Sheet Date") of the Company and its consolidated Subsidiaries (the "Latest Balance Sheet") and the unaudited consolidated statements of income, changes in shareholders' equity and cash flows of the Company and its consolidated Subsidiaries for the _____- month period then ended (such statements and the Latest Balance Sheet, the "Latest Financial Statements") and the audited consolidated balance sheet, as of _____ (the "Last Fiscal Year End") and for the each of the prior fiscal year ends, of the Company and its consolidated Subsidiaries and the audited consolidated statements of income, changes in shareholders' equity and cash flows, including the notes, of the Company and its consolidated Subsidiaries for each of the _____ years ended on the Last Fiscal Year End (collectively, the "Annual Financial Statements") are based upon the books and records of the Company and the Subsidiaries, have been prepared in accordance with GAAP consistently applied during the periods indicated and present fairly the financial position, results of operations and cash flows of the Company and its consolidated Subsidiaries on a consolidated basis at the respective dates and for the respective periods indicated, except that the Latest Financial Statements may not contain all notes and are subject to year-end adjustments, none of which are material.

4.7   Absence of Undisclosed Liabilities. Except as reflected or expressly reserved against in the Latest Balance Sheet, neither the Company nor any Subsidiary has any Liability, and there is no basis for any present or future Litigation, charge, complaint, claim or demand against any of them giving rise to any Liability, except (a) a Liability that has arisen after the date of the Latest Balance Sheet in the Ordinary Course of Business and that is not a Liability for breach of Contract, breach of warranty, tort, infringement, Litigation or violation of Governmental Order, Governmental Authorization or Law or (b) obligations under any Contract listed on a Schedule to this Agreement or under a Contract not required to be listed on such a Schedule.

4.8   Books and Records. The books of account of the Company and the Subsidiaries are complete and correct and have been maintained in accordance with sound business practices and the requirements of Section 13(b)(2) of the Exchange Act (regardless of whether the Company or any Subsidiary is subject to that section). Each transaction is properly and accurately recorded on the books and records of the Company or a Subsidiary, and each document upon which entries in the Company's or a Subsidiary's books and records are based is complete and accurate in all respects. The Company maintains a system of internal accounting controls adequate to insure that it maintains no off-the-books accounts and that its assets are used only in accordance with its management directives. The minute books and stock or equity records of each of the Company and the Subsidiaries, all of which have been made available to Buyer, are complete and correct. The minute books of each of the Company and the Subsidiaries contain accurate records of all meetings held and actions taken by the holders of stock or equity interests, the boards of directors and committees of the boards of directors or other governing body of each of the Company and the Subsidiaries, and no meeting of any such holders, boards of directors or other governing body or committees has been held for which minutes are not contained in such minute books. At the Closing, all such books and records will be in the possession of the Company.

4.9   Absence of Certain Developments. Since the Last Fiscal Year End, there has not been any Material Adverse Effect and:

   (a)   neither the Company nor any Subsidiary has sold, leased, licensed, transferred or assigned any of its assets, tangible or intangible, other than for a fair consideration in the Ordinary Course of Business;

(b)   neither the Company nor any Subsidiary has entered into any Contract (or series of related Contracts) either involving more than $_____ or outside the Ordinary Course of Business;

(c)   no party (including the Company or any Subsidiary) has accelerated, suspended, terminated, modified or canceled any Contract to which the Company or any Subsidiary is a party or by which any of them is bound that would have been a Material Contract at the time of any such action;

(d)   no Encumbrance has been imposed on any assets of the Company or any Subsidiary [except Permitted Encumbrances];

(e)   neither the Company nor any Subsidiary has made any capital expenditure (or series of related capital expenditures) either involving more than $_____ or outside the Ordinary Course of Business;

(f)   neither the Company nor any Subsidiary has made any capital investment in, any loan to, or any acquisition of the securities or assets of, any other Person (or series of related capital investments, loans and acquisitions) either involving more than $_____ or outside the Ordinary Course of Business or acquired (by merger, exchange, consolidation, acquisition of stock or assets or otherwise) any Person;

(g)   neither the Company nor any Subsidiary has issued any note, bond or other debt security or created, incurred, assumed or guaranteed any indebtedness for borrowed money (including advances on existing credit facilities) or Capital Lease either involving more than $_____ individually or $_____ in the aggregate;

(h)   neither the Company nor any Subsidiary has delayed, postponed or accelerated the payment of accounts payable or other

Liability or the receipt of any accounts receivable, in each case outside the Ordinary Course of Business;

(i)   neither the Company nor any Subsidiary has canceled, compromised, waived or released any right or claim (or series of related rights or claims) either involving more than $_____ or outside the Ordinary Course of Business;

(j)   except incidental to the sale of products or services, neither the Company nor any Subsidiary has granted any license or sublicense of any rights under or with respect to any Intellectual Property Rights;

(k)   there has been no change made or authorized in the Organizational Documents of the Company or any Subsidiary;

(l)   neither the Company nor any Subsidiary has issued, sold or otherwise disposed of any of its capital stock or equity interests, or granted any options, warrants or other rights to purchase or obtain (including upon conversion, exchange or exercise) any of its capital stock [(other than the issuance of shares of Company Common Stock upon exercise of outstanding Company Options or Company Warrants)];

(m)   neither the Company nor any Subsidiary has declared, set aside or paid any dividend or made any distribution with respect to its capital stock or equity interests (whether in cash or in kind) or redeemed, purchased or otherwise acquired any of its capital stock or split, combined or reclassified any outstanding shares of its capital stock;

(n)   neither the Company nor any Subsidiary has experienced any damage, destruction or loss (whether or not covered by insurance) to its property;

(o)   neither the Company nor any Subsidiary has entered into any employment or collective bargaining agreement, written or oral, or modified the terms of any such existing agreement;

(p)   neither the Company nor any Subsidiary has granted any increase in the base compensation or made any other change in employment terms of any of its directors, officers or employees outside the Ordinary Course of Business;

(q)   neither the Company nor any Subsidiary has adopted, amended, modified or terminated any Plan (or taken any such action with respect to any Plan);

(r)   neither the Company nor any Subsidiary has discharged or satisfied any Encumbrance or paid any liability, in each case with a value in excess of $_____ individually or $_____ in the aggregate, other than current liabilities paid in the Ordinary Course of Business;

(s)   neither the Company nor any Subsidiary has disclosed to any Person other than Buyer and authorized representatives of Buyer any proprietary confidential information, other than pursuant to a confidentiality agreement prohibiting the use or further disclosure of such information, which agreement is listed on Schedule 4.9 and is in full force and effect;

(t)   neither the Company nor any Subsidiary has made any change in accounting principles or practices from those utilized in the preparation of the Annual Financial Statements; and

(u)   neither the Company nor any Subsidiary has committed to take any of the actions described in this Section 4.9.

4.10   Property.

(a)   [Neither the Company nor any Subsidiary owns any real property.] The real properties [owned by the Company or any Subsidiary or] demised by the leases listed on Schedule 4.10 constitute all of the real property [owned,] leased (whether or not occupied and including any leases assigned or leased premises sublet for which the Company remains liable), used or occupied by the Company or any Subsidiary.

(b)   [The Company or a Subsidiary owns good and marketable title to each parcel of real property identified on Schedule 4.10 as being owned by the Company or a Subsidiary (the "Owned Real Property"), free and clear of all Encumbrances, except for [Permitted Encumbrances] Encumbrances listed on Schedule 4.10.]

(c)   The leases of real property listed on Schedule 4.10 as being leased by the Company or any Subsidiary (the "Leased Real Property" [and together with the Owned Real Property,] [or] the "Real Property") and are in full force and effect, and the Company or a Subsidiary holds a valid and existing leasehold interest under each of the leases for the term listed on Schedule 4.10. The Leased Real Property is subject to no ground lease, master lease, mortgage, deed of trust or other Encumbrance or interests that would entitle the holder thereof to interfere with or disturb use or enjoyment of the Leased Real Property or the exercise by the lessee of its rights under such lease so long as the lessee is not in default under such lease.

(d)   Each parcel of Real Property has access sufficient for the conduct of the business as conducted or as proposed to be conducted by the Company or any Subsidiary on such parcel of Real Property to public roads and to all utilities, including electricity, sanitary and storm sewer, potable water, natural gas, telephone, fiberoptic, cable television, and other utilities used in the operation of the business at that location. The zoning for each parcel of Real Property permits the existing improvements and the continuation of the business being conducted thereon as a conforming use. Neither the Company nor any Subsidiary is in violation of any applicable zoning ordinance or other Law relating to the Real Property, and neither the Company nor any Subsidiary has received any notice of any such violation or the existence of any condemnation or other proceeding with respect to any of the Real Property. The buildings and other improvements are located within the boundary lines of each parcel of Real Property and do not encroach over applicable setback lines.

(e)   There are no improvements made or contemplated to be made by any Governmental Entity, the costs of which are to be assessed as assessments, special assessments, special Taxes or charges against any of the Real Property, and there are no present assessments, special assessments, special Taxes or charges.

(f)   Each of the Company and the Subsidiaries has good and marketable title to, or a valid leasehold interest in, the buildings, machinery, equipment and other tangible assets and properties used by it, located on its premises or shown in the Latest Balance Sheet or acquired after the date thereof, free and clear of all Encumbrances, except for [Permitted Encumbrances] Encumbrances listed on Schedule 4.10 and properties and assets disposed of in the Ordinary Course of Business since the date of the Latest Balance Sheet.

(g)   The buildings, improvements, building systems, machinery, equipment and other tangible assets and properties used in the conduct of the business of each of the Company and the Subsidiaries are in good condition and repair, ordinary wear and tear excepted, and are usable in the Ordinary Course of Business. Each such asset is suitable for the purposes for which it is used and is proposed to be used, is free from defects (patent and latent), and has been maintained in accordance with normal industry practices. Each of the Company and the Subsidiaries owns, or leases under valid leases, all buildings, machinery, equipment and other tangible assets and properties necessary for the conduct of its respective business as conducted and as proposed to be conducted.

(h)   The fixed asset listing attached as Schedule 4.10(h) includes all buildings, machinery, equipment and other tangible assets and properties of the Company and its Subsidiaries as of __.

(i)   The Company owns or leases all of the assets, tangible and intangible, of any nature whatsoever, necessary to operate the Company's business in the manner operated by the Company.

4.11   Accounts Receivable. All notes and accounts receivable of each of the Company and the Subsidiaries are reflected properly on their books of account, are valid, have arisen from bona fide transactions in the Ordinary

Course of Business, are subject to no setoff or counterclaim, and are current and collectible. Such notes and accounts receivable will be collected in accordance with their terms (none of which is beyond 60 days) at their recorded amounts, subject only to the reserve for bad debts on the face of the Latest Balance Sheet as adjusted in the Company's books of account for the passage of time through the Closing Date in the Ordinary Course of Business.

4.12   Inventory. The inventory of raw materials, work in process, supplies and finished goods of each of the Company and the Subsidiaries consists of items of a quality and quantity usable and, with respect to finished goods only, salable at normal profit levels, in each case, in the Ordinary Course of Business. The inventory of finished goods is not slow-moving (as determined in accordance with past practices), obsolete, damaged or defective, subject only to any reserve for inventory on the face of the Latest Balance Sheet as adjusted in the Company's books of account for the passage of time through the Closing Date in the Ordinary Course of Business and is merchantable and fit for its particular use. Each of the Company and the Subsidiaries has on hand or has ordered and expects timely delivery of such quantities of raw materials and supplies and has on hand such quantities of work in process and finished goods as are reasonably required (and are not in excess) to fill current orders on hand in a timely manner and to maintain the manufacture and shipment of products at its normal level of operations.

4.13   Tax Matters.

(a)   Each of the Company and any Tax Affiliate has (i) timely filed (or has had timely filed on its behalf) each Return required to be filed or sent by it in respect of any Taxes or required to be filed or sent by it by any Governmental Entity, each of which was correctly completed and accurately reflected any liability for Taxes of the Company and any Tax Affiliate covered by such Return, (ii) timely and properly paid (or had paid on its behalf) all Taxes due and payable for all Tax periods or portions thereof whether or not shown on such Returns, (iii) established in the Company's books of account, in accordance with GAAP and consistent with past practices, adequate reserves for the payment of any Taxes not then due and payable and (iv) complied with all applicable Laws relating to the withholding of Taxes and the payment thereof.

(b)   Each of the Company and any Tax Affiliate has made (or caused to be made on its behalf) all estimated tax payments required to have been made to avoid any underpayment penalties.

(c)   There are no Encumbrances for Taxes upon any assets of the Company or any Tax Affiliate, except Encumbrances for Taxes not yet due.

(d)   Neither the Company nor any Tax Affiliate has requested any extension of time within which to file any Return, which Return has not since been filed.

(e)   No deficiency for any Taxes has been proposed, asserted or assessed against the Company or any Tax Affiliate that has not been resolved and paid in full. No waiver, extension or comparable consent given by the Company or any Tax Affiliate regarding the application of the statute of limitations with respect to any Taxes or any Return is outstanding, nor is any request for any such waiver or consent pending. There has been no Tax audit or other administrative proceeding or court proceeding with regard to any Taxes or any Return for any Tax year subsequent to the year ended _____, nor is any such Tax audit or other proceeding pending, nor has there been any notice to the Company or any Tax Affiliate by any Governmental Entity regarding any such Tax, audit or other proceeding, or, to the Knowledge of any Seller, is any such Tax audit or other proceeding threatened with regard to any Taxes or Returns. There are no outstanding subpoenas or requests for information with respect to any of the Returns of the Company or any Tax Affiliate. Neither the Company nor any Tax Affiliate has entered into a closing agreement pursuant to Section 7121 of the Code or any similar provision under any other Law.

(f)   To the Knowledge of any Seller, no additional Taxes will be assessed against the Company or any Tax Affiliate for any Tax period or portion thereof ending on or prior to the Closing Date, and there are no unresolved questions, claims or disputes concerning the liability for Taxes of the Company or any Tax Affiliate that would exceed the estimated reserves established on its books of account.

(g)   Schedule 4.13 lists all federal, state, local and foreign income Returns filed with respect to the Company or any Tax Affiliate for taxable periods ended on or after _____, indicates those Returns that have been audited and indicates those Returns that currently are the subject of audit.

(h)   Neither the Company nor any Tax Affiliate has any liability for Taxes in a jurisdiction where it does not file a Return, nor has the Company or any Tax Affiliate received notice from a taxing authority in such a jurisdiction that it is or may be subject to taxation by that jurisdiction.

(i)   Neither the Company nor any Tax Affiliate is a party to any Contract that would result, separately or in the aggregate, in the payment of any "excess parachute payments" within the meaning of Section 280G of the Code, and the consummation of the transactions contemplated by this Agreement will not be a factor causing payments to be made by the Company or any Tax Affiliate that are not deductible (in whole or in part) as a result of the application of Section 280G of the Code.

(j)   No property of the Company or any Tax Affiliate is (i) property that the Company or any Tax Affiliate is or will be required to treat as being owned by another Person under the provisions of Section 168(f)(8) of the Code (as in effect prior to amendment by the Tax Reform Act of 1986), (ii)"tax-exempt use property" within the meaning of Section 168(h) of the Code or (iii) "tax-exempt bond financed property" within the meaning of Section 168(g)(5) of the Code.

(k)   Neither the Company nor any Tax Affiliate is required to include in income any adjustment under either Section 481(a) or Section 482 of the Code (or an analogous provision of Law) by reason of a voluntary change in accounting method or otherwise, and the IRS has not proposed any such adjustment or change in accounting method.

(l)   All transactions that could give rise to an underpayment of tax (within the meaning of Section 6662 of the Code) were reported by the Company and each Tax Affiliate in a manner for which there is substantial authority or were adequately disclosed on the Returns as required in accordance with Section 6662(d)(2)(B) of the Code.

(m)   Neither the Company nor any Tax Affiliate is a party to any Tax allocation or sharing agreement.

(n)   Neither the Company nor any Subsidiary (i) has been a member of an affiliated group filing a consolidated Return (other than a group the common parent of which was the Company) or (ii) has any liability for the Taxes of any Person (other than the Company or any Subsidiary) under Treasury Regulations Section 1.1502-6 (or any similar provision of Law), as a transferee or successor, by Contract, or otherwise.

(o)   Neither the Company nor any Subsidiary constitutes either a "distributing corporation" or a "controlled corporation" (within the meaning of Section 355(a)(1)(A) of the Code) in a distribution of shares qualifying for tax-free treatment under Section 355 of the Code (i) that took place during the two-year period ending on the date of this Agreement or (ii) that could otherwise constitute part of a "plan" or "series of related transactions" (within the meaning of Section 355(e) of the Code) in conjunction with the purchase of the Shares.

(p)   None of the indebtedness of the Company or any Tax Affiliate constitutes (i) "corporate acquisition indebtedness" (as defined in Section 279(b) of the Code) with respect to which any interest deductions may be disallowed under Section 279 of the Code or (ii) an "applicable high yield discount obligation" under Section 163(i) of the Code, and none of the interest on any such indebtedness will be disallowed as a deduction under any other provision of the Code.

(q)   Neither the Company nor any Tax Affiliate has engaged in any transaction that is subject to disclosure under present or former Treasury Regulations Sections 1.6011-4 or 1.6011-4T, as applicable.

(r)   There is no Contract, plan or arrangement, including this Agreement, by which any current or former employee of the Company or any Subsidiary would be entitled to receive any payment from the Company or any Subsidiary as a result of the transactions contemplated by this Agreement that would not be deductible pursuant to Section 404 or 162(m) of the Code.

(s)   Neither the Company nor any Tax Affiliate has been a member of any partnership or joint venture or the holder of a beneficial interest in any trust for any period for which the statute of limitations for any Taxes potentially applicable as a result of such membership or holding has not expired.

(t)   [Neither the Company nor any Tax Affiliate is subject to accumulated earnings tax penalty or has received any notification regarding a personal holding company tax.]

(u)   [Foreign Company and Other Miscellaneous Reps & Warranties:

(v)   The Company and the Tax Affiliates have evidence of payment for all Taxes of a foreign country paid or accrued from the date of the formation of the Company or such Tax Affiliate.

(w)   Neither the Company nor any Tax Affiliate, to the extent they are "controlled foreign corporations" within the meaning of Section 957 of the Code, has had "subpart F income" within the meaning of Section 952 of the Code since the date of formation of the Company or such Tax Affiliate.

(x)   Neither the Company nor any Tax Affiliate has an "overall foreign loss" within the meaning of Section 904 of the Code or a "dual consolidated loss" within the meaning of Treasury Regulations Section 1.1503-2.

(y)   Neither the Company nor any Tax Affiliate is a "passive foreign investment corporation" as defined in Section 1297 of the Code or a "foreign personal holding company" as defined in Section 552 of the Code.

(z)   Neither the Company nor any Tax Affiliate participates in or cooperates with (or has at any time participated in or cooperated with) an international boycott within the meaning of Section 999(b)(3) of the Code.

(aa)   Since their formation, each of the Company and the Tax Affiliates has been a corporation or association taxable as a corporation for United States income tax purposes.

(bb)   All deductions claimed or reported on each Return of the Company and any Tax Affiliate on account of royalties or similar fees payable with respect to any Intellectual Property Rights are allowable in full.

(cc)   There is no indebtedness (or other obligation that might be characterized as debt for U.S. federal income Tax purposes) between the Company and any Subsidiary.]

4.14   Intellectual Property Rights.

(a)   Schedule 4.14(a)(i) lists and describes all Owned Intellectual Property Rights that are Registered Intellectual Property Rights and all other [material] Owned Intellectual Property Rights. Schedule 4.14(a)(ii) lists all Contracts relating to Licensed-In Intellectual Property Rights other than Software and describes the Intellectual Property Rights covered by such Contracts; to the extent there is no written Contract covering a Licensed-In Intellectual Property Right, Schedule 4.14(a)(ii) lists the licensor and describes the Intellectual Property Rights so licensed. Schedule 4.14(a)(iii) lists all Contracts relating to Licensed-In Intellectual Property Rights that are Software other than Off-the-Shelf Software and describes the Intellectual Property Rights covered thereby; to the extent there is no written Contract covering any Software, Schedule 4.14(a)(iii) lists the licensor and describes the Software so licensed. Schedule 4.14(a)(iv) lists and describes all materials otherwise protectable under Intellectual Property Rights used in the business of the Company or any Subsidiary as conducted or proposed to be conducted that are in the public domain. The Owned Intellectual Property Rights and the Licensed-In Intellectual Property Rights constitute all Intellectual Property Rights necessary for the business of the Company and its Subsidiaries as conducted or proposed to be conducted.

(b)   The Company owns all right, title and interest in the Owned Intellectual Property Rights free and clear of all Encumbrances (including royalty or other payments), except for those licenses of the Owned Intellectual Property Rights to Persons, payments for use of the Owned Intellectual Property Rights and other Encumbrances listed on Schedule 4.14(b). The Company is the official and sole owner of record of all Registered Intellectual Property Rights. No Owned Intellectual Property Right has been infringed by any Person. The Company or a Subsidiary owns all Intellectual Property Rights developed by its current and former employees and independent contractors during the period of their employment or within the scope of their contracting or consulting relationship, as the case may be, with the Company or any Subsidiary. No employee or former employee or independent contractor of the Company or any Subsidiary has any claim with respect to any Intellectual Property Right of the Company.

(c)   All Owned Intellectual Property Rights are valid and enforceable, and no Person has asserted that any Owned Intellectual Property Right is invalid or not enforceable. All Owned Intellectual Property Rights that are Registered Intellectual Property Rights are in full force and effect, and all actions required to keep such rights pending or in effect or to provide full available protection, including payment of filing, examination, annuity, and maintenance fees and filing of renewals, statements of use or working, affidavits of incontestability and other similar actions, have been taken, and no such Registered Intellectual Property Right is the subject of any interference, opposition, cancellation, nullity, re-examination or other proceeding placing in question the validity or scope of such rights. All products covered by Owned Intellectual Property Rights or Licensed-In Intellectual Property Rights that are Registered Intellectual Property Rights and all usages of Owned Intellectual Property Rights or Licensed-In Intellectual Property Rights that are Registered Intellectual Property Rights have been marked with the appropriate patent, trademark or other marking required or desirable to maximize available damage awards.

(d)   The documentation relating to all trade secrets listed on Schedule 4.14(a)(i) is current, accurate and sufficient in detail and content to identify and explain such trade secrets and to allow their full and proper use without reliance on the knowledge or memory of any individual. All reasonable precautions have been taken to protect the secrecy, confidentiality and value of the trade secrets and all other proprietary information used by the Company or any Subsidiary including the implementation and enforcement of policies requiring each employee or independent contractor who has access to trade secrets to execute proprietary information and confidentiality agreements substantially in a standard form, and each current and former employee and independent contractor of the Company or any Subsidiary has executed such an agreement. There has been no breach or other violation of such agreements. Each of the Company and its Subsidiaries has an unqualified right to use all trade secrets and other proprietary information currently used in its business, subject to any Contract relating to Licensed-In Intellectual Property Rights. No such trade secret or other proprietary information is part of the public knowledge or literature, and no trade secret or other proprietary information has been used, divulged or appropriated either for the benefit of any Person other than the Company or a Subsidiary or to the detriment of the Company or any Subsidiary.

(e)   Neither the Company nor any Subsidiary has taken action, or failed to take an action, that might have the effect of estopping or otherwise limiting its right to enforce Owned Intellectual Property Rights against any Person.

(f)   Neither the Company nor any Subsidiary has any present expectation or intention of not fully performing any obligation pursuant to any license, and there is no breach, anticipated breach or default by any other party to any license. There are no renegotiations of, attempts to renegotiate, demands for or outstanding rights to renegotiate any license. All rights under each license will be fully available to the Company or a Subsidiary after the Closing.

(g)   Each Licensed-in Intellectual Property Right for which the Company or any Subsidiary has an exclusive right is in full force and effect, all actions required to keep such right pending or in effect or to provide full protection, including payment of filing, examination, annuity, and maintenance fees and filing of renewals, statements of use or working, affidavits of incontestability and other similar actions, have been taken. No Licensed-in Intellectual Property Right that is a Registered Intellectual Property Right and for which the Company or any Subsidiary has an exclusive right is the subject of any interference, opposition, cancellation, nullity, re-examination or other proceeding placing in question the validity or scope of such right.

(h)   Neither the Company nor any Subsidiary has infringed, misappropriated or otherwise violated any Third-Party Intellectual Property Right, and neither the Company nor any Subsidiary has received any notice of any infringement, misappropriation or violation by the Company or any Subsidiary of any Third-Party Intellectual Property Right. No infringement, misappropriation or violation of any Third-Party Intellectual Property Right has occurred or will occur with respect to products or services sold by the Company or any Subsidiary or with respect to the products or services currently under development or with respect to the conduct of the business of the Company or any Subsidiary as conducted or proposed to be conducted.

(i)   All Software that is used by the Company or any Subsidiary or is present at any facility or on any equipment of the Company or any Subsidiary is owned by the Company or a Subsidiary or is subject to a current license agreement that covers all use of the Software in the business of the Company or any Subsidiary as conducted or as proposed to be conducted. Each of the Company and the Subsidiaries has the right to use the Software used in its business as it is being used, without any conflict with the rights of others. Neither the Company nor any Subsidiary is in breach of any license to, or license of, any Software. The Company and its Subsidiaries do not use, rely on or contract with any Person to provide service bureau, outsourcing or other computer processing services to the Company or any Subsidiary, in lieu of or in addition to their respective use of the Software. Following the Closing, each of the Company and the Subsidiaries will have sufficient rights to all necessary Software, to operate its business as it is conducted or as proposed to be conducted.

4.15   Material Contracts.

(a)   Schedule 4.15 lists the following Contracts to which the Company or any Subsidiary is a party or subject or by which it is bound (with the Contracts required to be listed on Schedule 4.14, the "Material Contracts"):

(i)   each employment, agency, collective bargaining or consulting Contract;

(ii)   each Contract (A) with any Insider or (B) between or among any Insiders relating in any way to the Company or any Subsidiary;

(iii)   each distributor, reseller, OEM, dealer, manufacturer's representative, broker, sales agency, advertising agency, finder's, manufacturing or assembly Contract;

(iv)   each franchise agreement;

(v)   each Contract or group of related Contracts with the same party for the purchase of products or services with a undelivered balance in excess of $_____;

(vi)   each Contract or group of related Contracts with the same party for the sale of products or services with an undelivered balance in excess of $_____;

(vii)   each lease of real or personal property with aggregate annual payments in excess of $_____;

(viii)   each Contract for the sale of any capital assets;

(ix)   each Contract for capital expenditures in excess of $_____;

(x)   each Contract relating to the borrowing of money or to mortgaging, pledging or otherwise placing an Encumbrance on any of the assets of the Company or any Subsidiary;

(xi)   each written warranty, guaranty or other similar undertaking with respect to contractual performance extended by the Company or any Subsidiary other than in the Ordinary Course of Business;

(xii)   each Contract relating to any surety bond or letter of credit required to be maintained by the Company or any Subsidiary;

(xiii)   each Contract that contains or provides for an express undertaking by the Company or any Subsidiary to be responsible for consequential damages;

(xiv)   each Contract concerning a partnership or joint venture;

(xv)   each Contract providing for the development of any products, Software or Intellectual Property Rights or the delivery of any services by, for or with any third party;

(xvi)   each Contract containing exclusivity, noncompetition or nonsolicitation provisions or that would otherwise prohibit the Company or any Subsidiary from freely engaging in business anywhere in the world or prohibiting the solicitation of the employees or contractors of any other entity;

(xvii)   each Contract pertaining to confidentiality or non-disclosure;

(xviii)   [each Capital Lease;]

(xix)   each Contract terminable by any other party upon a change of control of the Company or any Subsidiary or upon the failure of the Company or any Subsidiary to satisfy financial or performance criteria specified in such Contract;

(xx)   each stock purchase, stock option and stock incentive plan (other than a Plan);

(xxi)   each power of attorney that is currently in effect; and

(xxii)   each other Contract of the Company or any Subsidiary not entered into in the Ordinary Course of Business or that is material to the business, financial condition, results of operations or prospects of the Company and the Subsidiaries taken as a whole.

(b)   Each Material Contract is valid and binding, currently in force and enforceable in accordance with its terms, subject to the Remedies Exception. Each of the Company and the Subsidiaries has performed all obligations required to be performed by it in connection with each Material Contract. Neither the Company nor any Subsidiary has received any notice of any claim of default by it under or termination of any Material Contract. Neither the Company nor any Subsidiary has any present expectation or intention of not fully performing any obligation pursuant to any Material Contract, and there is no breach, anticipated breach or default by the Company or a Subsidiary or any other party to any Material Contract. There is no renegotiation of, attempt to renegotiate or outstanding right to renegotiate any material terms of any Material Contract and no Person has made written demand for such renegotiation. Each of the Company and the Subsidiaries can perform each Material Contract for the sale of products or services on time, at a profit and without unusual expenditures of time and money. Neither the Company nor any Subsidiary has any obligation to refund payments received for work not yet performed under a Material Contract where the percentage of work completed is less than the percentage of revenues received to date.

4.16   Litigation. No Litigation is pending or, to the Knowledge of any Seller, threatened against the Company or any Subsidiary and there is no reasonable basis for any Litigation against the Company or any Subsidiary. Neither the Company nor any Subsidiary is subject to any outstanding Governmental Order. [Alternative—Schedule 4.16 lists all Litigation pending or, to the Knowledge of any Seller, threatened against the Company or any Subsidiary and each Governmental Order to which the Company or any subsidiary is subject. None of the items listed on Schedule 4.16 could result in any Material Adverse Effect.]

4.17   Insurance.

(a)   Each of the Company and the Subsidiaries has at all times maintained insurance relating to its business and covering property, fire, casualty, liability, workers' compensation and all other forms of insurance customarily obtained by businesses in the same industry. Such insurance (i) is in full force and effect, (ii) is sufficient for compliance with all requirements of applicable Law and of any Contract to which the Company or any Subsidiary is subject, (iii) is valid and enforceable, (iv) insures against risks of the kind customarily insured against and in amounts customarily carried by businesses similarly situated and (v) provides adequate insurance coverage for the activities of each of the Company and the Subsidiaries. Schedule 4.17 lists each policy of insurance in effect.

(b)   Schedule 4.17 lists by year for the current policy year and each of the two preceding policy years a summary of the loss experience under each policy involving any claim in excess of

$\_\_\_\_\_$, setting forth (i) the name of the claimant, (ii) a description of the policy by insurer, type of insurance and period of coverage and (iii) the amount and a brief description of the claim. Schedule 4.17 also describes the loss experience for all claims in excess of $\_\_\_\_\_$ that were self-insured, including the aggregate cost of such claims.

4.18   <u>Compliance with Laws; Governmental Authorizations</u>.

(a)   Each of the Company and the Subsidiaries has complied with all applicable Laws and Governmental Orders. Neither the Company nor any Subsidiary is relying on any exemption from or deferral of any Law, Governmental Order or Governmental Authorization that would not be available to Buyer after the Closing.

(b)   Each of the Company and the Subsidiaries has in full force and effect all Governmental Authorizations necessary to conduct its business [the Business] and own and operate its properties. Schedule 4.18(b) lists each Governmental Authorization held by the Company or any Subsidiary. Each of the Company and the Subsidiaries has complied with all Governmental Authorizations applicable to it.

(c)   Neither the Company nor any Subsidiary has offered, authorized, promised, made or agreed to make any gifts, payments or transfers of property of any kind (other than incidental gifts of nominal value) in connection with any actual or proposed transaction, except as required or permitted by the Laws of each applicable jurisdiction and in each such case has complied with the U.S. Foreign Corrupt Practices Act.

(d)   Each of the Company and the Subsidiaries has complied with all applicable export control and trade embargo Laws in connection with any actual or proposed transaction.

(e)   Each of the Company and the Subsidiaries has complied with all applicable antiboycott Laws in connection with any actual or proposed transaction.

(f)   Neither the Company nor any Subsidiary has ever had a legal obligation to file any form, report, schedule, proxy statement or other document with the SEC, and neither the Company nor any Subsidiary has filed with the SEC any such form, report, schedule, proxy statement or other document.

4.19   Environmental Matters.

(a)   As used in this Section 4.19, the following terms have the following meanings:

(i)   "Environmental Costs" means any and all costs and expenditures, including any fees and expenses of attorneys and of environmental consultants or engineers incurred in connection with investigating, defending, remediating or otherwise responding to any Release of Hazardous Materials, any violation or alleged violation of Environmental Law, any fees, fines, penalties or charges associated with any Governmental Authorization, or any actions necessary to comply with any Environmental Law.

(ii)   "Environmental Law" means any Law, Governmental Authorization or Governmental Order relating to pollution, contamination, Hazardous Materials or protection of the environment.

(iii)   "Hazardous Materials" means any dangerous, toxic or hazardous pollutant, contaminant, chemical, waste, material or substance as defined in or governed by any Law relating to such substance or otherwise relating to the environment or human health or safety, including any waste, material, substance, pollutant or contaminant that might cause any injury to human health or safety or to the environment or might subject the owner or operator of the Property to any Environmental Costs or liability under any Environmental Law.

(iv)   "List" means the United States Environmental Protection Agency's National Priorities List of Hazardous

Waste Sites or any other list, schedule, log, inventory or record, however defined, maintained by any Governmental Entity with respect to sites from which there has been a Release of Hazardous Materials.

(v)   "Property" means real property owned, leased, controlled or occupied by the Company or any Subsidiary at any time.

(vi)   "Regulatory Action" means any Litigation with respect to the Company or any Subsidiary brought or instigated by any Governmental Entity in connection with any Environmental Costs, Release of Hazardous Materials or any Environmental Law.

(vii)   "Release" means the spilling, leaking, disposing, discharging, emitting, depositing, ejecting, leaching, escaping or any other release or threatened release, however defined, whether intentional or unintentional, of any Hazardous Material.

(viii)   "Third-Party Environmental Claim" means any Litigation (other than a Regulatory Action) based on negligence, trespass, strict liability, nuisance, toxic tort or any other cause of action or theory relating to any Environmental Costs, Release of Hazardous Materials or any violation of Environmental Law.

(b)   No Third-Party Environmental Claim or Regulatory Action is pending or, to the Knowledge of any Seller, threatened against the Company or any Subsidiary.

(c)   No Property is listed on a List.

(d)   All transfer, transportation or disposal of Hazardous Materials by the Company or any Subsidiary to properties not owned, leased or operated by the Company or any Subsidiary has been in compliance with applicable Environmental Law. The Company has not transported or arranged for the transportation of any Hazardous Materials to any location that is (i) listed on a List, (ii) listed for possible inclusion on any List or (iii) the subject of any Regulatory Action or Third-Party Environmental Claim.

(e)   No Property has ever been used as a landfill, dump or other disposal, storage, transfer, handling or treatment area for Hazardous Materials, or as a gasoline service station or a facility for selling, dispensing, storing, transferring, disposing or handling petroleum and/or petroleum products.

(f)   There has not been any Release of any Hazardous Material on, under, about, from or in connection with the Property, including the presence of any Hazardous Materials that have come to be located on or under the Property from another location.

(g)   The Property at all times has been used and operated in compliance with all applicable Environmental Law.

(h)   Each of the Company and the Subsidiaries has obtained all Governmental Authorizations relating to the Environmental Law necessary for operation of the Company, each of which is listed on Schedule 4.19. All Governmental Authorizations relating to the Environmental Law will be valid and in full force and effect upon consummation of the transactions contemplated by this Agreement. Each of the Company and the Subsidiaries has filed all reports and notifications required to be filed under and pursuant to all applicable Environmental Law.

(i)   No Hazardous Materials have been generated, treated, contained, handled, located, used, manufactured, processed, buried, incinerated, deposited or stored on, under or about any part of the Property. The Property contains no asbestos, urea, formaldehyde, radon at levels above natural background, PCBs or pesticides. No aboveground or underground storage tanks are located on, under or about the Property, or have been located on, under or about the Property and then subsequently been removed or filled. If any such storage tanks exist on, under or about the Property, such storage tanks have been duly registered with all appropriate Governmental

Entities and are otherwise in compliance with all applicable Environmental Law.

(j)   No expenditure will be required in order for Buyer, the Company or any Subsidiary to comply with any Environmental Law in effect at the time of Closing in connection with the operation or continued operation of the Property in a manner consistent with the present operation thereof.

(k)   All environmental reports and investigations that any Seller, the Company or any Subsidiary has obtained or ordered with respect to the Company, any Subsidiary or the Property are listed on Schedule 4.19.

(l)   No Encumbrance has been attached or filed against the Company or any Subsidiary in favor of any Person for (i) any liability under or violation of any applicable Environmental Law, (ii) any Release of Hazardous Materials or (iii) any imposition of Environmental Costs.

4.20   Warranties. Schedule 4.20 lists all claims pending or, to the Knowledge of any Seller, threatened for product liability or breach of any warranty relating to any products sold or services performed by the Company or any Subsidiary. Such claims in the aggregate are not in excess of the reserve for product warranty claims set forth on the face of the Latest Balance Sheet. Schedule 4.20 describes the warranties for products sold or services performed by each of the Company and the Subsidiaries. No product or service manufactured, sold, leased or delivered by the Company or any Subsidiary is subject to any guaranty, warranty or other indemnity other than such warranties. Except as listed on Schedule 4.20, none of the products manufactured, sold, leased or delivered by the Company or any Subsidiary has been the subject of any product recall or return (whether voluntary or involuntary) during the past five years.

4.21   Employees.

(a)   Schedule 4.21(a) lists each employee of the Company or any Subsidiary as of the date of this Agreement, states the total number of employees and indicates for each such employee, and in the aggregate, full-time, part-time and temporary status.

(b)   Schedule 4.21(b) lists each salaried employee of the Company or any Subsidiary as of the date of this Agreement and shows for each such employee annual salary, any other compensation payable (including compensation payable pursuant to bonus, incentive, deferred compensation or commission arrangements), date of employment and position. To the Knowledge of any Seller, no executive employee of the Company and no group of employees of the Company or any Subsidiary has any plans to terminate his, her or their employment. Each of the Company and the Subsidiaries has complied at all times with all applicable Laws relating to employment and employment practices and those relating to the calculation and payment of wages (including overtime pay, maximum hours of work and child labor restrictions), equal employment opportunity (including Laws prohibiting discrimination and/or harassment or requiring accommodation on the basis of race, color, national origin, religion, gender, disability, age, sexual orientation or otherwise), affirmative action and other hiring practices, occupational safety and health, workers' compensation, unemployment compensation, the payment of social security and other Taxes, and unfair labor practices under the National Labor Relations Act or applicable state law. Neither the Company nor any Subsidiary has any labor relations problem pending or, to the Knowledge of any Seller, threatened, and its labor relations are satisfactory. There are no workers' compensation claims pending against the Company or any Subsidiary, or, to the Knowledge of any Seller, any facts that would give rise to such a claim. No employee of the Company or any Subsidiary is subject to any secrecy or noncompetition agreement or any other agreement or restriction of any kind that would impede in any way the ability of such employee to carry out fully all activities of such employee in furtherance of the business of the Company.

(c)   Schedule 4.21(c), Part 1, lists each employee of the Company as of the date of this Agreement who holds a temporary work authorization, including H-1B, L-1, F-1 or J-1 visas or work authorizations (the "Work Permits"), and shows for each such employee the type of Work Permit and the length of time remaining on such Work Permit. With respect to each Work Permit, all of the information that the Company or any Subsidiary provided to the Department of Labor and the Immigration and Naturalization Service or the Department of Homeland Security (collectively, the "Department") in the application for such Work Permit was true and complete. The Company or a Subsidiary received the appropriate notice of approval from the Department with respect to each such Work Permit. Neither the Company nor any Subsidiary has received any notice from the Department that any Work Permit has been revoked. There is no action pending or, to the Knowledge of any Seller, threatened to revoke or adversely modify the terms of any Work Permit. Except as set disclosed in Schedule 4.21(c), Part 2, no employee of the Company or any Subsidiary is (a) a non-immigrant employee whose status would terminate or otherwise be affected by the transactions contemplated by this Agreement, or (b) an alien who is authorized to work in the United States in non-immigrant status. For each employee of the Company or any Subsidiary hired after November 6, 1986, the Company or such Subsidiary has retained an Immigration and Naturalization Service Form I-9, completed in accordance with applicable Law.

(d)   The employment of any terminated former employee of the Company or any Subsidiary has been terminated in accordance with any applicable Contract terms and applicable Law, and neither the Company nor any Subsidiary has any liability under any Contract or applicable Law toward any such terminated employee. The transactions contemplated by this Agreement will not cause the Company or any Subsidiary to incur or suffer any liability relating to, or obligation to pay, severance, termination or other payment to any Person.

(e)   Neither the Company nor any Subsidiary has made any loans (except advances for business travel, lodging or other expenses in the Ordinary Course of Business) to any employee of the Company or any Subsidiary.

(f)   Except as disclosed in Schedule 4.21(f), within the last five years, neither the Company nor any Subsidiary has experienced and, to the Knowledge of any Seller, there has not been threatened, any strike, work stoppage, slowdown, lockout, picketing, leafleting, boycott, other labor dispute, union organization attempt, demand for recognition from a labor organization or petition for representation under the National Labor Relations Act or applicable state law. Except as disclosed in Schedule 4.21(f), no grievance, demand for arbitration or arbitration proceeding arising out of or under any collective bargaining agreement is pending or, to the Knowledge of any Seller, threatened. Except as disclosed in Schedule 4.21(f), no Litigation is pending or, to the Knowledge of any Seller, threatened respecting or involving any applicant for employment, any current employee or any former employee, or any class of the foregoing, including:

(i)   the Equal Employment Opportunity Commission or any other corresponding state or local fair employment practices agency relating to any claim or charge of discrimination or harassment in employment;

(ii)   the United States Department of Labor or any other corresponding state or local agency relating to any claim or charge concerning hours of work, wages or employment practices;

(iii)   the Occupational Safety and Health Administration or any other corresponding state or local agency relating to any claim or charge concerning employee safety or health;

(iv)   the Office of Federal Contract Compliance or any corresponding state agency; and

(v)   the National Labor Relations Board or any corresponding state agency, whether relating to any unfair labor practice or any question concerning representation,

and there is no reasonable basis for any such Litigation.

(g)   No employee of the Company or any Subsidiary is covered by any collective bargaining agreement, and no collective bargaining agreement is being negotiated.

(h)   Each of the Company and the Subsidiaries has paid in full to all employees all wages, salaries, bonuses and commissions due and payable to such employees and has fully reserved in its books of account all amounts for wages, salaries, bonuses and commissions due but not yet payable to such employees.

(i)   There has been no lay-off of employees or work reduction program undertaken by or on behalf of the Company or any Subsidiary in the past two years, and no such program has been adopted by the Company or any Subsidiary or publicly announced.

4.22   Employee Benefits.

(a)   Schedule 4.22 lists all Plans by name and provides a brief description identifying (i) the type of Plan, (ii) the funding arrangements for the Plan, (iii) the sponsorship of the Plan, (iv) the participating employers in the Plan and (v) any one or more of the following characteristics that may apply to such Plan: (A) defined contribution plan as defined in Section 3(34) of ERISA or Section 414(i) of the Code, (B) defined benefit plan as defined in Section 3(35) of ERISA or Section 414(j) of the Code, (C) plan that is or is intended to be tax qualified under Section 401(a) or 403(a) of the Code, (D) plan that is or is intended to be an employee stock ownership plan as defined in Section 4975(e)(7) of the Code (and whether or not such plan has entered into an exempt loan), (E) nonqualified deferred compensation arrangement, (F) employee welfare benefit plan as defined in Section 3(1) of ERISA, (G) multiemployer plan as defined in Section 3(37) of ERISA or Section 414(f) of the Code, (H) multiple employer plan maintained by more than one employer as defined in Section 413(c) of the Code, (I) plan providing benefits after separation from service or termination of employment, (J) plan that owns any Company or other employer securities as an investment, (K) plan that provides benefits (or provides increased benefits or vesting) as a result of a change in control of the Company, (L) plan that is maintained pursuant to collective bargaining and (M) plan that is funded, in whole or in part, through a voluntary employees' beneficiary association exempt from Tax under Section 501(c)(9) of the Code.

(b)   Schedule 4.22 lists each corporation, trade or business (separately for each category below that applies): (i) that is (or was during the preceding five years) under common control with the Company within the meaning of Section 414(b) or (c) of the Code, (ii) that is (or was during the preceding five years) in an affiliated service group with the Company within the meaning of Section 414(m) of the Code, (iii) that is (or was during the preceding five years) the legal employer of Persons providing services to the Company as leased employees within the meaning of Section 414(n) of the Code and (iv) with respect to which the Company or any Subsidiary is a successor employer for purposes of group health or other welfare plan continuation rights (including Section 601 et seq. of ERISA) or the Family and Medical Leave Act.

(c)   Schedule 4.22 lists (i) the most recent determination letter received by the Company from the IRS regarding each Plan, (ii) the most recent determination or opinion letter ruling from the IRS that each trust established in connection with Plans that are intended to be tax exempt under Section 501(a) or (c) of the Code are so tax exempt, (iii) all pending applications for rulings, determinations, opinions, no action letters and the like filed with any governmental agency (including the Department of Labor, IRS, Pension Benefit Guaranty Corporation and the SEC), (iv) the financial statements for each Plan for the three most recent fiscal or plan years (in audited form if required by ERISA) and, where applicable, Annual Report/Return (Form 5500) with disclosure schedules, if any, and attachments for each Plan, (v) the most recently prepared actuarial valuation report for each Plan (including reports prepared for funding, deduction and financial accounting purposes), (vi) plan documents, trust agreements, insurance contracts, service agreements and all related contracts and documents (including any employee summaries and material employee communications) with respect to each Plan and (vii) collective bargaining agreements (including side agreements and letter agreements) relating to the establishment, maintenance, funding and operation of any Plan.

(d)   Schedule 4.22 lists each employee of the Company or any Subsidiary who is (i) absent from active employment due to short or long term disability, (ii) absent from active employment on a leave pursuant to the Family and Medical Leave Act or a comparable state Law, (iii) absent from active employment on any other leave or approved absence (together with the reason for each leave or absence) or (iv) absent from active employment due to military service (under conditions that give the employee rights to re-employment).

(e)   With respect to continuation rights arising under federal or state Law as applied to Plans that are group health plans (as defined in Section 601 et seq. of ERISA), Schedule 4.22 lists (i) each employee, former employee or qualifying beneficiary who has elected continuation and (ii) each employee, former employee or qualifying beneficiary who has not elected continuation coverage but is still within the period in which such election may be made.

(f)   (i) All Plans intended to be Tax qualified under Section 401(a) or Section 403(a) of the Code are so qualified, (ii) all trusts established in connection with Plans intended to be Tax exempt under Section 501(a) or (c) of the Code are so Tax exempt, (iii) to the extent required either as a matter of Law or to obtain the intended Tax treatment and Tax benefits, all Plans comply in all respects with the requirements of ERISA and the Code, (iv) all Plans have been administered in accordance with the documents and instruments governing the Plans, (v) all reports and filings with Governmental Entities (including the Department of Labor, the IRS, Pension Benefit Guaranty Corporation and the SEC) required in connection with each Plan have been timely made, (vi) all disclosures and notices required by Law or Plan provisions to be given to participants and beneficiaries in connection with each Plan have been properly and timely made and (vii) each of the Company and the Subsidiaries has made a good faith effort to comply with the reporting and taxation requirements for FICA taxes with respect to any deferred compensation arrangements under Section 3121(v) of the Code.

(g)   (i) All contributions, premium payments and other payments required to be made in connection with the Plans have been made, (ii) a proper accrual has been made on the books of account of the Company for all contributions, premium payments and other payments due in the current fiscal year, (iii) no contribution, premium payment or other payment has been made in support of any Plan that is in excess of the allowable deduction for federal income Tax purposes for the year with respect to which the contribution was made (whether under Section 162, Section 280G, Section 404, Section 419, Section 419A of the Code or otherwise) and (iv) with respect to each Plan that is subject to Section 301 et seq. of ERISA or Section 412 of the Code, the Company is not liable for any "accumulated funding deficiency" as that term is defined in Section 412 of the Code and the projected benefit obligations do not exceed the assets of the Plan.

(h)   The consummation of the transactions contemplated by this Agreement will not (i) cause any Plan to increase benefits payable to any participant or beneficiary, (ii) entitle any current or former employee of the Company or any Subsidiary to severance pay, unemployment compensation or any other payment, benefit or award or (iii) accelerate or modify the time of payment or vesting, or increase the amount of any benefit, award or compensation due any such employee.

(i)   (i) No Litigation is pending with regard to any Plan other than routine uncontested claims for benefits, (ii) no Plan is currently under examination or audit by the Department of Labor, the IRS or the Pension Benefit Guaranty Corporation, (iii) the Company has no actual or potential liability arising under Title IV of ERISA as a result of any Plan that has terminated or is in the process of terminating, (iv) the Company has no actual or potential liability under Section 4201 et seq. of ERISA for either a complete withdrawal or a partial withdrawal from a multiemployer plan and (v) with respect to the Plans, the Company has no liability (either directly or as a result of indemnification) for (and the transactions contemplated by this Agreement will not cause any liability for): (A) any excise Taxes under Section 4971 through Section 4980B, Section 4999, Section 5000 or any other Section of the Code, (B) any penalty under Section 502(i), Section 502(l), Part 6 of Title I or any other provision of ERISA or (C) any excise Taxes, penalties, damages or equitable relief as a result of any prohibited transaction, breach of fiduciary duty or other violation under ERISA or any other applicable Law, (vi) all accruals required under FAS 106 and FAS 112 have been properly accrued on the Latest Financial Statements, (vii) no condition, agreement or Plan provision limits the right of the Company to amend, cut back or terminate any Plan (except to the extent such limitation arises under ERISA) and (viii) the Company has no liability for life insurance, death or medical benefits after separation from employment other than (A) death benefits under the Plans and (B) health care continuation benefits described in Section 4980B of the Code.

4.23   Customers. Schedule 4.23 lists the 10 largest customers of the Company and the Subsidiaries on a consolidated basis for each of the last two fiscal years and for the interim period ended on the Latest Balance Sheet Date and sets forth opposite the name of each such customer the percentage of net sales by the Company and the Subsidiaries attributable to such customer for each such period. No customer listed on Schedule 4.23 has indicated that it will stop or decrease the rate of business done with the Company or any Subsidiary.

4.24   Suppliers. Schedule 4.24 lists the 10 largest suppliers of the Company and the Subsidiaries on a consolidated basis for each of the last two fiscal years and for the interim period ended on the Latest Balance Sheet Date and sets forth opposite the name of each such supplier the approximate percentage of purchases by the Company and the Subsidiaries attributable to such supplier for each such period. No supplier listed on Schedule 4.24 is a sole source of supply for the Company and the

Subsidiaries. No supplier listed on Schedule 4.24 has indicated that it will stop or decrease the rate of business done with the Company or any Subsidiary.

4.25   Affiliate Transactions. No Insider has any Contract with the Company or any Subsidiary (other than employment not represented by a written Contract and terminable at will), any loan to or from the Company or any interest in any assets (whether real, personal or mixed, tangible or intangible) used in or pertaining to the business of the Company or any Subsidiary (other than ownership of capital stock of the Company). No Insider has any direct or indirect interest in any competitor, supplier or customer of the Company or any Subsidiary or in any Person from whom or to whom the Company or any Subsidiary leases any property, or in any other Person with whom the Company or any Subsidiary otherwise transacts business of any nature. Schedule 4.25 lists all transactions between the Company or any Subsidiary and each Insider for each of the last three fiscal years and since the Last Fiscal Year End.

4.26   Brokerage. No Person will be entitled to receive any brokerage commission, finder's fee, fee for financial advisory services or similar compensation in connection with the transactions contemplated by this Agreement based on any Contract made by or on behalf of the Company for which Buyer or the Company is or could become liable or obligated.

4.27   Availability of Documents. Sellers have delivered to Buyer correct and complete copies of the items referred to in the Disclosure Schedule or in this Agreement (and in the case of any items not in written form, a written description thereof).

4.28   Solvency.

(a)   The Company is not insolvent and will not be rendered insolvent by any of the transactions contemplated by this Agreement. As used in this Section 4.28, "insolvent" means that the sum of the debts and other probable Liabilities of the Company exceeds the present fair saleable value of its assets.

(b)   Immediately after giving effect to the consummation of the transactions contemplated by this Agreement, (i) the Company will be able to pay its Liabilities as they become due in the usual course of its business; (ii) the Company will not have unreasonably small capital with which to conduct its present or proposed business; (iii) the Company will have assets (calculated at fair market value) that exceed its Liabilities; (iv) taking into account all pending and threatened litigation, final judgments against the Company in actions for money damages are not reasonably anticipated to be rendered at a time when, or in amounts such that, the Company will be unable to satisfy any such judgments promptly in accordance with their terms (taking into account the maximum probable amount of such judgments in any such actions and the earliest reasonable time at which such judgments might be rendered) as well as all other obligations of the Company; and (v) the cash available to the Company, after taking into account all other anticipated uses of the cash, will be sufficient to pay all such debts and judgments promptly in accordance with their terms.

4.29   Disclosure.

(a)   This Agreement, the exhibits, the Disclosure Schedule, the Annual Financial Statements or the Latest Financial Statements do not contain any untrue statement or omit any material fact necessary to make the statements contained herein or therein, in light of the circumstances in which they were made, not misleading.

(b)   Except as set forth in this Agreement or the Disclosure Schedule, there is no fact that has specific application to the Company (other than general economic or industry conditions) and that may materially adversely affect the assets, business, prospects, financial condition or results of operations of the Company.

V. Representations and Warranties of Buyer

Buyer represents and warrants to Sellers that as of the date of this Agreement and as of the Closing Date (as though made then and as though the Closing Date were substituted for the date of this Agreement):

5.1   Incorporation; Power and Authority. Buyer is a corporation duly organized, validly existing and in good standing under the Laws of its

391

jurisdiction of organization, with all necessary power and authority to execute, deliver and perform this Agreement [and the Ancillary Agreements to which it will become a party].

5.2   Valid and Binding Agreement. The execution, delivery and performance of this Agreement [and the Ancillary Agreements to which it will become a party] by Buyer have been duly and validly authorized by all necessary corporate action. This Agreement has been duly executed and delivered by Buyer and constitutes the valid and binding obligation of Buyer, enforceable against it in accordance with its terms, subject to the Remedies Exception. [Each Ancillary Agreement to which Buyer will become a party, when executed and delivered by Buyer, will constitute the valid and binding obligation of Buyer, enforceable against Buyer in accordance with its terms, subject to the Remedies Exception.]

5.3   No Breach; Consents. The execution, delivery and performance of this Agreement [and the Ancillary Agreements to which it will become a party] by Buyer will not (a) contravene any provision of the Organizational Documents of Buyer; (b) violate or conflict with any Law, Governmental Order or Governmental Authority; (c) conflict with, result in any breach of any of the provisions of, constitute a default (or any event that would, with the passage of time or the giving of notice or both, constitute a default) under, result in a violation of, increase the burdens under, result in the termination, amendment, suspension, modification, abandonment or acceleration of payment (or any right to terminate) or require a Consent, including any Consent under any Contract or Governmental Authorization that is either binding upon or enforceable against Buyer; or (d) require any Governmental Authorization.

5.4   Brokerage. No Person will be entitled to receive any brokerage commission, finder's fee, fee for financial advisory services or similar compensation in connection with the transactions contemplated by this Agreement based on any Contract made by or on behalf of Buyer for which any Seller is or could become liable or obligated.

5.5   Investment Intent. Buyer is acquiring the Shares for its own account for investment purposes, and not with a view to the distribution thereof.

5.6   [Buyer Notes. The Buyer Notes will, when issued and delivered in accordance with this Agreement, be duly authorized, validly issued and binding obligations of Buyer, enforceable against Buyer in accordance with their terms, subject to the Remedies Exception.]

5.7   [Buyer Common Stock. The shares of Buyer Common Stock will, when issued and delivered in accordance with this Agreement, be duly authorized, validly issued, fully paid and nonassessable.]

5.8   [Buyer Options. The Buyer Options will, when issued and delivered in accordance with this Agreement, be duly authorized, validly issued and binding obligations of Buyer, enforceable against Buyer in accordance with their terms, subject to the Remedies Exception, and any Buyer Common Stock issued upon exercise thereof in accordance with the terms of the relevant option plan and option agreement will, when issued, be duly authorized, validly issued, fully paid and nonassessable.]

5.9   [Buyer Warrants. The Buyer Warrants will, when issued and delivered in accordance with this Agreement, be duly authorized, validly issued and binding obligations of Buyer, enforceable against Buyer in accordance with their terms, subject to the Remedies Exception, and any Buyer Common Stock issued upon exercise thereof in accordance with the terms of the relevant warrant agreement will, when issued, be duly authorized, validly issued, fully paid and nonassessable.]

5.10   [SEC Filings; Financial Statements.

(a)   Buyer has filed all forms, reports, schedules, statements and other documents required to be filed by it during the 12 months immediately preceding the date of this Agreement (collectively, as supplemented and amended since the time of filing, the "Buyer SEC Reports") with the SEC. The Buyer SEC Reports (i) were prepared in all material respects in accordance with all applicable requirements of the Securities Act and the Exchange Act, as applicable, and (ii) did not, at the time they were filed, contain any untrue statement of a material fact or omit to state any material fact required to be stated therein or necessary in order to make the statements therein, in light of the circumstances under which they were made, not misleading. The representation in clause

(ii) of the preceding sentence does not apply to any misstatement or omission in any Buyer SEC Report that was superseded by subsequent Buyer SEC Reports.

(b)   The audited consolidated financial statements and unaudited consolidated interim financial statements of Buyer and its consolidated Subsidiaries included or incorporated by reference in the Buyer SEC Reports have been prepared in accordance with GAAP consistently applied during the periods indicated (except as may otherwise be indicated in the notes) and present fairly the financial position, results of operations and cash flows of Buyer and its consolidated Subsidiaries on a consolidated basis at the respective dates and for the respective periods indicated (except interim financial statements may not contain all notes and are subject to year-end adjustments).]

VI. Agreements of Sellers

Sellers, jointly and severally, agree with Buyer that:

6.1   <u>Conduct of the Business</u>. Sellers will cause each of the Company and the Subsidiaries to observe the following provisions to and including the Closing Date:

(a)   each of the Company and the Subsidiaries will conduct its business only in, and neither the Company nor any Subsidiary will take any action except in, the Ordinary Course of Business and in accordance with applicable Law;

(b)   neither the Company nor any Subsidiary will amend or modify any Material Contract or enter into any Contract that would have been a Material Contract if such Contract had been in effect on the date of this Agreement [except that the Company may enter into Contracts with vendors or customers in the Ordinary Course of Business];

(c)   each of the Company and the Subsidiaries will (i) use its best efforts to preserve its business organization and goodwill, keep available the services of its officers, employees and consultants and maintain satisfactory relationships with vendors, customers and others having business relationships with it, (ii), subject to applicable Laws, confer on a regular and frequent basis with representatives of Buyer to report operational matters and the general status of ongoing operations as requested by Buyer and (iii) not take any action that would render, or that reasonably may be expected to render, any representation or warranty made by Sellers in this Agreement untrue at the Closing as though then made and as though the Closing Date had been substituted for the date of this Agreement in such representation or warranty, including any actions referred to in Section 4.9;

(d)   except with the consent of Buyer or in the Ordinary Course of Business, neither the Company nor any Subsidiary will use extraordinary selling efforts that would have the effect of accelerating sales prior to the time reasonably expected, through offering of discounts, shipment of goods prior to anticipated shipping dates or otherwise;

(e)   [the Company will not (i) make or rescind any express or deemed election or take any other discretionary position relating to Taxes, (ii) amend any Return, (iii) settle or compromise any Litigation relating to Taxes or (iv) change any of its methods of reporting income or deductions for federal or state income Tax purposes from those employed in the preparation of the last filed federal or state income Tax Returns;]

(f)   the Company will not change any of its methods of accounting in effect on the Latest Balance Sheet Date, other than changes required by GAAP; and

(g)   neither the Company nor any Subsidiary will cancel or terminate its current insurance policies or allow any of the coverage thereunder to lapse, unless simultaneously with such termination, cancellation or lapse replacement policies providing coverage equal to or greater than the coverage under the canceled, terminated or lapsed policies for substantially similar premiums are in full force and effect.

6.2   Notice of Developments. Sellers will promptly notify Buyer of any emergency or other change in the Ordinary Course of Business of the Company or any Subsidiary or the commencement or threat of Litigation. Sellers will promptly notify Buyer in writing if any Seller should discover that any representation or warranty made by such Seller in this Agreement was when made, has subsequently become or will be on the Closing Date untrue in any respect. No disclosure pursuant to this Section 6.2 will be deemed to amend or supplement the Disclosure Schedule or to prevent or cure any inaccuracy, misrepresentation, breach of warranty or breach of agreement.

6.3   Pre-Closing Access. Through the Closing Date, Sellers will cause the Company and each of its Subsidiaries to afford to Buyer and its authorized representatives full access at all reasonable times and upon reasonable notice to the facilities, offices, properties, technology, processes, books, business and financial records, officers, employees, business plans, budgets, and projections, customers, suppliers and other information of each of the Company and the Subsidiaries, and the workpapers of _____, the Company's independent accountants, and otherwise provide such assistance as may be reasonably requested by Buyer in order that Buyer have a full opportunity to make such investigation and evaluation as it reasonably desires to make of the business and affairs of each of the Company and the Subsidiaries. In addition, Sellers will cause each of the Company and the Subsidiaries to cooperate fully (including providing introductions where necessary) with Buyer to enable Buyer to contact third parties, including employees, suppliers, customers and prospective customers of the Company, and to offer employment to employees of the Company and its Subsidiaries. Subject to Laws, Buyer will have full access to the personnel records (including performance appraisals, disciplinary actions, grievances and medical records) of the Company and the Subsidiaries for the purpose of preparing for and conducting employment interviews with all Active Employees. [The Company will provide such Plan documents and summary plan descriptions, employee data or other information as may be reasonably required to carry out the arrangements described in Section 7.8.] The Confidentiality Agreement, dated _____ (the "Confidentiality Agreement"), between the Company and Buyer will apply with respect to information obtained by Buyer under this Section 6.3.

6.4   Waivers; Payment of Indebtedness. To assure that Buyer obtains the full benefit of this Agreement, effective as of the Closing Date, each Seller waives any claim it might have against the Company or any Subsidiary, whether arising out of this Agreement or otherwise, and irrevocably offers to terminate any Contract between such Seller and the Company or any Subsidiary at no cost to the Company or any Subsidiary. Sellers will cause each Seller, the Members of the Immediate Family of each Seller and any Person controlled by any Seller to repay, in full, prior to the Closing, all indebtedness owed to the Company or any Subsidiary by such Person. Effective as of the Closing Date, each Seller agrees that such Seller will not make any claim for indemnification against the Company or any Subsidiary by reason of the fact that such Seller was a director, officer, employee or agent of any such entity or was serving at the request of any such entity as a partner, trustee, director, officer, employee or agent of another entity for any Loss (whether such claim is pursuant to any Law, Organizational Document, Contract or otherwise) with respect to any Litigation (whether such Litigation is pursuant to this Agreement, applicable Law or otherwise) and waives and releases any claim for indemnification such Seller may have against the Company or any Subsidiary. In order to assure that Buyer achieves the full benefit of this Agreement, effective as of the Closing, each Seller waives any claim it might have against the Company by virtue of the representations and warranties pertaining to the Company under this Agreement.

6.5   Conditions. Sellers will use their best efforts to cause the conditions set forth in Section 8.1 to be satisfied and to consummate the transactions contemplated by this Agreement as soon as reasonably possible and in any event prior to the Closing Date.

6.6   Consents and Authorizations; Regulatory Filings. Sellers will [use their best efforts to] obtain, and will cause each of the Company and the Subsidiaries [to use their best efforts] to obtain (at no cost or burden to the Company or any Subsidiary), within 30 days after the date of this Agreement, all Consents and Governmental Authorizations (the "Required Consents") necessary or reasonably desirable for the consummation of the transactions contemplated by this Agreement or that could, if not obtained, adversely affect the conduct of the business of the Company or any Subsidiary as it is conducted or proposed to be conducted, including those listed on Schedule 6.6[; provided that the Company will not be required to expend any more than $_____ to obtain such Consents]. The Company will keep Buyer reasonably advised of the status of obtaining the Required Consents [not less often than weekly]. [Without limiting the foregoing, no later than the second business day after the date of this Agreement, Sellers will make, and will cause each of the Company and the Subsidiaries to make, all filings and submissions required by them or it under the HSR Act and any other Law applicable to Sellers, or the Company or any Subsidiary, required for the consummation of the transactions contemplated by this Agreement. Sellers will use their best efforts, and will cause the Company to use its best efforts, to obtain an early termination of the applicable waiting period under, and will make any additional filings required pursuant to, the HSR Act.] [Buyer and the Sellers have previously established a program for obtaining the Required Consents, including cooperation and methodology for contacting third parties, the form of required notification and the form of consent (which provides that any Contract may be assigned to Buyer or any of its Affiliates).] [Sellers will cause the Company to pay off all Capital Leases prior to the Closing Date.]

6.7   No Sale. No Seller will sell, pledge, transfer or otherwise place any Encumbrance on any Shares owned by such Seller.

6.8   [Title Insurance and Surveys.

(a)   In preparation for the Closing, as soon as reasonably possible and in no event later than _____, Sellers will cause the Company to furnish to Buyer, at the Sellers' expense, with respect to each parcel of Owned Real Property a title commitment with respect to a title policy conforming to the following standards (i) the title policy will be an ALTA Form 1992 Owner's Policy of Title Insurance (or equivalent policy acceptable to Buyer if the Owned Real Property is located in a state in which an ALTA Owner's Policy of Title Insurance is not available) issued by a title insurer satisfactory to Buyer (and, if requested by Buyer, reinsured in whole or in part by one or more title insurance companies and pursuant to a direct access agreement acceptable to Buyer), in such amount as Buyer may determine to be the fair market value of the Owned Real Property, insuring marketable fee title in the Company or a Subsidiary as of the Closing, subject only to the exceptions shown on Schedule 4.10, (ii) each title policy will (A) insure title to (by including on Schedule A to such policy) all recorded easements or restrictions benefiting such Owned Real Property, (B) contain an "extended coverage endorsement" insuring over the so-called standard exceptions, (C) contain an ALTA 3.1 zoning endorsement (or equivalent), (D) contain an endorsement insuring access to adjacent public street(s), (E) contain a "contiguity" endorsement if the real property consists of more than one record parcel, (F) contain a "non-imputation" endorsement to the effect that title defects known to the officers, directors or shareholders of the Company or any Subsidiary prior to the Closing will not be deemed "facts known to the insured" for purposes of the policy, (G) contain an endorsement that the real property complies with all applicable subdivision Laws and (H) contain such other reasonable endorsements as Buyer may identify prior to Closing. Each commitment will include the title insurer's requirements for issuing its title policy, which requirements shall be met by the Sellers on or before the Closing Date (including those requirements that must be met by releasing or satisfying monetary Encumbrances (including assessments for public improvements levied, pending or deferred against any of the Owned Real Property), but excluding Encumbrances that the Sellers are not required by this Agreement to remove at or prior to Closing and those requirements that are to be met solely by Buyer).

(b)   With respect to each parcel of Real Property as to which a title insurance policy is to be procured pursuant to this Section 6.8, Sellers will cause the Company to furnish to Buyer a current survey of the Real Property certified to Buyer, the title insurer and Buyer's lender, if any, prepared by a licensed surveyor in the state in which such parcel is located and conforming to current ALTA/ACSM Minimum Detail Requirements for Land Title Surveys, disclosing the location of all improvements, easements, party walls, encroachments, sidewalks, roadways, utility lines, set back lines and other matters shown customarily on such surveys, and showing access affirmatively to public streets and roads.

(c)   If (i) any title commitment or other evidence of title or search of the appropriate real estate records discloses that any party other than the Company has title to any of the Owned Real Property; (ii) any title exception is disclosed in Schedule B to any title commitment that is not one of the Permitted Encumbrances or not one that Sellers specify when delivering the title commitment to Buyer that Sellers will cause to be deleted from the title commitment concurrently with the Closing, including (A) any exceptions that pertain to Encumbrances securing any loans that are required by this Agreement to be paid off before Closing and (B) any exceptions that Buyer reasonably believes could materially and adversely affect Buyer's use and enjoyment of the Real Property described therein; or (iii) any survey discloses any matter that Buyer reasonably believes could materially and adversely affect Buyer's use and enjoyment of the Real Property described therein (a "Title Objection"), Buyer will notify Sellers in writing ("Buyer Notice") of such matters within ten business days after receiving all of the title commitments or title evidence and surveys for the Real Property covered thereby. Sellers will use their best efforts to cure each Title Objection and take all steps required by the title insurer to eliminate each Title Objection as an exception to the title commitment. Any Title Objection that the title company is willing to insure over on terms acceptable to Sellers and Buyer is referred to as an "Insured Exception." The Insured Exceptions, together with any title exception or matters disclosed by the survey not objected to by Buyer in the manner aforesaid, will be deemed to be acceptable to Buyer.

6.9   [Post-Closing Access. After the Closing Date, Sellers will afford to Buyer, its accountants and counsel, during normal business hours, upon reasonable request, full access to the books and records of Sellers pertaining to each of the Company and the Subsidiaries.]

6.10   [Litigation Support. In the event and for so long as Buyer, the Company or any Subsidiary is actively contesting or defending against any Litigation in connection with any fact, situation, circumstance, status, condition, activity, practice, plan, occurrence, event, incident, action, failure to act or transaction existing or occurring on or prior to the Closing Date involving the Company or any Subsidiary, each Seller will cooperate in the contest or defense[, make available its personnel] and provide such testimony [and access to its books and records] as may be necessary in connection with the contest or defense, at the cost and expense of Buyer (unless and to the extent Buyer is entitled to indemnification therefor under Article X).]

6.11 [Nondisparagement. No Seller will take any action that is designed or intended to have the effect of discouraging any lessor, licensor, customer, supplier or other business associate of the Company or any Subsidiary from maintaining the same business relationship with each of the Company and the Subsidiaries after the Closing as it maintained with each of the Company and the Subsidiaries prior to the Closing. Each Seller will refer all customer inquiries relating to the business of the Company or any Subsidiary to Buyer from and after the Closing.]

6.12 [Non-Hire. During the period that commences on the Closing Date and ends on the _____ anniversary of the Closing Date, no Seller will[, and each Seller will cause each of its Affiliates not to,] employ (or attempt to employ or interfere with any employment relationship with) any employee of the Company or any Affiliate.]

6.13 [Confidentiality.

(a) Sellers will keep confidential and protect, and will not divulge, allow access to or use in any way, (i) Intellectual Property Rights, including product specifications, formulae, compositions, processes, designs, sketches, photographs, graphs, drawings, samples, inventions and ideas, past, current and planned research and development, current and planned manufacturing and distribution methods and processes, customer lists, current and anticipated customer requirements, price lists, market studies, business plans, Software, database technologies, systems, structures, architectures and data (and related processes, formulae, compositions, improvements, devices, know-how, inventions, discoveries, concepts, ideas, designs, methods and information) and _____ , (ii) any and all information concerning the business and affairs (including historical financial statements, financial projections and budgets, historical and projected sales, capital

401

spending budgets and plans, the names and backgrounds of key personnel, personnel training and techniques and materials and _____), however documented, and (iii) any and all notes, analyses, compilations, studies, summaries and other material containing or based, in whole or in part, on any information included in the foregoing ("Confidential Information") of the Company or any Subsidiary. Sellers acknowledge that such Confidential Information constitutes a unique and valuable asset of the Company or a Subsidiary and represents a substantial investment of time and expense by the Company or a Subsidiary, and that any disclosure or other use of such Confidential Information other than for the sole benefit of the Company or a Subsidiary would be wrongful and would cause irreparable harm to the Company or a Subsidiary. Each Seller will deliver promptly to Buyer or destroy, at the request and option of Buyer, all tangible and intangible embodiments (and all copies) of such Confidential Information that are in the possession of such Seller. The foregoing obligations of confidentiality will not apply to any Confidential Information that is or subsequently becomes generally publicly known, other than as a direct or indirect result of the breach of this Agreement by Sellers.

(b)   Sellers acknowledge that Buyer has required that Sellers make the agreements in this Section 6.13 as a condition to Buyer's purchase of the Shares and consummation of the transactions contemplated by this Agreement. Sellers agree that the agreements contained in this Section 6.13 are reasonable and necessary to protect the legitimate interests of Buyer and that any violation or breach of this Section 6.13 will result in irreparable injury to Buyer for which no adequate remedy would exist at law. Accordingly, in addition to any relief at law that may be available to Buyer for such violation or breach and regardless of any other provision contained in this Agreement, Buyer will be entitled to injunctive and other equitable relief restraining such violation or breach (without any requirement that Buyer provide any bond or other security).

(c)   In the event that any Seller is requested or required (by oral question or request for information or documents in any legal proceeding, interrogatory, subpoena, civil investigative demand or similar process) to disclose any Confidential Information, such Seller will notify Buyer promptly of the request or requirement so that Buyer may seek an appropriate protective order or waive compliance with the provisions of this Section 6.13. If, in the absence of a protective order or the receipt of a waiver from Buyer, such Seller is, on the advice of counsel, compelled to disclose any Confidential Information to any tribunal or else stand liable for contempt, such Seller may disclose the Confidential Information to the tribunal; provided, however, that the disclosing Seller will use such Seller's best efforts to obtain, at the request of Buyer, an order or other assurance that confidential treatment will be accorded to such portion of the Confidential Information required to be disclosed as Buyer designates.]

6.14   [Assignment of Confidentiality Agreements. Effective upon the Closing, each Seller will assign to the Company all of such Seller's right, title and interest in and to any confidentiality agreement to which such Seller or the agent of any such Seller may be a party pertaining to the confidentiality of information relating to the Company or the hiring of employees of the Company. Sellers will request the return or destruction of information covered by any such agreement within two business days of the date of this Agreement to the broadest extent permitted by such confidentiality agreement.]

6.15   [Covenant Not to Compete.

(a)   As an inducement for Buyer to enter into this Agreement and as additional consideration for the consideration to be paid to Sellers under this Agreement, for a period of [five] years from the Closing Date, no Seller [or any Affiliate of such Seller] will, directly or indirectly, engage in, acquire, own or hold a business [anywhere in [insert specific geographic territory, if appropriate] or in any geographic area in which the Company or any Subsidiary conducts business as of the Closing Date that competes with the business of the Company or any Subsidiary [the Business] as conducted prior to the Closing Date [include the following if the 20% exception is used below—including the business of _____ (the "Restricted Business")], including as a proprietor, principal, agent, partner, officer, director, shareholder, employee, member of any association, consultant or otherwise. Ownership by a Seller, as a passive investment, of less than one percent of the outstanding shares of capital stock of any corporation whose stock is listed on a national securities exchange or publicly traded on The NASDAQ National Market will not constitute a breach of this Section 6.15. [Exception to provide flexibility to corporate sellers that might make acquisitions that involve a competing business— Notwithstanding the foregoing, a Seller will not be restricted by the foregoing provisions from acquiring and thereafter owning and operating any business if the revenues attributable to the portion of the business thereof that consists of Restricted Business are less than 20% of the total revenues of such business; provided that within six months after such acquisition, such Seller will cause such business to divest that portion of its assets that constitutes Restricted Business.]

(b)   Sellers acknowledge that Buyer has required that Sellers make the agreements in this Section 6.15 as a condition to Buyer's consummation of the transactions contemplated by this Agreement. Sellers acknowledge that the agreements contained in this Section 6.15 are reasonable (including with respect to duration, geographical area and scope) and necessary to protect the legitimate interests of Buyer and the Company, including the preservation of the business of the Company, and that any violation or breach of this Section 6.15 will result in substantial and irreparable harm to Buyer and the Company for which no adequate remedy would exist at law. Accordingly, in addition to any relief at law that may be available to Buyer for such violation or breach and regardless of any other provision contained in this Agreement, Buyer will be entitled to injunctive and other equitable relief restraining such violation or breach (without any requirement that Buyer provide any bond or other security).

(c)   In the event of a violation or breach by any Seller of any agreement set forth in this Section 6.15, the term of such agreement will be extended by the period of the duration of such violation or breach.

(d)   If the final judgment of a court of competent jurisdiction declares that any term or provision of this Section 6.15 is invalid or unenforceable, the court making the determination of invalidity or unenforceability will have the power to reduce the scope, duration or area of the term or provision, to delete specific words or phrases or to replace any invalid or unenforceable term or provision with a term or provision that is valid and enforceable and that comes closest to expressing the intention of the invalid or unenforceable term or provision, and this Agreement will be enforceable as so modified after the expiration of the time within which the judgment may be appealed.]

6.16   [Use of Name. Seller may continue to use printed materials, signage, websites or similar identifying materials that contain the name or trademark of the Company or any of its affiliates for up to one year after the Closing Date.]

6.17   Release of Claims. Sellers and their successors and assigns waive, release and agree not to bring any claim, demand, cause of action or proceeding, including any cost recovery action, against Buyer under the Comprehensive Environmental Response, Compensation and Liability Act of 1980, as amended, or any state equivalent or any similar Law now existing or hereinafter enacted.

VII. Agreements of Buyer

Buyer agrees with Sellers that:

7.1   Conditions. Buyer will use its best efforts to cause the conditions set forth in Section 8.2 [other than Section 8.2(a) and, in the case of Section 8.2(c), subject to Section 7.2] to be satisfied and to consummate the transactions contemplated by this Agreement as soon as reasonably possible and in any event prior to the Closing Date.

7.2   [Regulatory Filings. No later than the second business day after the date of this Agreement, Buyer will make all filings and submissions required by it under the HSR Act and any other Law applicable to Buyer required for the consummation of the transactions contemplated by this Agreement. Buyer will use its best efforts to obtain an early termination of the applicable waiting period under, and will make any additional filings required pursuant to, the HSR Act; provided, that Buyer will not be required to dispose of, hold separately or make any change in, any portion of its business or assets (or the business or assets of the Company or any Subsidiary) or incur any other burden.]

7.3   [Buyer Shareholders' Meeting.

(a)   Buyer will take all action necessary under all applicable Laws to call, give notice of and hold a meeting of its shareholders to vote on a proposal to approve the issuance of the Buyer Common Stock to be issued pursuant to this Agreement (the "Buyer Shareholders' Meeting"). The Buyer Shareholders' Meeting will be held on a date selected by the Buyer as promptly as practicable [after the date of this Agreement] [after the Form S-4 Registration Statement is declared effective under the Securities Act]. Buyer will ensure that all proxies solicited in connection with the Buyer Shareholders' Meeting are solicited in compliance with all applicable Laws.

(b)   [The proxy statement for the Buyer Shareholders' Meeting will include a statement to the effect that the board of directors of the Buyer recommends that Buyer's shareholders vote to approve the issuance of the Buyer Common Stock to be issued pursuant to this Agreement at the Buyer Shareholders' Meeting.]

7.4   [Listing. Buyer will use its best efforts to cause the shares of Buyer Common Stock being issued in the Merger to be approved for listing (subject to notice of issuance) on the NASDAQ National Market [New York Stock Exchange].]

7.5   [Books and Records; Access. After the Closing Date, Buyer will cause the Company to hold all of the books and records of each of the Company and the Subsidiaries existing on the Closing Date in accordance with Buyer's retention policies in effect from time to time for a period of not less than two years from the Closing Date and, if it thereafter proposes to destroy or dispose of any such books and records, to offer first in writing at least 60 days prior to such proposed destruction or disposition to surrender them to Sellers' Representative at the sole expense of Sellers.

After the Closing Date, Buyer will cause each of the Company and the Subsidiaries to afford Sellers' Representative and its accountants and counsel, during normal business hours, upon reasonable request, full access to such books and records of each of the Company and the Subsidiaries. Buyer will make available to Sellers' Representative upon written request and at the expense of Sellers, but consistent with Buyer's business requirements, reasonable assistance of any of the Company's personnel whose assistance or participation is required by Sellers' Representative, in anticipation of, or preparation for, existing or future litigation or other matters in which Sellers are involved related to the Company.]

7.6   [Employee Matters. Employees of the Company and its Subsidiaries will continue as employees on the Closing Date, subject to the right to terminate the employment of such employees in accordance with law.]

7.7   [Indemnification of Officers and Directors.

(a)   All rights to indemnification existing in favor of those Persons who are, or were, directors and officers of the Company at or prior to the date of this Agreement (the "Indemnified Persons") will survive the Merger and will be observed by the Surviving Corporation to the fullest extent permitted by _____ law for a period of six years from the Closing Date.

(b)   From the Closing Date until the third anniversary of the Closing Date, the Surviving Corporation will maintain in effect, for the benefit of the Indemnified Persons with respect to acts or omissions occurring prior to the Closing Date, the existing policy of directors' and officers' liability insurance maintained by the Company as of the date of this Agreement in the form disclosed by the Company to Buyer prior to the date of this Agreement (the "Existing Policy"); provided, however, that (i) the Surviving Corporation may substitute for the Existing Policy a policy or policies of comparable coverage, and (ii) the Surviving Corporation will not be required to pay annual premiums for the Existing Policy (or for any substitute policies) in excess of $_____ in the aggregate [150% of current premium]. In the event any future annual premiums for the Existing Policy (or any substitute policies) exceeds $_____ in the aggregate [150% of current premium], the Surviving Corporation will be entitled to reduce the amount of coverage of the Existing Policy (or any substitute policies) to the amount of coverage that can be obtained for a premium equal to $_____ [150% of current premium].]

7.8   [Employee Matters. Employees of the Company and its Subsidiaries will continue as employees on the Closing Date, subject to the right to terminate the employment of such employees in accordance with law.]

7.9   [Employment; Employee Benefits.

(a)   Nothing in this Agreement will be construed to create a right in any employee of the Company or any Subsidiary to employment with Buyer, the Surviving Corporation or any other Subsidiary of Buyer (including this Company), and, subject to any agreement between an employee and Buyer, the Surviving Corporation or any other Subsidiary of Buyer (including this Company), the employment of each employee of the Company or any Subsidiary who continues employment with Buyer, the Surviving Corporation or any Subsidiary of the Surviving Corporation (including this Company) after the Closing Date (a "Continuing Employee") will be "at will" employment.

[Alternate—For the one-year period ending on the first anniversary of the Effective Date (the "Continuation Period"), except as otherwise provided in any employment agreement with the Company or any Subsidiary, Buyer will, or will cause the Surviving Corporation or its Subsidiaries to, (i) pay to the employees of the Surviving Corporation or its subsidiaries, during any portion of the Continuation Period that such employee is employed by the Surviving Corporation or any such subsidiary, an annual salary or hourly wage rate and bonus and annual incentives (other than equity-based awards), as applicable, that are no less than the annual salary or hourly wage rate and bonus and annual incentives (other than equity-based awards) payable to such employee immediately prior to the Closing Date and (ii) provide such employees with employee benefits, during any portion of the Continuation Period that such employees are employed by the Surviving Corporation or any such Subsidiary, that are substantially similar in the aggregate to the employee benefits provided to such employees pursuant to the Benefit Plans (other than equity-based benefits) immediately prior to the Closing Date, effective as of the Closing Date [Alternate— (ii) provide such employees in the aggregate with employee benefits, during any portion of the Continuation Period that such employees are employed by the Surviving Corporation or any such Subsidiary, equivalent to those provided to similarly situated employees of Buyer, effective as of the Closing Date]. Nothing in this Agreement will be construed to create a right in any employee of the Surviving Corporation or any Subsidiary to employment with Buyer, the Surviving Corporation or any other Subsidiary of Buyer (including the Company) and, subject to any agreement between an employee and Buyer, the Surviving Corporation or any other Subsidiary of Buyer (including the Company), the employment of each employee of the Surviving Corporation or any Subsidiary who continues employment with Buyer, the Surviving Corporation or any Subsidiary of the Surviving Corporation after the Closing Date (a "Continuing Employee") will be "at will" employment.

(b)   Each Continuing Employee will be eligible to continue to participate in the Surviving Corporation's health, vacation and other non-equity based employee benefit plans; provided, however, that (a) nothing in this Section 7.9(b) or elsewhere in this Agreement will limit the right of Buyer or the Surviving Corporation to amend or terminate any such health, vacation or other employee benefit plan at any time. Nothing in this Section 7.9(b) will be interpreted to require Buyer to provide for the participation of any Continuing Employee in any Buyer Plan. [Alternate—With respect to employee benefit plans, if any, of Buyer or its subsidiaries in which Continuing Employees become eligible to participate after the Closing Date (the "Buyer Plans"), Buyer will, or will cause the Surviving Corporation or its Subsidiaries to: (i) with respect to each Buyer Plan that is a medical or health plan, (x) waive any exclusions for pre-existing conditions under such Buyer Plan that would result in a lack of coverage for any condition for which the applicable Continuing Employee would have been entitled to coverage under the corresponding Benefit Plan in which such Continuing Employee was an active participant immediately prior to his or her transfer to the Buyer Plan; (y) waive any waiting period under such Buyer Plan, to the extent that such period exceeds the corresponding waiting period under the corresponding Benefit Plan in which such Continuing Employee was an active participant immediately prior to his or her transfer to the Buyer Plan (after taking into account the service credit provided for herein for purposes of satisfying such waiting period); and (z) provide each Continuing Employee with credit for any co-payments and deductibles paid by such Continuing Employee prior to his or her transfer to the Buyer Plan (to the same extent such credit was given under the analogous Benefit Plan prior to such transfer) in satisfying any applicable deductible or out-of-pocket requirements under such Buyer Plan for the plan year that includes such transfer and (ii) recognize service of the Continuing Employees with the Company (or their respective predecessors) for purposes of eligibility to participate and vesting credit, and, solely with respect to vacation and severance benefits, benefit accrual in any Buyer Plan in which the Continuing Employees are eligible to participate after the Closing Date, to the extent that such service was recognized for that purpose under the analogous Benefit Plan prior to such transfer; provided, however, that the foregoing will not apply to the extent it would result in duplication of benefits. Nothing in this paragraph will be interpreted to require Buyer to provide for the participation of any Continuing Employee in any Buyer Plan.

(c)   Buyer will cause the Surviving Corporation to honor the employment agreements (subject to the right of the Surviving Corporation to amend and/or terminate such agreements pursuant to the terms thereof) set forth in Schedule 7.9(c).

(d)   Buyer will cause the Surviving Corporation to honor the accrued benefits under each of the Company's non-qualified deferred compensation and retirement plans.

(e)   The Company and Buyer agree to the terms and conditions set forth on Schedule 7.9(e) with respect to certain employee benefits matters.]

VIII. Conditions to Closing

8.1   Conditions to Buyer's Obligations. The obligation of Buyer to take the actions required to be taken by it at the Closing is subject to the satisfaction or waiver, in whole or in part, in Buyer's sole discretion (but no such waiver will waive any rights or remedy otherwise available to Buyer), of each of the following conditions at or prior to the Closing:

(a)   The representations and warranties set forth in Articles III and IV will be true and correct [in all material respects] (without taking into account any supplemental disclosures after the date of this Agreement by Sellers or the Company or the discovery of information by Buyer); [Alternate—The representations and warranties set forth in Articles III and IV will be true and correct as of the Closing Date as though then made and as though the Closing Date had been substituted for the date of this Agreement in such representations and warranties (without taking into account any supplemental disclosures after the date of this Agreement by Sellers or the Company or the discovery of information by Buyer)] [Alternate—The representations and warranties set forth in Articles III and IV that are not subject to materiality or Material Adverse Effect qualifications will be true and correct in all material respects at and as of the Closing Date as though then made and as though the Closing Date had been substituted for the date of this Agreement in such representations and warranties, except that any representation or warranty expressly made as of a specified date will only need to have been true on and as of such date, and the representations and warranties set forth in Articles III and IV that are subject to materiality or Material Adverse Effect qualifications will be true and correct in all respects at and as of the Closing Date as though then made and as though the Closing Date had been substituted for the date of this Agreement in such representations and warranties, except that any representation or warranty expressly made as of a specified date will only need to have been true on and as of such date (without taking into account any

411

supplemental disclosures after the date of this Agreement by Sellers or the Company or the discovery of information by Buyer);] [Alternate—Except as would not have a Material Adverse Effect, the representations and warranties set forth in Articles III and IV, after the word or phrase "material" and "Material Adverse Effect" have been removed, will be true and correct at and as of the Closing Date as though then made and as though the Closing Date had been substituted for the date of this Agreement in such representations and warranties, except that any representation or warranty expressly made as of a specified date will only need to have been true on and as of such date (without taking into account any supplemental disclosures after the date of this Agreement by Sellers or the Company or the discovery of information by Buyer);].

(b)   Sellers will have performed and complied with each of their agreements contained in this Agreement [in all material respects];

(c)   [The applicable waiting periods under the HSR Act will have expired or will have been terminated;]

(d)   Each Required Consent will have been obtained and be in full force and effect and such actions as Buyer's counsel may reasonably require will have been taken in connection therewith;

(e)   Buyer will have obtained each Governmental Authorization required to operate the business of the Company in the manner it was operated prior to the Closing Date;

(f)   Buyer will have received evidence satisfactory to it that no Litigation is pending or threatened (i) challenging or seeking to prevent or delay consummation of any of the transactions contemplated by this Agreement, (ii) asserting the illegality of or seeking to render unenforceable any material provision of this Agreement [or any of the Ancillary Agreements], (iii) seeking to prohibit direct or indirect ownership, combination or operation by Buyer of any portion of the business or assets of the Company or any Subsidiary, or to compel Buyer or any of its Subsidiaries or the Company or any Subsidiary to dispose of, or to hold separately, or to make any change in any portion of the business or assets of Buyer or its Subsidiaries or of the Company or its Subsidiaries, as a result of the transactions contemplated by this Agreement, or incur any burden, (iv) seeking to require direct or indirect transfer or sale by Buyer of, or to impose material limitations on the ability of Buyer to exercise full rights of ownership of, any of the Shares or (v) imposing or seeking to impose material damages or sanctions directly arising out of the transactions contemplated by this Agreement on Buyer or the Company or any of their respective officers or directors;

(g)   No Law or Governmental Order will have been enacted, entered, enforced, promulgated, issued or deemed applicable to the transactions contemplated by this Agreement by any Governmental Entity that would reasonably be expected to result, directly or indirectly, in any of the consequences referred to in Section 8.1(f);

(h)   [After the date of this Agreement,] No Material Adverse Effect will have occurred;

(i)   No Person will have asserted or threatened that, other than as set forth in the Disclosure Schedule, such Person (i) is the owner of, or has the right to acquire or to obtain ownership of, any capital stock of, or any other voting, equity or ownership interest in, the Company or any Subsidiary or (ii) is entitled to all or any portion of the Purchase Price;

(j)   Buyer will have received from [counsel for Sellers and the Company] a written opinion, dated the Closing Date, addressed to Buyer and satisfactory to Buyer's counsel, in the form set forth in Exhibit H;

(k)   [Buyer, a Subsidiary or the Company will have entered into employment, consulting, noncompete or nonsolicitation agreements with such Persons as it may determine, on terms and conditions satisfactory to it, such agreements will be in full force and effect and none of such Persons will have indicated any intention of not fulfilling his or her obligations under any such agreement;]

(l)   Buyer will have entered into noncompetition agreements with _____, _____ and _____, in the form of Exhibit C, such agreements will be in full force and effect and none of such Persons will have indicated any intention of not fulfilling his or her obligations under any such agreement;

(m)   [Buyer will have entered into Affiliate Agreements with each Person who would reasonably be deemed an "affiliate" (as that term is used in Rule 145 under the Securities Act) of the Company, in the form of Exhibit I.]

(n)   Buyer will not have discovered any fact or circumstance existing as of the date of this Agreement not disclosed on the Disclosure Schedule that has a Material Adverse Effect; [Alternative—Buyer will have been satisfied (in its sole discretion) with the results of its continuing business, legal, environmental and accounting due diligence regarding the Company or any Subsidiary;]

(o)   Buyer will have received and will have been satisfied (in its sole and absolute discretion) with the title commitments and surveys described in Section 6.8. [Buyer shall have received unconditional and binding commitments to issue policies of title insurance consistent with Section 6.8, dated the Closing Date, deleting all requirements listed in ALTA Schedule B-1, amending the effective date to the date and time of recordation of the deed transferring title to the Owned Real Property to Buyer with no exception for the gap between closing and recordation, deleting or insuring over Title Objections as required pursuant to Section 6.8, attaching all endorsements required by Buyer in order to ensure provision of all coverage required pursuant to Section 6.8 and otherwise in form satisfactory to Buyer insuring the Company's interest in each parcel of Real Property or interest therein to the extent required by Section 6.8;]

(p)   The Company will have delivered each of the agreements, certificates, instruments and other documents that it is obligated to deliver pursuant to Section 2.8(c)(i), and such agreements so delivered will be in full force and effect;

(q)   [Buyer will have obtained on terms and conditions satisfactory to it the financing it needs in order to consummate the transactions contemplated by this Agreement and to fund the working capital requirements of the Company after the Closing;]

(r)   [Neither the Company nor any Subsidiary will have been, or threatened to be, materially adversely affected in any way as a result of fire, explosion, disaster, accident, labor dispute, any action by any Governmental Entity, flood, act of war, terrorism, civil disturbance or act of nature;]

(s)   [Not more than 5% of the full time employees of the Company and the Subsidiaries will have indicated that they will not continue their employment for an indefinite period after the Closing Date;]

(t)   [At least 90% of the Company's software engineers will have provided assurances to Buyer in a form acceptable to it that they will continue their employment with the Company after the Closing Date;]

(u)   [Other conditions designed to protect Buyer, such as the absence of the occurrence of war, terrorism, a precipitous drop in the market, price of Buyer's stock, general or specific economic conditions, defections of employees, customers or other;]

(v)   [Buyer's shareholders will have approved the issuance of the Buyer Common Stock to be delivered to Sellers;]

(w)   [The shares of Buyer Common Stock to be delivered to Sellers will have been authorized for listing on the [list appropriate market].]

(x)   Buyer will have received a statement from the holder of each note and mortgage listed on Schedule _____, if any, dated the Closing Date, setting forth the principal amount then outstanding on the indebtedness represented by such note or secured by such mortgage, the interest rate thereon and a statement to the effect that the Company, as obligor under such note or mortgage, is not in default under any of the provisions thereof;

(y)   Buyer will have received releases of all Encumbrances on the Real Property, other than Permitted Encumbrances, including releases of each mortgage of record and reconveyances of each deed of trust with respect to each parcel of real property included in the Real Property;

(z)   Buyer will have received certificates dated as of a date not earlier than the [third] business day prior to the Closing as to the good standing of the Company and payment of all applicable state Taxes by the Company, executed by the appropriate officials of the State of _____ and each jurisdiction in which the Company is licensed or qualified to do business as a foreign corporation as specified in Schedule 4.1; and

(aa)   Those key employees of the Company identified on Schedule 8.1(aa), or substitutes therefor who shall be acceptable to Buyer, in its sole discretion, shall have accepted employment with Buyer with such employment to commence on and as of the Closing Date.

8.2   Conditions to Sellers' Obligations. The obligation of Sellers to take the actions required to be taken by them at the Closing is subject to the satisfaction or waiver, in whole or in part, in the sole discretion of Sellers' Representative (but no such waiver will waive any right or remedy otherwise available under this Agreement), of each of the following conditions at or prior to the Closing:

(a)   The representations and warranties set forth in Article V will be true and correct [in all material respects] [Alternate—The representations and warranties set forth in Article V will be true and correct in all material respects as of the Closing Date as though then made and as though the Closing Date had been substituted for the date of this Agreement in such representations and warranties] [Alternate—The representations and warranties set forth in Article V that are not subject to materiality qualifications will be true and correct in all material respects at and as of the

Closing Date as though then made and as though the Closing Date had been substituted for the date of this Agreement in such representations and warranties, except that any representation or warranty expressly made as of a specified date will only need to have been true on and as of such date, and the representations and warranties set forth in Article V that are subject to materiality qualifications will be true and correct in all respects at and as of the Closing Date as though then made and as though the Closing Date had been substituted for the date of this Agreement in such representations and warranties, except that any representation or warranty expressly made as of a specified date will only need to have been true on and as of such date];

(b)　　Buyer will have performed and complied with each of its agreements contained in this Agreement [in all material respects];

(c)　　[The applicable waiting periods under the HSR Act will have expired or been terminated;]

(d)　　No Law or Governmental Order will have been enacted, entered, enforced, promulgated, issued or deemed applicable to the transactions contemplated by this Agreement by any Governmental Entity that prohibits the Closing;

(e)　　[After the date of this Agreement, no Buyer Material Adverse Effect will have occurred;]

(f)　　Buyer will have delivered each of the certificates, instruments and other documents that it is obligated to deliver pursuant to Section 2.8(c)(ii);

(g)　　[Sellers will have received from [counsel for Buyer] a written opinion, dated the Closing Date, addressed to Sellers and satisfactory to Sellers' counsel, in form set forth in Exhibit J;]

(h)　　[Buyer's shareholders will have approved the issuance of the Buyer Common Stock to be issued in connection with this Agreement;] and (i)　　[The shares of Buyer Common Stock to be delivered to Sellers will have been authorized for listing on the [list appropriate market].]

IX. Termination

9.1　　Termination. This Agreement may be terminated prior to the Closing:

(a)　　by the mutual written consent of Buyer and Sellers' Representative;

(b)　　by Sellers' Representative, if

(i)　　Buyer has or will have breached any representation, warranty or agreement contained in this Agreement [in any material respect];

(ii)　　the transactions contemplated by this Agreement will not have been consummated on or before [insert a date giving Buyer ample time to satisfy conditions within its control, such as financing, or insert "the Closing Date"] [; provided, that Sellers' Representative will not be entitled to terminate this Agreement pursuant to this Section 9.1(b)(ii) if Sellers' failure to comply fully with their obligations under this Agreement has prevented the consummation of the transactions contemplated by this Agreement];

(iii)　　a Law or Governmental Order will have been enacted, entered, enforced, promulgated, issued or deemed applicable to the transactions contemplated by this Agreement by any Governmental Entity that prohibits the Closing;

(iv)　　[after the date of this Agreement, a Buyer Material Adverse Effect will have occurred;]

(v) [the issuance of the Buyer Common Stock will not have been approved at the Buyer Shareholders' Meeting.]; or

(vi) any of the conditions set forth in Section 8.2 will have become impossible to satisfy;

(c) by Buyer, if

(i) any Seller has or will have breached any representation, warranty or agreement contained in this Agreement [in any material respect];

(ii) the transactions contemplated by this Agreement will not have been consummated on the Closing Date [Alternate—Insert a date long enough to clear HSR yet short enough so that Buyer may terminate if there has been a second request—perhaps 60 days (note that Buyer will still have a best efforts obligation prior to the termination) an alternative would be to provide that the second request itself creates a termination right] [; provided, that Buyer will not be entitled to terminate this Agreement pursuant to this Section 9.1(c)(ii) if Buyer's failure to comply fully with its obligations under this Agreement has prevented the consummation of the transactions contemplated by this Agreement;]

(iii) a Law or Governmental Order will have been enacted, entered, enforced, promulgated, issued or deemed applicable to the transactions contemplated by this Agreement by any Governmental Entity that would reasonably be expected to result directly or indirectly, in any of the consequences referred to in Section 8.1(d).

(iv) [after the date of this Agreement,] a Material Adverse Effect will have occurred;

(v) any of the conditions set forth in Section 8.1 will have become impossible to satisfy;

(vi) Buyer will have discovered any fact or circumstance existing as of the date of this Agreement that has not been previously disclosed on the Disclosure Schedule that has a Material Adverse Effect; [Alternative— if Buyer will not have been satisfied with the results of its continuing business, legal, environmental and accounting due diligence regarding each of the Company and the Subsidiaries;]

(vii) [Buyer will not have been able to obtain by [date], on terms and conditions satisfactory to it, the financing it needs in order to consummate the transactions contemplated in this Agreement and fund the working capital requirements of the Company after the Closing;]

(viii) [the Company or any Subsidiary will have been, or will have been threatened to be, materially adversely affected in any way as a result of fire, explosion, disaster, accident, labor dispute, any action by any Governmental Entity, flood, act of war, terrorism, civil disturbance or act of nature;]

(ix) [other termination rights designed to protect Buyer, such as the occurrence of war, terrorism, a precipitous drop in the market, price of Buyer's stock, general or specific economic conditions, defections of employees, customers or other]; or

(x) [the issuance of Buyer Common Stock will not have been approved at the Buyer Shareholders' Meeting.]

9.2 Effect of Termination. The right of termination under Section 9.1 is in addition to any other rights Buyer or Sellers may have under this Agreement or otherwise, and the exercise of a right of termination will not be an election of remedies and will not preclude an action for breach of this Agreement. If this Agreement is terminated, all continuing obligations of the parties under this Agreement will terminate except that Article XII and the Confidentiality Agreement will survive indefinitely unless sooner terminated or modified by the parties in writing.

X. Indemnification

10.1   Indemnification by Sellers.

(a)   Sellers will, jointly and severally, indemnify in full each of Buyer, the Company and the Subsidiaries (collectively, for purposes of this Article X only, "Buyer") and hold it harmless against any Loss, whether or not actually incurred prior to the applicable date referred to in Section 10.1(d), arising from, relating to or constituting (i) any breach or inaccuracy in any of the representations and warranties of Sellers contained in this Agreement or in the Disclosure Schedule as the same may be brought down to the Closing Date or any closing certificate delivered by or on behalf of Sellers pursuant to this Agreement (any such breach or inaccuracy to be determined without regard to any qualification for "materiality," "in all material respects" or similar qualification), (ii) any product sold, manufactured or licensed by, any services provided by, or the ownership, lease or control of property by the Company or any Subsidiary prior to the Closing Date, (iii) any matter disclosed on Schedule 10.1 or [reference other particular items for which indemnification is to be provided], (iv) [other consequences, such as failure to discharge indebtedness] of the Company or to effectuate the cancellation of Company Options, (v) any liability of the Company or any Subsidiary for Taxes incurred on or prior to the Closing Date; (vi) failure of Sellers to assume, pay and discharge the obligations of the Company and its Subsidiaries pursuant to Section _____; (vii) any claim by a customer of Buyer for a credit, discount or payment arising out of any sales made by the Company on or prior to the Closing Date; (viii) any liability under the WARN Act or any similar state or local Law that may result from an "Employment Loss," as defined by 29 U.S.C. 2101(a)(6), caused by any action of the Company prior to the Closing or by Buyer's decision not to retain employees of the Company; (ix) any Plan established or maintained by the Company; or (x) any breach of any of the agreements of any Seller contained in this Agreement (collectively, "Buyer Losses"). [The parties agree that, in determining the amount of any Buyer Loss, the basis for Buyer's formulation of the Purchase Price, including any multiple of earnings, cash flows or related measures, will be considered.]

(b)   Sellers will indemnify Buyer for Buyer Losses (i) resulting from breaches or inaccuracies of Sections 4.6 through 4.28 and (ii) pursuant to Section 10.1(a)(ii) only if the aggregate amount of all Buyer Losses attributable to clauses (i) and (ii) exceeds $_____ (the "Basket Amount"), in which case Sellers will be liable [only for the aggregate amount of all such Buyer Losses in excess of the Basket Amount] [or] [for the aggregate amount of all Buyer Losses].

(c)   [Sellers' liability will not exceed $_____ for Buyer Losses (i) resulting from breaches or inaccuracies of Sections 4.6 through 4.28, or (ii) pursuant to Section 10.1(a)(ii).]

(d)   If Buyer has a claim for indemnification under this Section 10.1, Buyer will deliver to Sellers' Representative one or more written notices of Buyer Losses (each a "Buyer Claim"), with a copy to the Escrow Agent, prior to the [third] anniversary of the Closing Date, except for Buyer Losses arising from a breach or inaccuracy in the representations and warranties made in Sections 4.13, 4.19 or 4.22 or any breach of any of the agreements by any Seller contained in this Agreement, for which Buyer will deliver a Buyer Claim prior to six months after the expiration of the applicable statute of limitations. Sellers will have no liability under this Section 10.1 unless the written notices required by the preceding sentence are given by the date specified. Any Buyer Claim will state in reasonable detail the basis for such Buyer Losses to the extent then known by Buyer and the nature of the Buyer Loss for which indemnification is sought, and it may state the amount of the Buyer Loss claimed. If such Buyer Claim (or an amended Buyer Claim) states the amount of the Buyer Loss claimed and Sellers' Representative notifies Buyer that Sellers' Representative does not dispute the claim described in such notice or fails to notify Buyer within 20 business days after delivery of such notice by Buyer whether Sellers disputes the claim described in such notice, the Buyer Loss in the amount specified in Buyer's notice will be admitted by Sellers (an "Admitted Claim"), and Sellers will pay the amount of such Buyer Loss to Buyer. If Sellers'

Representative has timely disputed the liability of Sellers with respect to a Buyer Claim (or an amended Buyer Claim) stating the amount of a Buyer Loss claimed, Sellers' Representative and Buyer will proceed in good faith to negotiate a resolution of such dispute. If a claim for indemnification has not been resolved within 30 days after delivery of the Sellers' Representative's notice, Buyer may seek judicial recourse. If a Buyer Claim does not state the amount of the Buyer Loss claimed, such omission will not preclude Buyer from recovering from Sellers the amount of the Buyer Loss described in such Buyer Claim if any such amount is subsequently provided in an amended Buyer Claim. In order to assert its right to indemnification under this Article X, Buyer will not be required to provide any notice except as provided in this Section 10.1(d).

(e)   Sellers will pay the amount of any Buyer Loss to Buyer within 10 days following the determination of Sellers' liability for and the amount of a Buyer Loss (whether such determination is made pursuant to the procedures set forth in this Section 10.1, by agreement between Buyer and Sellers' Representative, by arbitration award or by final adjudication).

(f)   [Buyer may elect to recoup all or any part of any Buyer Loss it suffers (in lieu of seeking any indemnification to which it is entitled under this Section 10.1) by notifying Sellers' Representative of such election and offsetting the amount of any payment required to be made pursuant to Section 2.5 or 2.9 or by offsetting principal or interest of the Buyer Notes [or payments to be made under any Ancillary Agreements.]. Such election will be considered a permitted prepayment (without premium or penalty) under the Buyer Notes as of the date of such notice.]

10.2   Indemnification by Buyer.

(a)   Buyer will indemnify in full Sellers and hold them harmless against any Loss, whether or not actually incurred prior to the date referred to in Section 10.2(d), arising from, relating to or constituting (i) any breach or inaccuracy in any of the representations and warranties of Buyer contained in this Agreement or in any certificate delivered by or on behalf of Buyer

423

pursuant to this Agreement (any such breach or inaccuracy to be determined without regard to any qualification as to "materiality," "in all material respects" or similar qualification) or (ii) any breach of any of the agreements of Buyer contained in this Agreement ("Sellers Losses").

(b)   Buyer will indemnify the Company for the Company Losses pursuant to Section 10.2(a)(i) only if the aggregate amount of all Sellers Losses attributable to Section 10.2(a)(i) exceeds $_____ (the "Sellers' Basket Amount"), in which case Buyer will be liable [only for the aggregate amount of all such Sellers Losses in excess of Sellers' Basket Amount] [or] [for the aggregate amount of all Sellers Losses].

(c)   [Buyer's liability will not exceed $_____ for Sellers Losses attributable to Section 10.2(a)(i).]

(d)   If Sellers have a claim for indemnification under this Section 10.2, Sellers will deliver to Buyer one or more written notices of Sellers Losses prior to the [third] anniversary of the Closing Date. Buyer will have no liability under this Section 10.2 unless the written notices required by the preceding sentence are given in a timely manner. Any written notice will state in reasonable detail the basis for such Sellers Losses to the extent then known by Sellers and the nature of Sellers Losses for which indemnification is sought, and it may state the amount of Sellers Losses claimed. If such written notice (or an amended notice) states the amount of Sellers Losses claimed and Buyer notifies Sellers that Buyer does not dispute the claim described in such notice or fails to notify Sellers within 20 business days after delivery of such notice by Sellers whether Buyer disputes the claim described in such notice, Sellers Losses in the amount specified in Sellers' notice will be admitted by Buyer, and Buyer will pay the amount of such Sellers Losses to Sellers. If Buyer has timely disputed its liability with respect to such claim, Buyer and Sellers' Representative will proceed in good faith to negotiate a resolution of such dispute. If a claim for indemnification has not been resolved within 30 days after delivery of Buyer's notice, the Sellers may seek judicial recourse. If a written notice does not state the amount of Sellers

Losses claimed, such omission will not preclude Sellers from recovering from Buyer the amount of Sellers Losses with respect to the claim described in such notice if any such amount is promptly provided once determined. In order to assert its right to indemnification under this Article X, Sellers will not be required to provide any notice except as provided in this Section 10.2.

(e)   Buyer will pay the amount of any Sellers Losses to Sellers within 10 days following the determination of Buyer's liability for and the amount of the Sellers Losses (whether such determination is made pursuant to the procedures set forth in this Section 10.2, by agreement between Sellers and Buyer, by arbitration award or by final adjudication).

10.3   Third-Party Actions.

(a)   Sellers will, jointly and severally, indemnify, defend and hold harmless each of Buyer, the Company and the Subsidiaries and their officers, directors, employees, agents, shareholders and Affiliates (collectively, the "Buyer Indemnified Parties") against any Loss arising from, relating to or constituting any Litigation instituted by any third party arising out of the actions or inactions of Sellers or the Company (or allegations thereof) whether occurring prior to, on or after the Closing Date [that are or may be Buyer Losses] (any such third party action or proceeding being referred to as a "Third-Party Action"). A Buyer Indemnified Party will give Sellers' Representative prompt written notice of the commencement of a Third-Party Action. The complaint or other papers pursuant to which the third party commenced such Third-Party Action will be attached to such written notice. The failure to give prompt written notice will not affect any Buyer Indemnified Party's right to indemnification unless such failure has materially and adversely affected Sellers' ability to defend successfully such Third-Party Action.

(b)   Sellers will contest and defend such Third-Party Action on behalf of any Buyer Indemnified Party that requests that they do so. Notice of the intention to so contest and defend will be given by Sellers' Representative to the requesting Buyer Indemnified

Party within 20 business days after the Buyer Indemnified Party's notice of such Third-Party Action (but, in all events, at least five business days prior to the date that a response to such Third-Party Action is due to be filed). Such contest and defense will be conducted by reputable attorneys retained by Sellers. A Buyer Indemnified Party will be entitled at any time, at its own cost and expense, to participate in such contest and defense and to be represented by attorneys of its own choosing. If the Buyer Indemnified Party elects to participate in such defense, the Buyer Indemnified Party will cooperate with Sellers in the conduct of such defense. A Buyer Indemnified Party will cooperate with Sellers to the extent reasonably requested by Sellers in the contest and defense of such Third-Party Action, including providing reasonable access (upon reasonable notice) to the books, records and employees of the Buyer Indemnified Party if relevant to the defense of such Third-Party Action; provided, that such cooperation will not unduly disrupt the operations of the business of the Buyer Indemnified Party or cause the Buyer Indemnified Party to waive any statutory or common law privileges, breach any confidentiality obligations owed to third parties or otherwise cause any confidential information of such Buyer Indemnified Party to become public.

(c)   If any Buyer Indemnified Party does not request that Sellers contest and defend a Third-Party Action[, on the basis that such Third-Party Action imposes a significant reputational or monetary risk to Buyer, as determined by Buyer in its sole discretion], or if after such request Sellers do not contest and defend a Third-Party Action or if any Buyer Indemnified Party reasonably determines that Sellers are not adequately representing or, because of a conflict of interest, may not adequately represent any interests of the Buyer Indemnified Party at any time after requesting Sellers to do so, such Buyer Indemnified Party will be entitled to conduct its own defense and to be represented by attorneys of its own choosing, all at Sellers' cost and expense. Sellers will pay as incurred (no later than 25 days after presentation) the fees and expenses of the counsel retained by such Buyer Indemnified Party.

(d)   Neither a Buyer Indemnified Party nor Sellers may concede, settle or compromise any Third-Party Action without the consent of the other party, which consents will not be unreasonably withheld. Notwithstanding the foregoing, (i) if a Third-Party Action seeks the issuance of an injunction, the specific election of an obligation or similar remedy or (ii) if the subject matter of a Third-Party Action relates to the ongoing business of any Buyer Indemnified Party, which Third-Party Action, if decided against any Buyer Indemnified Party, would materially adversely affect the ongoing business or reputation of any Buyer Indemnified Party, the Buyer Indemnified Party alone will be entitled to settle such Third-Party Action in the first instance and, if the Buyer Indemnified Party does not settle such Third-Party Action, Sellers will then have the right to contest and defend (but not settle) such Third-Party Action.

10.4   Escrow. To the extent funds are available in the Escrow Fund, Buyer will be entitled to have Sellers' obligation satisfied by transfer of monies in the Escrow Fund to Buyer. The availability of the Escrow Fund will not affect Buyer's rights under this Article X. [Sellers will remain responsible for any liability in excess of the Escrow Fund.] [The indemnification obligations of Sellers will be satisfied solely from the Escrow Fund.] [The costs and expenses of defense and the cost of any judgment or settlement pursuant to Section 10.3 may be paid from the Escrow Fund with the consent of Buyer.]

10.5   Sole and Exclusive Remedy. Prior to or in connection with the Closing, the parties will have available to them all remedies available at law or in equity, including specific performance or other equitable remedies. After the Closing, the rights set forth in Sections 10.1, 10.2 and, to the extent applicable, 10.3 will be the exclusive remedy for breach or inaccuracy of any of the representations and warranties contained in Article III through V of this Agreement and will be in lieu of contract remedies, but the parties otherwise will have available to them all other remedies available at law or in equity. Notwithstanding the foregoing, nothing in this Agreement will prevent any party from bringing an action based upon fraud or willful misconduct by the other party in connection with this Agreement.

In the event such action is brought, the prevailing party's attorneys' fees and costs will be paid by the nonprevailing party.

10.6   Tax Adjustment. Any payment to Buyer under this Article X will be, for Tax purposes, to the extent permitted by Law, an adjustment to the Purchase Price. In calculating any Loss, the amount will be increased to give effect to any Tax related to the receipt of any payment and the amount will be decreased to give effect to any benefit related to the increase of such Loss to the extent actually received by Buyer.

10.7   Indemnification in Case of Strict Liability or Indemnitee Negligence. THE INDEMNIFICATION PROVISIONS IN THIS ARTICLE X WILL BE ENFORCEABLE REGARDLESS OF WHETHER THE LIABILITY IS BASED UPON PAST, PRESENT OR FUTURE ACTS, CLAIMS OR LAWS (INCLUDING ANY PAST, PRESENT OR FUTURE BULK SALES LAW, ENVIRONMENTAL LAW, FRAUDULENT TRANSFER ACT, OCCUPATIONAL SAFETY AND HEALTH LAW OR PRODUCTS LIABILITY, SECURITIES OR OTHER LAW) AND REGARDLESS OF WHETHER ANY PERSON (INCLUDING THE PERSON FROM WHOM INDEMNIFICATION IS SOUGHT) ALLEGES OR PROVES THE SOLE, CONCURRENT, CONTRIBUTORY OR COMPARATIVE NEGLIGENCE OF THE PERSON SEEKING INDEMNIFICATION OR THE SOLE OR CONCURRENT STRICT LIABILITY IMPOSED UPON THE PERSON SEEKING INDEMNIFICATION.

XI. [Allocation of Taxes; Tax Return

11.1   Allocation of Tax Liabilities.

(a)   Seller will be responsible for all Taxes of each of the Company and the Subsidiaries regardless of when due and payable, (i) with respect to all Tax periods ending on or prior to the Closing Date and (ii) with respect to all Tax periods beginning before the Closing Date and ending after the Closing Date, but only with respect to the portion of such period up to and including the Closing Date; provided, however, Seller will not be responsible for the foregoing Taxes to the extent such Taxes are accrued on the books of the Company or any Subsidiary in the Ordinary Course of Business through the Closing Date.

(b)　　Buyer will be responsible for all Taxes of each of the Company and the Subsidiaries, regardless of when due and payable, (i) with respect to all Tax periods beginning after the Closing Date, (ii) with respect to all Tax periods beginning before the Closing Date and ending after the Closing Date, but only with respect to (A) the portion of such period commencing after the Closing Date or (B) to the extent such Taxes are accrued on the books of the Company or any Subsidiary in the Ordinary Course of Business through the Closing Date.

11.2　　Tax Return.

(a)　　Seller will include the income or loss of the Company and the Subsidiaries for all Tax periods ending on or before the Closing Date on Seller's timely filed income Return and will file all such Return when due (including extensions). Seller will cause to be prepared, and will cause to be filed when due (including any extensions), all other Return of the Company and the Subsidiaries for all Tax periods ending on or before the Closing Date for which Return have not been filed as of such date. Where such other Return must be filed by the Company or its Subsidiaries, upon the request of Seller, Buyer will cause such Return to be filed when due (including any extensions). Seller will submit copies (in the case of consolidated Return, the consolidating portion thereof applicable to the Company and the Subsidiaries) to Buyer at least 30 days prior to the due date, as it may be extended, for Buyer's review and approval. Seller will cause all such Return to be accurate and complete in accordance with applicable Laws and to be prepared on a basis consistent with the Return filed by or on behalf of the Company and the Subsidiaries for the preceding Tax period.

(b)　　Buyer will prepare and file when due (including any extensions) all Return of the Company and the Subsidiaries for Tax periods ending after the Closing Date; provided, however, that Seller will have the right to review and approve prior to filing all

Return for any Tax period that includes the Closing Date or any period prior to the Closing Date.

11.3   Income and Loss Allocation. For purposes of this Article XI, in the case of any Taxes that are imposed on a periodic basis and are payable for a Tax period that includes (but does not end on) the Closing Date, the portion of such Tax related to the Tax period ending on the Closing Date will (i) in the case of Taxes other than Taxes based upon or related to income, sales, gross receipts, wages, capital expenditures, expenses or any similar Tax base, be deemed to be the amount of such Tax for the entire period multiplied by a fraction, the numerator of which is the number of days in the Tax period ending on the Closing Date and the denominator of which is the number of days in the entire Tax period and (ii) in the case of any Tax based upon or related to income, sales, gross receipts, wages, capital expenditures, expenses or any similar Tax base, be deemed equal to the amount that would be payable if the relevant Tax period had ended on the Closing Date. All determinations necessary to give effect to the foregoing allocations will be made in a manner consistent with prior practice of the Company and the Subsidiaries.

11.4   Cooperation. After the Closing Date, Buyer and Seller will make available to the other, as reasonably requested, all information, records or documents (including state apportionment information) relating to Tax liabilities or potential Tax liabilities of the Company or any Subsidiary with respect to (i) Tax periods ending on or prior to the Closing Date and (ii) Tax periods beginning before the Closing Date and ending after the Closing Date, but only with respect to the portion of such period up to and including the Closing Date. Buyer and Seller will preserve all such information, records and documents until the expiration of any applicable statute of limitations thereof. Buyer will prepare and provide to Seller any information or documents reasonably requested by Seller for Seller's use in preparing or reviewing the Return referred to in Section 11.2. Notwithstanding any other provision hereof, each party will bear its own expenses in complying with the foregoing provisions.

11.5   [Audits. Each party will promptly notify the other in writing upon receipt by such party (or any of its Tax Affiliates) of notice of any pending or threatened Tax liabilities of the Company or its Subsidiaries for any (i) Tax period ending on or before the Closing Date or (ii) Tax Period ending after the Closing Date but which includes the Closing Date. Seller will have the sole right to represent the interests of the Company and the Subsidiaries in any Tax audit or administrative or court proceeding for Tax periods ending on or prior to the Closing Date and to employ counsel of its choice at its expense, and Buyer and Seller agree to cooperate in the defense of any claim in such proceeding. Seller will have the right to participate at its expense in representing the interests of the Company and the Subsidiaries in any Tax audit or administrative or court proceeding for any Tax period ending after the Closing Date, if and to the extent that such period includes any Tax Period before the Closing Date, and to employ counsel of its choice at its expense. Seller and Buyer agree to cooperate in the defense of any claim in such proceeding.]

11.6   Tax Refunds.

(a)   All refunds of Taxes relating to the Company or any Subsidiary received by Seller or any of its Tax Affiliates with respect to Tax periods ending on or before the Closing Date and involving Seller's consolidated returns will be for the account of Seller. At Seller's request, Buyer will pay over to Seller any such refunds that Buyer may receive immediately upon receipt of such request.

(b)   All other refunds of Taxes with respect to the Company or any Subsidiary will be for the account of Buyer. At Buyer's request, Seller will take such action as reasonably requested by Buyer to obtain such refunds and will pay over to Buyer any such refunds immediately upon receipt thereof.

11.7   Tax Sharing Agreements. All tax sharing agreements between Seller, on the one hand, and the Company or any Subsidiary, on the other hand, will be terminated [without further liability]as of the Closing Date after normal operations [but before the "deemed sale of assets" under Section 338(h)(10)].

11.8   [Section 338(h)(10) Election.

(a)   Buyer and Seller will make an election under Section 338(h)(10) of the Code (and any comparable election under state or local law) with respect to the acquisition of the Company by Buyer. Buyer and Seller will cooperate fully with each other in the making of such election including the filing of all required IRS forms and related forms under state and local Law. Buyer and Seller will endeavor in good faith to agree on an allocation of the Purchase Price among the assets of the Company and the Subsidiaries for purposes of Section 338 of the Code prior to the Closing Date to be evidenced by a written schedule signed and dated by Buyer and Seller, and Buyer and Seller will each file their Tax Return in a manner consistent with such allocation.

(b)   Seller will pay all Taxes attributable to the making of the Section 338(h)(10) election, including any federal, state, local or foreign Tax attributable to an election under federal, state, local or foreign law similar to the election available under Section 338(h)(10) of the Code.

(c)   Seller will cause each partnership or limited liability company that is at least 50% owned, either directly or indirectly, by the Company, to make an election under Section 754 of the Code and Treasury Regulations Section 1.754-1(b) to adjust the basis of the partnership or limited liability company property in the manner provided in Sections 734(b) and 743(b) of the Code to be effective for the tax year that includes the deemed asset sale under Section 338(h)(10) of the Code.

(d)   Buyer will initially prepare a complete set of IRS Forms 8023 (and any comparable forms required to be filed under state, local or foreign tax law) and any additional data or materials required to be attached to Form 8023 pursuant to the Treasury Regulations promulgated under Section 338 of the Code ("Section 338 Forms"). Buyer will deliver such forms to Seller for review no later than 60 days prior to the date the Section 338 Forms are required to be filed. In the event Seller reasonably objects to the manner in which the Section 338 Forms have been prepared, Seller will notify Buyer within 15 days of receipt of the Section 338 Forms of such objection, and the parties will endeavor within the next 15 days to resolve such dispute in good faith. If the parties are unable to resolve such dispute within such 15-day period, Buyer and Seller will submit such dispute to an independent accounting firm of recognized national standing (the "Allocation Arbiter") selected by Buyer or Seller, which firm will not be the regular accounting firm of Buyer or Seller. Promptly, but not later than 15 days after its acceptance of appointment under this Agreement, the Allocation Arbiter will determine (based solely on representations of Buyer and Seller and not by independent review) only those matters in dispute and will render a written report as to the disputed matters and the resulting preparation of the Section 338 Forms will be conclusive and binding upon the parties.]]

XII. General

12.1   Press Releases and Announcements. Any public announcement, including any announcement to employees, customers, suppliers or others having dealings with the Company or any Subsidiary, or similar publicity with respect to this Agreement or the transactions contemplated by this Agreement, will be issued, if at all, at such time and in such manner as Buyer determines and approves. Buyer will have the right to be present for any in-person announcement by the Company. Unless consented to by Buyer or required by Law, Sellers will keep, and Sellers will cause each of the Company and the Subsidiaries to keep, this Agreement and the transactions contemplated by this Agreement confidential.

12.2   Expenses. Except as otherwise expressly provided for in this Agreement, Sellers, on the one hand, and Buyer, on the other hand, will each pay all expenses incurred by each of them (and, in the case of Sellers, the expenses incurred by the Company and Sellers' Representative) in connection with the transactions contemplated by this Agreement, including legal, accounting, investment banking and consulting fees and expenses incurred in negotiating, executing and delivering this Agreement and the other agreements, exhibits, documents and instruments contemplated by this Agreement (whether the transactions contemplated by this Agreement are consummated or not). Sellers agree that neither the Company nor any Subsidiary has borne or will bear any of Sellers' expenses in connection with the transactions contemplated by this Agreement. Sellers will pay all amounts payable to the title insurer in respect of the title commitments, copies of exceptions and title policies, including premiums (including premiums for endorsements), search fees and closing fees, and amounts payable to surveyors. Buyer will pay one-half and the Sellers will pay one-half of (a) the HSR Act filing fee and (b) the fees and expenses of the escrow agent under the Escrow Agreement.

12.3   Amendment and Waiver. This Agreement may not be amended, a provision of this Agreement or any default, misrepresentation or breach of warranty or agreement under this Agreement may not be waived, and a consent may not be rendered, except in a writing executed by the party against which such action is sought to be enforced. Neither the failure nor any delay by any Person in exercising any right, power or privilege under this Agreement will operate as a waiver of such right, power or privilege, and no single or partial exercise of any such right, power or privilege will preclude any other or further exercise of such right, power or privilege or the exercise of any other right, power or privilege. In addition, no course of dealing between or among any Persons having any interest in this Agreement will be deemed effective to modify or amend any part of this Agreement or any rights or obligations of any Person under or by reason of this Agreement. The rights and remedies of the parties to this Agreement are cumulative and not alternative.

12.4   Notices. All notices, demands and other communications to be given or delivered under or by reason of the provisions of this Agreement will be in writing and will be deemed to have been given (i) when delivered if personally delivered by hand (with written confirmation of receipt), (ii) when received if sent by a nationally recognized overnight courier service (receipt requested), (iii) five business days after being mailed, if sent by first class mail, return receipt requested, or (iv) when receipt is acknowledged by an affirmative act of the party receiving notice, if sent by facsimile, telecopy or other electronic transmission device (provided that such an acknowledgement does not include an acknowledgment generated automatically by a facsimile or telecopy machine or other electronic transmission device). Notices, demands and communications to Buyer, Sellers and Sellers' Representative will, unless another address is specified in writing, be sent to the address indicated below:

If to Buyer:

> [Name
>
> Address
>
> Attn:
>
> Facsimile No.]

With a copy to:

> [Counsel
>
> Address
>
> Attn:
>
> Facsimile No.]

If to Sellers or Sellers' Representative:

> [Name of Sellers' Representative
>
> Address
>
> Attn:
>
> Facsimile No.]

With a copy to:

> [Counsel
>
> Address
>
> Attn:
>
> Facsimile No.]

12.5   Assignment. Neither this Agreement nor any of the rights, interests or obligations under this Agreement may be assigned by any party to this Agreement without the prior written consent of the other parties to this Agreement, except that Buyer may assign any of its rights under this Agreement to one or more Subsidiaries of Buyer, so long as Buyer remains responsible for the performance of all of its obligations under this Agreement. Subject to the foregoing, this Agreement and all of the provisions of this Agreement will be binding upon and inure to the benefit of the parties to this Agreement and their respective successors and permitted assigns.

12.6   No Third-Party Beneficiaries. [Except as provided in Sections _____, _____ and _____,] Nothing expressed or referred to in this Agreement confers any rights or remedies upon any Person that is not a party or permitted assign of a party to this Agreement.

12.7   Severability. [If the Agreement contains a noncompetition provision that itself has a severability clause, use the following lead-in—In addition to the severability provisions of Section 6.15, whenever] Whenever possible, each provision of this Agreement will be interpreted in such manner as to be effective and valid under applicable Law, but if any provision of this Agreement is held to be prohibited by or invalid under applicable Law, such provision will be ineffective only to the extent of such prohibition or invalidity, without invalidating the remainder of such provision or the remaining provisions of this Agreement.

12.8   Complete Agreement. This Agreement, the Confidentiality Agreement and, when executed and delivered, the Ancillary Agreements contain the complete agreement between the parties and supersede any prior understandings, agreements or representations by or between the parties, written or oral. Sellers acknowledge that Buyer has made no representations, warranties, agreements, undertakings or promises except for those expressly set forth in this Agreement or in agreements referred to herein that survive the execution and delivery of this Agreement

12.9   Schedules. The Disclosure Schedule contains a series of schedules corresponding to the sections contained in Articles III and IV. Nothing in the Disclosure Schedule is deemed adequate to disclose an exception to a representation or warranty made in this Agreement unless the Disclosure

Schedule identifies in the corresponding schedule the exception with particularity and describes the relevant facts in detail. Without limiting the generality of the foregoing, the mere listing (or inclusion of a copy) of a document or other item is not deemed adequate to disclose an exception to a representation or warranty unless the representation or warranty relates solely to the existence of the document or other item itself. The schedules in the Disclosure Schedule relate only to the representations and warranties in the section and subsection of this Agreement to which they correspond and not to any other representation or warranty in this Agreement. In the event of any inconsistency between the statements in this Agreement and statements in the Disclosure Schedule, the statements in this Agreement will control and the statements in the Disclosure Schedule will be disregarded.

12.10   Signatures; Counterparts. This Agreement may be executed in one or more counterparts, any one of which need not contain the signatures of more than one party, but all such counterparts taken together will constitute one and the same instrument. A facsimile signature will be considered an original signature.

12.11   Governing Law. THE DOMESTIC LAW, WITHOUT REGARD TO CONFLICTS OF LAWS PRINCIPLES, OF THE STATE OF DELAWARE WILL GOVERN ALL QUESTIONS CONCERNING THE CONSTRUCTION, VALIDITY AND INTERPRETATION OF THIS AGREEMENT AND THE PERFORMANCE OF THE OBLIGATIONS IMPOSED BY THIS AGREEMENT.

12.12   Specific Performance. Each of the parties acknowledges and agrees that the subject matter of this Agreement, including the business, assets and properties of the Company and the Subsidiaries, is unique, that the other parties would be damaged irreparably in the event any of the provisions of this Agreement are not performed in accordance with their specific terms or otherwise are breached, and that the remedies at law would not be adequate to compensate such other parties not in default or in breach. Accordingly, each of the parties agrees that the other parties will be entitled to an injunction or injunctions to prevent breaches of the provisions of this Agreement and to enforce specifically this Agreement and the terms and provisions of this Agreement in addition to any other remedy to which they may be entitled, at law or in equity (without any requirement that Buyer provide any bond or other security). The parties waive any defense that a remedy at law is adequate and any requirement to post bond or provide similar security in connection with actions instituted for injunctive relief or specific performance of this Agreement.

12.13 Jurisdiction. Subject to the procedures specified in Article II, each of the parties submits to the exclusive jurisdiction of any state or federal court sitting in Wilmington, Delaware, in any action or proceeding arising out of or relating to this Agreement and agrees that all claims in respect of the action or proceeding may be heard and determined in any such court. Each party also agrees not to bring any action or proceeding arising out of or relating to this Agreement in any other court. Each of the parties waives any defense of inconvenient forum to the maintenance of any action or proceeding so brought and waives any bond, surety or other security that might be required of any other party with respect to any such action or proceeding. Each party appoints CT Corporation System (the "Process Agent") as its agent to receive on its behalf service of copies of the summons and complaint and any other process that might be served in the action or proceeding. Any party may make service on any other party by sending or delivering a copy of the process (i) to the party to be served or (ii) to the party to be served in care of the Process Agent at the following address:_____, _____. The parties agree that either or both of them may file a copy of this paragraph with any court as written evidence of the knowing, voluntary and bargained agreement between the parties irrevocably to waive any objections to venue or to convenience of forum. [Alternative—Process in any proceeding referred to in the first sentence of this section may be served on any party anywhere in the world.] [Nothing in this Section 12.13 will affect the right of any party to serve legal process in any other manner permitted by law or in equity.]

12.14 Waiver of Jury Trial. EACH PARTY ACKNOWLEDGES AND AGREES THAT ANY CONTROVERSY THAT MAY ARISE UNDER THIS AGREEMENT IS LIKELY TO INVOLVE COMPLICATED AND DIFFICULT ISSUES, AND THEREFORE IT IRREVOCABLY AND UNCONDITIONALLY WAIVES ANY RIGHT IT MAY HAVE TO A TRIAL BY JURY IN RESPECT OF ANY LITIGATION DIRECTLY OR INDIRECTLY ARISING OUT OF OR RELATING TO THIS AGREEMENT OR THE TRANSACTIONS

CONTEMPLATED BY THIS AGREEMENT. EACH PARTY CERTIFIES AND ACKNOWLEDGES THAT (I) NO REPRESENTATIVE, AGENT OR ATTORNEY OF ANY OTHER PARTY HAS REPRESENTED, EXPRESSLY OR OTHERWISE, THAT SUCH OTHER PARTY WOULD NOT, IN THE EVENT OF LITIGATION, SEEK TO ENFORCE THE FOREGOING WAIVER, (II) IT UNDERSTANDS AND HAS CONSIDERED THE IMPLICATIONS OF SUCH WAIVER, (III) IT MAKES SUCH WAIVER VOLUNTARILY AND (IV) IT HAS BEEN INDUCED TO ENTER INTO THIS AGREEMENT BY, AMONG OTHER THINGS, THE MUTUAL WAIVER AND CERTIFICATIONS IN THIS SECTION 12.14.

12.15   Construction. The parties and their respective counsel have participated jointly in the negotiation and drafting of this Agreement. In addition, each of the parties acknowledges that it is sophisticated and has been advised by experienced counsel and, to the extent it deemed necessary, other advisors in connection with the negotiation and drafting of this Agreement. In the event an ambiguity or question of intent or interpretation arises, this Agreement will be construed as if drafted jointly by the parties and no presumption or burden of proof will arise favoring or disfavoring any party by virtue of the authorship of any of the provisions of this Agreement. The parties intend that each representation, warranty and agreement contained in this Agreement will have independent significance. If any party has breached any representation, warranty or agreement in any respect, the fact that there exists another representation, warranty or agreement relating to the same subject matter (regardless of the relative levels of specificity) that the party has not breached will not detract from or mitigate the fact that the party is in breach of the first representation, warranty or agreement. Any reference to any Law will be deemed to refer to all rules and regulations promulgated thereunder, unless the context requires otherwise. The headings preceding the text of articles and sections included in this Agreement and the headings to the schedules and exhibits are for convenience only and are not be deemed part of this Agreement or given effect in interpreting this Agreement. References to sections, articles, schedules or exhibits are to the sections, articles, schedules and exhibits contained in, referred to or attached to this Agreement, unless otherwise specified. The word "including" means "including without limitation." A statement that an action has not occurred in the past means that it is also not presently occurring. When any party may take any permissive action, including the granting of a consent, the waiver of any provision of this Agreement or otherwise, whether to take such action is in its sole and absolute discretion. The use of the masculine, feminine or neuter gender or the singular or plural form of words will not limit any provisions of this Agreement. A statement that an item is listed, disclosed or described means that it is correctly listed, disclosed or described, and a statement that a copy of an item has been delivered means a true and correct copy of the item has been delivered.

12.16   Time of Essence. With regard to all dates and time periods set forth or referred to in this Agreement, time is of the essence.

IN WITNESS WHEREOF, Buyer, Sellers and Sellers' Representative have executed this Stock Purchase Agreement as of the date first above written.

BUYER:

[COMPANY NAME]

By: _____

Name: _____

Title: _____

SELLERS' REPRESENTATIVE

[NAME]

By: _____

Name: _____

Title: _____

[or]

Name: _____

Title: _____

SELLERS:

[COMPANY NAME]

By: _____

Name: _____

Title: _____

[GENERAL PARTNERSHIP NAME]

By: _____

Name: _____

Title: General Partner

[LIMITED PARTNERSHIP NAME]

By: [GENERAL PARTNER NAME]

By: _____

Name: _____

Title: _____

[LLC NAME]

By: _____

Name: _____

Title: _____

Name: _____

Title: _____

Name: _____

Title: _____

EXHIBIT G

Allocation of Purchase Price

The Purchase Price will be allocated among all Sellers in proportion to the number of Shares owned by each of them.

EXHIBIT H

Form of Opinion of Counsel for Seller

1.   The Company is a corporation duly incorporated, validly existing and in good standing under the laws of the State of [State], with corporate power to conduct any lawful business activity.

2.   Each of A, B and C [names of significant subsidiaries] is a corporation duly incorporated, validly existing and in good standing under the laws of the State of _____, with corporate power to conduct any lawful business activity. Based solely on our review of the stock registers of A, B and C, respectively, the Company owns all of the issued and outstanding capital stock of each of A, B and C.

3.   [To be customized—] The Company's authorized capital stock consists of _____ Nonvoting Common Shares, par value $_____ per share, _____ Voting Common Shares, par value $_____ per share (collectively, the "Common Shares"), and _____ Class A Preferred Shares, par value $_____ per share ("Preferred Shares"). Based solely on our review of Company minutes, actions by written consent, stock registers, certificates of officers of the Company and exercises of options shown to be outstanding on a schedule to the Agreement, (i) the Common Shares listed on Exhibit A, which constitute all of the outstanding Common Shares, have been duly authorized and validly issued and are fully paid and nonassessable, (ii) there are no Common Shares [or Preferred Shares] held in the treasury of the Company and (iii), to our knowledge, there are no outstanding shares of capital stock or options or rights to purchase shares of capital stock of the Company, other than the Common Shares listed on Exhibit A.

4.   Assuming that the Buyer has purchased the Common Shares listed on Exhibit A for value in good faith and without notice of any adverse claim, the Buyer has acquired all the rights of the Sellers therein free of any adverse claim, except as otherwise created by Buyer and other than restrictions arising under federal and applicable state securities law.

5.   Each of the Agreement, the Escrow Agreement and the [other agreement] (collectively, the "Documents") has been duly executed and delivered by each Seller and, assuming the due execution and delivery by the

other parties thereto, constitutes the valid and binding obligation of such Seller, enforceable against him[her][it] in accordance with their respective terms.

6.   The execution, delivery and performance of the Documents by the Sellers do not (a) violate any provision of the Company's [Constituent Documents or other appropriate defined term], (b) materially violate any federal or _____ statute, rule or regulation to which the Company is subject or (c) violate any judgment, order or decree known to us applicable to the Company of any court or governmental authority.

7.   To our knowledge, there is no lawsuit or other proceeding pending or overtly threatened that seeks to prevent, enjoin, alter or materially delay the transactions contemplated by the Agreement [and there are no material legal proceedings or governmental investigations pending or threatened against the Company or its assets].

8.   To our knowledge, no consent, approval, authorization or order of, and no notice to or filing with, any governmental authority or any court is required to be obtained or made by the Company or the Sellers in connection with the valid authorization, execution, delivery and performance of the Documents by the Sellers other than such consents, approvals, authorizations, orders, notices and filings as have been made or obtained.

EXHIBIT J

Form of Opinion of Counsel for Buyer

1.   Buyer is a corporation duly organized, validly existing and in good standing under the laws of the State of _____, with corporate power to conduct any lawful business activity.

2.   Buyer has the corporate power to execute, deliver and perform the Agreement. The execution, delivery and performance of the Agreement by Buyer have been duly and validly authorized by all requisite corporate action.

3.   The Agreement has been duly executed and delivered by Buyer and, assuming the due execution and delivery by the other parties thereto, constitutes the valid and binding obligation of Buyer, enforceable against Buyer in accordance with its terms.

4.   Buyer or [name of subsidiary], as the case may be, has the corporate power to execute, deliver and perform each Ancillary Agreement and other employment and consulting agreements delivered in connection with the Closing. The execution, delivery and performance of each such agreement by Buyer or [name of subsidiary], as the case may be, have been duly and validly authorized by all requisite corporate action. Each such agreement has been duly executed and delivered by Buyer or [name of subsidiary], as the case may be, and, assuming the due execution and delivery by the other parties thereto, constitutes the valid and binding obligation of Buyer or [name of subsidiary], as the case may be, enforceable against it in accordance with its terms.

5.   [The Buyer Notes have been duly authorized and validly issued, and are binding obligations of Buyer, enforceable against Buyer in accordance with their terms.]

6.   [The shares of Buyer Common Stock have been duly authorized and validly issued, and are fully paid and nonassessable].

7.   [The Buyer Options have been duly authorized and validly issued, and are binding obligations of Buyer, enforceable against Buyer in accordance with their terms, and any Buyer Common Stock issued upon

exercise thereof in accordance with the terms of the relevant option plan and option agreement will, when issued, be duly authorized, validly issued, fully paid and nonassessable.]

8.   [The Buyer Warrants have been duly authorized and validly issued, and are binding obligations of Buyer, enforceable against Buyer in accordance with their terms, and any Buyer Common Stock issued upon exercise thereof in accordance with the terms of the relevant warrant agreement will, when issued, be duly authorized, validly issued, fully paid and nonassessable.]

Courtesy of William B. Payne, Dorsey & Whitney LLP

APPENDIX D

ARBITRATION CLAUSE FOR
STOCK PURCHASE AGREEMENT

12.11 Governing Law. THE DOMESTIC LAW, WITHOUT REGARD TO CONFLICTS OF LAWS PRINCIPLES, OF THE STATE OF DELAWARE WILL GOVERN ALL QUESTIONS CONCERNING THE CONSTRUCTION, VALIDITY AND INTERPRETATION OF THIS AGREEMENT AND THE PERFORMANCE OF THE OBLIGATIONS IMPOSED BY THIS AGREEMENT.

12.12 Specific Performance. Each of the parties acknowledges and agrees that the subject matter of this Agreement, including the business, assets and properties of the Company and the Subsidiaries, is unique, that the other parties would be damaged irreparably in the event any of the provisions of this Agreement are not performed in accordance with their specific terms or otherwise are breached, and that the remedies at law would not be adequate to compensate such other parties not in default or in breach. Accordingly, each of the parties agrees that the other parties will be entitled to an injunction or injunctions to prevent breaches of the provisions of this Agreement and to enforce specifically this Agreement and the terms and provisions of this Agreement in addition to any other remedy to which they may be entitled, at law or in equity (without any requirement that Buyer provide any bond or other security). The parties waive any defense that a remedy at law is adequate and any requirement to post bond or provide similar security in connection with actions instituted for injunctive relief or specific performance of this Agreement.

12.13 Jurisdiction. Other than for matters contemplated by Section 2.9, for which the procedures in that section shall be applicable[, by Section 11.8(d), for which the procedures in that section shall be applicable] [and by Section 2.15], each of the parties submits to the exclusive jurisdiction of any state or federal court sitting in Wilmington, Delaware, in any action or proceeding arising out of or relating to this Agreement and agrees that all claims in respect of the action or proceeding may be heard and determined in any such court. Each party also agrees not to bring any action or proceeding arising out of or relating to this Agreement in any other court.

Each of the parties waives any defense of inconvenient forum to the maintenance of any action or proceeding so brought and waives any bond, surety or other security that might be required of any other party with respect to any such action or proceeding. Each party appoints CT Corporation System (the "Process Agent") as its agent to receive on its behalf service of copies of the summons and complaint and any other process that might be served in the action or proceeding. Any party may make service on any other party by sending or delivering a copy of the process (i) to the party to be served or (ii) to the party to be served in care of the Process Agent at the following address: ___, ____. The parties agree either or both of them may file a copy of this paragraph with any court as written evidence of the knowing, voluntary and bargained agreement between the parties irrevocably to waive any objections to venue or to convenience of forum. [Alternative—Process in any proceeding referred to in the first sentence of this section may be served on any party anywhere in the world.] [Nothing in Section 12.13 will affect the right of any party to serve legal process in any other manner permitted by law or in equity.]

12.14 Waiver of Jury Trial. EACH PARTY ACKNOWLEDGES AND AGREES THAT ANY CONTROVERSY THAT MAY ARISE UNDER THIS AGREEMENT IS LIKELY TO INVOLVE COMPLICATED AND DIFFICULT ISSUES, AND THEREFORE IT IRREVOCABLY AND UNCONDITIONALLY WAIVES ANY RIGHT IT MAY HAVE TO A TRIAL BY JURY IN RESPECT OF ANY LITIGATION DIRECTLY OR INDIRECTLY ARISING OUT OF OR RELATING TO THIS AGREEMENT OR THE TRANSACTIONS CONTEMPLATED BY THIS AGREEMENT. EACH PARTY CERTIFIES AND ACKNOWLEDGES THAT (I) NO REPRESENTATIVE, AGENT OR ATTORNEY OF ANY OTHER PARTY HAS REPRESENTED, EXPRESSLY OR OTHERWISE, THAT SUCH OTHER PARTY WOULD NOT, IN THE EVENT OF LITIGATION, SEEK TO ENFORCE THE FOREGOING WAIVER, (II) IT UNDERSTANDS AND HAS CONSIDERED THE IMPLICATIONS OF SUCH WAIVER, (III) IT MAKES SUCH WAIVER VOLUNTARILY AND (IV) IT HAS BEEN INDUCED TO ENTER INTO THIS AGREEMENT BY, AMONG OTHER THINGS, THE MUTUAL WAIVER AND CERTIFICATIONS IN THIS SECTION 12.14.

12.15   Dispute Resolution.

(a)   [One form (agreement to arbitrate all matters other than the true-up and allocation)—Other than for matters contemplated by Section 2.9, for which the procedures in that section shall be applicable[, and by Section 11.8(d), for which the procedures in that section shall be applicable], any dispute arising out of or relating to this Agreement will be settled by binding arbitration and, except as specifically stated otherwise in this Agreement, in accordance with the Rules for Non-Administered Arbitration ("CPR Rules") of the International Institute for Conflict Prevention and Resolution ("CPR") then in effect.][Another form (agreement to arbitrate all matters other than the true-up and allocation and other than post-closing covenants)—Other than for matters contemplated by Section 2.9, for which the procedures in that section shall be applicable[, and by Section 11.8(d), for which the procedures in that section shall be applicable], and other than any matter arising out of or relating to the covenants in Sections 6.11 through 6.15 after the Closing, for which all legal and equitable remedies are preserved, any dispute arising out of or relating to this Agreement will be settled by binding arbitration and, except as specifically stated otherwise in this Agreement, in accordance with the Rules for Non-Administered Arbitration ("CPR Rules") of the International Institute for Conflict Prevention and Resolution ("CPR") then in effect.][Yet another form (agreement to arbitrate only contract law matters)—If there is a closing for the transactions contemplated by this Agreement, other than matters contemplated by Section 2.9, for which the procedures in that section shall be applicable[, by Section 11.8(d), for which the procedures in that section shall be applicable], any matter arising out of or relating to the covenants in Sections 6.11 through 6.15 arising after the Closing, for which all legal and equitable remedies are preserved, or any claim based other than on the law of contracts, any dispute arising out of or relating to this Agreement will be settled by binding arbitration and, except as specifically stated otherwise in this Agreement, in accordance with the Rules for Non-Administered Arbitration ("CPR Rules") of the International Institute for Conflict Prevention and Resolution

("CPR") then in effect.][Another form agreeing only to arbitrate breach of rep/indemnification claims—Any claim arising under Articles III , IV or X, including the interpretation of those Articles, will be settled by binding arbitration and, except as specifically stated otherwise in this Agreement, in accordance with the Rules for Non-Administered Arbitration ("CPR Rules") of the International Institute for Conflict Prevention and Resolution ("CPR") then in effect.]

(b)   Any party proposing to arbitrate a matter pursuant to this Agreement shall serve notice on the other party, specifying in reasonable detail the facts giving rise to the claim and the relief sought. For a period of one month, the parties may discuss such matter. After such one-month period, the party proposing to arbitrate a matter may commence arbitration by a demand for arbitration served on the other party as provided in Section 12.4. [Another from without mediation—Any party proposing to arbitrate a matter may commence arbitration by a demand for arbitration served on the other party as provided in Section 12.4.]

(c)   Such arbitration will be conducted before a single arbitrator who shall be an admitted lawyer knowledgeable in the negotiation of agreements for the purchase of businesses who has not performed services for any party within the prior three years selected by the parties. If the parties cannot agree on an arbitrator by the end of the 14th day after the demand for arbitration is deemed given, the CPR shall select the arbitrator upon request of either party from a list of at least five potential qualified arbitrators that it shall develop. The CPR shall establish procedures by which each potential arbitrator shall furnish information on his or her qualifications and any relationship to either party. A party may object to the qualifications of any potential arbitrator, and the CPR shall disqualify any potential arbitrator not qualified. The CPR shall choose the arbitrator from the remaining potential arbitrators. The arbitrator will be paid a fee or rate determined by the parties. If the parties cannot agree, the fee will be determined by the CPR based on the reasonable hourly or daily rates. The parties agree to execute an engagement letter in the customary form required by the arbitrator.

(d)   The parties intend that the arbitrator will have the power to conduct an arbitration procedure to the greatest extent provided by law, including the determination of the scope of arbitration. Except as specifically provide by the CPR Rules or this Agreement, the arbitrator shall establish all rules for the arbitration. The arbitration will be conducted in _____. Each party shall bear the portion of any deposit, advance or other expense as determined by the arbitrator. A record shall be kept of all hearings and all evidence (including exhibits, deposition transcripts and affidavits admitted into evidence) in the arbitration proceeding. The award of the arbitrator shall be based on a preponderance of the evidence. The arbitrator shall reach a decision in compliance with the applicable law and shall render a written decision setting forth the factual and legal bases of the award. The arbitrator may award any type of relief including monetary damages and equitable relief, including any provisional relief. [Alternate—The arbitrator may award only monetary damages and not equitable or provisional relief.] The arbitrator will award to the prevailing party all costs, fees and expenses related to the arbitration. Judgment upon the award may be entered in any court of competent jurisdiction.

(e)   An appeal may be taken under the Arbitration Appeal Procedure of CPR from any final award of the arbitration panel. Unless otherwise agreed by the parties and the appeal tribunal, the appeal shall be conducted at the place of the original arbitration.

(f)   Neither party nor the arbitrator shall disclose to any person any information about the arbitration, including the fact of arbitration, the status thereof or any documents or other information disclosed in connection therewith. The parties and the arbitrator will take reasonable precautions to keep all such information confidential.

12.16   Construction. The parties and their respective counsel have participated jointly in the negotiation and drafting of this Agreement. In addition, each of the parties acknowledges that it is sophisticated and has been advised by experienced counsel and, to the extent it deemed necessary, other advisors in connection with the negotiation and drafting of this Agreement. In the event an ambiguity or question of intent or interpretation arises, this Agreement will be construed as if drafted jointly by the parties and no presumption or burden of proof will arise favoring or disfavoring any party by virtue of the authorship of any of the provisions of this Agreement. The parties intend that each representation, warranty and agreement contained in this Agreement will have independent significance. If any party has breached any representation, warranty or agreement in any respect, the fact that there exists another representation, warranty or agreement relating to the same subject matter (regardless of the relative levels of specificity) that the party has not breached will not detract from or mitigate the fact that the party is in breach of the first representation, warranty or agreement. Any reference to any Law will be deemed to refer to all rules and regulations promulgated thereunder, unless the context requires otherwise. The headings preceding the text of articles and sections included in this Agreement and the headings to the schedules and exhibits are for convenience only and are not be deemed part of this Agreement or given effect in interpreting this Agreement. References to sections, articles, schedules or exhibits are to the sections, articles, schedules and exhibits contained in, referred to or attached to this Agreement, unless otherwise specified. The word "including" means "including without limitation." A statement that an action has not occurred in the past means that it is also not presently occurring. When any party may take any permissive action, including the granting of a consent, the waiver of any provision of this Agreement or otherwise, whether to take such action is in its sole and absolute discretion. The use of the masculine, feminine or neuter gender or the singular or plural form of words will not limit any provisions of this Agreement. A statement that an item is listed, disclosed or described means that it is correctly listed, disclosed or described, and a statement that a copy of an item has been delivered means a true and correct copy of the item has been delivered.

12.17 Time of Essence. With regard to all dates and time periods set forth or referred to in this Agreement, time is of the essence.

Courtesy of William B. Payne, Dorsey & Whitney LLP

APPENDIX E

DUE DILIGENCE CHECKLISTS

OPERATIONS DUE DILIGENCE

TASK:

General Operations Information

ITEMS TO REVIEW:

List of personal property (machinery and equipment), including location and summary of condition.

List of owned or lease transportation equipment:

- over-the-road tractors;
- semi-trailers;
- railcars;
- barges and vessels.

List of major suppliers, prices charged, and volumes purchased for last three years.

Computer hardware purchase or lease agreements, software licenses, service arrangements, and maintenance contracts.

Marketing price lists.

List of five largest customers for each product line.

List of five largest competitors for each product line.

SPECIFIC ACTIONS:

1. Identify fitness and ability of assets to operate for intended purposes.

2. Identify any obsolete machinery and equipment.

3. Examine and count inventory, spare parts, and supplies.

4. Prepare a summary of computer information systems (equipment and software compatibility, transferability, license conditions) for administration and operations systems.

5. Obtain a description of any relationships between any officer, director or shareholder of the seller and any major supplier, customer, or competitor.

6. Obtain a description of all non-U.S. operations and assets and export licensing matters.

TASK:

Major Contracts

ITEMS TO REVIEW:

Purchase or sales agreements relating to the assets (including purchase orders).

Agreements for the purchase or sale of electricity for division operations.

List of purchases of supplies and raw materials (other than logs and pulpwood) for the division's operations for the last three years, by supplier and location.

List of purchases of logs and pulpwood for the division's operations for the last three years, by supplier and location.

Supply agreements

Equipment leases and rental agreements (including telephone system and office equipment and transportation equipment).

Railroad and other transportation agreements.

Waste disposal and treatment agreements.

Dealer, distribution, or franchise agreements.

Agency or manufacturer's representation agreements.

Conditional sales contracts relating to the assets.

Consignment agreements relating to the assets.

Confidentiality or secrecy agreements.

Contracts or commitments for capital expenditures.

Partnership or joint venture agreements, including foreign joint ventures.

Promissory notes, indentures, loan, credit, revolving credit, subordination, financing, guarantee, or other agreements relating to indebtedness for borrowed money that relate to or are secured by the assets or the division.

Standard terms of purchase and sale (including product warranties), quotation forms, purchase orders, and invoices used for the past three years.

Recent and pending acquisitions and divestitures involving the assets or division.

Computer hardware purchase or lease agreements, software licenses, service arrangements, and maintenance contracts.

Intercompany agreements.

Summary of pending transactions.

Services contracts.

Copies or summaries of any other contracts, agreements, or commitments, verbal or written, that are material to (or the loss of which would have a materially adverse effect upon) the operation of the division or use of the assets.

SPECIFIC ACTIONS:

1. Determine business plan for each facility to be transferred.

2. Review contracts and identify any necessary price adjustments or other modifications.

3. Review all major agreements and identify the following:

- term;
- termination charges;

- change of control provisions;
- price adjustment and pricing options; and
- need for notice to or approval from governmental authorities or other parties.

4. Determine whether Buyer prefers to assume the existing agreements or negotiate new agreements.

TASK:

Real Estate Materials

SPECIFIC ACTIONS:

1. Determine whether to order title reports for the real property to be transferred.

2. Determine whether to order title insurance for the real property to be transferred.

3. Determine whether to order surveys or appraisals for the real property to be transferred and, if so, determine the level of detail desired.

4. Determine whether to obtain current floor plan drawings of facilities to be transferred.

TASK:

Litigation Materials and Governmental Approvals

ITEMS TO REVIEW:

Documentation or correspondence related to any charges, investigations, and inquiries brought against Target by any government agency or third party in the last five years related to the assets or the division.

Documentation relating to all judgments, settlements, arbitrations, injunctions, decrees, suits, actions, claims, proceedings, or investigations, pending or threatened, against Target (which could affect the division or the transferred assets) in the last five years.

SPECIFIC ACTIONS:

1. Obtain a summary of all closed, pending, or threatened product liability claims against Target for the last five years.

2. Obtain a summary of all closed, pending, or threatened workers' compensation claims against Target for the last five years.

3. Obtain a summary of all other closed, pending, or threatened claims against Target for the last five years that are not covered in the documents provided above and that relate to or could affect the division or the assets to be purchased.

4. Obtain the details of any termination within the last five years of any franchise, distribution, or marketing representative of the division.

5. Obtain a summary of warranty costs and returns for the last five years.

TASK:

Intellectual Property Materials

ITEMS TO REVIEW:

To the extent held or used by the division or necessary for the use of the assets to be purchased:

- List of all issued patents (with title, number, country, filing date, issue date, and status).
- List of all patent applications (with title, number, country, filing date, and status).
- List of all trademarks used by Target.
- List of all trademark registrations and applications.
- Copies of all license agreements, including settlement agreements

SPECIFIC ACTIONS:

To the extent related to intellectual property held or used by the division or necessary for the use of the assets to be purchased:

1. Determine the status of all claims against the division (including predecessors in interest) and the potential effect on Buyer going forward.

2. Obtain a summary of Target's use of each patent and patent application and the products covered.

3. Obtain a summary of any rights or encumbrances granted or imposed with respect to any patent.

4. Obtain a summary of all known or suspected or claimed infringement of Target's intellectual property rights by any third parties or challenge to the enforceability of Target's intellectual property rights.

5. Obtain a summary of Target's use of each trademark.

TAX AND ACCOUNTING DUE DILIGENCE

TASK:

ITEMS TO REVIEW:

Forms 10-K, Forms 10-Q, and Forms 8-K of Target for each of the last three years.

Annual [audited] financial statements of the division for the last three years.

Interim financial statements of Target and its affiliates for the current year.

List of assets of the division, listed by subsidiary whenever applicable.

Depreciation and amortization schedules for assets of the division.

List of assets subject to capital leases, listed by subsidiary whether applicable, and identification of whether division is lessor or lessee under such leases.

Schedule of operating leases, listed by subsidiary whenever applicable, including:

- description of leased equipment;
- term;
- payments;
- purchase option information.

Debt financing and credit agreements of any kind relating to or secured by the assets to be sold.

Securitization agreement for accounts receivable line.

Letters of credit, guarantees, and indemnity agreements.

Proxy statements, annual reports, prospectuses, and registration statements of Target for the last three years.

Press releases of Target for the last two years.

Outside auditors' reports and management letters for the past three years.

Summary of internal audit reports for the prior two years; sample of internal audit workpapers.

Key management reports, financial projections, budgets, operating plans and long-range plans for the division or its business units.

Record of general, administrative, and marketing expenses for the last five years and year-to-date for the division.

Record of research and development expenses for the division for the last five years.

List of capital expenditures for each of the last three years by major category for the division.

List of swap agreements, future contracts, and similar agreements related to the division.

Aging of trade receivables as of the end of most recent quarter with respect to the division.

Audit committee reports to the board of directors of Target for the last five fiscal years that relate to the division.

Federal and state income tax returns for the last five years for subsidiaries being acquired (and any applicable audit information relating to the division or the assets).

Amounts of all real and personal property taxes and assessments paid, due, or pending for the last five years, listed by site or location, with respect to property to be acquired.

Payroll tax data for the division, organized by state and country.

State sales and use tax returns related to activities of the division for the last three years.

State payroll tax returns related to the division for the last three years.

Correspondence with revenue authorities related to the division or the assets.

Record of foreign sales of the division, by product category and country.

Transfer pricing policies and any transfer pricing agreements or audits applicable to the division.

Information on the foreign sales corporations used by the division.

Tax rulings or closing agreements applied for or materially affecting the division.

Analysts' reports and industry surveys relating to the business of the division.

SPECIFIC ACTIONS:

1. Determine willingness to utilize IRC Section 338(h)(10) election in connection with the transaction.

2. Quantify sales and use taxes that will be triggered by the transaction.

3. Quantify real estate excise or transfer taxes that will be triggered by the transaction.

4. Examine information regarding any tax audits of each owner of the assets for the last five years and copies of any notices or inquiries (including real estate tax audits, business tax audits, inspections of customs filing requirements, etc.). Obtain information on sales tax audits.

5. Determine whether any issues involved in tax audits of Target relate to the division or its assets and are of a recurring or ongoing nature or could affect the future tax liability of the division.

6. Obtain a summary of supplies, spare parts, and product inventory of the division by product and location (including description of conditions, valuation accounts, valuation and pricing methodology, turnover, and items and categories identified as obsolete).

7. Identify the amounts and composition of all rental income received with respect to purchased assets and identify the amounts of all rental expense on leased assets of the division.

8. Obtain operating income statements for the division and identify any unusual operating expenses or operating expense savings from prior operation of the division.

9. Propose purchase price allocation (tax and book).

10. Confirm details of all tax incentives, government grants and subsidies received by Target in connection with the operation of the division (including criteria for continued receipt of such incentives, grants, and subsidies, and any obligations to repay). Any special property tax programs? Any deferred taxes? Fee-in-lieu of tax agreements?

11. Compare depreciation list with list of assets being purchased.

12. Obtain a summary of or written agreements for any services provided by any parent or affiliate of Target (and allocated costs) for the last three years with respect to the division.

13. Obtain a description of current capital expenditure status through the most recent quarterly period for the division.

14. Obtain a description of commitments for capital expenditure projects in excess of $100,000 relating to the division.

15. Obtain a description of product category sales and gross profit contribution by product for the last five years and year-to-date with respect to the division.

16. Obtain a summary of third-party debt to be assumed at latest year-end and as of end of latest quarter.

17. Analyze results required for remainder of year to achieve the budget for the current fiscal year for the division.

18. Obtain a description of differences between tax and book income applicable to the division.

19. Obtain a description of capitalized policies used in connection with the division and the assets.

20. Obtain summaries of accruals related to the division.

21. Obtain a description of the internal periodic financial reporting process.

22. Obtain a description of the method applied within the division of applying significant accounting policies.

23. Obtain a description of the method of accounting for slow-moving or obsolete inventory of the division.

24. Obtain a description of the treatment of intercompany profits.

25. Obtain a description of the tax basis of the assets to be acquired; address Section 338(h)(10) election with respect to each subsidiary.

26. Obtain a summary of income statement and balance sheet acquisition adjustment items for the most recent fiscal year and for the most recent quarter with respect to the division.

27. Obtain a description of receivable write-offs and bad debt reserves at latest year-end relating to the division.

28. Prepare capital lease and operating lease analysis for the division.

29. Determine whether to continue (or how to terminate) accounts receivable securitization to the extent applicable to the division.

30. Determine foreign (export) sales tax strategies to be implemented by Buyer.

FOREIGN OPERATIONS AND SUBSIDIARIES
DUE DILIGENCE

TASK:

[Identify each foreign country in which the division does business (including through any subsidiary) and prepare individual due diligence checklists for each such country. Such checklists will substantially mirror the primary due diligence checklists with modifications particular to the countries involved.]

INSURANCE ADVISER DUE DILIGENCE

TASK:

SPECIFIC ACTIONS:

1. Obtain agreements and policies with respect to all necessary insurance (including vehicle insurance, products liability, export insurance, general liability insurance, casualty insurance, property insurance, and health and welfare insurance).

2. Identify any third parties who require coverage with respect to the division or its operation and identify any third parties that maintain insurance benefiting Target or the assets.

3. Identify any need for flood or earthquake insurance.

4. As required, negotiate terms of insurance protection (waivers of subrogation, etc.) for Buyer with respect to products liability and environmental claims and other areas of potential successor liability.

5. Review claims history and report on any pending claims.

6. Review and analyze premium payment information, loss runs for the last five years under the insurance policies, and information pertaining to all pending claims.

7. Confirm adequacy of Buyer's existing insurance coverage.

8. Obtain a summary description of the insurance policies regarding properties and operations of the division for which Target or the division is self-insured.

ENVIRONMENTAL DUE DILIGENCE

TASK:

ITEMS TO REVIEW:

Building, occupancy, zoning, environmental, operating, or other licenses, permits, and authorizations pertaining to the division and the assets (past and present), including with respect to:

- water quality;
- air quality;
- noise levels;
- solid and hazardous waste treatment and disposal;
- fire and hazard safety standards;
- fuel requirements;
- production volumes;
- underground storage tanks.

List of each "hazardous waste" generated by the division or the assets in the past or present.

Records of inspection, notices of violations, correspondence with governmental agencies, internal correspondence or engineering reports regarding the release, threat of release, or clean-up of hazardous substances with respect to the division or the assets.

Records of inspection, notices of violations, correspondence with governmental agencies, internal correspondence or engineering reports regarding compliance with any material environmental law in connection with the ownership or operation of the division or the assets.

Copies of environmental or safety inspection surveys, audits, and reports for the last five years that are related to or could affect the division or the assets.

Former and pending safety or environmental citations relating to or affecting the division or the assets.

Any logs or copies of soil borings, geotechnical reports, environmental assessment reports, or well information for the properties where assets are located.

Any information showing the condition of the groundwater at or near any of the assets to be acquired.

Quality certification documents, indicating the quality of manufactured products of the division.

Air and water pollutant discharge monitoring reports relating to the division or the assets.

Neighbor and other third-party complaints with respect to environmental matters relating to the division or the assets.

Copies of Target's safety procedures and guidelines related to the division or the assets.

Results of noise tests and industrial hygiene test for the last three years related to the division or the assets.

Records of OSHA compliance and any occupational injury or illness occurring within the division.

SPECIFIC ACTIONS:

1. Identify any type of asbestos or asbestos-containing materials utilized in processes or used as insulation or building materials included in or related to the assets to be acquired, including:

- type of material; and
- condition of material.

2. Identify any hazardous products included in or related to the assets to be acquired.

3. Identify all past and present uses of the real property to be acquired.

4. Identify all past and present industrial processes conducted on the real property to be acquired.

5. Obtain a summary of any pending or threatened changes in permit requirements or regulations and any breaches or potential breaches of applicable permit requirements or regulations. Conduct an historical review of permit compliance.

6. Obtain an historical PSD (prevention of significant deterioration) review from 1980 to present in connection with the assets to be acquired.

7. Obtain a description of sites to be acquired that have been identified as Superfund sites or are currently being monitored or are subject to clean-up or other action in connection with CERCLA and similar state laws.

8. Identify all past and present storage of chemicals, raw materials, fuels or liquid in tank in connection with the assets to be acquired, including:

- material stored;
- size of tanks;
- age of tanks;
- construction of tanks;
- spill containment methods;
- evidence of spills;
- method of corrosion protection;
- dates and results of tests for tank tightness; and
- documents or notices filed with any government agency regarding tanks.

9. Identify all past and present storage of chemicals, raw materials, fuels, liquids or washes in drums or other containers at any facility to be acquired, including:

- type of material stored;
- normal quantity in storage;
- type of container;
- size of storage area;
- type of base materials under container;
- spill containment; and
- evidence of spills.

10. Identify past or present septic systems, dry wells, or leach beds utilized to dispose of washes and wastes at each facility to be acquired, including:

- type of system;
- processes discharging to system; and
- any written analyses of discharges to system.

11. Identify past or present equipment or processing containing or utilizing PCBs or PCB-containing fluids at each facility to be acquired, including:

- type of equipment;
- type of fluid utilized; and
- disposal practices.

12. Identify past and present practices for the disposal of spent solvents, oils, other solutions and materials, and other wastes at the facility to be acquired, including:

- material disposed;
- quantity disposed;
- name and address of disposal firm; and
- method of disposal.

13. Identify any waste or other liquid (other than uncontaminated water) applied to or disposed of on any of the sites to be acquired.

14. Identify source of drinking water at each of the facilities to be acquired.

473

15. Identify all wells at each of the facilities to be acquired.

16. Obtain a description of any unusual occurrences of environmental significance that have occurred on the properties to be acquired or adjacent sites (spills, fires, releases, etc.).

17. Identify all water treatment facilities at each of the facilities to be acquired, including:

- type of treatment;
- basic flow diagram;
- discharge requirements; and
- any written analyses of discharges.

18. Identify any stack emissions at any of the facilities to be acquired, including:

- process used;
- method of control;
- monitoring requirements; and
- compliance with permit conditions.

19. Review the following agreements with respect to environmental issues and concerns relating to the assets to be acquired:

- agreements for purchase or sale of utilities;
- raw material supply agreements;
- equipment lease agreements;
- transportation agreements; and
- labor agreements.

20. Determine whether additional environmental assessments or auditing is needed.

21. Obtain and review a summary of any environmental work, clean-up, analysis or inspections that have taken place on the properties to be acquired.

22. Determine whether any environmental mitigation plans affect any of the sites to be acquired.

23. Obtain a description of the basis for and amount of any fines levied or threatened and any injunctive relief required for violation of environmental laws, regulations, or permits that relates to or affects the division or the assets to be acquired.

24. Identify use restrictions, transfer restrictions, and applicable standards contained in all material permits and licenses related to the assets to be acquired.

HUMAN RESOURCES DUE DILIGENCE

TASK:

ITEMS TO REVIEW:

List of all salaried and hourly employees of the division, with date of hire, job title, prior year's earnings, current rate of pay, function, location, number of employees per area, and identification of where employees are charged on the profit and loss statement.

List of employees that are part-time, temporary, on probation, laid off, or on a leave of absence (with the reason for each).

List of leased employees and independent contractors.

Employment policies, manuals and handbooks applicable to employees of the division.

Bonus/profit sharing plans applicable to the division and its employees.

Severance and settlement agreement regarding departed employees or departing employees of the division for the last five years.

Documentation regarding labor disputes, requests for arbitration, grievance proceedings, etc., involving employees of the division.

Complete personnel files and management notes and data on each employee of the division fired or laid off within the last five years.

Employment contracts and consulting agreements applicable to employees and consultants of the division.

Collective bargaining agreement and labor contracts in effect for the division.

Benefit and vacation policies applicable to division employees for the last five years.

Information given to division employees to comply with Family Medical Leave Act requirements.

Documentation of Form I-9 compliance for the division and its employees for the last five years.

For all single-employer qualified pension plans (defined benefit and defined contribution) maintained for employees of the division:

- plan and trust documents (or insurance contracts), with amendments;
- latest IRS determination letter;
- current summary plan description, with amendments;
- Forms 5500 for the last five years;
- FAS 87 determinations, letters, reports or other communications;
- any SEC filing for any plan;
- actuarial valuation reports for the last three years for any defined benefit plan;
- PBGC forms for each defined benefit plan for the most recent full plan year;
- documentation pertaining to 401(k) accounts and retiree medical or life coverage within any plan;
- investment results of the fund(s) for any defined contribution plan for the last three years;
- copies of any QDROs, with relevant documentation;
- other related communications and manuals.

For any multiemployer plan or multiple employer plan (past or present) to which contributions are or were made on behalf of employees of the division:

- plan and trust documents, with amendments;
- any withdrawal liability notices;
- financial information regarding each plan for the last five years;
- contribution amounts for the last five years;
- the withdrawal liability, if any, of the controlled group.

For any VEBA (trust fund) maintained to provide welfare benefits for employees of the division:

- plan and trust documents, with amendments;
- Forms 1024 submitted to IRS;
- IRS determination letter regarding status of VEBA;
- any available financial information regarding VEBA;
- any other IRS or DOL filings with respect to VEBA (Forms 5500, etc.).

For each medical benefit plan for division employees:

- plan documents and insurance contracts for major medical, comprehensive, HMO, PPO, or other
- medical coverage or managed care arrangements;
- dental plan documents and insurance contracts;
- flexible spending account (health or dependent) plan documents;
- documents for plans "carved out" of major medical or comprehensive medical plans (e.g.,
- prescription drugs);
- summary plan description and employee communications regarding the plan;
- Forms 5500 with respect to each plan for the last three years;
- insurance contract or administrative services contract with the provider or claim administrator for each plan.

COBRA notification and election forms and manuals used in connection with the division and its employees and former employees.

Plan documents and insurance contracts used in connection with the division relating to:

- group term life insurance plans and programs;
- universal life insurance plans and programs;
- accidental death and dismemberment plans and programs;
- business and travel accident plans and programs; and

- dependent life insurance plans and programs.

Forms 5500 with respect to each life insurance plan applicable to any division employee for the last three years.

Plan documents for each long-term disability and short-term disability plan applicable to any division employee.

Forms 5500 with respect to each disability plan applicable to any employee of the division for the last three years.

Plan documents and Form 5500 for any employee assistance program applicable to any division employee.

For any post-retirement plans (retiree medical, dental, life insurance, etc.) applicable to retirees of the division:

- plan documents;
- summary plan descriptions and communications;
- Forms 5500 for each plan for the last three years;
- actuarial valuation for the last three years;
- information relating to FAS 106 calculations, reserves, liabilities;
- trust agreement for any funded plan;
- list of retirees currently covered.

Documents setting forth any deferred compensation arrangements, executive compensation, employment agreements, or other arrangements covering any executives of the division, including "top-hat" plans described in ERISA § 20 1(2).

Stock option plans or stock purchase plans applicable to division employees.

SPECIFIC ACTIONS:

1. Identify the number of employees to be retained, wages and seniority of each, and whether each employee is hourly or salaried.

2. Review labor agreements and job training and hiring agreements for the division and its facilities.

3. Obtain a description of liabilities and obligations under workers' compensation, disability, and employee benefit plans for division employees.

4. Obtain a summary of obligations to retirees of the division upon retirement (including under any existing pension plans or ERISA).

5. Obtain information pertaining to any general increase in the rate of compensation paid to the division's employees during the last 12 months.

6. Obtain information pertaining to any outstanding loan or advance to any division employee.

7. Identify any employee fidelity or bond policy or practice within the division.

8. Obtain a description of bonus, sales commission, and incentive compensation policies and history within the division for the last five years.

9. Obtain a description of any union organizing activity involving the division.

10. Obtain a description of layoff and leave of absence policies applicable to employees to be hired by Buyer, including any extension of benefits.

11. Determine the level of plan participation for any single-employer qualified pension plan for employees of the division that requires employee contributions.

12. Identify the number of outstanding loans for any 40 1(k) plan available to division employees with a loan provision.

13. Identify any contribution limits for highly compensated employees of the division.

14. Obtain the names and addresses of law firms, pension consultants, trustees, auditors, record keepers, insurance companies, and agents responsible for each benefit plan applicable to division employees.

15. Determine the employer's experience with the cost of each medical benefit plan for division employees for the last three years.

16. Determine breakdown of experience with each medical benefit plan for division employees for the last three years (e.g., hospital usage, prescription drugs, in-patient/outpatient services).

17. Compare experience of hourly employees and salaried employees in connection with each medical benefit plan for division employees.

18. Determine if there is a stop-loss arrangement in place with respect to the division and if it is insured or self-insured. Review related documentation.

19. Conduct a census of any COBRA participants for the division and determine the division's experience under COBRA and rates under COBRA for the last three years.

20. Determine whether each medical benefit plan for division employees is part of a flexible benefit program and, if so, identify or review:

- election patterns for the last three years;
- experience of each option;
- structure of credits/price tags; and
- administration manual.

21. Obtain a description and history of any salary continuation program in lieu of or in addition to a disability plan or program utilized with respect to division employees.

22. Determine funding arrangements and information relating to FAS 87 calculations, reserves, and liabilities for each employment agreement, severance agreement, and deferred compensation arrangement for executive employees of the division.

23. Determine any fringe benefits afforded to division employees, such as key-man life insurance, company cars, reimbursement for club memberships, educational expense reimbursement, etc.

24. Determine whether any employee benefit plan for division employees has not been maintained in compliance with the Internal Revenue Code, ERISA, and other laws, and whether any prohibited transaction or reportable event has occurred with respect to any such plan.

25. Identify any division employees who have U.S. citizenship and are working in foreign countries and any separate benefit plans for such employees.

26. Identify any division employees who are foreign citizens and confirm immigration status.

27. Confirm whether any WARN Act notifications have been given with respect to the division and determine need for further WARN Act notifications.

28. Obtain a description of any and all strikes, lockouts, slow downs and other disruptions at the division's facilities and any claim of unfair labor practices.

LEGAL DUE DILIGENCE

TASK:

General Corporate Documents

ITEMS TO REVIEW:

List of all subsidiaries and affiliates of Target through which Target operates the division, including state of incorporation or organization.

List of officers and directors for all subsidiaries and affiliates through which Target operates the division.

List of any minority ownership interests in any subsidiaries or affiliates of Target.

TASK:

Financial and Tax Documents

ITEMS TO REVIEW:

Forms 10-K, Forms 10-Q, and Forms 8-K of Target for each of the last three years.

Annual [audited] financial statements of the division for the last three years.

Interim financial statements of Target and affiliates for the current year.

Promissory notes, indentures, loan, credit, revolving credit, subordination, financing, or other agreements relating to indebtedness for borrowed money that relate to or are secured by the assets or the division and that will be assumed by Buyer.

Letters of credit, guarantees, and indemnity agreements that Buyer will assume.

SPECIFIC ACTIONS:

1. Examine debt financing and other financial instruments to be assumed (including payment schedules and "change of control" provisions).

2. Determine if the transaction will trigger sales or use taxes in each state where Target's assets are located.

3. Determine the amount of real property transfer taxes triggered by the transaction; confirm that such taxes are Target's obligations in each applicable jurisdiction.

4. Complete fraudulent conveyance analysis.

TASK:

Security Interest and Liens

ITEMS TO REVIEW:

UCC search reports.

Local lien and litigation reports that could affect the assets to be purchased.

Successor liability reports.

SPECIFIC ACTIONS:

1. Identify creditors with recorded security interests in the assets to be purchased; examine related documents.

2. Obtain reports on successor liability under relevant state laws (bulk sales laws and otherwise).

TASK:

Major Contracts

ITEMS TO REVIEW:

(See Operations Due Diligence checklist for Major Contracts below.)

SPECIFIC ACTIONS:

1. Confirm whether each contract requires consent to transfer or contains other limitations on assignability.

2. Confirm that no obligation is owed to any third party or professional in connection with the proposed transaction.

3. Confirm that there are no outstanding obligations under any monetized timber sales agreements.

4. Confirm that there are no outstanding proxies or powers of attorney granted to any third party by the division or by Target that relates to the division or the assets.

TASK:

Real Estate Materials

ITEMS TO REVIEW:

Lease agreements for real property to be transferred.

Property tax statements for real property to be transferred.

Recorded mortgages, easements, and encumbrances on real property to be transferred.

Deeds for real property to be transferred.

Subleases for real property to be transferred.

Construction contracts relating to real property to be transferred.

SPECIFIC ACTIONS:

1. Examine terms of any purchase options and remaining obligations on leases to be assumed by Buyer.

2. Determine whether to order title reports, surveys, title insurance, appraisals, or current floor plan drawings with respect to each facility to be acquired.

3. Confirm that Target holds legal title to all of the property to be transferred. Identify any encumbrances or clouds on title.

4. Identify issues relating to any property adjacent to property to be transferred (e.g., rights of access, lot line disputes, etc.).

5. Identify any agreements or understandings with public bodies or agencies regarding real property to be transferred.

6. Obtain information regarding flood, fire, and other natural disasters history at all mill sites to be transferred.

7. Review historical compliance with zoning laws and similar regulations applicable to real property to be transferred.

8. Review adequacy of existing title insurance policies on real property to be transferred.

TASK:

Litigation Materials and Governmental Approvals

ITEMS TO REVIEW:

Documentation or correspondence related to any charges, investigations, and inquiries brought against Target by any government agency or third party in the last five years related to the assets or the division.

Documentation relating to all judgments, settlements, arbitrations, injunctions, decrees, suits, actions, claims, proceedings, or investigations pending or threatened, against Target (which could affect the division or the transferred assets) in the last five years, including wood products consent decree.

Copies of the most recent three legal representation letters sent to Target's auditors.

Opinions or other assessments (other than audit response letters) of Target's or the division's attorneys as to any pending or threatened litigation against Target or any of its affiliates (with respect to the division).

SPECIFIC ACTIONS:

1. Complete Hart-Scott Rodino Act filings.

2. Obtain a summary of all closed, pending, or threatened product liability claims against Target for the last five years that relate the division or its assets.

3. Obtain a summary of all closed, pending, or threatened workers' compensation claims against Target for the last five years that relate to the division.

4. Obtain a summary of all other closed, pending, or threatened claims against Target for the last five years that are not covered in the documents

provided above and which relate to or could affect the division or the assets to be purchased.

5. Examine licenses, permits, documentation regarding violations or potential violations that relate to the division or its assets, and related correspondence.

6. Obtain the details of any termination with the last five years of any franchise, distribution, or marketing representative of the division.

7. Obtain a summary of warranty costs and returns for the division for the last five years.

Courtesy of J. Franklin Cable, Miller Nash LLP

APPENDIX F

ASSET PURCHASE AGREEMENT LETTER OF INTENT

_____, 20_____

Company
[Address]

Re: Proposal to Purchase Assets of the Company

Dear [Chairman/President]:

This letter will confirm that Buyer is interested in acquiring substantially all of the assets of the Company, and assuming certain of its liabilities and obligations, on terms that would be mutually agreeable. In this letter, (a) Buyer and the Company are sometimes called singularly a "Party" and collectively the "Parties;" (b) the shareholders of the Company are sometimes called the "Shareholders;" and (c) Buyer's possible acquisition of the assets of the Company is sometimes called the "Possible Acquisition."

[PART ONE]

The Parties wish to commence negotiating a definitive written acquisition agreement providing for the Possible Acquisition (a "Definitive Agreement"). To facilitate the negotiation of a Definitive Agreement, the Parties request that Buyer's counsel prepare an initial draft. The execution of any such Definitive Agreement would be subject to the satisfactory completion of Buyer's ongoing investigation of the Company's business and would also be subject to approval by Buyer's board of directors.

Based upon the information currently known to Buyer, it is proposed that the Definitive Agreement include the following terms:

[BASIC TRANSACTION]

1.   The Company would sell all of its operating assets, property, rights, good-will and business to Buyer at the price (the "Purchase Price") set forth

in Paragraph 2 below. The closing of this transaction (the "Closing") would occur as soon as possible after the termination of the applicable waiting period under the Hart-Scott-Rodino Antitrust Improvements Act of 1976 (the "HSR Act").

[PURCHASE PRICE]

2.   The Purchase Price would be _____ dollars ($_____) (subject to adjustment as described below) and would be paid in the following manner:

(a) at the Closing, Buyer would pay the Company the sum of $_____ in cash;

(b) at the Closing, Buyer would deposit with a mutually acceptable escrow agent the sum of _____ dollars ($_____), which would be held in escrow for a period of at least _____ (_____) years in order to secure the performance of the Company's obligations under the Definitive Agreement and related documents; and

(c) at the Closing, Buyer would execute and deliver to the Company an unsecured, nonnegotiable, subordinated promissory note. The promissory note to be delivered to the Company by Buyer would have a principal amount of _____ dollars ($_____), would bear interest at the rate of _____ percent (_____%) per annum, would mature on the _____ (_____) anniversary of the Closing, and would provide for _____ (_____) equal [annual] [quarterly] payments of principal along with [annual] [quarterly] payments of accrued interest.

The Purchase Price assumes that the Company will transfer working capital at the Closing at least equal to _____ dollars ($_____), its working capital as of its most recent balance sheet prior to execution of this letter. For this purpose, working capital shall be determined by subtracting current liabilities to be assumed (consisting of accounts and notes payable, accrued expenses, provisions for taxes and current maturity on long-term debt) from current assets to be acquired (consisting of cash and cash equivalents, accounts receivable, inventory and pre-paid expenses). The Purchase Price would be increased or decreased based upon the amount by which the working capital transferred at the Closing exceeds or falls short of the initial working capital as reflected on the Company's most recent balance sheet on a dollar-for-dollar basis.

[EMPLOYMENT AND NON-COMPETITION AGREEMENTS]

3.	At the Closing:

(a) Buyer and A would enter into a _____-year (_____-year) employment agreement under which A would agree to serve as Buyer's [Vice President and Chief Operating Officer] and would be entitled to receive a salary of _____ dollars ($_____) per year; and(b)	each Shareholder would execute a _____-year (_____-year) non-competition agreement in favor of Buyer.

[OTHER TERMS]

4.	The Company and the Shareholders would make comprehensive representations and warranties to Buyer and would provide comprehensive covenants, indemnities and other protections for the benefit of Buyer. The consummation of the contemplated transactions by Buyer would be subject to the satisfaction of various conditions, including:

(a)	_____

(b)	_____

[PART TWO]

The following paragraphs of this letter (the "Binding Provisions") are the legally binding and enforceable agreements of Buyer, the Company and the Shareholders.

[ACCESS]

5.	During the period from the date this letter is signed on behalf of the Company and the Shareholders (the "Signing Date") until the date on which either Party provides the other Party with written notice that negotiations toward a Definitive Agreement are terminated (the "Termination Date"), the Company will afford Buyer full and free access to the Company, its personnel, properties, contracts, books and records and all other documents and data, subject to the confidentiality provisions referred to or described in paragraph 9 of this letter.

[EXCLUSIVE DEALING]

6.   Until the later of (a) [90] days after the Signing Date or (b) the Termination Date:

(a) Neither the Company nor the Shareholders will, directly or indirectly, through any representative or otherwise, solicit or entertain offers from, negotiate with or in any manner encourage, discuss, accept or consider any proposal of any other person relating to the acquisition of the Company, its assets or business, in whole or in part, whether directly or indirectly, through purchase, merger, consolidation or otherwise (other than sales of inventory in the ordinary course); and

(b) Either the Company or any Shareholder will, as the case may be, immediately notify Buyer regarding any contact between the Company, such Shareholder or their respective representatives and any other person regarding any such offer or proposal or any related inquiry.

[BREAK-UP FEE]

7.   If (a) either the Company or any Shareholder breaches Paragraph 6 of this letter or the Company provides to Buyer written notice that negotiations toward a Definitive Agreement are terminated, and (b) within [six] months after the date of such breach or the Termination Date, as the case may be, either the Company or any Shareholder signs a letter of intent or other agreement relating to the acquisition of a material portion of the Company or its capital stock, assets or business, in whole or in part, whether directly or indirectly, through purchase, merger, consolidation or otherwise (other than sales of inventory or immaterial portions of the Company's assets in the ordinary course) and such transaction is ultimately

consummated, then, immediately upon the closing of such transaction, the Company will pay to Buyer the sum _____ dollars ($_____). This fee will not serve as the exclusive remedy to Buyer under this letter in the event of a breach by the Company or any Shareholder of Paragraph 6 of this letter or any other of the Binding Provisions, and Buyer will be entitled to all other rights and remedies provided by law or in equity.

[CONDUCT OF BUSINESS]

8.   During the period from the Signing Date until the Termination Date, the Company shall operate its business in the ordinary course and refrain from any extraordinary transactions.

[CONFIDENTIALITY]

9.   Except as expressly modified by the Binding Provisions, the Confidentiality Agreement entered into between the Company and Buyer on _____, 20_____, shall remain in full force and effect.

or

9.   Except as and to the extent required by law, Buyer will not disclose or use, and will direct its representatives not to disclose or use to the detriment of the Company, any Confidential Information (as defined below) with respect to the Company furnished, or to be furnished, by either the Company or the Shareholders or their respective representatives to Buyer or its representatives at any time or in any manner other than in connection with its evaluation of the transaction proposed in this letter. For purposes of this Paragraph, "Confidential Information" means any information about the Company stamped "confidential" or identified in writing as such to Buyer by the Company promptly following its disclosure, unless (a) such information is already known to Buyer or its representatives or to others not bound by a duty of confidentiality at the time of its disclosure or such information becomes publicly available through no fault of Buyer or its representatives; (b) the use of such information is necessary or appropriate in making any filing or obtaining any consent or approval required for the consummation of the Possible Acquisition; or (c) the furnishing or use of such information is required by or necessary or

appropriate in connection with legal proceedings. Upon the written request of the Company, Buyer will promptly return to the Company or destroy any Confidential Information in its possession and certify in writing to the Company that it has done so.

[DISCLOSURE]

10.   Except as and to the extent required by law, without the prior written consent of the other Party, none of Buyer, the Company or its Shareholders will, and each will direct its representatives not to make, directly or indirectly, any public comment, statement or communication with respect to, or otherwise to disclose or to permit the disclosure of the existence of discussions regarding, a possible transaction between the Parties or any of the terms, conditions or other aspects of the transaction proposed in this letter. If a Party is required by law to make any such disclosure, it must first provide to the other Party the content of the proposed disclosure, the reasons that such disclosure is required by law, and the time and place that the disclosure will be made.

[COSTS]

11.   Buyer and the Company will be responsible for and bear all of their respective costs and expenses (including any broker's or finder's fees and the expenses of its representatives) incurred at any time in connection with pursuing or consummating the Possible Acquisition. Notwithstanding the preceding sentence, Buyer will pay one-half and the Company will pay one-half of the HSR Act filing fee.

[CONSENTS]

12.   During the period from the Signing Date until the Termination Date, Buyer and the Company will cooperate with each other and proceed, as promptly as is reasonably practical, to prepare and to file the notifications required by the HSR Act.

[ENTIRE AGREEMENT]

13.   The Binding Provisions constitute the entire agreement between the Parties and supersede all prior oral or written agreements, understandings, representations and warranties and courses of conduct and dealing between the Parties on the subject matter thereof. Except as otherwise provided herein, the Binding Provisions may be amended or modified only by a writing executed by all of the Parties.

[GOVERNING LAW]

14.   The Binding Provisions will be governed by and construed under the laws of the State of _____ without regard to conflicts-of-laws principles.

[JURISDICTION; SERVICE OF PROCESS]

15.   Any action or proceeding seeking to enforce any provision of, or based on any right arising out of, the Binding Provisions may be brought against any of the Parties in the courts of the State of _____, County of _____, or, if it has or can acquire jurisdiction, in the United States District Court for the_____ District of _____, and each of the Parties consents to the jurisdiction of such courts (and of the appropriate appellate courts) in any such action or proceeding and waives any objection to venue laid therein. Process in any action or proceeding referred to in the preceding sentence may be served on any Party anywhere in the world.

[TERMINATION]

16.   The Binding Provisions will automatically terminate on _____, 20_____, and may be terminated earlier upon written notice by either Party to the other Party unilaterally, for any reason or no reason, with or without cause, at any time, provided, however, that the termination of the Binding Provisions will not affect the liability of a Party for breach of any of the Binding Provisions prior to the termination. Upon termination of the Binding Provisions, the parties will have no further obligations hereunder, except as stated in Paragraphs 6, 7, 9, 10, 11, 13, 14 and 15, which will survive any such termination.

[COUNTERPARTS]

17.   This letter may be executed in one or more counterparts, each of which will be deemed to be an original of this letter and all of which, when taken together, will be deemed to constitute one and the same letter.

[NO LIABILITY]

18.   The provisions of paragraphs 1 through 4 of this letter are intended only as an expression of intent on behalf of Buyer, are not intended to be legally binding on Buyer, the Company or the Shareholders and are expressly subject to the execution of an appropriate Definitive Agreement. Moreover, except as expressly provided in paragraphs 5 through 18 (or as expressly provided in any binding written agreement that the Parties may enter into in the future), no past or future action, course of conduct or failure to act relating to the Possible Acquisition, or relating to the negotiation of the terms of the Possible Acquisition or any Definitive Agreement, will give rise to or serve as a basis for any obligation or other liability on the part of Buyer, the Company or the Shareholders.

If you are in agreement with the foregoing, please sign and return one copy of this letter, which thereupon will constitute our understanding with respect to its subject matter.

Very truly yours,

BUYER:

By: _____

Name: _____

Title: _____

Agreed to as to the Binding Provisions on _____, 20_____.

COMPANY:

By: _____

Name: _____

Title: _____

_____
Shareholder
[address]

_____
Shareholder
[address]

Courtesy of Barry J. Siegel, Klehr, Harrison, Harvey, Branzburg & Ellers LLP

APPENDIX G

LETTER OF INTENT AND ACQUISITION PROPOSAL

DATE

Addressee

Re: Acquisition Proposal

Dear _____:

This letter of intent sets forth the basic terms upon which _____or its designee ("Buyer") proposes to acquire XYZ Corp (the "Company"). Based upon the information provided to Buyer, Buyer proposes the following terms:

I.

1.   Basic Transaction. The Company would sell all of its assets to Buyer at the price (the "Purchase Price") set forth in Paragraph 2 below.

2.   Purchase Price. The Purchase Price would be $_____ (subject to adjustment as described below) and would be paid at the closing in immediately available funds, with [an escrow of $_____] [a reasonable escrow] to be deposited with a mutually acceptable escrow agent to secure the performance of the Company's obligations under the Definitive Agreements (as defined below). The Purchase Price assumes that the Company will satisfy at or prior to the closing all outstanding indebtedness and other liabilities and all other fees and expenses related to the transaction incurred by or on behalf of the Company and that the Company will transfer working capital at the closing of at least $_____ ("Target Working Capital"). For this purpose, working capital shall be determined by subtracting current liabilities from current assets. The Purchase Price would be decreased if working capital at the closing falls short of the Target Working Capital [or increased if working capital exceeds Target Working Capital], on a dollar-for-dollar basis. In addition, the Purchase Price would be decreased by an amount equal to the

outstanding balance as of the closing of any indebtedness or other liabilities not accounted for in the working capital adjustment.

3.   Employment And Noncompetition Agreements. As a condition to Buyer's obligation to close, at the closing (a) Buyer shall have secured the support of incumbent management and shall have entered into mutually acceptable consulting or employment agreements with certain key personnel of the Company, such key personnel to be identified by Buyer in due diligence and in consultation with the Company, and (b) the Company and _____ ("Parent") would execute a five-year noncompetition and nonsolicitation agreement in favor of Buyer.

4.   Other Terms. The Company and Parent would make representations and warranties to Buyer and would provide covenants, indemnities and other protections for the benefit of Buyer as are reasonable and customary for transactions of this nature. The consummation of the contemplated transactions by Buyer would be subject to the satisfactory completion of Buyer's due diligence and other customary closing conditions. Counsel for Buyer shall draft definitive agreements (the "Definitive Agreements") containing the terms of this letter of intent and other appropriate and customary terms not inconsistent herewith.

5.   Access. During the period from the date this letter of intent has been signed by Buyer, the Company and Parent (the "Signing Date") until the date on which either Buyer or the Company provides the other party with written notice that negotiations toward Definitive Agreements are terminated (the "Termination Date"), the Company and Parent will afford Buyer access to the Company, its personnel, properties, contracts, books and records and all other documents and data upon reasonable notice and without unreasonable disruption to the Company's business.

6.   Conduct Of Business. During the period from the Signing Date until the Termination Date, the Company shall operate its business in the ordinary course and refrain from any extraordinary transactions.

II.

The following Paragraphs 7 through 16 of this letter of intent (the "Binding Provisions") are the legally binding and enforceable agreements of Buyer, the Company and the Shareholders.

7.   Exclusive Dealing. For a period of 90 days after the Signing Date (the "Exclusivity Period"): (a) neither the Company nor Parent will, directly or indirectly, through any representative or otherwise, solicit or entertain offers from, negotiate with or in any manner encourage, discuss, accept or consider any proposal of any other person relating to the acquisition of the Company, its assets or business, in whole or in part, whether directly or indirectly, through purchase of stock or assets, merger, consolidation or otherwise (other than sales of inventory in the ordinary course); and (b) either the Company or Parent, as the case may be, will immediately notify Buyer regarding any contact between the Company, Parent or their respective representatives and any other person regarding any such offer or proposal or any related inquiry. If the parties have not consummated the transactions contemplated by this letter of intent within the Exclusivity Period and Buyer is negotiating in good faith the terms of the Definitive Agreements, Buyer may at its election by written notice to the Company, extend the Exclusivity Period for up to an additional 30 days.

8.   Expense Reimbursement. If the Company or Parent breaches Paragraph 7 of this letter of intent, the Company or Parent provides to Buyer notice that negotiations toward Definitive Agreements are terminated or the Company or Parent determines for any reason not to execute Definitive Agreements or consummate the transactions contemplated by this letter of intent (whether during or after the period described above in Paragraph 7) notwithstanding Buyer's good faith efforts to negotiate Definitive Agreements or consummate the transaction on the terms set forth in this letter of intent (and other terms not inconsistent herewith as are customary in transactions of this nature), then, in any such case, within 30 days of a demand therefore by the Buyer, the Company and Parent shall have the joint and several obligation to pay to Buyer an amount equal to all of Buyer's actual costs and expenses incurred in connection with its investigation and due diligence review of the Company and the preparation and negotiation of this letter of intent and the Definitive Agreements

(including without limitation, fees of attorneys, accountants and consultants). This provision will not serve as the exclusive remedy to Buyer under this letter of intent in the event of a breach by the Company or Parent of Paragraph 7 of this letter of intent or any other of the Binding Provisions, and Buyer will be entitled to all other rights and remedies provided by law or in equity.

9. Disclosure. Except as and to the extent required by law, without the prior written consent of the other party, none of Buyer on the one hand, or the Company or Parent on the other, will, and each will direct its representatives not to, make, directly or indirectly, any public comment, statement or communication with respect to, or otherwise to disclose or to permit the disclosure of the existence of discussions regarding, a possible transaction among the parties or any of the terms, conditions or other aspects of the transaction proposed in this letter of intent. If a party is required by law to make any such disclosure, it must first provide to the other party the content of the proposed disclosure, the reasons that such disclosure is required by law, and the time and place that the disclosure will be made.

10. Confidentiality. The Confidentiality Agreement, dated as of _____, shall remain in full force and effect.

11. Costs. Except as otherwise expressly provided herein, Buyer, the Company and Parent will be responsible for and bear all of their respective costs and expenses (including any broker's or finder's fees and the expenses of its representatives) incurred at any time in connection with pursuing or consummating the transactions contemplated by this letter of intent.

12. Entire Agreement. The Binding Provisions constitute the entire agreement among the parties and supersede all prior oral or written agreements, understandings, representations and warranties and courses of conduct and dealing among the parties on the subject matter thereof. Except as otherwise provided herein, the Binding Provisions may be amended or modified only by a writing executed by all of the parties to this letter of intent.

13.   Governing Law. The Binding Provisions will be governed by and construed under the laws of the State of Delaware without regard to conflicts-of-laws principles.

14.   Jurisdiction; Service Of Process. Any action or proceeding seeking to enforce any provision of, or based on any right arising out of, the Binding Provisions may be brought against any of the parties hereto solely in the state or federal courts located in Wilmington, Delaware, and each of the parties consents to the exclusive jurisdiction of such courts (and of the appropriate appellate courts) in any such action or proceeding and waives any objection to venue laid therein. Process in any action or proceeding referred to in the preceding sentence may be served on any party anywhere in the world.

15.   Counterparts. This letter of intent may be executed in one or more counterparts, each of which will be deemed to be an original of this letter of intent and all of which, when taken together, will be deemed to constitute one and the same letter of intent.

16.   No Liability. The provisions of Paragraphs 1 through 6 of this letter of intent are intended only as an expression of intent on behalf of the parties hereto, are not intended to be legally binding on Buyer, the Company or Parent and are expressly subject to completion by Buyer of its due diligence review and the execution of Definitive Agreements, in each case satisfactory to Buyer in its sole discretion. Moreover, except as expressly provided in Paragraphs 7 through 15 (or as expressly provided in any binding written agreement that the parties may enter into in the future), no past or future action, course of conduct or failure to act relating to transactions contemplated hereby, or relating to the negotiation of the terms of the Definitive Agreements, will give rise to or serve as a basis for any obligation or other liability on the part of Buyer, the Company or Parent.

If you are in agreement with the foregoing, please sign and return one copy of this letter of intent by no later than 5 p.m. on _____, which thereupon will constitute our understanding with respect to its subject matter.

Very truly yours,

_____

By: _____

Name: _____

Title: _____

Agreed to as to the Binding Provisions on _____.

XYZ Corp.

By: _____

Name: _____

Title: _____

[Parent]

By: _____

Name: _____

Title: _____

Courtesy of Barry J. Siegel, Klehr, Harrison, Harvey, Branzburg & Ellers LLP

APPENDIX H

ASSET PURCHASE AGREEMENT

BY AND AMONG

_____

[SHAREHOLDERS]

and

_____

DATED _____, 200___

THIS AGREEMENT, made this ___ day of _____, 200___, is by and among _____, a _____ corporation ("Seller"), [Seller's Shareholders] (each a "Shareholder" and collectively, the "Shareholders"), and _____, a _____ limited liability company ("Buyer").

RECITALS

A.   Seller is engaged in the business of [_____] at its [office/plan/facility] located in or near _____, _____ (the "Business"); and

B.   Seller and the Shareholders desires to sell, transfer and assign to Buyer, and Buyer desires to purchase and acquire from Seller and the Shareholders, certain assets relating to the operation of the Business, and in connection therewith Buyer has agreed to assume certain of the liabilities of Seller relating to the Business, all on the terms set forth herein.

NOW, THEREFORE, in consideration of the mutual covenants and agreements hereinafter contained, the parties hereto agree as follows:

ARTICLE I.
PURCHASE AND SALE OF ASSETS

1.01   Purchase and Sale. Subject to the terms and conditions of this Agreement, at a closing to be held at the offices of Buyer's counsel contemporaneously with the execution and delivery of this Agreement, or such other time and place as may be agreed upon among Buyer and Seller (the "Closing"), Seller and the Shareholders shall sell and Buyer shall purchase the Assets (as hereinafter defined), free and clear of all liens, claims, encumbrances, restrictions and security interests (other than "Permitted Encumbrances" as defined herein), and Buyer shall pay to Seller the consideration specified in Section 1.04.

1.02   Assets to be Transferred by Seller. The following is an identification of the assets being transferred by Seller and/or the Shareholders to Buyer (the "Assets") at Closing pursuant to a bill of sale and such other appropriate instruments of transfer as are agreed among the parties:

(a)   Tangible Assets. All of the tangible property of Seller, other than any "Real Property" and "Inventory," as each such term is defined below, including, without limitation, all of Seller's equipment, tools, furnishings, books and records (computerized and hard copy, including, without limitation, all supplier files, customer order and inquiry files, brochures, catalogs and standards books) pertaining to the Business or the Assets and all other items described on Schedule 1.02(a) hereto (the "Tangible Assets"). Notwithstanding the foregoing, Seller may retain the original copies of its accounting and financial records, provided that the Purchaser is provided with true, complete and correct photocopies of such items. For the purposes hereof, "Real Property" shall mean all land and any buildings or improvements thereon owned by Seller, but does not include fixtures and leasehold improvements owned by Seller, which shall constitute Tangible Assets.

(b)   Intangible Assets. All the intangible assets of Seller, including, without limitation, all registered and unregistered patents, copyrights, trademarks, trade names (including the name

"_____" and any similar names), service marks, domain names, web sites and content therein, logos and other proprietary designs, vendor and client lists, computer software, engineering drawings, technical specifications and ratings data, know-how, trade secrets and the goodwill of Seller, and including, without limitation, those items set forth on Schedule 1.02(b) attached hereto (the "Intangible Assets"). Notwithstanding the foregoing, the bank accounts of Seller (other than prepaid receipts and deposits described in Section 1.02(d)) and all amounts held therein shall not be considered an Asset for the purposes of this Agreement and shall remain the property of Seller.

(c)   Inventory. All inventory of Seller including, without limitation, finished products, work in process, raw materials, parts and supplies, and all other inventory or goods held for sale, in all forms, wherever located, now or hereafter existing (the "Inventory"), but excluding therefrom "Excluded Inventory" as defined below; all of such Inventory which exists as of date hereof and its book value, to be listed and enumerated with specificity on Schedule 1.02(c) attached hereto and incorporated herein. For the purposes hereof, unless otherwise agreed among the parties and specified with a book value on Schedule 1.02(c), inventory meeting any of the following criteria will be valued at zero and not included in the Inventory transferred to Buyer hereunder (the "Excluded Inventory"): (i) all quantities of any item of inventory not in the current standard catalogues or price or parts listings of the selling vendor, (ii) all inventory that is damaged, appears worn or otherwise in a non-saleable condition or only saleable at a substantial discount in accordance with applicable industry standards, (iii) any inventory that is not new and contained in its original packaging, (iv) any inventory that does not have a current manufacturer's part number, and (v) any items in quantity greater than amounts historically used by Seller in one year.

(d)   Contracts. Those leases, contracts (including, but not limited to, vendor and supplier agreements) and outstanding customer orders and vendor purchase orders to which Seller is a party or by which Seller or the properties of Seller is or may be bound that are identified on Schedule 1.02(d) attached hereto, and all prepaid amounts for customer invoices or orders paid to Seller and other prepaid amounts for items and deposits made or received by Seller with respect to any and all of the foregoing (the "Contracts").

(e)   Accounts Receivable. All accounts receivable from customers and other trade debtors of Seller as well as any and all receivables or reimbursements relating to purchase warranty and other claims and purchase rebates from vendors of Seller (such items relating to purchase rebates from vendors, the "Vendor Rebates," and all such items, collectively the "Accounts Receivable"); all of such Accounts Receivable and their Book Value that exist as of the date hereof to be listed and enumerated with specificity on Schedule 1.02(e) attached hereto and incorporated herein. Notwithstanding the foregoing, any Accounts Receivable other than Vendor Rebates that have been outstanding for 90 days or more or are otherwise known to be uncollectible shall not be considered an Asset for the purposes of this Agreement and shall remain the property of Seller.

1.03   Liabilities to be Assumed. At Closing, Buyer shall assume, pursuant to an agreed upon form of assignment and assumption agreement, and become responsible to pay, perform and discharge, as and when they become due, the obligations of Seller (i) accruing under the Contracts from and after the date hereof and (ii) those other specified liabilities of Seller that are listed and enumerated with specificity on Schedule 1.03 attached hereto and incorporated herein (collectively, the "Assumed Liabilities"). Buyer shall not assume any liabilities of Seller other than the Assumed Liabilities listed and enumerated on Schedule 1.03.

1.04   Consideration to be Paid by Buyer.

(a)   Purchase Price for the Assets. Except as stipulated below, the purchase price for the Assets, shall be $_____, plus or minus agreed upon adjustments from estimated to actual net realizable book value of the Tangible Assets, Inventory, Accounts Receivable and Assumed Liabilities (the "Purchase Price"), as reflected on the closing statement to be prepared and delivered at Closing (the "Closing Statement").

(b)   Payment Schedule. The Purchase Price shall be paid as follows:

(i)   Contemporaneously with the execution and delivery of this Agreement, Buyer shall pay to Seller an amount equal to $_____; and

(ii)   The balance of the Purchase Price shall be paid by promissory note with a term of ____ years, with interest at a rate of ____% per annum.

(c)   Allocation of Purchase Price. Prior to the Closing, Buyer and Seller shall agree on the manner in which the Purchase Price shall be allocated for state and federal income tax purposes. Such allocation shall be set forth on the Closing Statement. Buyer and Seller further agree that an Internal Revenue Service Form 8594 shall be timely filed in accordance with such allocation.

(d)   Manner of Payments. All cash payments required hereunder shall be in U. S. funds and made by certified or bank official check or by wire transfer at the paying party's option.

1.05   Excluded Inventory and Assets. Seller, at its own expense, shall remove all Excluded Inventory, and any other assets of Seller that Buyer has specifically agreed to exclude from the Assets and which are enumerated on Schedule 1.05 (the "Excluded Assets"), from the Buyer's facilities as soon as practicable following the Closing and in no event more than thirty (30) days following the Closing; and, if Seller fails to do so, Buyer may dispose thereof, at the expense of Seller (and without notice to Seller) in any manner that Buyer deems appropriate and without any obligations to account to Seller or to remit to Seller amounts, if any, received by Buyer in connection with the disposition of such Excluded Inventory.

ARTICLE II.
REPRESENTATIONS AND WARRANTIES
OF SELLER AND SHAREHOLDERS

Seller and the Shareholders, jointly and severally, represent and warrant to Buyer that:

2.01   Corporate Standing and Authority; Binding Agreement. Seller is a corporation duly organized, validly existing and in good standing under the laws of the State of _____ and has full corporate power to own all of its properties and assets and to conduct its business as it is now being conducted, and neither its ownership or leasing of property nor the conduct of its business requires it to be qualified as a foreign corporation in any jurisdiction. The execution of this Agreement and consummation of the transactions contemplated herein shall not violate any provision of Seller's Articles of Incorporation or Bylaws, and Seller has obtained all necessary authorization and approval from its board of directors and shareholders for the execution, delivery and performance of this Agreement and the consummation of the transactions contemplated hereby. This Agreement is a legal, valid and binding agreement of Seller and the Shareholders, enforceable against each in accordance with its terms.

2.02   Stock Ownership. Attached hereto as Schedule 2.02 is a complete and accurate list of all authorized capital stock including the number of shares of each class of capital stock and the number of shares of each class held by each owner. All outstanding shares of Seller have been duly issued and are fully paid and non-assessable. The shareholders identified on Schedule 2.02 own all of the outstanding equity interests of Seller. Seller has no equity interest in and has not made advances to any corporation, association, partnership, joint venture or other entity.

2.03   Absence of Conflicting Agreements or Required Consents. Except as set forth in Schedule 2.03, the execution, delivery and performance of this Agreement by Seller and the Shareholders, including, without limitation, the assignment of the Contracts to Buyer, do not and will not: (i) conflict with or violate any law, rule, regulation, order, judgment or decree applicable to Seller or the Shareholders or by which any of Seller's or the Shareholders' assets are bound or affected, (ii) result in any breach of or constitute a default under any Contract or other agreement or note, bond, mortgage, indenture, lease, license, franchise or other instrument or obligation to which Seller or any Shareholder is a party or by which any of Seller's or the Shareholders' assets are bound or affected, or (iii) require any consent, approval, authorization or permit of, or filing with or notification to, any governmental or regulatory authority, domestic or foreign, or any person or entity not a party to this Agreement.

2.04   Title to Assets; Permitted Encumbrances. Seller has good and marketable title to all of the Assets free and clear of all liens, claims, security interests, mortgages, easements, restrictions, charges and encumbrances other than those listed as "Permitted Encumbrances" on Schedule 2.04. No condemnation or other appropriation proceeding is in existence concerning any of the Assets and Seller is not aware of and has not received any notice concerning the possible commencement of such a proceeding.

2.05   Operations and Use of Properties and Assets. Seller's operations, business and properties, including leased properties, have at all times been and are in full conformity with all applicable laws, orders, ordinances and regulations, including without limitation zoning, land use and building codes and motor vehicle registration, permitting, inspection and operation. All of the Tangible Assets are in good operating condition and repair and are usable in the normal course of business. The Assets constitute all assets, property and rights of any nature whatsoever, necessary to operate the Business in the manner it is operated presently and has been operated prior to the date hereof, and there are no material capital expenditures of Seller which Seller now anticipates will be required to be made in connection with the Business as now conducted in order to comply with any existing laws, regulations or other governmental requirements applicable to the Business, including without limitation requirements relating to occupational health and safety or the environment. Seller knows of no facts or circumstances that might reasonably be expected to have an adverse effect on Buyer's continuance of the Business after the Closing in the same manner as such business was conducted by Seller prior to Closing.

2.06   Licenses. Seller has all licenses, permits, approvals and other governmental authorizations necessary to own all of its assets and carry on the Business as now being conducted (collectively, the "Licenses") all of which Licenses are listed in Schedule 2.06. Except as disclosed on Schedule 2.06, the continuation, validity and effectiveness of each License will in no way be affected by the consummation of the transactions contemplated by this Agreement, including the transfer of same to Buyer. Seller has not breached any provision of, is not in default under the terms of, and has not engaged in any activity that would cause revocation or suspension of, any License and no action or proceeding looking to or contemplating the revocation or suspension of any License is pending or threatened.

2.07   Financial Statements. Seller has furnished Buyer with: (i) Seller's financial statements for Seller's most recently completed fiscal year ended December 31, 200___, and each of the four previous fiscal years ended December 31, 200__, 200__, 200__, and 200__, all of which have been compiled by Seller's accountants, _____, and (ii) Seller's interim balance sheets and statements of profit and loss and supporting schedules of expenses for the period ended _____, 200__ (the "Balance Sheet Date"), prepared from Seller's books and records (collectively, the "Financial Statements"). The Financial Statements have been prepared in accordance with generally accepted accounting principles and procedures consistently applied throughout the periods indicated except as set forth in the notes to the Financial Statements, and fairly, accurately and completely present the results of the operations of Seller, and Seller's financial position, for the periods indicated except, with respect to the interim financial statements, for non-material changes resulting from normal year-end adjustments.

2.08   Absence of Changes. Since the Balance Sheet Date, there has not been (i) any adverse change in the financial condition, assets, liabilities, business or properties of Seller, (ii) any damage to, destruction of or loss of property, whether or not covered by insurance, adversely affecting the property, assets or business of Seller, (iii) any material changes in compensation or bonus payments or arrangements for any employees of Seller, (iv) any sale or transfer of any assets of Seller other than in the ordinary course of business, (v) any cancellation or compromise of any debts or claims owed to Seller other than in the ordinary course of business, (vi) any transaction not in the ordinary course of business, or (vii) any amendment or termination of any contract or agreement which adversely affects the Assets or the Business. Since the Balance Sheet Date, there have been no material changes in the Assets other than with respect to the sale or acquisition of Inventory in the usual and ordinary course of business.

2.09   Liabilities. There are no debts, liabilities, commitments or obligations of Seller of any kind or character, whether accrued, fixed, absolute, contingent, matured, unmatured, liquidated, due, to become due or otherwise, except (i) as indicated in the Financial Statements and (ii) liabilities or obligations arising since the Balance Sheet Date which (A) were incurred in the ordinary and usual course of business, (B) are in types and amounts consistent with past practices and experience, and (C) will not have an adverse impact either individually or in the aggregate upon Seller, the Business or the Assets. No such liabilities or obligations of Seller will become liabilities of Buyer other than the Assumed Liabilities.

2.10   Taxes. Seller has filed all tax returns and reports that are required by law to have been filed and has fully paid any and all taxes (including, but not limited to, income, franchise, property, sales, use and employment taxes) required to be paid in respect of the periods covered by those returns and reports. Schedule 2.10 lists all such tax returns and reports which have been filed for the past five (5) years, true and correct copies of which have been provided to Buyer, and sets forth the most recent years for which income, sales and use and employment tax returns have been examined by the Internal Revenue Service of the Federal Government and any taxation agency or authority of any other jurisdiction, as the case may be. All filed tax returns and reports of Seller are correct and true in all respects and there is no outstanding claimed deficiency with respect to any tax period, no formal or informal notice of a proposed deficiency, no notification of any pending audit of tax returns and reports and no waiver or extension granted by Seller with respect to any period of limitations affecting assessment of any tax.

2.11   Inventories. The listing and enumeration of the Inventory on Schedule 1.02(c) is true, accurate and complete and fairly and accurately represent in all respects the subject matter required to be contained therein pursuant to Section 1.02(c). The Inventory: (i) complies with all applicable federal laws and regulations and with all applicable laws and regulations of each of the states of the United States into which any product would be shipped; (ii) does not contain any Hazardous Material, as defined below, or any substance that was the subject of a pre-manufacturing notice filed with the United States Environmental Protection Agency under the Toxic Substance Control Act, as amended, 15 U.S.C. §§2601 et seq.; and (iii) does not consist of any damaged or obsolete items. Each item of Inventory is usable and saleable in the normal and ordinary course of business.

2.12   Accounts Receivables. The listing and enumeration of Accounts Receivable contained on Schedule 1.02(e) is true, accurate and complete and fairly and accurately represent in all respects the subject matter required to be contained therein pursuant to Section 1.02(e).All Accounts Receivable of Seller have been properly recorded on Seller's books and arose in connection with the bona fide sale of goods or services in the ordinary course of business.

2.13   Insurance. Seller is covered by valid and currently effective insurance policies issued in favor of Seller with coverages in amounts that are typical within Seller's industry for a company of Seller's size and that are, in Seller's best judgment, sufficient for its businesses and operations. Such insurance policies include, but are not necessarily limited to, general liability, casualty and products liability coverages and Seller has been insured with all such coverages continuously since its incorporation. All of Seller's policies of insurance are listed and described on Schedule 2.13 hereto.

2.14   Environmental Matters. Seller has at all times been and remains in full compliance with all Environmental Laws (as hereinafter defined). Except as set forth in Schedule 2.14: (a) Seller has not manufactured, processed, distributed, used, treated, stored, disposed of, transported or handled any Hazardous Material (as hereinafter defined) at any property or facility ever owned, leased or used by Seller (collectively, "Seller's Facilities") in violation of any applicable law, and to the best of Seller's and each Shareholder's knowledge, no such event occurred at any of Seller's Facilities prior to Seller's ownership or leasing of same; (b) with respect to any disposal of Hazardous Material, Seller has at all times disposed of Hazardous Material off site of Seller's Facilities and in accordance with all Environmental Laws; (c) to the best of Seller's and each Shareholder's knowledge there is no ambient air, surface water, groundwater or land contamination within building structures, within, under, originating from or relating to Seller's Facilities or any other location adjacent to Seller's

515

Facilities; (d) there is no underground or above ground storage tanks located at Seller's Facilities and Seller has never used nor owned any such storage tanks at Seller's Facilities; and (e) with respect to any storage tanks disclosed in Schedule 2.14, there is not now and never has been any leakage or loss of any contents of any such tanks. There are no pending or threatened claims with respect to Hazardous Material relating to any of Seller's Facilities or arising in connection with or relating to any operations of Seller, and Seller nor any Shareholder knows of any basis for a claim being made against Seller with respect to any Hazardous Material under any Environmental Law.

For purposes of this Agreement, "Hazardous Material" shall mean (a) any hazardous substance as now defined in or regulated by the federal Comprehensive Environmental Response, Compensation and Liability Act of 1980 and the regulations promulgated thereunder, all as amended; (b) any hazardous waste, pollutant or contaminant as now defined in or regulated by the federal Resource Conservation and Recovery Act; (c) any petroleum, including crude oil and any fraction thereof; natural or synthetic crude oil and any fraction thereof; (d) any natural or synthetic gas usable for fuel; (e) any hazardous chemical as defined in or regulated by the federal Occupational Safety and Health Act; (f) any asbestos, polychlorinated biphenyl or isomer of dioxin, or any material or thing containing or composed of such substance or substances; and (g) any other substance, regardless of physical form that is subject to any Environmental Laws. For purposes of this Agreement, "Environmental Laws" shall mean all statutes, regulations, requirements, orders, ordinances, rules of liability or standards of conduct of any federal, state or local government, or common law relating to the protection of human health, plant life, animal life, natural resources, the environment or property from the presence in the environment of any solid, liquid, gas, odor or any form of energy, from whatever source, including, without limitation, any emissions, discharges, releases, or threatened releases of Hazardous Material into the environment (including, without limitation, ambient air, surface water, groundwater, land surface or subsurface or building structures).

2.15   Employees. Attached hereto as Schedule 2.15 is a list of all employees of Seller showing their names, whether they are employed full-time or part-time, their positions, current annual salaries or rate of compensation (including bonus and incentive compensation), and all benefits they are eligible to receive.

2.16   Employees and Labor Laws. Except as disclosed in Schedule 2.15, there have been no strikes, lockouts, or other material labor disputes or demands for recognition of a union as collective bargaining agent for all or any part of Seller's employees, and Seller is not a party to any collective bargaining or other labor agreement. Seller has no written agreements of employment and no oral agreements or understandings with any employee as to any specific period of employment. Seller is in compliance with all federal, state and local governmental laws and regulations relating to employment or labor, including provisions relating to wages, fringe benefits, hours, working conditions, occupational safety and health, safety of the premises, collective bargaining, payment of social security and unemployment taxes, civil rights and discrimination in hiring, retention, promotion, pay and other conditions of employment; and Seller is not liable for arrears on wages or any tax or penalties for failure to comply with those laws or regulations. There are no oral agreements or understandings with Seller's employees except as to current salary or wage rates and no other oral agreements or understandings which will affect Seller's employment practices or operations. Seller is, and at all times has been, in compliance with the Immigration Reform and Control Act of 1986.

2.17   Employee Benefit Plans. Schedule 2.17 sets forth and briefly describes all of the Seller's employee pension benefit plans (as defined in section 3(2) of the Employee Retirement Income Security Act of 1974, as amended ("ERISA")), all employee welfare benefit plans (as defined in section 3(1) of ERISA), all specified fringe benefit plans (as defined in section 6039D(d) of the Internal Revenue Code of 1986, as amended (the "Code")), and all executive compensation, retirement, supplemental retirement, deferred compensation, incentive, bonus, severance, compensation associated with change in control, perquisite, health care, death benefit, medical insurance, disability insurance, life insurance, vacation pay, sick pay or other plans, programs, and arrangements to which Seller is or has been a party, with respect to which Seller has an obligation, or that have been or are maintained, contributed to, or sponsored by Seller for the benefit of any current or former employee (such plans, programs, and arrangements to be referred to collectively as "Employee Benefit

517

Plans"). Seller has delivered to Buyer a true and complete copy of each Employee Benefit Plan listed on Schedule 2.17, which copies accurately reflect the understanding of Seller with respect to those instruments. Neither Seller nor any officer, director, employee or fiduciary of Seller or any plan administrator has committed any breach under any Employee Benefit Plan which would subject Buyer or any of its directors, officers or employees to liability under ERISA, the Code or any other applicable law. Seller has no written or oral plan, arrangement, obligation or understanding to pay severance or change of control benefits to any employee.

2.18   WARN Statute. Seller has fewer than 50 employees in total, including all active employees together with all employees on layoff, leave of absence, and any other non-active categories; Seller has never been an "employer" within the meaning of that term under the Worker Adjustment Retraining and Notification Act ("WARN"), 29 U.S.C. §2101 et seq.; and Seller at all times has been completely independent of all other entities and business enterprises within the meaning of 20 C.F.R. § 639.3(a)(2), and has never been and cannot be considered part of or combined with any "employer" covered by WARN.

2.19   Product Labeling and Product Liability. Seller is in compliance with all federal, state and local laws and regulations relating to product labeling, product safety and public health and safety. Seller has not received any notice of any claim that any product now or heretofore offered for sale or sold by it or distributed by it in connection with product sales is injurious to the health and safety of any person or is not in conformity with its specifications or not suitable for any purpose or application for which it is offered for sale, sold or distributed.

2.20   Exports. Seller (whether through the Business or otherwise) does not and has not ever exported any goods from the United States to foreign nations.

2.21   Validity and Existence of Agreements; Related Party Contracts. Schedule 2.21 sets forth and briefly describes all written or oral agreements, contracts, arrangements, commitments, understandings or obligations to which Seller is a party or by which it or its properties is or may be bound, including, but not limited to, the Contracts being transferred to Buyer hereunder. With respect to the Contracts, Schedule 2.21 also includes the following information: (i) all prepayments or deposits made to Seller on unfulfilled orders, and (ii) all prepayments or deposits made by Seller for goods or services not yet received. No affiliates of the Seller or the Shareholders have any interest, direct or indirect, in any agreement, contract, arrangement, commitment, understanding or obligation, oral or written, relating to Seller, its business, operations, prospects, properties, assets or condition (financial or otherwise) except as described on Schedule 2.21. Seller has delivered to Buyer (a) a true and complete copy of each written contract, lease, agreement, instrument or other document listed on Schedule 2.21, which copies accurately reflect the understanding of Seller with respect to those instruments, and (b) a fair and accurate written summary of the material terms of each oral contract, agreement or understanding listed on Schedule 2.21. Each of the Contracts being transferred to Buyer hereunder is a valid and binding obligation of the parties thereto in accordance with its respective terms. Seller has performed and complied in all material respects with all the provisions of each of the Contracts, and no party is in default or would be in default with the lapse of time or notice under the terms of any of the Contracts.

2.22   Non-Infringement of Patents, Trademarks and Other Intellectual Property. Schedule 1.02(b) contains a complete and correct list of all of the registered and unregistered patents, copyrights, trademarks, trade names, service marks and domain names owned or used by Seller in connection with the Business (such items, along with any trade secrets, industrial designs and technical know how owned or used by Seller in connection with the Business, hereinafter referred to collectively as the "Intellectual Property"). Schedule 1.02(b) also contains a list of Seller's applications and registrations in any governmental office or registry with respect to any Intellectual Property. Except as disclosed in Schedule1.02(b), the Intellectual Property is owned by Seller and is free and clear of any license, sublicense, lien, charge or encumbrance. The Intellectual Property being transferred to Buyer pursuant to this Agreement, constitutes all intellectual property rights necessary to conduct the Business as it is currently conducted. None of the Intellectual Property has a material defect or has been misappropriated from any third party. Seller is not infringing upon or otherwise violating any intellectual property rights of any third party, and Buyer's continued use of any and all of the Intellectual Property after the

Closing in a manner consistent with Seller's past practices shall not result in any such infringement or violation. Seller is not in default under any license or sublicense agreement with any third party. Neither Seller nor any Shareholder knows of (i) any claim by a third party that the use of the Intellectual Property infringes or violates the intellectual property rights of said third party, or (ii) any infringement or violation by a third party of Seller's rights in the Intellectual Property or any default by a third party under a license or sublicense agreement with Seller.

2.23   Litigation. Except as disclosed in Schedule 2.23, there are no (i) claims, suits, actions, citations, administrative or arbitration or other proceedings or governmental investigations pending or, to the best knowledge of Seller and each Shareholder, threatened against Seller or to which Seller is a party or relating to any of the Assets, the Business, or other properties, businesses or business practices of Seller, or the transactions contemplated by this Agreement (including without limitation proceedings and investigations related to Environmental Laws, civil rights, discrimination in employment and occupational safety and health) or (ii) judgments, orders, writs, injunctions or decrees of any court or administrative agency involving Seller or affecting the Assets or the Business.

ARTICLE III.
REPRESENTATIONS AND WARRANTIES OF BUYER.

Buyer represents and warrants to Seller and the Shareholders that:

3.01   Organization and Authority. Buyer is a limited liability company duly organized, validly existing and in good standing under the laws of the State of _____, and has full power and authority to carry on its current business operations and consummate the transactions contemplated by this Agreement. The execution of this Agreement and consummation of the transactions contemplated herein shall not violate any provision of Buyer's Articles of Organization or Operating Agreement, and Buyer has obtained all necessary authorization and approval by its board of governors and members for the execution, delivery and performance of this Agreement and the consummation of the transactions contemplated hereby. This Agreement is a legal, valid and binding agreement of Buyer enforceable against Buyer in accordance with its terms, subject to the laws of bankruptcy, insolvency and moratorium and other laws or equitable principles generally affecting creditors' rights.

3.02   Absence of Conflicting Agreements or Required Consents. The execution, delivery and performance of this Agreement by Buyer do not and will not: (i) conflict with or violate any law, rule, regulation, order, judgment or decree applicable to Buyer or by which any of Buyer's assets are bound or affected, (ii) result in any breach of or constitute a default under any contract or other agreement or note, bond, mortgage, indenture, lease, license, franchise or other instrument or obligation to which Buyer is a party or by which any of Buyer's assets are bound or affected, or (iii) require any consent, approval, authorization or permit of, or filing with or notification to, any governmental or regulatory authority, domestic or foreign, or any person or entity not a party to this Agreement.

3.03   Litigation. There is no litigation pending or, to the best knowledge of Buyer after due inquiry of its officers, threatened against Buyer which seeks to prevent, or if successful would prevent, Buyer from consummating the purchase contemplated by this Agreement.

ARTICLE IV.
COVENANTS

4.01   Indemnification of Buyer. Seller and the Shareholders, jointly and severally, shall defend, indemnify and hold Buyer harmless from and against any liabilities, losses, claims, damages, costs and expenses (including, but not limited to, reasonable attorneys' fees) resulting from: (i) any breach of any representation, warranty, covenant or agreement (including but not limited to the covenant contained in Section 4.05) on the part of Seller and/or the Shareholders made herein or pursuant to any other document, certificate or agreement delivered pursuant hereto, (ii) the assertion against Buyer of any liability of Seller, other than the Assumed Liabilities (including, but not limited to, any assertion that Buyer is liable as a successor in interest to Seller under the continuity of enterprise doctrine, under COBRA or otherwise), (iii) any claims from former or existing shareholders of Seller other than the Shareholders, or (iv) the existence or operation of the Business on or prior to the Closing (including, without limitation, (x)liabilities arising out of Seller's employment of its employees or the termination of such employment, whether in connection with the transactions contemplated herein or otherwise, (y) liabilities arising out of circumstances pertaining to laws regarding the environment or worker health or safety or to the environment in general on or prior to the Closing, and (z) liabilities arising from the failure of Seller to pay any taxes).

(a)   Without limiting the generality of the foregoing, with respect to any measurement of damages or costs or expenses owing to Buyer hereunder, the Buyer shall have the right to be put in the same financial position as it would have been had the matter leading to the claim of indemnification never occurred or arose. Buyer shall be reimbursed by Seller and the Shareholders, jointly and severally, for all liabilities and damages incurred by Buyer and all reasonable costs and reasonable expenses incurred in enforcing this indemnity.

(b)   Buyer shall have the right to set-off against any amounts owing by it to Seller or any Shareholder under this Agreement or any other document, certificate or agreement delivered pursuant hereto, the amount of any liabilities, losses, claims, damages, costs and expenses for which Buyer is entitled to indemnification hereunder. Notwithstanding any other provision herein, Buyer shall be entitled to obtain equitable relief in any appropriate indemnification claim. Buyer shall use reasonable efforts to provide prompt notice to Seller of each indemnifiable claim it believes it has suffered; provided, however, no delay in providing any such notice shall affect the rights of Buyer to recover damages or equitable relief as appropriate under this Agreement.

4.02   Indemnification of Seller and Shareholders. Buyer shall defend, indemnify and hold Seller and the Shareholders harmless from and against any liabilities, losses, claims, damages, costs and expenses (including, but not limited to, reasonable attorneys' fees) resulting from any breach of any representation, warranty, agreement or covenant on the part of Buyer made herein or pursuant hereto, including without limitation the failure to pay, perform or discharge the Assumed Liabilities.

(a)   Without limiting the generality of the foregoing, with respect to any measurement of damages or costs or expenses owing to Seller and the Shareholders hereunder, Seller and the Shareholders shall have the right to be put in the same financial position as such parties would have been had the matter leading to the claim of indemnification never occurred or arose. Seller and the Shareholders shall be reimbursed by Buyer for all liabilities and damages incurred by Seller and the Shareholders and all reasonable costs and reasonable expenses incurred in the defense of the claim and all expenses incurred in enforcing this indemnity.

(b)   Seller and the Shareholders shall use reasonable efforts to provide prompt notice to Buyer of each indemnifiable claim they believe they have suffered; provided, however, no delay in providing any such notice shall affect the rights of Seller or the Shareholders to recover damages or equitable relief as appropriate hereunder.

4.03   Announcements. No press releases, announcements, or other disclosure related to this Agreement or the transactions contemplated herein shall be issued or made to the press, employees, customers, suppliers or any other person without the approval of Buyer.

4.04   Name Change. Following the Closing, Buyer and its successors and assigns may utilize the name "_____" or such other similar names as Buyer may select (the "Names"). As of the Closing and thereafter, Seller and the Shareholders shall cease all use of the Names and any other similar names and shall adopt a corporate name dissimilar to the Names and such similar names. As soon as practicable following the Closing, Buyer shall prepare and file with all appropriate governmental bodies, such documentation as is necessary to change Seller's corporate name, and deliver proof of such filing to the Buyer.

4.05   Warranty Claims. Without limiting the indemnification obligation set forth under Section 4.01above, Seller shall be responsible for and covenants that it shall satisfy all warranty claims asserted by customers of Seller both before and after the Closing in connection with products and services provided to such customers by Seller prior to the Closing. Buyer shall administer and service any and all such warranty claims on behalf of Seller. Seller and each Shareholder, jointly and severally, shall pay Buyer, on demand, Buyer's costs incurred in connection with any and all such administration and service (consisting of Buyer's labor costs and out-of-pocket expenses), and Buyer shall be entitled to set-off against any amounts owing by it to Seller under this Agreement or any other document, certificate or agreement delivered pursuant hereto, any amounts owing to Buyer by Seller or any Shareholder under this Section 4.05. In addition, Buyer shall have no liability in connection with such warranty claims or the administration and service of the same and Seller and each Shareholder shall indemnify and hold Buyer harmless from and against any losses, liabilities, costs or expenses (including attorneys' fees) incurred by Buyer in connection therewith.

ARTICLE V.
MISCELLANEOUS

5.01   Survival of Representations, Warranties and Covenants. Except as otherwise provided in this Agreement: (a) all covenants and agreements of the parties contained in this Agreement shall survive the Closing in accordance with their terms, and (b) the representations and warranties of each of the parties contained in this Agreement or contained in any document or certificate given under this Agreement as well as the right of the other party to rely thereon shall survive the Closing for a period of three (3) years, provided that with respect to any claim made in writing within such three (3) year period, such representations and warranties shall survive until a final and binding resolution of such claim has been determined. Notwithstanding the Closing, nor any investigation made by or on behalf of any party, such representations and warranties shall continue in full force and effect for such period. Further, notwithstanding the foregoing, (i) the representations and warranties contained in Section 2.04 herein (title to the Assets), Section 2.14 (environmental laws), and Section 2.10 (taxes), shall survive until the expiration of any and all applicable statutes of limitations periods on the subject matter of the representation or warranty (or in the event of a claim or an assessment or reassessment, until a final and binding resolution of all matters in relation thereto is made) and (ii) the representations and warranties contained in Section 2.01 (due authority and organization) shall continue indefinitely.

5.02   No Broker. Buyer represents to Seller, and Seller represents to Buyer, that neither has engaged, or incurred any unpaid liability to, any broker, finder or consultant in connection with this transaction. Seller shall indemnify the Buyer and its directors, officers, shareholders and employees and will hold them harmless from and against any claims by any broker, finder or consultant deemed to be engaged by Seller for a brokerage fee, finder's fee or the like. Buyer shall indemnify Seller and will hold it harmless from and against any claims by any broker, finder or consultant deemed to be engaged by Buyer for a brokerage fee, finder's fee or the like.

5.03   Expense. Except as otherwise provided herein, the parties shall each pay all of their respective legal, accounting and other expenses incurred in connection with the transactions contemplated by this Agreement.

5.04   Notices. Any notice or other communication required or permitted hereunder shall be in writing and delivered personally or by a recognized international overnight courier service, addressed as follows or to such other address as a party shall specify for this purpose in a notice given in the same manner:

(a)   To Seller and the Shareholders:

_____

_____

_____

Attn: _____

Facsimile: _____

with copies to:

_____

_____

_____

Attn: _____

Facsimile: _____

(b)   To Buyer:

_____

_____

_____

Attn: _____
Facsimile: _____

with copies to:

_____

_____

_____

Attn: _____
Facsimile: _____

Any notice given pursuant to this Section shall be deemed given when delivered.

5.05   Binding Effect; Assignment. This Agreement shall be binding upon and shall inure to the benefit of the parties hereto and their respective successors and assigns, but may not be assigned or otherwise transferred by any party without the written consent of all the other parties.

5.06   Entire Agreement. This Agreement, the schedules hereto and the other exhibits, documents and instruments expressly contemplated hereby contain the entire understanding of the parties relating to the subject matter hereof and supersede all prior written or oral and all contemporaneous oral agreements and understandings relating to the subject matter hereof. All statements of the Seller and the Shareholders contained in any schedule, certificate or other document required under this Agreement to be delivered in connection with the transactions contemplated hereby will constitute representations and warranties of the Seller and Shareholders under this Agreement. The recitals to this Agreement, the schedules hereto and such other documents and instruments contemplated hereby are hereby incorporated by reference into and made a part of this Agreement for all purposes.

5.07   Choice of Law. This Agreement shall be interpreted under the internal laws of the State of _____ without regard to any conflicts of law rule or principle that might result in the application of the law of another jurisdiction.

5.08   Amendment; Waiver. This Agreement may be amended, supplemented or modified, and any provision hereof may be waived, only by written instrument making specific reference to this Agreement signed by the party against whom enforcement is sought. No waiver of any of the provisions of this Agreement shall be deemed to or shall constitute a waiver of any other provision, whether or not similar, nor shall any waiver constitute a continuing waiver unless so specified in writing.

5.09   Post-Closing Cooperation. Following the Closing, upon the reasonable request of any other party or parties, each of the parties agrees to take such actions and furnish such additional documents and instruments as may be necessary or reasonably desirable to better effectuate the transactions contemplated by this Agreement and the smooth transition of the Business to the Buyer.

5.10   Counterparts. This Agreement may be executed in counterparts and will be effective when at least one counterpart has been executed by each party hereto. This Agreement may be executed in duplicate originals, each of which shall be deemed to be an original instrument. All such counterparts and duplicate originals together shall constitute but one Agreement.

5.11   Certain Taxes. The Purchase Price includes, and Seller shall be responsible for paying, any and all _____ or local sales or use tax payable on the transfer of the Assets from Seller to Buyer.

5.12   Bulk Sales Law. Without admitting that the bulk sales law of any state is applicable to the transactions contemplated by this Agreement, the parties waive and agree not to comply with the bulk sales law of any state. Buyer shall have no liability in connection with such noncompliance and Seller shall indemnify and hold Buyer, its shareholders, directors, employees and affiliates harmless from and against any losses, liabilities, costs or expenses (including attorneys' fees) incurred by Buyer or such other parties in connection therewith; and Buyer shall be entitled to setoff against any amounts owing by it to Seller under this Agreement or any other document, certificate or agreement delivered pursuant hereto, any such losses, liabilities, costs or expenses Buyer or such other indemnified parties incur in connection with such aforementioned noncompliance.

5.13   Interpretation. The article and section headings contained in this Agreement are solely for the purpose of reference, are not part of the agreement of the parties and will not in any way affect the meaning or interpretation of this Agreement. Whenever the singular form of a word is used in this Agreement, that word will include the plural form of that word. The term "or" will not be interpreted as excluding any of the items described. The term "include" or any derivative of such term does not mean that the items following such term are the only types of such items. Neither this Agreement nor any provision contained in this Agreement will be interpreted in favor of or against any party hereto because such party or its legal counsel drafted this Agreement or such provision. Whenever the plural form of a word is used in this Agreement, that word will include the singular form of that word.

[The remainder of this page is intentionally left blank.]

IN WITNESS WHEREOF, this Agreement has been executed the day and year first above written.

SELLER: _____

By: _____

Name: _____

Title: _____

SHAREHOLDERS: _____
[Name]

_____
[Name]

_____
[Name]

BUYER: _____

By: _____

Name: _____

Title: _____

Schedules

1.02(a)	-	Tangible Assets
1.02(b)	-	Intangible Assets
1.02(c)	-	Inventory
1.02(d)	-	Contracts Being Transferred
1.02(e)	-	Accounts Receivable
1.04	-	Assumed Liabilities
2.15	-	Employees
2.03	-	Required Consents
2.04	-	Permitted Encumbrances
2.10	-	Tax Filings & Inspections
2.06	-	Licenses
2.13	-	Insurance
2.14	-	Environmental Matters
2.15	-	Labor Matters
2.21	-	Contracts and Agreements
2.23	-	Legal Proceedings
2.22	-	Intellectual Property

Courtesy of Stephen M. Quinlivan and Marci K. Winga, Leonard, Street and Deinard PA

APPENDIX I

AGREEMENT AND PLAN OF MERGER

AGREEMENT AND PLAN OF MERGER (this "Agreement"), dated as of _____, 200__, by and among _____, Inc., a Delaware corporation ("Parent"), _____ Acquisition Corp., a _____ corporation and a wholly-owned Subsidiary of Parent (the "Purchaser"), and _____, a _____ corporation (the "Company" and, together with Purchaser, hereinafter sometimes referred to as the "Constituent Corporations").

WHEREAS, the Board of Directors of Parent (the "Parent Board"), the Board of Directors of Purchaser, Parent as the sole shareholder of Purchaser, and the Board of Directors of the Company, based upon the recommendation of a special committee of its independent directors (the "Company Special Committee"), have approved this Agreement, and determined that it is in the best interests of their respective companies and shareholders to consummate this Agreement and the transactions provided for herein;

WHEREAS, Parent has proposed acquiring the Company by effecting the Merger (as defined herein) pursuant to this Agreement, whereby the shares of the outstanding common stock, par value $.01 per share, of the Company (the "Shares" or "Company Common Stock"), except as otherwise provided herein, will be converted into cash at a price of $1.00 per Share;

WHEREAS, Parent is the owner of a majority of the issued and outstanding shares of the Company Common Stock and all of the issued and outstanding shares of the preferred stock of the Company, consisting of 200,000 shares of Series A Preferred Stock, par value $1.00 per share, of the Company (the "Series A Preferred Stock"), which shares of Series A Preferred Stock are entitled to vote, together with the shares of Company Common Stock, as a single class with respect to this Agreement and the Merger (with each share of Series A Preferred Stock being entitled to cast 100 votes per share); and

531

WHEREAS, the Company, Parent and Purchaser desire to make certain representations, warranties, covenants and agreements in connection with the Merger.

NOW, THEREFORE, in consideration of the foregoing premises and the respective representations, warranties, covenants and agreements set forth herein, the parties hereto agree as follows:

ARTICLE I.
THE MERGER

Section 1.01   Company Actions.

(a)   The Company hereby approves of the Merger and represents that, upon the recommendation of the Company Special Committee, its Board of Directors, at a meeting duly called and held, has (i) approved this Agreement (including all terms and conditions set forth herein) and the transactions contemplated hereby, including the Merger, determining that the Merger is advisable and that the terms of the Merger are fair to, and in the best interests of, the Company and its shareholders, (ii) directed that this Agreement and the Merger be submitted to a vote of the shareholders of the Company, and (iii) resolved to recommend that the shareholders of the Company approve and adopt this Agreement and the Merger. The Company represents that Section 302A.673 of the _____ Business Corporation Act, as amended (the "__BCA"), does not limit in any respect the transactions contemplated by this Agreement. The Company hereby consents to the inclusion in the Proxy Documents (as defined herein) of the recommendation of its Board of Directors described in clause (iii) of the first sentence of this Section 1.01.

(b)   In connection with the Merger, the Company shall promptly furnish or cause to be furnished to the Parent mailing labels, security position listings and any available listing or computer file containing the names and addresses of the record holders of the Shares as of a recent date, and shall furnish the Parent with such information and assistance as the Parent or its agents may reasonably request in communicating with the shareholders of the Company with respect to the Merger. Except for such steps as are necessary to disseminate the Proxy Documents and subject to the requirements of applicable law, Parent shall, and shall cause the Purchaser to, hold in confidence the information contained in any of such labels and lists and the additional information referred to in the preceding sentence and shall use such information only in connection with the Merger.

Section 1.02   The Merger. Subject to the terms and conditions of this Agreement and the provisions of the __BCA, at the Effective Time (as defined herein), the Company and the Purchaser shall consummate a merger (the "Merger") pursuant to which (a) the Purchaser shall be merged with and into the Company and the separate corporate existence of the Purchaser shall thereupon cease, (b) the Company shall be the surviving corporation in the Merger (the "Surviving Corporation"), its name shall continue to be "_____" and it shall continue to be governed by the laws of the State of _____, and (c) the separate corporate existence of the Company with all its rights, privileges, immunities, powers and franchises shall continue unaffected by the Merger. Pursuant to the Merger, (x) the Articles of Incorporation of the Purchaser, in the form attached as Exhibit A hereto, shall be the Articles of Incorporation of the Surviving Corporation until thereafter amended as provided by law and such Articles of Incorporation, provided, that Article I of the Articles of Incorporation of the Surviving Corporation shall be amended at the Effective Time, without any further action of the shareholders of the Company or Purchaser, to read in its entirety as follows: "The name of the Corporation is _____" and (y) the By-laws of the Purchaser, as in effect immediately prior to the Effective Time, shall be the By-laws of the Surviving Corporation until thereafter amended as provided by law, the Articles of Incorporation and such By-laws. The Merger shall have the effects set forth in the __BCA.

Section 1.03   Effective Time. Parent shall cause the Purchaser to, and the Company shall, execute and file on the Closing Date (as defined in Section 1.04) (or on such later date as Parent and the Company may agree) with the Secretary of State of the State of _____ (the "Secretary of State") appropriate Articles of Merger (the "Articles of Merger") as provided in the __BCA. The Merger shall become effective on the date on which the Articles of Merger are duly filed with the Secretary of State or such later date and time as is agreed upon by the Constituent Corporations and specified in the Articles of Merger, and such date and time is hereinafter referred to as the "Effective Time."

Section 1.04   Closing. The closing of the Merger (the "Closing") shall take place at 10:00 a.m., on a date to be specified by the parties, which shall be as soon as practicable, but in no event later than the third business day, after satisfaction or waiver of all of the conditions set forth in Article VI hereof (the "Closing Date"), at the offices of _____ _____, unless another date, time or place is agreed to in writing by the parties hereto.

Section 1.05   Directors and Officers of the Surviving Corporation. The directors of the Purchaser and the officers of the Company immediately prior to the Effective Time shall, from and after the Effective Time, be the directors and officers, respectively, of the Surviving Corporation until their successors shall have been duly elected or appointed or qualified or until their earlier death, resignation or removal in accordance with the Surviving Corporation's Articles of Incorporation and By-laws.

Section 1.06   Shareholders' Meeting.

(a)   As required by applicable law in order to consummate the Merger, the Company, acting through its Board of Directors, shall, in accordance with applicable law: (i) use its reasonable efforts to duly call, give notice of, convene and hold a special meeting of its shareholders (the "Special Meeting") as soon as practicable following the date of this Agreement for the purpose of considering and taking action upon this Agreement; (ii) prepare and file with the Securities and Exchange Commission ("SEC") a preliminary proxy or information statement relating to the Merger and this Agreement and use its reasonable efforts (x) to obtain and furnish the information required to be included by the federal securities laws (and the rules and regulations thereunder) in the Proxy Statement (as hereinafter defined) and, after consultation with Parent, to respond promptly to any comments made by the

SEC with respect to the preliminary proxy or information statement and cause a definitive proxy or information statement (the "Proxy Statement") to be mailed to its shareholders, and (y) to obtain the necessary approvals of the Merger and this Agreement by its shareholders; and (iii) include in the Proxy Statement the recommendation of the Board that shareholders of the Company vote in favor of the approval of the Merger and this Agreement (the Proxy Statement, together with such related materials sent to the Company shareholders, collectively, the "Proxy Documents"). The Company shall submit this Agreement and the Merger to a vote of the shareholders of the Company at the Special Meeting whether or not the Board of Directors of the Company or the Company Special Committee determines at any time after its approval of this Agreement that this Agreement is no longer advisable and recommends that the shareholders of the Company reject this Agreement.

(b)   Parent shall provide the Company with the information concerning Parent and Purchaser required to be included in the Proxy Statement. Parent shall vote, or cause to be voted, all of the shares of Company Common Stock and Series A Preferred Stock then owned by it, the Purchaser or any of its other Subsidiaries and affiliates in favor of the approval of the Merger and of this Agreement.

ARTICLE II.
CONVERSION OF SECURITIES

Section 2.01   Conversion of Capital Stock.

The manner and basis of converting the shares of capital stock of each of the Constituent Corporations is set forth in this Section 2.01. As of the Effective Time, by virtue of the Merger and without any action on the part of the holders of any shares of Company Common Stock or common stock, par value $.01 per share, of the Purchaser (the "Purchaser Common Stock"):

(a)   <u>Purchaser Common Stock</u>. Each issued and outstanding share of the Purchaser Common Stock shall be converted into and become one validly issued, fully paid and nonassessable share of common stock, $.01 par value per share, of the Surviving Corporation, which shall constitute the only issued and outstanding shares of capital stock of the Surviving Corporation immediately after the Effective Time.

(b)   <u>Cancellation of Certain Shares</u>. All shares of Company Common Stock owned by any Subsidiary (as defined in Section 3.01) of the Company and any shares of Company Common Stock or Series A Preferred Stock owned by Parent, the Purchaser or any other wholly owned Subsidiary of Parent shall be cancelled and retired and shall cease to exist and no consideration shall be delivered in exchange therefor.

(c)   <u>Conversion of Shares of Company Common Stock</u>. Each issued and outstanding share of Company Common Stock (other than Shares to be cancelled in accordance with Section 2.01(b) and any Dissenting Common Stock (as defined in Section 2.03 hereof)), shall be converted into the right to receive cash in the amount of $1.00, without interest, payable to the holder thereof (the "Merger Consideration"), prorated for fractional shares, upon surrender of the certificate formerly representing such share of Company Common Stock in the manner provided in Section 2.02 hereof. All such shares of Company Common Stock, when so converted, shall no longer be outstanding and shall automatically be cancelled and retired and shall cease to exist, and each holder of a certificate representing any such shares shall cease to have any rights with respect thereto, except the right to receive the Merger Consideration therefor upon the surrender of such certificate in accordance with Section 2.02 hereof, without interest.

Section 2.02   <u>Exchange of Certificates</u>.

(a)   <u>Paying Agent</u>. Parent shall designate a bank or trust company (the "Paying Agent") reasonably acceptable to the Company to make the payments of the funds to which holders of shares of Company Common Stock shall become entitled pursuant to Section 2.01(c) hereof. Prior to the Effective Time, Parent shall take all steps necessary to deposit or cause to be deposited with the Paying Agent such funds for timely payment thereunder. Such funds shall be invested by the Paying Agent as directed by Parent or the Surviving Corporation.

(b)   Exchange Procedures. As soon as practicable after the Effective Time, but in no event more than three (3) business days thereafter, Parent shall cause the Paying Agent to mail to each holder of record of a certificate or certificates, which immediately prior to the Effective Time represented outstanding shares of Company Common Stock (the "Certificates"), whose shares were converted pursuant to Section 2.01(c) hereof into the right to receive the Merger Consideration, (i) a letter of transmittal (which shall specify that delivery shall be effected, and risk of loss and title to the Certificates shall pass, only upon delivery of the Certificates to the Paying Agent and shall be in such form and have such other provisions as Parent and the Surviving Corporation may reasonably specify), and (ii) instructions for use in effecting the surrender of the Certificates in exchange for payment of the Merger Consideration. Upon surrender of a Certificate for cancellation to the Paying Agent, together with such letter of transmittal, duly executed, the holder of such Certificate shall be entitled to receive in exchange therefor the Merger Consideration (subject to subsection (f) below), for each share of Company Common Stock (prorated for fractional shares) formerly represented by such Certificate and the Certificate so surrendered shall forthwith be cancelled; provided, however, that such aggregate amount shall be rounded up to the nearest whole cent. If payment of the Merger Consideration is to be made to a person other than the person in whose name the surrendered Certificate is registered, it shall be a condition of payment that the Certificate so surrendered shall be properly endorsed or shall be otherwise in proper form for transfer and that the person requesting such payment shall have paid any transfer and other taxes required by reason of the payment of the Merger Consideration to a person other than the registered holder of the Certificate surrendered or shall have established to the satisfaction of the Surviving Corporation that such tax either has been paid or is not applicable. Until surrendered as contemplated by this Section 2.02, each Certificate shall be deemed at any time after the Effective Time to represent only the right to receive the Merger Consideration in cash as contemplated by this Section 2.02.

(c)   Lost, Stolen or Destroyed Certificates. In the event that any Certificate or Certificates shall have been lost, stolen or destroyed, upon the making of an affidavit of that fact by the person claiming such Certificate or Certificates to have been lost, stolen or destroyed, the amount to which such person would have been entitled under Section 2.02(b) hereof but for failure to deliver such Certificate or Certificates to the Paying Agent shall nevertheless be paid to such person; provided, however, that the Surviving Corporation may, in its sole discretion and as a condition precedent to such payment, require such person to give the Surviving Corporation an indemnity agreement in form and substance satisfactory to the Surviving Corporation and if reasonable deemed advisable by the Surviving Corporation, a bond in such sum as it may reasonably direct as indemnity against any claim that may be had against the Surviving Corporation or Parent with respect to the Certificate or Certificates alleged to have been lost, stolen or destroyed.

(d)   Transfer Books; No Further Ownership Rights in Company Common Stock. At the Effective Time, the stock transfer books of the Company shall be closed and thereafter there shall be no further registration of transfers of shares of Company Common Stock on the records of the Company. From and after the Effective Time, the holders of Certificates evidencing ownership of shares of Company Common Stock outstanding immediately prior to the Effective Time shall cease to have any rights with respect to such Shares, except as otherwise provided for herein or by applicable law. If, after the Effective Time, Certificates for Shares subject to Section 2.01(c) are presented to the Surviving Corporation for any reason, they shall be cancelled in exchange for the Merger Consideration for each Share represented by such Certificate as provided in this Article II.

(e)   Termination of Fund; No Liability. At any time following six months after the Effective Time, the Surviving Corporation shall be entitled to require the Paying Agent to deliver to it any funds (including any interest received with respect thereto) which had been made available to the Paying Agent and which have not been disbursed to holders of Certificates, and thereafter such holders shall be entitled to look only to the Surviving Corporation (subject to abandoned property, escheat or other similar laws) as general creditors thereof with respect to the payment of any Merger Consideration that may be payable upon surrender of any Certificates such shareholder holds, as determined pursuant to this Agreement, without any interest thereon. Notwithstanding the foregoing, neither the Surviving Corporation nor the Paying Agent shall be liable to any holder of a Certificate for Merger Consideration delivered to a public official pursuant to any applicable abandoned property, escheat or similar law.

(f)   Withholding Taxes. As specified in the Proxy Documents or otherwise required by law, Parent, the Purchaser, the Surviving Corporation and the Paying Agent shall be entitled to deduct and withhold from the consideration otherwise payable to a holder of Shares pursuant to the Offer or Merger such amounts as Parent, the Purchaser, the Surviving Corporation or the Paying Agent is required to deduct and withhold with respect to the making of such payment under the Internal Revenue Code of 1986, as amended (the "Code"), or any provision of state, local or foreign tax law. To the extent amounts are so withheld by Parent, the Purchaser, the Surviving Corporation or the Paying Agent, the withheld amounts (i) shall be treated for all purposes of this Agreement as having been paid to the holder of the Shares in respect of which the deduction and withholding was made, and (ii) shall be promptly paid over to the applicable taxing authority.

Section 2.03   Dissenting Common Stock. Notwithstanding any provision of this Agreement to the contrary, if and to the extent required by the __BCA, shares of Company Common Stock which are issued and outstanding immediately prior to the Effective Time and which are held by holders of such shares of Company Common Stock who have properly exercised dissenters' rights with respect thereto in accordance with Sections 302A.471 and 302A.473 of the __BCA and have not withdrawn or lost such rights (the "Dissenting Common Stock"), shall not be converted into or represent the right to receive the Merger Consideration, and holders of such shares of Dissenting Common Stock shall be entitled to receive payment of the fair value of such shares of Dissenting Common Stock in accordance with the provisions of Section 302A.473 of the __BCA unless and until such holders fail to perfect or effectively withdraw or otherwise lose their rights to dissent and payment under Sections 302A.471 and 302A.473 of the __BCA. If, after the Effective Time, any such holder fails to perfect or effectively withdraws or loses such right, such shares of Dissenting Common Stock shall thereupon be treated as if they had been converted into and to have become, for each such share, at the Effective Time, the right to receive the Merger Consideration, without any interest thereon. Notwithstanding anything to the contrary contained in this Section 2.03, if (i) the Merger is rescinded or abandoned or (ii) the shareholders of the Company do not approve the Merger and the Merger Agreement, then the right of any shareholder to be paid the fair value of such shareholder's shares of Dissenting Common Stock pursuant to Section 302A.473 of the __BCA shall cease. The Company shall give Parent prompt notice of any notice of intent to demand payment of fair value of any shares of Company Common Stock under Section 302A.473 of the __BCA received by the Company with respect to shares of Dissenting Common Stock, and Parent shall have the right to participate in all negotiations and proceedings with respect to such demands. The Company shall not, except with the prior written consent of Parent, make any payment with respect to any dissenters' rights or offer to settle or settle any demands made by holders of any shares of Dissenting Common Stock.

Section 2.04   Company Option Plans. Parent and the Company shall take all actions necessary (including, without limitation, the execution and delivery by the Company and each of the holders of employee stock options to purchase shares of Company Common Stock ("Options") of one or more agreements of the type described in Section 6.02(g)) to provide that, effective as of the Effective Time, (i) each outstanding Option granted under the Company's 1987 Stock Option Plan and 1995 Stock Option Plan (collectively, the "Stock Plan"), whether or not then exercisable or vested, shall be cancelled, and (ii) in consideration of such cancellation, the

Company (or, at Parent's option, the Purchaser) shall pay to such holders of Options an amount in cash in respect thereof equal to the sum of (A) _____ Dollars ($_____); plus (B) the number of shares of Company Common Stock subject to the unexercised Options to be surrendered by the holder thereof with a purchase or exercise price less than $1.00 per share, multiplied by the difference, if any, between $1.00 and the purchase or exercise price for such Option as set forth in the applicable option agreement; plus (C) the number of shares of Company Common Stock subject to the unexercised Options to be surrendered by the holder thereof with a purchase or exercise price of at least $1.00 per share multiplied by $_____ (such payment to be net of applicable withholding taxes). As of the Effective Time, the Stock Plan shall terminate and all rights under any provision of any other plan, program or arrangement providing for the issuance or grant of any other interest in respect of the capital stock of the Company or any Subsidiary of the Company shall be cancelled. The Company shall take all action necessary to ensure that, after the Effective Time, no person shall have any right under the Stock Plan or any other plan, program or arrangement with respect to equity securities of the Company, or any direct or indirect Subsidiary of the Company.

ARTICLE III.
REPRESENTATIONS AND WARRANTIES OF THE COMPANY

The Company represents and warrants to each of Parent and the Purchaser, as of the date hereof and at the Closing Date, as follows:

Section 3.01   Corporate Organization. Each of the Company and its Subsidiaries is a corporation duly organized, validly existing and in good standing under the laws of the jurisdiction of its organization and has the corporate power and authority to own or lease all of its properties and assets and to carry on its business as it is now being conducted. Each of the Company and its Subsidiaries is duly licensed or qualified to do business in each jurisdiction in which the nature of the business conducted by it or the character or location of the properties and assets owned or leased by it makes such licensing or qualification necessary, except where the failure to be so licensed or qualified would not reasonably be expected to have, when aggregated with all other such failures, a Material Adverse Effect (as defined below) on the Company ("Company Material Adverse Effect"). As used in this Agreement, (a) the term "Material Adverse Effect" means, (i) a material adverse effect on the business, results of operations, financial condition or prospects of such party or any of its Subsidiaries, either individually or in the aggregate, including, without limitation, any adverse effect that results in or gives rise to, or is reasonably likely to result in or give rise to, the creation, incurrence or imposition of any liability, individually or in the aggregate, in excess of $250,000, with respect to such party (including, in the case of the Company, the Surviving Corporation), or (ii) a material adverse effect on the party's ability to consummate the transactions contemplated hereby, and (b) the term "Subsidiary" when used with respect to any party means any corporation, partnership or other organization, whether incorporated or unincorporated, of which (i) at least a majority of the securities or other interests having by their terms voting power to elect a majority of the board of directors or others performing similar functions with respect to such corporation or other organization is directly or indirectly beneficially owned or controlled by such party or by any one or more of its subsidiaries, or by such party and one or more of its subsidiaries, or (ii) such party or any subsidiary of such party is a general partner of a partnership or a manager of a limited liability company. The copies of the Articles of Incorporation and Bylaws (or similar organizational documents) of the Company, which have previously been made available to Parent, are true, complete and correct copies of such documents as in effect as of the date of this Agreement and as of the Closing Date.

Section 3.02   Capitalization.

(a)   The authorized capital stock of the Company consists of _____ shares of Company Common Stock and 1,000,000 shares of preferred stock, of which 200,000 shares have been designated as Series A Preferred Stock. At the close of business on _____, 200__, there were _____ shares of Company Common Stock issued and outstanding and 200,000 shares of Series A Preferred Stock issued and outstanding, all of which issued and outstanding Series A Preferred Stock is owned of record by Parent. As of _____, 200__,, there were _____ shares of Company Common Stock issuable upon the exercise of outstanding Options pursuant to the Stock Plan. Except as set forth in Section 3.02(a) of the disclosure schedule of the Company delivered to Parent concurrently herewith (the "Company Disclosure Schedule"), all of the issued and outstanding shares of Company Common Stock and Series A Preferred Stock have been duly authorized and validly issued and are fully paid, nonassessable and free of preemptive rights, with no personal liability attaching to the ownership thereof. Except as set forth in Section 3.02(a) of the Company Disclosure Schedule, since _____, 200__, the Company has not issued any shares of its capital stock or any securities convertible into or exercisable for any shares of its capital stock, other than pursuant to the exercise of stock options referred to above and as disclosed in Section 3.02(a) of the Company Disclosure Schedule. Except as set forth above or in Section 3.02(a) of the Company Disclosure Schedule or as otherwise contemplated or permitted by Section 5.01(a) hereof, as of the date of this Agreement there are not and, as of the Effective Time there will not be, any shares of capital stock issued and outstanding or any subscriptions, options, warrants, calls, commitments or agreements of any character calling for the purchase or issuance of any securities of the Company, including any securities representing the right to purchase or otherwise receive any shares of Company Common Stock or Series A Preferred Stock.

(b)   Except as set forth in Section 3.02(b) of the Company Disclosure Schedule, the Company owns, directly or indirectly, all of the issued and outstanding shares of capital stock of each of its Subsidiaries, free and clear of any liens, charges, encumbrances, pledges, hypothecations, adverse rights or claims and security interests whatsoever (collectively, "Liens"), and all of such shares are duly authorized and validly issued and are fully paid, nonassessable and free of preemptive rights, with no personal liability attaching to the ownership thereof. None of the Company's Subsidiaries has or is bound by any outstanding subscriptions, options, warrants, calls, commitments or agreements of any character calling for the purchase or issuance of any security of such Subsidiary, including any securities representing the right to purchase or otherwise receive any shares of capital stock or any other equity security of such Subsidiary.

Section 3.03   Authority.

(a)   The Company has full corporate power and authority to execute and deliver this Agreement and to consummate the transactions contemplated hereby, subject to obtaining the approval of holders of a majority of the outstanding shares of Company Common Stock and Series A Preferred Stock, voting together as a single class (with each share of Series A Preferred Stock being entitled to cast 100 votes per share) prior to the consummation of the Merger in accordance with Section 302A.613 of the __BCA. The execution, delivery and performance by the Company of this Agreement, and the consummation by it of the transactions contemplated hereby, have been duly authorized by its Board of Directors and, except for obtaining the approval of its shareholders as contemplated by Section 1.06 hereof, no other corporate action on the part of the Company is necessary to authorize the execution and delivery by the Company of this Agreement and the consummation by it of the transactions contemplated hereby. This Agreement has been duly executed and delivered by the Company and, assuming due and valid authorization, execution and delivery hereof by the other parties hereto, is a valid and binding obligation of the Company enforceable against the Company in accordance with its terms.

(b)   The Company Special Committee and Board of Directors of the Company have approved and taken all corporate action required to be taken by the Company Special Committee and Board of Directors, respectively, for the consummation of the transactions contemplated by this Agreement.

Section 3.04   Consents and Approvals; No Violations.

(a)   Except for (i) the consents and approvals set forth in Section 3.04(a) of the Company Disclosure Schedule, (ii) the filing with the SEC of the Proxy Documents relating to the meeting of the Company's shareholders to be held in connection with this Agreement and the transactions contemplated hereby, (iii) the filing of the Articles of Merger with the Secretary of State pursuant to the __BCA, (iv) the adoption of this Agreement by approval of holders of a majority of the shares of outstanding Company Common Stock and Series A Preferred Stock, voting together as a single class (with each share of Series A Preferred Stock being entitled to cast 100 votes per share) and (v) filings, permits, authorizations, consents and approvals as may be required under, and other applicable requirements of, the Securities Exchange Act of 1934, as amended (the "Exchange Act"), no consents or approvals of, or filings, declarations or registrations with, any federal, state or local court, administrative or regulatory agency or commission or other governmental authority or instrumentality, domestic or foreign (each a "Governmental Entity"), are necessary for the consummation by the Company of the transactions contemplated hereby, except for such consents, approvals, filings, declarations or registrations which, if not obtained prior to or at the Closing would not, either individually or in the aggregate, result in or give rise to a Company Material Adverse Effect.

(b)   Except as set forth in Section 3.04(b) of the Company Disclosure Schedule, neither the execution and delivery of this Agreement by the Company nor the consummation by the Company of the transactions contemplated hereby, nor compliance by the Company with any of the terms or provisions hereof, will (i) conflict with or violate any provision of the Articles of Incorporation or Bylaws of the Company or any of the similar organizational documents of any of its Subsidiaries, or (ii) assuming that the consents and approvals referred to in Section 3.04(a) and the authorization hereof by the Company's shareholders are duly obtained in accordance with the __BCA prior to the Closing Date, (x) violate any statute, code, ordinance, rule, regulation, judgment, order, writ, decree or injunction applicable to the Company or any of its Subsidiaries, or any of their respective properties or assets, or (y) violate, conflict with, result in a breach of any provision of or the loss of any benefit under, constitute a default (or an event which, with notice or lapse of time, or both, would constitute a default) under, result in the termination of or a right of termination or cancellation under, accelerate the performance required by, or result in the creation of any Lien upon any of the respective properties or assets of the Company or any of its Subsidiaries under, any of the terms, conditions or provisions of any note, bond, mortgage, indenture, deed of trust, license, lease, agreement or other instrument or obligation to which the Company or any of its Subsidiaries is a party, or by which they or any of their respective properties or assets may be bound or affected, except for such conflict, violation, breach or default that would not, either individually or in the aggregate, result in or give rise to a Company Material Adverse Effect.

Section 3.05   SEC Reports. Since _____, 200__, the Company has filed, and will at all times prior to the Effective Time file, all required forms, notices, reports, schedules and documents (including all exhibits, schedules, annexes, amendments and supplements thereto) with the SEC (collectively, the "Company Reports"), and no such form, notice, report, schedule or document, at the time it was filed or is filed, contained or will contain any untrue statement of a material fact or omitted or will omit to state any material fact required to be stated therein or necessary in order to make the statements therein, in light of the circumstances in which they were made, not misleading. As of their respective dates, all Company Reports complied (and all SEC Reports filed after the date hereof will comply) in all material respects with all applicable provisions of the Securities Act of 1933, as amended (the "Securities Act"), and the Exchange Act, and the rules and regulations promulgated thereunder.

Section 3.06   Financial Statements. Each consolidated balance sheet of the Company (including the related notes and schedules) included in the Company Reports fairly presents, in all material respects, the consolidated financial position of the Company and its Subsidiaries as of the date thereof, and the other financial statements included in the Company Reports (including the related notes, where applicable) fairly present, in all material respects (subject, in the case of the unaudited statements, to audit adjustments normal in nature and amount), the results of the consolidated operations and changes in shareholders' equity and consolidated financial position of the Company and its Subsidiaries for the respective periods or dates therein set forth. Each of such statements has been prepared in accordance with the requirements of the SEC and GAAP consistently applied during the periods involved, except in each case as specifically indicated in such statements or in the notes thereto. The books and records of the Company and its Subsidiaries have been, and will at all times prior to the Effective Time be, maintained in all material respects in accordance with GAAP and any other applicable legal and accounting requirements, except with respect to normal and recurring period end accruals that are made only at the end of each fiscal quarter.

Section 3.07 <u>Broker's Fees</u>. Neither the Company nor any Subsidiary of the Company nor any of their respective officers or directors on behalf of the Company or such Subsidiaries has employed any financial advisor, broker or finder or incurred any liability for any broker's fees, commissions or finder's fees in connection with any of the transactions contemplated hereby, except, in the case of the Company Special Committee, _____ ("_____"). The Company has delivered to Parent a true and complete copy of the engagement letter, dated _____, 200__, pursuant to which _____ has been engaged by the Special Committee, and _____ is not entitled to any payments from the Company (or the Surviving Corporation) except as specifically provided therein.

Section 3.08 <u>Absence of Certain Changes or Events</u>. Except as disclosed in the Company Reports filed or press releases of the Company (the "Company Releases") issued prior to the date hereof or as set forth in Section 3.08 of the Company Disclosure Schedule, since _____, 200__, (i) the Company and its Subsidiaries have carried on and operated their respective businesses in all material respects in the ordinary course of business consistent with past practice, and (ii) there has not occurred, nor has the Company or any of its Subsidiaries effected, permitted, authorized or taken any action that has resulted in, or is reasonably likely to result in:

(a)   any event, occurrence or development of a state of circumstances or facts which has had or reasonably would be expected to have a Company Material Adverse Effect;

(b)   any amendment of any material term of any outstanding security of the Company or any of its Subsidiaries;

(c)   any incurrence, assumption or guarantee by the Company or any of its Subsidiaries of any indebtedness for borrowed money other than in the ordinary course of business and in amounts and on terms consistent with past practices;

(d)   any creation or assumption by the Company or any of its Subsidiaries of any Lien on any material asset other than in the ordinary course of business consistent with past practices;

(e)   any making of any loan, advance or capital contributions to or investment in any Person other than loans, advances or capital contributions to or investments in wholly-owned Subsidiaries made in the ordinary course of business consistent with past practices;

(f)   any damage, destruction or other casualty loss (whether or not covered by insurance) affecting the business or assets of the Company or any of its Subsidiaries which, individually or in the aggregate, has had or would reasonably be expected to have a Company Material Adverse Effect;

(g)   any transaction or commitment made, or any contract or agreement entered into, by the Company or any of its Subsidiaries relating to its assets or business (including the acquisition or disposition of any assets) or any relinquishment by the Company or any of its Subsidiaries of any contract or other right, in either case, material to the Company and any of its Subsidiaries taken as a whole, other than transactions and commitments in the ordinary course of business consistent with past practice and those contemplated by this Agreement;

(h)   any change in any method of accounting or accounting practice by the Company or any of its Subsidiaries, except for any such change required by reason of a concurrent change in generally accepted accounting principles;

(i)   any termination, cancellation, acceleration or amendment to any contract, lease, plan or agreement referred to in Section 3.19 of the Company Disclosure Schedule to which the Company or any Subsidiary is a party or pursuant to which any of its assets or properties is bound;

(j)   any (i) grant of any new severance or termination arrangement to any director, officer or employee of the Company or any of its Subsidiaries, (ii) entering into of any employment, deferred compensation or other similar agreement (or any amendment to any such existing agreement) with any director or officer of the Company or any of its Subsidiaries, (iii) increase in benefits payable under any existing severance or termination pay policies or employment agreements or (iv) increase in compensation, bonus or other benefits payable to directors or officers of the Company or any of its Subsidiaries, other than, in the case of this clause (iv), in the ordinary course of business consistent with past practice;

(k)   any labor dispute, other than routine individual grievances, or any activity or proceeding by a labor union or representative thereof to organize any employees of the Company or any of its Subsidiaries, or any lockouts, strikes, slowdowns, work stoppages or threats thereof by or with respect to such employees;

(l)   the opening or closure, whether on a permanent or temporary basis, of any office or facility owned, operated or managed, or to be owned, operated or managed, by the Company or any Subsidiary, or any renewals, terminations, or extensions of any lease with respect thereto;

(m)   any cancellation of any licenses, sublicenses, franchises, permits or agreements to which the Company or any of its Subsidiaries is a party, or any notification to the Company or any of its Subsidiaries that any party to any such arrangements intends to cancel or not renew such arrangements beyond its expiration date as in effect on the date hereof, which cancellation or notification, individually or in the aggregate, has had or reasonably could be expected to have a Company Material Adverse Effect; or

(n)   any event, occurrence or development of the type that, had such event, occurrence or development occurred following the date hereof, would require the consent of Parent pursuant to the second sentence of Section 5.01 hereof.

Section 3.09   <u>Legal Proceedings; Liabilities.</u>

(a)   Except as set forth in the Company Reports, the Company Releases or in Section 3.09 of the Company Disclosure Schedule, neither the Company nor any of its Subsidiaries is a party to and there are not pending or, to the best of the Company's knowledge, threatened, any legal, administrative, arbitral or other proceedings, claims, actions or governmental or regulatory investigations of any nature against the Company or any of its Subsidiaries which, in the aggregate, would reasonably be expected to have a Company Material Adverse Effect, or which challenge the validity or propriety of the transactions contemplated.

(b)   Except as set forth in the Company Reports, the Company Releases or in Section 3.09 of the Company Disclosure Schedule, there is no injunction, order, judgment, decree or regulatory restriction imposed upon the Company, any of its Subsidiaries or the assets of the Company or any of its Subsidiaries which, when aggregated with all other such injunctions, orders, judgments, decrees and restrictions, would reasonably be expected to have a Company Material Adverse Effect.

(c)   Neither the Company nor any of its Subsidiaries has any liabilities (absolute, accrued, contingent or otherwise), except (i) liabilities described in the Company's SEC Reports filed prior to the date hereof or reflected on the Company's consolidated balance sheet (and related notes thereto) as of the end of its most recently completed fiscal quarter filed in the Company SEC Reports, (ii) liabilities incurred since the end of the Company's most recently completed fiscal year in the ordinary course of its business consistent with past practice, and (ii) liabilities disclosed in Section 3.09(c) of the Company Disclosure Schedule.

Section 3.10   Compliance with Applicable Law.

(a)   Except as disclosed in Section 3.10(a) of the Company Disclosure Schedule, the Company and each of its Subsidiaries hold, and have at all applicable times held, all material licenses, franchises, permits and authorizations necessary for the lawful conduct of their respective businesses and have complied with, and are not in default in any material respect under any, applicable law, statute, order, rule, regulation, and/or written policy or guideline of any Governmental Entity relating to the Company or any of its Subsidiaries.

(b)   Except as disclosed in Section 3.10(b) of the Company Disclosure Schedule, the Company and each of its Subsidiaries has complied in all material respects and is currently in material compliance with each law, license, permit, certificate of need ("CON"), ordinance, or governmental or regulatory rule ("Regulations") to which its business, operations, assets or properties is subject, including any Regulations related to reimbursement for services rendered or goods provided and including any applicable federal or state health care program laws, rules, or regulations, including, but not limited to, those pertaining to improper inducements, gratuitous payments, fraudulent or abusive practices, excessive or inadequate services, false claims and/or false statements, civil money penalties, prohibited referrals, and/or financial relationships, excluded individuals, controlled substances and licensure. Each Facility (as hereinafter defined) holds, possesses or lawfully uses in the operation of its business the licenses, permits, CONs, provider agreements and certifications under Titles XVIII and XIX of the Social Security Act (the "Social Security Act," Titles XVIII and XIX of the Social Security Act are hereinafter referred to collectively as the "Medicare and Medicaid Programs"), which licenses, permits, CONs, provided agreements and certifications are in substantial compliance with all Regulations. None of the Company or any of its Subsidiaries is in default under any order of any court, governmental authority or arbitration board or tribunal specifically applicable to the Company or any of its Subsidiaries. As of the date hereof, no action has been taken or recommended by any governmental or regulatory official, body or authority, either to: (i) revoke, withdraw or suspend any CON or any license, permit or other authority to operate any of the Facilities; (ii) terminate or decertify any participation of any of the Facilities in the Medicare and Medicaid Programs; or (iii) reduce or propose to reduce the number of licensed beds in any category, nor, as of the date hereof, has there been any decision not to renew any provider agreement related to any Facility. In the event that any such action shall have been taken or recommended subsequent to the date hereof, or if any decision shall have been made not to renew any such provider agreements, the Company hereby agrees to provide notice to Parent of the same and to diligently and in good faith take prompt corrective or remedial action to cure the same. As used in this Agreement, "Facility" or "Facilities" refers to any office, nursing home, assisted living facility, home health agency, health care center, clinic or pharmacy or other facility or owned, operated, leased or managed by the Company, Parent or any of their respective Subsidiaries.

(c)   All cost reports ("Cost Reports") required to be filed by the Company or any Subsidiary with respect to the Facilities under the Medicare and Medicaid Programs (or any other applicable governmental or private provider regulations) have been prepared and filed in accordance with applicable laws, rules and regulations. The Company has paid, has caused a Subsidiary to have paid, or has made provision to pay through proper recordation of any net liability, any material overpayments received from the Medicare and Medicaid Programs and any similar obligations with respect to other reimbursement programs in which the Company and its Subsidiaries participate. Section 3.10(c) of the Company Disclosure Schedule sets forth for each Facility the years for which Cost Reports remain to be settled.

Section 3.11   Company Information. The information relating to the Company and its Subsidiaries to be provided by the Company to be contained in the Proxy Documents, or in any other document filed with any other Governmental Entity in connection herewith, shall not contain any untrue statement of a material fact or omit to state a material fact necessary to make the statements therein, in light of the circumstances in which they are made, not misleading.

Section 3.12   Opinion of Financial Advisor. The Company Special Committee has received the opinion of _____, financial advisor to the Company Special Committee, to the effect that, as of the date of such opinion, the consideration to be received in the Merger is fair to the holders, other than Parent, of shares of Company Common Stock from a financial point of view.

Section 3.13   Intellectual Property.

(a)   As used herein, the term "Intellectual Property" means all trademarks, service marks, trade names, Internet domain names, e-mail addresses, designs, logos, slogans and general intangibles of like nature, together with goodwill, registrations and applications relating to the foregoing; patents and patent applications, copyrights, including registrations and applications; proprietary computer programs, including any and all software implementations of algorithms, models and methodologies whether in source code or object code form, proprietary databases and compilations, including any and all data and collections of data, all documentation, including user manuals and training materials, related to any of the foregoing and the content and information contained on any website (excluding any off-the-shelf, commercially available shrink-wrapped or pre-installed word processing, spreadsheet, e-mail and similar programs, collectively, "Software"); confidential information, customer and supplier lists, price and discount lists, technology, know-how, inventions, processes, formulae, algorithms, models and methodologies (such confidential items, collectively, "Trade Secrets") held for use or used in the business of the Company as conducted as of the Closing Date or as presently contemplated to be conducted and any licenses to use any of the foregoing, including those for the benefit of the Company and those granted by the Company to third parties.

(b)   Section 3.13(b) of the Company Disclosure Schedule sets forth, for all Intellectual Property owned by the Company or any Subsidiary of the Company, a complete and accurate list, of all United States and foreign: (i) patents and patent applications; (ii) trademark and service mark registrations (including Internet domain name registrations), trademark and service mark applications and material unregistered trademarks and service marks; and (iii) copyright registrations, copyright applications and material unregistered copyrights.

(c)   Section 3.13(c) of the Company Disclosure Schedule lists all contracts for material Software which is licensed, leased or otherwise used by the Company or any Company Subsidiary, and all Software which is owned by the Company or any Company Subsidiary, and identifies which Software is owned, licensed, leased, or otherwise used, as the case may be.

(d)   Section 3.13(d) of the Company Disclosure Schedule sets forth a complete and accurate list of all agreements granting or obtaining any right to use or practice any rights under any Intellectual Property, to which the Company or any Company Subsidiary is a party or otherwise bound, as licensee or licensor thereunder, including, without limitation, license agreements, settlement agreements and covenants not to sue (collectively, the "License Agreements").

(e)   Except as set forth on Section 3.13(e) of the Company Disclosure Schedule: (i) the Company or Subsidiaries of the Company own or have the right to use all Intellectual Property, free and clear of all Liens; (ii) any Intellectual Property owned or used by the Company or Subsidiary of the Company has been duly maintained, is valid and subsisting, in full force and effect and has not been cancelled, expired or abandoned; (iii) the Company has not received written notice from any third party regarding any actual or potential infringement by the Company or any Subsidiary of the Company of any intellectual property of such third party, and the Company has no knowledge of any basis for such a claim against the Company or any Subsidiaries of the Company; (iv) the Company has not received written notice from any third party regarding any assertion or claim challenging the validity of any Intellectual Property owned or used by the Company or any Subsidiary of the Company and the Company has no knowledge of any basis for such a claim; (v) neither the Company nor any Subsidiary of the Company has licensed or sublicensed its rights in any Intellectual Property, or received or been granted any such rights, other than pursuant to the License Agreements; (vi) to the Company's knowledge, no third party is misappropriating, infringing, diluting or violating any Intellectual Property owned by the Company or any Subsidiary of the Company; (vii) the License Agreements are valid and binding obligations of the Company or any Subsidiary of the Company, enforceable in accordance with their terms, and there exists no event or condition which will result in a violation or breach of, or constitute a default by the Company or any Subsidiary of the Company or, to the knowledge of the Company, the other party thereto, under any such License Agreement; and (viii) the Company and each of the Subsidiaries of the Company takes reasonable measures to protect the confidentiality of Trade Secrets including requiring third parties having access thereto to execute written nondisclosure agreements.

Section 3.14   Takeover Statutes. The Company has taken all actions necessary such that no restrictive provision of any "fair price," "moratorium," "control share acquisition," "interested shareholder" or other similar anti-takeover statute or regulation (including, without limitation, Section 302A.671 or Section 302A.673 of the __BCA) (each a "Takeover Statute") or restrictive provision of any applicable anti-takeover provision in the governing documents of the Company limits or otherwise affects, or at or after the Effective Time will limit or otherwise affect, in any respect, Parent, the Purchaser, the Merger or any other transaction contemplated by this Agreement, the voting by Parent of its shares of Company Common Stock or Series A Preferred Stock with respect to this Agreement or the Merger, or any business combination between the Company and Parent or any affiliate thereof (other than stock purchases following any tender offer by the Parent or any affiliate thereof after the date of this Agreement which would be subject to the Section 302A.675 of the __BCA).

Section 3.15   No Other Agreements to Sell the Company. Except pursuant to this Agreement, the Company has no legal obligation, absolute or contingent, to any other person to sell any material portion of the assets of the Company or any of its Subsidiaries, to sell any material portion of the capital stock or other ownership interest of the Company or any of its Subsidiaries, or to effect any merger, consolidation or other reorganization of the Company or any of its Subsidiaries, or to enter into any agreement or arrangement with respect thereto.

Section 3.16   No Shareholders Rights Plan. The Company has not entered into, and its Board of Directors has not adopted or authorized the adoption of, a shareholder rights plan or similar agreement.

Section 3.17   Tax Returns and Tax Payments. The Company and its Subsidiaries have timely filed (or, as to Subsidiaries, the Company has filed on behalf of such Subsidiaries) all Tax Returns (as defined below) required to be filed by it or obtained valid extensions, which extensions have not yet expired. The Company and its Subsidiaries have paid (or, as to Subsidiaries, the Company has paid on behalf of such Subsidiaries) all Taxes (as defined below) shown to be due on such Tax Returns or has provided (or, as to Subsidiaries, the Company has made provision on behalf of such Subsidiaries for) reserves in its financial statements for any Taxes that have not been paid, whether or not shown as being due on any Tax Returns. Neither the Company nor any of its Subsidiaries has requested any extension of time within which to file any Tax Returns in respect of any taxable year which have not since been filed, except for such extensions that have not yet expired, nor made any request for waivers of the time to assess any Taxes that are pending or outstanding. No claim for unpaid Taxes has been asserted against the Company or any of its Subsidiaries in writing by a Governmental Entity which, if resolved in a manner unfavorable to the Company or any of its Subsidiaries, as the case may be, would result, individually or in the aggregate, in a material Tax liability to the Company and its Subsidiaries taken as a whole. There are no material Liens for Taxes upon the assets of the Company or any Subsidiary except for Liens for Taxes not yet due and payable or for Taxes that are being disputed in good faith by appropriate proceedings and with respect to which adequate reserves have been provided for. No audit of any Tax Return of the Company or any of its Subsidiaries is being conducted by a Governmental Entity. None of the Company or any of its Subsidiaries has made an election under Section 341(f) of the Code. Neither the Company nor any of its Subsidiaries has any liability for Taxes of any individual or entity, including, but not limited to, any corporation, partnership, limited liability company, trust or unincorporated organization (other than the Company and its Subsidiaries) under Treasury Regulation Section 1.1502-6 (or any comparable provision of state, local or foreign law) or by other reason of law (including transferee or successor liability), or as a result of any contractual obligation to indemnify any person or entity. As used herein, (a) "Taxes" shall mean all taxes of any kind, including, without limitation, those on or measured by or referred to as income, gross receipts, sales, use, ad valorem, franchise, profits, license, withholding, value added, property or windfall profits taxes, customs, duties or similar fees, assessments or charges of any kind whatsoever, together with any interest and any penalties, additions to tax or additional amounts imposed by any Governmental Entity, domestic or foreign, and (b) "Tax Return" shall mean any return, report or statement required to be filed with any governmental authority with respect to Taxes.

Section 3.18   ERISA.

(a)   Section 3.18 of the Company Disclosure Schedule contains a correct and complete list identifying each material "employee benefit plan," as defined in Section 3(3) of the Employee Retirement Income Security Act of 1974 ("ERISA"), each employment, severance or similar contract, plan, arrangement or policy and each other plan or arrangement (written or oral) providing for compensation, bonuses, profit-sharing, stock option or other stock related rights or other forms of incentive or deferred compensation, vacation benefits, insurance (including any self-insured arrangements), health or medical benefits, employee assistance program, disability or sick leave benefits, workers' compensation, supplemental unemployment benefits, severance benefits and post-employment or retirement benefits (including compensation, pension, health, medical or life insurance benefits) which is maintained, administered or contributed to by the Company or any ERISA Affiliate and covers any employees or former employee of the Company or any of its Subsidiaries, or with respect to which the Company or any of its Subsidiaries has any liability. Copies of such plans (and, if applicable, related trust or funding agreements or insurance policies) and all amendments thereto and written interpretations thereof have been made available to Parent together with the most recent annual report (Form 5500) including, if applicable, related trust or funding agreements or insurance policies) and all amendments thereto and written interpretations thereof have been made available to Parent together with the most recent annual report (Form 5500 including, if applicable, Schedule B thereto) and tax return (Form 990) prepared in connection with any such plan or trust. Such plans are referred to collectively herein as the "Employee Plans." For purposes of this Section 3.18, "ERISA Affiliate" of any person or entity means any other person or entity which, together with such person or entity, would be treated as a single employer under Section 414 of the Code.

(b)   Neither the Company nor any ERISA Affiliate nor any predecessor thereof sponsors, maintains or contributes to, or has any actual or reasonably likely potential liability under, any Employee Plan subject to Title IV of ERISA (other than a Multiemployer Plan, as defined below). Neither the Company nor any ERISA Affiliate nor any predecessor thereof contributes to, or has any actual or reasonably likely potential liability under, any multiemployer plan, as defined in Section 3(37) of ERISA (a "Multiemployer Plan").

(c)   A current favorable Internal Revenue Service determination letter is in effect with respect to each Employee Plan which is intended to be qualified under Section 401(a) of the Code (or the relevant remedial amendment period has not expired with respect to such Employee Plan), and the Company knows of no circumstance giving rise to a likelihood that such Employee Plan would be treated as other than qualified by the Internal Revenue

Service. The Company has made available to Parent copies of the most recent Internal Revenue Service determination letters with respect to each such Plan. Each Employee Plan has been maintained in compliance with its terms and with the requirements prescribed by any and all statutes, orders, rules and regulations, including but not limited to ERISA and the Code, which are applicable to such Plan.

(d)   Except as set forth in Section 3.18 of the Company Disclosure Schedule, the consummation of the transactions contemplated by this Agreement will not (either alone or together with any other event) entitle any employee or independent contractor of the Company or any of its Subsidiaries to severance pay or accelerate the time of payment or vesting or trigger any payment of funding (through a grantor trust or otherwise) of compensation or benefits under, increase the amount payable or trigger any other material obligation pursuant to, any Employee Plan. To the knowledge of the Company, there is no contract, agreement, plan or arrangements covering any employee or former employee of the Company or any Affiliate that, individually or collectively, could give rise to the payment of any amount that would not be deductible by the Company pursuant to the terms of Sections 162(m) or 280G of the Code.

(e)   Except as set forth in Section 3.18 of the Company Disclosure Schedule, or as reflected on the Balance Sheet, neither the Company nor any Subsidiary has any liability in respect of post-retirement health, medical or life insurance benefits for retired, former or current employees of the Company or its Subsidiaries except as required to avoid excise tax under Section 4980B of the Code.

(f)   There has been no amendment to, written interpretation or announcement (whether or not written) by the Company or any of its affiliates relating to, or change in employee participation or coverage under, any Employee Plan which would increase the expense of maintaining such Employee Plan above the level of the expense incurred in respect thereof for the fiscal year ended

September 30, 1999, unless such increase would not individually or in the aggregate, have a Company Material Adverse Effect.

(g)   Neither the Company nor any of its Subsidiaries is a party to or subject to, or is currently negotiating in connection with entering into, any collective bargaining agreement or other contract or understanding with a labor union or labor organization.

(h)   Except as set forth in Section 3.18 of the Company Disclosure Schedule, all contributions and payments accrued under each Employee Plan, determined in accordance with prior funding and accrual practices, as adjusted to include proportional accruals for the period ending as of the date hereof, have been discharged and paid on or prior to the date hereof except to the extent reflected as a liability on the most recent balance sheet filed by the Company with the SEC.

(i)   Except as set forth in Section 3.18 of the Company Disclosure Schedule, there is no action, suit, investigation, audit or proceeding pending against or involving or, to the knowledge of the Company, threatened, against or involving, any Employee Plan before any court or arbitrator or any state, federal or local governmental body, agency or official which would, individually or in the aggregate, have a Company Material Adverse Effect.

Section 3.19   Material Contracts.

(a)   Except as expressly disclosed in the Company Reports filed prior to the date hereof or in Section 3.19 of the Company Disclosure Schedule, neither the Company nor any of its Subsidiaries is a party to any oral or written (i) agreement, contract, indenture or other instrument relating to the incurrence or guarantee of indebtedness for borrowed money in an amount exceeding $100,000, (ii) partnership, joint venture or limited liability agreement or management with any person, (iii) agreement, contract, or other instrument relating to any merger, consolidation, business combination, share exchange, business acquisition, or for the purchase, acquisition, sale or disposition of any assets of the

Company or any of its Subsidiaries outside the ordinary course of business, (iv) other contract, agreement or commitment to be performed after the date hereof which would be a material contract (as defined in Item 601(b)(10) of Regulation S-K of the SEC), (v) contract, agreement or commitment which materially restricts the conduct of any line of business by the Company or any of its Subsidiaries), or (vi) contract, agreement, plan, policy or commitment which requires any payment by the Company or the Surviving Corporation following a change in control of the Company, the termination of any employee of the Company or otherwise in connection with or upon consummation of the transactions contemplated hereby (such contracts, agreements and commitments described in clauses (i) through (vi) are collectively referred to as the "Material Contracts").

(b)   Except as expressly disclosed in the Company Reports filed prior to the date hereof, (i) each of the Material Contracts is a valid and binding obligation of the Company in accordance with its terms and is in full force and effect and (ii) there is no material breach or violation of or default by the Company or any of its Subsidiaries under any of the Material Contracts, whether or not such breach, violation or default has been waived, and no event has occurred which, with notice or lapse of time or both, would constitute a material breach, violation or default, or give rise to a right of termination, modification, cancellation, foreclosure, imposition of a lien, prepayment or acceleration under any of the Company Material Contracts, which breach, violation or default referred to in clauses (i) or (ii), alone or in the aggregate with other such breaches, violations or defaults referred to in clauses (i) or (ii), would be reasonably likely to have a Company Material Adverse Effect.

Section 3.20   Insurance. All fire and casualty, general liability, business interruption and product liability insurance policies maintained by the Company or any of its Subsidiaries are in character and amount at least equivalent to that carried by persons engaged in similar businesses and subject to the same or similar perils or hazards.

Section 3.21   Environmental Matters.

(a)   No notice, notification, demand, request for information, citation, summons, complaint or order has been received by or is pending, or, to the knowledge of the Company or any of its Subsidiaries, threatened by any person against, the Company or any of its Subsidiaries nor has any material penalty been assessed against the Company or any of its Subsidiaries with respect to any (1) alleged violation of any Environmental Law or liability thereunder, (2) alleged failure to have any permit, certificate, license, approval, registration or authorization required under any Environmental Law, (3) generation, treatment, storage, recycling, transportation or disposal of any Hazardous Substance or (4) discharge, emission or release of any Hazardous Substance, that in the case of (1), (2), (3) and/or (4), would, either individually or in the aggregate, reasonably be expected to result in a Company Material Adverse Effect.

(b)   No Hazardous Substance has been discharged, emitted, released or, to the knowledge of the Company, is present at any property now or previously owned, leased or operated by the Company or any Subsidiary of the Company, which circumstance, individually or in the aggregate, would reasonably be expected to result in a Company Material Adverse Effect; and

(c)   To the knowledge of the Company, there are no Environmental Liabilities that have had or would reasonably be expected to have a Company Material Adverse Effect.

(d)   There has been no environmental investigation, study, audit, test, review or other analysis conducted of which the Company has knowledge in relation to the current or prior business of the Company or any property or facility now or previously owned or leased by the Company or any of its Subsidiaries which has not been delivered to Parent at least five (5) days prior to the date hereof.

(e)   Except as set forth in Section 3.21 of the Company Disclosure Schedule, neither the Company nor any Subsidiary owns or leases or has owned or leased any real property, or conducts or has conducted any operations, in

_____.

(f)   For purposes of this Section 3.21, the following items shall have the meaning set forth below:

(i)   "Environmental Laws" means any and all federal, state, local and foreign statutes, laws, judicial decisions, regulations, ordinances, rules, judgments, orders, decrees, codes, plans, injunctions, permits, concessions, grants, franchises, licenses, agreements and governmental restrictions, relating to human health, the environment or to emissions, discharge or releases of pollutants, contaminants or other hazardous substance or wastes into the environment, including without limitation ambient air, surface water, ground water or land, or otherwise relating to the manufacture, processing, distribution, use, treatment, storage, disposal, transport or handling of pollutants, contaminants or other hazardous substances or wastes or the clean-up or other remediation thereof.

(ii)   "Environmental Liabilities" means any and all liabilities of or relating to the Company or any of its Subsidiaries, whether contingent or fixed, actual or potential, known or unknown, which (i) arise under or relate to matters covered by Environmental Laws and (ii) relate to actions occurring or conditions existing on or prior to the Effective Time; and

(iii)   "Hazardous Substances" means any pollutant, contaminant, toxic, radioactive, corrosive or otherwise hazardous substance, material or waste, including petroleum, its derivatives, by-products and other hydrocarbons, or any substance having any constituent elements displaying any of the foregoing characteristics, which in any event is regulated under Environmental Laws.

ARTICLE IV.
REPRESENTATIONS AND WARRANTIES
OF PARENT AND PURCHASER

Parent and the Purchaser, jointly and severally, represent and warrant to the Company, as of the date hereof and at the Closing Date, as follows:

Section 4.01   Corporate Organization. Each of Parent and the Purchaser is a corporation duly organized, validly existing and in good standing under the laws of the jurisdiction of its organization and has the corporate power and authority to own or lease all of its properties and assets and to carry on its business as it is now being conducted. Each of Parent and the Purchaser is duly licensed or qualified to do business in each jurisdiction in which the nature of the business conducted by it or the character or location of the properties and assets owned or leased by it makes such licensing or qualification necessary, except where the failure to be so licensed or qualified would not reasonably be expected to have, when aggregated with all other such failures, a Material Adverse Effect on the Parent ("Parent Material Adverse Effect"). The copies of the Articles or Certificate of Incorporation and Bylaws (or similar organizational documents) of the Parent and Purchaser, which have previously been made available to Company, are true, complete and correct copies of such documents as in effect as of the date of this Agreement and as of the Closing Date.

Section 4.02   Authority. Each of Parent and the Purchaser has full corporate power and authority to execute and deliver this Agreement and to consummate the transactions contemplated hereby. The execution, delivery and performance by Parent and the Purchaser of this Agreement, and the consummation of the transactions contemplated hereby, have been duly authorized by their Boards of Directors and by Parent as the sole shareholder of Purchaser and no other corporate action on the part of Parent and the Purchaser is necessary to authorize the execution and delivery by Parent and the Purchaser of this Agreement and the consummation by them of the transactions contemplated hereby. This Agreement has been duly executed and delivered by Parent and the

Purchaser, as the case may be, and, assuming due and valid authorization, execution and delivery hereof by the Company, is a valid and binding obligation of each of Parent and the Purchaser, as the case may be, enforceable against them in accordance with its terms.

Section 4.03   Consents and Approvals; No Violation.

(a)   Except for (i) the consents and approvals set forth in Section 4.03(a) of the disclosure schedule of the Parent delivered to the Company concurrently herewith (the "Parent Disclosure Schedule"), (ii) the filing with the SEC of the Proxy Documents, (iii) the filing of the Articles of Merger with the Secretary of State pursuant to the __BCA, and (iv) filings, permits, authorizations, consents and approvals as may be required under, and other applicable requirements of, the Exchange Act and the Securities Act, no consents or approvals of, or filings, declarations or registrations with, any Governmental Entity are necessary for the consummation by Parent and the Purchaser of the transactions contemplated hereby, other than such other consents, approvals, filings, declarations or registrations that, if not obtained, made or given, would not reasonably be expected to have, in the aggregate, a Parent Material Adverse Effect.

(b)   Except as set forth in Section 4.03(b) of the Parent Disclosure Schedule, neither the execution and delivery of this Agreement by Parent or the Purchaser, nor the consummation by Parent or the Purchaser of the transactions contemplated hereby, nor compliance by Parent or the Purchaser with any of the terms or provisions hereof, will (i) conflict with or violate any provision of the Restated Certificate of Incorporation or Bylaws of Parent, or (ii) assuming that the consents and approvals referred to in Section 4.03(a) are obtained prior to the Closing Date, (x) violate any statute, code, ordinance, rule, regulation, judgment, order, writ, decree or injunction applicable to Parent or the Purchaser, or any of their respective properties or assets, or (y) violate, conflict with, result in a breach of any provision of or the loss of any benefit under, constitute a default (or an event which, with notice or lapse of time, or both, would constitute a default) under, result in the termination of or a right of termination or cancellation under, accelerate the performance required by, or result in the creation of any Lien upon any of the respective properties or assets of Parent or the Purchaser under, any of the terms, conditions or provisions of any note, bond, mortgage, indenture, deed of trust, license, lease, agreement or other instrument or obligation to which Parent or any of its Subsidiaries is a party, or by which they or any of their respective properties or assets may be bound or affected.

Section 4.04   Legal Proceedings; Liabilities.

(a)   Except as set forth in the any of the forms, notices, reports, schedules or documents (including all exhibits, schedules, annexes, amendments and supplements thereto) filed by Parent, Purchaser or any of their affiliates with the SEC, or any press releases made by any of such entities (collectively, the "Parent Reports and Releases"), neither Parent nor Purchaser is a party to and there are not pending or, to the best of Parent's knowledge, threatened, any legal, administrative, arbitral or other proceedings, claims, actions or governmental or regulatory investigations of any nature against the Parent or the Purchaser which, in the aggregate, would reasonably be expected to challenge the validity or propriety of the transactions contemplated.

(b)   Except as set forth in the Parent Reports and Releases, there is no injunction, order, judgment, decree or regulatory restriction imposed upon the Parent, Purchaser or their respective assets which, when aggregated with all other such injunctions, orders, judgments, decrees and restrictions, would reasonably be expected to have a Parent Material Adverse Effect.

Section 4.05   Broker's Fees. Except as set forth in Section 4.05 of the Parent Disclosure Schedule, neither Parent nor any Subsidiary of Parent nor any of their respective officers or directors on behalf of Parent or such Subsidiaries has employed any financial advisor, broker or finder or incurred any liability for any broker's fees, commissions or finder's fees in connection with any of the transactions contemplated hereby.

Section 4.06   Purchaser's Operations. The Purchaser was formed solely for the purpose of engaging in the transactions contemplated hereby and has not engaged in any business activities or conducted any operations other than in connection with the transactions contemplated hereby.

Section 4.07   Available Funds. Parent currently has available cash and/or the ability to borrow funds under existing credit arrangements in the ordinary course of business that are adequate to fund Parent's payment obligations pursuant to Section 2.01 and 2.02 of this Agreement.

Section 4.08   Parent Information. The information relating to Parent and its Subsidiaries and affiliates to be provided by Parent to be contained in the Proxy Documents, or in any other document filed with any other Governmental Entity in connection herewith, will not contain any untrue statement of a material fact or omit to state a material fact necessary to make the statements therein, in light of the circumstances in which they are made, not misleading. The Proxy Documents (except that no representation is made as to such portions thereof that relate only to the Company or any of its Subsidiaries) shall comply in all material respects with the provisions of the Exchange Act and the rules and regulations thereunder and the Securities Act and the rules and regulations thereunder, respectively.

ARTICLE V.
COVENANTS

Section 5.01   Conduct of Businesses Prior to the Effective Time. Except as set forth in Section 5.01 of the Company Disclosure Schedule, as expressly contemplated or permitted by this Agreement, or as required by applicable law, rule or regulation, during the period from the date of this Agreement to the Effective Time, unless Parent otherwise agrees in writing, the Company shall, and shall cause its Subsidiaries to (i) conduct its business in the usual, regular and ordinary course consistent with past practice (ii) maintain and preserve intact its business organization, employees and advantageous business relationships and retain the services of its officers and key employees, and (iii) refrain from taking, authorizing or permitting any action of the type that would be required to be disclosed pursuant to Section 3.08. Without limiting the generality of the foregoing, and except as set forth in Section 5.01 of the Company Disclosure

Schedule, as expressly contemplated or permitted by this Agreement, or as required by applicable law, rule or regulation, during the period from the date of this Agreement to the Effective Time, the Company shall not, and shall not permit any of its Subsidiaries to, without the prior written consent of Parent: (a) (i) issue, sell, grant, dispose of, pledge or otherwise encumber, or authorize or propose the issuance, sale, disposition or pledge or other encumbrance of (A) any additional shares of its capital stock or any securities or rights convertible into, exchangeable for, or evidencing the right to subscribe for any shares of its capital stock, or any rights, warrants, option, calls, commitments or any other agreements of any character to purchase or acquire any shares of its capital stock or any securities or rights convertible into, exchangeable for, or evidencing the right to subscribe for, any shares of its capital stock or (B) any other securities in respect of, in lieu of, or in substitution for, any shares of its capital stock outstanding on the date hereof other than pursuant to the proper exercise of stock options or warrants outstanding as of the date hereof; (ii) redeem, purchase or otherwise acquire, or propose to redeem, purchase or otherwise acquire, any of its outstanding shares of capital stock; or (iii) split, combine, subdivide or reclassify any shares of its capital stock or declare, set aside for payment or pay any dividend, or make any other actual, constructive or deemed distribution in respect of any shares of its capital stock or otherwise make any payments to its shareholders in their capacity as such; (b) other than in the ordinary course of business consistent with past practice, incur any indebtedness for borrowed money or guarantee any such indebtedness or make any loans, advances or capital contributions to, or investments in, any other person other than the Company or its Subsidiaries; (c) sell, transfer, mortgage, encumber, lease, license or otherwise dispose of any of its properties or assets to any individual, corporation or other entity other than a direct or indirect wholly owned Subsidiary, or cancel, release or assign any indebtedness to any such person or any claims held by any such person, (i) pursuant to contracts or agreements in force at the date of this Agreement or (ii) pursuant to plans disclosed in writing prior to the execution of this Agreement to the Parent; (d) except for transactions in the ordinary course of business consistent with past practice, make any acquisition or investment either by purchase of stock or securities, merger or consolidation, contributions to capital, property transfers, or purchases of any property or assets of any other individual, corporation or other entity other than a wholly owned Subsidiary thereof; (e) amend its Articles of

Incorporation, Bylaws or similar governing documents; (f) enter into, amend, accelerate, vest or modify any employee benefit plan, employment agreement or any other agreement, understanding or arrangement providing for payments by or on behalf of the Company or any of its Subsidiaries; or (g) make any commitment to, take any of the actions prohibited by, or requiring the consent of Parent under, this Section 5.01.

Section 5.02   No Solicitation.

(a)   The Company shall immediately cease and terminate any existing solicitation, initiation, encouragement, activity, discussion or negotiation with any person or entity conducted heretofore by the Company, its Subsidiaries or any of their respective officers, directors, employees, agents or representatives (collectively, "Representatives") with respect to any proposed, potential or contemplated Acquisition Proposal (as defined herein).

(b)   From and after the date hereof, without the prior written consent of the Purchaser, the Company will not, and will not authorize or permit any of its Subsidiaries or Representatives to, directly or indirectly, solicit, initiate or encourage (including by way of furnishing information) or take any other action reasonably designed to facilitate any inquiries or the making of any proposal which constitutes or would reasonably be expected to lead to an Acquisition Proposal.

(c)   Notwithstanding any other provision hereof, the Company may engage in discussions or negotiations with a third party who (without any solicitation, initiation or encouragement, directly or indirectly, by or with the Company or any of its Representatives) seeks to initiate such discussions or negotiations and may furnish such third party information concerning the Company and its business, properties and assets if, and only to the extent that, (i)(A) the third party has first made a bona fide Acquisition Proposal to the Board of Directors of the Company in writing prior to the date upon which this Agreement and the Merger shall have been approved by the required vote of the shareholders of the Company, (B) the Company's Board of Directors concludes in good faith (after consultation with its financial advisor) that the transaction contemplated by such Acquisition Proposal is reasonably capable of being completed, taking into account all legal, financial, regulatory and other aspects of the Acquisition Proposal and the party making such Acquisition Proposal, and could, if consummated, reasonably be expected to result in a transaction more favorable to the Company's shareholders from a financial point of view than the Merger contemplated by this Agreement (any such Acquisition Proposal, a "Company Superior Proposal"), and (C) the Company's Board of Directors shall have concluded in good faith, after considering applicable provisions of state law, and after consultation with outside counsel, that such action is required for the Board of Directors to act in a manner consistent with its fiduciary duties under applicable law; (ii) the Company (A) shall as promptly as practicable notify Parent and the Purchaser (1) that the Company has received a bona fide Acquisition Proposal from a third party, (2) that the Company is permitted to furnish information to, or to enter into discussions or negotiations with, such third party pursuant to clause (i) of this Section 5.02(c), and (3) of the identity of the third party making such Acquisition Proposal and of all the terms and conditions of such proposal, and (B) shall keep Parent and the Purchaser reasonably informed of the status and material terms of such Acquisition Proposal; and (iii) the Company shall promptly advise the third party making such Acquisition Proposal that the Company will not participate in negotiations or discussions with or provide information to such Person, unless and until such person authorizes the Company to comply with clause (ii) of this Section 5.02(c).

(d)   Without limiting the foregoing, it is understood that any violation of the restrictions set forth in the preceding sentence by a director or an officer of the Company or any of its Subsidiaries, or any investment banker, attorney or other Representative of the Company or any of its Subsidiaries, whether or not such person is purporting to act on behalf of the Company or any of its Subsidiaries or otherwise, shall be deemed to be a breach of this Section 5.02 by the Company.

(e)   The term "Acquisition Proposal" shall mean any proposal or offer (other than by Parent or the Purchaser) for a tender or exchange offer, merger, consolidation or other business combination involving the Company or any Subsidiary of the Company, or any proposal to acquire in any manner an equity interest which could result in such party having a direct or indirect equity interest in or acquiring all or material portion of the assets of the Company or any Subsidiary of the Company, other than the transactions contemplated by this Agreement.

Section 5.03   Regulatory Matters. The Company and Parent shall, and Parent shall cause the Purchaser to, take all actions necessary to comply promptly with all legal requirements which may be imposed on it with respect to this Agreement and the transactions contemplated hereby (which actions shall, as applicable, include, without limitation, filing the notification and report form and furnishing all other information required in connection with approvals of or filings with any other Governmental Entity) and shall promptly cooperate with and furnish information to each other in connection with any such requirements imposed upon any of them or any of their Subsidiaries in connection with this Agreement and the transactions contemplated hereby. Each of the Company, Parent and the Purchaser shall, and shall cause its Subsidiaries to, use its best efforts to take all actions necessary to obtain (and shall cooperate with each other in obtaining) any consent, authorization, order or approval of, or any exemption by, any Governmental Entity or other public or private third party required to be obtained or made by Parent, the Purchaser, the Company or any of their respective Subsidiaries in connection with the Merger or the taking of any action contemplated thereby or by this Agreement.

Section 5.04   Financing. At the Effective Time, Parent and the Purchaser shall have sufficient funds available (through cash on hand and existing credit arrangements or otherwise) to pay the Merger Consideration in respect of all Shares (other than Shares held by Parent of the Purchaser or any of their Subsidiaries or affiliates) outstanding and to pay all fees and expenses related to the transactions contemplated by this Agreement.

Section 5.05   Publicity. The initial press release with respect to the execution of this Agreement shall be a joint press release reasonably acceptable to Parent and the Company. Thereafter, so long as this Agreement is in effect, neither the Company, Parent nor any of their respective affiliates shall issue or cause the publication of any press release or other announcement with respect to the Merger, this Agreement or the other transactions contemplated hereby without the prior approval of the other party, except as may be required by law, by any listing agreement with a national securities exchange or by any rule or regulation of the NASD (in which event, the non-disclosing party shall nevertheless have the opportunity to review and consult with the disclosing party regarding such disclosure prior to the making thereof).

Section 5.06   Notification of Certain Matters. The Company shall give prompt notice to Parent, and Parent shall give prompt notice to the Company, of (i) the occurrence, or non-occurrence of any event the occurrence or non-occurrence of which would cause any representation or warranty contained in this Agreement to be untrue or inaccurate in any material respect at or prior to the Effective Time, or is of the type which would be required to be disclosed under Section 3.08, and (ii) any material failure of the Company or Parent, as the case may be, to comply with or satisfy any covenant, condition or agreement to be complied with or satisfied by it hereunder; provided, however, that the delivery of any notice pursuant to this Section 5.06 shall not limit or otherwise affect the remedies available hereunder to the party receiving such notice.

Section 5.07   Access to Information. Upon prior notice and subject to applicable laws relating to the exchange of information, the Company shall, and shall cause each of its Subsidiaries to, afford to the officers, employees, accountants, counsel and other representatives of the Parent, and the Purchaser during the period prior to the Effective Time, access to all its properties, books, contracts, commitments and records, and to its officers, employees, accountants, counsel and other representatives and, during such period, the Company shall, and shall cause its Subsidiaries to, make available to the Parent and the Purchaser (i) a copy of each report, schedule, registration statement and other document filed or received by it during such period pursuant to the requirements of Federal securities laws and (ii) all other information concerning its business, properties and personnel as the Parent or the Purchaser may reasonably request.

Section 5.08   Further Assurances. Subject to the terms and conditions of this Agreement, each of Parent and the Company shall use all reasonable efforts to take, or cause to be taken, all actions, and to do, or cause to be done, all things necessary, proper or advisable to consummate and make effective, as soon as practicable after the date of this Agreement, the transactions contemplated hereby, including, without limitation, using all reasonable efforts to lift or rescind any injunction or restraining order or other order adversely affecting the ability of the parties to consummate the transactions contemplated hereby and using all reasonable efforts to defend any litigation seeking to enjoin, prevent or delay the consummation of the transactions contemplated hereby or seeking material damages.

Section 5.09   Indemnification; Directors' and Officers' Insurance.

(a)   Parent agrees that all rights to indemnification (including advancement of expenses) from the Company existing under _____ law on the date hereof in favor of the persons who are officers or directors of the Company and its Subsidiaries on the date hereof or immediately prior to the Effective Time (the "D&O's") with respect to actions taken in their capacity as directors and officers prior to or at the Effective Time as provided in the respective Articles of Incorporation or by-laws of the Company and its Subsidiaries in effect as of the date hereof shall survive the Merger and shall continue in full force and effect following the Effective Time. To the extent, if any, not provided by a right under one of the parties' directors and officers liability insurance policies, from and after the Effective Time, Parent shall, to the fullest extent permitted by applicable law, indemnify, defend and hold harmless each D&O against all losses, expenses (including reasonable attorneys' fees and expenses), claims, damages or liabilities or amounts paid in settlement arising out of actions or omissions occurring prior to the Effective Time, and whether asserted or claimed prior to, at or after the Effective Time, that are in whole or in part (i) based on or arising out of the fact that such person is or was a director or officer of the Company, or (ii) based on, arising out of or pertaining to the transactions contemplated by this Agreement. In the event of any such loss, claim, damage or liability (whether or not arising before the Effective Time), in addition to any indemnification and hold harmless hereunder, Parent shall pay the reasonable fees and expenses of counsel selected by the D&O's (including counsel selected prior to the date hereof), promptly after statements therefore are received and otherwise advance to such D&O's upon request documented expenses reasonably incurred. Nothing contained herein shall entitle any D&O to any duplicate recovery of any loss, expense, claim, damage or liability. Parent shall not be liable for any settlement incurred without its prior written consent, which consent shall not be unreasonably withheld.

(b)   For a period of six (6) years after the Effective Time, Parent shall cause to be maintained in effect by or on behalf of the Surviving Corporation for the benefit of the D&O's policies of directors' and officers' liability insurance or "run-off" or "tail" coverage at least equivalent in scope and limits of coverage to the current policies maintained by the Company with respect to claims arising from facts or events which occurred prior to or at the Effective Time; provided, however, that in no event shall _____, a Delaware corporation and the owner of all the issued and outstanding equity interests of Parent, Parent or the Surviving Corporation be obligated to expend, in order to maintain or procure such insurance coverage, (i) if such insurance is purchased as "run off" or "tail" coverage, an amount exceeding twelve (12) times the annual premium of the Company's directors' and officers' insurance policy in effect on the date hereof (the "Current Premium") or (ii) if such insurance is purchased annually, an amount annually more than two (2) times the Current Premium, but in either such case Parent or the Surviving Corporation shall be obligated to purchase a policy with the greatest coverage available for a cost not exceeding such amount.

(c)   For a period of six (6) years after the Effective Time, Parent shall cause _____ to maintain in effect for the benefit of the D&O's policies of directors' and officers' liability insurance, or "run-off" or "tail" coverage, pursuant to which directors and officers of majority-owned Subsidiaries of _____ are entitled to coverage (it being acknowledged that such policies currently cover the D&O's), equivalent in scope and limits of coverage to the current policies maintained by Parent with respect to claims arising from facts or events which occurred during the period prior to the Effective Time during which Parent owned a majority of the voting stock of the Company; provided, however, that in no event shall _____ or Parent be obligated to expend, in order to maintain or procure such insurance coverage, (i) if such insurance is purchased as "run off" or "tail" coverage, an amount exceeding twelve (12) times the annual premium of the Parent's directors' and officers' insurance policy in effect on the date hereof (the "Current Parent Premium"), or (ii) if such insurance is purchased annually, an amount annually more than two (2) times the Current Parent Premium, but in either such case Parent shall be obligated to purchase a policy with the greatest coverage available for a cost not exceeding such amount.

(d)   The covenants contained in this Section 5.09 shall survive the Closing, shall continue without time limit and are intended to benefit the Company and each of the indemnified parties.

(e)   No provision in this Section 5.09 shall prohibit or restrict the Parent or the Purchaser from merging the Surviving Corporation with or into another entity for the purpose of changing the jurisdiction of incorporation, organization or formation thereof.

Section 5.10   Additional Agreements. In case at any time after the Effective Time any further action is necessary or desirable to carry out the purposes of this Agreement or to vest the Surviving Corporation with full title to all properties, assets, rights, approvals, immunities and franchises of any of the parties to the merger, the proper officers and directors of each party to this Agreement and their respective Subsidiaries shall take all such necessary action as may be reasonably requested by Parent.

Section 5.11   Actions by Company. Except as otherwise required by applicable law, any actions contemplated to be taken under this Agreement by the Board of Directors of the Company or the Company may be taken by the Company Special Committee on behalf of the Company or its Board of Directors. Notwithstanding any other provisions contained herein, (i) any amendment or modification of, or supplement to, this Agreement that is adverse to the holders of the Company Common Stock shall require the consent of the Company Special Committee and (ii) the waiver of any obligation, covenant, agreement or condition herein, or the giving of any consent or the exercise of any material right thereunder by the Company or its Board of Directors shall require the consent of the Company Special Committee

Section 5.12   Continuation of Certain Employee Benefits. Except as otherwise required by applicable law, Parent covenants and agrees that it shall cause the Company to continue in full force and effect all employee health and welfare benefits of the Company (but not equity-based employee benefits), as the same are currently in effect, until _____, 200__.

ARTICLE VI.
CONDITIONS

Section 6.01   Conditions to Each Party's Obligation To Effect the Merger. The respective obligation of each party to effect the Merger shall be subject to the satisfaction on or prior to the Closing Date of each of the following conditions:

(a)   Shareholder Approval. This Agreement shall have been approved and adopted by the requisite vote of the holders of Company Common Stock and the Series A Preferred Stock required by applicable law and the Articles of Incorporation of the Company in order to consummate the Merger;

(b)   Statutes; Consents. No statute, rule, order, decree or regulation shall have been enacted or promulgated by any foreign or domestic Governmental Entity or authority of competent jurisdiction which prohibits the consummation of the Merger and all foreign or domestic governmental consents, orders and approvals required for the consummation of the Merger and the transactions contemplated hereby shall have been obtained and shall be in effect at the Effective Time; and

(c)   Injunctions. There shall be no order or injunction of a foreign or United States federal or state court or other Governmental Entity of competent jurisdiction in effect precluding, restraining, enjoining or prohibiting consummation of the Merger.

Section 6.02   Additional Conditions to Parent's and Purchaser's Obligation to Effect the Merger. In addition to the conditions set forth in Section 6.01, Parent's and Purchaser's obligation to effect the Merger shall also be subject to the satisfaction on the Closing Date of each of the following additional conditions:

(a)   Representations and Warranties of the Company. The representations and warranties of the Company shall be true and correct in all material respects, except for representations and warranties that are qualified by materiality or Material Adverse Effect, which shall be true and correct in all respects.

(b)   Compliance With Covenants. The Company and each Subsidiary of the Company shall have complied with or performed all covenants to be complied with or performed by the Company or such Subsidiary pursuant to the terms of this Agreement, including without limitation, those set forth in Article V hereof.

(c)   Dissenting Common Stock. The holders of not more than five percent (5%) of the issued and outstanding shares of Company Common Stock immediately prior to the Effective Time shall have purported to exercise, or delivered notice to the Company of their intention to exercise, dissenters' rights with respect to such Shares (which purported exercise shall include notice of intent to demand payment of fair value of shares of Company Common Stock under Section 302A.473 of the __BCA).

(d)   No Outstanding Options. All Options shall have been cancelled in accordance with the provisions of Section 2.04 hereof.

(e)   No Material Adverse Effect. There shall not have occurred any change, event, development or circumstance that has had, or could reasonably be expected to have, a Company Material Adverse Effect.

(f)   Withdrawal of Recommendation. The Special Committee shall not have withdrawn or rescinded its recommendation that the shareholders vote in favor of this Agreement and the Merger.

(g)   Agreements Regarding Stock Options. The Company shall have entered into written agreements regarding stock options, in form and substance reasonably satisfactory to Parent, with each employee of the Company who currently holds options to purchase shares of Company Common Stock.

Section 6.03   Additional Conditions to Company's Obligation to Effect the Merger. In addition to the conditions set forth in Section 6.01, the Company's obligation to effect the Merger shall also be subject to the satisfaction on the Closing Date of each of the following additional conditions:

(a)   Representations and Warranties of Parent and Purchaser. The representations and warranties of the Parent and Purchaser shall be true and correct in all material respects, except for representations and warranties that are qualified by materiality or Material Adverse Effect, which shall be true and correct in all respects.

(b)   Compliance With Covenants. The Parent and Purchaser shall have complied with or performed all covenants to be complied with or performed by them pursuant to the terms of this Agreement, including without limitation, those set forth in Article V hereof.

(c)   Deposit of Funds. Parent shall have deposited sufficient funds with the Paying Agent to permit the exchange of all eligible Certificates for Merger Consideration pursuant to Section 2.02 hereof.

(d)   No Withdrawal of Opinion of Financial Advisor. _____ _____, financial advisor to the Company Special Committee, shall not have withdrawn their opinion referred to in Section 3.12 prior to the Closing Date.

ARTICLE VII.
TERMINATION

Section 7.01   Termination. Anything herein or elsewhere to the contrary notwithstanding, this Agreement may be terminated and the Merger contemplated herein may be abandoned at any time prior to the Effective Time, whether before or after shareholder approval thereof:

(a)   by the mutual consent of the Parent Board and the Company Special Committee;

(b)   by either of the Company Special Committee or the Parent: (i) if any Governmental Entity shall have issued an order, decree or ruling or taken any other action (which order, decree, ruling or other action the parties hereto shall use their respective reasonable best efforts to lift), in each case permanently restraining, enjoining or otherwise prohibiting the transactions contemplated by this Agreement and such order, decree, ruling or other action shall have become final and non-appealable; provided that the party seeking to terminate this Agreement shall have used all reasonable efforts to challenge such order, decree or ruling; or (ii) if the Effective Time shall not have occurred by _____, 200__, unless the Effective Time shall not have occurred because of a material breach of this Agreement by the party seeking to terminate this Agreement;

(c)   by the Parent Board if any of the conditions specified in Sections 6.01 or 6.02 shall not have been satisfied on or prior to the earlier to occur of (i) the Closing Date, or (ii) _____, 200__; or

(d)   by the Company (but only after the Company has made such payments as are provided for in Section 7.02 and only prior to the approval of this Agreement and the Merger by the Company's shareholders), if (i) the Board of Directors of the Company shall conclude in good faith, after considering applicable state law and consulting with outside legal counsel, that failure to enter into a definitive agreement with respect to a Company Superior Proposal would result in the non-compliance by the Board of Directors of the Company with its fiduciary duties to the shareholders of the Company under applicable law, (ii) simultaneously with such termination, the Company shall enter into a definitive and binding acquisition or similar agreement with respect to such Company Superior Proposal and (iii) the Company shall have notified Parent and the Purchaser in writing at least five (5) business days prior to the earlier of such determination by the Board of Directors of the Company and the entering into such definitive and binding agreement; provided, however, that such termination under this Section 7.01(d) shall not be effective until the Company shall have made payment of such amounts as are provided for in Section 7.02).

Section 7.02   Effect of Termination. In the event of the termination of this Agreement as provided in Section 7.01, written notice thereof shall forthwith be given to the other party or parties specifying the provision hereof pursuant to which such termination is made in accordance with the terms thereof, and this Agreement shall forthwith become null and void, and there shall be no liability on the part of the Parent or the Company; provided, however, that nothing in this Section 7.02 shall relieve any party of liability for fraud or for breach of this Agreement (other than a breach of this Agreement arising solely out of the inaccuracy of a representation or warranty of the Company that was accurate when made on the date hereof and which inaccuracy was not caused by any willful and intentional actions or omissions by the Company); provided, further, that in the event that the Company terminates this Agreement pursuant to Section 7.01(d), then, simultaneously with, and as condition precedent to, such termination, the Company shall pay to Parent, by wire transfer of immediately available funds, cash in an amount equal to the sum of (a) all reasonable out of pocket costs and expenses (including, without limitation, all fees, expenses and disbursements of counsel, accountants, investment bankers, experts and other consultants and advisors to Parent and/or the Purchaser) incurred by or on behalf of Parent and/or the Purchaser in connection with or related to this Agreement and the transactions contemplated hereby, including, without limitation, the Merger, plus (b) $100,000 (which amount the parties agree are reasonable liquidated damages and not a penalty).

ARTICLE VIII.
MISCELLANEOUS

Section 8.01   Amendment and Modification. Subject to applicable law, this Agreement may be amended, modified and supplemented in any and all respects, whether before or after any vote of the shareholders of the Company contemplated hereby, by written agreement of the parties hereto (which, in the case of the Company, shall require approval of its Board of Directors upon the recommendation of the Company Special Committee), at any time prior to the Closing Date with respect to any of the terms contained herein, provided that after approval of the Agreement by the shareholders of the Company, the amount of the Merger Consideration shall not be decreased and the form of the Merger Consideration shall not be altered without the approval of the shareholders of the Company.

Section 8.02   Nonsurvival of Representations and Warranties. None of the representations and warranties in this Agreement, the Company Disclosure Schedule, the Parent Disclosure Schedule or in any other schedule, instrument or other document delivered pursuant to this Agreement shall survive the Effective Time.

Section 8.03   Notices. All notices and other communications hereunder shall be in writing and shall be deemed given if delivered personally, telecopied (which is confirmed) or sent by an overnight courier service, such as Federal Express, to the parties at the following addresses (or at such other address for a party as shall be specified by like notice):

    (a)   if to Parent or the Purchaser, to:

        _____

        _____

        _____

with a copy to:

_____

_____

_____

(b)   if to the Company, to:

_____

_____

_____

with a copy to:

_____

_____

_____

Section 8.04   Entire Agreement; Third Party Beneficiaries. This Agreement (including the Company Disclosure Schedule, the Parent Disclosure Schedule and each other schedule, instrument and other document delivered pursuant hereto) and that certain confidentiality agreement, dated as of _____, 200__, between the Company and the Parent (including the documents and the instruments referred to herein and therein): (a) constitutes the entire agreement and supersedes all prior agreements and understandings, both written and oral, among the parties with respect to the subject matter hereof, and (b) except as provided in Sections 1.02, Section 2.04 and Section 5.09, are not intended to confer upon any person other than the parties hereto any rights or remedies hereunder.

Section 8.05   Severability. If any term, provision, covenant or restriction of this Agreement is held by a court of competent jurisdiction or other authority to be invalid, void, unenforceable or against its regulatory policy, the remainder of the terms, provisions, covenants and restrictions of this Agreement shall remain in full force and effect and shall in no way be affected, impaired or invalidated.

Section 8.06   Governing Law. This Agreement shall be governed and construed in accordance with the laws of the State of _____ without giving effect to the principles of conflicts of law thereof or of any other jurisdiction.

Section 8.07   Assignment. Neither this Agreement nor any of the rights, interests or obligations hereunder shall be assigned by any of the parties hereto (whether by operation of law or otherwise) without the prior written consent of the other parties, except that the Purchaser may assign, in its sole discretion, any or all of its rights, interests and obligations hereunder to Parent or to any direct or indirect wholly owned Subsidiary of Parent. Subject to the preceding sentence, this Agreement shall be binding upon, inure to the benefit of and be enforceable by the parties and their respective successors and assigns.

Section 8.08   Headings; Construction. The descriptive headings used herein are inserted for convenience of reference only and are not intended to be part of or to affect the meaning or interpretation of this Agreement. "Include," "includes," and "including" shall be deemed to be followed by "without limitation" whether or not they are in fact followed by such words or words of like import.

Section 8.09   Waiver. Any party hereto may waive any condition to its obligations hereunder, or any breach, default or misrepresentation of any other party hereunder (which, in the case of a waiver by the Company, shall require the approval of its Board of Directors upon the recommendation of the Company Special Committee); provided, however, that no waiver by any party of any default, misrepresentation, or breach of warranty or covenant hereunder, whether intentional or not, shall be deemed to extend to any prior or subsequent default, misrepresentation, or breach of warranty or covenant hereunder or affect in any way any rights arising by virtue of any prior or subsequent such occurrence.

Section 8.10   Counterparts. This Agreement may be executed in one or more counterparts, all of which shall be considered one and the same agreement and shall become effective when two or more counterparts have been signed by each of the parties and delivered to the other parties, it being understood that all parties need not sign the same counterpart.

[SIGNATURE PAGE FOLLOWS]

IN WITNESS WHEREOF, Parent, the Purchaser and the Company have caused this Agreement to be signed by their respective officers thereunto duly authorized as of the date first written above.

[PARENT]

_____

By: _____

Name: _____

Title: _____

[PURCHASER]

_____

By: _____

Name: _____

Title: _____

[COMPANY]

_____

By: _____

Name: _____

Title: _____

Courtesy of Stephen M. Quinlivan and Marci K. Winga, Leonard, Street and Deinard PA

APPENDIX J

STOCK PURCHASE AGREEMENT

THIS PURCHASE AGREEMENT (this "Agreement") is made as of [ ] between [ ], a [ ] corporation or its designee ("Buyer"), and [ ], a resident of [ ] ("Seller").

RECITALS:

WHEREAS, [ ], a [ ] corporation (together with (i) any predecessor, by merger or otherwise, including [ ], a [ ] corporation, and (ii) any past or present subsidiary, the "Company") is engaged in the Business;

WHEREAS, Buyer desires to acquire all of the issued and outstanding equity capital of the Company so that the Company will become wholly owned by Buyer;

WHEREAS, Buyer desires Seller to cause the Company to undertake the transactions set forth herein and to purchase from Seller the Purchased Shares so that Buyer owns all of the equity capital of the Company, subject to the terms and conditions set forth herein, and upon reliance of each and every representation made by Seller; and

WHEREAS, Seller desires to sell to Buyer all stockholder-owned intangible assets related to the Business (the "Seller Intangible Assets") so that the Company has all the rights and privileges related to the Business available to the Company.

NOW, THEREFORE, in consideration of the premises and mutual agreements hereinafter set forth, the parties hereto hereby agree as follows:

ARTICLE I
DEFINITIONS

1.1   Defined Terms. As used herein, the terms defined below shall have the following meanings. Any of these terms, unless the context otherwise requires, may be used in the singular or plural depending on the reference.

"Adjusted Net Worth" means the excess (or deficit) of the book value of the Company's assets, over the book value of the Company's liabilities, after giving effect to the full payment and satisfaction of the Retired Debt by Seller as required by this Agreement (but only to the extent such Retired Debt is in fact so satisfied), in each case computed in accordance with GAAP and calculated as of the close of business on [ ].

"Affiliate" means, as to any party, any Person which directly or indirectly, is in control of, is controlled by, or is under common control with, such party, including any Person who would be treated as a member of a controlled group under Section 414 of the Code, and any officer or director of such party and, as to a party who is a natural Person, such Person's spouse, parents, siblings and lineal descendants and any relative having the same home as such Person. For purposes of this definition, an entity shall be deemed to be "controlled by" a Person if the Person possesses, directly or indirectly, power either to (i) vote ten percent (10%) or more of the securities (including convertible securities) having ordinary voting power or (ii) direct or cause the direction of the management or policies of such Person, whether by contract or otherwise.

"Assets" means (i) all assets related to the Business, (ii) all strategic data, such as marketing development plans, forecasts, and forecast assumptions and volumes, and future plans and potential strategies of the Company which are being discussed, and all financial data, such as price and price objectives, price lists, pricing and quoting policies, and procedures, (iii) all accounts receivable, notes receivable and installment receivables existing as of the Closing Date (the "Accounts Receivable"), (iv) all inventory, work in progress, raw materials, returned goods inventory, evaluation systems inventory, warranty returns inventory, service inventory, finished products, supplies, packaging and shipping containers and materials (on-site, off-site and consigned) as of the Closing Date (the "Inventory"), (v) all machinery, equipment, furniture and fixtures, including without limitation, the items set forth in Schedule 4.13 (the "Fixed Assets"), (vi) all database information and software, (vii) all information necessary to bill customers for license usage, service contracts and all other revenue items, (viii) all of the Company's rights under any personal property leases and other agreements, supply agreements, licenses, end user agreements, contracts (including customer contracts, OEM contracts, lease contracts, commitment contracts, and all agreements for the testing, modification, development, trial, license, lease, rental or sale or other use of the product), insurance policies and commitments, including without limitation, the leases, agreements, contracts and commitments relating to or necessary to the conduct and operation of the Business set forth on Schedule 4.12 (the "Contracts"), (ix) all backlog and orders, (x) all permits, approvals, qualifications, and the like issued by any government or governmental unit, agency, board, body, or instrumentality, whether, federal, state, local or otherwise relating to or necessary to the conduct and operation of the Business, (xi) all of the Company's Intellectual Property, and (xii) all other tangible or intangible personal or mixed property of the Company, if any, of every kind and description, wherever located together with any customer relationships, employee relationships and any other intangible assets related to the Business owned by Seller.

"Business" means all of the business products, support and services of the Company related to the Company's system integration, consulting, implementation, and managed services business, including network operating centers, SSP, MSP, ERSM storage architecture and business continuance businesses.

"Environmental Lien" means any encumbrance, whether recorded or unrecorded, in favor of any governmental or regulatory authority, relating to any Liability of the Company or Seller under any Environmental and Safety Requirements.

"Environmental and Safety Requirements" means all federal, state and local statutes, regulations, ordinances and other provisions having the force or effect of law, all judicial and administrative orders and determinations, all contractual obligations and all common law, in each case concerning public health and safety, worker health and safety and pollution or protection of the environment (including, without limitation, all those relating to the presence, use, production, generation, handling, transport, treatment, storage, disposal, distribution, labeling, testing, processing, discharge, Release, threatened Release, control or cleanup of any hazardous or otherwise regulated materials, substances or wastes, chemical substances or mixtures, pesticides, pollutants, contaminants, toxic chemicals, petroleum products or byproducts, asbestos, polychlorinated biphenyls, noise or radiation).

"GAAP" means United States generally accepted accounting principles.

"Intellectual Property" means on a world-wide basis, any and all: (i) patents, patent disclosures, designs, algorithms and other industrial property rights, (ii) trademarks, service marks, trade dress, trade names, logos and corporate names, together with all of the goodwill associated therewith, (iii) copyrights (registered or unregistered), together with all authors' and moral rights (whether choate or inchoate, published or unpublished), (iv) mask works, (v) computer software (including, without limitation, source code (with all comments and remarks, if any), object code, macros, scripts, objects, routines, modules and other components), data, data bases and documentation thereof, (vi) trade secrets and other confidential or proprietary information (including, without limitation, ideas, formulas, compositions, inventions (whether patentable or unpatentable and whether or not reduced to practice), know-how, products, processes, techniques, methods, research and development information and results, drawings, specifications, designs, technical and development plans and proposals, technical data and customer, prospect and supplier lists and information), (vii) all other intellectual and industrial property rights of every kind and nature and however designated, whether arising by operation of law, contract, license or otherwise, (viii) "technical data" as defined in 48 CFR § 27.401, (ix) copies and tangible embodiments thereof (in whatever form or medium), and (x) all registrations, applications (pending and in-process), renewals, extensions, continuations, divisions or reissues of any of the foregoing rights, now or hereafter in force (including all rights therein).

As used herein, "knowledge of the Company," "known by the Company" and the like means the knowledge of [ ].

"Liability" shall mean, without limitation, any direct or indirect liability, indebtedness, guaranty, endorsement, claim, loss, damage, deficiency, cost, expense, obligation or responsibility, whether accrued, absolute, contingent, mature, unmature or otherwise and whether known or unknown, fixed or unfixed, choate or inchoate, liquidated or unliquidated, secured or unsecured.

"Lien" shall mean any claim, lien, pledge, option, charge, easement, security interest, right-of-way, mortgage or other right or encumbrance of any kind.

"Permitted Legal Fees" means Ten Thousand Dollars ($10,000) of legal fees and expenses related to employees entering into employment agreements referred to in Section 7.2(d) and Fifteen Thousand Dollars ($15,000) in the aggregate related to legal fees and expenses for settlements with respect to leases in default, employee option transactions required for the closing and termination of the 401(k) and profit sharing plans.

"Permitted Liens" means (i) mechanics, materialmens, and purchase money security interests in amounts less than Fifteen Thousand Dollars ($15,000) individually and Fifty Thousand Dollars ($50,000) in the aggregate (but only to the extent such Liens secure Permitted Liabilities), (ii) Liens for property Taxes not yet due and payable, and (iii) only those Liens specifically set forth on Schedule 1.1(a) hereto.

"Person" shall mean any person, limited liability company, partnership, trust, unincorporated organization, corporation, association, joint stock company, business, group, governmental authority or other entity.

"Release" shall have the meaning set forth in CERCLA.

"Retired Debt" shall mean any debt or Liability of the Company on the Closing Date, all or part of which would be classified as a noncurrent liability of the Company on any financial statements prepared as of the Closing Date in accordance with GAAP, and also includes all amounts due to Sovereign Bank (f/k/a Fleet National Bank), regardless of the balance sheet classification of such debt.

"[ ] Case" means [ ] presently pending in [ ] and any similar case commenced by Mr. [ ] in a different court arising out of the same facts and circumstances.

"Seller Costs" shall mean all costs, expenses and funding necessary (i) to discharge the Retired Debt in full (except to the extent satisfied by Buyer pursuant to Section 6.12), (ii) to discharge any Lien on the Assets other than the Permitted Liens (except to the extent satisfied by Buyer pursuant to Section 6.12), (iii) to provide for full payment of all of Seller's and the Company's investment banking, legal (other than Permitted Legal Fees), accounting (expressly excluding any costs directly related to the audit and preparation of the Company's Tax returns) and other costs and expenses of the Company and Seller with respect to the transactions contemplated hereby (or any similar transaction with another party), (iv) to pay in full all sale and discretionary bonuses earned by employees of the Company prior to the Closing Date or granted in connection with the Closing (other than bonuses previously accrued in the ordinary course of business which do not breach any representation and warranty), (v) to pay in full any payment required by any change in control provision (other than any usual and ordinary consent fees) resulting from the transaction, (vi) to pay in full all remaining costs under the Company's "[ ]" and deferred compensation plans, (vii) to pay one-half of cash severance payments due to [ ] after giving effect to the amendment to be made pursuant to Section 7.2.(m)(ix), (viii) to discharge and pay off or extinguish any other equity interest in the Company other than the Purchased Shares, including all costs associated with Company options outstanding (except to the extent satisfied by Buyer pursuant to Section 6.12), (ix) to settle all past due obligations for any lease of the Company set forth on Schedule 4.12, except to the extent such costs have previously been accrued on the Company's books, (x) to pay any vacation and severance pay due employees of the Company which were previously terminated that was not paid when due, and (xi) to pay retention bonuses to key employees pursuant to the employment contracts entered into pursuant to Section 7.2(d) (other than [ ]) and all payroll Taxes associated therewith (except to the extent satisfied by Buyer pursuant to Section 6.12).

"Software" means any and all (i) computer programs, including any and all software implementations of algorithms, models and methodologies, whether in source code or object code, (ii) databases and compilations, including any and all data and collections of data, whether machine readable or otherwise, (iii) descriptions, flow-charts and other work product used to design, plan, organize and develop any of the foregoing, (iv) the technology (other than hardware) supporting any Internet site(s) operated by or on behalf of the Company, and (v) all documentation, including user manuals and training materials, relating to any of the foregoing.

"Tax" means any tax imposed by any federal, state, local or foreign governmental authority relating to income, sales, payroll, property, duty, excise, gross receipts, severance, stamp, occupation, franchise, withholding, unemployment, use, transfer, registration or like tax or other governmental charge of any kind, including any interest, penalty, or addition thereto.

"Transaction Documents" means this Agreement, the Escrow Agreement, the Employment Agreement entered into by Seller and any document or agreement executed in connection therewith.

1.2   Index of Other Defined Terms. In addition to the terms defined above, the following terms shall have the respective meanings given to them in the Sections set forth below:

Defined Term	Section
Accounts Receivable	1.1
Additional Purchase Price	3.3
Bonus Payout Date	8.4
Bonus Plan	6.11
Bonus Pool	6.11
CERCLA	4.14
Claims	8.1
Claim Notice	8.3
Closing	7.1
Closing Date	7.1
Closing Date Statement	3.2
Company	Recitals
Contracts	1.1
Code	4.21
Company Material Adverse Effect	4.1
Contingent Workers	4.20
Customers	4.18
Disclosure Schedule	Article 4
ERISA	4.21
Escrow Agent	3.1
Escrow Agreement	3.1
Escrow Amount	3.1

ARTICLE 2
TRANSFER OF STOCK AND PROPERTIES

2.1   Purchase of Shares. On the terms and subject to conditions hereof, Seller covenants and agrees to sell, assign and transfer to Buyer all of his right, title and interest in, and Buyer covenants and agrees to purchase from Seller effective the Closing Date all of the issued and outstanding shares of capital stock of the Company, which consists of [ ] (the "Purchased Shares") free and clear of any and all Liens.

2.2   Purchase of Seller Intangible Assets. On the terms and subject to the conditions hereof, Seller covenants and agrees to sell, assign and transfer to Buyer all of his right, title and interest in, and Buyer covenants and agrees to purchase from Seller effective as of the Closing Date, all of the Seller Intangible Assets.

2.3   Instruments of Transfer. On the Closing Date Seller shall deliver or cause to be delivered to Buyer (i) duly executed stock powers, accompanied by certificates representing the Purchased Shares and such other instruments of transfer and assignment as may be reasonably necessary to vest in Buyer good and valid title to, and all of Seller's right title and interest in, the Purchased Shares, free and clear of all Liens, and (ii) to execute instruments assigning to Buyer all Seller Intangible Assets. Seller also agrees to take all such other action as Buyer may reasonably request to put Buyer in possession and operating control of the Assets and Business of the Company. All such stock powers and other instruments shall be in form and substance reasonably satisfactory to Buyer.

ARTICLE 3
PURCHASE PRICE

3.1   Initial Purchase Price. Subject to adjustment pursuant to Section 3.2, and subject to increase for the Additional Purchase Price set forth in Section 3.3 below, the aggregate consideration to be paid by Buyer to Seller for the Purchased Shares, all of the issued and outstanding equity capitalization (including cancellation of vested and unvested options and any other equity interest in the Company of whatever kind, which, except as set forth in Section 6.12, shall be at Seller's expense) of the Company and the Seller Intangible Assets shall be [ ] (the "Initial Purchase Price"). Except as set forth in Section 6.12, it is also agreed that Seller is solely responsible for the Seller Costs and such amounts shall either be funded by Seller from the Initial Purchase Price, or if paid by the Company with the consent of Buyer, the Initial Purchase Price shall be reduced by the amount of such payment. The Initial Purchase Price shall be payable as follows:

(a)   On the Closing Date Buyer shall, by wire transfer or bank check of immediately available funds, pay to Seller [ ] (it being understood that Buyer shall direct payment of such funds in a manner satisfactory to Buyer, so that the Seller Costs are discharged in full except as set forth in Section 6.12); and

(b)   On the Closing Date Seller shall deposit with [ ], a national banking association, ("Escrow Agent") [ ] (the "Escrow Amount") to be disbursed pursuant to the terms of the escrow agreement (the "Escrow Agreement") attached hereto as Exhibit A.

(c)   Subsequent to the Closing, the Initial Purchase Price shall be allocated among the Purchased Shares, the Seller Intangible Assets and the covenant not to compete entered into by Seller pursuant to the employment agreement referred to in Section 7.2(d). The foregoing allocation shall be agreed between Buyer and Seller based upon an independent appraisal by [ ]. Each party agrees not to assert, in connection with any Tax return, audit or similar proceeding, any allocation to the Initial Purchase Price which differs from the allocation described above. Any subsequent adjustment to the Initial Purchase Price pursuant to Section 3.2 shall be allocated to the Purchased Shares and the Seller Intangible Assets.

3.2   Adjustment.

(a)   As promptly as practicable following the Closing Date, Buyer shall prepare a statement (the "Closing Date Statement") calculating Adjusted Net Worth in accordance with the assumptions and methodology set forth on Schedule 3.2. The Closing Date Statement shall be delivered to Seller upon the later of (i) sixty (60) days after the Closing and (ii) twenty (20) days after completion of the audit of the Company for the fiscal year ended [ ]. When calculating Adjusted Net Worth, Buyer shall take into account any adjustments made in the audit for the year ended [ ], but Buyer shall not increase allowances for doubtful accounts or reserves for obsolete inventory in excess of those shown on the [ ] balance sheet of the Company; provided that the foregoing sentence shall not in any way limit any other representation, warranty or covenant in this Agreement, including the representations and warranties in Sections 4.10 or 4.29.

(b)   Upon receipt of the Closing Date Statement, Seller (and at Seller's expense, its independent certified public accountants) shall be permitted during the succeeding fifteen (15) day period to examine, and Buyer shall make available, the books and records relied upon by Buyer in preparing the Closing Date Statement. As promptly as practicable, and in no event later than the last day of such fifteen (15) day period, Seller shall either inform Buyer in writing that the Closing Date Statement is acceptable or object to the Closing Date Statement by delivering to Buyer a written statement setting forth a specific description of Seller's objection to the Closing Date Statement (the "Statement of Objections") and Seller's calculation of any disputed amounts.

If Seller shall fail to deliver a Statement of Objections within such fifteen (15) day period, the Closing Date Statement shall be deemed to have been accepted by Seller. If a Statement of Objections is delivered, Buyer and Seller shall attempt in good faith to resolve any dispute within fifteen (15) days after delivery. If Seller and Buyer are unable to resolve the dispute within such fifteen (15) days, Buyer and Seller shall engage a "Big 5" accounting firm reasonably acceptable to Buyer and Seller to resolve any unresolved objections. The fees of such firm shall be paid by Seller if Buyer's calculation of disputed amounts as set forth in the Statement of Objections is closer to such accountant's final determination than the Seller's determination, and otherwise such fees shall be paid by Buyer. Such firm's resolution of the dispute shall be conclusive and binding upon the parties and nonappealable and shall not be subject to further review under the dispute resolution provisions of Article 10 (in the event no "Big 5" accounting firm acceptable to Seller and Buyer is willing to undertake such engagement, or Buyer and Seller cannot agree on a "Big 5" accounting firm, the dispute resolutions provisions in Article 10 shall be used (provided that if Buyer and Seller cannot agree on a Big 5 accounting firm, the arbitrators appointed pursuant to Article 10 may make such appointment)).

(c)   Except as otherwise provided in this Paragraph (c), "Minimum Adjusted Net Worth" shall equal a deficit of [ ]. However, Schedule 3.2 sets forth certain orders the Company anticipates will be received within five business days of the Closing Date and the anticipated gross profit (revenue less cost of goods sold) from each such order. If such orders are not received within such five (5) business days from the Closing so that the gross profit in the aggregate from such orders is less than [ ], the Minimum Adjusted Net Worth deficit shall be reduced dollar for dollar to the extent such gross profit is less than [ ]. In no event shall Minimum Adjusted Net Worth be less than a deficit of [ ] after giving effect to such adjustment, and if no such orders are received within such five (5) business days, Minimum Adjusted Net Worth shall be equal to a deficit of [ ].

(d)   If Adjusted Net Worth on the Closing Date Statement is less than Minimum Adjusted Net Worth (i.e., the actual deficit is greater than the deficit anticipated by Minimum Adjusted Net Worth) by more than [ ], the Initial Purchase Price shall be decreased by the amount by which the actual deficit reflected in Adjusted Net Worth exceeds the deficit anticipated by Minimum Adjusted Net Worth plus [ ].

(e)   Any reduction in purchase price required pursuant to Section 3.2(d) shall be effected as set forth herein. If the adjustment is less than [ ], Buyer shall be entitled to withdraw such amounts from the Escrow Amount pursuant to the terms of the Escrow Agreement. If the reduction in purchase price is greater than[ ], Seller shall remit such funds to Buyer as set forth in Section 3.2(f), or Buyer at its option may withdraw all or portion of such funds from the Escrow Amount pursuant to the terms of the Escrow Agreement.

(f)   Seller shall make any payment required by Section 3.2(e) within five (5) business days of the date of determination in accordance with Section 3.2, and if no Statement of Objections is delivered, the amount shall be delivered on the 15th day following delivery of the Closing Date Statement. In the event Seller delivers a Statement of Objections, Buyer shall be entitled to withdraw the undisputed portion from the Escrow Amount, if such amounts are to be remitted from the Escrow Amount pursuant to Section 3.2(e), or, if applicable, Seller shall pay the undisputed portion to Buyer if Seller is required to pay such amount pursuant to Section 3.2(e).

3.3   Additional Purchase Price.

(a)   Buyer shall pay Seller an additional purchase price calculated as set forth in Exhibit B hereto (the "Additional Purchase Price"), but not in excess of [ ], paid as set forth therein. Such payment shall be made no later than [ ]. In the event of a dispute regarding the amount of the Additional Purchase Price, Buyer shall pay the undisputed amount not later than such date, and the balance shall be payable when the amount is finally determined, whether by agreement of Buyer and Seller, or pursuant to a determination by the arbitration panel pursuant to Article 10.

(b)   In the event Buyer has made a claim for indemnification pursuant to Article 8 prior to payment of the Additional Purchase Price, the payment of the Additional Purchase Price shall be deposited into escrow pursuant to the Escrow Agreement to the extent the Escrow Amount may not, in the reasonable judgment of Buyer, be satisfactory to satisfy the indemnification claim.

ARTICLE 4
REPRESENTATIONS, WARRANTIES AND AGREEMENTS
OF SELLER

Seller hereby represents and warrants to Buyer that the statements contained in this Article 4 are true and correct, except as set forth in the disclosure schedule provided by Seller on the date hereof (the "Disclosure Schedule"), and Seller also represents and warrants the statements in the Disclosure Schedule are true and correct. The Disclosure Schedule shall be arranged in sections and paragraphs corresponding to the numbered and lettered sections and paragraphs contained in this Article 4. The disclosures in any section or paragraph of the Disclosure Schedule (including any specific cross reference referred to therein) shall qualify as disclosures with respect to the numbered and lettered paragraphs in that section to which the disclosures specifically relate. Any reference in this Article 4 to an agreement being "enforceable" shall be deemed to be qualified to the extent such enforceability is subject to (i) laws of general application relating to bankruptcy, insolvency, moratorium and the relief of debtors, and (ii) the availability of specific performance, injunctive relief and other equitable remedies.

4.1 <u>Organization, Good Standing, Power, Etc.</u> The Company is a corporation duly organized and validly existing under the laws of the jurisdiction of its incorporation. The Company is qualified to do Business and is in corporate good standing in each jurisdiction in which the character and location of the assets or the nature of the business transacted by the Company makes such qualification necessary, except where the failure to qualify would not have a material adverse effect on the business, operations or financial condition of the Company (a "Company Material Adverse Effect"). Schedule 4.1 lists each state in which the Company is currently qualified to do Business and the Company is in corporate good standing in each such state. The Company has all the requisite corporate power and authority to own or lease and operate the Assets and its Business and to carry on its Business and to consummate the transactions contemplated hereby.

4.2 <u>Certificate of Incorporation and Bylaws; Capitalization.</u>

(a) The Company and Seller have furnished Buyer with (i) the Certificate of Incorporation of the Company, as amended to date, and (ii) the Bylaws of the Company, as amended to date. Such Certificate of Incorporation and Bylaws are in full force and effect.

(b) With respect to the capitalization of the Company:

(i) The authorized capital stock of the Company consists of (x) [ ] shares of common stock, par value $0.01 per share, of which only the Purchased Shares are issued and are outstanding, (y) [ ] shares of preferred stock, par value $0.01 per share, of which no shares are issued and outstanding, and (z) [ ] shares of common stock held in the Company's treasury;

(ii) The Purchased Shares have been issued as fully paid and non-assessable shares, and not in violation of any pre-emptive rights, to Seller;

(iii)   All of the Purchased Shares are owned by Seller as the legal and beneficial owner of record, with a good and valid title thereto, free and clear of all Liens;

(iv)   Other than as contemplated by this Agreement, no Person has any agreement or option or warrant or any right or privilege, whether by law, pre emptive or contractual, for the purchase from Seller of any of the Purchased Shares;

(v)   Except as set forth on Schedule 4.2 (all of which rights shall be cancelled prior to Closing at Seller's expense), no Person has any agreement or option or warrant or any right or privilege to subscribe for or otherwise acquire any shares of the capital stock or any other securities of the Company, whether by law, pre emptive or contractual or conversion right; and

(vi)   The documents to be delivered pursuant to Section 7.2(a)(iii) are sufficient to extinguish all outstanding equity securities of the Company, and from and after the Closing, Buyer will own all of the Purchased Shares and equity of the Company and there will be no options, warrants, convertible securities or other equity securities of the Company outstanding.

(c)   Except as set forth on Schedule 4.2, Seller has at all times owned all of the issued and outstanding capital stock of the Company. Any such shares not owned by Seller were either acquired by Seller free and clear of all Liens or were acquired by the Company free and clear of all Liens.

(d)   Schedule 4.2 includes a true and accurate list of all outstanding options for capital stock of the Company, the number of vested and unvested shares immediately prior to the Closing, the exercise price, and vesting schedule (including a description of any accelerated vesting which will occur as a result of this Agreement) with respect to each such option. All options granted by the

Company and any deferred compensation plan maintained by the Company were granted or maintained in full compliance with federal and state securities laws.

4.3   Other Information. None of the documents which have been or may be furnished by the Company or Seller or any representatives of the Company or Seller to Buyer, or any of their representatives in connection with the transactions contemplated hereby, or in or pursuant to this Agreement or any Transaction Document, or in connection with Buyer's and its representative's review of the Business of the Company, is or will be materially false or misleading or contains or will contain any material misstatement of fact or omit to state any fact necessary to make the same not misleading in light of the circumstances and the purposes for which the documents were furnished.

4.4   Execution and Validity of Agreement; Spousal Consent, Etc.

(a)   This Agreement has been, and the Transaction Documents will be, duly executed and delivered by Seller. This Agreement is, and the Transaction Documents when executed and delivered will be, the valid and binding obligation of Seller enforceable in accordance with its terms, except that such enforcement may be limited by (i) bankruptcy, insolvency or other similar laws affecting the enforcement of creditors' rights generally, and (ii) general principles of equity, regardless of whether enforcement is sought in a proceeding in equity or at law.

(b)   Seller has the sole and exclusive right to take all actions with respect to the Purchased Shares (including actions with respect to execution of the Agreement), free from any community property laws, spousal consent, divorce proceeding, property settlement made or pending in connection with a divorce, judgments, decrees, shareholders agreement, Liens, equitable liens, bank or contractual covenants and the like.

4.5   Effect of Agreement, Etc. The execution, delivery and performance of this Agreement and the Transaction Documents by Seller and consummation by Seller and the Company of the transactions contemplated hereby and thereby will not, with or without the giving of notice and the lapse of time, or both, (a) violate any provision of law, statute, rule or regulation which is material to the Business of the Company or any material law to which the Seller is subject, (b) violate any judgment, order, writ or decree of any court specifically naming the Company or Seller, (c) violate any material permits, licenses, orders or approvals of the Company or Seller or the ability of Buyer to make use of such permits, licenses, orders or approvals, (d) result in a breach of or conflict with any term or provision of, or result in the creation or imposition of any Lien pursuant to, the Company's Certificate of Incorporation or Bylaws, or (e) result in a material breach of, or material conflict with, any term, covenant, condition or provision of, result in a material modification or termination of, constitute a material default under, or result in the creation or imposition of any Lien, security interest, restriction, charge or encumbrance upon any of the Assets (other than Permitted Liens) or the Purchased Shares pursuant to any material contract or other agreement or instrument to which the Company or Seller is a party or by which any of the Assets is or may be bound or affected or from which the Company or Seller derives benefit.

4.6   Consents and Approvals. No permit, application, notice, transfer, consent, approval, order, qualification, waiver from, or authorization of, or declaration, filing or registration with, any governmental authority is necessary in connection with the execution and delivery by Seller of this Agreement or the consummation by Seller and the Company of the transactions contemplated hereby, and no consent of any third party is required to consummate any of the transactions contemplated hereby.

4.7   Financial Statements.

(a)   Seller has delivered to Buyer copies of the Company's audited balance sheets and related statements of operations as of [ ], and [ ] and [ ] and for each of the years then ended and the unaudited financial statements as of and for the year ended [ ] (together, all such balance sheets and related statements of operations shall be hereinafter referred to as the "Financial Statements"). The Financial Statements (i) are in accordance with the books and records of the Company, (ii) reflect fairly and accurately in all material respects the operations and financial condition of the Company for the periods or as of the dates indicated, and were prepared in accordance with GAAP, uniformly applied on a basis consistent with that of prior years or periods, (iii) contain and reflect all necessary adjustments and reserves for a fair and accurate presentation in all material respects of the results of operations for the periods covered by such Financial Statements, and (iv) reflect fairly and accurately in all material respects all of the Liabilities and obligations of the Company (whether direct or indirect, accrued, absolute, contingent or otherwise).

(b)   The books and records of the Company are auditable, have been kept in conformity with GAAP and are sufficient to permit the preparation of pro forma information and audited financial statements with an unqualified opinion that comply with applicable Securities and Exchange Commission ("SEC") requirements within seventy (70) days of the Closing Date. To the knowledge of Seller and the Company, there exist no material weaknesses in the internal controls of the Company.

4.8   No Undisclosed Liabilities, Claims, Etc. The Company does not have any outstanding Liabilities or obligations, except (a) as set forth on Schedule 4.8, (b) to the extent recorded in the most recent Financial Statements (other than general references to commitments and contingent liabilities) and (c) incurred in the ordinary course of business since the date of the most recent Financial Statements. As of the Closing Date the Company does not have any Liabilities except those set forth in the previous sentence, those incurred in the ordinary course of business in accordance with this Agreement and those described on the Schedule delivered pursuant to Section 7.2(m)(ii) (such Liabilities, to the extent included in calculating Adjusted Net Worth, but excluding any Liability which would be a breach of any representation or warranty of this Agreement, or which relate to Seller Costs, or any litigation against the Company, are referred to as "Permitted Liabilities").

4.9   Taxes.

(a)   The Company has timely prepared and filed, with the appropriate foreign, federal, state and local tax authorities, all Tax returns required to be filed by the Company or Seller. All such Tax returns are correct and complete and have been prepared in accordance with applicable law. All Taxes required to have been paid by the Company and Seller have been paid on a timely basis. No claim has ever been made by a governmental authority in a jurisdiction where the Company or Seller do not file Tax returns that Company or Seller are or may be subject to taxation by that jurisdiction.

(b)   There are no claims pending or, to the knowledge of Seller or the Company, threatened for Taxes against the Company or attributable to the Company in excess of the amounts reflected on the Financial Statements for such Taxes and no basis for any such claim exists.

(c)   The Company has not agreed to any waiver or extension of statutes of limitations related to Taxes.

(d)   The Company has paid or provided adequate reserves for all Taxes attributable to the Company.

(e)   No deficiencies on any of the Company's Tax returns or reports attributable to or otherwise allocable to the Company have been threatened as of the date hereof. The Company made a valid "Subchapter S" Tax election on [ ], which election remained in full force and effect until [ ].

(f)   The Company (i) is not a party to any Tax allocation or Tax sharing arrangement, (ii) has not been a member of any consolidated group for Tax reporting purposes, and (iii) has no liability for Taxes owing by any other Person.

(g)   The Company has not taken any action that would have the effect of deferring a measure of Tax or income from a period prior to the Closing Date to a period after the Closing Date.

(h)   The Company has delivered complete and accurate copies of (i) all of the Company's federal Tax returns for each of the last three years, (ii) all examination reports issued regarding, and statements of deficiencies related to, such federal income Tax returns assessed or agreed to during such five-year period and (iii) any agreement with a governmental authority relating to any Tax that could be payable by the Company. The Company has made available copies of all state Tax returns of the Company during the preceding three (3) years and any examination reports with respect thereto. Schedule 4.9 identifies all foreign, federal, state and local Tax returns with respect to income, sales, payroll, excise and other taxes required to be filed by the Company or Seller in each of the last three years and the periods covered by such returns.

(i)   The Company is not a party to any agreement, plan, contract or arrangement that could result, separately or in the aggregate, in any "excess parachute payments" within the meaning of Section 280G of the Code.

4.10   Inventory and Backlog. The Inventory is (a) except to the extent of reserves therefor in the Financial Statements, salable or usable in the normal course of the Business, (b) at levels consistent with past practices of the Business, and (c) carried on the books of the Company at the lower of cost or market and pursuant to the normal inventory valuation policies of the Company, as reflected in the Financial Statements. All of the Inventory is located at [ ], except as set forth on Schedule 4.10. At [ ], the backlog of firm orders for the Company was [ ].

4.11   Absence of Certain Changes or Events. Except as set forth on Schedule 4.11 or as contemplated by this Agreement, since [ ], the Company and Seller have conducted the Business only in the ordinary course and consistent with past practices and neither the Company nor Seller has, with respect to the Company:

(a)   Suffered any damage, destruction or loss of any of the Assets, whether or not covered by insurance, in excess of Twenty-Five Thousand Dollars ($25,000);

(b)   Suffered any change in its financial condition, assets, Liabilities or business or suffer any other event or condition of any character which individually or in the aggregate had any Company Material Adverse Effect or is reasonably likely to result in a Company Material Adverse Effect;

(c)   Paid, discharged or satisfied any claims, Liabilities or obligations (absolute, accrued, contingent or otherwise) of the Company except in each case in the ordinary course of business;

(d)   Waived any claims or rights with a value greater than Twenty-Five Thousand Dollars ($25,000) individually;

(e)   Pledged or permitted the imposition of any Lien (other than Permitted Liens) on or sell, assign, transfer or otherwise dispose of any of the Assets used in or relating to the Business, except the sale or disposition of inventory and Assets in the ordinary course of business;

(f)   Sold, assigned, encumbered, licensed, pledged, abandoned or otherwise transferred any patents, applications for patent, trademarks, trade names, copyrights, licenses, or other intangible assets;

(g)   Made any material change in any method of accounting or accounting principle or practice;

(h)   Except for de minimus adjustments, written up or down the value of the inventory or determined as collectible any notes or accounts receivable that were previously considered to be uncollectible, except for write-ups or write-downs and other determinations in the ordinary course of business;

(i)   Granted any general increase in the compensation payable or to become payable to its officers or employees or any special increase in the compensation payable or to become payable to any such officer or employee, or make any bonus payments to any such officer or employee, except for normal merit and cost of living increases in the ordinary course of business and in accordance with past practice (which details of such ordinary course actions have been disclosed to Buyer);

(j)   Lost or learned of the prospective loss of any Customer or Vendor listed on Schedule 4.18;

(k)   Made capital expenditures on behalf of or relating to the Business in excess of Twenty-Five Thousand Dollars ($25,000) in the aggregate;

(l)   Failed in any material respect to maintain records for accounts receivable, inventory, accounts payable and other accounts;

(m)   Issued any capital stock or any options, warrants for, or securities convertible into, the equity capital of the Company;

(n)   Paid any Seller Costs from funds of the Company without the consent of Buyer;

(o)   Agreed, whether in writing or otherwise, to take any action described in this Section 4.11.

4.12   Contracts and Commitments.

(a)   Schedule 4.12 sets forth an accurate and complete list of each Contract of the Company in effect as of the date of this Agreement to which the Company is a party or which affects the Company or its assets, (i) with a dealer, broker, sales agency, advertising agency or other Person engaged in sales or promotional activities, (ii) which requires aggregate payments by or to the Company, or involves an unperformed commitment or service, having a value in excess of Twenty-Five Thousand Dollars ($25,000), (iii) pursuant to which the Company has made or will make loans or advances, or has or will incur debts or become a guarantor or surety or pledged its credit on or otherwise become responsible with respect to any undertaking of another, (iv) which is an indenture, credit agreement, loan agreement, note, mortgage, security agreement, lease of real property or personal property or agreement for financing, (v) involving a partnership, joint venture or other cooperative undertaking, (vi) involving material restrictions relating to any business conducted or proposed to be conducted by the Company, (vii) which is a power of attorney or agency agreement or written arrangement with any Person pursuant to which such Person is granted the authority to act for or on behalf of the Company, (viii) with respect to which the requirements for performance extend beyond one (1) year from the date of this Agreement, (ix) which contains warranties with respect to products manufactured and/or sold or services rendered by the Company other than those warranties expressly made in the literature accompanying such products, (x) which is a consulting or professional advisor agreement, (xi) which cannot be terminated without penalty or payment or on at least ninety (90) days' notice, (xii) with any of the Company's Affiliates, or (xiii) which is not made in the ordinary course of business and which is to be performed at or after the date of this Agreement (the "Material Contracts").

(b)   Except as set forth on Schedule 4.12, to the knowledge of the Company or Seller, no Material Contract has been materially breached or cancelled by the other party, and neither the Company nor Seller has knowledge of any anticipated material breach by any other party to any Material Contract. The Company and Seller have performed all the material obligations required to be performed by them in connection with each Material Contract and are not in material default under or in breach of any Material Contract, and no event has occurred which with the passage of time or the giving of notice or both would result in a material default or breach thereunder. Neither the Company nor Seller has a present expectation or intention of not fully performing any material obligation pursuant to any Material Contract. Each Material Contract is legal, valid, binding, enforceable and in full force and effect. Except as set forth on Schedule 4.12, to the knowledge of Seller and the Company, no Material Contract obligates the Company to process, manufacture or deliver products or perform services that shall result in a loss upon completion of performance.

(c)   Seller has made available all Material Contracts disclosed pursuant to Section 4.12(a)(ii), which have a value of less than One Hundred Thousand Dollars ($100,000) and has provided Buyer with a true and correct copy of all other written Material Contracts that are required to be disclosed on Schedule 4.12, and has furnished to Buyer all amendments, waivers or any material changes thereto (all of which are disclosed on Schedule 4.12). Schedule 4.12 contains an accurate and correct description of all material terms of all oral Material Contracts. Except as set forth on Schedule 4.12, no consent is required, and no change of control provisions are triggered, with respect to any of the Material Contracts in connection with the execution, delivery and performance of this Agreement and the consummation of the transactions contemplated hereby.

(d)   Schedule 4.12 sets forth a list of each location where the Company leases real property, the applicable lease agreement, whether the Company still occupies the property, the status of past due obligations under the lease and a summary of any litigation threatened or commenced by the landlord. Schedule 4.12 lists each lease for real property terminated by the landlord in the last twelve months and the status of any past due obligations under such leases and a summary of any related litigation.

4.13   Fixed Assets; Absence of Liens and Encumbrances, Etc. Schedule 4.13 contains a complete and accurate list of all of the Company's Fixed Assets as of [ ]. As of the Closing Date, the Company will own all right, title and interest in and to the Assets, free and clear of all Liens, encumbrances, security interests, options, pledges, restrictions on transfer and other claims of any kind, other than Permitted Liens. All of the Company's personal property is in good working condition, normal wear and tear excepted. The list of Fixed Assets to be delivered at the Closing Date pursuant to Section 7.2(m)(ii) will be complete and accurate at the Closing.

4.14   Environmental and Safety Matters. Except as disclosed on Schedule 4.14, (a) the Company has materially complied and is in material compliance with all Environmental and Safety Requirements (including without limitation all permits and licenses required there under), (b) neither the Company nor Seller has received any oral or written notice of any material violation of, or any Liabilities (other than Permitted Liabilities), investigatory, corrective or remedial obligation under, any Environmental and Safety Requirements, (c) neither this Agreement nor the consummation of the transactions contemplated hereby will result in any obligations for site investigation or cleanup, or notification to or consent of governmental or regulatory authority or third parties, pursuant to any so-called "transaction-triggered" or "responsible property transfer" Environmental and Safety Requirements, (d) neither the Company, nor Seller with respect to the Business, has released, disposed of or transported or arranged for the disposal of any hazardous substance or to Seller's and the Company's knowledge owned or operated any property or facility (and to the knowledge of Seller and the Company no such property or facility is contaminated by any such substance) in a manner that has given or would give rise to material Liabilities (other than Permitted Liabilities) under the Comprehensive Environmental Response, Compensation and Liability Act of 1980, as amended ("CERCLA"), the Resource Conservation and Recovery Act, as amended or any other Environmental and Safety Requirements, (e) to the knowledge of the Company and Seller, there are no underground storage tanks, asbestos-containing material in any form and condition, polychlorinated biphenyls or landfills, surface impoundments or disposal areas at any property or facility owned or operated by the Company, or Seller with respect to the Business, and (f) no Environmental Lien (other than Permitted Liens) has attached to any property owned, leased or operated by the Company, or Seller with respect to the Business. No facts or circumstances with respect to the past or current operation or facilities of the Company, or Seller with respect to the Business, or any predecessor or Affiliate thereof (including, without limitation any onsite or offsite disposal or release of hazardous materials, substances or wastes) would give rise to any material Liability (other than a Permitted Liability) or corrective or remedial obligation under any Environmental and Safety Requirements. Neither the Company, nor Seller with respect to the Business, has, either expressly or by operation of law, assumed or undertaken any material Liability or material obligation (other than a Permitted Liability) of any other Person relating to Environmental and Safety Requirements.

4.15   Intellectual Property.

(a)   The Company (i) is the owner of, with all right, title and interest in and to (free and clear of any Liens other than Permitted Liens), or otherwise possesses the right to use the Intellectual Property used in its Business as conducted or proposed to be conducted by Seller.

(b)   Schedule 4.15(b) sets forth a list of all of the Company's material Intellectual Property and federal, state and foreign patents, registered copyrights, registered trademarks, domain registrations, and any applications therefore included in the Intellectual Property, and specifies, where applicable, the jurisdictions in which each such item of Intellectual Property has been issued or registered or in which an application for such issuance or registration has been filed, including the respective registration or application numbers and the names of all registered owners. Schedule 4.15(b) sets forth a list of all licenses, sublicenses and other agreements having a value of at least Twenty-Five Thousand Dollars ($25,000), to which the Company is a party and pursuant to which the Company or any other Person is authorized to use or license the use of any (i) Intellectual Property or trade secret of the Company and (ii) third-party patents, copyrights, trademarks, and applications for registration thereof, schematics, technology, know-how, computer software programs or applications (in both source code and object code form), and tangible or intangible proprietary information or material that are, are incorporated in, or form a part of the Intellectual Property. The execution and delivery of this Agreement by Seller, and the consummation of the transactions contemplated hereby, will not cause the Company to be in violation or default under any such license, sublicense or agreement, nor entitle any other party to any such license, sublicense or agreement to terminate or modify such license, sublicense or agreement.

(c)   No claims with respect to the Intellectual Property have been asserted in writing or are, to the Company's or Seller's knowledge, threatened by any Person (i) to the effect that the Business of the Company infringes on any copyright, patent, trademark, service mark, trade secret or other proprietary right of any third party, (ii) against the use by the Company of any trademarks, service marks, trade names, trade secrets, copyrights, patents, technology, know-how or computer software programs and applications used in the Business as currently conducted or under development for use in such business or (iii) challenging the ownership by the Company, or the validity or effectiveness, of any of the Intellectual Property. The Company has not infringed, and the Business of the Company does not infringe, any copyright or patent or, to the knowledge of Seller and the Company, any trade secret or other proprietary right of any third party. To the knowledge of the Company and Seller, there is no material unauthorized use, infringement or misappropriation of any of the Intellectual Property by any third party, including any employee or former employee of the Company. No Intellectual Property or product of the Company is subject to any outstanding decree, order, judgment or stipulation restricting in any manner the licensing thereof by the Company.

(d)   Schedule 4.15(d) lists all Software (other than Software acquired in the ordinary course of business or having an acquisition price of less than Fifteen Thousand Dollars ($15,000)) owned, licensed, leased, or otherwise used by the Company, and identifies which Software is owned, licensed, leased, or otherwise used, as the case may be. Schedule 4.15(d) lists all Software sold, licensed, leased or otherwise distributed by the Company to any third party, and identifies which Software is sold, licensed, leased, or otherwise distributed as the case may be. With respect to the Software set forth in Schedule 4.15(d), which the Company purports to own, such Software was either developed (i) by employees of the Company within the scope of their employment, or (ii) by independent contractors who have assigned their rights to the Company pursuant to written agreements. In each agreement pursuant to which the Company has licensed its Software to third parties, the Company has not (x) failed to limit its Liability to the amount of the fees paid pursuant to the agreements or (y) warranted as to the performance or functionality of the Software other than to state that the Software would perform in accordance with its documentation and/or specifications

4.16   Warranties; Service Commitments. True and correct copies of the form of all written warranties and guaranties and written service warranties and commitments applicable to products sold and services rendered are attached hereto as Schedule 4.16. The amounts reflected as warranty reserves and Liabilities related to the service commitments reflected in the Financial Statements and to be reflected in the Closing Statement are not less than the amount required by GAAP. Any products sold or services rendered by the Company meet, in all material respects, the specifications and the standards set forth in the Company's written descriptions of the products and services in its representations and warranties to customers and distributors of the products, including those set forth on Schedule 4.16.

4.17   Litigation. Except as set forth in Schedule 4.17, there is no claim, action, suit, proceeding, arbitration, investigation or hearing or notice of hearing pending against the Company or Seller affecting the Company or any of the Assets, the Purchased Shares, or, with respect to any employment matter, an employee, or the transactions contemplated by this Agreement and, to the knowledge of the Company and Seller no such action is threatened; nor are any facts known to the Company or Seller, which may give rise to any such claim, action, suit, proceeding, arbitration, investigation or hearing. No such claim, action, suit, proceeding, arbitration, investigation or hearing will prevent the closing of this Agreement or the consummation of the transaction contemplated hereby.

4.18   Customers and Vendors. Schedule 4.18 sets forth correct and complete lists of the customers ("Customers") and vendors ("Vendors") of the Company during the most recently completed fiscal year, indicating the existing contractual arrangements, if any, with each such Customer or Vendor. Except as set forth in Schedule 4.18, there are no outstanding disputes with any Customer or Vendor listed thereon and no Customer or Vendor listed thereon has refused to continue to do business with the Company or has stated its intention not to continue to do business with the Company. Since [ ], there has not been any material shortage or unavailability of the raw materials necessary to manufacture the products sold by the Business, and, to the knowledge of Seller and the Company, there is no current shortage or unavailability which leads it to believe that any such shortages will occur.

4.19   Books and Records. The books of account and other financial and corporate records of the Company related to the Accounts Receivable, Inventory and Fixed Assets and operations of the Company are in all material respects substantially complete and correct and are maintained in accordance with good business practices. All of the minutes of all the Company's Board of Directors and Stockholder meetings have been provided to Buyer.

4.20   Employment Matters.

(a)   Except as provided in Schedule 4.20, the Company is in material compliance with all laws, rules and regulations respecting employment and employment practices, terms and conditions of employment and wages and hours with respect to employees of the Business. The Company has withheld all amounts required by law or agreement to be withheld from the wages or salaries of, and other payments to, its employees and any former employees and is not liable for any arrearage of wages, salaries or other payments to such employees and any former employees (excluding wages and bonuses accrued in the ordinary course of business and not yet due) or any Taxes or penalties for failure to comply with any of the foregoing. Except as provided on Schedule 4.20, to the knowledge of the Company and Seller, no executive or key employee or group of employees has any plans to terminate his, her or their employment with the Company.

(b)   There (i) is no material labor strike, picketing of any nature, stoppage or lockout pending or material labor dispute, slowdown or other concerted interference with normal operations or, to the knowledge of the Company or Seller, threatened against or affecting the Business, (ii) are no union claims or demands to represent the employees of the Business, (iii) to the knowledge of the Company and Seller, are no current union organizing activities among the employees of the Company, and (iv) are no labor or collective bargaining agreements that pertain to or cover employees of the Company or to which the Company is a party or by which the Company is bound.

(c)   None of the Company's employment policies or practices is currently being audited or investigated, or, to the knowledge of the Company or Seller, subject to imminent audit or investigation, by any governmental body. The Company is not subject to any consent decree, court order or settlement in respect of any labor or employment matters. No claim, arbitration or similar proceeding with respect to employment matters is pending or, to the knowledge of the Company or Seller, threatened. The Company is, and at all times since November 6, 1986 has been, in material compliance with the requirements of the Immigration Reform Control Act of 1986. The transaction contemplated by this Agreement will not adversely effect the authority of any employee to work in the United States.

(d)   Except as set forth on Schedule 4.20, the Company does not employ or use any independent contractors, temporary employees, leased employees or any other servants or agents compensated other than through reportable wages paid by the Company (collectively, "Contingent Workers"). To the extent that Company employs or uses Contingent Workers, it has properly classified and treated them in accordance with applicable law and for purposes of all benefit plans and perquisites.

(e)   The Company has not taken any action that would require any notice to be given pursuant to the Worker Adjustment Retraining and Notification Act ("WARN Act") or any similar state law. Schedule 4.20 sets forth a list of all dismissals of employees by location during the last sixty (60) days (and with respect to [ ] state law, six (6) months), which when aggregated, could cause a WARN

Act notice (or notice or Liability under any similar state law) to be given, if further dismissals were made with respect to such site.

4.21   Employee Benefit Plans.

(a)   Schedule 4.21 is a true and complete list of all written and oral, formal and, to the knowledge of the Company and Seller, informal annuity, bonus, cafeteria, stock option, stock purchase, profit sharing, savings, pension, retirement, incentive, group insurance, disability, employee welfare, prepaid legal, non-qualified deferred compensation including, without limitation, excess benefit plans, top-hat plans, deferred bonuses, rabbi trusts, secular trusts, non-qualified annuity contracts, insurance arrangements, non-qualified stock options, phantom stock plans, or golden parachute payments, or other similar fringe benefit plans, and all other employee benefit plans, funds, arrangements or programs (whether or not within the meaning of Section 3(3) of Employee Retirement Income Security Act of 1974 and of the regulations adopted pursuant thereto (collectively "ERISA"), covering employees or former employees of the Company (the "Plans"). Except as set forth on Schedule 4.21, the Company is not a party to any employee agreement, understanding, plan, policy, procedure or arrangement, whether written or oral, which provides compensation or fringe benefits to employees of the Company engaged or formerly engaged in the operation of the Business or which applies to former employees of the Company who were engaged in the Business, and the Company is in compliance in all material respects with its obligations under all such Plans. Except for changes required by applicable law, there are no negotiations, demands, commitments or proposals that are pending or that have been made that concern matters now covered or that would be covered by the type of agreements described on Schedule 4.21 or this Section 4.21(a). The Company has no any direct or indirect, actual or contingent liability for any Plan, other than to make payments for contributions, premiums or benefits when due, all of which payments have been timely made. None of the Assets are subject to any existing lien or security interest under Section 302(f), 306(a), 307(a) or 4068 of ERISA or Section 401(a)(29), 412(n) or

615

6321 of the Internal Revenue Code of 1986 and the regulations adopted pursuant thereto (collectively the "Code").

(b)   With respect to each employee benefit plan listed on Schedule 4.21, true and complete copies of (i) all Plan documents (including all amendments and modifications thereof), and related agreements, including, without limitation, the trust agreement and amendments thereto, insurance contracts, third party administration contracts and investment management agreements, (ii) the last three (3) filed Form 5500 series and applicable schedules, SSA, and Forms PBGC-l, if any, (iii) summary plan descriptions, (iv) summary of material modifications, if any, (v) the most recent auditor's report, (vi) copies of any and all Tax qualification correspondence, including, without limitation, private letter rulings, applications for determination and determination letters issued with respect to the Plans, and applications, correspondence, and internal documentation, in whatever form held, relating to operational, documentation or other errors or failures with respect to the Plans, and (vii) the most recent annual and periodic accounting of related Plan assets, have also been delivered to Buyer.

(c)   With respect to the Plans listed on Schedule 4.21 which are subject to ERISA:

(i)   The Plans are in compliance in all material respects with the applicable provisions of ERISA and each of the employee pension benefit plans, within the meaning of Section 3(2) of ERISA (the "Pension Plans"), which are intended to be qualified under Section 401(a) of the Code have been determined by the Internal Revenue Service ("IRS") to be so qualified or a request for such determination has been timely filed with the IRS (and to the knowledge of the Company and Seller, nothing has occurred to cause the IRS to revoke such determination and the IRS has not indicated any disapproval of any request for such a determination) or there is time remaining within which to file such a request;

(ii)   Each Plan has been operated in accordance with its terms and all required filings that are due prior to the date hereof, including, without limitation, the Forms 5500 for all Plans have been made;

(iii)   No prohibited transactions as defined by Section 406 of ERISA or Section 4975 of the Code, for which exemptions are not available, have occurred with respect to any of the Plans which would result in a material liability to the Company;

(iv)   The Company has not engaged in any transaction in connection with which the Company could be subjected to a criminal or material civil penalty under ERISA;

(v)   None of the Plans, nor any trust which serves as a funding medium for any of such Plans, nor any issue relating thereto is currently under examination by or pending before the IRS, the Department of Labor, the PBGC or any court, other than applications for determinations pending before the IRS;

(vi)   None of the Pension Plans is a defined benefit plan within the meaning of Section 414(j) of the Code; or an employee stock ownership plan within the meaning of Section 4975(e)(7) of the Code which has not been satisfied;

(vii)   None of the Plans is a "multiemployer plan" as that term is defined in Section 3(37) of ERISA and Section 411(f) of the Code, nor a plan maintained by more than one employer (hereinafter referred to as a "multiple employer plan"), nor a single employer plan under a multiple controlled group within the meaning of Section 4063 of ERISA, and neither Seller nor any entity required to be aggregated with Seller under Section 414(b), (c), (m), or (o) of the Code has incurred any withdrawal liability with respect to any single plan, multiemployer or multiple employer plan which have not been satisfied;

(viii)   No benefit claims (except those submitted in the ordinary course of administration of such Plan) are currently pending against any Plan;

(ix)   No Plan provides for retiree medical or retiree life insurance benefits for former employees of the Company except as may be required under the continuation coverage provisions of Sections 601-608 of ERISA and Section 4980B of the Code or comparable provision of state law to the extent applicable, and there is no liability for Taxes with respect to disqualified benefits under Section 4976 of the Code; and

(x)   Except as set forth on Schedule 4.21, no Pension Plan covering, or formerly covering, employees of Seller has been terminated and there is no liability for Taxes with respect to a reversion of qualified plan assets under Section 4980 of the Code.

(d)   There have been no material failures to comply with the continuation coverage provisions required by Sections 601-608 of ERISA and Section 4980B of the Code or comparable provision of state law to the extent applicable. There is no liability for Taxes under Section 4980B of the Code with respect to any Plan.

(e)   There have been no material failures to comply with the portability, access and renewability provisions required by Sections 701-734 of ERISA and chapter 100 of the Code, as amended, or comparable provision of state law to the extent applicable. There is no liability for Taxes under Section 4980D of the Code with respect to any Plan.

(f)   There are no employee benefit plans which cover employees of Seller which are required to comply with the provisions of any foreign law.

(g)   All excess contributions (as defined in Section 4979(c) of the Code), if any (together with any income allocable thereto), have been distributed (or, if forfeitable, forfeited) before the close of the first two and one half (2½) months of the following Plan year; and there is no liability for excise Taxes under Section 4979 of the Code with respect to such excess contributions, if any, for any Plan.

(h)   There is no liability for Taxes with respect to: (i) an accumulated funding deficiency under Section 4971 of the Code; and/or (ii) nondeductible contributions under Section 4972 of the Code.

(i)   The Company's deferred compensation plan (Shared Harvest) has been irrevocably terminated by the Company and no former participant in such plan has any further rights under such plan except as set forth on Schedule 4.21.

(j)   Except as set forth on Schedule 4.21, each employee which has been terminated by the Company has been paid in full for all accrued vacation and severance pay.

4.22   No Subsidiaries; Prior Names, Addresses and Businesses.   Except as set forth on Schedule 4.22, the Company does not now have, nor has it ever had, any subsidiaries. The Company has not (i) merged or consolidated with, (ii) acquired the stock or assets of or (iii) assumed the Liabilities of any other Person in connection with a business combination transaction except as set forth on Schedule 4.22. The Company has not conducted business under any other name except as set forth on Schedule 4.22 and the principal office of the Company has always been located at the address set forth on Schedule 4.22. The Company has not conducted any business other than the Business conducted as it substantially exists on the date hereof.

4.23   Finder.   There is no Person or entity that is entitled to a finder's fee or any type of commission in relation to or in connection with the transactions contemplated by this Agreement as a result of any agreement or understanding with the Company or Seller (other than [ ], which fees and expenses shall be paid by Seller) and Seller agrees to indemnify Buyer and to hold it harmless against all claims, damages, costs or expenses of or for any other such fees or commissions resulting from Seller's actions or agreements regarding the execution or performance of this Agreement, and will pay all costs of defending any action or lawsuit brought to recover any such fees or commissions incurred by Buyer, including reasonable attorneys' fees.

4.24   Sufficiency of Assets. Except as set forth in Schedule 4.24, the Assets of the Company at the Closing Date will include all of the Company's and Seller's Assets used in the ordinary course of Business as presently conducted.

4.25   Employees.

(a)   Schedule 4.25 sets forth a complete and accurate list of all employees (including leased employees) of the Company, showing for each: name, hire date, current job title or description, current salary level (including any bonus or deferred compensation arrangements) and any bonus, commission or other remuneration paid during the most recently completed fiscal year, and describing any existing contractual arrangement (including any severance arrangement). Except as specifically contemplated by this Agreement or as set forth on Schedule 4.25, no employee (including leased employees) shall receive any compensation as a result of the consummation of the transactions contemplated by this Agreement (all of which shall be considered Seller Costs). Except as set forth on Schedule 4.25, none of the employees (including leased employees) is currently on short-term or long-term disability, absence, sabbatical, maternity, parenting, Family and Medical Act (FMLA) leave or other leave of absence. Except as set forth on Schedule 4.25, since [ ], no salaried employee (including leased employees) of the Business who has been compensated at an annual rate in excess of One Hundred Thousand Dollars ($100,000) has terminated his or her employment or had such employment terminated for any reason or for no reason; no such employee has given written notice (or to the knowledge of the Seller and the Company, oral notice) of his or her intent to terminate such employment; and no notice of termination has been given to any such employee by the Company. No employee is a party to any contract which provides for change of control benefits or, except as set forth on Schedule 4.25 severance benefits or which would provide for increased compensation or permit termination as a result of the transactions to be consummated hereby.

(b)   Schedule 4.25 sets forth the name of each employee who requires an immigration visa and the type of visa.

4.26   Condition of Assets. The Assets (a) are in good condition and repair, normal wear and tear excepted, and (b) are in substantial compliance with all applicable laws, ordinances, regulations, orders and other requirements relating thereto.

4.27   Governmental Authorizations. The Company has all material licenses, permits or other authorizations from governmental, regulatory or administrative agencies or authorities required for the operation of its business in the manner presently conducted and proposed to be conducted, each of which will be in full force and effect on the Closing Date and all such material authorizations will be in full force and effect on the Closing Date. A list of all such material governmental authorizations is set forth on Schedule 4.27 and all such authorizations will remain in full force and effect following the Closing Date. No registrations, filings, applications, notices, transfers, consents, approvals, orders, qualifications, waivers or other actions of any kind are required by virtue of the execution and delivery of this Agreement or the consummation of the transactions contemplated hereby to enable Buyer and the Company to continue the operation of the Business as presently conducted in all material respects following the Closing.

4.28   Compliance with Applicable Laws. The Company has been, is, and on the Closing Date will continue to be, in compliance in all material respects with all applicable laws (including duties imposed by common law), rules, regulations, orders, ordinances, judgments and decrees of all governmental authorities (federal, state, local and foreign) applicable to the Business, Assets, products, services and employees of the Company.

4.29   Accounts Receivable, Installment Receivables, and Accounts Payable. All accounts receivable, notes receivable and installment receivables of the Company, whether reflected on the Financial Statements, or to be reflected of the Closing Statement, represent sales actually made or leases entered into in the ordinary course of business or valid claims as to which full performance has been rendered. Except to the extent reserved against, the accounts receivable, notes receivable and installment receivables, are fully collectible within the later of (i) ninety (90) days of the related invoice date and (ii) forty-five (45) days from the Closing Date. Except to the extent reserved against, and as set forth on Schedule 4.29, no counterclaims or offsetting claims with respect to the accounts receivable, notes receivable and installment receivables are pending or, to the knowledge of the Seller, threatened. The listing of accounts receivable, notes receivable and installment receivables provided by the Company dated [ ] was true and correct (including the aging thereon) as of such date and no material change has occurred since that date. Schedule 4.29 sets forth the amounts the Company owes to or is owed by Seller or any of his Affiliates as of the date hereof. The accounts payable of the Company reflected on the Financial Statements and to be reflected on the Closing Statement arose, or will arise, from bona fide transactions in the ordinary course of business, and all such accounts payable have been paid, are not yet due and payable under the Company's payment policies and procedures or are being contested by the Company in good faith. Any debit balance in accounts payable are valid offsets to amounts due vendors. The listing of Accounts Payable provided by the Company dated [ ] was true and correct as of such date and no material change has occurred since that date.

4.30   Insurance.

(a)   Schedule 4.30 lists each insurance policy currently maintained by or on behalf of the Company and each general liability policy and workers' compensation policy maintained in the last three years. The Company has delivered copies to Buyer of all such insurance policies. All of such current insurance policies are in full force and effect, and the Company is not in default with respect to its obligations under any such insurance policies. The Company is current in all of its premiums for its current insurance policies. Neither the Company nor Seller knows of any threatened termination of, or material premium increase with respect to, any of such policies.

(b)   Schedule 4.30 lists (i) each claim which has been made against the Company's insurance policies during the last two (2) years, (ii) any other currently pending claim, and (iii) the status of such claim.

ARTICLE 5
REPRESENTATIONS AND WARRANTIES OF BUYER

Buyer hereby represents, warrants and covenants to and agrees with Seller as follows, all of which representations, warranties and agreements are made as of the date of this Agreement and as of the Closing Date:

5.1   Organization, Etc. Buyer is a corporation duly organized, validly existing and in good corporate standing under the laws of the state of [ ]. Buyer has all the requisite corporate power and authority to execute, deliver and perform this Agreement and consummate the transactions contemplated hereby.

5.2   Authorization of Agreement. This Agreement has been, and the Transaction Documents will be, duly executed and delivered by Buyer. The execution, delivery and performance of this Agreement and the Transaction Documents has been duly authorized and approved by all requisite corporate action. This Agreement is, and the Transaction Documents when executed and delivered will be, valid and binding obligations of Buyer enforceable in accordance with their respective terms, except that such enforcement may be limited by (a) bankruptcy, insolvency or other similar laws affecting the enforcement of creditors' rights generally, and (b) general principles of equity, regardless of whether enforcement is sought in a proceeding in equity or at law.

5.3   Approvals. No consent or approval is required of any Person or entity, private or governmental, for the execution, delivery and performance of this Agreement and the Transaction Documents by Buyer, and neither will such execution, delivery or performance, nor the consummation of the transactions contemplated herein, breach any provision of Buyer's Articles of Incorporation or Bylaws or any law, rule, regulation, judgment, order, decree, agreement, instrument or arrangement that would have a material adverse effect on Buyer's ability to perform its obligations hereunder.

5.4   Finder. There is no Person or entity that is entitled to a finder's fee or any type of commission in relation to or in connection with the transactions contemplated by this Agreement as a result of any agreement or understanding with Buyer; and Buyer agrees to indemnify Seller and to hold it harmless against all claims, damages, costs or expenses of or for any other such fees or commissions resulting from Buyer's actions or agreements regarding the execution or performance of this Agreement, and will pay all costs of defending any action or lawsuit brought to recover any such fees or commissions incurred by the Company, including reasonable attorneys' fees.

5.5   Effect of Agreement, Etc. The execution, delivery and performance of this Agreement and the Transaction Documents by Buyer and consummation by Buyer of the transactions contemplated hereby and thereby will not, with or without the giving of notice and the lapse of time, or both, (a) violate any material provision of law, statute, rule or regulation to which Buyer is subject, (b) violate any judgment, order, writ or decree of any court applicable to Buyer, or (c) result in the material breach of or material conflict with any material term, covenant, condition or provision of, result in the material modification or termination of, constitute a material default under, or result in the creation or imposition of any material Lien, security interest, restriction, charge or encumbrance upon any of the material assets of Buyer pursuant to the Articles of Incorporation or Bylaws of Buyer, or any commitment, contract or other agreement or instrument to which Buyer is a party.

ARTICLE 6
COVENANTS OF SELLER AND BUYER

Seller covenants and agrees with Buyer as follows:

6.1   [Intentionally Omitted.]

6.2   Approvals, Consents, Etc. Seller shall, or shall cause the Company to, use its reasonable efforts to obtain in writing prior to the Closing Date all approvals, consents and waivers required to be obtained by the Company or Seller (and Seller shall use its reasonable efforts to obtain any such approvals, consents and waivers after the Closing Date, it being understood that no waiver of such items is intended by the parties hereto) in order to effectuate the transactions contemplated hereby and shall deliver to Buyer copies of such approvals and consents in form and substance reasonably satisfactory to Buyer and counsel for Buyer. In the event Buyer elects to close prior to the time all option holders execute the forms to be delivered pursuant to Section 7.2(a)(iii), Buyer is not waiving delivery of such forms and Seller shall use its best efforts to obtain the rest of such forms after the Closing.

6.3   Further Assurances. After the Closing Date, the Company and Seller shall, at the request of Buyer, execute, acknowledge and deliver to Buyer without further consideration, all such further assignments, conveyances, endorsements, consents and other documents and take such other action as Buyer may reasonably request to (a) transfer to and vest in Buyer and protect its right, title and interest in, all of the Assets and Purchased Shares and (b) otherwise to consummate the transactions contemplated by this Agreement.

6.4   Seller's Employment Agreement. Seller acknowledges the noncompetition, nondisclosure and other covenants in his employment agreement entered into in connection with this transaction were given to induce Buyer to acquire the Purchased Shares and such covenants are enforceable as if set forth in this Agreement in full, and any breach thereof shall be deemed a breach of this Agreement.

6.5   Financial Statements. Seller shall cause the Company to immediately engage [ ] to perform an audit of its financial statements for the most recently completed fiscal year on terms acceptable to Buyer. Seller shall cause the Company to expeditiously complete such audit within sixty (60) days of the date hereof, and Seller shall, and shall cause the Company to, render all needed assistance to cause such audit to be completed.

6.6.   [Intentionally Omitted.]

6.7   Tax Returns; Tax Audits.

(a)   Seller shall provide Buyer with the Company's [ ] federal and state income Tax returns prior to filing thereof (if such tax returns are filed prior to the Closing Date) and such Tax returns shall be satisfactory to Buyer (including any allocation of income and expenses between the periods covered by the "Subchapter S" and "C corporation" returns). If such Tax returns are filed after the Closing Date, such Tax returns shall be prepared by Buyer and furnished to Seller for his approval, which shall not be unreasonably withheld or delayed.

(b)   Any party who receives any written notice of a pending or threatened Tax audit, assessment or adjustment with respect to the Company or Seller which affects any period prior to the Closing Date shall promptly notify the other parties hereto. Failure to provide timely notice of such pending or threatened action shall not release any party who failed to receive such notice from liability to the party failing to give timely notice unless such failure precluded the defense of such pending or threatened action. Each party shall allow the other party an opportunity of it and its counsel to participate (at its own expense) in any audits of the Company or any audit of Seller which could affect the Company. Seller will not settle any such audit in a manner which would impose any Tax liability on the Company or Buyer.

6.8   Litigation. Seller shall assist the Company and Buyer with respect to any litigation involving the Company relating in any way to periods prior to the Closing Date; provided that Buyer shall reimburse Seller for its reasonable out-of-pocket expenses related thereto.

6.9   Authorization and Grant of Stock Options. No later than thirty (30) days after the Closing Date, the Buyer agrees to grant non-qualified options to purchase at least [ ] and not more than [ ] shares of its common stock to the employees of the Company recommended by Seller and approved by Buyer, at a per share exercise price equal to the fair market value of the Buyer's common stock on the grant date and pursuant to an established stock option plan of the Buyer, the shares of which will be registered with the SEC on Form S-8. Such options shall have such terms consistent with stock options granted to Buyer's employees generally.

6.10   401(k) Plan. As soon as practicable following the Closing Date, Buyer will cause its 401(k) plan to accept contributions from those employees of the Company otherwise eligible to participate in Buyer's 401(k) plan, taking into account as service with Buyer, service with the Company completed on or before the Closing Date by employees employed by the Company on the Closing Date. As soon as practicable following the Closing Date (which may be later than the date for acceptance of plan contributions and which may occur after receipt of a favorable determination letter on the termination of the Company's 401(k) plan), Buyer will cause its 401(k) plan to accept a direct rollover from the Company's 401(k) plan of account balances, including outstanding loans, of electing plan participants who are employed by Buyer at the time of the rollover.

6.11   Bonus Plan. As of the Closing Date, the Company shall adopt a bonus pool in the aggregate amount of [ ] (the "Bonus Pool"), which amount includes [ ] of employer payroll taxes which will not be distributed to participants. The Bonus Pool shall be administered by the Company in accordance with and pursuant to the terms of the bonus plan (the "Bonus Plan") set forth on Exhibit C. Buyer hereby unconditionally and irrevocably guarantees the payment and performance of the Company under the Bonus Plan, provided that Buyer's maximum liability is limited to [ ]. Buyer covenants and agrees to cause the Company to administer the Bonus Plan in accordance with its terms and further covenants and agrees that the Bonus Plan shall remain in effect and shall not be terminated by Buyer or the Company, for any reason, except in accordance with the terms thereof.

6.12   Payments by Buyer's Undisbursed Funds.

(a)   [ ] Bank. Concurrently with the Closing, Buyer shall advance to [ ] Bank, as a contribution to capital to the Company, the amount set forth on Schedule 6.12.

(b)   Option Holder Termination and Release Agreement. Buyer shall advance on behalf of the Company, the amount set forth on Schedule 6.12, which shall be used to fund payments for executed Option Holder Termination and Release Forms delivered pursuant to Section 7.2(a)(iii). Such amounts shall be advanced prior to the time payment under such agreements are due and shall be increased with respect to which any executed Option Holder Termination and Release Forms are received after the Closing but prior to the time payment is due.

(c)   Retention Bonuses. Buyer shall advance, on behalf of the Company, the amounts set forth on Schedule 6.12 to pay retention bonuses to [ ]. If such amounts are in excess of those necessary to satisfy such payments, or if such payments are not made, such excess amounts shall be paid to Seller when it can reasonably be determined such payments will not be made.

(d)   Options. Seller is withholding [ ] to reserve against option holders which have not signed Option Holder Termination and Release Agreements as set forth on Schedule 7.2(a)(iii). Buyer shall disburse such funds when such persons execute documents reasonably satisfactory to Buyer, and upon such execution, by all such persons, Buyer shall remit excess funds to Seller. Seller remains fully liable for all claims to equity interests.

(e)   Undisbursed Funds. Undisbursed funds and other Seller costs shall be directed by Seller as set forth on Schedule 6.12(e). No funds shall be paid to [ ] until statutory waiting periods necessary to effect the release of employment claims have expired. Seller shall reimburse Buyer for any employer related taxes as a result of such disbursements.

ARTICLE 7
CLOSING

7.1   Closing. The Closing of the transactions contemplated hereby shall occur on [ ] (the "Closing") or as soon as practicable following such date as all of the conditions to Closing as set forth herein have been satisfied or waived. The Closing will be held at the offices of Leonard, Street and Deinard Professional Association, Suite 2300, 150 South Fifth Street,

Minneapolis, MN 55402 at 10:00 a.m. or at such other time and place as the parties mutually agree. The date upon which the Closing occurs is referred to herein as the "Closing Date."

7.2   Buyer's Conditions to Closing. The obligations of Buyer under this Agreement are subject to the satisfaction of the following conditions as of the Closing Date, any or all of which conditions may be waived by Buyer in writing in its sole discretion:

    (a)   Changes in Benefit Plans.

        (i)   Except as set forth herein (including clause (ii) and (iii) hereof and Section 7.3(f)), the Company shall not enter into, adopt or amend in any material respect or terminate any Plan or any other agreement, arrangement, plan or policy involving any employee to be employed by Buyer or increase the compensation of any such employee or pay any benefit or amount not required by a plan or arrangement as in effect on the date of this Agreement, or enter into any arrangement or commitment to do any of the foregoing.

        (ii)   The Company shall have terminated its 401(k) and profit sharing plans prior to the Closing in a manner satisfactory to Buyer.

        (iii)   Except as set forth on Schedule 7.2(a)(iii), all past and present employees and other persons who have vested or unvested options (which have not expired by their terms) shall have executed the Option Holder Termination and Release Agreement in the form set forth in the form set forth in Exhibit D. All amounts required to be withheld by law from any payment to option holders shall have been withheld.

    (b)   [Intentionally omitted.]

(c)   Consents and Approvals. Buyer shall have received (i) from governmental and administrative authorities all permits and licenses required for it to carry on the business of the Company, and (ii) all consents or approvals required on the part of Seller, the Company or Buyer for the transfer of the Purchased Shares (including the consent of all landlords) all in form and substance reasonably satisfactory to Buyer.

(d)   Employment Agreements. The Company and Seller and each of the employees of the Company listed on Schedule 7.2(d) shall have entered into employment agreements in the form set forth in Exhibit E attached hereto.

(e)   Good Standing Certificates, Etc. Buyer shall have received a certificate dated within two (2) business days before the Closing Date from the office of the Secretary of State of Delaware certifying that the Company is validly existing and in good standing under the laws of its state of incorporation.

(f)   Lien Search. Seller, at its expense, shall have arranged for and Buyer shall have received the report or reports, reasonably satisfactory to Buyer and its counsel, of a reputable search company indicating that there are no Liens, mortgages, encumbrances, charges or other rights of third parties of record (other than Permitted Liens) as of a date not more than ten (10) days before the Closing Date in each jurisdiction where Assets are located, other than any Lien for which a Lien release, satisfactory to Buyer, is delivered pursuant to Section 7.2(m).

(g)   Opinion of Counsel to the Company. Buyer shall have received the opinion of [ ], counsel to Seller and the Company, addressed to Buyer, dated the Closing Date, in the form set forth in Exhibit F attached hereto.

(h)   [Intentionally Omitted.]

(i)   Adverse Change; Litigation. There shall not have occurred (x) any material adverse change in the financial condition, results of operation or business of the Company since the date of this Agreement or any event reasonably likely to result in a Company Material Adverse Effect, (y) commencement of litigation or any threat of litigation not set forth on Schedule 4.17, or (z) any adverse change in the status of the [ ] Case, including any ruling on appeal contrary to the trial court ruling or any amendment or threatened amendment by [ ] of the related complaint alleging new causes of action.

(j)   Audit. Seller shall have delivered an engagement letter of [ ] to perform the audit referred to in Section 6.5. Seller shall deliver the consent of its independent certified public accountant wherein such firm's opinion on the financial statements may be included in Buyer's SEC filings and such firm may be named as an expert in such filings and that such firm will use reasonable efforts to prepare any comfort letters requested by Buyer (with such comfort letters to be at Buyer's expense).

(k)   Retired Debt; Costs and Expenses. Except to the extent to be discharged by Buyer pursuant to Section 6.12, the Retired Debt shall be repaid in full in full concurrently with the Closing and all Seller Costs shall be discharged, either by Seller from the Initial Purchase Price, or if paid by the Company with the consent of Buyer, the Initial Purchase Price shall be reduced by the amount of such payment.

(l)   Leases. The Company shall have reached a settlement with respect to all leases in default set forth on Schedule 4.12 and such settlement shall be satisfactory to Buyer in its sole discretion.

(m)   Other. The Company and Seller shall execute and/or deliver to Buyer the following:

(i)   An assignment conveying to Buyer the Seller Intangible Assets in form reasonably satisfactory to Buyer and its counsel, free and clear of all Liens and encumbrances;

(ii)   A list of the Inventory, Accounts Receivable, Fixed Assets, deposits and payables as of a date not more than three (3) days prior to the Closing Date, which lists shall be satisfactory to Buyer, in its sole discretion;

(iii)   The Escrow Agreement;

(iv)   Lien releases (including UCC termination statements) in form satisfactory for recording or filing, with respect to any Lien on any Asset (other than Permitted Liens), including [ ] Bank and [ ];

(v)   Resignations from each member of the Company's Board of Directors and any officers requested by Buyer;

(vi)   Seller shall provide a release in a form satisfactory to Buyer signed by each person who is owed funds under the "[ ]" or "Deferred Compensation" plan as of [ ] that such amounts have been paid in full;

(vii)   [ ] shall have released the Company from all obligations under the letter agreement dated [ ];

(viii)   [Intentionally omitted];

(ix)   The employment agreements with each of [ ] shall have been amended to reduce cash severance payments obligations by one third (1/3) and that upon payment of such severance all claims (other than salary, benefit plans and the like) against the Company are released;

(x)   Seller and his Affiliates shall have repaid all amounts owed to the Company and released all claims against the Company;

(xi)   The minute book of the Company; and

(xii)   Such other and further documents and certificates of Seller, the Company's officers and others as Buyer shall reasonably request to evidence compliance with the conditions set forth in this Agreement.

7.3   Seller's Conditions to Closing. The obligations of Seller under this Agreement are subject to the satisfaction of the following conditions as of the Closing Date, any or all of which may be waived by Seller in its sole discretion:

(a)   [Intentionally Omitted.]

(b)   Consents and Approvals. Seller shall have received all consents or approvals required on the part of Seller, the Company or Buyer for the transfer of the Purchased Shares (including the consent of all landlords), all in form and substance reasonably satisfactory to Seller.

(c)   Secretary's Certificate. Seller shall have received a certificate of the Secretary of Buyer with respect to the resolutions adopted by the Board of Directors of Buyer approving this Agreement and the transactions contemplated hereby.

(d)   Good Standing Certificates, Etc. Seller shall have received a certificate dated within two days before the Closing Date from the office of the Secretary of State of [ ] certifying that Buyer is validly existing and in good standing under the laws of its state of incorporation.

(e)   Opinion of Counsel to Buyer. Seller shall have received the opinion of Leonard, Street and Deinard Professional Association, counsel to Buyer, addressed to Seller, dated at the Closing Date, in the form set forth in Exhibit G attached hereto.

(f)   Bonus Plan. The Company shall have adopted the bonus plan in the form attached hereto as Exhibit C.

(g)   Employment Agreements. The Company and Seller and each of the employees of the Company listed on Schedule 7.2(d) shall have entered into employment agreements in the form set forth in Exhibit E attached hereto.

(h)   Other. Buyer shall execute and/or deliver to Seller the following:

(i)   The Purchase Price, by wire transfer, or in certified funds in accordance with Article 3 of this Agreement (including depositing relevant amounts pursuant to the Escrow Agreement) (it being understood that Seller shall direct payment of such funds, in a manner satisfactory to Buyer, so that Seller Costs are discharged in full, it being understood Buyer shall deposit a portion of the Purchase Price in escrow pursuant to Section 3.1(b));

(ii)   An Escrow Agreement; and

(iii)   Such other documents and certificates to evidence compliance with the conditions set forth in this Article as may be reasonably requested by Seller.

ARTICLE 8
INDEMNIFICATION

8.1   Indemnification by Seller. Seller covenants and agrees with Buyer that it shall indemnify Buyer and its directors, officers, employees, agents and stockholders, and their successors and assigns, heirs and legal representatives, and the owners, directors, and officers, employees, agents and stockholders of any such successors and assigns or any other Person indemnified hereunder, and hold them harmless from, against and in respect of any and all judgments, awards, costs, losses, claims, Liabilities, fines, payments (including payments to discharge the Retired Debt, Seller Costs and any Lien on any Asset, and any Liability which is not a Permitted Liability), penalties, damages and expenses of any kind, whether actual, threatened or alleged, contingent or liquidated (including interest which may be imposed in connection therewith and court costs and fees and disbursements of counsel) (hereinafter referred to as "Claims") arising out of or with respect to:

(a)   Any Liabilities or obligations of the Company as of the Closing Date which are not Permitted Liabilities;

(b)   The Retired Debt, the Seller Costs and any Lien on any Asset (other than Permitted Liens) or the Purchased Shares to the extent such items are not satisfied in full at Closing or by Buyer pursuant to Section 6.12;

(c)   Any claim to any equity interest in the Company other than the Purchased Shares;

(d)   Any breach of any of the representations, warranties or covenants in this Agreement or in any other agreement or certificate executed and delivered by the Company or Seller pursuant hereto;

(e)   Any litigation or threatened litigation commenced by any Person relating to the period prior to the Closing Date, including the Company's employees and any litigation to which the Company or Seller is a party or threatened to be made a party on the Closing Date, including the litigation set forth on Schedule 4.17 (including all costs of further defense and settlement of any such litigation) except to the extent reserved in the most recent Financial Statements and other than any litigation commenced by any vendor which was commenced solely to collect a past due accounts payable owed to such vendor which is a Permitted Liability;

(f)   Any income, sales, payroll, excise or other Tax imposed on the Company by any federal, state, local or foreign authority with respect to a period prior to the Closing Date, except to the extent any such Tax is accrued on the books and records of the Company and reflected on the most recent Financial Statements; and

(g)   Any excise Tax under Section 4979 of the Code for failure to complete discrimination testing on any benefit plan.

Seller waives any right Seller may have for contribution or reimbursement or the like from the Company with respect to any matters indemnified hereunder. If any representation, warranty or covenant which is qualified by materiality or Company Material Adverse Effect is breached, the amount indemnified hereunder shall include all damages related to such breach, and not just damages in excess of material amounts.

8.2   Indemnification by Buyer. Buyer hereby covenants and agrees with Seller that it shall indemnify Seller and his heirs and legal representatives, and hold them harmless from, against and in respect of any and all Claims, arising out of or with respect to:

(a)   The operation of the Company on and following the Closing Date; and

(b)   Any breach of any of the representations, warranties, covenants or agreements made by Buyer in this Agreement or in any ancillary documents delivered pursuant hereto.

8.3   Indemnification Procedures. All Claims or demands for indemnification under this Article 8 shall be asserted and resolved as follows:

(a)   In the event that Buyer (on the one hand) or Seller (on the other hand) (each an "Indemnified Party") has a claim against Seller (on the one hand) or Buyer (on the other hand) (each an "Indemnifying Party") hereunder, which does not involve a Claim being asserted against or sought to be collected by a third party, the Indemnified Party shall with reasonable promptness send a notice (a "Claim Notice") with respect to such claim to the Indemnifying Party. If the Indemnifying Party does not notify the Indemnified Party within ten (10) days whether the Indemnifying Party disputes such claim, the Indemnified Party may arbitrate such claim in accordance with the terms of Section 10.3 hereof. In case the Indemnifying Party shall deliver a Notice of Dispute, then the procedures set forth in Section 10.1 and 10.2 shall apply.

(b)   In the event that any Claim, which may give rise to damages for which an Indemnifying Party would be liable to an Indemnified Party hereunder is asserted against an Indemnified Party by a third party (a "Third Party Claim"), the Indemnified Party shall with reasonable promptness send a Claim Notice to the Indemnifying Party, specifying the nature of such claim and the amount or the estimated amount thereof to the extent then feasible (which estimate shall not be conclusive of the final amount of any such Claim arising from such Third Party Claim). The Indemnifying Party shall have fifteen (15) days from the receipt of the Claim Notice (the "Notice Period") to notify the Indemnified Party (i) whether or not the Indemnifying Party disputes the Indemnifying Party's liability to the Indemnified Party hereunder with respect to damages arising from such Claim and (ii) if the Indemnifying Party does not dispute such liability, whether or not the Indemnifying Party desires, at the sole cost and expense of the Indemnifying Party, to defend against such Third Party Claim. In the event that the Indemnifying Party notifies the Indemnified Party within the Notice Period that the Indemnifying Party does not dispute the Indemnifying Party's obligation to indemnify hereunder and desires to defend the Indemnified Party against such Third Party Claim, then the Indemnifying Party shall have the right to defend such Third Party Claim by appropriate proceedings, which proceedings shall be promptly settled or prosecuted by the Indemnifying Party to a final conclusion; provided that, unless the Indemnified Party otherwise agrees in writing, the Indemnifying Party may not settle any matter (in whole or in part), unless such settlement includes a complete and unconditional release of the Indemnified Party. If the Indemnified Party desires to participate in, but not control, any such defense or settlement, the Indemnified Party may do so at the Indemnified Party's sole cost and expense. If the Indemnifying Party elects not to defend the Indemnified Party against such Claim, whether by failure of the Indemnifying Party to give the Indemnified Party timely notice as provided above or otherwise, then the Indemnified Party, without waiving any rights against the Indemnifying Party, may settle or defend against any such Claim in the Indemnified Party's sole discretion, after giving ten days prior written notice to the

Indemnifying Party. The Indemnifying Party shall be entitled to participate in (but not control) the defense of such action, with its counsel and at its own expense.

8.4   Limitations on Indemnification.

(a)   Seller shall not be obligated to make any payment for indemnification under Article 8 hereof in excess of the sum of (i) [ ] plus (ii) an amount equal to the Additional Purchase Price paid pursuant to Section 3.3, in the aggregate, except with respect to any claim for indemnification arising from or related to fraud or breach of the representations, warranties and covenants contained in Sections 4.2 (Certificate of Incorporation and Bylaws; Capitalization), 4.9 (Taxes) and 4.21 (Employee Benefit Plans) and indemnification under Section 8.1(e) (Litigation) related to the [ ] Case, for which there is no limit. Except with regard to any claim for indemnification arising out of or relating to fraud or intentional breach of an obligation, breach of the representations, warranties and covenants in Sections 3.2 (Adjustments), 4.2 (Certificate of Incorporation and Bylaws; Capitalization), 4.9 (Taxes), and indemnification under Sections 8.1(b) (Retired Debt) and 8.1(e) (Litigation), Seller shall not be obligated to pay any amounts for indemnification under Article 8 until Seller's aggregate indemnification obligations under Article 8 equal or exceed [ ], whereupon Seller shall be obligated to pay all such indemnification including the [ ].

(b)   Buyer shall not be obligated to make any payment for indemnification under Article 8 hereof in excess of [ ] in the aggregate, except with respect to any claim for fraud or indemnification arising from or related to breach of the representations, warranties and covenants contained in Sections 5.1 (Organization, Etc.) and 5.2 (Authorization of Agreement) for which there is no limit. Except with respect to any claim for indemnification arising out of or relating to fraud or intentional breach of an obligation, Buyer shall not be obligated to pay any amounts for indemnification under Article 8 until the Buyer's aggregate indemnification obligations under Article 8 equal or exceed [ ], whereupon Buyer shall be obligated to pay all such indemnification including the [ ].

(c)   Except as set forth in Section 3.2, Buyer shall seek to satisfy any claim for indemnification from the Escrow Amount before proceeding against Seller's other assets; provided that nothing herein shall prevent Buyer from proceeding against Seller (including any injunction to prevent dissipation of assets) for indemnification for Claim amounts in excess of the Escrow Amount in the event it reasonably believes the Escrow Amount is inadequate.

(d)   With respect to any claim for indemnification:

(i)   If made prior to [ ], Buyer may proceed against Seller and the Escrow Amount, in accordance with Section 8.4(c), and at Buyer's option Buyer may seek to satisfy sixty-five percent (65%) of such amounts by reduction of payments under the Bonus Plan;

(ii)   If made on or after [ ], but prior to the earlier of (x) the date of distribution of bonuses under the Bonus Plan or (y) expiration or termination of the Bonus Plan in accordance with its terms (the "Bonus Payout Date"), except as set forth herein, Buyer shall seek to satisfy thirty-five percent (35%) of such claim from Seller and the Escrow Amount and sixty-five percent (65%) of such claim by reduction of the payments to be made pursuant to the Bonus Plan. Notwithstanding the foregoing, Buyer shall not be required to seek compensation for such indemnification from the Bonus Plan: (A) with respect to the [ ] Case, (B) with respect to any breach of the representations and warranties in Section 4.2 (Certificate of Incorporation and Bylaws; Capitalization) or (C) in the event that the payout under the Bonus Plan is inadequate to satisfy the allocated portion of the claim, or if Buyer reasonably believes that based on current operating results, there will be no distribution under the Bonus Plan or the distribution will be inadequate to cover the payment. Seller remains fully liable for all amounts for which the Bonus Plan is sought to satisfy indemnification to the extent the amounts to be distributed under the Bonus Plan are inadequate;

(iii)   If made after the Bonus Payout Date, Buyer may proceed against Seller and the Escrow Amount, in accordance with Section 8.4(c).

8.5.   Sole and Exclusive Remedy. The rights set forth in this Article 8 and Section 4.23 shall be Buyer's sole and exclusive remedy against the Seller for misrepresentations or breaches of covenants contained in this Agreement and the Transaction Documents. Notwithstanding the foregoing, nothing herein shall prevent Buyer from bringing an action based upon allegations of fraud or other intentional misrepresentation or breach of any representation or obligation of or with respect to the Company or Seller in connection with this Agreement and the Transaction Documents.

ARTICLE 9
[Intentionally Omitted.]

ARTICLE 10
DISPUTE RESOLUTION

10.1   Initial Meeting. In the event that there is a dispute arising out of or relating to this Agreement or the documents and instruments executed in connection therewith, the parties shall attempt in good faith to resolve such disputes promptly by negotiation between the parties. Any party may give the other parties written notice that a dispute exists (a "Notice of Dispute"). The Notice of Dispute shall include a statement of such party's position. Within ten (10) days of the delivery of the Notice of Dispute, the parties shall meet at a mutually acceptable time and place, and thereafter as long as they reasonably deem necessary, to attempt to resolve the dispute. All documents and other information or data on which each party relies concerning the dispute shall be furnished or made available on reasonable terms to the other party at or before the first meeting of the parties as provided by this Section 10.1.

10.2   Mediation. If the dispute has not been resolved by negotiation within thirty (30) days of the delivery of a Notice of Dispute, or if the parties have failed to meet within ten (10) days of the Notice of Dispute, the parties shall endeavor to settle the dispute by mediation under the then current CPR Model Mediation Procedure for Business Disputes. Unless otherwise agreed, the parties shall select a mediator from the CPR Panels of Neutrals and shall notify CPR to initiate the selection process.

10.3   Binding Arbitration. Unless a different venue is required by the Escrow Agreement, any controversy or claim arising out of or relating to this Agreement or any agreement or document in connection therewith, the breach, termination or validity thereof, or the transactions contemplated herein (including any question arising as to whether or not any dispute falls within the terms of this Section or the selection of arbitrators) if not settled by negotiation or mediation as provided in Section 10.1 and Section 10.2, shall be settled by arbitration if commenced by Buyer, in [ ], and if commenced by Seller, in [ ], in accordance with the CPR Rules for Non-Administrative Arbitration of Business Disputes by three arbitrators. Any party may initiate arbitration from and after sixty (60) days following the delivery of a Notice of Dispute if the dispute has not then been settled by negotiation or mediation. The arbitrators shall be appointed by the parties as provided by CPR Rule 5, Selection of Arbitrators. The arbitration procedure shall be governed by the United States Arbitration Act, 9 U.S.C. §§ 1-16, and the award rendered by the arbitrators shall be final and binding on the parties and may be entered in any court having jurisdiction thereof.

10.4   Discovery. Each party shall have discovery rights as provided by the Federal Rules of Civil Procedure; provided, however, that all such discovery shall be commenced and concluded within ninety (90) days of the initiation of arbitration.

10.5   Expeditious Proceedings. It is the intent of the parties that any arbitration shall be concluded as quickly as reasonably practicable. Unless the parties otherwise agree, once commenced, the hearing on the disputed matters shall be held four (4) days a week until concluded, with each hearing date to begin at 9:00 a.m. and to conclude at 5:00 p.m. The arbitrators shall use all reasonable efforts to issue the final award or awards within a period of five (5) business days after closure of the proceedings. Failure of the arbitrators to meet the time limits of this Section 10.5 shall not be a basis for challenging the award.

10.6   Arbitration Costs. Each party shall bear its own costs in connection with the arbitration and shall share equally the fees and expenses of the arbitrators.

10.7   Enforcement of Awards. Each party agrees that any legal proceeding instituted to enforce an arbitration award hereunder will be brought in a court of competent jurisdiction (either state or federal) in the venue of the arbitration set forth in Section 10.3 and hereby submits to personal jurisdiction therein and irrevocably waives any objection as to venue therein, and further agrees not to plead or claim in any such court that any such proceeding has been brought in an inconvenient forum.

10.8   Equitable Relief. Nothing herein shall be construed to prevent any party from seeking equitable relief in any court of competent jurisdiction to restrain or prohibit any breach or threatened breach of any covenant of the parties set forth in this Agreement or any document executed in connection herewith, whether or not the parties have first sought to resolve the dispute through negotiation, mediation or arbitration pursuant to this Article 10.

ARTICLE 11
GENERAL

11.1   Expenses, Taxes. Buyer and Seller shall pay their own respective expenses and the fees and expenses of their respective counsel and accountants and other experts, and Seller shall pay the fees and expenses of the Company (other than Permitted Legal Fees which will be paid by Buyer). Seller shall bear all transfer Taxes, gains Taxes, recording Taxes and similar Taxes payable or determined to be payable in connection with the execution, delivery and performance of this Agreement and the transfer of the Purchased Shares contemplated hereby.

11.2   Survival of Representations and Warranties. Each covenant and agreement contained in this Agreement or in any agreement or other document delivered pursuant hereto shall survive the Closing and be enforceable until such covenant or agreement has been fully performed. All representations and warranties contained in this Agreement shall survive for a period of eighteen (18) months after the Closing and shall thereafter expire, except that (a) any representation or warranty with respect to which a claim has been made for a breach thereon prior to the expiration of such eighteen (18) month period shall survive until such claim is resolved; (b) any breach of the representations and warranties set forth in Sections 4.9 (Taxes) and 4.21 (Employee Benefit Plans) shall survive for the applicable statute of limitations), and (c) any claim related to fraud, intentional misrepresentation, intentional breach of an obligation, and breach of the representations and warranties set forth in Sections 4.2 (Certificate of Incorporation and Bylaws; Capitalization), 4.4 (Execution and Validity of Agreement; Spousal Consent etc.) and any claim related to the litigation set forth on Schedule 4.17 shall survive without limitation. The representations and warranties in this Agreement shall not be affected by any knowledge of Buyer with respect to any breach thereof or any investigation performed by Buyer.

11.3   Waivers. No action taken pursuant to this Agreement, including any investigation by or on behalf of any party, shall be deemed to constitute a waiver by the party taking such action, or compliance with any representation, warranty, covenant or agreement contained herein. The waiver by any party hereto of a breach of any provision of this Agreement shall not operate or be construed as a waiver of any subsequent breach.

11.4   Binding Effect; Benefits; Assignment. This Agreement shall inure to the benefit of and be binding upon the parties hereto and their respective successors and permitted assigns, heirs and legal representatives. Nothing in this Agreement, express or implied, is intended to confer on any Person other than the parties hereto or their respective successors and permitted assigns any rights, remedies, obligations, or Liabilities under or by reason of this Agreement. Seller may not assign his rights hereunder or in any agreement or instrument executed in connection herewith, whether by operation of law or otherwise. Buyer may assign this Agreement and any agreement or instrument executed in connection herewith to any of its

Affiliates, or pursuant to a merger, consolidation of sale of substantially all of its assets or to any Person which acquires an interest in the Business as conducted by Buyer. Signatures delivered by facsimile on this Agreement or any document executed in connection herewith shall be binding to the same extent as an original.

11.5   Notices. All notices, requests, demands and other communications which are required to be or may be given under this Agreement shall be in writing and shall be deemed to have been duly given when delivered in Person or three (3) days after deposit by certified or registered first class mail, postage prepaid, return receipt requested, to the party to whom the same is so given or made:

(a)   If to Buyer, to:

_____

_____

_____

With a copy to:

_____

_____

_____

(b)   If to Seller to:

_____

_____

_____

With a copy to:

_____

_____

_____

or to such other address as such party shall have specified by notice to the other party hereto.

11.6   Entire Agreement. This Agreement (including the Schedules and Exhibits hereto) constitutes the entire agreement and supersedes all prior agreements and understandings, oral and written, between the parties hereto with respect to the subject matter hereof and cannot be changed or terminated orally.

11.7   Headings. The Section and other headings contained in this Agreement are for reference purposes only and shall not be deemed to be a part of this Agreement or to affect the meaning or interpretation of this Agreement.

11.8   Governing Law. This Agreement shall be construed as to both validity and performance and enforced in accordance with and governed by the laws of the State of [ ], without giving effect to the choice of law principles thereof.

11.9   Amendments. This Agreement may not be modified or changed except by an instrument or instruments in writing signed by the party against whom enforcement of any such modification or amendment is sought.

11.10   Severability. The invalidity of all or any part of any representation, warranty, covenant or indemnification section of this Agreement shall not render invalid the remainder of this Agreement or the remainder of such section. If any representation, warranty, covenant or indemnification section of this Agreement or portion thereof is so broad as to be unenforceable, it shall be interpreted to be only so broad as is enforceable.

[Remainder of page is blank.]

IN WITNESS WHEREOF, the parties hereto have caused this Agreement to be signed in their respective names by an officer thereunto duly authorized on the date first above written.

SELLER: **BUYER:**

By: _____   By: _____

Its: _____   Its: _____

Courtesy of Stephen M. Quinlivan and Marci K. Winga, Leonard, Street and Deinard PA

APPENDIX K

AGREEMENT AND PLAN OF MERGER
BY AND AMONG MDU RESOURCES GROUP INC., FIREMOON ACQUISITION INC., AND CASCADE NATURAL GAS CORPORATION

This Agreement and Plan of Merger, is made and entered into as of July 8, 2006 (this "Agreement"), by and among MDU RESOURCES GROUP, INC., a Delaware corporation ("Buyer"), FIREMOON ACQUISITION, INC., a Washington corporation and a wholly-owned subsidiary of Buyer ("Merger Sub"), and CASCADE NATURAL GAS CORPORATION, a Washington corporation (the "Company").

WITNESSETH:

WHEREAS, the parties desire that Merger Sub be merged with and into the Company (the "Merger") pursuant to which the Company will become a wholly-owned Subsidiary of Buyer; and

WHEREAS, the respective Boards of Directors of Buyer, Merger Sub and the Company have approved this Agreement and the Merger.

NOW, THEREFORE, in consideration of the foregoing and the mutual covenants and agreements herein contained, and intending to be legally bound hereby, the parties hereto hereby agree as follows:

ARTICLE I
THE MERGER

Section 1.1   The Merger. Upon the terms and subject to the conditions hereof, and in accordance with the Washington Business Corporation Act (the "WBCA"), Merger Sub will be merged with and into the Company at the Effective Time. Following the Effective Time, the separate corporate existence of Merger Sub will cease and the Company will continue as the surviving corporation (the "Surviving Corporation") and will succeed to and assume all the rights and obligations of Merger Sub and the Company in accordance with the WBCA.

Section 1.2   Closing. The closing of the Merger will take place at 9:00 a.m. on a date mutually agreed to by Buyer and the Company, which will be no later than the business day after satisfaction or waiver of the conditions set forth in Article VII (the "Closing Date"), at the offices of Preston Gates & Ellis LLP, Seattle, Washington, unless another date, time or place is agreed to in writing by Buyer and the Company.

Section 1.3   Effective Time. The Merger will become effective (the "Effective Time") upon the later of (a) the date of filing of properly executed Articles of Merger (the "Articles of Merger") relating to the Merger with the Secretary of State of Washington in accordance with the WBCA, and (b) at such other time as Buyer and the Company agree and set forth in the Articles of Merger.

Section 1.4   Effects of the Merger. The Merger will have the effects set forth in this Agreement and in the WBCA.

Section 1.5   Articles of Incorporation and Bylaws; Officers and Directors.

(a)   The Articles of Incorporation of the Company, as in effect immediately prior to the Effective Time, will be the Articles of Incorporation of the Surviving Corporation until thereafter changed or amended as provided therein and by applicable law.

(b)   The bylaws of the Company, as in effect immediately prior to the Effective Time, will be the bylaws of the Surviving Corporation until thereafter changed or amended as provided by the Surviving Corporation's Articles of Incorporation, bylaws and by applicable law.

(c)   The directors and officers of Merger Sub immediately prior to the Effective Time will be the directors and officers of the Surviving Corporation, until their respective successors have been duly elected or appointed and qualified or until their earlier death, resignation or removal in accordance with the Surviving Corporation's Articles of Incorporation and bylaws and by applicable law.

ARTICLE II
EFFECT OF THE MERGER; CONVERSION OF SHARES

Section 2.1 <u>Effect on Company Stock</u>. As of the Effective Time, by virtue of the Merger and without any action on the part of any of Buyer or the Company or the holders of any securities thereof:

(a) <u>Cancellation of Certain Shares</u>. Each share of Common Stock, $1.00 par value per share, of the Company ("Company Common Stock,") that (i) has been reacquired by the Company and is held as authorized but unissued Company Common Stock, (ii) is owned by any Subsidiary of the Company or (iii) is owned by Buyer or any Subsidiary of Buyer, will automatically be cancelled and retired and will cease to exist, and no consideration will be delivered in exchange therefor. "Subsidiary" of any Person means another Person, an amount of the voting securities, other voting ownership or voting partnership interests of which is sufficient to elect at least a majority of its Board of Directors or other governing body (or, if there are no such voting interests, greater than 50% of the equity interests of which) is owned directly or indirectly by such first Person.

(b) <u>Conversion of Company Common Shares</u>. Each share of Company Common Stock issued and outstanding, including Company Stock Options deemed exercised pursuant to Section 2.2, (but not Dissenting Shares and shares of Company Common Stock to be cancelled in accordance with Section 2.1(a)) (the "Company Common Shares") will be converted into the right to receive $26.50 in cash, without interest (the "Merger Consideration") on the terms set forth in this Agreement. All such Company Common Shares, when so converted, will no longer be outstanding and will automatically be cancelled and retired, and each holder of a certificate representing any such Company Common Shares will cease to have any rights with respect thereto, except the right to receive Merger Consideration without interest upon the surrender of the proper documentary evidence to the Paying Agent in accordance with Section 2.4(c).

Section 2.2   Effect on Company Options and Other Company Securities; Suspension of DRIP and Employee Savings Plans.

(a)   Immediately prior to the Effective Time, contingent on consummation of the Closing, each outstanding option to purchase Company Common Stock (a "Company Stock Option") that is outstanding immediately prior to the Effective Time pursuant to the Company's 1998 Stock Incentive Plan (including the Company's 2000 Director Stock Award Plan (the "Director Stock Plan")) (collectively, the "Company Option Plan") that is not vested, will immediately vest and become exercisable by the holder. If this Agreement is terminated, all Company Stock Options that were otherwise unvested will revert to their original status. The Company will exercise reasonable efforts to cause all holders of Company Stock Options to either exercise such options or irrevocably waive his or her rights to do so. At the Effective Time, each Company Stock Option with respect to which the holder has delivered to the Company a proper exercise notice will be considered exercised. The Common Stock issuable in respect of such exercise will be deemed issued without the necessity of issuing a stock certificate and will be treated as Company Common Shares in the Merger. The Paying Agent, on Buyer's behalf, will deduct the exercise price payable in connection with the exercise of Company Stock Options from the Merger Consideration otherwise payable in respect of the Company Common Shares deemed issued in respect of the exercised option; it will not be necessary for holders of Company Stock Options to tender the exercise price. Any Company Stock Options with respect to which the Payment Agent has not received notice of exercise before termination of the Payment Fund will be cancelled.

(b)   At the Effective Time, all remaining restrictions with respect to shares of Company restricted stock issued pursuant to the Company Option Plan (the "Company Restricted Shares") will expire and all of the Company Restricted Shares will be fully vested and will be treated as Company Common Shares in the Merger, provided, however, that the amount payable by the Paying Agent in respect of such Company Common Shares shall be reduced by all applicable federal, state and local Taxes required to be withheld by the Company or otherwise with respect thereto.

(c)   Prior to the record date for the Company Shareholders Meeting, the Company will take such actions and enter into such agreements to cause (i) all outstanding Stock Units (as defined in the Director Stock Plan) (the "Company Stock Units") to be cancelled and (ii) to be issued to each holder of Company Stock Units a number of Company Common Shares equal to number of Company Stock Units such Person holds, which will be treated as Company Common Shares in the Merger, in each case to be effective immediately prior to the Effective Time.

(d)   Prior to the Effective Time, the Company will cause the Company's Automatic Dividend Reinvestment Plan (the "Company DRIP") and all rights thereunder to be suspended immediately following the Investment Date (as defined in the Company DRIP) ending immediately prior to the Effective Time, with the effect of such suspension being that no offering period will commence or continue under such plan during the period of such suspension.

(e)   Prior to the Effective Time, the Company will cause the Company's Employee Retirement Savings Plan (2002 Restatement) (the "Company Employee Savings Plan" and, collectively with the Company Option Plan and the Company DRIP, the "Company Stock Plans"), to be amended to suspend investments in Qualifying Employer Securities (as defined therein) effective as of the last business day prior to the Effective Time.

Section 2.3   Conversion of Merger Sub Common Shares. Each share of common stock, no par value, of Merger Sub issued and outstanding immediately prior to the Effective Time will, by virtue of the Merger and without any action on the part of the holder thereof, be converted into and exchangeable for one (1) share of common stock of the Surviving Corporation and each certificate evidencing ownership of any shares of common stock of Merger Sub shall evidence ownership of the same number of shares of common stock of the Surviving Corporation.

Section 2.4   Payment Procedures.

(a)   Payment Agent; Payment Fund. Not less than five business days prior to the Effective Time, Buyer will authorize a banking or other financial institution selected by Buyer and reasonably satisfactory to the Company to act as Payment Agent hereunder (the "Payment Agent") with respect to the Merger. At or prior to the Effective Time, Buyer will deposit, or will cause to be deposited, with the Payment Agent, for the benefit of the holders of Company Common Shares, for exchange in accordance with this Article II, the aggregate Merger Consideration payable in connection with the Merger (the "Payment Fund"). Such funds shall be invested by the Payment Agent as directed by the Surviving Corporation, provided that such investments shall be in obligations of or guaranteed by the United States of America or any agency or instrumentality thereof, in commercial paper obligations rated A-1 or P-1 or better by Moody's Investors Services, Inc. or Standard & Poor's Corporation, respectively, or in certificates of deposits, bank repurchase agreements or banker's acceptances of commercial banks with capital exceeding $500,000,000; provided however that (i) none of the foregoing will affect Buyer's obligation to pay the Merger Consideration as set forth in this Section 2.4 and (ii) Buyer and the Surviving Corporation will promptly replace any losses relating to the aggregate Merger Consideration. Any net profit resulting from, or interest or income produced by, such investments will be payable to Buyer. The Payment Agent will, pursuant to irrevocable instructions of the Buyer, deliver the applicable Merger Consideration pursuant to this Article II out of the Payment Fund. At or prior to the Effective Time, the Company will provide to the Payment Agent a certified ledger setting forth the names and amounts held by the holders of all Company Stock Options. The Payment Fund will not be used for any purpose other than as set forth in this Section 2.4(a).

(b)   Instructions. Promptly after the Effective Time, the Surviving Corporation will cause the Payment Agent to mail to each holder of record of Company Common Shares (i) a letter of transmittal (which will specify that delivery will be effected, and risk of loss and title to the Certificates will pass, only upon delivery of the Certificates to the Payment Agent and will be in a form and have such other provisions as Buyer may specify and that are acceptable to the Company) and (ii) instructions for use in effecting the surrender of the Certificates and shares that are held in book-entry form ("Book-Entry Shares") in exchange for the consideration contemplated hereby, if not previously surrendered. "Certificate" means a stock certificate representing the applicable holder's Company Common Shares or, in the case of Company Stock Options exercised for Company Common Shares pursuant to Section 2.2, the holder's applicable stock option agreement together with the proper executed exercise notice.

(c)   Procedures. Upon surrender of a Certificate for cancellation to the Payment Agent, together with such letter of transmittal, duly executed, and such other documents as may reasonably be required by the Payment Agent, the holder of such Certificate or Book-Entry Shares will be entitled to receive in exchange therefor the Merger Consideration that such holder has the right to receive in respect of the Certificate or Book-Entry Shares surrendered pursuant to the provisions of this Article II, after giving effect to any required withholding Tax. In the event of a transfer of ownership of Company Common Shares that is not registered in the Company's transfer records, a check for the Merger Consideration to be paid pursuant to this Section 2.4, if applicable, may be issued to such a transferee if such Certificate or Book-Entry Shares are properly endorsed (as applicable) or otherwise be in proper form for transfer and the transferee will pay any transfer or other Taxes required by reason of the payment to any person, employee, individual, corporation, limited liability company, partnership, trust, or any other non-governmental entity (including any foreign entity) or any governmental or regulatory authority or body (including any foreign entity) (each a "Person"), other than the registered holder of such Certificate or Book-Entry Shares, or establish to the satisfaction of the Surviving Corporation that such Tax has been paid or is not applicable.

(d)   Tax Withholding. Each of the Surviving Corporation, Buyer, Merger Sub and the Payment Agent will be entitled to deduct and withhold from the consideration otherwise payable pursuant to this Agreement (without duplication) such amounts as it is required to deduct and withhold with respect to the making of such payment under the Internal Revenue Code of 1986, as amended (the "Code") or under any provision of state, local or foreign Tax law and to pay such amounts to the applicable taxing authority. To the extent that amounts are so withheld by the Surviving Corporation, Buyer, Merger Sub or the Payment Agent, as the case may be, such withheld amounts will be treated for all purposes of this Agreement as having been paid to the Person in respect of which such deduction and withholding was made. "Tax" means: (i) any federal, state, local or foreign net income, gross income, gross receipts, windfall profit, severance, property, production, sales, use, license, excise, franchise, employment, payroll, estimated, withholding, alternative or add-on minimum, ad valorem, value-added, transfer, stamp, or environmental (including taxes under Section 59A of the Code) tax, or any other tax, custom, duty, governmental fee or other like assessment or charge of any kind whatsoever, together with any interest or penalty, addition to tax or additional amount imposed by any governmental authority and (ii) any liability in respect of any items described in clause (i) payable by reason of contract, assumption, transferee liability, operation of law, Treasury Regulation 1.1502-6(a) (or any predecessor or successor thereof or any analogous or similar provision under law) or otherwise.

(e)   No Further Ownership Rights in Shares. All Merger Consideration paid upon the surrender of Certificates in accordance with the terms of this Article II will be deemed to have been issued in full satisfaction of all rights pertaining to the Company Common Shares theretofore represented by such Certificates or Book-Entry Shares. At the Effective Time, the Company's stock transfer books will be closed, and there will be no further registration of transfers on the stock transfer books of the Surviving Corporation of the Company Common Shares that were outstanding immediately prior to the Effective Time. If, after the

Effective Time, Certificates are presented to the Surviving Corporation or the Payment Agent for any reason, they will be cancelled as provided in this Article II.

(f)   Termination of Payment Fund. Any portion of the Payment Fund (including the proceeds of any investments thereof) which remains undistributed to the holders of Company Common Shares for 12 months after the Effective Time may be delivered to Buyer upon its demand, and any holder of Company Common Shares who has not theretofore exchanged such holder's Certificate(s) or Book-Entry Shares in accordance with this Article II and the instructions set forth in the letter of transmittal mailed to such holders after the Effective Time will thereafter look only to Buyer or its agent (subject to abandoned property, escheat or other similar laws) for payment of their Merger Consideration deliverable in respect of each Company Common Share such shareholder holds as determined pursuant to this Agreement.

(g)   No Liability. None of Buyer, the Surviving Corporation, the Company or the Payment Agent will be liable to any Person in respect of any amount properly delivered or deliverable to a public official pursuant to any applicable abandoned property, escheat or other similar law.

Section 2.5   Dissenting Shares. Shares of Company Common Stock issued and outstanding immediately prior to the Effective Time (but not Company Common Shares deemed issued for exercised Company Stock Options pursuant to Section 2.2) that are held by a holder who (a) has not voted such shares in favor of the adoption of this Agreement and the Merger, (b) is entitled to, and who has, properly demanded and perfected dissenter's rights for such Company Common Shares in accordance with the WBCA and (c) has not effectively withdrawn or forfeited such dissenter's rights prior to the Effective Time (the "Dissenting Shares"), will not be converted into a right to receive Merger Consideration at the Effective Time. If, after the Effective Time, such holder fails to perfect or withdraws, forfeits or otherwise loses such holder's dissenter's rights, (i) such Company Common Shares will be treated as if they had been converted as of the Effective Time pursuant to Section 2.1(b), without any interest therefor, and (ii) the procedures in Section 2.4 will apply with respect to the payment of Merger Consideration with regard to such Company Common Shares. The Company will give Buyer prompt notice of any written notice received by the Company for dissenter's rights with respect to Company Common Shares, and Buyer will have the right to participate in all negotiations and proceedings with respect to such demands. The Company will not, except with the prior written consent of Buyer, make any payment with respect to, or settle or offer to settle, any such demands.

Section 2.6   Lost Certificates. If any Certificate has been lost, stolen or destroyed, upon the making of an affidavit of that fact by the Person claiming such Certificate to be lost, stolen or destroyed and, if required by the Surviving Corporation or the Payment Agent, the posting by such Person of a bond, in such reasonable amount as Surviving Corporation or the Payment Agent may direct as indemnity against any claim that may be made against them with respect to such Certificate, the Payment Agent will issue in exchange for such lost, stolen or destroyed Certificate the Merger Consideration in respect thereof pursuant to this Agreement.

Section 2.7   Adjustment of Merger Consideration. In the event that the Company changes, or establishes a record date for changing, the number of shares of Company Common Stock issued and outstanding as a result of a stock split, stock dividend, recapitalization, subdivision, reclassification, combination or similar transaction and the record date therefor is or will be prior to the Effective Time, the Merger Consideration will be appropriately, equitably and proportionately adjusted in light of such stock split, stock dividend, recapitalization, subdivision, reclassification, combination or similar transaction.

ARTICLE III
REPRESENTATIONS AND WARRANTIES OF THE COMPANY

The Company represents and warrants to Buyer, except as set forth in the Company Disclosure Schedules dated as of the date hereof (the "Company Disclosure Schedules"), and except as disclosed in the documents (excluding any exhibits or portions thereof) filed with or furnished to the Securities and Exchange Commission (the "SEC") by the Company and publicly available on the Electronic Data Gathering, Analysis and Retrieval System prior to the date of this Agreement (the "Company Filed SEC Documents") (it being understood that any matter set forth in the Company Filed SEC Documents will be deemed to qualify any representation or warranty in this Article III only to the extent that the description of such matter in the Company Filed SEC Documents is made in such a way as to make its relevance to the information called for by such representation or warranty readily apparent), as follows:

Section 3.1   Organization. The Company is validly existing under the laws of the State of Washington and has all requisite power and authority to carry on its businesses as now being conducted, except where the failure to be so existing or to have such power and authority would not, individually or in the aggregate, have a Company Material Adverse Effect. The Company is duly qualified or licensed to do business and in good standing (as applicable) in each jurisdiction in which the nature of its businesses or the ownership or leasing of its properties makes such qualification or licensing necessary, except in such jurisdictions where the failure to be so duly qualified or licensed and in good standing (as applicable) would not, individually or in the aggregate, have a Company Material Adverse Effect. The Company has made available to Buyer complete and correct copies of its Articles of Incorporation and bylaws. "Company Material Adverse Effect" means any event, effect, change or development that, individually or in the aggregate with other events, effects, changes or developments (i) is, or would reasonably be expected to be, material and adverse to the financial condition, business, assets, liabilities (contingent or otherwise), operations or results of operations of the Company and its Subsidiaries taken as a whole or (ii) has, or would reasonably be expected to have, a material and adverse effect on the ability of the Company to perform its obligations under this Agreement or to consummate the transactions contemplated hereby by the End Date; provided, however, that to the extent any event, effect, change or development is caused by or results from any of the following, in each case, it will not be taken into account in determining whether there has been (or would reasonably be expected to be) a Company Material Adverse Effect: (A) general economic, legal or regulatory conditions affecting the gas utility industry as a whole, except to the extent the Company and its Subsidiaries, taken as a whole, are materially and adversely affected in a disproportionate manner as compared to comparable gas utilities; (B) the announcement of the execution of this Agreement; (C) any failure by the Company to meet any revenue or earnings predictions prepared by the Company or revenue or earnings predictions of equity analysts or the receipt by the Company or any of its Subsidiaries of any credit ratings downgrade (it being understood that the facts or occurrences giving rise or contributing to any such effect, event, change or development which affect or otherwise relate to or result from the failure to meet revenue or earnings predictions prepared by the Company or revenue or earnings predictions of equity analysts or to the receipt of any credit ratings downgrade may be deemed to constitute, or be taken into account in determining whether there has been, or would reasonably be expected to be, a Company Material Adverse Effect); (D) changes in laws, rules or regulations of any Governmental Entity affecting the energy market as a whole except to the extent the Company and its Subsidiaries, taken as a whole, are materially and adversely affected in a disproportionate manner as compared to comparable participants in the energy market; (E) any orders or decisions by the Washington Utilities and Transportation Commission (the "WUTC") or Oregon Public Utility Commission (the "OPUC") regarding the Company or the transactions contemplated hereby; (F) any change in generally accepted accounting principles ("GAAP") by the Financial Accounting Standards Board, the SEC or any other regulatory body; (G) any change in the price of the Company Common Shares (it being understood that the facts or occurrences giving rise or contributing to any such change in the price of the Company Common Shares may be deemed to constitute, or be taken into account in determining whether there has been, or would reasonably be expected to be, a Company Material Adverse Effect); (H) any outbreak or escalation of hostilities, terrorism or war (whether or not declared), or the declaration by the United States of a national emergency or war or the occurrence of any other calamity or crisis or natural disaster, in each case that does not directly affect the assets or properties of, or communities served by, the Company and its Subsidiaries, taken as a whole; (I) the effects of weather or other meteorological events; or (J) the compliance of any party hereto with the terms of this Agreement.

Section 3.2   Subsidiaries.

(a)   Section 3.2(a) of the Company Disclosure Schedules lists each Subsidiary of the Company and its jurisdiction of organization. No Subsidiary of the Company is a Significant Subsidiary. "Significant Subsidiary" of any Person means a Subsidiary of such Person that would constitute a "significant subsidiary" of such Person within the meaning of Rule 1.02(w) of Regulation S-X as promulgated by the SEC.

(b)   All of the outstanding Capital Stock of each Subsidiary of the Company is owned by the Company, by one or more Subsidiaries of the Company or by the Company and one or more Subsidiaries of the Company. Except for the Capital Stock of its Subsidiaries, the Company does not own, directly or indirectly, any Capital Stock of any corporation, partnership, joint venture, limited liability company or other entity. Neither the Company nor any of its Subsidiaries is a party to, or has any commitment to become a party to, any joint venture, off-balance sheet partnership or any similar written or oral agreement, undertaking, contract, commitment, lease, license, permit, franchise, concession, deed of trust, contract, note, bond, mortgage, indenture, arrangement or other instrument or obligation ("Contract"). "Capital Stock" means, as applicable any capital stock of a corporation or any other equity interest (including preferred interests) in any Person including any equity interest (including preferred interests) in any partnership, limited liability company or limited liability partnership.

Section 3.3   Capital Structure.

(a)   The authorized Capital Stock of the Company consists of 15,000,000 shares of Company Common Stock, 96,560 shares of 55 cents Cumulative Preferred Stock, no par value ("Company Cumulative Preferred Stock"), and 1,000,000 shares of preferred stock, $1.00 par value per share ("Company Preferred Stock"). At the close of business on June 30, 2006, (i) 11,498,571 shares of Company Common Stock (which includes 5,000 Company

Restricted Shares for which restrictions have not lapsed) were issued and outstanding, (ii) 3,501,429 shares of Company Common Stock were held by the Company as authorized but unissued Company Common Stock, (iii) 326,730 shares of Company Common Stock were reserved for issuance pursuant to the Company Option Plan (including 33,000 shares of Company Common Stock reserved for issuance pursuant to outstanding Company Stock Options and 14,750 shares of Company Common Stock reserved for issuance pursuant to outstanding Long-Term Incentive Award Agreements), (iv) 22,112 shares of Company Common Stock were reserved for issuance pursuant to the Director Stock Plan (including 10,702.8352 shares of Common Stock reserved for issuance pursuant to outstanding Company Stock Units), (v) 170,113 shares of Company Common Stock were reserved for issuance pursuant to the Company Employee Savings Plan, (vi) 113,834 shares of Company Common Stock were reserved for issuance pursuant to the Company DRIP, (vii) 2,027,054 shares of Company Common Stock were reserved for issuance for other matters (including 2,012,300 shares reserved for issuance pursuant to a previously anticipated offering that the Company has since abandoned) and (viii) no shares of Company Cumulative Preferred Stock or Company Preferred Stock were outstanding. As of the close of business on the date of this Agreement, except as set forth above, no shares of Company Common Stock or shares of Company Cumulative Preferred Stock or Company Preferred Stock are issued, reserved for issuance or outstanding, and there are no phantom stock or other contractual rights the value of which is determined in whole or in part by the value of any Capital Stock of the Company ("Company Stock Equivalents"). There are no outstanding stock appreciation rights with respect to the Capital Stock of the Company. Each outstanding share of Company Common Stock is, and each share of Company Common Stock which may be issued pursuant to the Company Stock Plans and any awards thereunder will be, when issued, duly authorized, validly issued, fully paid and nonassessable and not subject to preemptive rights. There are no outstanding bonds, debentures, notes or other indebtedness of the Company having the right to vote (or convertible into, or exchangeable for, securities having the right to vote) on any matter on which the Company's shareholders may vote ("Company Voting Debt").

(b)   As of the date of this Agreement, other than as contemplated by Section 3.3(a), there are no securities, options, warrants, calls, rights, commitments, agreements, arrangements or undertakings of any kind to which the Company is a party or by which it is bound obligating the Company to issue, deliver or sell or create, or cause to be issued, delivered or sold or created, additional Capital Stock, Company Stock Options, Company Voting Debt or other securities or Company Stock Equivalents of Company or obligating the Company to issue, grant, extend or enter into any such security, option, warrant, call, right, commitment, agreement, arrangement or undertaking. As of the date of this Agreement, there are no outstanding contractual obligations of the Company to repurchase, redeem or otherwise acquire any Capital Stock of the Company. There are no outstanding agreements to which the Company, or to its Knowledge any of its officers or directors, is a party concerning the voting of any Capital Stock of the Company.

Section 3.4   Authority. On or prior to the date of this Agreement, the Board of Directors of the Company unanimously approved this Agreement, declared this Agreement and the Merger advisable and in the best interest of the Company and its shareholders, resolved to recommend the approval of this Agreement by the Company's shareholders, directed that this Agreement be submitted to the Company's shareholders for approval and adoption (all in accordance with the WBCA) and approved the other agreements to be entered into by the Company as contemplated hereby. The Company has all requisite corporate power and authority to execute and deliver this Agreement and, subject to the satisfaction of the conditions set forth in Sections 7.1 and 7.2, to consummate the transactions contemplated hereby. The execution, delivery and performance of this Agreement by the Company and the consummation by the Company of the Merger and of the other transactions contemplated hereby have been duly authorized by all necessary corporate action on the part of the Company, subject to the satisfaction of the conditions set forth in Sections 7.1 and 7.2. This Agreement has been, and any agreements contemplated herein to which the Company is or will be a party will be, duly executed and delivered by the Company and (assuming the valid authorization, execution and delivery hereof and thereof by Buyer and the other Persons party thereto) constitutes, or upon execution will constitute, the valid and binding obligation of the Company enforceable against the Company in accordance with their respective terms, except that such enforceability (i) may be limited by bankruptcy, insolvency, moratorium or other similar laws affecting or relating to the enforcement of creditors' rights generally and (ii) is subject to general principles of equity.

Section 3.5   <u>Consents and Approvals; No Violations.</u>

(a)   Except for filings, permits, authorizations, consents and approvals contemplated by Section 3.5(b), neither the execution, delivery or performance of this Agreement by the Company nor the consummation by the Company of the transactions contemplated hereby will (i) subject to the receipt of Company Shareholder Approval, conflict with or result in any breach of any provision of the Company's Articles of Incorporation or bylaws, (ii) result in a violation or breach of, or constitute (with or without due notice or lapse of time or both) a default (or give rise to any right of termination, guaranteed payment, loss of rights, cancellation or acceleration) under any of the terms, conditions or provisions of any material Contract to which the Company is a party or by which it or any of its properties or assets may be bound or any material Company Permit, (iii) violate any order, writ, injunction, decree, statute, rule or regulation applicable to the Company or any of its properties or assets or (iv) result in the creation of any material pledges, liens and security interests of any kind or nature whatsoever ("Liens") upon any of the properties or assets of the Company, except in the case of clauses (ii) through (iv) for such matters that would not, individually or in the aggregate, have a Company Material Adverse Effect.

(b)   No filing or registration with, or authorization, consent or approval of, any Governmental Entity (other than filings, registrations, authorizations, consents and approvals the failure of which to make or obtain would not, individually or in the aggregate, have a Company Material Adverse Effect or, after giving effect to the Merger, on Buyer) is required by or with respect to the Company in connection with the execution and delivery of this Agreement by the Company or is necessary for the consummation by the Company of the Merger and the other transactions contemplated by this Agreement, except (i) receipt from the WUTC of approvals and orders, as applicable, pertaining to the Merger (excluding any approvals or orders relating to the Rate Case, the "WUTC Approval"), (ii) receipt from the OPUC of approvals and orders, as applicable, pertaining to the Merger (the "OPUC Approval"), (iii) in connection, or in compliance, with the provisions of the Hart-Scott-Rodino Antitrust Improvements Act of 1976, as amended (the "HSR Act"), (iv) the filing of the Articles of Merger with the Secretary of State of Washington, and appropriate documents with the similar relevant authorities of other states in which the Company is qualified to do business, (v) as may be required by state takeover laws and foreign or supranational laws relating to antitrust and competition clearances disclosed on Section 3.5(b) of the Company Disclosure Schedules, (vi) such filings as may be required in connection with the Taxes described in Section 6.6, (vii) as may be required under the Securities Act of 1933, as amended, together with the rules and regulations promulgated thereunder (the "Securities Act") or the Securities Exchange Act of 1934, as amended, together with the rules and regulations promulgated thereunder (the "Exchange Act") and (viii) such other filings, registrations, authorizations, consents and approvals as set forth on Section 3.5(b) of the Company Disclosure Schedules (collectively, whether or not legally required to be made or obtained, the "Company Required Statutory Approvals"). References to "obtained" with respect to Company Required Statutory Approvals will include the making of all filings and registrations and the giving of all applicable notices. "Governmental Entity" means any federal, state, local or foreign government or any court, tribunal, administrative agency or commission or other governmental or other regulatory authority or agency, domestic, foreign or supranational.

Section 3.6   SEC Documents; Financial Statements; and Other Reports.

(a)   The Company has timely filed with or furnished to the SEC the documents required to be filed or furnished by it since December 31, 2001 under the Securities Act or the Exchange Act. As of their respective filing or furnishing dates, the Company Filed SEC Documents complied in all material respects with the requirements of the Securities Act or the Exchange Act, as the case may be, each as in effect on the date so filed or furnished, and at the time filed with the SEC, none of the Company Filed SEC Documents so filed contained any untrue statement of a material fact or omitted to state a material fact required to be stated therein or necessary to make the statements therein, in light of the circumstances under which they were made, not misleading. The consolidated financial statements of the Company included in the Company Filed SEC Documents complied as of their respective dates in all material respects with the then applicable accounting requirements and the published rules and regulations of the SEC with respect thereto, were prepared in accordance with GAAP (except in the case of the unaudited statements, as permitted by Form 10-Q under the Exchange Act) applied on a consistent basis during the periods involved (except as may be indicated therein or in the notes thereto) and fairly present in all material respects the consolidated financial position of the Company and its consolidated Subsidiaries as at the dates thereof and the consolidated results of their operations and their consolidated cash flows for the periods then ended all in accordance with GAAP (subject, in the case of unaudited statements, to normal year-end audit adjustments and to any other adjustments described therein that were not or are not expected to be, individually or in the aggregate, materially adverse to the Company).

(b)   (i) The Company has filed with the WUTC and the OPUC or the appropriate public utilities commission, as the case may be, all material documents required to be filed by it under applicable state public utility laws and regulations, and (ii) all such documents complied, as of the date so filed or, if amended, as of the date of the last amendment prior to the date hereof, in all material respects with all applicable requirements of the applicable statute and rules and regulations thereunder, except for filings the failure of which to make, or the failure of which to make in compliance with all applicable requirements of the applicable statute and the rules and regulations thereunder, individually or in the aggregate, have not had and could not reasonably be expected to have a Company Material Adverse Effect.

Section 3.7   Absence of Material Adverse Effect. Between September 30, 2005 and the date hereof the Company has conducted its business in all material respects only in the ordinary course, and there has not been (i) any Company Material Adverse Effect, (ii) any declaration, setting aside or payment of any dividend or other distributions with respect to its Capital Stock (other than (a) regular quarterly cash dividends paid by the Company on Company Common Stock with usual record and payment dates and consistent with the Company's past dividend policy and (b) material dividends and distributions by a direct or indirect Subsidiary of the Company to its parent or another Subsidiary of the Company), (iii) any split, combination or reclassification of any of its Capital Stock or any issuance or the authorization of any issuance of any other securities in respect of, in lieu of or in substitution for shares of its Capital Stock, (iv) any change in accounting methods, principles or practices by the Company, (v) any material damage, destruction or other casualty loss with respect to any material asset or property owned, leased or otherwise used by the Company, whether or not covered by insurance or (vi) any increase in the compensation payable or that could become payable by the Company to officers or key employees or any amendment of any of the Benefit Plans of the Company other than increases or amendments in the ordinary course. "Benefit Plan" means any bonus, pension, profit sharing, deferred compensation, incentive compensation, stock ownership, stock purchase, stock option, restricted stock, phantom stock, stock appreciation or other equity-based compensation, retirement, vacation, severance, disability, death benefit, hospitalization, medical, dental, vision care, life insurance or other plan, program or arrangement providing compensation or benefits to or in respect of any current or former employee, officer or director of the Company or Buyer, as the case may be, or any of their respective Subsidiaries.

Section 3.8   Information Supplied. None of the information supplied or to be supplied by the Company specifically for inclusion or incorporation by reference in the proxy statement (together with any amendments or supplements thereto, the "Proxy Statement") relating to the Company Shareholders Meeting to be filed by the Company with the SEC, will, at the time it is first mailed to the shareholders of the Company and at the time of the Company Shareholders Meeting, contain any untrue statement of a material fact or omit to state any material fact required to be stated therein or necessary in order to make the statements therein, in light of the circumstances under which they are made, not misleading. No representation or warranty is made by the Company with respect to statements made or incorporated by reference in the Proxy Statement based on information supplied by Buyer or any of its representatives specifically for inclusion or incorporation by reference therein.

Section 3.9   Compliance with Laws; Permits.

(a)   The business of the Company is not being and has not been conducted in material violation of any law, ordinance or regulation of any Governmental Entity, except for violations that would not, individually or in the aggregate, have a Company Material Adverse Effect. The Company is in possession of all franchises, authorizations, licenses, permits, easements, exceptions, consents, certificates, approvals and orders of any Governmental Entity necessary for the Company to own, lease and operate its properties or to carry on its business as it is now being conducted (the "Company Permits"), except where the failure to have any of the Company Permits would not, individually or in the aggregate, have a Company Material Adverse Effect. The Company has not received notice of any suspension or cancellation of any of the Company Permits, except where such suspension or cancellation would not, individually or in the aggregate, have a Company Material Adverse Effect. Notwithstanding the foregoing, no representation or warranty is made in this Section 3.9(a) with respect to Environmental Laws, which are covered exclusively by Section 3.14.

(b)   The Company is in compliance in all material respects with (i) the applicable provisions of the Sarbanes-Oxley Act of 2002 and the related rules and regulations promulgated thereunder or under the Exchange Act (the "Sarbanes-Oxley Act") and (ii) the applicable listing and corporate governance rules and regulations of the New York Stock Exchange, Inc. Except as permitted by the Exchange Act, including Sections 13(k)(2) and (3), since the enactment of the Sarbanes-Oxley Act, neither the Company nor any of its Affiliates has made, arranged or modified (in any material way) personal loans to any executive officer or director of the Company. "Affiliate" has the meaning as defined in Rule 12b-2 under the Exchange Act.

(c)   Each of the principal executive officer of the Company and the principal financial officer of the Company (or each former principal executive officer of the Company and each former principal financial officer of the Company) has made all certifications required by Rule 13a-14 or 15d-14 under the Exchange Act or Sections 302 and 906 of the Sarbanes-Oxley Act and the rules and regulations of the SEC promulgated thereunder with respect to Company Filed SEC Documents. For purposes of the preceding sentence, "principal executive officer" and "principal financial officer" have the meanings given to such terms in the Sarbanes-Oxley Act.

(d)   The Company has (i) designed disclosure controls and procedures to ensure that material information relating to it and its consolidated Subsidiaries is made known to its management by others within those entities and (ii) to the extent required by applicable laws, disclosed, based on its most recent evaluation, to its auditors and the audit committee of its Board of Directors (A) any significant deficiencies and material weaknesses in the design or operation of internal controls over financial reporting which are reasonably likely to adversely affect its ability to record, process, summarize and report financial information and (B) to the Knowledge of the Company, any fraud, whether or not material, that involves management or other employees who have a significant role in its internal control over financial reporting.

"Knowledge" means the actual knowledge of the Persons set forth on Section 1.1(a) of the Company Disclosure Schedules, in the case of the Company, and the actual knowledge of the Persons set forth on Section 1.1(a) of the Buyer Disclosure Schedules, in the case of Buyer.

(e)   Through the date hereof the Company has delivered to Buyer copies of any written notifications it has received since December 31, 2002 of a (i) "reportable condition" or (ii) "material weakness" in the Company's internal controls. For purposes of this Agreement, the terms "reportable condition" and "material weakness" have the meanings assigned to them in the Statements of Auditing Standards No. 60, as in effect on the date hereof.

(f)   Section 3.9(f) of the Company Disclosure Schedules lists any Off-Balance Sheet Arrangements of the Company. "Off-Balance Sheet Arrangement" has the meaning given to "off-balance sheet arrangement" in Section 303(a) of Regulation S-K of the SEC.

(g)   Section 3.9(g) of the Company Disclosure Schedules contains a description of all non-audit services performed by the Company's auditors for the Company and its Subsidiaries for the fiscal year ended September 30, 2005 and the fees paid for such services. All such non-audit services, and any non-audit services performed by the Company's auditors for the Company and its Subsidiaries since September 30, 2005, have been approved as required by Section 202 of the Sarbanes-Oxley Act.

Section 3.10   Tax Matters.

(a)   (i) The Company, each Subsidiary of the Company and each Company Group has timely filed all Tax Returns required to be filed, except where the failure to timely file would not, individually or in the aggregate, have a Company Material Adverse Effect, (ii) all such Tax Returns are true, correct and complete and disclose all Company Material Taxes required to be paid by the Company, each Subsidiary of the Company and each Company

Group for the periods covered thereby, except where the failure to be true, correct and complete or to disclose all Company Material Taxes would not, individually or in the aggregate, have a Company Material Adverse Effect, (iii) none of the Company, any Subsidiary of the Company or any Company Group is currently the beneficiary of any extension of time within which to file any Tax Return, (iv) all Taxes (whether or not shown on any Tax Return) due and payable by the Company, any Subsidiary of the Company or any Company Group have been timely paid, except where the failure to timely pay would not, individually or in the aggregate, have a Company Material Adverse Effect, (v) neither the Company nor any Subsidiary of the Company has waived or been requested in writing to waive any statute of limitations in respect of Company Material Taxes which waiver is currently in effect, (vi) the Tax Returns referred to in clause (i) have been examined by the appropriate taxing authority or the period for assessment of the Taxes in respect of which each such Tax Return was required to be filed (taking into account all applicable extensions and waivers) has expired, (vii) there is no action, suit, proceeding, audit, claim or assessment pending, and to the Knowledge of the Company there is no action, suit, proceeding, inquiry, investigation, audit, claim or assessment proposed in writing or threatened in writing with respect to Taxes of the Company, any Subsidiary of the Company or any Company Group, except for such actions, suits, proceedings, audits, claims or assessments that would not singularly or in the aggregate have a Company Material Adverse Effect, (viii) all deficiencies asserted or assessments made as a result of any examination of any Tax Returns required to be filed by the Company, any Subsidiary of the Company or any Company Group have been paid in full or finally settled, (ix) there are no Liens for Taxes upon the assets of the Company or any Subsidiary of the Company except Liens relating to current Taxes not yet due or except to the extent such Liens would not, individually or in the aggregate, have a Company Material Adverse Effect, (x) all material Taxes which the Company or any Subsidiary of the Company are required by law to withhold have been duly withheld and paid to the appropriate tax authorities, (xi) to the Knowledge of the Company, neither the Company nor any Subsidiary of the

Company has any material liability for Taxes of another Person under Treasury Regulation §1.1502-6 (or any similar provision of state, local or foreign law), (xii) to the extent the Company, any Subsidiary of the Company or any Affiliate thereof has participated in a transaction that is a "reportable transaction" within the meaning of Section 6707A(c)(1) of the Code, information with respect to such transaction has been adequately disclosed to the Internal Revenue Service ("IRS") in compliance with applicable reporting requirements and (xiii) neither the Company nor any Subsidiary of the Company has constituted either a "distributing corporation" or a "controlled corporation" (within the meaning of Section 355(a)(1)(A) of the Code) in a distribution of stock qualifying for tax-free treatment under Section 355 of the Code (i) in the two years prior to the date of this Agreement or (ii) in a distribution which could otherwise constitute part of a "plan" or "series of related transactions" (with the meaning of Section 355(e) of the Code) in conjunction with the transactions contemplated by this Agreement. For purposes of the representations and warranties contained in this Section 3.10(a), references to the Company or any Subsidiary of the Company includes, except where the context requires otherwise, any predecessor thereof. "Company Group" means (a) any "affiliated group" (as defined in Section 1504(a) of the Code without regard to the exceptions set forth in Section 1504(b) of the Code) that, at any time on or before the Closing Date, includes or included the Company (or any predecessor), any Subsidiary of the Company (or any predecessor) or any combination thereof or that, at any time on or before the Closing Date, has or had the Company (or any predecessor) or any Subsidiary of the Company (or any predecessor) as the common parent corporation, and (b) any other group of entities that, at any time on or before the Closing Date, files or has filed, or is or has been required to file, Tax Returns on a combined, consolidated or unitary basis and includes or included the Company (or any predecessor), any Subsidiary of the Company (or any predecessor) or any combination thereof or that, at any time on or before the Closing Date, files or has filed or is, or has been required to file, Tax Returns on a combined, consolidated or unitary basis and has or had the Company (or any predecessor) or any Subsidiary of the Company (or any predecessor) as the common parent corporation.

(b)   No transaction contemplated by this Agreement is subject to withholding under Section 1445 of the Code.

(c)   Neither the Company nor any Subsidiary of the Company is a party to any indemnification, allocation or sharing agreement with respect to Taxes that could give rise to a material payment or indemnification obligation (other than agreements among the Company and its Subsidiaries and other than customary Tax indemnifications contained in credit or other commercial lending agreements).

(d)   Each of the Company and its Subsidiaries and their respective successors will not be required to include any item of income in, exclude any item of deduction from, or otherwise adjust, taxable income for any taxable period ending after the Closing Date as a result of any: (i) change in method of accounting for a taxable period (or portion thereof) ending on or prior to the Closing Date; (ii) agreement by the Company or any Subsidiary with a tax authority relating to Taxes executed on or prior to the Closing Date; (iii) installment sale or open transaction disposition or intercompany transaction made or deemed to be made on or prior to the Closing Date; (iv) the completed contract method of accounting or other method of accounting applicable to long-term contracts (or any comparable provisions of state, local or foreign law); (v) prepaid amount received on or prior to the Closing Date; or (vi) other Tax positions, elections or methods taken, made, or used by the Company or any of its Subsidiaries having the effect of either deferring taxable income to taxable periods or portions thereof ending after the Closing Date or accelerating deductions to taxable periods or portions or thereof ending on or prior to the Closing Date.

(e)   None of the Company or any of its Subsidiaries has received written notice from any governmental entity in a jurisdiction in which such entity does not file a Tax Return stating that such entity is or may be subject to taxation by that jurisdiction.

(f)   Neither Company nor any of the Subsidiaries is party to any agreement, contract or arrangement or plan that resulted or will result, separately or in the aggregate in the payment of any amount that is not deductible pursuant to Code section 404 or 162 (or any corresponding provision of state, local or foreign Tax law).

(g)   "Tax Return" means any return, report or similar document filed or required to be filed with respect to any Tax (including any attached schedules), including any information return, claim for refund, amended return or declaration of estimated Tax. "Company Material Taxes" means (i) federal income Taxes imposed on the Company, any Subsidiary of the Company or any Company Group, (ii) material state income Taxes imposed on the Company, any Subsidiary of the Company or any Company Group and (iii) material foreign Taxes imposed on the Company, any Subsidiary of the Company or any Company Group (including, in the case of each reference to the Company or any Subsidiary of the Company, any predecessor thereof).

Section 3.11   Litigation. There is no suit, action, order or proceeding pending, and to the Knowledge of the Company no suit, action, order, proceeding or investigation is threatened, against the Company that would, individually or in the aggregate, have a Company Material Adverse Effect. The Company is not subject to any outstanding judgment, order, writ, injunction or decree that would, individually or in the aggregate, have a Company Material Adverse Effect. Notwithstanding the foregoing, no representation or warranty is made in this Section 3.11 with respect to Environmental Laws, which are covered exclusively by Section 3.14.

Section 3.12   Benefit Plans.

(a)   Section 3.12(a) of the Company Disclosure Schedules sets forth a true and complete list of each Benefit Plan (including each Benefit Plan maintained as of the date of this Agreement which is also an "employee pension benefit plan" (as defined in Section 3(2) of ERISA) or which is also an "employee welfare benefit plan" (as defined in Section 3(1) of ERISA) (an "ERISA Benefit Plan")) maintained by the Company. Except as required by law, the Company has not adopted or amended in any material respect any Benefit Plan since the date of the most recent audited financial statements included in the Company Filed SEC Documents. As of the date of this Agreement (i) none of the Company or any trade or business which is treated as a single employer ("ERISA Affiliate") with the Company under Section 414(b), (c), (m) or (o) of the Code contributes to any ERISA Benefit Plan that is a "multiemployer plan" (as defined in Section 3(37) of the Employee Retirement Income Security Act of 1974, as amended, together with the rules and regulations promulgated thereunder ("ERISA")) or maintains any ERISA Benefit Plan that is subject to Title IV of ERISA or Section 412 of the Code, (ii) there exists no material Contract, commitment, understanding, plan, policy or arrangement of any kind, whether written or oral, with or for the benefit of any current or former officer, director, employee or consultant, including each employment, compensation, deferred compensation, severance, pension, supplemental pension, life insurance, termination or consulting Contract or arrangement and any Contracts or arrangements associated with a change in control between the Company and any current or former employee, officer, director or consultant of the Company ("Compensation Commitments") and (iii) neither the Company nor any ERISA Affiliate maintains or contributes to any Benefit Plan or employ any employees outside of the United States.

(b)   With respect to each Benefit Plan listed on Section 3.12(a) of the Company Disclosure Schedules, correct and complete copies, where applicable, of the following documents have been made available to Buyer: (i) all Benefit Plan documents and amendments, trust agreements and insurance and annuity contracts and policies, (ii) the most recent IRS determination letter or opinion letter if the Benefit Plan is intended to satisfy the requirements for Tax favored treatment pursuant to Sections 401-417 or 501(c)(9) of the Code, (iii) the Annual Reports (Form 5500 Series) and accompanying schedules, as filed, for the three most recently completed plan years, (iv) any discrimination or coverage tests performed during the last two plan years and (v) the current summary plan description. True and complete copies of all written Compensation Commitments and of all related insurance and annuity policies and contracts and other documents with respect to each Compensation Commitment have been made available to Buyer. Section 3.12(b) of the Company Disclosure Schedules contains a true and complete description of all material oral Compensation Commitments.

(c)   Each Benefit Plan listed on Section 3.12(a) of the Company Disclosure Schedules which is intended to be a Benefit Plan that is intended to be qualified and exempt from federal income Taxes under Sections 401(a) and 501(a) of the Code (a "Qualified Plan") has received a favorable determination letter from the IRS that such plan is so qualified under the Code (or an application for such letter has been or will be submitted to the IRS within the applicable remedial amendment period) or has been established pursuant to a prototype plan that has received a favorable opinion letter from the IRS, and no circumstance exists which, might cause such plan to cease being so qualified except for any circumstance that would not, individually or in the aggregate, have a Company Material Adverse Effect. Each Benefit Plan listed on Section 3.12(a) of the Company Disclosure Schedules complies and has been maintained in all respects with its terms and all requirements of law and regulations applicable thereto, and there has been no notice issued by any Governmental Entity questioning or challenging such compliance, except for any circumstance that would not, individually or in the aggregate, have a Company Material Adverse Effect. Neither the Company nor any ERISA Affiliate has taken any action within the 12-month period ending on the date hereof to take corrective action or make a filing under any voluntary correction program of the IRS, Department of Labor or any other Governmental Entity with respect to any Benefit Plan or Compensation Commitment, and neither the Company nor any ERISA Affiliate has any Knowledge of any plan defect which would qualify for correction under any such program, except for any action, filing or plan defect that would not, individually or in the aggregate, have a Company Material Adverse Effect. There is no dispute, arbitration, grievance, action, suit or claim (other than routine claims for benefits) pending or, to the Knowledge of the Company, threatened involving such Benefit Plans or the assets of such plans that would, individually or in the aggregate, have a Company Material Adverse Effect. Neither the Company nor any ERISA Affiliate has any obligation under any welfare plans or otherwise to provide health or death benefits to or in respect of former employees of the Company, except as specifically required by the continuation requirements of Part 6 of Title I of ERISA or applicable state law. No plan or arrangement disclosed on Section 3.12(c) of the Company Disclosure Schedules that provides health or death benefits to or in respect of former employees of the Company or an ERISA Affiliate contains provisions that by their terms prohibit the Company or an ERISA Affiliate from amending or terminating such plan or arrangement at any time without the consent of any other Person and without incurring liability thereunder other than in respect of claims incurred prior to such amendment or termination. Neither the Company nor any ERISA Affiliate has, directly or indirectly, any liability (i) on account of any violation of the health care requirements of Part 6 of Title I of ERISA or Section 4980B of the Code, (ii) under Section 406, Section 502(c), Section 502(i) or Section 502(l) of ERISA or Section 4975 of the Code, (iii) under Section 302 of ERISA or Section 412 of the Code, (iv) under Sections 511, 4971, 4972, 4976, 4977, 4978, 4979, 4979A, 4980B or 5000 of the Code or (v) under Title IV of ERISA that would, individually or in the aggregate, have a Company Material Adverse Effect.

(d)   Neither the Company nor any ERISA Affiliate has, within the 12-month period ending on the date hereof, incurred and does not expect to incur any material withdrawal liability with respect to a "multiemployer plan" (within the meaning of Section 3(3) of ERISA) (a "Multiemployer Plan") (regardless of whether based on contributions of an ERISA Affiliate of the Company). No notice of a "reportable event," within the meaning of Section 4043 of ERISA for which the 30-day reporting requirement has not been waived or extended, has been required to be filed for any pension plan or by any ERISA Affiliate of the Company within the 12-month period ending on the date hereof or will be required to be filed in connection with the transactions contemplated by this Agreement.

(e)   All contributions or premiums required to be paid under the terms of any Benefit Plan maintained by the Company, collective bargaining agreement or by any applicable laws as of the date hereof have been timely made or have been reflected on the most recent consolidated balance sheet filed or incorporated by reference in the Company Filed SEC Documents. No Benefit Plan maintained by the Company that is subject to Section 412 of the Code or Section 302 of ERISA has an "accumulated funding deficiency" (whether or not waived) within the meaning of Section 412 of the Code or Section 302 of ERISA and the Company does not have an outstanding funding waiver. The Company has not provided, and is not required to provide, security to any Benefit Plan pursuant to Section 401(a)(29) of the Code.

(f)   Under each Benefit Plan maintained by the Company which is a single-employer plan (as defined in Section 4001(a)(15) of ERISA), as of the last day of the most recent plan year ended prior to the date hereof, the actuarially determined present value of all "benefit liabilities," within the meaning of Section 4001(a)(16) of ERISA (as determined on the basis of the actuarial assumptions contained in the Benefit Plan's most recent actuarial valuation), did not exceed the then current value of the assets of such Benefit Plan by more than $16,000,000 as of the date hereof, and there has been no material adverse effect in the financial condition of such Benefit Plan since the last day of the most recent plan year.

(g)   None of the execution and delivery of this Agreement, approval of this Agreement, or consummation of the transactions contemplated by this Agreement will: (i) entitle any employees of the Company to severance pay or any increase in severance pay upon termination of employment, (ii) accelerate the time of payment or vesting or trigger any payment of compensation or benefits under, increase the amount payable or trigger any other material obligation pursuant to, any of the Benefit Plans or Compensation Commitments, (iii) result in any breach or violation of, or a default under, any of the Benefit Plans or Compensation Commitments or (iv) limit or restrict the right of the Company or, after the consummation of the transactions contemplated hereby, Buyer or any of its Subsidiaries to merge, amend or terminate any of the Benefit Plans maintained by the Company or Compensation Commitments.

(h)   The Company is not a party to any agreement, plan or arrangement that, individually or considered collectively with such other agreements, plans or arrangements, could reasonably be expected to result in payments, in connection with the transactions contemplated by this Agreement, that would constitute a "parachute payment" to a "disqualified individual" as those terms are defined in Section 280G of the Code and the Treasury Regulations thereunder.

(i)   To the extent applicable, each Benefit Plan has complied with the "secondary payor" requirements of Section 1862(b)(2) of the Social Security Act and Section 1860D-13(b)(6) of the Social Security Act.

(j)   Neither the Company nor any ERISA Affiliates maintains, sponsors, or contributed to (or has at any time maintained, sponsored or contributed to, or been obligated to maintain, sponsor or contribute to): any welfare benefit fund within the meaning of Section 419 of the Code.

(k)   The Company and each ERISA Affiliate are not subject to any legal, contractual, equitable, or other obligation to (1) establish as of any date any employee benefit plan of any nature, including, without limitation, any pension, profit sharing, welfare, post-retirement welfare, stock option, stock or cash award, non-qualified deferred compensation or executive compensation plan, policy or practice; or (2) continue any Benefit Plan listed hereunder or otherwise (or to continue their participation in any such Benefit Plan) after the Closing Date; The Company may, in any manner, subject to the limitations imposed by applicable law or any applicable collective bargaining agreement, and without the consent of any employee, beneficiary or other Person, prospectively terminate, modify or amend any Benefit Plan, whether or not listed hereunder (or its participation in any such Benefit Plan) effective as of any date; and has made no representations or communications (directly or indirectly, orally, in writing or otherwise) with respect to participation, eligibility for benefits, vesting, benefit accrual coverage or other material terms of any Benefit Plan prior to the Closing Date to any employee, beneficiary or other Person other than any such representations or communications which are in accordance with the terms and provisions of each such Benefit Plan as in effect immediately prior to the Closing Date.

(l)   Any "nonqualified deferred compensation plan" (within the meaning of Section 409A of the Code) to which the Company is a party has at all times since the effective date of Section 409A of the Code, complied in operation with the requirements of Section 409A of the Code as set forth in regulatory guidance available as of the Closing Date, except for any circumstance that would not, individually or in the aggregate, have a Company Material Adverse Effect.

Section 3.13   Labor Matters.

(a)   The Company has complied with all applicable requirements of law which relate to prices, wages, hours, discrimination in employment and collective bargaining and to the operation of its business and is not liable for any arrears of wages or any withholding Taxes or penalties for failure to comply with any of the foregoing, except as would not, individually or in the aggregate, reasonably be expected to have a Material Adverse Effect on the Company. The collective bargaining agreements and labor Contracts to which the Company is a party, and all union organizing activities related to the Company of which the Company has Knowledge, are set forth on Section 3.13 of the Company Disclosure Schedules. The Company has not engaged in any unfair labor practice with respect to any Persons employed by or otherwise performing services primarily for the Company (the "Company Business Personnel"), and the Company has not received written notice of any unfair labor practice charge or complaint against the Company by the National Labor Relations Board or any comparable state agency pending or threatened in writing with respect to Company Business Personnel, except, in each case, as would not, individually or in the aggregate, reasonably be expected to have a Material Adverse Effect on the Company.

(b)   There is (i) no labor strike, dispute, slowdown or stoppage pending, or to the Knowledge of the Company threatened against or affecting the Company, that could interfere with the respective business activities of the Company, except as would not, individually or in the aggregate, reasonably be expected to have a Material Adverse Effect on the Company and (ii) no pending, or to the Knowledge of the Company threatened, employee or governmental claim or investigation regarding employment matters, including any charges to the Equal Employment Opportunity Commission or state employment practice agency or investigations regarding Fair Labor Standards Act or similar state law or other wage and hour compliance, or audits by the Office of Federal Contractor Compliance Programs, except as would not, individually or in the aggregate, reasonably be expected to have a Material Adverse Effect on the Company.

Section 3.14   Environmental Matters. Except for matters that would not, individually or in the aggregate, have a Company Material Adverse Effect:

(a)   the Company has materially complied at all times with all applicable Environmental Laws and all Company Permits issued pursuant to Environmental Laws;

(b)   the Company has not received any notice, demand, letter, claim or request for information alleging that the Company is or may be in violation of or subject to liability under any Environmental Law (including claims of exposure, personal injury or property damage); and

(c)   the Company is not party to any proceeding, or subject to any order, decree, injunction, indemnity or other agreement with any Governmental Entity or any third party resolving or relating to violations of or liability under any Environmental Law or liability with respect to Hazardous Substances.

(d)   "Environmental Law" means any federal, state, local or foreign statute, law, regulation, order, decree, permit, authorization, common law or agency requirement relating to: (i) the protection, investigation or restoration of the environment, health, safety or natural resources, (ii) the handling, use, presence, disposal, release or threatened release of any Hazardous Substance or radioactive material or (iii) noise, odor, indoor air, employee exposure, wetlands, pollution, contamination or any injury or threat of injury to persons or property relating to any Hazardous Substance or nuclear and radioactive materials. "Hazardous Substance" means any substance of a type or quantity which would reasonably be expected to require remediation pursuant to any Environmental Law that is (A) any petroleum product or by-product, asbestos-containing material, lead-containing paint, polychlorinated biphenyls or radioactive material or (B) any other substance which is regulated by or for which liability or standards of care are imposed by any Environmental Law.

Section 3.15   Regulation as a Utility. The Company is regulated as a public utility by the States of Washington and Oregon and by no other state. Except as set forth above, neither the Company nor any "subsidiary company" or "affiliate" of the Company is subject to regulation as a public utility or public service company (or similar designation) by any other state in the United States or any foreign country. The Company is a "gas utility company" as defined by the Public Utility Holding Company Act of 2005 ("PUHCA 2005").

Section 3.16   Title to Properties. The Company has good title in and to each material parcel of real property owned in fee by the Company, subject to no Liens that would, individually or in the aggregate, have a Company Material Adverse Effect or materially impair the Company's rights to or ability to use any such property. Section 3.16 of the Company Disclosure

Schedules lists all Contracts pursuant to which the Company leases real property.

Section 3.17   Regulatory Proceedings. Section 3.17 of the Company Disclosure Schedules sets forth each rate proceeding pending before a Governmental Entity with respect to rates charged by the Company. Other than fuel adjustment or purchase gas adjustment or similar adjusting rate mechanisms, the Company (a) does not have rates in any amounts that have been or are being collected subject to refund, pending final resolution of any rate proceeding pending before a Governmental Entity or on appeal to a court or (b) is not a party to any Contract with any Governmental Entity entered into other than in the ordinary course consistent with past practice imposing conditions on rates or services in effect as of the date hereof or which, to the Knowledge of the Company, are as of the date hereof scheduled to go into effect at a later time, except in each case as would not, individually or in the aggregate, have a Company Material Adverse Effect. No representation or warranty with respect to the Company Permits is made by this Section 3.17.

Section 3.18   Hedging Transactions. Section 3.18 of the Company Disclosure Schedules sets forth all agreements or arrangements which are related to hedges, forwards, derivatives or similar transactions (collectively "Hedging Transactions") to which the Company is a party as of the date noted on such Company Disclosure Schedules.

Section 3.19   Intellectual Property. The Company owns or has a valid right to use all patents, trademarks, trade names, service marks, domain names, copyrights, and any applications and registrations therefor, technology, trade secrets, know-how, computer software and tangible and intangible proprietary information and materials (collectively, "Intellectual Property Rights") used in connection with the business of the Company except as would not, individually or in the aggregate, have a Company Material Adverse Effect. No Person has notified the Company that its use of such Intellectual Property Rights infringes, misappropriates or violates any rights of any third party except where such infringement, misappropriation or violation would not, individually or in the aggregate, have a Company Material Adverse Effect. To the Company's Knowledge, no third party infringes, misappropriates or violates any Intellectual

Property Rights owned or exclusively licensed by or to the Company, except where such infringement, misappropriation or violation would not, individually or in the aggregate, have a Company Material Adverse Effect.

Section 3.20   Required Vote of the Company Shareholders. The affirmative vote of the holders of two-thirds of the issued and outstanding shares of Company Common Stock (the "Company Shareholder Approval") is the only vote of the holders of any class or series of the Company's Capital Stock necessary to approve this Agreement and the transactions contemplated by this Agreement.

Section 3.21   State Takeover Statutes. Assuming Buyer does not beneficially own 10% or more of the Company Common Stock on the date hereof, the action of the Board of Directors of the Company in approving the Merger, this Agreement and the transactions contemplated by this Agreement is sufficient to render inapplicable to Buyer, the Merger and this Agreement the provisions of Section 23B.19 of the WBCA and Article XII of the Company's Articles of Incorporation.

Section 3.22   Brokers. No broker, investment banker, financial advisor or other Person, other than J.P. Morgan Securities Inc. ("JPMorgan"), the fees and expenses of which will be paid by the Company (and are reflected in an agreement between JPMorgan and the Company, complete copies of which have been furnished to Buyer), is entitled to any broker's, finder's, financial advisor's or other similar fee or commission in connection with the transactions contemplated by this Agreement based upon arrangements made by or on behalf of the Company.

Section 3.23   Material Contracts.

(a)   As of the date hereof, the Company is not a party to or bound by any Contract that (i) is a "material contract" (as such term is defined in Section 601(b)(10) of Regulation S-K promulgated by the SEC) as to the Company, (ii) would, after giving effect to the Merger, limit or restrict the Surviving Corporation or any successor thereto, from engaging or competing in any line of business or in any geographic area or that contains restrictions on pricing (including most favored nation provisions) or exclusivity or non-solicitation provisions with respect to customers, (iii) limits or otherwise restricts the ability of the Company to pay dividends or make distributions to its shareholders, (iv) provides for the operation or management of any operating assets of the Company by any Person other than the Company and its Subsidiaries or (v) is a material guarantee or contains a material guarantee by the Company of any indebtedness or other obligations of any Person (each Contract referred to in (i) through (v) is a "Company Material Contract").

(b)   Each Company Material Contract is a valid and binding obligation of the Company enforceable against the Company in accordance with its terms and, to the Company's Knowledge, each other party thereto, and is in full force and effect, and the Company has performed in all material respects all obligations required to be performed by it to the date hereof under each Company Material Contract and, to the Company's Knowledge, each other party to each Company Material Contract has performed in all material respects all obligations required to be performed by it under such Company Material Contract, except, in each case, as would not, individually or in the aggregate, have a Company Material Adverse Effect. The Company has not received notice of any violation of or default under (or any condition which with the passage of time or the giving of notice would cause such a violation of or default under) any Company Material Contract to which it is a party or by which it or any of its properties or assets is bound, except for violations or defaults that would not, individually or in the aggregate, have a Company Material Adverse Effect or, after giving effect to the Merger, on Buyer. "Company Indebtedness" means (i) indebtedness for borrowed money of the Company, (ii) obligations of the Company evidenced by notes, bonds, debentures or other similar instruments or by letters of credit agreements, including purchase money obligations or other obligations relating to the deferred purchase price of property and (iii) direct or indirect guarantees by the Company of indebtedness for borrowed money of any Person.

ARTICLE IV
REPRESENTATIONS AND WARRANTIES
OF BUYER AND MERGER SUB

Buyer and Merger Sub hereby jointly and severally represent and warrant to the Company, other than as set forth in the Buyer Disclosure Schedules dated as of the date hereof (the "Buyer Disclosure Schedules") and except as disclosed in the documents (excluding any exhibits or portions thereof) filed with or furnished to the SEC by Buyer and publicly available on the Electronic Data Gathering, Analysis and Retrieval System prior to the date of this Agreement (the "Buyer Filed SEC Documents") (it being understood that any matter set forth in the Buyer Filed SEC Documents will be deemed to qualify any representation or warranty in this Article IV only to the extent that the description of such matter in the Buyer Filed SEC Documents is made in such a way as to make its relevance to the information called for by such representation or warranty readily apparent), as follows:

Section 4.1   Organization. Each of Buyer and Merger Sub is duly organized, validly existing and in good standing under the laws of the jurisdiction of its organization and has all requisite power and authority to carry on its businesses as now being conducted, except where the failure to be so organized, existing and in good standing or to have such power and authority would not, individually or in the aggregate, have a Buyer Material Adverse Effect. Buyer is duly qualified or licensed to do business and in good standing in each jurisdiction in which the nature of its business or the ownership or leasing of its properties makes such qualification or licensing necessary, except in such jurisdictions where the failure to be so duly qualified or licensed and in good standing would not, individually or in the aggregate, have a Buyer Material Adverse Effect. Buyer has delivered to the Company complete and correct copies of its Certificate of Incorporation and bylaws and the Articles of Incorporation and bylaws of Merger Sub. "Buyer Material Adverse Effect" means any event, effect, change or development that, individually or in the aggregate with other events, effects, changes or developments) has, or would reasonably be expected to have, a material and adverse effect on the ability of Buyer or Merger Sub to perform its obligations under this Agreement or to consummate the transactions contemplated hereby by the End Date. Merger Sub has been organized solely for the purpose of consummating the Merger and has conducted no business or engaged in any operations of any kind.

Section 4.2   Authority. On or prior to the date of this Agreement, the Board of Directors of each of Buyer and Merger Sub, and the sole shareholder of Merger Sub, approved the Merger and this Agreement. Each of Buyer and Merger Sub has all requisite corporate power and authority to execute and deliver this Agreement. Merger Sub has all requisite corporate power and authority to consummate the Merger. The execution, delivery and performance of this Agreement by Buyer and Merger Sub and the consummation by Merger Sub of the Merger and of the other transactions contemplated hereby have been duly authorized by all necessary corporate action on the part of Buyer and Merger Sub. This Agreement has been duly executed and delivered by Buyer and Merger Sub and (assuming the valid authorization, execution and delivery of this Agreement by the Company) constitutes the valid and binding obligation of Buyer and Merger Sub enforceable against them in accordance with its terms, except that such enforceability (i) may be limited by bankruptcy, insolvency, moratorium or other similar laws affecting or relating to the enforcement of creditors' rights generally and (ii) is subject to general principles of equity.

Section 4.3   Consents and Approvals; No Violations.

(a)   Except for filings, permits, authorizations, consents and approvals contemplated by Section 4.3(b) and as set forth on Section 4.3(a) of the Buyer Disclosure Schedules, neither the execution, delivery or performance of this Agreement by Buyer and Merger Sub nor the consummation by Buyer and Merger Sub of the transactions contemplated hereby will (i) conflict with or result in any breach of any provision of the Certificate of Incorporation or bylaws of Buyer or the Articles of Incorporation or bylaws of Merger Sub, (ii) result in a violation or breach of, or constitute (with or without due notice or lapse of time or both) a default (or give rise to any right of termination, guaranteed payment, loss of rights, cancellation or acceleration) under any of the terms, conditions or provisions of any Contract to which Buyer is a party or by which it or any of its properties or assets may be bound or any Buyer Permit, (iii) violate any order, writ, injunction, decree, statute, rule or regulation applicable to Buyer or Merger Sub or any of its properties or assets or (iv) result in the creation of any Lien upon any of the properties or assets of Buyer except in the case of clauses (ii) through (iv) for such matters that would not, individually or in the aggregate, have a Buyer Material Adverse Effect.

(b)   No filing or registration with, or authorization, consent or approval of, any Governmental Entity (other than filings, registrations, authorizations, consents and approvals the failure of which to make or obtain would not, individually or in the aggregate, have a Buyer Material Adverse Effect) is required by or with respect to Buyer in connection with the execution and delivery of this Agreement by Buyer and Merger Sub or is necessary for the consummation by Buyer and Merger Sub of the Merger and the other transactions contemplated by this Agreement, except (i) the WUTC Approval, (ii) the OPUC Approval, (iii) in connection, or in compliance, with the provisions of the HSR Act, (iv) the filing of the Articles of Merger with the Secretary of State of Washington and appropriate documents with the relevant authorities of other states in which Buyer or any of its Subsidiaries is qualified to do business, (v) as may be required by state takeover laws and foreign or supranational laws relating to antitrust and competition clearances disclosed on Section 4.3(b) of the Buyer Disclosure Schedules, (vi) such filings as may be required in connection with the Taxes described in Section 6.6, (vii) as may be required under the Exchange Act and (viii) such other filings, registrations, authorizations, consents and approvals as set forth on Section 4.3(b) of the Buyer Disclosure Schedules (collectively, whether or not legally required to be made or obtained, except for those items set forth on Section 4.3(b)(1) of the Buyer Disclosure Schedules, the "Buyer Required Statutory Approvals"). References to "obtained" with respect to Buyer Required Statutory Approvals will include the making of all filings and registrations and the giving of all applicable notices.

Section 4.4   Available Funds. Buyer has or will have available to it all funds necessary to deliver the Merger Consideration and satisfy all of its obligations hereunder.

Section 4.5   Information Supplied. None of the information supplied or to be supplied by Buyer specifically for inclusion or incorporation by reference in the Proxy Statement relating to the Company Shareholders Meeting will, at the time it is first mailed to the shareholders of the Company and at the time of the Company Shareholders Meeting, contain any untrue statement of a material fact, or omit to state any material fact required to be stated therein or necessary in order to make the statements therein, in light of the circumstances under which they are made, not misleading.

Section 4.6   Ownership of Company Common Shares. None of Buyer or its Subsidiaries owns any shares of Company Common Stock.

Section 4.7   Brokers. No broker, investment banker, financial advisor or other Person, other than UBS Securities LLC ("Buyer's Banker"), the fees and expenses of which will be paid by Buyer, is entitled to any broker's, finder's, financial advisor's or other similar fee or commission in connection with the transactions contemplated by this Agreement based upon arrangements made by or on behalf of Buyer.

Section 4.8   SEC Documents and Other Reports.

(a)   Buyer has timely filed with or furnished to the SEC all documents required to be filed or furnished by it since December 31, 2001 under the Securities Act or the Exchange Act. As of their respective filing or furnishing dates, the Buyer Filed SEC Documents complied in all material respects with the requirements of the Securities Act or the Exchange Act, as the case may be, each as in effect on the date so filed or furnished, and at the time filed with the SEC, none of the Buyer Filed SEC Documents so filed contained any untrue statement of a material fact or omitted to state a material fact required to be stated therein or necessary to make the statements therein, in light of the circumstances under which they were made, not misleading. The consolidated financial statements of Buyer included in the Buyer Filed SEC Documents complied as of their respective dates in all material respects with the then applicable accounting requirements and the published rules and regulations of the SEC with respect thereto, were prepared in accordance with GAAP (except in the case of the unaudited statements, as permitted by Form 10-Q under the Exchange Act) applied on a consistent basis during the periods involved (except as may be indicated therein or in the notes thereto) and fairly present in all material respects the consolidated financial position of Buyer and its consolidated Subsidiaries as at the dates thereof and the consolidated results of their operations and their consolidated cash flows for the periods then ended all in accordance with GAAP (subject, in the case of unaudited statements, to normal year-end audit adjustments and to any other adjustments described therein that were not or are not expected to be, individually or in the aggregate, materially adverse to Buyer).

(b)   The financial statements of each of the deconsolidated Subsidiaries of Buyer, if any, for each of the last three fiscal years fairly present in all material respects the financial position of such deconsolidated Subsidiary of Buyer as at the dates thereof and the results of their operations and their cash flows for the periods then ended (subject, in the case of unaudited statements, to normal year-end audit adjustments and to any other adjustments described therein).

Section 4.9   Litigation.   There is no suit, action, order or proceeding pending, and to the Knowledge of Buyer there is no suit, action, order, proceeding investigation threatened, against Buyer or any of its Subsidiaries that would, individually or in the aggregate, have a Buyer Material Adverse Effect. Neither Buyer nor any of its Subsidiaries is subject to any outstanding judgment, order, writ, injunction or decree that would, individually or in the aggregate, have a Buyer Material Adverse Effect.

ARTICLE V
COVENANTS RELATING TO CONDUCT OF BUSINESS

Section 5.1   Conduct of Business Pending the Merger.

(a)   Conduct of Business by the Company Pending the Merger. During the period from the date of this Agreement until the Effective Time, except as expressly permitted by this Agreement or as set forth on Section 5.1(a) of the Company Disclosure Schedules or as Buyer otherwise agrees in writing, the Company will and will cause each of its Subsidiaries to carry on its business in the ordinary course consistent with past practice and, to the extent consistent therewith, use reasonable efforts to preserve its business organization intact, maintain in full force and effect the Company Permits and maintain its existing relations and goodwill with Governmental Entities, customers, suppliers, distributors, creditors, lessors, licensors, licensees, employees and business associates to the end that their goodwill and ongoing businesses will not be impaired in any material respect at the Effective Time. Without limiting the generality of the foregoing, and except (i) as otherwise expressly permitted by this Agreement, (ii) as contemplated by the Confidential Evaluation Material, dated March 2006, previously provided by the Company to Buyer (the "CEM"), except as otherwise set forth below in this Section 5.1(a), or (iii) as set forth on Section 5.1(a) of the Company Disclosure Schedules, during the period from the date of this Agreement to the Effective Time, the Company will not, and will not permit any of its Subsidiaries to, without the prior written consent of Buyer (which consent will not be unreasonably withheld or delayed), take any of the following actions:

(i)   (A) declare, set aside or pay any dividends on, or make any other distributions in respect of, any of its Capital Stock, other than (1) dividends and distributions by a direct or indirect Subsidiary of the Company to its parent and (2) regular quarterly cash dividends and distributions with respect to the Company Common Stock, not to exceed $0.24 per share of Company Common Stock per quarter, and otherwise in accordance with the Company's dividend policy as set forth on Section 5.1(a)(i)(A)(2) of the Company Disclosure Schedules (regardless of any assumptions regarding dividends set forth in the CEM), with record dates and payment dates consistent with the Company's past dividend practice, (B) split, combine or reclassify any of its Capital Stock or issue or authorize the issuance of any other securities in respect of, in lieu of or in substitution for its Capital Stock or (C) purchase, redeem or otherwise acquire any Capital Stock of the Company or any of its Subsidiaries or any other securities thereof or any rights, warrants or options to acquire any Capital Stock or other securities thereof, other than purchases of shares of Company Common Stock for issuance to participants in the Company DRIP and the Company Employee Savings Plan;

(ii) issue, deliver, pledge, encumber, sell, dispose of or grant (A) any of its Capital Stock or any Capital Stock in any of its Subsidiaries, (B) any Company Voting Debt, Company Stock Equivalents or other voting securities, (C) any securities convertible into or exchangeable for, or any options, warrants or rights to acquire, any Capital Stock referred to in clause (A), Company Voting Debt, Company Stock Equivalents, voting securities or convertible or exchangeable securities or (D) any "phantom" stock, "phantom" stock rights, stock appreciation rights or stock-based performance units, other than (1) the issuance of Company Common Stock upon the exercise or conversion of awards made under the Company Stock Plans that are outstanding on the date of this Agreement and in accordance with their present terms, upon the exercise or conversion of awards granted under the Company Stock Plans awarded in accordance with Section 5.1(a)(ii)(D)(2) or pursuant to the terms of any Compensation Commitment as in effect on the date of this Agreement or as amended in accordance with or as permitted by this Agreement, (2) issuances by a direct or indirect Subsidiary of the Company of its Capital Stock to its parent, (3) the reissuance of shares of Company Common Stock that have been purchased in accordance with Section 5.1(a)(i)(C) pursuant to the Company DRIP and the Company Employee Savings Plan or (4) the annual issuance of 8,000 shares (in the aggregate) of Company Common Stock in accordance with Section 6.1 of the 2000 Director Stock Award Plan (as amended), as in effect on the date hereof.

(iii)   amend the Company's Articles of Incorporation or bylaws;

(iv)   (A) acquire or agree to acquire by merging or consolidating with, or by purchasing a substantial equity interest in or portion of the assets of, or by any other manner, any business or any corporation, partnership, joint venture, association or other business organization or division thereof, (B) acquire or agree to acquire any assets, other than in the ordinary course of business consistent with past practice or pursuant to capital expenditures made in accordance with Section 5.1(a)(ix) or (C) make any investment in the Capital Stock of, or other instrument convertible into or exchangeable for the Capital Stock of, any other Person (other than direct or indirect Subsidiaries of the Company that are direct or indirect Subsidiaries of the Company as of the date hereof);

(v)   except to the extent required by applicable law or by the terms of any Benefit Plan maintained by the Company, Compensation Commitment or collective bargaining agreement in effect as of the date of this Agreement, (A) grant to any current or former employee, officer or director of the Company or any of its Subsidiaries any increase in compensation or benefits or new incentive compensation grants except in the ordinary course of business consistent with past practice (including annual salary and compensation increases in respect of any fiscal year regardless of when such increases were approved), provided that such compensation and benefits increases, in the aggregate, do not result in an increase of more than 5% when compared to the prior year (excluding the effect of increases due to actuarial assumptions), (B) grant to any current or former employee, officer or director of the Company or any of its Subsidiaries any increase in severance, pay to stay or termination pay except to the extent consistent with past practice and that, in the aggregate, does not result in a material increase in benefits or compensation expenses, (C) enter into or amend any Compensation Commitment with any such current or former employee, officer or director, (D) establish, adopt, enter into or amend in any material respect any collective bargaining agreement or Benefit Plan, except with respect to any Benefit Plan maintained by the Company that is a Qualified Plan, as may be required to facilitate or obtain a determination from the IRS that such Benefit Plan is a Qualified Plan or (E) take or permit to be taken any action to accelerate any rights or benefits or the funding thereof, or make or permit to be made any material determinations not in the ordinary course of business consistent with past practice, under any collective bargaining agreement, Benefit Plan or Compensation Commitment; provided, however, that notwithstanding anything in this Section 5.1(a)(v) to the contrary, the foregoing will not restrict the Company or its Subsidiaries from entering into or making available to newly hired officers, or employees hired to fill existing positions or up to ten newly created positions, or to officers or employees in the context of promotions based on job performance or workplace requirements in the ordinary course of business consistent with past practice, plans, agreements (except employment, severance or change of control agreements), benefits and compensation arrangements (excluding equity grants) that have, consistent with past practice, been made available to newly hired or promoted officers or employees;

(vi)   make any material change in accounting methods, principles or practices except as required by GAAP, by regulatory authorities of competent jurisdiction or by law;

(vii)   sell, lease (as lessor), license or otherwise dispose of or subject to any Lien (other than Liens as required by after acquired property covenants in Contracts evidencing Company Indebtedness and Liens created in connection with the refinancing of Company Indebtedness in accordance with Section 5.1(a)(viii) that are no less favorable to the Company and its Subsidiaries than those Liens that were created in connection with the Company Indebtedness that is being refinanced) any properties or assets that are material, individually or in the aggregate, to the Company and its Subsidiaries, taken as a whole, other than sales of excess or obsolete assets in the ordinary course of business consistent with past practice;

(viii)   except with respect to indebtedness incurred under the Company's Amended and Restated Loan Agreement, dated as of September 30, 2004, with U.S. Bank National Association and the Company's uncommitted line of credit with The Bank of New York in the ordinary course of business consistent with past practice (A) incur any indebtedness for borrowed money or guarantee any such indebtedness of another Person, issue or sell any debt securities or warrants or other rights to acquire any debt securities of the Company or any of its Subsidiaries, guarantee any debt securities of another Person, enter into any "keep well" or other agreement to maintain any financial statement condition of another Person or enter into any arrangement having the economic effect of any of the foregoing, in each case, other than (1) in connection with any refinancing on commercially reasonable terms any borrowings of the Company or its Subsidiaries outstanding on the date hereof (or under any extensions or replacements thereof), including any revolving credit agreements or similar credit facilities and the Company's 8.50% medium term notes due October 2006, and (2) indebtedness incurred by any Subsidiary of the Company under any loan permitted by clause (B), or (B) make any loans, advances or capital contributions to, or investments in, any other Person, other than to or in the Company or any Subsidiary;

(ix)   make or agree to make any capital expenditure or expenditures, other than (A) expenditures in accordance with Section 5.1(a)(ix) of the Company Disclosure Schedules, (B) expenditures contemplated in the CEM and (C) expenditures to the extent made or agreed to be made in order to ensure compliance with the rules and regulations or an order of the WUTC or OPUC or any other Governmental Entity or to ensure compliance with the terms of any Permit, in which case, to the extent permissible under applicable law, the Company will consult with Buyer prior to making or agreeing to make any such expenditure;

(x)   engage in any activities not engaged in on the date hereof which would cause a change in the Company's status as a local distribution company under PUHCA 2005;

(xi)   enter into any Contract for the purchase and/or sale of natural gas ("Gas Supply Agreement") other than any Gas Supply Agreement entered into in the ordinary course of business consistent with past practice unless the Company consults with Buyer regarding such Gas Supply Agreement and the Company has obtained the prior written consent of Buyer to such Gas Supply Agreement or such Gas Supply Agreement is fully compliant with criteria to which Buyer has previously given a generic consent, in each case, which consent will not be unreasonably withheld or delayed, it being understood that in such consultation process Buyer and the Company will comply with all applicable laws and any applicable confidentiality or similar third party agreement;

(xii)   pay, discharge, settle, compromise or satisfy any material claims, liabilities, litigation or other obligations (absolute, accrued, asserted or unasserted, contingent or otherwise), or waive, release or assign any such material rights or claims, other than the payment, discharge or satisfaction (A) in the ordinary and usual course of business consistent with past practice or (B) in accordance with their terms, with respect to liabilities or other obligations reserved against in the financial statements in the Company Filed SEC Documents (in amounts not to exceed such reserves).

(xiii)   enter into any Hedging Transactions other than in the ordinary course of business consistent with past practice as set forth in Section 5.1(a)(xiii) of the Company Disclosure Schedule, provided, however, that all such Hedging Transactions (including those set forth in Section 5.1(a)(xiii) of the Company Disclosure Schedule) shall qualify for hedge accounting treatment under current accounting guidelines set forth in Statement of Financial Accounting Standards No. 133, "Accounting for Derivative Instruments and Hedging Activities";

(xiv)   adopt a plan of complete or partial liquidation or a dissolution or resolutions providing for or authorizing such a liquidation or a dissolution, restructuring, recapitalization or reorganization;

(xv)   commit or agree to take any of the foregoing actions; or

(xvi)   (A) make any change (or file any such change) in any method of Tax accounting for a material amount of Taxes, (B) make, change or rescind any material Tax election with respect to the Company or any Subsidiary of the Company (except as required by law), (C) settle or compromise any material Tax liability or otherwise pay or consent to any material assessment as the result of an audit, (D) file any amended Tax Return involving a material amount of additional Taxes (except as required by law), (E) enter into any closing agreement relating to a material amount of Taxes, or (F) waive or extend the statute of limitations in respect of Taxes (other than pursuant to extensions of time to file Tax Returns obtained in the ordinary course of business), other than, in each case, in the ordinary course of business and consistent with past practice.

(b)   Conduct of Business by Buyer Pending the Merger. During the period from the date of this Agreement until the Effective Time, except as expressly permitted by this Agreement or as the Company otherwise agrees in writing, Buyer agrees that it will not acquire or agree to acquire any asset or to make any investment in any Person to the extent such agreement, acquisition or investment would reasonably be expected to have a material adverse effect on the ability of Buyer or the Company to obtain any Buyer Required Statutory Approval or Company Required Statutory Approval, respectively, or to delay by a material period the receipt thereof.

Section 5.2   No Solicitation.

(a)   From the date hereof until the earlier of the Effective Time or the date on which this Agreement is terminated in accordance with the terms hereof, the Company will not, nor will it permit any of its Subsidiaries to, nor will it or its Subsidiaries authorize or permit any of their respective officers, directors, employees, representatives or agents to, directly or indirectly, (i) solicit, initiate or knowingly encourage or facilitate (including by way of furnishing non-public information regarding the Company or its Subsidiaries) any inquiries regarding, or the making of any proposal which constitutes or that may reasonably be expected to lead to, any Takeover Proposal, (ii) enter into any letter of intent or agreement related to any Takeover Proposal (each, an "Acquisition Agreement") or (iii) participate in any discussions or negotiations regarding, or that may reasonably be expected to lead to, any

Takeover Proposal; provided, however, that if, at any time after the date hereof and prior to the receipt of the Company Shareholder Approval the Company receives an unsolicited bona fide written Takeover Proposal from any third Person that in the good faith judgment of the Company's Board of Directors constitutes, or is reasonably likely to constitute, a Superior Proposal and the Board of Directors of the Company determines in good faith, after consultation with outside counsel, that the failure to take any of the following actions in (A) through (C) with respect to such Takeover Proposal would be reasonably likely to result in a breach of its fiduciary duties under applicable law, the Company may, in response to such Superior Proposal, (A) furnish information with respect to the Company to any such Person and its representatives pursuant to a confidentiality agreement no more favorable to such Person than the Confidentiality Agreement is to Buyer, (B) participate in discussions and negotiations with such Person regarding such Superior Proposal and (C) enter into, approve or recommend (or propose any of the foregoing) any letter of intent or agreement involving the Company or any Subsidiary of the Company related to any Takeover Proposal or Superior Proposal if (1) prior to furnishing such non-public information to such third Person the Company provides at least two business days advance written notice to Buyer of the identity of the third Person making, and the proposed material terms and conditions of, such Superior Proposal and (2) the Company continues to comply with this Section 5.2. "Takeover Proposal" means any proposal or offer from any Person (other than Buyer and its Affiliates) that contemplates, or could reasonably be expected to lead to, a Takeover Transaction. "Takeover Transaction" means a proposal or offer relating to (x) any direct or indirect acquisition or purchase of 10% or more of the assets of the Company and its Subsidiaries, taken as a whole (other than a proposal to acquire or purchase the building in which the Company's principal executive offices are located on the date hereof) or 10% or more of the voting power of the Capital Stock of the Company then outstanding, (y) any tender offer or exchange offer that if consummated would result in any Person beneficially owning 10% or more of the voting power of the Capital Stock of the Company then outstanding, or (x) any merger, consolidation, business combination, recapitalization, liquidation, dissolution or similar transaction involving the Company, as a result of which a third party or the shareholders of a third party would acquire 10% or more of the voting power of the Capital Stock of the Company then outstanding, other than the transactions with Buyer contemplated by this Agreement. "Superior Proposal" means any bona fide written offer made by any Person (other than Buyer and its Affiliates) to acquire, directly or indirectly, for consideration consisting of cash and/or securities, more than 50% of the voting power of the Capital Stock of the Company then outstanding or all or substantially all the assets of the Company and otherwise on terms which the Board of Directors of the Company determines in good faith (after consultation with its financial and other advisors) to be more favorable (taking into account (I) all financial and strategic considerations, including relevant legal, financial, regulatory and other aspects of such Takeover Proposal and the Merger and the other transactions contemplated by this Agreement deemed relevant by the Board of Directors, (II) the identity of the third party making such Takeover Proposal and (III) the conditions and prospects for completion of such Takeover Proposal) to the Company's shareholders than the Merger (and any revised proposal made by Buyer), which is reasonably capable of being completed on the terms proposed (taking into account the ability to deliver any consideration to be paid in connection with such transaction and obtain required regulatory approvals).

(b)   Except as contemplated in Section 5.2(a) and otherwise in this Agreement, neither the Board of Directors of the Company nor any committee thereof will (i) withdraw, qualify or modify, in a manner adverse to Buyer, the approval by such Board of Directors of the Merger and this Agreement and the transactions contemplated hereby or the recommendation by such Board of Directors of this Agreement, (ii) approve or recommend, or propose to approve or recommend, any Takeover Proposal or (iii) authorize or permit the Company or any of its Subsidiaries to enter into any Acquisition Agreement.

(c)   Nothing contained in this Section 5.2 will prohibit the Company and its Board of Directors from complying with Rules 14d-9 or 14e-2 promulgated under the Exchange Act with respect to a Takeover Proposal; provided, however, that compliance with such rules will not in any way limit or modify the effect that any action taken pursuant to such rules has under any other provision of this Agreement, including Section 8.1(d).

(d)   The Company agrees that it and its Subsidiaries will, and the Company will direct and cause its and its Subsidiaries' respective officers, directors, employees, representatives and agents to, immediately cease and cause to be terminated any activities, discussions or negotiations with any Persons with respect to any Takeover Proposal. The Company agrees that it will notify Buyer in writing as promptly as practicable (and in any event within two business days) after any Takeover Proposal is received by, any information is requested by any Person who the Board of Directors in good faith believes is reasonably likely to make a Takeover Proposal from, or any discussions or negotiations relating to a Takeover Proposal are sought to be initiated or continued with, the Company, its Subsidiaries, or their officers, directors, employees, representatives or agents. The notice will indicate the name of the Person making such Takeover Proposal or taking such action and the material terms and conditions of any proposals or offers, and thereafter the Company will keep Buyer informed, on a current basis, of the status and materials terms of any such proposals or offers and the status of any such discussions or negotiations.

Section 5.3   <u>Rate and Regulatory Matters</u>. To the extent permitted by applicable law, the Company will cause each of its Subsidiaries to deliver to Buyer a copy of each principal filing or agreement (other than filings or agreements related to a fuel adjustment or purchase gas adjustment or similar adjusting rate mechanism) related to its generally applicable rates, charges, standards of service, accounting or regulatory policy which could lead to a material change in any of those areas as soon as practicable and in any event no later than five business days prior to the filing or execution thereof so that Buyer may comment thereon. The Company will, and will cause its respective Subsidiaries to, make all such filings only in the ordinary course of business consistent with past practice or as required by a Governmental Entity or regulatory agency with appropriate jurisdiction or under existing settlement agreements to which the Company is a party.

Section 5.4   Disclosure of Certain Matters; Delivery of Certain Filings.

(a)   The Company will promptly notify Buyer if, to the Knowledge of the Company, there exists a material breach of a representation or warranty made by the Company contained herein or if there occurs, to the Knowledge of the Company, any change or event which results in the executive officers of the Company having a good faith belief that such change or event has resulted in, or is reasonably likely to result in, a material breach of a representation or warranty made by the Company contained herein. Buyer will promptly notify the Company if, to the Knowledge of Buyer, if there exists a material breach of a representation or warranty made by Buyer contained herein or if there occurs, to the Knowledge of Buyer, any change or event which results in the executive officers of Buyer having a good faith belief that such change or event has resulted in, or is reasonably likely to result in, a material breach of a representation or warranty made by Buyer contained herein. The Company will provide to Buyer, and Buyer will provide to the Company, copies of all filings made by the Company or Buyer, as the case may be, with any Governmental Entity in connection with this Agreement and the transactions contemplated hereby.

(b)   To the extent permitted by applicable law, the Company will, and will cause its Subsidiaries to, promptly notify Buyer of any written communication with or notice from any taxing authority relating to any material Tax audit or examination relating to any material Taxes, any extension of any statute of limitations relating to Taxes or any change in method of accounting relating to material Taxes.

(c)   To the extent permitted by applicable law, the Company will, and will cause its Subsidiaries to, consult with Buyer with respect to negotiations relating to the renewal of any collective bargaining agreement. No consultation in accordance with this Section 5.4(c) will be deemed to be a consent by either party to any action proposed by the other party with respect to renewal of a collective bargaining agreement.

(d) The Company and Buyer each will give prompt notice to the other of any proposed change that is reasonably likely to result in a Company Material Adverse Effect and Buyer Adverse Effect, respectively.

ARTICLE VI
ADDITIONAL AGREEMENTS

Section 6.1   Employee Benefits; Workforce Matters.

(a) From and after the Effective Time, the Surviving Corporation will, or will cause one of its Subsidiaries to, honor and perform in accordance with their respective terms (as in effect on the date of this Agreement or as amended in accordance with or as permitted by this Agreement), all the collective bargaining agreements to which the Company or one of its Subsidiaries is a party and is set forth on Section 3.13(a) of the Company Disclosure Schedules. Nothing in this Section 6.1(a) will be interpreted to prevent the Surviving Corporation or any of its Subsidiaries from enforcing such agreements in accordance with their respective terms, including enforcement of any reserved right to amend, modify, suspend, revoke or terminate any such agreement.

(b) Subject to applicable law and obligations under each applicable collective bargaining agreement, Compensation Commitment and Benefit Plan, and except as provided in Section 2.3, the Surviving Corporation will, or will cause one of its Subsidiaries to, assume, maintain in effect, honor and perform in accordance with their respective terms (as in effect on the date of this Agreement or as amended or established in accordance with or as permitted by this Agreement) each Benefit Plan and Compensation Commitment listed on Section 3.12(a) of the

Company Disclosure Schedules and in effect on the date of this Agreement (or established as permitted by this Agreement), with respect to the current and former employees, officers or directors of the Company and its Subsidiaries who are covered by such plans or commitments immediately prior to the Effective Time. Nothing in this Section 6.1(b) will be interpreted to limit any reserved right contained in any such Benefit Plan or Compensation Commitment to amend, modify, suspend, revoke or terminate any such plan or commitment in accordance with its terms. As soon as practicable after the execution of this Agreement, the Company will provide Buyer with the documentation and information requested by Buyer to determine whether a merger of the Company Employee Savings Plan into the Buyer's 401(k) Plan would require amendment of the Buyer's 401(k) Plan in order to satisfy Section 411(d)(6) of the Code and applicable IRS regulations and rulings. If Buyer determines that the Company Employee Savings Plan should instead be terminated and gives the Company timely notice of that determination, the Company's Board of Directors will ensure that appropriate resolutions terminating the plan are passed by the Company's Board of Directors at least three (3) business days before the Closing Date, with such resolutions conditioned upon the Closing occurring.

(c)   Following the Effective Time, subject to the terms of this Agreement, applicable law and applicable collective bargaining agreements: (i) the Surviving Corporation will, in good faith and consistent with business needs, consider reductions in work force in a fair and equitable manner and in light of the circumstances and the objectives to be achieved, giving consideration to previous work history, job experience and qualifications and (ii) all employees of the Surviving Corporation will be entitled to fair and equitable consideration in connection with any job opportunities with the Surviving Corporation and its Subsidiaries, in each case without regard to whether employment prior to the Effective Time was with the Company and its Subsidiaries or the Surviving Corporation and its Subsidiaries.

(d)   Nothing contained in this Section 6.1 will be deemed to constitute an employment Contract between the Surviving Corporation or any Subsidiary of the Surviving Corporation and any individual, or a waiver of the Surviving Corporation's or any of its Subsidiaries' right to discharge any employee at any time, with or without cause.

Section 6.2   Shareholder Approval; Preparation of Proxy Statement; Other Actions.

(a)   As soon as practicable following the date of this Agreement the Company will duly call, give notice of, convene and hold a meeting of its shareholders (including any adjournments or postponements thereof, the "Company Shareholders Meeting") for the purpose of obtaining the Company Shareholder Approval. The Company will, through its Board of Directors, recommend to its shareholders that the Company Shareholder Approval be given and will not withdraw, qualify or modify, or propose to withdraw, qualify or modify, in a manner adverse to Buyer, the approval or recommendation by such Board of Directors of the Merger and this Agreement and the transactions contemplated hereby or the recommendation by such Board of Directors of the approval of the Merger and this Agreement or take any other action or make any other statement in connection with the Company Shareholders Meeting inconsistent with such recommendation or approval except to the extent expressly permitted in Section 5.2.

(b)   The Company, with Buyer's reasonable assistance, will promptly prepare and file with the SEC the Proxy Statement. The Company will distribute the Proxy Statement to its shareholders.

(c)   No filing of, or amendment or supplement to, the Proxy Statement (other than filings of Annual Reports on Form 10-K, Quarterly Reports on Form 10-Q and Current Reports on Form 8-K) will be made by the Company without providing Buyer the opportunity to review and comment thereon. If at any time prior to the Effective Time any information relating to Buyer or the Company, or any of their respective Affiliates or officers or directors, should be discovered by Buyer with respect to Buyer or any of its Subsidiaries or any of its Affiliates, officers or directors or the Company with respect to the Company or any of its Subsidiaries or any of its Affiliates, officers or directors which should be set forth in an amendment or supplement to the Proxy Statement, so that any of such documents would not include any misstatement of a material fact or omit to state any material fact necessary to make the statements therein, in light of the circumstances under which they were made, not misleading, the party which discovers such information will promptly notify the other parties hereto and an appropriate amendment or supplement describing such information will be promptly filed with the SEC and, to the extent required by law, disseminated to the shareholders of the Company.

Section 6.3   Access to Information.

(a)   Upon reasonable notice and subject to the terms of the Confidentiality Agreement, dated as of February 28, 2006, between the Company and Buyer, as the same may be amended, supplemented or modified (the "Confidentiality Agreement"), and applicable laws relating to the exchange of information, the Company will, and will cause its Subsidiaries to, afford to the Buyer and its officers, employees, accountants, counsel, financial advisors, consultants and other representatives reasonable access, during normal business hours during the period prior to the Effective Time, to all its properties, books, contracts and records and personnel and, during such period, the Company will (and will cause its Subsidiaries to) make available to Buyer or its designated advisors (i) a copy of each report, schedule, registration statement and other document filed or received by it during such period pursuant to the requirements of the federal or state securities laws or the federal Tax laws, (ii) all other information concerning its business, properties and personnel as Buyer may reasonably request and (iii) copies of any written notifications it has received after the date hereof of a (A) "reportable condition" or (B) "material weakness" in the Company's internal controls.

(b)   No investigation or exchange of information or other action pursuant to this Section 6.3 will be deemed to affect any representation or warranty made by any party hereto in this Agreement.

Section 6.4   Fees and Expenses. Except as provided in this Section 6.4 and Section 8.2, all fees and expenses incurred in connection with the Merger, this Agreement and the transactions contemplated hereby will be paid by the party incurring such fees or expenses, whether or not the Merger is consummated; provided, however, that Buyer and the Company will share equally up to $2,000,000 in the aggregate of (i) all fees and expenses (but excluding fees and expenses of legal counsel and investment bankers) incurred in relation to the preparing, printing, filing and mailing of the Proxy Statement (including any related preliminary materials) and any amendments or supplements thereto, and (ii) if the Company Shareholder Approval is obtained, all fees and expenses incurred by the Company (including fees and expenses of legal counsel, consultants, accountants and investment bankers, excluding, however, the Company's fees for its investment bankers in connection with the Merger) related to any efforts to obtain the Company Required Statutory Approvals (including, for the purposes of this sentence, any efforts in connection with the Rate Case).

Section 6.5   Public Announcements; Employee Communications. Buyer and the Company will consult with each other before issuing any press release or otherwise making any public statements with respect to the transactions contemplated by this Agreement and will not issue any such press release or make any such public statement prior to such consultation, except as may be required by applicable law, fiduciary duties or by obligations pursuant to any listing agreement with any national securities exchange, and each party hereto will use reasonable efforts to provide copies of such release or other announcement to the other party, and give due consideration to such comments as such other party may have, prior to such release or announcement.

Section 6.6   Transfer Taxes. The Company and Buyer will cooperate in the preparation, execution and filing of all returns, questionnaires, applications or other documents regarding any real property transfer or gains, sales, use, documentary, transfer, value added, stock transfer and stamp Taxes, any transfer, recording, registration and other fees and any similar Taxes which become payable under applicable law in connection with the transactions contemplated by this Agreement. Notwithstanding the foregoing, the Surviving Corporation will be responsible for any pay any real estate transfer tax under Chapter 82.45 of the Revised Code of Washington in connection with the transactions contemplated hereby and will hold the holders of the Company Common Shares harmless therefrom.

Section 6.7   State Takeover Laws. If any "fair price" or "control share acquisition" statute or other similar statute or regulation is or becomes applicable to the transactions contemplated hereby, the Company and its Board of Directors will use its reasonable best efforts to grant such approvals and take such actions as are necessary so that the transactions contemplated hereby may be consummated as promptly as practicable on the terms contemplated hereby and otherwise act to minimize the effects of any such statute or regulation on the transactions contemplated hereby.

Section 6.8   Indemnification; Directors and Officers Insurance.

(a)   All rights to indemnification and exculpation from liabilities for acts or omissions occurring at or prior to the Effective Time now existing in favor of the current or former directors, officers, employees, or agents, or fiduciaries under benefit plans, currently indemnified by the Company and its Subsidiaries (each an "Indemnified Person"), as provided in their respective articles of incorporation, bylaws (or comparable organizational documents) or other agreements providing indemnification, will survive the Merger and will continue in full force and effect in accordance with their terms. In addition, from and after the Effective Time, Indemnified Persons who become directors, officers or employees, or fiduciaries under benefit plans, of the Surviving Corporation will be entitled to the indemnity rights and protections afforded to directors, officers, employees and fiduciaries under benefit plans of the Surviving Corporation. Without limiting the generality of the preceding sentence, in the event that any Indemnified Person becomes involved in any actual or threatened action, suit, claim, proceeding or investigation covered by this Section 6.8 after the Effective Time, the Surviving Corporation will promptly advance to such Indemnified Person his or her legal and other expenses (including the cost of any investigation and preparation incurred in connection therewith), subject to the receipt by the Surviving Corporation of an undertaking by or on behalf of such Indemnified Party to reimburse all amounts so advanced in the event of a non-appealable determination of a court of competent jurisdiction that such Indemnified Person is not entitled thereto.

(b)   The Surviving Corporation will purchase officers' and directors' liability insurance with an insurer substantially comparable to the insurer under the Company's current policy of at least the same coverage and amounts, containing terms and conditions no less favorable to the insured for a period of at least six years after the Effective Time and, prior to the Effective Time, Buyer will provide evidence to the Company of such insurance.

(c)   The provisions of this Section 6.8 are intended to be for the benefit of, and will be enforceable by, each Indemnified Person, his or her heirs and his or her personal representatives and will be binding on all successors and assigns of the Surviving Corporation and the Company.

Section 6.9   Appropriate Actions; Consents; Filings.

(a)   The Company and Buyer will cooperate with each other and use (and will cause their respective Subsidiaries to use) reasonable best efforts to take or cause to be taken all actions, and do or cause to be done all things, necessary, proper or advisable on its part under this Agreement and applicable laws to consummate and make effective the Merger and the other transactions contemplated by this Agreement as soon as reasonably practicable, including preparing and filing as promptly as reasonably practicable all documentation to effect all necessary notices, reports and other filings and to obtain as promptly as reasonably practicable all consents, registrations, approvals, permits and authorizations necessary or advisable to be obtained from any third party and/or any Governmental Entity in order to consummate the Merger or any of the other transactions contemplated by this Agreement, including obtaining the Buyer Required Statutory Approvals and the Company Required Statutory Approvals and other actions requested in order to satisfy the conditions to the parties' obligations set forth in Article VII.

(b)   Subject to applicable laws relating to the exchange of information, Buyer and the Company will have the right to review in advance, and to the extent practicable each will consult the other on, all the material information relating to Buyer or the Company, as the case may be, and any of their respective Subsidiaries, that appear in any filing made with, or material written materials submitted to, any third party and/or any Governmental Entity in connection with the Merger and the other transactions contemplated by this Agreement. In exercising the foregoing right, each of the Company and Buyer will act reasonably and as promptly as practicable.

(c)

(i)   Promptly after the date hereof, Buyer and the Company will establish a regulatory approval team (the "Regulatory Approval Team"), the chairperson (the "Chairperson") of which will be Bruce Imsdahl or such other person as may be designated by Buyer and the other members of which (the "Regulatory Approval Coordinators") will consist of representatives designated by the Company (the "Company Coordinators") and representatives designated by Buyer (the "Buyer Coordinators"), which will be equal in number unless Buyer and the Company otherwise agree. The Chairperson will assign areas of responsibility to the Regulatory Approval Coordinators. Subject to the terms and conditions of this Agreement, the Regulatory Approval Team will formulate the approach to be taken with respect to obtaining the Company Required Statutory Approvals and coordinate filings for such approvals as set forth below. The primary responsibility for formulating the approach to be taken with respect to obtaining the

Company Required Statutory Approvals will reside with the entire Regulatory Approval Team and not a committee thereof. The responsibility for formulating the approach to be taken with respect to all required approvals from Governmental Entities (including but not limited to the Buyer Required Statutory Approvals) other than the Company Required Statutory Approvals will reside with Buyer, unless Buyer otherwise agrees; provided, however, that Buyer will (A) regularly consult with the Company regarding such approvals and (B) not agree to any terms or conditions contained in or relating to such approvals without the Company's prior written consent, which consent shall not be unreasonably withheld.

(ii)   No committee of the Regulatory Approval Team or any member thereof or of the Regulatory Approval Team will make or commit to make any concessions, agreements or other undertakings with or to any Governmental Entity or other Person in connection with obtaining the Company Required Statutory Approvals or otherwise consummating the Merger and the other transactions related to the Merger without the prior approval of Buyer and the Company.

(d)   The Company and Buyer each will, through the Regulatory Approval Team, keep the other apprised of the status of matters relating to completion of the transactions contemplated hereby, including: (i) promptly furnishing the other with copies of notice or other material communications received by Buyer or the Company, as the case may be, or any of its Subsidiaries, from any third party and/or any Governmental Entity and (ii) providing the other with copies of any materials to be provided to any Governmental Entities, in each case with respect to the Merger and the other transactions contemplated by this Agreement.

(e)   Subject to applicable laws relating to the exchange of information, the Company and Buyer each will, upon request by the other, furnish the other with all information concerning itself, its Subsidiaries, directors, officers and shareholders and such other matters as may be reasonably necessary or advisable in connection with the Proxy Statement or any other material statement, filing, notice or application made by or on behalf of Buyer, the Company or any of their respective Subsidiaries to any third party and/or any Governmental Entity in connection with the Merger and the transactions contemplated by this Agreement.

(f)   The Company agrees to provide, and shall use commercially reasonably efforts to cause its officers, employees and advisors to provide, all cooperation reasonably requested by Buyer in connection with Buyer's arrangement of financing in connection with the Merger, including (x) participation in meetings, drafting sessions, due diligence sessions, management presentation sessions, road shows and meetings with rating agencies, (y) preparation of business projections or financial or other information required to be included in offering memoranda, prospectuses or similar documents and (z) using commercially reasonable efforts to obtain, at Buyer's expense, comfort letters of accountants and consents of accountants for use of their reports in connection with such financing and legal opinions with respect to the Company required to be delivered in connection with such financing. Buyer shall provide copies of any materials that contain information provided to Buyer by the Company that are to be provided to third parties in connection with any such financing efforts.

(g)   No investigation or exchange of information or other action pursuant to this Agreement will be deemed to modify any representation or warranty made by any party to this Agreement. In the event of a termination of this Agreement for any reason (other than because of a breach by the other party), each party will promptly return or destroy, or cause to be returned or destroyed, all nonpublic information obtained from the other party or any of its Subsidiaries.

(h)   The Company will be solely responsible with respect to all matters related to the Company's general rate application with the

WUTC (docket number UG-060256) (the "Rate Case"), including all communications and filings with the WUTC or any other third parties related thereto; provided that the Company will (i) regularly consult with Buyer regarding the Rate Case, (ii) promptly furnish Buyer with copies of notice or other material communications received by the Company from any third party with respect to the Rate Case, (iii) provide Buyer with copies of any materials to be provided to the WUTC with respect to the Rate Case and (iv) not settle or compromise all or any portion of the Rate Case without Buyer's prior written consent, which consent shall not be unreasonably withheld, provided, however, that such consent will not constitute a waiver of, otherwise have any effect on the rights of Buyer regarding, the condition set forth in Section 7.1(c)(ii).

Section 6.10   Charitable Contributions. Following the Effective Time, the Surviving Corporation will honor and pay all commitments of the Company and its Subsidiaries with respect to charitable contributions and local community support that are set forth on Section 6.10(a) of the Company Disclosure Schedules.

Section 6.11   Further Assurances. If at any time after the Effective Time the Surviving Corporation will consider or be advised that any deeds, bills of sale, assignments or assurances or any other acts or things are necessary, desirable or proper (a) to vest, perfect or confirm, of record or otherwise, in the Surviving Corporation its right, title or interest in, to or under any of the rights, privileges, powers, franchises, properties, permits, licenses or assets of the Company, or (b) otherwise to carry out the purposes of this Agreement, the Surviving Corporation and its proper officers and directors or their designees will be authorized to execute and deliver, in the name and on behalf the Company, all such deeds, bills of sale, assignments and assurances and to do, in the name and on behalf of the Company, all such other acts and things as may be necessary, desirable or proper to vest, perfect or confirm the Surviving Corporation's right, title or interest in, to or under any of the rights, privileges, powers, franchises, properties or assets of the Company and otherwise to carry out the purposes of this Agreement.

ARTICLE VII
CONDITIONS PRECEDENT

Section 7.1   Conditions to Each Party's Obligation to Effect the Merger. The respective obligations of each party to effect the Merger will be subject to the fulfillment at or prior to the Effective Time of the following conditions:

(a)   Shareholder Approval. The Company Shareholder Approval will have been obtained.

(b)   No Prohibition. No Governmental Entity of competent jurisdiction will have enacted, issued, promulgated, enforced or entered any statute, law, ordinance, rule, regulation, judgment, decree, injunction or other order (whether temporary, preliminary or permanent) that is in effect and restrains, enjoins or otherwise prohibits consummation of the Merger or the other transactions contemplated by this Agreement (collectively, an "Order"), and no federal or state Governmental Entity will have instituted any action, suit or proceeding that is pending seeking any such Order.

(c)   Regulatory Consents.

(i)   The waiting period (and any extension thereof) applicable to the consummation of the Merger under the HSR Act will have expired or been terminated.

(ii)   Other than as set forth in Section 7.1(c)(i), the Buyer Required Statutory Approvals and Company Required Statutory Approvals (including solely for the purpose of this Section 7.1(c)(ii), a Final Order relating to the Rate Case) will have been obtained and will have become Final Orders and such Final Orders will not impose terms or conditions that, in the aggregate, have had or could reasonably be expected to have a Company Material Adverse Effect (but excluding, solely for the purposes of this Section 7.1(c)(ii), matters described in clause (E) of the definition of "Company Material Adverse

Effect"). "Final Order" means any action by the relevant Governmental Entity which has not been reversed, stayed, enjoined, set aside, annulled or suspended, with respect to which any waiting period prescribed by law before the transactions contemplated hereby may be consummated has expired, and as to which all conditions to the consummation of such transactions prescribed by law, regulation or order have been satisfied.

(iii)   Other than the filings provided for in Section 1.3, Section 7.1(c)(i) and (ii), and in Section 4.3(b)(1) of the Buyer Disclosure Schedules, all other notices, reports and other filings required to be made prior to the Effective Time by the Company or Buyer or any of their respective Subsidiaries with, and all other consents, registrations, approvals, permits and authorizations required to be obtained prior to the Effective Time by the Company or Buyer or any of their respective Subsidiaries from, any Governmental Entity in connection with the execution and delivery of this Agreement and the consummation of the Merger and the other transactions contemplated hereby by the Company and Buyer will have been made or obtained, as the case may be, except for those the failure to be made or obtained would not, individually or in the aggregate, have a Company Material Adverse Effect or Buyer Material Adverse Effect (in each case considering the operations of Buyer and the Company separately).

Section 7.2   Conditions to the Obligations of the Company to Effect the Merger. The obligation of the Company to effect the Merger will be subject to the fulfillment at or prior to the Effective Time of the following additional conditions:

(a)   Accuracy of Representations and Warranties. The representations and warranties of Buyer and Merger Sub set forth in this Agreement (i) will be true and correct with respect to those matters that are qualified by Material Adverse Effect or materiality and (ii) will be true and correct in all material respects with respect to those matters that are not so qualified, in each case as of the date of this Agreement and as of the Effective Time as though made on and as of the Effective Time (except that any representation and warranty that expressly speaks as of a specified date will be determined as of such specified date). The Company will have received a certificate signed by Buyer's Chief Executive Officer and Chief Financial Officer to such effect.

(b)   Performance of Obligations. Buyer and Merger Sub will have performed in all material respects all obligations and complied in all material respects with all agreements and covenants of Buyer and Merger Sub to be performed and complied with by them under this Agreement at or prior to the Effective Time.

(c)   Material Adverse Effect. From the date hereof through the Effective Time, there will not have been any event, effect, change or development that, individually or in the aggregate with other such events, effects, changes or developments, has had, or would reasonably be expected to have, a Buyer Material Adverse Effect.

(d)   Consents Under Agreements. Buyer will have obtained the consent or approval of each Person whose consent or approval will be required under any Contract to which Buyer or any of its Subsidiaries is a party, except those to be obtained pursuant to Section 7.1(c), and those for which the failure to obtain such consent or approval would not, individually or in the aggregate, have a Buyer Material Adverse Effect.

Section 7.3   Conditions to the Obligations of Buyer and Merger Sub to Effect the Merger. The obligation of Buyer and Merger Sub to effect the Merger will be subject to the fulfillment at or prior to the Effective Time of the following additional conditions:

(a)   Accuracy of Representations and Warranties. The representations and warranties of the Company set forth in this Agreement (i) will be true and correct with respect to those matters that are qualified by Material Adverse Effect or materiality, (ii) will, except with respect to Section 3.10(d), be true and correct in all material respects with respect to those matters that are not so qualified and (iii) with respect to Section 3.10(d), will be true and correct except where the failure to be so true and correct would in the aggregate not have a Company Material Adverse Effect, in each case as of the date of this Agreement and as of the Effective Time as though made on and as of the Effective Time (except that any representation and warranty that expressly speaks as of a specified date will be determined as of such specified date). Buyer will have received a certificate signed on behalf of the Company by the Company's Chief Executive Officer and Chief Financial Officer to such effect.

(b)   Performance of Obligations. The Company will have performed in all material respects all obligations and complied in all material respects with all agreements and covenants of the Company to be performed and complied with by it under this Agreement at or prior to the Effective Time.

(c)   Material Adverse Effect. From the date hereof through the Effective Date, there will not have been any event, effect, change or development that, individually or in the aggregate with other such events, effects, changes or developments, has had, or would reasonably be expected to have, a Company Material Adverse Effect.

(d)   Consents Under Agreements. The Company will have obtained the consent or approval of each Person whose consent or approval will be required under any Contract to which the Company or any of its Subsidiaries is a party, except those to be obtained pursuant to Section 7.1(c), and those for which the failure to obtain such consent or approval would not, individually or in the aggregate, have a Company Material Adverse Effect or, after giving effect to the Merger, a material adverse effect on Buyer.

(e)   FIRPTA. Prior to the Closing on the Closing Date, the Company shall cause to be delivered to Buyer an executed affidavit, in accordance with Treasury Regulation Section 1.897-2(h)(2), certifying that an interest in the Company is not a U.S. real property interest within the meaning of Section 897(c) of the Code and sets forth the Company's name, address and taxpayer identification number.

ARTICLE VIII
TERMINATION

Section 8.1   Termination. This Agreement may be terminated at any time prior to the Effective Time, whether before or after the Company Shareholder Approval (the date of any such termination, the "Termination Date"):

(a)   by mutual written consent of Buyer and the Company;

(b)   by either Buyer or the Company if (i) any Government Authority of competent jurisdiction has issued a Final Order denying the grant of a Required Buyer Statutory Approval or a Company Required Statutory Approval, in each case as a result of which the condition set forth in Section 7.1(c) cannot be satisfied, or (ii) any Governmental Entity will have enacted, issued, promulgated or entered any statute, law, ordinance, regulation, judgment, injunction, order, decree or ruling or taken any other action which is a Final Order permanently enjoining, restraining or otherwise prohibiting the transactions contemplated by this Agreement; provided, that the party seeking to terminate this Agreement under this Section 8.1(b) shall otherwise have performed or observed the covenants and agreements of such party set forth herein;

(c)   by Buyer if there has been a breach of any representation, warranty, covenant or other agreement made by the Company in this Agreement, or any such representation and warranty will have become untrue after the date of this Agreement, in each case such that Section 7.3(a) or Section 7.3(b) would not be satisfied, and such breach or condition is not curable or, if curable, is not cured within 60 days after written notice thereof is given by Buyer to the Company;

(d)   by Buyer if (i) the Company's Board of Directors has not recommended, or has withdrawn or qualified or modified in any manner adverse to Buyer its recommendation of, this Agreement or the Merger, (ii) the Company's Board of Directors (or any committee thereof) has entered into a definitive agreement for or recommended any Takeover Proposal, (iii) the Company has breached Section 5.2 in any material respect or (iv) a tender offer or exchange offer for 50% or more of the outstanding shares of Capital Stock of the Company is commenced, and the Company's Board of Directors fails to recommend against acceptance of such tender offer or exchange offer by its shareholders within ten days after such commencement (including by taking no position with respect to the acceptance of such tender offer or exchange offer by its shareholders);

(e)   by the Company prior to obtaining the Company Shareholder Approval if (i) the Board of Directors of the Company authorizes the Company, subject to complying with the terms of this Agreement, to enter into a definitive agreement concerning a transaction that constitutes a Superior Proposal and the Company notifies Buyer in writing that it intends to enter into such an agreement, attaching the most current version of such agreement to such notice, (ii) Buyer does not make, within five business days of receipt of the Company's written notification of its intention to enter into a definitive agreement for a Superior Proposal, an offer that the Board of Directors of the Company determines, in its reasonable good faith judgment after consultation with its financial and other advisors, is at least as favorable (taking into account (A) all financial and strategic considerations, including relevant legal, financial, regulatory and other aspects of such Takeover Proposal and the Merger and the other transactions contemplated by this Agreement deemed relevant by the Board of Directors, (B) the identity of the third party making such Takeover Proposal and (C) the conditions and prospects for completion of such Takeover Proposal) to the shareholders of the Company as the Superior Proposal and (iii) the Company prior to or concurrently with such termination pays to Buyer in immediately available funds the amount required by Section 8.2(b). The Company agrees (1) that it will not enter into a definitive agreement referred to in clause (i) above until at least the sixth business day after it has provided the notice to Buyer required thereby and (2) to notify Buyer promptly in writing if its intention to enter into a definitive agreement referred to in its notification changes at any time after giving such notification;

(f)   by the Company if there has been a breach of any representation, warranty, covenant or other agreement made by Buyer in this Agreement, or any such representation and warranty will have become untrue after the date of this Agreement, in each case such that Section 7.2(a) or Section 7.2(b) would not be satisfied, and such breach or condition is not curable or, if curable, is not cured within 60 days after written notice thereof is given by the Company to Buyer;

(g)   by either the Company or Buyer if at the Company Shareholders Meeting (including any adjournment or postponement thereof), the Company Shareholder Approval is not obtained; or

(h)   by either Buyer or the Company if the Merger has not been consummated by the date which is nine months after the date of this Agreement (the "End Date"); provided, however, that if all other conditions set forth in Article VII (other than conditions that by their nature are to be satisfied on the Closing Date) are satisfied except that the WUTC Approval and the OPUC Approval have not been obtained, either Buyer or the Company, by written notice delivered to the other party prior to the End Date, may extend such period by six months after the End Date; provided, further, that the right to terminate this Agreement under this Section 8.1(i) will not be available to any party whose failure to fulfill any obligation under this Agreement has been the cause of or resulted in the failure of the Merger to occur on or before the End Date.

Section 8.2   Effect of Termination.

(a)   In the event of a termination of this Agreement by either the Company or Buyer as provided in Section 8.1, this Agreement will forthwith become void and there will be no liability or obligation on the part of Buyer or the Company or their respective officers or directors, except with respect to Section 3.22, Section 4.10, Section 6.4, this Section 8.2 and Article IX; provided, however, that nothing herein will relieve any party for liability for any willful or knowing breach hereof.

(b)   If this Agreement is terminated by Buyer pursuant to Section 8.1(c), then the rights of Buyer to pursue all legal remedies available will survive such termination unimpaired and no election of remedies will be deemed to be made, and further, if (i) at or prior to the Termination Date a Takeover Proposal shall have been publicly announced, commenced or otherwise communicated or made known to the Company's Board of Directors (or any person shall have publicly announced, commenced or otherwise communicated or made known an intention to the Company's Board of Directors, whether or not conditional, to make a Takeover Proposal) and (ii) within 12 months after the Termination Date, the Company or any of its Subsidiaries either becomes a party to any definitive, binding agreement with respect to a Takeover Proposal (which need not be the same Takeover Proposal described in clause (i)) or consummates a transaction that would constitute a Takeover Proposal (which need not be the same Takeover Proposal described in clause (i)), then, in either case, the Company will pay to Buyer an amount equal to the Termination Fee.

(c)   If this Agreement is terminated (i) by Buyer pursuant to Section 8.1(d) or (ii) by the Company pursuant to Section 8.1(e), then the Company will pay to Buyer, an amount equal to the Termination Fee.

(d)   If this Agreement is terminated by the Company pursuant to Section 8.1(f), the rights of the Company to pursue all legal remedies available will survive such termination unimpaired and no election of remedies will be deemed to have been made.

(e)   If this Agreement is terminated by either the Company or Buyer pursuant to Section 8.1(b), Section 8.1(g) (other than a termination of this Agreement by reason of the issuance of a Final Order by the North Dakota Public Service Commission or the Minnesota Public Utilities Commission denying the grant of a Buyer Required Statutory Approval) or Section 8.1(h), and (i) at or prior to the Termination Date a Takeover Proposal shall have been publicly announced, commenced or otherwise communicated or made known to an executive officer or the Board of Directors of the Company (or any person shall have publicly announced, commenced or otherwise communicated or made known an intention to an executive officer or the Board of Directors of the Company, whether or not conditional, to make a Takeover Proposal) and (ii) within twelve months after the binding Termination Date, the Company or any of its Subsidiaries either became a party to any definitive, binding agreement, with respect to a Takeover Proposal (which need not be the same Takeover Proposal described in clause (i)) or consummates a transaction that would constitute a Takeover Proposal (which need not be the same Takeover Proposal described in clause (i)), then, in either case, the Company will pay to Buyer an amount equal to the Termination Fee.

(f)   The Company shall pay the Termination Fee to Buyer by wire transfer of immediately available funds within two business days after the date giving rise to the obligations to make such payment.

(g)   As used in this Agreement, "Termination Fee" shall mean $9,000,000.

(h)   The Company and Buyer acknowledge that the agreements contained in Section 8.2 are an integral part of the transactions contemplated by this Agreement, and that, without these agreements, Buyer or the Company, as applicable, would not enter into this Agreement. If the Company fails to promptly pay the amount due pursuant to this Section 8.2 and, in order to obtain such payment, Buyer commences a suit which results in a judgment against the Company for any of the amounts set forth in this Section 8.2, the Company will pay to Buyer, its costs and expenses (including attorneys' fees) in connection with such suit.

(i)   Neither the Company nor Buyer, as the case may be, may terminate this Agreement, and receive any applicable fees pursuant to this Section 8.2, under more than one subsection of Section 8.1.

ARTICLE IX
GENERAL PROVISIONS

Section 9.1   Non-Survival of Representations and Warranties and Agreements. None of the representations and warranties in this Agreement or in any instrument delivered pursuant to this Agreement will survive the Effective Time. Any covenant or agreement of the parties which by its terms contemplates performance after the Effective Time of the Merger will survive the Effective Time.

Section 9.2   Notices. All notices and other communications hereunder will be in writing addressed as follows:

(a)   if to Buyer or Merger Sub, to:

MDU Resources Group, Inc.
1200 West Century Avenue
P.O. Box 5650
Bismarck, ND 58506-5650
Attn: Paul K. Sandness, General Counsel and Secretary
Fax: (701) 530-1731
Email: Paul.Sandness@MDUResources.com

with a copy (which will not constitute notice) to:

Thelen Reid & Priest LLP
875 Third Avenue

New York, NY 10022-6225
Attn: Richard S. Green
Fax: (212) 829-2006
Email: rgreen@thelenreid.com

(b)   if to the Company, to:

Cascade Natural Gas Corporation
222 Fairview Avenue N
Seattle, WA 98109
Attn: David W. Stevens, Chief Executive Officer
Fax: (206) 654-4052
Email: dstevens@cngc.com

Cascade Natural Gas Corporation
222 Fairview Avenue N
Seattle, WA 98109
Attn: Rick A. Davis, Chief Financial Officer
Fax: (206) 654-4052
Email: rdavis@cngc.com

with a copy (which will not constitute notice) to:

Preston Gates & Ellis LLP
925 Fourth Avenue, Suite 2900
Seattle, Washington 98104
Attn: Kent Carlson
Fax: (206) 623-7022
Email: kentc@prestongates.com

Any such notice or communication will be deemed given (i) when made, if made by hand delivery, (ii) when sent, if delivered via email, provided, however, that the party sending such notice or communication shall also concurrently telephone the intended recipient of such notice or communication that such a notice or communication has been sent by email, (iii) upon confirmation of receipt, if made by facsimile between the hours of 9:00 A.M. and 5:00 P.M. in the recipient party's time zone, (iv) one business day after being deposited with a next-day courier, postage prepaid, or (v) three business days after being sent certified or registered mail, return receipt requested, postage prepaid, in each case addressed as above (or to such other address as such party may designate in writing from time to time). For the purposes of this Agreement, delivery or transmission of (A) a writing, a copy of a writing, or a physical reproduction, on paper or on other tangible material, or (B) an email, in each case pursuant to this Section 9.2, constitutes delivery "in writing."

Section 9.3   Counterparts. This Agreement may be executed in counterparts, all of which will be considered one and the same agreement, and will become effective when one or more counterparts have been signed by each of the parties and delivered to the other parties, it being understood that all parties need not sign the same counterpart.

Section 9.4   Entire Agreement; No Third-Party Beneficiaries. Except for the Confidentiality Agreement and all documents contemplated herein to be executed and/or delivered at or in connection with the Merger, this Agreement (and the schedules and exhibits hereto) constitute the entire agreement and supersede all prior agreements and understandings, both written and oral, among the parties with respect to the subject matter hereof. This Agreement, except for the provisions of Section 6.8, is not intended to confer upon any Person other than the parties hereto any rights or remedies hereunder.

Section 9.5   Governing Law and Venue; Waiver of Jury Trial.

(a) THIS AGREEMENT WILL BE DEEMED TO BE MADE IN AND IN ALL RESPECTS WILL BE INTERPRETED, CONSTRUED AND GOVERNED BY AND IN ACCORDANCE WITH THE LAW OF THE STATE OF WASHINGTON WITHOUT GIVING EFFECT TO THE CONFLICT OF LAW PRINCIPLES THEREOF THAT WOULD REQUIRE THE APPLICATION OF THE LAW OF ANOTHER JURISDICTION. Each of the parties irrevocably submits to the exclusive jurisdiction of any state or federal court sitting in the State of Washington for the purposes of any suit, action or other proceeding arising out of this Agreement or any transaction contemplated hereby. Each of the parties hereto

INSIDE THE MINDS

irrevocably and fully waives the defense of an inconvenient forum to the maintenance of such suit, action or proceeding. Each of the parties hereto irrevocably and unconditionally waives any objection to the laying of venue of any action, suit or proceeding arising out of this Agreement or the transactions contemplated hereby in any state or federal court sitting in the State of Washington, and hereby further irrevocably and unconditionally waives and agrees not to plead or claim in any such court that any such action, suit or proceeding brought in any such court has been brought in an inconvenient forum.

(b)   EACH PARTY HERETO HEREBY IRREVOCABLY AND UNCONDITIONALLY WAIVES ANY RIGHT SUCH PARTY MAY HAVE TO A TRIAL BY JURY IN RESPECT OF ANY ACTION, SUITE OR PROCEEDING DIRECTLY OR INDIRECTLY ARISING OUT OF OR RELATING TO THIS AGREEMENT, OR THE TRANSACTIONS CONTEMPLATED BY THIS AGREEMENT.

Section 9.6   Assignment. Neither this Agreement nor any of the rights, interests or obligations hereunder may be assigned by any of the parties hereto (whether by operation of law or otherwise) without the prior written consent of the other parties. Subject to the preceding sentence, this Agreement will be binding upon, inure to the benefit of, and be enforceable by, the parties and their respective successors and assigns.

Section 9.7   Severability. If any term or other provision of this Agreement is invalid, illegal or incapable of being enforced by any rule of law or public policy, all other conditions and provisions of this Agreement will nevertheless remain in full force and effect so long as the economic and legal substance of the transactions contemplated hereby are not affected in any manner materially adverse to any party. Upon such determination that any term or other provision is invalid, illegal or incapable of being enforced by any rule of law or public policy, the parties will negotiate in good faith to modify this Agreement so as to effect the original intent of the parties as closely as possible in a mutually acceptable manner in order that the transactions contemplated by this Agreement may be consummated as originally contemplated to the fullest extent possible.

724

Section 9.8   Enforcement of this Agreement. In addition to any remedy to which any party hereto is specifically entitled by the terms hereof, each party will be entitled to pursue any other remedy available to it at law or in equity (including damages, specific performance or other injunctive relief) in the event that any of the provisions of this Agreement were not performed in accordance with their terms or were otherwise breached; provided that, notwithstanding the foregoing, if a termination fee or any expenses in connection with the transactions contemplated by this Agreement are payable pursuant to Section 8.2, then, subject to Section 8.2(a), such termination fee or expenses will be the sole remedy with respect to the failure or failures to perform or other breach or breaches giving rise to such obligation to pay such termination fee or expenses. The parties hereto agree that (a) irreparable damage would occur and that the parties hereto would not have an adequate remedy at law if any of the provisions of this Agreement were not performed in accordance with their specific terms or were otherwise breached and (b) they will be entitled to an injunction or injunctions to prevent breaches of this Agreement and to enforce specifically this Agreement in any court having jurisdiction over the parties and the matter, subject to Section 9.5, in addition to any other remedy to which they may be entitled at law or in equity.

Section 9.9   Obligations of Subsidiaries. Whenever this Agreement requires any Subsidiary of Buyer or of the Company to take any action, such requirement will be deemed to include an undertaking on the part of Buyer or the Company, as the case may be, to cause such Subsidiary to take such action.

Section 9.10   Amendment. This Agreement may be amended by the parties hereto at any time before or after obtaining the Company Shareholder Approval, but if the Company Shareholder Approval has been obtained, thereafter no amendment will be made which by law requires further approval by the Company's shareholders without obtaining such further approval. This Agreement may not be amended except by an instrument in writing signed on behalf of each of the parties hereto.

Section 9.11   Extension; Waiver. At any time prior to the Effective Time, the parties hereto, by action taken or authorized by their respective Board of Directors, may, to the extent legally allowed, (i) extend the time for the performance of any of the obligations or other acts of the other parties hereto, (ii) waive any inaccuracies in the representations and warranties contained herein or in any document delivered pursuant hereto or (iii) waive compliance with any of the agreements or conditions contained herein; provided, however, that such extension or waiver will not operate as a waiver of, or estoppel with respect to, any subsequent or other failure. Any agreement on the part of a party hereto to any such extension or waiver will be valid only if set forth in a written instrument signed on behalf of such party. The failure of any party to this Agreement to assert any of its rights under this Agreement or otherwise will not constitute a waiver of those rights.

Section 9.12   Disclosure Schedules. The disclosures made on the Company Disclosure Schedules and the Buyer Disclosure Schedules, with respect to any representation or warranty hereunder, will be deemed to be made with respect to any other representation or warranty requiring the same or similar disclosure to the extent that the relevance of such disclosure to other representations and warranties is reasonably evident from the face of such disclosure. The inclusion of any matter on the Company Disclosure Schedules and the Buyer Disclosure Schedules will not be deemed an admission by any party that such matter is material or that such matter has or could reasonably be expected to have a Material Adverse Effect with respect to the Company or Buyer, as applicable.

Section 9.13   Construction. The table of contents, index of defined terms and headings contained in this Agreement are for reference purposes only and will not affect in any way the meaning or interpretation of this Agreement. Whenever the words "include," "includes" or "including" are used in this Agreement, they will be deemed to be followed by the words "without limitation." Words in the singular form will be construed to include the plural and vice versa, unless the context requires otherwise. Any reference to the Surviving Corporation or to the Company after giving effect to the Merger means Buyer as the Surviving Corporation. Any agreement referred to herein means such agreement as amended, supplemented or modified from time to time to the extent permitted by the applicable provisions thereof and by this Agreement.

[Remainder of page intentionally left blank]

IN WITNESS WHEREOF, Buyer, Merger Sub and the Company have caused this Agreement to be signed by their respective officers thereunto duly authorized all as of the date first written above.

Buyer:
MDU RESOURCES GROUP, INC.

By: _____
Martin A. White
Chairman of the Board and
Chief Executive Officer

Merger Sub:
FIREMOON ACQUISITION, INC.

By: _____
Terry D. Hildestad
Chairman of the Board and
Chief Executive Officer

Company:
CASCADE NATURAL GAS CORPORATION

By: _____
David W. Stevens
President and Chief Executive Officer

Courtesy of Richard S. Green, Thelen Reid Brown Raysman & Steiner LLP

APPENDIX L

AGREEMENT AND PLAN OF REORGANIZATION AND MERGER BY AND AMONG MDU RESOURCES GROUP INC., CONNPAC ACQUISITION CORP., L.G. EVERIST INC., AND CONNOLLY-PACIFIC CO.

AGREEMENT AND PLAN OF REORGANIZATION AND MERGER (this "Agreement"), dated as of the 24th day of January, 2000, by and among MDU RESOURCES GROUP, INC., a Delaware corporation ("MDU"), CONNOLLY-PACIFIC CO., a California corporation ("CP"), CONNPAC ACQUISITION CORP., a California corporation and a wholly-owned subsidiary of MDU ("Acquisition Subsidiary"), and L.G. EVERIST, INCORPORATED, an Iowa corporation and holder of a majority of the capital stock of CP ("LGE"). LGE and RALPH LARISON, an individual resident of the State of California and a holder of capital stock of CP ("Larison"), are sometimes referred to herein each as a "Stockholder" and together as the "Stockholders."

WHEREAS, MDU, CP, Acquisition Subsidiary, and LGE desire to enter into a business combination transaction pursuant to which MDU will acquire all of the issued and outstanding capital stock of CP through the merger of Acquisition Subsidiary with and into CP, with CP being the surviving corporation in such merger and with each issued and outstanding share of capital stock of CP being converted into the right to receive shares of common stock, par value $1.00 per share, of MDU, and the associated preference share purchase rights, subject to the terms and conditions contained herein.

WHEREAS, MDU, CP, and LGE intend for the transactions provided for herein to qualify as a reorganization pursuant to Section 368(a) of the Internal Revenue Code of 1986, as amended.

NOW, THEREFORE, in consideration of the covenants and agreements contained herein, and for other good and valuable consideration, the receipt and sufficiency of which is hereby acknowledged, the parties hereto, intending to be legally bound hereby, agree as follows:

ARTICLE 1.

DEFINITIONS; HEADINGS

1.01   Defined Terms. As used in this Agreement, terms defined in the preamble and recitals of this Agreement have the meanings set forth therein, and the following terms have the meanings set forth below:

(1)   "Adjusted Current Liabilities" means Current Liabilities excluding the current portion of Long Term Debt and capital leases payable.

(2)   "Arbitrating Accountants" means a nationally recognized firm of independent public accountants with offices in California mutually selected by MDU and LGE.

(3)   "Business Day" means any day other than Saturday, Sunday and any day that is a legal holiday or a day on which banking institutions in New York are authorized or required by law or other action of a Governmental Authority to close.

(4)   "Closing" has the meaning ascribed to such term in Section 2.08.

(5)   "Closing Balance Sheet" means the audited special purpose balance sheet of CP as of the Closing Date.

(6)   "Closing Date" has the meaning ascribed to such term in Section 2.08.

(7)   "Code" means the Internal Revenue Code of 1986, as amended.

(8)   "Consideration" means 2,826,087 shares of MDU Common Stock.

(9)   "CP Common Stock" means the common stock, $1.00 par value of CP.

(10)   "CP Financial Statements" means the Existing CP Financial Statements and the Updated CP Financial Statements.

(11)   "Consideration Adjustment" means the amount, if any, that, when added to Current Assets, would increase a Current Ratio of less than 1.0:1.0 to 1.0:1.0, or, when subtracted from Current Assets would decrease a Current Ratio of greater than 1.0:1.0 to 1.0:1.0. If the Current Ratio, as computed based upon the Current Assets and Adjusted Current Liabilities on the Closing Balance Sheet, is greater than 1.0:1.0, then the Consideration Adjustment shall be deemed to be a positive amount. If the Current Ratio, as computed based upon the Current Assets and Adjusted Current Liabilities on the Closing Balance Sheet, is less than 1.0:1.0, then the Consideration Adjustment shall be deemed to be a negative amount.

(12)   "Controlled Group" has the meaning ascribed to such term in Section 3.21(a).

(13)   "Current Assets" means those assets determined to be current in accordance with GAAP.

(14)   "Current Liabilities" means those liabilities determined to be current in accordance with GAAP.

(15)   "Current Ratio" means an amount, expressed as a ratio, equal to Current Assets divided by Adjusted Current Liabilities.

(16)   "Debt" means the amount of the aggregate principal and accrued or unpaid interest on indebtedness for borrowed money or capital lease obligations of CP outstanding on the Closing Date, other than the current portion of long-term indebtedness for borrowed money and capitalized lease obligations included in Current Liabilities.

(17)   "Effective Time" has the meaning ascribed to such term in Section 2.01.

(18)   "Employee Benefit Plan" has the meaning ascribed to such term in Section 3.21(a).

(19) "Employment Agreement" means that certain Employment Agreement dated as of the Closing Date, between CP and Larison substantially in the form of Exhibit 7.03(a) hereof.

(20) "Environmental Laws" means all Laws relating to pollution or protection of human health or the environment (including, without limitation, ambient air, threatened or endangered species surface water, groundwater, land surface or subsurface strata), including, without limitation, laws and regulations relating to Releases or threatened Releases of Hazardous Materials, or otherwise relating to the manufacture, processing, distribution, use, treatment, storage, disposal, transport or handling of Hazardous Materials.

(21) "ERISA" means the Employee Retirement Income Security Act of 1974, as amended.

(22) "Existing CP Financial Statements" means the unaudited income statements of CP for each of the years ended March 31, 1995, March 31, 1996, March 31, 1997, March 31, 1998, and March 31, 1999 and the unaudited balance sheets of CP as of March 31, 1998, March 31, 1999 and December 31, 1999.

(23) "GAAP" means generally accepted accounting principles consistently applied.

(24) "Governmental Authority" means any federal, state or local court, arbitration tribunal or governmental department, board, commission, bureau, agency, authority or instrumentality.

(25) "HSR Act" means the Hart-Scott Rodino Antitrust Improvements Act of 1976, as amended.

(26) "Hazardous Materials" means (a) any petroleum or petroleum products, radioactive materials, asbestos in any form that is friable, urea-formaldehyde foam insulation, and transformers or other equipment that contain dielectric fluid containing polychlorinated biphenyls (PCBs); (b) any chemicals, materials or substances which are now defined as or included in the definition

of "hazardous substances," "hazardous wastes," "hazardous materials," "extremely hazardous wastes," "restricted hazardous wastes," "toxic substances," "toxic pollutants," or words of similar import, under any Environmental Law; and (c) any other chemical, material, substance or waste, exposure to which is prohibited, limited or regulated by any Governmental Authority in a jurisdiction in which the Company operates.

(27) "Indemnified Purchaser Group" means MDU, any subsidiary or affiliate thereof (including, without limitation, CP), and each of their respective successors, assigns, directors, officers, employees, attorneys, accountants and other affiliates, representatives and controlling persons.

(28) "Indemnified Seller Group" means Larison, LGE, any subsidiary or affiliate of LGE, and each of their respective successors, assigns directors, officers, employees, attorneys, accountants and other affiliates, representatives and controlling persons.

(29) "Intellectual Property" means all trademarks, trademark registrations and trademark applications, trade names, assumed names, service marks, service names, copyrights, copyright registrations, patents and patent applications, patent, trademark and copyright licenses, proprietary business techniques and non-public customer information, and rights relating thereto, including without limitation all rights to sue for past infringements, owned by CP or used by CP in the conduct of its business.

(30) "IRS" means the United States Internal Revenue Service.

(31) "Knowledge" as used with respect to (i) MDU, LGE or CP, as the case may be, shall mean those facts that are actually known to an officer or director of MDU, LGE or CP, as the case may be, or those facts that, after due inquiry in the exercise of reasonable diligence, taking into account the scope and nature of the responsibilities of the officer or director in question, should have been know to such officer or director and (ii) Larison shall mean those facts that are actually known by Larison or those facts

that, after due inquiry in the exercise of reasonable diligence, taking into account the scope and nature of Larison's responsibilities as an officer and as a shareholder of CP, should have been known to Larison.

(32)   "KRC" means KRC Holdings, Inc, a wholly-owned subsidiary of MDU.

(33)   "Laws" means all (i) federal, state, or local or foreign laws, rules and regulations, (ii) orders, (iii) Permits, and (iv) agreements with federal, state, local or foreign regulatory authorities to which MDU, either Stockholder or CP, as the case may be, is a party or by which any of them is bound.

(34)   "LGE's Accountants" means independent public accountants selected by LGE.

(35)   "LGE Stockholder Approval" means the affirmative vote of a majority of the total number of votes cast by holders of shares of issued and outstanding voting stock of LGE with respect to the transactions contemplated by this Agreement at the LGE Stockholders' Meeting.

(36)   "LGE Stockholders' Meeting" has the meaning ascribed to such term in Section 5.06.

(37)   "Long Term Debt" means all Debt reflected, or required to be reflected, as long term debt, including capitalized lease obligations, on the Closing Balance Sheet, determined in accordance with GAAP and, in each case, including the current portion thereof.

(38)   "Liens" means all liens, liabilities, claims, security interests, mortgages, pledges, agreements, obligations, restrictions, or other encumbrances of any nature whatsoever, whether absolute, legal, equitable, accrued, contingent or otherwise, including, without limitation, any rights of first refusal.

(39)   "Major Customers" means the ten (10) largest customers of CP.

(40)   "Material Adverse Effect" with respect to CP or MDU shall mean a material adverse effect upon the assets, liabilities, condition (financial or other), business or operations of such entity and its subsidiaries (including, with respect to MDU, CP) taken as a whole or on the ability of such entity to consummate the Merger.

(41)   "Material Contracts" has the meaning ascribed to such term in Section 3.23.

(42)   "MDU's Accountants" means MDU's independent public accountants and/or MDU's internal auditors.

(43)   "MDU Common Stock" means the common stock, par value $1.00 per share, of MDU and the associated preference share purchase rights.

(44)   "MDU Preference Stock" means the Cumulative Preference Stock, without par value, of MDU.

(45)   "MDU Preferred Stock" means the Cumulative Preferred Stock, par value $100 per share, of MDU.

(46)   "MDU Preferred Stock A" means the Cumulative Preferred Stock A, without par value, of MDU.

(47)   "MDU SEC Reports" has the meaning ascribed to such term in Section 4.06.

(48)   "MDU Stockholders' Meeting" has the meaning ascribed to such term in Section 5.05.

(49)   "MDU Stockholder Approval" means the affirmative vote of a majority of the total number of votes cast with respect to the proposal to approve this Agreement and the Merger and the transactions contemplated thereby at the MDU Stockholders' Meeting, provided that the total number of votes cast with respect to the proposal represents more than 50% of the total number of outstanding shares of MDU Common Stock.

(50) "MDU Stock Price" means the sum of the closing prices of the MDU Common Stock in New York Stock Exchange Composite Transactions as reported in The Wall Street Journal for the ten (10) trading days preceding the tenth (10th) day preceding the day of the Closing, divided by ten (10), appropriately adjusted, in any case, for any stock split, reverse stock split, stock dividend, or like event. The parties to this Agreement acknowledge that this definition applies only to Section 2.07 hereof.

(51) "Merger" means the merger of Acquisition Subsidiary with and into CP, as contemplated by Section 2.01.

(52) "1933 Act" means the Securities Act of 1933, as amended.

(53) "1934 Act" means the Securities Exchange Act of 1934, as amended.

(54) "Noncompetition Agreement" means that certain Noncompetition and Proprietary Information Agreement, dated as of the Closing Date, by and between LGE and MDU, substantially in the form of Exhibit 7.03(b) hereto.

(55) "NYSE" means The New York Stock Exchange, Inc.

(56) "PBGC" means the Pension Benefit Guaranty Corporation.

(57) "Permits" means all permits, licenses, franchises, orders, certificates and approvals.

(58) "Permitted Liens" means all (a) liens for Taxes or governmental assessments, charges or claims the payment of which is not yet due, (b) liens imposed by applicable law, rule or regulation such as mechanics', materialmen's, landlords', warehousemen's and carriers' liens, and other similar liens, securing obligations incurred in the ordinary course of business consistent with past practice, (c) liens under workers' compensation unemployment insurance, Social Security, or similar legislation and (d) liens incurred in the ordinary course of business consistent with

past practice for sums not yet delinquent or immaterial in amount and being contested in good faith.

(59)   "PE" means the Pacific Exchange, Inc.

(60)   "Proxy Statement" has the meaning ascribed to such term in Section 5.07.

(61)   "PUHCA" means the Public Utility Holding Company Act of 1935, as amended.

(62)   "Quarry Agreement" means that certain Quarry Agreement, dated as of March 30, 1992, between Santa Catalina Island Co. and CP, as amended by Amendment No. 1, dated as of August 31, 1994, Amendment No. 2, dated as of December 31, 1995, and Amendment No. 3, dated as of July 1, 1997, and as it may be further amended prior to the Closing Date, including the sublease contained therein of Tidelands Lease No. PRC 7030.1 between the State of California State Lands Commission and the Santa Catalina Island Co.

(63)   "Real Property" has the meaning ascribed to such term in Section 3.12(a).

(64)   "Related Agreements" means all of the other agreements to be executed in connection with and pursuant to this Agreement, including, without limitation, the Restricted Stock Agreement, the Noncompetition Agreement and the Stockholder's Agreement.

(65)   "Release" means any spilling, leaking, pumping, pouring, emitting, emptying, discharging, injecting, escaping, leaching, dumping, or disposing into the environment.

(66)   "Restricted Stock Agreement" means that certain Restricted Stock Agreement, dated as of January 24, 2000, between CP and Larison.

(67)   "SEC" means the United States Securities and Exchange Commission.

(68) "SEC Documents" means all registration statements, proxy statements, periodic reports and schedules filed by MDU or any of its subsidiaries with the SEC under the Securities Laws.

(69) "Securities Laws" means the 1933 Act, the 1934 Act, the Investment Company Act of 1940, as amended, the Trust Indenture Act of 1939, as amended, and the rules and regulations of the SEC promulgated thereunder.

(70) "Stockholder's Agreement" means that certain Stockholder's Agreement, dated as of the Closing Date, by and between MDU and LGE, substantially in the form of Exhibit 7.03(c) hereto.

(71) "Surviving Corporation" has the meaning ascribed to that term in Section 2.02.

(72) "Taxes" means (i) any and all federal, state, local, foreign and other taxes, assessments and other governmental charges, duties, impositions and liabilities, including taxes based upon or measured by gross receipts, income, profits, sales, use and occupation, and value added, ad valorem, transfer, gains, franchise, capital stock, severance, withholding, payroll, recapture, employment, excise, unemployment insurance, social security, business license, occupation, business organization, stamp, environmental and property taxes, together with all interest, penalties and additions imposed with respect to such amounts; (ii) any liability for the payment of any amounts described in clause (i) as a result of being a successor to or transferee of any individual or entity or a member of an affiliated, consolidated or unitary group for any period (including pursuant to Treas. Reg. § 1.1502 6 or comparable provisions of state, local or foreign tax law); and (iii) any liability for the payment of amounts described in clause (i) or clause (ii) as a result of any express or implied obligation to indemnify any person or entity or as a result of any obligations under agreements or arrangements with any person or entity.

(73) "Tax Reports" means all returns, estimates, information statements and reports relating to Taxes.

(74) "Thomas Everist Stockholder's Agreement" means that certain Stockholder's Agreement, dated the date hereof, between MDU and Thomas Everist, an individual resident of the State of South Dakota, pursuant to which Thomas Everist agrees, among other things, to vote the shares of LGE beneficially owned by him as set forth in such Stockholder's Agreement.

(75) "Updated CP Financial Statements" means the following financial statements prepared after the date hereof and to be included in the Proxy Statement: (i) the unaudited financial statements of CP for the years ended March 31, 1997 and March 31, 1998 and the nine months ended December 31, 1998 and December 31, 1999 and (ii) the audited financial statements of CP for the year ended March 31, 1999.

1.02   Other Definitional Provisions. Wherever the context so requires, words used herein in the masculine gender shall be deemed to include the feminine and neuter. A definition of any term shall be equally applicable to both the singular and plural forms of the term defined.

1.03   Titles; Headings. All titles and headings appearing in this Agreement are for identification only and are not to be used for interpretive purposes.

ARTICLE 2.

THE MERGER; CLOSING

2.01   Merger. The acquisition of CP shall be effected through the merger of Acquisition Subsidiary with and into CP (the "Merger"). The Merger shall be effective upon the filing of the agreement of merger and an officers' certificate of each constituent corporation, consistent with the terms of this Agreement and the provisions of the General Corporation Law of the State of California, together with any other documents required by law to effectuate the Merger with the Secretary of State of the State of California and the California Franchise Tax Board. Unless otherwise agreed, the Merger shall become effective on the Closing Date. The time at which the Merger becomes effective pursuant to the terms of this Agreement is hereinafter referred to as the "Effective Time."

2.02   Surviving Corporation in the Merger; Effect of the Merger. CP shall be the surviving corporation in the Merger. CP, as the surviving corporation in the Merger, is referred to herein as the "Surviving Corporation." At the Effective Time (i) the separate existence of Acquisition Subsidiary shall cease and Acquisition Subsidiary shall be merged into CP, and (ii) the Merger shall have the effects provided in Section 1108 of the General Corporation Law of the State of California. The Surviving Corporation shall continue its existence under the laws of the state of its incorporation from and after the Effective Time.

2.03   Governing Documents of Surviving Corporation. The Articles of Incorporation of CP, as in effect immediately prior to the Effective Time, shall be the Articles of Incorporation of the Surviving Corporation, without change or amendment until thereafter amended as provided therein or in accordance with the laws of the state of incorporation of the Surviving Corporation. The By-laws of CP, as in effect immediately prior to the Effective Time, shall be the By-laws of the Surviving Corporation, without change or amendment until thereafter amended as provided therein or in accordance with the laws of the state of incorporation of the Surviving Corporation.

2.04   Directors and Officers of the Surviving Corporation. From and after the Effective Time, the individuals identified on Schedule 2.04 as Post-Merger Directors of the Surviving Corporation shall be the directors of the Surviving Corporation, each to hold office in accordance with the Articles of Incorporation and By-Laws of the Surviving Corporation. From and after the Effective Time, the individuals identified on Schedule 2.04 as Post-Merger Officers of the Surviving Corporation shall be the officers of the Surviving Corporation, each to hold office in accordance with the Articles of Incorporation and By-Laws of the Surviving Corporation.

2.05   Additional Actions. If, at any time after the Effective Time, the Surviving Corporation shall consider, or be advised that, any further assignments or assurances in law or any other acts are necessary or desirable to vest, perfect or confirm, of record or otherwise, in the Surviving Corporation, title to and possession of any property or right of Acquisition Subsidiary acquired by reason of, or as a result of, the Merger, Acquisition Subsidiary shall be deemed to have granted to the Surviving Corporation an irrevocable power of attorney to execute and deliver all such deeds, assignments and assurances in law and to do all acts necessary or proper to vest, perfect or confirm title to, and possession of, such property or rights in the Surviving Corporation, and the proper directors and officers of the Surviving Corporation are fully authorized in the name of Acquisition Subsidiary to take any and all such actions.

2.06   Conversion of Shares.

(a)   MDU shall make available for conversion and exchange, by delivery to LGE and to Larison or, if and to the extent required pursuant to the Restricted Stock Agreement or the Employment Agreement, to the Escrow Agent, as defined in the Restricted Stock Agreement or the Employment Agreement, the Consideration provided for herein.

(b)   Each of the shares of common stock of Acquisition Subsidiary outstanding immediately prior to the Effective Time shall be converted into and exchangeable for one share of common stock of the Surviving Corporation. From and after the Effective Time, each outstanding certificate representing shares of common stock of Acquisition Subsidiary shall be deemed for all purposes to evidence ownership of, and to represent the number of shares of, common stock of the Surviving Corporation. Promptly after the Effective Time, the Surviving Corporation shall issue to MDU a stock certificate representing the appropriate number of shares of common stock of the Surviving Corporation in exchange for the certificate or certificates that formerly represented shares of common stock of Acquisition Subsidiary which shall be immediately canceled.

(c)   Each of the shares of CP Common Stock issued and outstanding immediately prior to the Effective Time shall, by virtue of the Merger and without any action on the part of the Stockholders, be converted into and exchangeable for the right to receive a pro-rata share of the Consideration, subject to adjustment with respect to LGE pursuant to Section 2.07 hereof, as provided herein.

(d)   At the Effective Time, LGE shall surrender the certificate or certificates representing all of the issued and outstanding shares of CP Common Stock owned, beneficially or of record, by LGE as set forth on Schedule 3.03 in exchange for a certificate or certificates, registered in the name of LGE representing LGE's share of the Consideration as set forth on Schedule 3.03. Each certificate representing CP Common Stock owned by LGE shall be duly endorsed in blank by LGE, with all necessary transfer tax and other revenue stamps, acquired at LGE's expense, affixed and canceled. LGE agrees to cure any deficiencies with respect to the endorsement of the certificates representing the CP Common Stock owned by LGE or with respect to the stock power accompanying any such certificate. As promptly as practicable after the Closing, MDU shall deliver to each Stockholder (or, if and to the extent required pursuant to the Restricted Stock Agreement or the Employment Agreement, to the Escrow Agent, as defined in the Restricted Stock Agreement or the Employment Agreement) the certificates representing such Stockholder's share of the Consideration, as set forth on Schedule 3.03.

2.07   Consideration Adjustment.

(a)   Not later than sixty (60) calendar days after the Closing Date, MDU shall cause to be prepared and delivered via overnight courier, to LGE and LGE's Accountants the Closing Balance Sheet, prepared in accordance with GAAP. LGE's Accountants may, at the sole cost and expense of LGE, observe any physical count of the inventory when taken and participate in its evaluation.

(b)   LGE and LGE's Accountants shall have a period of thirty (30) calendar days after the delivery to LGE of the Closing Balance Sheet to examine the Closing Balance Sheet, and to present any objections that LGE may have to any of the matters set forth therein, which objections shall be set forth in writing and in reasonable detail. Thereafter, LGE and representatives of MDU shall meet to discuss any of the objections raised by LGE, with a view to resolving such objections. If LGE does not deliver any written objection to MDU within such thirty (30) calendar day period, LGE shall be deemed to have accepted the Closing Balance Sheet and waived any objection thereto.

(c)   If all of such objections cannot be resolved by MDU and LGE within thirty (30) calendar days after the commencement of the discussions pursuant to Section 2.07(b), then, not later than forty (40) calendar days after the commencement of such discussions, either MDU or LGE shall have the right, by the delivery of written notice to the other party to such effect, to cause matters in dispute to be submitted to an Arbitrating Accountant for determination. The Arbitrating Accountant shall be instructed to deliver a decision with respect to the matters referred to it for determination within thirty (30) calendar days after the submission of such matters. Unless otherwise agreed, any meetings or proceedings deemed necessary by the Arbitrating Accountant in order to resolve the matters referred to the Arbitrating Accountant for determination will be conducted in California. The decision of the Arbitrating Accountant shall be binding and conclusive upon MDU and LGE for all purposes under this Agreement. MDU shall pay the fees and expenses of MDU's Accountants, and LGE shall pay the fees and expenses of LGE's Accountants. The fees and expenses of the Arbitrating Accountant shall be paid one half by MDU and one half by LGE.

(d)   If the Consideration Adjustment is a positive amount, then not later than ten (10) calendar days after the amount of the Consideration Adjustment has been finally determined, MDU shall deliver to LGE a certificate or certificates, issued in the name of LGE, representing a number of shares of MDU Common Stock (rounded to the nearest whole share, with 0.5 of a share being rounded upward) equal to the quotient of (A) the Consideration Adjustment divided by (B) the MDU Stock Price; provided, that, in no event shall the aggregate number of shares of MDU Common Stock comprising the Consideration Adjustment, determined as set forth herein, exceed the aggregate number of shares of MDU Common Stock issued to the Stockholders on the Closing Date. If the Consideration Adjustment is a negative amount, then not later than ten (10) calendar days after the Consideration Adjustment has been finally determined, LGE shall deliver to MDU an aggregate amount in cash equal to the Consideration Adjustment, by wire transfer of immediately available funds to an account designated by MDU in writing.

2.08   Closing. Upon the terms and subject to the satisfaction of the conditions contained in Article 6, the closing of the transactions provided for herein (the "Closing") shall take place at the offices of Faegre & Benson LLP, 2200 Norwest Center, 90 South Seventh Street, Minneapolis, Minnesota, at 11:00 A.M., local time, as soon as practicable, but no later than two Business Days, following the date on which all of the conditions set forth in Article 6 have been satisfied or waived, or such other date as may be mutually agreed upon by the parties hereto (the "Closing Date").

ARTICLE 3.

REPRESENTATIONS AND WARRANTIES OF LGE

LGE represents, warrants and covenants to MDU , as follows:

3.01   Organization and Existence of LGE and CP.

(a)   LGE is a corporation duly organized and validly existing under the laws of its jurisdiction of incorporation, with all requisite corporate power and authority to own, operate and lease its properties and assets and to carry on its business as now being conducted.

(b)   CP is a corporation duly organized and validly existing under the laws of its jurisdiction of incorporation, with all requisite corporate power and authority to own, operate and lease its properties and assets and to carry on its business as now being conducted. CP is duly qualified to do business and is in good standing in each jurisdiction where the conduct of its business or the ownership of its property requires such qualification, except where the failure to so qualify would not have a Material Adverse Effect on CP. The jurisdictions in which CP is qualified to do business, and the names and addresses of CP's registered agents in such jurisdictions, are set forth on Schedule 3.01 hereto. Schedule

3.01 hereto sets forth all names under which CP has conducted or purported to conduct business since the date of its incorporation.

3.02   Capital Stock. CP has an authorized capitalization consisting solely of 10,000 shares of CP Common Stock of which 1,036.6826 shares are issued and outstanding. Other than the CP Common Stock, there is no class or series of equity security of CP authorized, issued or outstanding. All such outstanding shares of CP Common Stock have been duly authorized and validly issued and are fully paid and nonassessable. There are no outstanding options, warrants, rights, calls, commitments, conversion rights, rights of exchange, plans or other agreements of any character providing for the purchase, issuance or sale of any shares of any equity security of CP, including any CP Common Stock, other than as contemplated by this Agreement.

3.03   Ownership of Shares.

(a)   Each Stockholder is the lawful owner, beneficially and of record, of all of the issued and outstanding shares of CP Common Stock set forth opposite such Stockholder's name on Schedule 3.03, free and clear of all Liens (other than restrictions imposed by Securities Laws applicable to unregistered securities generally and other than restrictions on transfer pursuant to the Restricted Stock Agreement),

(b)   the aggregate number of shares of CP Common Stock set forth opposite Stockholders' names on Schedule 3.03 constitutes all of the issued and outstanding shares of CP Common Stock,

(c)   Schedule 3.03 sets forth the address and tax identification number of each Stockholder,

(d)   Each Stockholder's share of the Consideration is set forth next to such Stockholder's name on Schedule 3.03.

3.04   Subsidiaries. CP does not have any subsidiaries or hold any equity or ownership interest of any kind, whether beneficially or of record, in any corporation, partnership, limited liability company, joint venture, or other enterprise or entity of any nature whatsoever.

3.05   Authority of LGE and CP. Each of LGE and CP has the corporate power and authority to execute, deliver, and perform its obligations under this Agreement and the Related Agreements to which it is a party and to consummate the transactions contemplated hereby and thereby. Each of CP and, subject to the LGE Stockholder Approval, LGE has taken all necessary corporate action to authorize the execution, delivery and performance of this Agreement and the consummation of the Merger. The LGE Stockholder Approval constitutes the only vote of any class or series of LGE capital stock necessary to approve this Agreement and the Merger.

3.06   Due Execution and Enforceability as to LGE. This Agreement has been duly executed and delivered by each of LGE and CP and is a valid and binding obligation of each of LGE and CP, enforceable against each of LGE and CP in accordance with its terms, except as limited by applicable bankruptcy, insolvency, reorganization, moratorium or other laws of general application referring to or affecting enforcement of creditors' rights and general principles of equity.

3.07   No Restrictions Against Performance. Except as set forth on Schedule 3.07 hereto, neither the execution, delivery nor performance of this Agreement or the Related Agreements, nor the consummation of the transactions contemplated in this Agreement or in the Related Agreements will, with or without the giving of notice or the passage of time, or both, violate any provisions of, conflict with, result in a breach of, constitute a default under, or result in the creation or imposition of any Lien on any property or asset of CP under:

> (i)   the Articles of Incorporation or By-Laws of LGE or CP;

> (ii)   any Law which is applicable to either Stockholder or CP or any of their respective properties or assets;

> (iii)   (x) any Material Contract of CP or (y) any contract, indenture, instrument, agreement, mortgage, lease, right or other obligation or restriction to which LGE is a party or by which LGE or any of its properties or assets is or may be bound; or

(iv)   any order, judgment, writ, injunction, decree, license, franchise, permit or other authorization of any Governmental Authority by which either CP, either Stockholder or any of their respective properties or assets is or may be bound;

except, in the case of clauses (ii) through (iv) above, for circumstances that, taken in the aggregate, could not reasonably be expected to have a Material Adverse Effect on CP.

3.08   Historical Financial Information.

(a)   True and complete copies of the Existing CP Financial Statements are attached hereto as Exhibit 3.08. The Existing CP Financial Statements present fairly the financial position, assets and liabilities of CP as of the dates thereof and the revenues, expenses and results of operations of CP for the periods covered thereby. The Existing CP Financial Statements are in accordance with the books and records of CP and do not reflect any transactions which are not bona fide transactions. The books and records of CP have been maintained in accordance with applicable laws, rules and regulations, and in the ordinary course of business. The accounts and notes receivable of CP reflected in the Existing CP Financial Statements are valid, existing and genuine and represent sales actually made or services actually delivered by CP in bona fide transactions in the ordinary course of business consistent with past practice; and there is no material right of set-off or counterclaim or threat thereof that would jeopardize the collectability of such accounts and notes receivable at the aggregate recorded amounts thereof.

(b)   The Updated CP Financial Statements will be prepared in accordance with GAAP. The Updated CP Financial Statements will present fairly the financial position, assets and liabilities of CP as of the dates thereof and the revenues, expenses, results of operations and cash flows of CP for the periods covered thereby, all in accordance with GAAP (subject, in the case of interim financial statements, to normal recurring year end adjustments and the absence of footnotes). The Updated CP Financial Statements will be in accordance with the books and records of CP and will not reflect any transactions which are not bona fide transactions. Between the date hereof and the Closing Date, the books and records of CP will be maintained in accordance with applicable laws, rules and regulations, and in the ordinary course of business. The accounts and notes receivable of CP reflected in the Updated CP Financial Statements will be valid, existing and genuine and will represent sales actually made or services actually delivered by CP in bona fide transactions in the ordinary course of business consistent with past practice; and there will be no material right of set-off or counterclaim or threat thereof that would jeopardize the collectability of such accounts and notes receivable at the aggregate recorded amounts thereof.

3.09   No Undisclosed Liabilities. CP has no liabilities or obligations of any nature (whether absolute, accrued, contingent or otherwise) that would be required to be accrued or reflected on the CP Financial Statements in accordance with GAAP, that are not (i) reflected or reserved against in the CP Financial Statements, (ii) incurred in the ordinary course of business consistent with past practice since the respective dates thereof, or (iii) disclosed in this Agreement. To the Knowledge of LGE and CP, no basis exists on the date hereof for assertions against CP of any material claim or liability of any nature other than those which have been disclosed in the CP Financial Statements. For purposes of this Section 3.09, a claim or liability shall be deemed to be "material" if it involves an amount in excess of $50,000, individually or in the aggregate, as the context requires.

3.10   No Adverse Effects or Changes. Except as listed and described in detail on Schedule 3.10, since December 31, 1999, CP has not experienced an event that reasonably could be expected to have had a Material Adverse Effect on it or:

(a)   made any change in its authorized capital or outstanding securities;

(b)   issued, sold or delivered, or agreed to issue, sell or deliver, any capital stock, bonds or other corporate securities (whether authorized and unissued or held in the treasury), or granted or agreed to grant any options, warrants or other rights calling for the issue, sale or delivery thereof;

(c)   borrowed or agreed to borrow any funds, guaranteed the repayment of any indebtedness or incurred any other contingent financial obligations, including any counter-claim, cross-complaint or set-off raised in any action to collect receivables outstanding at the Closing Date, except borrowings incurred in the ordinary course of business consistent with past practice;

(d)   satisfied any obligation or liability (absolute or contingent), other than obligations and liabilities incurred in the ordinary course of business consistent with past practice that are in excess of $50,000 individually or $50,000 in the aggregate;

(e)   declared or made, or agreed to declare or make, any payment of dividends or distributions of any assets of any kind whatsoever in respect of its capital stock, or purchased, redeemed or otherwise acquired, or agreed to purchase, redeem or otherwise acquire, any of its outstanding capital stock;

(f)   sold, transferred or otherwise disposed of, or agreed to sell, transfer or otherwise dispose of, any material assets, properties or rights, except inventory and equipment in the ordinary course of business consistent with past practice, or canceled or otherwise terminated, or agreed to cancel or otherwise terminate, any debts or claims other than accounts receivable write-offs and writedowns in the ordinary course of business consistent with past practice;

(g)   other than in the ordinary course of business consistent with past practice, entered, or agreed to enter, into any agreement or arrangements to sell any of its assets, properties or rights, including inventories and equipment, or requiring the consent of any party to the transfer or assignment of any of its assets, properties or rights;

(h)   other than change orders on construction contracts made in the ordinary course of business consistent with past practice, made or permitted any amendment or termination of any Material

Contract, agreement, permit or license to which it is a party or by which it or any of its properties are bound;

(i)   made, directly or indirectly, any accrual or arrangement for or payment of any bonuses or special compensation of any kind or any severance or termination pay to any present or former officer, director or executive employee;

(j)   except for customary raises granted in the ordinary course of business consistent with past practice, increased the rate of compensation payable, or to become payable, by it to any of its officers, directors or employees or adopted any new, or made any increase in, any profit sharing, bonus, deferred compensation, savings, insurance, pension, retirement or other employee benefit plan payment or arrangement made to, for or with any present or former such officers, directors or executive employees;

(k)   incurred, or become subject to, any uninsured claim or liability of any damages in excess of $50,000 individually or in the aggregate for any negligence or other tort or breach of contract;

(l)   made any capital expenditures (or commitments therefor) which in the aggregate exceed $100,000;

(m)   suffered any damages, destruction or casualty losses in excess of $50,000 individually or in the aggregate; or

(n)   entered into any other transaction involving more than $50,000 individually or in the aggregate, other than in the ordinary course of business consistent with past practice.

3.11   Third-Party and Governmental Consents. Except for the filing of the agreement of merger and an officers' certificate of each constituent corporation, together with any other documents required by law to effectuate the Merger, with the Secretary of State of the State of California and the California Franchise Tax Board, as contemplated under Section 2.01, and except for the LGE Stockholder Approval, and except for filings required under the HSR Act with respect to (i) the acquisition by LGE of the shares of MDU Common Stock constituting its share of the

Consideration and (ii) the Merger, and except as set forth on Schedule 3.11 hereto, no approval, consent, waiver, order or authorization of, or registration, qualification, declaration, or filing with, or notice to, any Governmental Authority or other third party is required on the part of any Stockholder or CP in connection with the execution and delivery of this Agreement or the Related Agreements by any Stockholder or CP or the consummation of the transactions contemplated hereby or thereby, including, without limitation, the Merger.

3.12   Real and Personal Property.

(a)   Real Property. CP does not own any real property. Schedule 3.12(a) sets forth a list and a description of all real properties leased or subject to any contract or purchase and sale or lease commitment by CP, written or oral (collectively "Real Property"). Except as set forth in Schedule 3.12(a), the buildings, premises and equipment that are leased by CP are in good operating condition and repair, subject only to ordinary wear and tear customary within the local trade. Except as set forth on Schedule 3.12(a) there is not any pending or, to the Knowledge of LGE or CP, threatened change in the zoning or building ordinances affecting the Real Property or leasehold interests of CP or the real property subject to the Quarry Agreement. To the Knowledge of LGE or CP, none of the Real Property, or the operation and maintenance thereof as now operated or maintained, contravenes any zoning ordinance or other similar governmental or administrative regulation (whether or not permitted because of a prior nonconforming use) or violates any restrictive covenant, the effect of which in any material respect would interfere with or prevent the continued use of any of the Real Property or any of the real property subject to the Quarry Agreement for the purposes for which it is now being used or would materially affect the value thereof. There is no pending or, to the Knowledge of LGE or CP, contemplated eminent domain or similar proceeding pursuant to which any portion of any Real Property or any real property subject to the Quarry Agreement would be acquired for public use or the right of CP to use such property as presently used would be restricted in any material respect.

(b)   Real Property Leases. Schedule 3.12(b) sets forth a true, correct and complete list of all real property leases to which CP is a party, whether as lessor or lessee. The Quarry Agreement and all leases listed on such Schedule are valid and subsisting and in full force and effect, and all rent and other payments now due have been paid. CP enjoys and is in peaceful and undisturbed possession under the Quarry Agreement and under each lease so listed in which it is a lessee. Except as set forth on Schedule 3.12(b),CP has not received any notice of, and there does not exist any event of default or, to the Knowledge of LGE or CP, any event, occurrence or act which, with the giving of notice or the lapse of time or both, would become a default, under the Quarry Agreement or under any such lease and CP has not violated any of the terms or conditions under the Quarry Agreement or under any such lease in any material respect. Such real property and the buildings, fixtures and equipment situated thereon or attached or appurtenant thereto are in good operating condition and repair, are adequate and suitable for the purposes for which they are presently being used, and, to the Knowledge of LGE or CP, are in compliance with all applicable Laws, except for such matters which in the aggregate would not have a Material Adverse Effect on CP. Schedule 3.12(b) also sets forth a true, correct and complete list of all notices issued pursuant to the Quarry Agreement or pursuant to such leases within the six months prior to the date hereof by CP regarding the Quarry Agreement or such leases. Except as set forth in Schedule 3.12(b), such notices were timely made and in accordance with the Quarry Agreement or the applicable lease agreement, as the case may be.

(c)   Personal Property. CP has good, valid, marketable, legal and beneficial title to all of its owned assets, free and clear of all Liens, other than Permitted Liens. There are no outstanding options, warrants, commitments, agreements or any other rights of any character entitling any person or entity other than MDU or any of its subsidiaries to acquire any interest in all, or any part of, the assets of CP.

3.13   Accounts and Notes Receivable. Schedule 3.13 sets forth a list as of December 31, 1999 of all accounts and notes receivable of CP, together with:

(i)   an aging schedule setting forth all such accounts receivable (other than intercompany receivables);

(ii)   the identity of any asset in which CP holds a security interest to secure payment of the underlying indebtedness; and

(iii)   a description of the nature and amount of any liens on or security interest in such accounts and notes receivable.

3.14   Payables and Promissory Notes. Schedule 3.14 sets forth a list of

(i)   all accounts payable of as of December 31, 1999 together with an appropriate aging schedule;

(ii)   all long-term and short-term promissory notes, installment contracts, loan agreements and credit agreements to which CP is a party or to which any of its properties are subject; and

(iii)   all indentures, mortgages, security agreements, pledges, and any other agreements, pledges, and any other agreements of CP relating thereto or with respect to collateral securing the same.

3.15   Insurance and Bonds. Schedule 3.15 sets forth a list of all insurance policies and bonds (except group health and life policies listed on Schedule 3.21(a) and any title insurance policies), held by CP, including those covering its properties, buildings, equipment, fixtures, employees and operations. Such list specifies with respect to each such policy:

(i)   the insurer and agent,

(ii)   the amount of coverage,

(iii)   the dates of premiums or payments due thereunder, and

(iv)   the expiration date, as applicable.

Each such policy identified is currently in full force and effect. All insurance premiums due according to the applicable payment schedules reflected in such policies have been timely paid. Except as set forth on Schedule 3.15, to the Knowledge of LGE or CP, there are no facts or circumstances under which any claims for uninsured losses or damages are likely to be asserted against CP in an amount in excess of $50,000 nor are there any such claims pending against CP. The insurance policies currently maintained by CP provide coverage believed by LGE and CP to be adequate for its properties, assets, products and operations. CP has not requested cancellation of any material policy of insurance at any time during the previous two years. CP has not sought and been denied any insurance coverage during the two-year period prior to the Closing Date. All bonds issued to secure performance of or payment by CP under any Material Contract in progress or yet to be completed are in force and effect and are identified on Schedule 3.15. Neither LGE nor CP has made any representations or undertaken any other act which would give rise to a viable claim that any such existing bond is invalid or unenforceable. To the Knowledge of LGE or CP, there are no facts or circumstances under which the validity or enforceability by CP of any such existing bond could be successfully challenged. The transactions contemplated by this Agreement will have no adverse effect on any such existing bond.

3.16   Bank Accounts. Schedule 3.16 sets forth a list of: (i) the name of each bank or other financial institution in which CP has an account or safe deposit box; (ii) the names of all persons authorized to draw thereon or to have access thereto; and (iii) the names of all persons other than the officers of CP who are authorized to incur liabilities on behalf of CP for borrowed funds.

3.17   Compliance with Laws. CP has complied with and is not in default under any Laws the violation of which could reasonably be expected to have a Material Adverse Effect on CP.

3.18   Litigation. Except as set forth in Schedule 3.18, there is no judicial or administrative claim, action, suit, proceeding or, to the Knowledge of LGE or CP, investigation pending or, to the Knowledge of LGE or CP, threatened, against or relating to either Stockholder or CP or the officers or directors of LGE or CP in their capacities as officers or directors, the business, properties or assets of CP or the transactions contemplated by this Agreement or the Related Agreements, including, but not limited to, actions or proceedings alleging any violation of any Environmental Law, before any federal, state or local court, arbitration tribunal or Governmental Authority, which could reasonably be expected, individually or in the aggregate, to have a Material Adverse Effect on CP, or to materially adversely effect the transactions contemplated by this Agreement or the Related Agreements and to the Knowledge of LGE or CP there does not exist any valid basis for any such claim, action, suit, proceeding or investigation. There are no claims, actions, suits, proceedings or, to the Knowledge of LGE or CP, investigations pending or, to the Knowledge of LGE or CP, threatened, by or against either Stockholder or CP with respect to this Agreement or the Related Agreements, or in connection with the transactions contemplated hereby or thereby and to the Knowledge of LGE or CP there does not exist any valid basis for any such claim, action, suit, proceeding or investigation.

3.19   Permits. Schedule 3.19 hereto sets forth a true, correct and complete list of all material Permits of any federal, state or local regulatory or Governmental Authority relating to the business properties or assets of CP. The Permits constitute all material permits, licenses, franchises, orders, certificates and approvals which are required for the lawful operation of the business, properties and assets of CP. CP is in compliance in all material respects with all such Permits and owns or has owned or had valid Permits to use all properties, tangible or intangible, necessary for the conduct of its business and the operation of its properties and assets in the manner in which they are now conducted and operated.

3.20   Taxes. Except as described in Schedule 3.20, which Schedule 3.20 also lists all jurisdictions in which Tax Reports are required to be filed by CP (or have been required since the inception of CP) and the types of Tax Reports required to be filed in each such jurisdiction:

(a)   CP has filed all material Tax Reports required to be filed prior to the Closing Date, and such Tax Reports are true and correct 'and completed in accordance with applicable law and no claim has been made by a taxing authority in any jurisdiction in which CP does not file Tax Reports that CP is or may be subject to taxation by that jurisdiction;

(b)   CP has (i) timely paid all Taxes due and payable as shown on the Tax Reports, (ii) timely paid all Taxes for which a notice of assessment or collection has been received (other than amounts properly accrued on the CP Financial Statements and described on Schedule 3.20), (iii) accrued on the CP Financial Statements all Taxes attributable to periods covered by such statements that are not yet due and payable, and (iv) properly reserved, in accordance with GAAP, for all Taxes not yet due but which are expected to become due and payable in the future;

(c)   Neither the IRS nor any other taxing authority has asserted any claim for Taxes in writing, or to the Knowledge of CP or LGE, is threatening to assert any claims for Taxes;

(d)   No Tax deficiency notice or notice of assessment or collection has been received in writing by CP;

(e)   No audit or other examination of any Tax Report of CP is presently in progress, nor has CP been notified in writing of any request for such an audit or other examination;

(f)   No power of attorney to deal with Tax matters or waiver of any statute of limitations with respect to Taxes has been granted by CP;

(g)   The relevant statute of limitations for the assessment or proposal of a deficiency against CP for Taxes has expired for all years before 1996;

(h)   CP has not availed itself of any tax amnesty, tax holiday or similar relief in any jurisdiction;

INSIDE THE MINDS

(i)   CP has withheld or collected and paid over to the appropriate governmental authorities (or is properly holding for such payment) all Taxes required by law to be withheld or collected with respect to its operations, including withholdings on payments to CP for sales and use taxes or payments by CP to employees or independent contractors on account of federal, state, and foreign income Taxes, the Federal Insurance Contribution Act, and the Federal Unemployment Tax Act;

(j)   There are no liens for Taxes upon the assets of CP (other than Permitted Liens);

(k)   There is no contract, agreement, plan or arrangement, including but not limited to the provisions of this Agreement, covering any employee or former employee of CP that, individually or collectively, could give rise to the payment of any amount that would not be deductible pursuant to Sections 280G, 404 or 162 of the Code;

(l)   CP has not filed any consent agreement under Section 341(f) of the Code or agreed to have Section 341(f)(2) of the Code apply to any disposition of a subsection (f) asset (as defined in Section 341(f)(4) of the Code) owned by CP;

(m)   CP is not and has not been a member of an affiliated group of corporations filing a consolidated federal income tax return (or a group of corporations filing a consolidated, combined or unitary income tax return under comparable provisions of state, local or foreign tax law);

(n)   CP has no obligation under any agreement or arrangement with any other person or entity with respect to Taxes of such other person or (including pursuant to Treas. Reg. §1.1502 6 or comparable provisions of state, local or foreign tax law) and including any liability for Taxes of any predecessor entity;

(o)   CP has made available to MDU true copies of all Tax Reports that CP has filed since December 31, 1993 and true copies

756

of all correspondence and other written submissions to or communications with any Tax authorities;

(p)   None of the assets of CP is "tax exempt use property" within the meaning of Section 168(h) of the Code;

(q)   CP has not agreed to make, nor is it required to make, any adjustment under Section 481 of the Code by reason of a change in accounting method or otherwise;

(r)   CP is not and has not been a member of a limited liability company or a party to any joint venture, partnership, or other arrangement or contract that is or could be treated as a partnership for federal income tax purposes;

(s)   CP has not indemnified any person against Taxes in connection with any arrangement for the leasing of real or personal property, except for indemnity with respect to acts of CP; and

(t)   Neither Stockholder nor any of LGE's shareholders is a "foreign person" within the meaning of Section 1445 of the Code.

3.21   Employee Benefit Plans and Employment Agreements.

(a)   Set forth on Schedule 3.21(a) is a list of each employee benefit plan (within the meaning of Section 3(3) of ERISA), written or oral employment or consulting agreement, severance pay plan or agreement, employee relations policy (or practice, agreement or arrangement), agreements with respect to leased or temporary employees, vacation plan or arrangement, sick pay plan, stock purchase plan, stock option plan, fringe benefit plan, incentive plan, bonus plan, cafeteria or flexible spending account plan and any deferred compensation agreement (or plan, program, or arrangement) covering any present or former employee of CP and which is, or at any time during the six year period preceding the Closing Date was, sponsored or maintained by (or to which contributions are, were, or at any time during the six year period preceding the Closing Date were required to have been, made by) either (1) CP or (2) any other organization which is a member of a controlled group of organizations (within the meaning of Code Sections 414(b), (c), (m) or (o)) of which CP is a member (the "Controlled Group"). Each and every such plan, program, policy, practice, arrangement and agreement included on the list set forth under Schedule 3.21(a) is hereinafter referred to as an "Employee Benefit Plan."

(b)   With respect to each Employee Benefit Plan that is not a multi-employer plan as defined under 3(37) or Section 4001(a)(3) of ERISA, there has been delivered to MDU, (i) current, accurate and complete copies of each such Employee Benefit Plan (including all trust agreements, insurance or annuity contracts, summary plan descriptions, general notices to employees or beneficiaries and any other material documents or instruments relating thereto); (ii) the most recent audited financial statement with respect to each such Employee Benefit Plan that is required to have an audited financial statement; (iii) copies of the most recent determination letters with respect to any such Employee Benefit Plan which is an employee pension benefit plan (as such term is defined in Section 3(2) of ERISA) intended to qualify under the Code; and (iv) copies of the three most recent actuarial reports with respect to each such Employee Benefit Plan that is required to have an actuarial report; and (v) copies of the three most recent annual reports (Forms 5500) with respect to each LGE Employee Benefit Plan in which any CP employee participates and which is required to file an annual report.

(c)   With respect to each Employee Benefit Plan that is not a multi-employer plan as defined under 3(37) or Section 4001(a)(3) of ERISA:

(i)   each such Employee Benefit Plan which is an employee pension benefit plan (as such term is defined in ERISA Section 3(2)) intended to qualify under the Code so qualifies and has received a favorable determination letter as to its qualification under the Code, and no event has occurred that will or could be expected to give rise to disqualification or loss of tax-exempt status of any such plan or related trust;

(ii)   Each Stockholder, CP and each member of the Controlled Group has complied with all provisions of ERISA, the Code and other applicable law, and no act or omission by any Stockholder, CP, each member of the Controlled Group, or any fiduciary of any Employee Benefit Plan, has occurred that will or could be expected to give rise to liability to CP for a breach of fiduciary responsibilities under ERISA or to any fines or penalties under ERISA Section 502(l);

(iii)   no Employee Benefit Plan provides for any post retirement life, medical, dental or other welfare benefits (whether or not insured) for any current or former employee of CP except as required under Code Section 4980B, Part 6 of Title I of ERISA or applicable state or local Law or as set forth in Schedule 3.21(c);

(iv)   all contributions, insurance and annuity premiums and salary deferrals elected by an employee or required to have been made by CP, any Stockholder or any member of the Controlled Group under law or under the terms of any contract, agreement or Employee Benefit Plan for all complete and partial periods up to and including the Closing Date have been made or will be made to the appropriate plan on or before such date;

(v)   the transactions contemplated by this Agreement will not be the direct or indirect cause of any amount paid or payable from such Employee Benefit Plan being classified as an excess parachute payment under Code Section 280G;

(vi)   there are no matters pending before the IRS, the United States Department of Labor or the PBGC;

(vii)   there have been no claims or notice of claims filed under any fiduciary liability insurance policy covering any Employee Benefit Plan; and

(viii) each and every such Employee Benefit Plan which is a group health plan (as such term is defined under the Code or ERISA Section 607(1)) complies, and in each and every case has complied in all material respects with the applicable requirements of Code Section 4980B, Part 6 of Title I of ERISA, the applicable requirements of the Health Insurance Portability and Accountability Act of 1996, and all other applicable federal, state or local Laws or ordinances requiring the provision or continuance of health or medical benefits.

(d) With respect to any Employee Benefit Plan that is an employee benefit plan within the meaning of Section 3(3) of ERISA, stock purchase plan, stock option plan, fringe benefit plan, bonus plan or any deferred compensation agreement, plan or program (whether or not any such plan, program or agreement is currently in effect):

(i) there are no actions, suits or claims (other than routine claims for benefits in the ordinary course) pending or, to the Knowledge of LGE or CP, threatened, and neither LGE nor CP has any Knowledge of any facts which could give rise to any such actions, suits or claims (other than routine claims for benefits in the ordinary course), which could subject CP to any liability;

(ii) neither Stockholder, nor CP, nor any member of the Controlled Group or any other person has engaged in a prohibited transaction, as such term is defined in Code Section 4975 or ERISA Section 406, which would subject CP to any taxes, penalties or other liabilities resulting from prohibited transactions under Code Section 4975 or under ERISA Sections 409 or 502(i);

(iii) no event has occurred and no condition exists that could subject CP to any tax or penalty under Code Sections 511, 4971, 4972, 4976, 4977, 4978, 4979, 4979A, 4980B, or 5000, or to a fine under ERISA Section 502(c);

(iv)   CP is not subject to (1) any liability, lien or other encumbrance under any agreement imposing secondary liability on CP as a seller of the assets of a business in accordance with Section 4204 of ERISA or under any other provision of Title IV of ERISA or Code Section 412, (2) contingent liability under Title IV of ERISA to the PBGC or to any plan, participant, or other person or (3) a lien or other encumbrance under Section 4068 of ERISA; and

(v)   CP is not subject to any liability pursuant to Section 4069 of ERISA.

(e)

(i)   CP is not subject to any legal, contractual, equitable, or other obligation to (1) establish as of any date any employee benefit plan of any nature, including, without limitation, any pension, profit sharing, welfare, post retirement welfare, stock option, stock or cash award, non qualified deferred compensation or executive compensation plan, policy or practice or (2) continue any employee benefit plan of any nature, including, without limitation any Employee Benefit Plan that is not a multi-employer plan as defined under 3(37) or Section 4001(a)(3) of ERISA or any other pension, profit sharing, welfare, or post retirement welfare plan, or any stock option, stock or cash award, non qualified deferred compensation or executive compensation plan, policy or practice (or to continue their participation in any such benefit plan, policy or practice) on or after the Closing Date except in connection with any collective bargaining agreement;

(ii)   CP and each member of the Controlled Group may, in any manner, subject to the limitations imposed by applicable law or restrictions imposed under any collective bargaining agreement or by the collective bargaining process, and without the consent of any employee, beneficiary or other person, prospectively terminate, modify or amend any such Employee Benefit Plan or any other plan, program or practice (or its participation in such Employee Benefit Plan that is not a multi-employer plan as defined under 3(37) or Section 4001(a)(3) of ERISA or any other plan, program or practice) effective as of any date on or after the Closing Date; and

(iii)   no representations or communications by LGE or CP (directly or indirectly, orally, in writing or otherwise) with respect to participation, eligibility for benefits, vesting, benefit accrual coverage or other material terms of any Employee Benefit Plan have been made prior to the Closing to any employee, beneficiary or other person other than those which are in accordance with the terms and provisions of each such Employee Benefit Plan as in effect immediately prior to the Closing.

(f)   With respect to each pension plan that is a multi-employer plan (within the meaning of Section 3(37) or 4001(a)(3) of ERISA) in which CP or any member of the Controlled Group participates or has participated: (i) no such company has withdrawn, partially withdrawn, or received any notice of any claim or demand for withdrawal liability or partial withdrawal liability, (ii) no such company has received any notice that any such plan is in reorganization, that increased contributions may be required to avoid a reduction in plan benefits or the imposition of any excise tax, or that any such plan is or may become insolvent, (iii) no such company has failed to make any required contributions, (iv) to the Knowledge of LGE or CP, no such multi-employer plan is a party to any pending merger or asset or liability transfer, (v) to the Knowledge of LGE or CP, there are no proceedings of the PBGC against or affecting any such multi-employer plan, (vi) no such company has (or will have as a result of the transactions contemplated hereby) any withdrawal liability by reason of a sale of assets pursuant to Section 4204 of ERISA; and (vii) Schedule 3.21(f) includes for each such multi-employer plan, as of its last valuation date, an estimate of the amount of potential withdrawal liability of each such company, calculated according to the information made available pursuant to ERISA Section 4221(e), and identifies the specific obligor, and nothing has occurred or is expected to occur that would materially increase the amount of the total potential withdrawal liability of a specified obligor for any such plan over the amount shown in Schedule 3.21(f), in each case, to the extent such information is available on the date hereof.

(g)   With respect to each and every Employee Benefit Plan that is not a multi-employer plan as defined under 3(37) or Section 4001(a)(3) of ERISA subject to Title IV of ERISA other than a multiemployer pension plan: (i) no such Employee Benefit Plan or related trust has been terminated or partially terminated; (ii) no liability to the PBGC has been or is expected to be incurred with respect to such a Employee Benefit Plan; (iii) the PBGC has not instituted and is not expected to institute any proceedings to terminate such a Employee Benefit Plan; (iv) there has been no reportable event (within the meaning of Section 4043 of ERISA); (v) there exists no condition or set of circumstances that presents a material risk of the termination of such a Employee Benefit Plan by the PBGC; (vi) no accumulated funding deficiency (as defined in Section 302 of ERISA and Section 412 of the Code), whether or not waived, exists with respect to such a Employee Benefit Plan; and (vii) the current value of all vested accrued benefits under each such Employee Benefit Plan did not as of the last day of the most recently ended fiscal year of such Employee Benefit Plan, and will not as of the Closing, exceed the current value of the assets of each such Employee Benefit Plan allocable to such vested accrued benefits.

3.22   Certain Employees and Salaries. Schedule 3.22 sets forth a list of the names and salary rates of all present officers and executive employees of CP whose current regular annual salary rate is $100,000 or more, together with any bonuses paid or payable to each such officer or executive employee of CP for the preceding or current fiscal year, and, to the extent existing on the Closing Date, all arrangements with respect to any bonuses or other payments to be paid to such officers and executive employees by CP from and after the Closing Date. Schedule 3.22 also identifies the company cars, club memberships and other like benefits, if any, paid or payable by CP on behalf of such officers and executive employees.

3.23   Material Contracts. Schedule 3.23 lists all contracts and arrangements, written, electronic, oral or otherwise, of the following types ("Material Contracts") to which CP is a party or by which it is bound, or to which any of its assets or properties is subject:

(a)   any contract or arrangement of any kind with either Stockholder or with any employee, officer or director of CP or LGE or any of their affiliates;

(b)   any contract or arrangement with a sales representative, dealer, broker, marketing, sales agency, advertising agency or other person engaged in sales, distributing, marketing, servicing or promotional activities, or any contract to act as one of the foregoing on behalf of any person;

(c)   any contract or arrangement of any nature which involves the payment or receipt of cash or other property, an unperformed commitment, or goods or services, having a value in excess of $50,000;

(d)   any contract or arrangement pursuant to which CP has made or will make loans or advances, or has or will have incurred debts or become a guarantor or surety or pledged its credit on or otherwise become responsible with respect to any undertaking of another (except for the negotiation or collection of negotiable instruments in transactions in the ordinary course of business consistent with past practice);

(e)   any indenture, credit agreement, loan agreement, note, mortgage, security agreement, lease of real property (to the extent not addressed in Section 3.12) or personal property or agreement or arrangement for financing;

(f)   any contract or arrangement involving a partnership, joint venture or other cooperative undertaking;

(g)   any contract or arrangement involving any restrictions with respect to the geographical area of operations or scope or type of business of CP;

(h)   any power of attorney or agency agreement or arrangement with any person pursuant to which such person is granted the authority to act for or on behalf of CP, or CP is granted the authority to act for or on behalf of any person;

(i)   any real property leases or licenses, or similar arrangements, to which CP is a party, whether as lessor, lessee, licensor or licensee, which relate to the business of CP;

(j)   any contract or arrangements, other than this Agreement and the Related Agreements, not made in the ordinary course of business consistent with past practice which is to be performed at or after the date of this Agreement;

(k)   any contract or arrangement providing for guaranteed maximum prices, guaranteed completion time, guaranteed general conditions, a lump sum price or surety bond contract; and

(l)   any contract or arrangement not specified above that is material to the business, properties, prospects or assets of CP.

There has been delivered to MDU, true, correct and complete copies of each document listed on Schedule 3.23 and a written description of each oral arrangement so listed. There has been delivered to MDU accurate copies of each form which has been used in the business of CP and is in effect with respect to any third party on the Closing Date.

Except as set forth on Schedule 3.23 hereto, each Material Contract is valid and in full force and effect and constitutes the legal, valid and binding obligation of CP and the other parties thereto, enforceable against CP and the other parties thereto in accordance with their respective terms, and there are no existing material violations or defaults by CP (including, but not limited to, the subcontracting or delegation by CP of duties to third parties) or, to the Knowledge of LGE or CP, by any other party thereto and, to the Knowledge of LGE or CP, no event, act or omission has occurred which (with or without notice, lapse of time or the happening or occurrence of any other event) would result in a material violation or default thereunder. No other party to any such contract has in writing or, to the Knowledge of LGE or CP, otherwise asserted the right, and, to the Knowledge of LGE or CP, no basis exists for the assertion of any enforceable right, to renegotiate, or cancel or terminate prior to the full term thereof, any of the terms or conditions of any such contract, nor do LGE or CP have any Knowledge that any party to any such contract intends to not renew any such contract upon termination of its current term. Except as set forth on Schedule 3.11 hereto, no consent of any party to such contracts is required for the execution, delivery or performance of this Agreement or the Related Agreements or the consummation of the transactions contemplated hereby or thereby.

3.24   Intellectual Property. Schedule 3.24 hereto sets forth a true, correct and complete list of all Intellectual Property. Except as disclosed on Schedule 3.24 hereto:

(a)   all of the Intellectual Property owned by CP is owned free and clear of all Liens and is not subject to any license, royalty or other agreement;

(b)   none of the Intellectual Property owned by CP has been or is the subject of any pending litigation or claim of infringement and, to the Knowledge of LGE or CP, none of the Intellectual Property has been or is the subject of any pending or threatened litigation or claim of infringement;

(c)   no license or royalty agreement to which CP is a party is in breach or default by any party thereto or the subject of any notice of termination given or, to the Knowledge of LGE or CP, threatened;

(d)   CP has not received any written or, to the Knowledge of LGE or CP, other notice contesting its right to use any Intellectual Property and, to the Knowledge of LGE and CP, the properties and assets of CP do not infringe any confidential or proprietary rights of any other person or entity,

(e)   CP has not granted any license or agreed to pay or receive any royalty in respect of any Intellectual Property; and

(f)   CP owns or possesses adequate rights in and to all Intellectual Property necessary to conduct its business.

(g)   CP has taken all actions, including any filings, necessary to perfect its interests and rights in and to the Intellectual Property, except for such actions the failure to take which, in the aggregate, could not reasonably be expected to have a Material Adverse Effect CP.

3.25   Labor Matters. CP has conducted, and currently is conducting its business in full compliance with all applicable federal and state laws relating to employment and employment practices, terms and conditions of employment, wages and hours, and nondiscrimination in employment, except for violations which in the aggregate could not reasonably be expected to have a Material Adverse Effect on CP. Except as set forth on Schedule 3.25, the relationships of CP with its employees are good and there is, and during the past five years there has been, no labor strike, dispute, slow-down, work stoppage or other labor difficulty actually pending or threatened against or involving CP. Except as set forth on Schedule 3.25, to the Knowledge of LGE or CP, there are no facts or circumstances that could give rise to a claim for wrongful termination or discrimination on any basis. Except as set forth on Schedule 3.25, none of the employees of CP is covered by any collective bargaining agreement, no collective bargaining agreement is currently being negotiated and, to the Knowledge of LGE or CP, no attempt is currently being made or during the past three years has been made to organize any employees of CP to form or enter a labor union or similar organization. LGE has have delivered to MDU a true and complete copy of each collective bargaining agreement to which CP is a party or by which CP is bound.

3.26   Customers and Suppliers.

(a)   Schedule 3.26 sets forth a list of the Major Customers in terms of revenue during each of the years ended March 31, 1998 and 1999 showing the approximate total revenue received in each such period from each such Major Customer.

(b)   Except as set forth on Schedule 3.26, no customer represented in excess of 5% of the total revenue of CP during the year ended March 31, 1999. Except to the extent set forth in Schedule 3.26, since March 31, 1999, there has not been any adverse change in the business relationship, and there has been no dispute involving more than $100,000 individually or in the aggregate, between CP and any Major Customer, and neither LGE nor CP has any Knowledge of any indications that any Major Customer intends to adversely change its servicing arrangements with CP.

3.27   Environmental Matters. Except as set forth in Schedule 3.27:

(a)   CP is currently in compliance with all applicable Environmental Laws, has cured any past violations or alleged violations of Environmental Laws to the satisfaction of Governmental Authorities, is not currently in receipt of any notice of violation, is not currently in receipt of any notice of any potential liability for cleanup of Hazardous Materials and is not now subject to any investigation or information request by a Governmental Authority concerning Hazardous Materials or any Environmental Laws. CP holds and is in compliance with all governmental permits, licenses, and authorizations necessary to operate those aspects of its business that relate to siting, zoning, wetlands, coastal zone management, threatened or endangered species, air emissions, discharges to surface or ground water, discharges to any sewer or septic system, noise emissions, solid waste disposal or the generation, use, transportation or other management of Hazardous Materials. CP has never generated, manufactured, refined, recycled, discharged, emitted, released, buried, processed, produced, reclaimed, stored, treated, transported, or disposed of any Hazardous Materials except in compliance with all applicable Laws, including applicable Permit requirements;

(b)   No assets of CP are subject to any Lien in favor of any person as a result of any Hazardous Material or response thereto;

APPENDICES

(c)   To the actual knowledge of LGE or CP, all facilities where any person has treated, stored, disposed of, reclaimed, or recycled any Hazardous Material on behalf of CP are in compliance with Environmental Laws.

3.28   Necessary Property. The assets of CP include all of the tangible and intangible assets (including goodwill) which are required for the operation by CP of its business as now conducted.

3.29   Minute Books and Charter Documents. All corporate records and books (including stock transfer ledgers) of CP have been made available to MDU for its review.

3.30   Broker's Fees. Other than any fees or commission payable to KPMG LLP, which fees or commission shall be the responsibility solely of LGE, no agent, broker or other person is or may be entitled to a commission or finder's fee in connection with the transactions contemplated by this Agreement, or is or may be entitled to make any claim against either Stockholder or CP or against MDU or any of its subsidiaries or affiliates as a result of any actions by either Stockholder or CP. LGE shall indemnify MDU and its subsidiaries against any claim for any such commission or finder's fee made by any agent, broker or other person as a result of any actions by either Stockholder or CP.

3.31   Investment Representation. LGE acknowledges that the issuance to each Stockholder by MDU of the shares of MDU Common Stock constituting the Consideration pursuant to this Agreement has not been registered under the 1933 Act or any state securities Law, and that such shares may not be sold or transferred other than pursuant to an effective registration statement under the 1933 Act or pursuant to an available exemption from such registration, and further acknowledges that the certificates representing the Consideration will bear a restrictive legend to the foregoing effect. Each Stockholder is acquiring such shares of MDU Common Stock for investment purposes only, for its or his own account (and not for the account(s) of others) and not with a view to the distribution thereof. LGE confirms that each Stockholder (i) is familiar with the business of MDU and has had the opportunity to ask questions of appropriate executive officers of MDU (and has received responses thereto to his or its satisfaction) and to obtain such information about the business

769

and financial condition of MDU as it or he has reasonably requested, and (ii) has such knowledge and experience in financial and business matters that it or he is capable of evaluating the merits and risks of an investment in MDU Common Stock. LGE represents that each Stockholder is an "accredited investor" as such term is defined in Regulation D under the 1933 Act.

3.32   Questionable Payments. Neither CP nor any executive, employee, shareholder, agent, or representative of CP (including each Stockholder) has made, directly or indirectly, any (a) bribes, kickbacks or illegal payments, (b) payments that were falsely recorded on the books and records of CP, or (c) payments to governmental officials for improper purposes.

3.33   No Misstatements or Omissions. No representation or warranty made in this Agreement or on any Schedule hereto by either LGE or CP is false or misleading as to any material fact, or omits to state a material fact required to make any of the statements made herein or therein not misleading in any material respect. Notwithstanding the foregoing, except as set forth or contemplated in this Agreement, neither LGE nor CP makes any representation or warranty with respect to any projections, estimates or budgets previously delivered or made available to MDU or Acquisition Subsidiary or any of their affiliates concerning future revenues, expenses, expenditures, or results of operations.

3.34   Proxy Statement. None of the information to be supplied by either Stockholder or CP or any of their accountants, counsel or other authorized representatives for inclusion in the Proxy Statement will, at the time of the mailing of the Proxy Statement and any amendments or supplements thereto, and at the time of the MDU Stockholders' Meeting contain any untrue statement of a material fact required to be stated therein or necessary in order to make the statements therein, in light of the circumstances under which they are made, not misleading. If at any time prior to the Closing Date any event with respect to either Stockholder or CP, or their officers and directors or any of the subsidiaries of LGE or CP shall occur which is or should be described in an amendment of, or a supplement to, the Proxy Statement, LGE will notify MDU in writing of such event.

3.35   Regulatory Status. Neither Stockholder nor CP is a "public utility" or a "holding company" or a "subsidiary company" for purposes of PUHCA.

3.36   Thomas Everist Stockholder's Agreement. The Thomas Everist Stockholder's Agreement has been duly and validly executed and delivered by Thomas Everist as of the date hereof and is enforceable against Thomas Everist in accordance with its terms.

ARTICLE 4.

REPRESENTATIONS AND WARRANTIES OF MDU

MDU represents and warrants to LGE as follows:

4.01   Organization; Good Standing. Each of MDU and Acquisition Subsidiary is a corporation duly organized, validly existing and in good standing under the laws of its jurisdiction of incorporation with all requisite corporate power and authority and legal right to own, operate and lease its properties and assets and to carry on its business as now being conducted and to enter into this Agreement and perform its obligations hereunder, and is duly qualified to do business and is in good standing as a foreign corporation in each jurisdiction where the conduct of its business or the ownership of its property requires such qualification, except where the failure to so qualify would not have a Material Adverse Effect on MDU.

4.02   Authority. Each of MDU and Acquisition Subsidiary has the corporate power and authority to execute, deliver, and perform its obligations under this Agreement and the Related Agreements to which it is a party and to consummate the transactions contemplated hereby and thereby, and, subject to the MDU Stockholder Approval, has taken all necessary corporate action to authorize the execution, delivery and performance of this Agreement. MDU has the power and authority to deliver the Consideration, and, subject to the MDU Stockholder Approval, all necessary corporate action to authorize the delivery of the Consideration has been taken. The MDU Stockholder Approval constitutes the only vote of any class or series of MDU capital stock necessary to approve the issuance and delivery of the Consideration.

4.03   Due Execution and Enforceability. This Agreement has been duly executed and delivered by each of MDU and Acquisition Subsidiary and constitutes a valid and binding obligation of each of MDU and Acquisition Subsidiary, enforceable in accordance with its terms, except as limited by applicable bankruptcy, insolvency, reorganization, moratorium or other laws of general application referring to or affecting enforcement of creditors' rights and general principles of equity.

4.04   No Restrictions Against Performance. Neither the execution, delivery, authorization or performance of this Agreement, nor the consummation of the transactions contemplated hereby will, with or without the giving of notice or the passage of time, or both, violate any provisions of, conflict with, result in a breach of, constitute a default under, or result in the creation or imposition of any Lien on any property or asset of MDU or Acquisition Subsidiary under (i) the respective Certificates of Incorporation or By-Laws of MDU or Acquisition Subsidiary; (ii) any federal, state or local Law, which is applicable to MDU or Acquisition Subsidiary; (iii) any material contract, indenture, instrument, agreement, mortgage, lease, right or other obligation or restriction to which MDU or Acquisition Subsidiary is a party or by which either of them is bound; or (iv) any order, judgment, writ, injunction, decree, license, franchise, permit or other authorization of any Governmental Authority by which MDU or Acquisition Subsidiary is bound, any of which, when taken as a whole, would have a Material Adverse Effect upon MDU.

4.05   Capital Stock of MDU. The authorized capital stock of MDU consists of (i) 150,000,000 shares of MDU Common Stock, (ii) 500,000 shares of MDU Preferred Stock, (iii) 1,000,000 shares of MDU Preferred Stock A, and (iv) 500,000 shares of MDU Preference Stock. The issued and outstanding shares of each class or series of capital stock of MDU as of January 1, 2000, are set forth on Schedule 4.05 hereto. All of the issued and outstanding shares of MDU Common Stock are, and all of the shares of MDU Common Stock, when issued in accordance with the terms of this Agreement are or will be, duly and validly authorized and issued and outstanding, fully paid and nonassessable. None of the outstanding shares of MDU Common Stock to be issued pursuant to this Agreement will be issued in violation of any preemptive rights of the current or past holders of MDU Common Stock.

Except as disclosed on Schedule 4.05 hereto, as of the date of this Agreement, there are no shares of capital stock or other equity securities of MDU outstanding and no outstanding options, warrants, rights, calls, commitments, conversion rights, rights of exchange, plans or other agreements of any character providing for the purchase, issuance or sale of any shares of the capital stock of MDU, other than as contemplated by this Agreement

4.06   SEC Filings; Financial Statements of MDU. MDU has timely filed and made available to the Stockholders all SEC Documents required to be filed by MDU since December 31, 1996 (the "MDU SEC Reports"). Since the date of the most recent MDU SEC Report, MDU has not experienced an event that reasonably could be expected to have a Material Adverse Effect on MDU. The MDU SEC Reports (i) at the time filed, complied in all material respects with the applicable requirements of the Securities Laws and other applicable laws, and (ii) did not, at the time they were filed (or, if amended or superseded by a filing prior to the date of this Agreement, then on the date of such filing), contain any untrue statement of a material fact or omit to state a material fact required to be stated in such MDU SEC Reports, or necessary in order to make the statements in such MDU SEC Reports in light of the circumstances under which they were made, not misleading.

Each of the MDU financial statements (including, in each case, any related notes) contained in the MDU SEC Reports complied as to form in all material respects with the applicable published rules and regulations of the SEC with respect thereto, was prepared in accordance with GAAP (except to the extent required by changes in GAAP, as may be indicated in the notes to such financial statements or, in the case of unaudited interim statements, as permitted by Form 10-Q under the 1934 Act, as amended), and fairly presented in all material respects the consolidated financial positions of MDU and its subsidiaries as at the respective dates and the consolidated results of operations and cash flows for the periods indicated, except that the unaudited interim financial statements were or are subject to normal and recurring year-end adjustments which were not or are not expected to be material in amount or effect.

4.07   Proxy Statement. None of the information to be supplied by MDU or Acquisition Subsidiary or any of their accountants, counsel or other authorized representatives for inclusion in the Proxy Statement will, at the time of the mailing of the Proxy Statement and any amendments or supplements thereto, and at the time of the MDU Stockholders' Meeting contain any untrue statement of a material fact required to be stated therein or necessary in order to make the statements therein, in light of the circumstances under which they are made, not misleading, it being understood and agreed that no representation or warranty is made by MDU with respect to any information supplied by either Stockholder or CP or their accountants, counsel or other authorized representatives. If at any time prior to the Closing Date any event with respect to MDU or Acquisition Subsidiary, or their officers and directors or any of its subsidiaries shall occur which is or should be described in an amendment of, or a supplement to, the Proxy Statement, such event shall be so described and the presentation in such amendment or supplement of such information will not contain any statement which, at the time and in light of the circumstances under which it is made, is false or misleading in any material respect or omits to state any material fact required to be stated therein or necessary in order to make the statements therein in light of the circumstances under which they were made, not false or misleading. The Proxy Statement will comply as to form in all material respects with all applicable laws, including the provisions of the 1934 Act and the rules and regulations promulgated thereunder.

4.08   Valuation Report. MDU has received the written report of Rohrer & Associates, Inc., consultant to KRC, which report sets forth a current business value for CP, and such report has not been withdrawn as of the date hereof. MDU has delivered a copy of such report to LGE.

4.09   Third-Party and Governmental Consents. Except for the filing of the agreement of merger and an officers' certificate of each constituent corporation, together with any other documents required by law to effectuate the Merger, with the Secretary of State of the State of California and the California Franchise Tax Board, as contemplated under Section 2.01, and except for the MDU Stockholder Approval, and except for filings required under the HSR Act with respect to (i) the acquisition by LGE of the shares of MDU Common Stock constituting its portion of the Consideration, and (ii) the Merger, and except for the authorization for listing of MDU Common Stock constituting the Consideration on the

NYSE and the PE, and except as set forth on Schedule 4.09 hereto, and other than the delivery by MDU of notice to the Federal Energy Regulatory Commission not later than 30 days after the Closing Date of the issuance of shares of MDU Common Stock constituting the Consideration, no approval, consent, waiver, order or authorization of, or registration, qualification, declaration, or filings with, or notice to, any Governmental Authority or other third party is required on the part of MDU or Acquisition Subsidiary in connection with the execution of this Agreement, the Related Agreements, or the consummation of the transactions contemplated hereby or thereby, including, but not limited to, the Merger.

4.10   Litigation. There are no claims, actions, suits, proceedings or, to the Knowledge of MDU, investigations pending or, to the Knowledge of MDU, threatened, by or against MDU with respect to this Agreement or the Related Agreements, or in connection with the transactions contemplated hereby or thereby and, to the Knowledge of MDU, there does not exists any valid basis for any such claim, action, suit, proceeding or investigation.

4.11   Broker's Fees. No agent, broker or other person is or may be entitled to a commission or finder's fee in connection with the transactions contemplated by this Agreement, or is or may be entitled to make any claim against either Stockholder or CP or against MDU or any of its subsidiaries or affiliates as a result of any actions by MDU. MDU shall indemnify Stockholders against any claim for any such commission or finder's fee made by any agent, broker or other person as a result of any actions by MDU.

4.12   Acquisition Subsidiary.

(a)   Acquisition Subsidiary was organized for the purpose of effectuating the Merger and at no time has engaged in the conduct of any business.

(b)   The assets of Acquisition Subsidiary consist solely of a nominal amount of cash. Acquisition Subsidiary has no liabilities.

4.13   Preference Share Purchase Rights. The preference share purchase rights (the "Rights") described in the agreement dated as of November 12, 1998 between MDU Resources Group, Inc., and Norwest Bank Minnesota, N.A., as Rights Agent ("Rights Agreement"), are not currently represented by separate Rights certificates and are not currently exercisable or separately tradable. Further, at the Effective Time, no event will have occurred that would result in a "Distribution Date" being established under the Rights Agreement or require the issuance of separate certificates for the Rights.

ARTICLE 5.

CERTAIN COVENANTS

5.01   Conduct of CP's Business Pending Closing. From the date hereof until the Closing, except as otherwise expressly permitted or contemplated by this Agreement or specifically disclosed in the Schedules hereto, and except as otherwise expressly consented to or approved by MDU in writing:

(a)   Regular Course of Business. CP shall, and LGE shall cause CP to, carry on its business in the ordinary course of business consistent with past practice, including without limitation, the performance by CP of its obligations under Material Contracts.

(b)   Amendments. CP shall not, and LGE shall cause CP not to, change, amend or propose any changes or amendments to its Certificate of Incorporation or By-Laws.

(c)   Capital Changes; Dividends; Redemptions. Except as provided in Schedule 5.01(c), CP shall not, and LGE shall cause CP not to, issue or sell any shares of its capital stock or other securities; acquire directly or indirectly, by redemption or otherwise, any such capital stock; reclassify or split-up any such capital stock; declare or pay any dividends thereon in cash, securities or other property or make any other distribution with respect thereto; grant or enter into any options, warrants, calls or commitments of any kind with respect thereto; or amend any material term of any outstanding securities.

(d)   Subsidiaries. CP shall not, and LGE shall cause CP not to, organize any new subsidiary, acquire any capital stock or other equity securities of any other corporation or acquire any entity or ownership interest in any business.

(e)   Organization. CP shall use its reasonable best efforts to, and LGE shall use its reasonable best efforts to cause CP to, preserve its corporate existence and business organization substantially intact, including its present relationships with material customers, suppliers and other third parties and keep available the services of its present officers and employees.

(f)   Certain Changes. Except as expressly provided for elsewhere in this Agreement, CP shall not, and LGE shall cause CP not to:

> (i)   Borrow or agree to borrow any funds or incur, or assume or become subject to, whether directly or by way of guarantee or otherwise, any obligation or liability (absolute or contingent), except obligations and liabilities incurred in the ordinary course of business consistent with past practice;

> (ii)   Pay, discharge or satisfy any claim, liability or obligation (absolute, accrued, contingent or otherwise), other than the payment, discharge or satisfaction in the ordinary course of business consistent with past practice;

> (iii)   Prepay any obligation having a fixed maturity of more than 90 days from the date such obligation was issued or incurred;

> (iv)   Permit or allow any of its property or assets (personal or mixed, tangible or intangible) to be subjected to any pledge, lien or encumbrance in an amount exceeding $50,000 in the aggregate, other than inchoate liens incurred in the ordinary course of business consistent with past practice;

(v)   Cancel any debts or waive any claims or rights of substantial value or sell, transfer, or otherwise dispose of any of its properties or assets, except in the ordinary course of business consistent with past practice;

(vi)   Except as required by contractual commitments set forth on Schedule 5.01(f)(vi), (A) increase the compensation payable or to become payable to its officers or employees (except for increases in the ordinary course of business consistent with past practice in salaries or wages of officers or employees of CP), (B) establish, adopt, enter into or amend any collective bargaining, bonus, profit sharing, thrift, compensation, employment, termination, severance or other plan, agreement, trust, fund, policy or arrangement for the benefit of any director, officer or employee, (C) increase the benefits payable under any existing severance or termination pay policies or employment or other agreements or (D) take any affirmative action to accelerate the vesting of any stock based compensation;

(vii)   Make any single capital expenditure or commitment in excess of $50,000 for additions to its property, plant or equipment or make aggregate capital expenditures and commitments in excess of $100,000 for additions to its property, plant or equipment;

(viii)   Pay, loan or advance any amount to, or sell, transfer or lease its properties or assets to, or enter into any agreement or arrangement with or for the benefit of, any of its officers, directors or shareholders or any affiliate or associate of any of its officers, directors or shareholders, except for directors' fees and compensation to officers and employees at rates not exceeding the rates of compensation paid during the fiscal year ended March 31, 1999 and except as otherwise permitted in clause (vi) above;

(ix)   Take any action with respect to accounting policies or procedures, other than actions in the ordinary course of business consistent with past practice or except as required by changes in GAAP;

(x)   Settle or compromise any claim or lawsuit or institute any action or proceeding involving CP or any of its properties or assets in excess of $50,000; or

(xi)   Agree, whether in writing or otherwise, to do any of the foregoing.

(g)   Contracts. CP shall not, and LGE shall cause CP not to, terminate, cancel, waive any rights under or request any material change in, or agree to any change in, any Material Contract or, except in the ordinary course of business consistent with past practice, or enter into any contract or arrangement of the type that would constitute a Material Contract.

(h)   Insurance; Property. CP shall use its reasonable best efforts to, and LGE shall use its reasonable best efforts to cause CP to, continue to insure, at individual and aggregate limits and scope of coverage not less than those contained in CP's current insurance policies, its business and operations and all property, real, personal and mixed, owned or leased by CP, with financially responsible insurance companies against all ordinary and insurable risks consistent with past practice. All such property shall be used, operated, maintained and repaired in a customary manner. CP shall not, and LGE shall cause CP not to, terminate, cancel, waive any rights under or request any material change in, or agree to any material change in, any material insurance policy.

(i)   Taxes. CP shall not, and LGE shall cause CP not to, make any material election relating to Taxes or take any position on any Tax Report filed on or after the date of this Agreement or adopt any method therefor that is inconsistent with elections made, positions taken or methods used in preparing or filing similar Tax Reports in prior periods. For the period from the date of this Agreement to the Closing Date, CP shall, and LGE shall cause CP to, timely file all material tax returns and other material reports required to be filed by it and duly and timely pay in all material respects all Taxes for such period.

(j) Collection of Accounts Receivable. CP shall use its reasonable best efforts to, and LGE shall use its reasonable best efforts to cause CP to, collect its accounts receivable outstanding as of December 31, 1999 in the ordinary course of business, consistent with past practice.

(k) Representations and Warranties. Neither CP nor any Stockholder shall intentionally take any action that, individually or in the aggregate would reasonably be expected to result in a material breach of any provision of this Agreement or to make any representation and warranty of CP or LGE hereunder untrue in any material respect at or as of any time prior to the Closing, as though such representation or warranty were made at and as of such time.

(l) Agreements. CP shall not, and LGE shall cause CP not to, agree or commit to do anything that would be prohibited under this Section 5.01.

(m) Termination of 401(k) Plan. The Board of Directors of CP shall adopt resolutions terminating the participation of CP in the L.G. Everist, Incorporated and Subsidiaries 401(k) Plan effective as of the Closing Date.

5.02 Full Access. CP shall, and LGE shall cause CP to, until the earlier to occur of the Closing Date or the termination of this Agreement pursuant to Section 8.01 hereof, afford to MDU, its counsel, accountants and other representatives and advisors full access to the operations, offices, properties, books and records of CP. CP shall, and LGE shall cause CP to, permit two MDU designees to attend senior management and board meetings of CP. MDU shall have the right to review any and all work papers of CP's accountants, and shall have full opportunity to make such investigations as it shall desire to make of the affairs of CP; provided, however, that any such investigation shall occur upon reasonable notice and during normal business hours and shall be conducted in a manner as not to interfere unreasonably with operation of CP's business; LGE and CP shall cause the officers and accountants of CP to furnish such additional financial, operating and other information as MDU shall from time to time reasonably request.

5.03   Obtaining Consents. Each of LGE and CP shall use commercially reasonable efforts to obtain, prior to the Closing, all consents, approvals and authorizations required to be obtained by either LGE or CP necessary to the consummation of the transactions contemplated by this Agreement or the Related Agreements and will deliver to MDU copies of each such consent, approval and authorization promptly after it is obtained.

5.04   Covenant to Satisfy Conditions.

(a)   Each of LGE and CP shall use its commercially reasonable efforts to insure that the conditions set forth in Sections 6.01 and 6.03 of this Agreement are satisfied.

(b)   MDU shall use its commercially reasonable efforts to insure that the conditions set forth in Sections 6.01 and 6.02 of this Agreement are satisfied.

5.05   MDU Stockholders' Meeting. MDU shall, promptly after the date of this Agreement, take all action necessary in accordance with the Delaware General Corporation Law and its Restated Certificate of Incorporation and By-Laws to convene a meeting of MDU's stockholders to act on the Agreement and the Merger and the transactions contemplated thereby (the "MDU Stockholders' Meeting"), and MDU shall consult with LGE in connection therewith. MDU shall use its reasonable best efforts to solicit from shareholders of MDU proxies in favor of the approval and adoption of the Agreement and the Merger and the transactions contemplated thereby and to secure the vote or consent of stockholders to approve this Agreement and the Merger and the transactions contemplated thereby unless otherwise required by the applicable fiduciary duties of the directors of MDU, as determined by such directors in good faith after consultation with independent legal counsel (which may include MDU's regularly engaged legal counsel).

5.06   LGE Stockholders' Meeting. LGE shall, promptly after the date of this Agreement, take all action necessary in accordance with the General Corporation Law of the State of Iowa and its Restated Articles of Incorporation and By-Laws to convene a meeting of LGE's stockholders to act on the Agreement and the Merger (the "LGE Stockholders' Meeting"), and LGE shall consult with the MDU in connection therewith. LGE shall use its reasonable best efforts to secure the vote or consent of stockholders to approve this Agreement and the Merger unless otherwise required by the applicable fiduciary duties of the directors of LGE, as determined by such directors in good faith after consultation with independent legal counsel (which may include LGE's regularly engaged legal counsel).

5.07   Proxy Statement. As promptly as practicable after the execution of this Agreement, MDU shall prepare and file with the SEC a proxy statement and form of proxy, in connection with the vote of MDU's stockholders with respect to this Agreement and the Merger (such proxy statement, together with any amendments thereof or supplements thereto, in each case in the form or forms mailed to MDU's stockholders, being the "Proxy Statement"). Each of MDU, on the one hand, and each Stockholder and CP, on the other hand, shall furnish all information concerning it and the holders of its capital stock, if any, as the other may reasonably request in connection with such actions. As promptly as practicable MDU shall mail the Proxy Statement to its stockholders. The Proxy Statement shall include the recommendation of MDU's Board of Directors in favor of the approval of this Agreement and the Merger unless otherwise required by the applicable fiduciary duties of the Board of Directors of MDU, as determined by such directors in good faith after consultation with legal counsel.

5.08   Updated CP Financial Statements. CP shall, and LGE shall cause CP to, as soon as practicable after the date of execution of this Agreement, prepare the Updated CP Financial Statements, which shall be prepared in accordance with GAAP and shall contain all of the information required to be contained in financial statements furnished pursuant to paragraph (b)(3)(ii) of Item 14 of Rule 14A-101 under the 1934 Act and shall comply as to form with the applicable requirements under Rule 14A-101 under the 1934 Act. CP shall, and LGE shall cause CP to, deliver copies of the

Updated CP Financial Statements to MDU as soon as practicable after the preparation thereof and, in any case, before the Closing Date.

5.09   HSR Filing. To the extent required by law, the respective ultimate parent entities of MDU and LGE shall file Notification and Report Forms under the HSR Act with the Federal Trade Commission and the Antitrust Division of the Department of Justice. The parties shall cooperate and consult with each other with respect to the preparation of the Notification and Report Forms and any other submissions, including, but not limited to, responses to written or oral comments or requests for additional information or documenting material by the Federal Trade Commission or the Antitrust Division of the Department of Justice, required to be made pursuant to the HSR Act in connection with the transactions contemplated hereby. The filing fee associated with such filings shall be borne equally by MDU and LGE.

5.10   Certificates. At the Closing, LGE and CP will furnish MDU with such certificates to evidence compliance with the covenants set forth in this Article 5 as MDU may reasonably request.

5.11   Other Transactions. Neither Stockholder nor CP, or any of their representatives, agents, officers, employees, shareholders or boards of directors, shall enter into or continue any discussions or transactions concerning, or approve or recommend to the holders of any shares of capital stock of CP or LGE, any merger, consolidation, disposition of any significant portion of CP's business, properties or assets, acquisition or other business combination or like transaction or proposal therefor relating to CP (other than pursuant to this Agreement), or furnish or cause to be furnished any information concerning the business, properties or assets of CP to any party in connection with any transaction or proposed transaction involving the merger, consolidation or acquisition of CP or any substantial part of its business by or with any person other than MDU.

5.12   Information as to Violation of Representations and Warranties. LGE shall promptly inform and advise MDU of any fact or situation that, after reasonable inquiry, is or could be reasonably expected to result in a violation of any representation or warranty contained in Article 3 of this Agreement.

5.13   Tax-Free Reorganization.

(a)   MDU, CP, Acquisition Subsidiary and each Stockholder shall each use its best efforts to cause the Merger to be treated as a reorganization within the meaning of Section 368(a) of the Code (a "Reorganization").

(b)   To the extent permitted under applicable tax laws, the Merger shall be reported as a Reorganization in all federal, state, and local tax returns filed after the Effective Time.

(c)   Following the Merger and for a period sufficient to qualify the Merger as a Reorganization, MDU will cause the Surviving Corporation to hold at least 90% of the fair market value of CP's net assets and 70% of the fair market value of CP's gross assets held by CP immediately prior to the Merger and at least 90% of the fair market value of Acquisition Subsidiary's net assets and at least 70% of the fair market value of Acquisition Subsidiary's gross assets held by Acquisition Subsidiary immediately prior to the Merger.

(d)   Following the Merger and for a period sufficient to qualify the Merger as a Reorganization, MDU will cause the Surviving Corporation to continue the historic business of CP or use a significant portion of CP's historic business assets in a business.

(e)   Following the Merger and for a period sufficient to qualify the Merger as a Reorganization, MDU will retain control of the Surviving Corporation, within the meaning of Section 368(c) of the Code; provided, that MDU may transfer some or all of the stock of the Surviving Corporation to the extent permitted by Treasury Regulation Section 1.368-2(k).

(f)   Following the Merger and for a period sufficient to qualify the Merger as a Reorganization, MDU will not reacquire any of its stock issued in the Merger, whether directly or through a partnership, successor, or a person related to MDU within the meaning of Treasury Regulation Section 1.368-1(e)(3) if such reacquisition would cause the Merger to fail to qualify as a Reorganization.

(g)   Following the Merger and for a period sufficient to qualify the Merger as a Reorganization, MDU will not liquidate the Surviving Corporation, merge the Surviving Corporation with or into another corporation. sell or dispose of the stock of the Surviving Corporation (except for transfers described in Section 368(a)(2)(C) of the Code), or cause the Surviving Corporation to sell or dispose of any of its assets, except for dispositions in the ordinary course of business.

(h)   At the Effective Time, none of MDU, CP or Acquisition Subsidiary will be an investment company as defined in Sections 368(a)(2)(F)(iii) and (iv) of the Code.

(i)   At the Effective Time, no indebtedness between MDU and CP or between Acquisition Subsidiary and CP will have been issued, acquired, or settled at a discount.

(j)   At the Effective Time, MDU will own all of the issued and outstanding shares of stock of Acquisition Subsidiary, and Acquisition Subsidiary will have no liabilities.

(k)   As contemplated by Section 10.01 of this Agreement, each of the parties will pay its own expenses, if any, incurred in connection with the Merger.

5.14   Tax Audits or Controversies. LGE shall promptly notify and advise MDU of the beginning of any audit or examination by any tax authority of any tax Report of LGE in which any of the income or operations of CP have been included. LGE shall also advise MDU if in the course of any such audit a tax authority proposes any adjustments or assessments ("Proposed Adjustments") that, if accepted, could have, in the aggregate, a material effect on the tax liabilities of the Surviving Corporation or of MDU with respect to the Surviving Corporation for periods after the Closing Date. MDU shall have the right to receive copies of any written materials that LGE received from the taxing authority with respect to the Proposed Adjustments and, at MDU's own expense, to review any written materials proposed to be submitted to a taxing authority with respect to any such Proposed Adjustments. LGE shall not concede or settle any such Proposed Adjustments without the written consent of MDU, which shall not be unreasonably withheld. In the event that LGE desires to settle or concede such Proposed Adjustments, but MDU shall withhold its written consent, MDU shall bear the expense of contesting such Proposed Adjustments. MDU shall in such event be entitled to control the contest of the Proposed Adjustments and be present at any conferences with tax authorities with respect to such Proposed Adjustments; provided however, that MDU shall have no right to participate in the contest of any adjustment or assessment that is not a Proposed Adjustment. For the purpose of this Section, Proposed Adjustments shall be considered to have a material effect on the tax liability of the Surviving Corporation or MDU if the present value (using a discount rate equal to the applicable Federal mid-term rate determined under Code Section 1274(d) in effect on the date of notice of the beginning of the audit or examination) of the additional taxes that could be imposed on the Surviving Corporation or MDU for periods after the Closing Date as a result of the Proposed Adjustments is more than $500,000.

5.15   Books and Records; Tax Matters. LGE will retain its books and records relating to CP for at least seven (7) years following the Closing Date. LGE will cooperate with and make available to MDU or its designated representative, during normal business hours, the books and records relating to CP retained by LGE and remaining in existence after the Effective Time that are necessary or useful in connection with any tax inquiry, audit, investigation or any other matter reasonably requiring the use of any books and records for any reasonable business purpose.

5.16   Tax Reports. LGE will prepare and file all consolidated, combined or unitary Tax Reports that will include the operations of CP with LGE's operations for periods ending on or before the Closing Date and that are due after the Closing Date. LGE will furnish MDU with a schedule of such returns at the Closing. MDU will, or will cause CP to, prepare and file all other Tax Reports that are due after the Closing Date with respect to Taxes for CP for any taxable period ending on or before the Closing Date. LGE and MDU will each prepare and file such Tax Reports on a basis that is consistent with the basis upon which similar Tax Reports for prior periods have been prepared and filed (including any material elections on such Tax Reports), unless the party preparing the Tax Report obtains an opinion from a reputable national law firm or accounting firm to the effect that continued reporting on such basis would be contrary to law.

5.17   Amendment of Schedule 3.21(f). As soon as practicable after the date hereof, and in any case at least two (2) Business Days prior to the Closing Date, LGE shall supplement or amend Schedule 3.21(f) hereto to include all information that would have been required to be included on such Schedule 3.21(f) on the date of execution of this Agreement had such information been available at that time.

ARTICLE 6.

CONDITIONS TO CLOSING

6.01   Conditions to Each Party's Obligations. The respective obligations of each party to this Agreement to consummate the transactions contemplated by this Agreement and the Related Agreements shall be subject to the satisfaction or waiver of the following conditions:

(a)   Stockholder Approvals. The MDU Stockholder Approval and the LGE Stockholder Approval shall have been obtained.

(b)   Waiting Periods; Approvals. The waiting periods applicable to the consummation of the transactions contemplated by this Agreement under the HSR Act shall have expired or been terminated and all other approvals required under applicable laws shall have been obtained, except where the failure to obtain such approval would not, individually or in the aggregate, be reasonably expected to have a Material Adverse Effect on MDU.

(c)   No Governmental Proceeding or Litigation. No suit, action, investigation, inquiry or other proceeding by any Governmental Authority shall have been instituted or, to the Knowledge of any party, threatened, which questions the validity or legality of the transactions contemplated by this Agreement and the Related Agreements.

(d)   Listing on NYSE and PE. The shares of MDU Common
Stock comprising the Consideration shall have been authorized for
listing on the NYSE and the PE, subject to official notice of
issuance.

6.02   Additional Conditions to Obligations of MDU. The obligations of
MDU to consummate the transactions contemplated by this Agreement
and the Related Agreements shall be subject to the satisfaction or waiver of
the following additional conditions:

(a)   Representations and Warranties. The representations and
warranties of LGE set forth in this Agreement shall be true and
correct in all material respects as of the Closing Date as though
such representations and warranties were made on and as of the
Closing Date (except to the extent any such representation or
warranty expressly speaks as of an earlier date); and MDU shall
have received a certificate executed by LGE to such effect.

(b)   Performance. Each Stockholder and CP shall have
performed and complied in all material respects with all covenants,
obligations and conditions required by this Agreement to be
performed or complied with by it on or prior to the Closing Date.

(c)   Consents Obtained. All consents, approvals and
authorizations required to be obtained by either Stockholder or CP
pursuant to this Agreement, including, without limitation, consents
and approvals referred to in Section 3.11, shall have been obtained,
except to the extent the failure to obtain any such consents,
approvals and authorizations could not reasonably be expected to
have a Material Adverse Effect on CP.

(d)   No Material Adverse Change. Since the date of this
Agreement, no change in the business, financial condition, assets or
liabilities or results of operations of CP shall have occurred, which
change could reasonably be expected to result in a Material
Adverse Effect on CP; provided, that, for the purposes of this
Section 6.02(d), the failure of LGE to win any current bid on any
project shall not be deemed to be a change that could reasonably
be expected to result in a Material Adverse Effect.

(e)   Larison. At the Effective Time, Larison shall surrender the certificate or certificates representing all of the issued and outstanding shares of CP Common Stock owned, beneficially or of record, by Larison as set forth on Schedule 3.03 in exchange for a certificate or certificates, registered in the name of Larison representing Larison's share of the Consideration as set forth on Schedule 3.03. Each certificate representing CP Common Stock owned by Larison shall be duly endorsed in blank by Larison, with all necessary transfer tax and other revenue stamps, acquired at Larison's expense, affixed and canceled. Larison shall have cured any deficiencies with respect to the endorsement of the certificates representing the CP Common Stock owned by Larison or with respect to the stock power accompanying any such certificate. Larison shall have delivered to MDU, if requested by MDU, a waiver of any dissenters or appraisal rights under the laws of the State of California, in form and substance reasonably satisfactory to MDU. Larison shall have delivered to MDU a waiver of any rights to any portion of the Consideration Adjustment, in form and substance reasonably satisfactory to MDU. By its execution of this Agreement, LGE hereby consents to such waiver.

(f)   Additional Deliveries. All documents required to have been delivered by or on behalf of either Stockholder or CP pursuant to Section 7.01 or Section 7.03 shall have been delivered.

6.03   Additional Conditions to Obligations of LGE and CP. The obligations of LGE and CP to consummate the transactions contemplated by this Agreement and the Related Agreements shall be subject to the satisfaction or waiver of the following additional conditions:

(a)   Representations and Warranties. The representations and warranties of MDU set forth in this Agreement shall be true and correct in all material respects as of the Closing Date as though such representations and warranties were made on and as of the Closing Date (except to the extent any such representation or warranty expressly speaks as of an earlier date); and LGE shall have received a certificate executed by MDU to such effect.

(b)   Performance. Each of MDU and Acquisition Subsidiary shall have performed and complied in all material respects with all covenants, obligations and conditions required by this Agreement to be performed or complied with by it on or prior to the Closing Date.

(c)   Consents Obtained. All consents, approvals and authorizations required to be obtained by MDU or Acquisition Subsidiary pursuant to this Agreement, including, without limitation, consents and approvals referred to in Section 4.09, shall have been obtained, except to the extent the failure to obtain any such consents, approvals and authorizations could not reasonably be expected to have a Material Adverse Effect on MDU.

(d)   Releases of LGE's Liability. LGE shall have received releases of liability for post-Closing activities with respect to the following transactions: (i) the Quarry Agreement, including the sublease from the Santa Catalina Island Company contained therein, and (ii) any performance and payment bonds relating to post-Closing activities that are listed on Schedule 6.03, all of which are also listed on Schedule 3.23. LGE shall prepare and deliver Schedule 6.03 to MDU as soon as practicable after the execution of this Agreement, but in no case later than seven days preceding the Closing Date.

(e)   Additional Deliveries. All documents required to have been delivered by or on behalf of MDU pursuant to Section 7.02 or Section 7.03 shall have been delivered.

ARTICLE 7.

ADDITIONAL DELIVERIES

7.01   Deliveries by LGE and CP. At the Closing, in addition to any other certificates, documents or items required to be delivered under the terms of this Agreement, LGE and CP shall deliver the following:

(a)   A certificate of the President of LGE and Thomas Everist, as a Vice President of CP, dated the Closing Date, certifying that all consents, approvals and authorizations required to be obtained by LGE or CP pursuant to Section 6.02(c) have been obtained, together with copies of such consents and approvals.

(b)   Copies of the Articles of Incorporation of (i) LGE and (ii) CP, certified as of a recent date by the Secretary of State of the States of Iowa and California, respectively.

(c)   Copies of the By-Laws of (i) LGE and (ii) CP, including all amendments thereto, certified by the Secretary or an Assistant Secretary of LGE or CP, as the case may be.

(d)   Certificates, dated not earlier than seven (7) calendar days prior to the Closing Date, of the Secretary of State of the States of Iowa and California, respectively, as to the valid existence of (i) LGE and (ii) CP, together with other assurances reasonably acceptable to MDU dated the Closing Date bringing down such certificates to the Closing Date.

(e)   Certificates of authority, dated not earlier than seven (7) calendar days prior to the Closing Date, of the Secretary of State of each of the states in which CP is qualified to do business, as to the due qualification or license of CP as a foreign corporation in such state.

(f)   Resolutions adopted by the Board of Directors of LGE and resolutions adopted by the Board of Directors and by the stockholders of CP, in each case authorizing this Agreement and the transactions contemplated hereby, including, without limitation, the Merger, certified by the Secretary or an Assistant Secretary of LGE or CP, as the case may be.

(g)   Resolutions adopted by the stockholders of LGE evidencing the LGE Stockholder Approval, certified by the Secretary or an Assistant Secretary of LGE

(h)   A preliminary draft of the Closing Balance Sheet accompanied by a certificate of Thomas Everist, as Vice President of CP, and by the Treasurer of CP and by the President of LGE to the effect that such Closing Balance Sheet has been prepared in accordance with GAAP, and is true, accurate and complete in all material respects.

(i)   A certificate of Thomas Everist, as Vice President of CP, and by the Treasurer of CP and the President of LGE as to the amount of Debt.

(j)   The opinions of Faegre & Benson LLP and Lillick & Charles LLP, counsel to LGE and CP, substantially in the form of Exhibit 7.01(j)-1 and Exhibit 7.01(j)-2 hereto.

(k)   Evidence in form and substance satisfactory to MDU of the completion of the notices described in Schedule 3.12(b) hereto.

(l)   A certificate from each Stockholder, substantially in the form of Exhibit 7.01(l) hereto, stating that such Stockholder is not a nonresident alien for purposes of U.S. federal income taxation.

(m)   Duly executed resignations of each of the directors of CP, in form and substance reasonably satisfactory to MDU.

(n)   Each of LGE and CP shall deliver to MDU Uniform Commercial Code financing statement searches for the State of California and any other state in which CP does business, dated within 15 calendar days prior to the date of the Closing, showing that there are no security interests, judgments, taxes, other liens or encumbrances outstanding either Stockholder or CP or their respective assets.

(o)   Certificates of CP and LGE, in a form satisfactory to MDU, evidencing incumbency of the officers of CP and LGE, respectively, executing this Agreement, any Related Documents or any certificate or document in connection with the Agreement or the Related Agreements or the transactions contemplated thereby.

(p)   The following documents or items:

(i)   Amended and Restated Lease between LGE, as lessor, and CP, as lessee, relating to the premises located at

1925 Pier "D" Street, Long Beach, in the County of Los Angeles, State of California, substantially in the form attached here to as Exhibit 7.01(p)(i), duly executed and delivered by LGE and CP;

(ii)   Lease between LGE, as lessor, and CP, as lessee, relating to the premises located at Berth 44, Pier "D" Street, Long Beach, in the County of Los Angeles, State of California, substantially in the form attached here to as Exhibit 7.01(p)(ii), duly executed and delivered by LGE and CP; and

(iii)   a legal description of the real properties leased under, or subject to, either of the documents referred to in Section 7.01(p)(i) or (ii) above.

7.02   Deliveries by MDU. At the Closing, in addition to any other certificates, documents or items required to be delivered under the terms of this Agreement, MDU shall have deliver the following:

(a)   A certificate of the President or a Vice President of MDU, dated the Closing Date, certifying that all consents and approvals referred to in Section 4.09 have been obtained, together with copies of such consents and approvals or evidence thereof.

(b)   A copy of the Certificate of Incorporation of each of MDU and Acquisition Subsidiary, certified as of a recent date by the Secretary of State of the States of Delaware and California, respectively

(c)   A copy of the By-Laws of MDU, including all amendments thereto, certified by the Secretary or an Assistant Secretary of MDU.

(d)   Certificate, dated as of a recent date, of the Secretary of State of the State of Delaware, as to the valid existence and good standing of MDU, together with other assurances reasonably acceptable to LGE dated the Closing Date bringing down such certificate to the Closing Date.

(e)   Resolutions adopted by the respective Boards of Directors of MDU and Acquisition Subsidiary (or, to the extent applicable, a duly appointed and authorized committee thereof) authorizing this Agreement and the transactions contemplated hereby, including, without limitation, the Merger, certified by the Secretary or an Assistant Secretary of MDU or Acquisition Subsidiary, as the case may be.

(f)   Resolutions adopted by the Board of Directors of MDU (or, to the extent applicable, a duly appointed and authorized committee thereof), authorizing the delivery of the Consideration, certified by the Secretary or an Assistant Secretary of MDU.

(g)   Resolutions adopted by the stockholders of MDU evidencing the MDU Stockholder Approval, certified by the Secretary or an Assistant Secretary of MDU.

(h)   The opinions of Thelen Reid & Priest LLP, counsel to MDU, and Lester H. Loble, II, Vice President and General Counsel of MDU, substantially in the forms of Exhibit 7.02(h)-1 and Exhibit 7.02(h)-2 hereto.

(i)   Certificate of MDU, in a form satisfactory to LGE, evidencing incumbency of the officers of MDU executing this Agreement, any Related Documents or any certificate or document in connection with the Agreement or the Related Agreements or the transactions contemplated thereby.

7.03   Joint Deliveries. At the Closing, in addition to any other certificates, documents or items required to be delivered under the terms of this Agreement, the following documents shall be delivered:

(a)   Employment Agreement, dated as of the Closing Date, between CP and Larison substantially in the form of Exhibit 7.03(a) hereto.

(b)   A Noncompetition Agreement, dated as of the Closing Date, by and between MDU and LGE, substantially in the form of Exhibit 7.03(b) hereto.

(c)   A Stockholder's Agreement, dated as of the Closing Date, by and between MDU and LGE, substantially in the form of Exhibit 7.03(c) hereto.

ARTICLE 8.

TERMINATION

8.01   Termination. This Agreement may be terminated at any time prior to the Closing by written notice by the terminating party to the other parties:

(a)   by mutual written consent of MDU and LGE; or

(b)   by MDU or LGE after June 1, 2000, if the Closing Date has not occurred on or prior to such date.

8.02   Effect of Termination. In the event of termination as provided in this Article 8, such termination shall be without liability of any party to any other party to this Agreement, except that (i) if such termination results from the willful failure of MDU or Acquisition Subsidiary to fulfill a condition to the Agreement or from a material and willful breach by MDU or Acquisition Subsidiary, MDU shall be fully liable for any and all damages, costs and expenses (including but not limited to reasonable counsel fees) sustained or incurred by the other parties hereto, and (ii) if such termination results from the willful failure of either Stockholder or CP to fulfill a condition to the Agreement or from a material and willful breach by either LGE or CP, then LGE and CP shall, jointly and severally, be fully liable for any and all damages, costs and expenses (including but not limited to reasonable counsel fees) sustained or incurred by MDU and Acquisition Subsidiary. The provisions of Sections 8.02, 10.06 and 10.09 of this Agreement shall remain in full force and effect and survive any termination of this Agreement.

8.03   Confidentiality Following Termination. In the event of termination of this Agreement for any reason, MDU shall immediately return to LGE all information and data (regardless of the form in which such information or data is kept) of LGE and MDU's use or disclosure of such information or data shall be governed by the terms and provisions of the Confidentiality

Agreement between KRC and LGE. The confidentiality and other obligations of MDU contained in such Confidentiality Agreement shall expire two (2) years after the termination of this Agreement.

ARTICLE 9.

INDEMNIFICATION

9.01   Survival of Representations, Warranties and Covenants. Regardless of any investigation by any party hereto, the representations, warranties and covenants contained in this Agreement or any document delivered hereunder shall survive the Closing and remain in full force and effect until two (2) years after the Closing Date, other than (i) any representation, warranty or covenant by LGE contained herein which relates to Taxes or ERISA matters, including without limitation, any representation, warranty or covenant contained in Sections 3.20 or 3.21, which shall survive until the date on which the relevant statute of limitations expires (giving effect to any waiver, mitigation or extension thereof) and (ii) any representation, warranty or covenant contained in Sections 3.01(a), 3.01(b) (first two sentences only), 3.02, 3.03, 3.05, 3.06, 3.07, 4.12, 4.13, 5.13, 5.14, 5.16 or 9.03(b) which shall survive indefinitely.

9.02   Indemnification by and on Behalf of LGE.

(a)   LGE agrees to defend, indemnify and hold the Indemnified Purchaser Group harmless from and against any and all losses, liabilities, damages, costs or expenses (including reasonable attorneys' fees, penalties and interest) payable to or for the benefit of, or asserted by, any party, resulting from, arising out of, or incurred as a result of:

(i)   the breach of any representation made by either LGE or CP herein or in accordance herewith; or

(ii)   the breach of any warranty or covenant made by either LGE or CP herein or in accordance herewith.

(b)   If LGE, at the time it is required to make any payment for indemnification pursuant to this Section 9.02, holds shares of MDU Common Stock that are subject to the restrictions on transfer contained in the Stockholder's Agreement, then LGE's obligations to make any such payment for indemnification shall be deferred until such time as LGE holds shares of MDU Common Stock that are not subject to the restrictions on transfer contained in the Stockholder's Agreement; provided, that, if, at the time LGE is required to make any payment for indemnification pursuant to this Section 9.02, it holds any shares of MDU Common Stock that are not subject to the restrictions on transfer contained in the Stockholder's Agreement, then, to the extent of the then current market value of such MDU Common Stock, LGE's obligations to make any such payment for indemnification shall not be deferred.

9.03   Indemnification by MDU.

(a)   MDU agrees to defend, indemnify and hold the Indemnified Seller Group harmless from and against any and all losses, liabilities, damages, costs, or expenses (including reasonable attorneys' fees, penalties and interest) payable to or for the benefit of, or asserted by, any party, resulting from, arising out of, or incurred as a result of (a) the breach of any representation made by MDU herein or in accordance herewith; (b) the breach of any warranty or covenant made by MDU herein or in accordance herewith, and (c) any liabilities of CP or the Stockholders arising from ownership or operation of CP or CP's business after the Closing Date (including, without limitation, all actions, suits and claims of any nature arising from such ownership or operation after the Closing Date).

(b)   MDU will, to the extent required in order to assure that the Merger will qualify as a tax-free reorganization, take all reasonable steps necessary to pay the following amounts in MDU Common Stock: (x) any amounts due for indemnification pursuant to this Section 9.03 in MDU Common Stock, or (y) any attorneys' fees payable by MDU pursuant to Section 10.11 hereof, in each case subject to MDU's receipt of (i) any necessary regulatory approvals relating to the issuance of such MDU Common Stock, (ii) authorization for listing of such MDU Common Stock on the NYSE and the PE, (iii) the approval of the MDU Board of Directors relating to the issuance of such MDU Common Stock and (iv) any necessary approval of the stockholders of MDU relating to the issuance of such MDU Common Stock. For the purposes of this Section 9.03(b), the value of the MDU Common Stock to be issued to make any of the payments described in this Section 9.03(b), shall be deemed to be the sum of the closing prices of the MDU Common Stock in New York Stock Exchange Composite Transactions as reported in The Wall Street Journal for the ten (10) trading days preceding the date on which all of the authorizations and approvals referred to in (i) through (iv) above have been obtained, divided by ten (10) (appropriately adjusted, in any case, for any stock split, reverse stock split, stock dividend, or similar event).

9.04   Limitations on Indemnification.

(a)   Neither the Indemnified Seller Group, on the one hand, nor the Indemnified Purchaser Group, on the other hand, shall be entitled to make any claim for indemnification under this Article 9 with respect to (i) the breach of any representation, warranty or covenant contained herein (other than those representations, warranties or covenants by LGE that relate to Taxes or ERISA matters, including without limitation, any representation, warranty or covenant contained in Sections 3.20 or 3.21, and other than those representations, warranties or covenants contained in Sections 3.01(a), 3.01(b) (first two sentences only), 3.02, 3.03, 3.05, 3.06, 3.07, 4.12, 4.13, 5.13, 5.14, 5.16 or 9.03(b)) after two (2) years after the Closing Date, or (ii) the breach by LGE of any representation and warranty contained herein which relates to Taxes or ERISA matters, including without limitation, any representation, warranty or covenant contained in Sections 3.20 or 3.21, after the date on which the relevant statute of limitations expires (giving effect to any waiver, mitigation or extension thereof), unless the Indemnified Seller Group or the Indemnified Purchaser Group, as the case may be, shall assert such claim for indemnification, and shall specify, in reasonable detail to the extent known, the specific facts constituting the basis for such claim for indemnification prior to the date on which such representation and warranty cease to survive.

(b)   Except as hereinafter expressly provided, no claim for indemnification under Section 9.02 shall he made by members of the Indemnified Purchaser Group unless and until the aggregate amount of all losses, liabilities, damages, costs and expenses suffered by the members of the Indemnified Purchaser Group exceeds $500,000 in the aggregate, and then only to the extent that the aggregate amount of such losses, liabilities, damages, costs and expenses exceeds $500,000. In addition, LGE shall not be liable for indemnification under Section 9.02 in an aggregate amount in excess of $15 million.

(c)   In no event shall LGE have any liability hereunder for any breach of a representation or warranty of either LGE or CP of which an officer or director of MDU (other than Thomas Everist) or an employee of KRC who has devoted substantial attention to the transactions contemplated hereby had actual conscious awareness prior to the execution hereof or the Closing, as the case may be.

(d)   Notwithstanding the foregoing, there shall be no limitation on indemnification under this Article 9 with respect to breach of any representation, warranty or covenant contained in Sections 3.01(a), 3.01(b) (first two sentences only), 3.02, 3.03, 3.05, 3.06, 3.07, 3.20, 3.21, 5.13, 5.14, 5.16 or 9.03(b).

(e)   Notwithstanding the foregoing, (i) no indemnified party shall be entitled to be indemnified hereunder for any portion of the amount of any losses, liabilities, damages, costs, or expenses with respect to which such party receives final, irrevocable payment from any insurer; and (ii) the amount of any losses, liabilities, damages, costs, or expenses with respect to which an indemnified party is entitled to indemnification hereunder shall be reduced by an amount equal to the quantifiable tax benefits to such party associated with such losses, liabilities, damages, costs or expenses.

9.05   Supplements to Disclosure Schedules. Prior to the Closing Date, LGE will promptly supplement or amend the Schedules delivered pursuant to Article 3 hereof with respect to any matter arising after the date hereof which if existing or occurring at the date hereof would have been required to be set forth or described in such Schedules. Any such supplement or amendment shall be provided to MDU in writing and certified by the Secretary or an Assistant Secretary of LGE before the Closing Date and shall not be effective unless and until so provided. For purposes of the indemnifications set forth in Article 9 (but not for purposes of determining the accuracy of representations and warranties of LGE contained in Article 3 hereof with respect to the fulfillment of the conditions set forth in Section 6.02 for which the Schedules hereto shall be deemed to include only that information contained therein on the date of this Agreement), the Schedules hereto shall be deemed to include all information contained in any supplement or amendment.

9.06   Remedies Exclusive. Except as specifically provided for herein, each of MDU, on behalf of the Indemnified Purchaser Group and LGE, on behalf of the Indemnified Seller Group, acknowledge and agree that, should the Closing occur, the sole and exclusive remedy of each party hereto against any other party hereto with respect to any and all claims arising under this Agreement shall be pursuant to the indemnification provisions set forth in this Article 9. In furtherance of the foregoing, except as set forth in this Agreement (including but not limited to Article 9 hereof) MDU, Acquisition Subsidiary and LGE, on behalf of the Stockholders, hereby waive, from and after the Closing, to the fullest extent permitted under applicable law, any and all rights, claims and causes of action arising out of this Agreement that the members of the Indemnified Purchaser Group may have against LGE or the members of the Indemnified Seller Group may have against MDU, in each case arising under or based upon any federal, state, local or foreign statute, law, ordinance, rule or regulation or otherwise; provided, however, that no party waives its rights to pursue any legal or equitable remedy available to it, whether by statute or at common law, for intentional fraud or intentional misrepresentation.

9.07   Notice of Claims. LGE, on the one hand, and MDU, on the other hand, agree to give prompt written notice to each other of any claim by any party which might give rise to a claim by it or them against the other parties hereto based upon the indemnity provisions contained herein, stating the nature and basis of the claim and the actual or estimated amount thereof; provided, however, that failure to give such notice will not affect the obligation of the indemnifying party to provide indemnification in accordance with the provisions of this Article 9 unless, and only to the extent that, such indemnifying party is actually prejudiced thereby. In the event that any action, suit or proceeding is brought by a third party against any member of the Indemnified Seller Group or the Indemnified Purchaser Group with respect to which any party hereto may have liability under the indemnification provisions contained herein, the indemnifying party shall have the right, at its sole cost and expense, to defend such action in the name or on behalf of the indemnified party and, in connection with any such action, suit or proceeding, the parties hereto agree to render to each other such assistance as may reasonably be required in order to ensure the proper and adequate defense of any such action, suit or proceeding; provided, however, that an indemnified party shall have the right to retain its own counsel, with the fees and expenses to be paid by the indemnifying party (subject to Section 9.03(b)), if representation of such indemnified party by the counsel retained by the indemnifying party would be inappropriate because of actual or potential differing interests between such indemnified party and any other party represented by such counsel. No party hereto shall make any settlement of any claim which might give rise to liability of any other party under the indemnification provisions contained herein without the written consent of such other party, which consent such other party covenants shall not be unreasonably withheld.

ARTICLE 10.

GENERAL PROVISIONS

10.01   Expenses. Except as otherwise expressly provided herein, LGE and MDU shall each pay their own expenses (including, without limitation, the fees and expenses of its agents, representatives, counsel, and accountants) incurred in connection with the negotiation, drafting, execution, delivery and performance of this Agreement and the Related Agreements and the transactions contemplated hereby and thereby, it being understood that any expenses incurred by CP in connection with the negotiation, drafting, execution, delivery and performance of this Agreement and the Related Agreements will be borne by LGE. LGE will cause CP to estimate and accrue on the Closing Balance Sheet all such expenses incurred by CP, to the extent not previously paid by CP.

10.02   Successors and Assigns. This Agreement shall be binding upon and inure to the benefit of LGE and MDU and their respective, successors, representatives and assigns.

10.03   Waiver. No provision of this Agreement shall be deemed waived by course of conduct, including the act of closing, unless such waiver is made in a writing signed by all then existing or surviving parties hereto, stating that it is intended specifically to modify this Agreement, nor shall any course of conduct operate or be construed as a waiver of any subsequent breach of this Agreement, whether of a similar or dissimilar nature.

10.04   Entire Agreement. This Agreement (together with the Schedules and Exhibits hereto) supersedes any other agreement, whether written or oral, that may have been made or entered into by MDU or any of its subsidiaries, either Stockholder or CP (or by any director, officer, employee, shareholder, agent, or other representative of such parties) relating to the matters contemplated hereby. This Agreement (together with the Schedules and Exhibits hereto) constitutes the entire agreement between the parties and there are no agreements or commitments except as expressly set forth herein.

10.05   Further Assurances. Each of the parties hereto agrees to execute all further documents and instruments and to take or to cause to be taken all reasonable actions which are necessary or appropriate to complete the transactions contemplated by this Agreement.

10.06   Notices. All notices, demands, requests, and other communications hereunder shall be in writing and shall be deemed to have been duly given and shall be effective upon receipt if delivered by hand, or sent by certified or registered United States mail, postage prepaid and return receipt requested, or by prepaid overnight express service or facsimile transmission (with receipt confirmed). Notices shall be sent to the parties at the following addresses (or at such other addresses for a party as shall be specified by like notice; provided that such notice shall be effective only upon receipt thereof):

(a)   If to LGE:
L. G. Everist, Incorporated
300 S. Phillips Avenue
Suite 200
P.O. Box 5829
Sioux Falls, South Dakota
57117-5829
Telephone: 605-334-5000
Facsimile: 605-334-3656
Attn: Thomas Everist, President

with a copy (which shall not constitute notice) to:
Faegre & Benson LLP
2200 Norwest Center
90 South Seventh Street
Minneapolis, MN 55402-3901
Telephone: 612-336-3000
Facsimile: 612-336-3026
Attn: Bruce M. Engler, Esq.

(b)   If to MDU:
MDU Resources Group, Inc.
Schuchart Building
918 East Divide Avenue
P.O. Box 5650
Bismarck, North Dakota, 58506-5650
Telephone: (701) 222-7900
Facsimile: (701) 222-7607
Attn: Corporate Secretary

with a copy (which shall not constitute notice) to:
Thelen Reid & Priest LLP
40 West 57th Street
New York, New York 10019-4097
Telephone: (212) 603-2000
Facsimile: (212) 603-2001
Attn: Richard S. Green, Esq.

10.07   Amendments, Supplements, Etc. This Agreement may be amended or modified only by a written instrument executed by all then existing or surviving parties hereto which states specifically that it is intended to amend or modify this Agreement.

10.08   Severability. In the event that any provision contained in this Agreement shall for any reason be held to be invalid, illegal or unenforceable in any respect, such invalidity, illegality or unenforceability shall not affect any other provision hereof and this Agreement shall be construed as if such invalid, illegal or unenforceable provisions had never been contained herein and, in lieu of each such illegal, invalid or unenforceable provision, there shall be added automatically as a part of this Agreement a provision as similar in terms to such illegal, invalid or unenforceable provision as may be possible but still be legal, valid and enforceable.

10.09   Governing Law. This Agreement and the legal relations between the parties hereto shall be governed by and construed in accordance with the substantive laws of the State of California without giving effect to the conflicts of laws principles thereof.

10.10   Execution in Counterparts. This Agreement may be executed in one or more counterparts, each of which shall be deemed an original, but all of which together shall constitute one and the same instrument.

10.11   Attorney Fees. In any litigation, arbitration, or other proceeding by which one party either seeks to enforce its rights under this Agreement (whether in contract, tort, or both) or seeks a declaration of any rights or obligations under this Agreement, the prevailing party shall be awarded reasonable attorney fees, together with any costs and expenses, including expert witness fees, to resolve the dispute and to enforce the final judgment.

10.12   Disclosure Schedules.

(a)   Matters set forth in the Schedules to this Agreement may include matters not required by this Agreement to be set forth in such Schedules. The inclusion of any such non-required matter shall not of itself imply any obligation on the part of MDU, LGE or CP to set forth any other non-required matter.

(b)   A disclosure made by LGE, CP or MDU in any particular Section of this Agreement or any particular Schedule to this Agreement that is set forth in sufficient detail to reasonably inform the other parties of information required to be disclosed in another Section of this Agreement or another such Schedule (taking into account the context in which the disclosure was made) shall be deemed, for the purposes of this Agreement to have been made with respect to such other Section of this Agreement or such other Schedule. In no event shall the mere listing in a Schedule to this Agreement (or the mere provision by LGE or CP to MDU of a copy) of a document or other item be deemed adequate to disclose an exception to a representation or warranty made herein, unless such representation or warranty has to do with the existence of the document or other item itself.

IN WITNESS WHEREOF, the parties hereto have executed this Agreement as of the date first above written.

MDU RESOURCES GROUP, INC.

By: _____

Name: Lester H. Loble, II
Title: Vice President, General Counsel, and Secretary

CONNPAC ACQUISITION CORP.

By: _____

Name: Terry D. Hildestad
Title: President

L.G. EVERIST, INCORPORATED

By: _____

Name: _____

Title: _____

CONNOLLY-PACIFIC CO.

By: _____

Name: _____

Title: _____

Courtesy of Richard S. Green, Thelen Reid Brown Raysman & Steiner LLP